basic research methods in social science

Consulting Editor

Hanan C. Selvin

State University of New York at Stony Brook

Julian L. Simon

University of Illinois

Basic Research Methods in Social Sciences

The Art of Empirical Investigation

Second edition

 Random House, New York

Second Edition
98765432

Copyright © 1969, 1978 by Random House, Inc.
All rights reserved under International and Pan-American
Copyright Conventions. No part of this book may be reproduced in any
form or by any means, electronic or mechanical, including
photocopying, without permission in writing from the publisher. All
inquiries should be addressed to Random House, Inc., 201 East
50th Street, New York, N.Y. 10022. Published in the United States
by Random House, Inc., and simultaneously in Canada by Random House
of Canada Limited, Toronto.

Library of Congress Cataloging in Publication Data
Simon, Julian Lincoln, 1932–
Basic research methods in social science.
Bibliography: p.
Includes index.
1. Social science research. 2. Social sciences
Methodology. I. Title.
H62.S475   1978   300'.1'8   77–17286
ISBN 0-394-32049-2

Manufactured in the United States of America

I am grateful for the privilege of quoting from "voices to voices" in *Complete Poems 1913–1962* by E. E. Cummings. Reprinted by permission of Harcourt Brace Jovanovich, Inc.; from *Argonauts of the Western Pacific* by Branislaw Malinowski. Published in the United States by E. P. Dutton, and reprinted with their permission and with permission of Routledge & Kegan Paul Ltd.; from "Freud in Research Is a Rising Problem in Science" by Boyce Rensberger. © 1977 by The New York Times Company. Reprinted by permission; from a by-lined article by Ward Cannel, copyrighted January 26, 1964 by Newspaper Enterprise Association. Reprinted by permission; from *The Nature of Statistics* by Allen Wallis and Harry Roberts. Reprinted by permission of The Macmillan Company. © The Free Press of Glencoe, a Corporation 1956; from *The Essential Works of Pavlov* by Ivan Pavlov (edited by Michael Kaplan). Copyright © 1927 by Oxford University Press. Copyright © 1966 by Bantam Books. Reprinted by permission of the Oxford University Press; from *Memory: A Contribution to Experimental Psychology* by Hermann Ebbinghaus. Copyright © 1913 by Dover Publications, Inc.; from "Obesity's Problem Child Demands Rewards" by Arthur J. Snider. Copyright © 1964 by *The Chicago Daily News*. Reprinted by permission; from "Phobias in Britons Fall into 130 types." Copyright © 1969 by The New York Times Company. Reprinted by permission; from *Readings in the Philosophy of the Social Sciences* by May Brodbeck. Copyright © 1968 by The Macmillan Publishing Company, Inc. Reprinted by permission; excerpt from the *Champaign-Urbana Courier* February 21, 1965. Reprinted with permission; from *The Ambassador* by Morris West. Copyright © 1965 by William Morrow & Company, Inc. Reprinted by permission; from *The Human Meaning of the Social Sciences* by Daniel Lerner. Copyright © 1959 by Peter Smith. Reprinted by permission; from *The Conduct of Inquiry* by Abraham Kaplan. Copyright © 1974 by Thomas Y. Crowell, Inc. Reprinted by permission; from Paul F. Lazarsfeld, *The People's Choice: How the Voter Makes up His Mind in a Presidential Campaign,* third edition, New York: Columbia University Press, 1968. Reprinted by permission; from *Printer's Ink,* August 27, 1965; from *Anthropology* by A. L. Kroeber. Copyright 1923, 1948 by Harcourt Brace Jovanovich, Inc.; renewed 1951 by A. L. Kroeber. Reprinted by permission of the publishers; from *The Economics of Seller's Competition* by Fritz Machlup. Copyright © 1952 by The Johns Hopkins University Press. Reprinted by permission; from "Evaluation of Alternate Rating Devices for Consumer Research," from *Journal of Marketing Research,* published by the American Marketing Association; from *An Introduction to Scientific Research* by E. Bright Wilson. Copyright © 1952 by McGraw-Hill, Inc. Used with permission of McGraw-Hill Book Company; from Lawrence R. Klein (ed): *Contributions of Survey Methods to Economics,* New York: Columbia University Press, 1954. Reprinted by permission; from "Land Price Set by Jury." Copyright © 1965 by the *Champaign-Urbana Courier.* Excerpt from *Illinois Business Review,* April 1966, p. 9. Copyright © 1966. Reprinted by permission; from "Hired Hand Research," by Julius A. Roth. Copyright © 1966 by the American Sociological Association. Reprinted by permission of publisher and author; from *Experimenter Effects in Behavioral Research* by Robert Rosenthal. Copyright © 1966. Reprinted by permission; Selections from Stanley L. Payne, *The Art of Asking Questions* (copyright 1951 by Princeton University Press), pp. 7, 11 and 16. Reprinted by permission of Princeton University Press; from "A Middle Way Out of Vietnam" by Arthur Schlesinger, Jr. in *The New York Times Magazine.* © 1966 by The New York Times Company. Reprinted by permission; from "A Psuedo Experiment in Parapsychology" by L. W. Alvarez. Copyright 1965 by the American Association for the Advancement of Science. Reprinted by permission of the author; from "Privacy and Behavioral Research" by K. E. Clark et al. Copyright 1967 by the American Association for the Advancement of Science. Reprinted by permission of the authors.

preface

The aim of this second edition is the same as that of the first: to help you get started doing empirical research. The book has been reorganized considerably to better serve that purpose. The chapters on research decisions and procedures now come early in the book (Part II), followed by chapters on the obstacles to research (Part III). And now there are complete chapters on sampling (Chapter 9), experiments (Chapters 10 and 11), surveys (Chapter 13), and scaling (Chapters 15 and 16), plus independent appendices on questionnaire construction (Chapter 20) and interviewing (Chapter 19); in the first edition this material was scattered throughout the book. There is also a new chapter on the relationship between theory and empirical research (Chapter 5).

The first edition of this book is not intellectually obsolete. The practice of good science has changed little since the first edition—or in the last half century, for that matter; this explains why most of the examples have not been changed from the first edition. But the organization of the second edition should be more convenient for you to read. And over the years I've learned how to express some ideas better. In addition, the new material fills some needs that readers of the first edition said needed filling. Last but not least, chapter summaries and other pedagogical devices should ease your studying.

Though this is a practical how-to-do-it book, it aims also to teach the basic concepts in the philosophy of science. In my view this is not a contradiction, because the philosophy of science at its best is also a very practical subject, composed of ideas that clarify the nature and meaning of research and help the researcher better understand how to proceed when faced with difficult choices and decisions.

This book may be deceptively easy to read. I have always hated obscurantism and have been emotionally committed to simplicity, perhaps because of the coincidence of my name with the nursery rhyme "Simple Simon met a pieman. . . ." But simplicity has its drawbacks, such as: (1) Some students concluded that the first edition was so simple to read that it was insufficiently "challenging." Simplicity has a basic psychological difficulty, as expressed by T. S. Eliot about poetry: "A successful poem must be sufficiently simple so it can be understood, but sufficiently difficult so that it cannot be understood immediately." But I am unwilling to make my writing hard to understand so as to be more appealing. (2) Simplicity of *expression* may fool you into thinking that the *ideas* discussed here are simple ones. They are not. (3) As someone has said: Seek simplicity—but distrust it.

On the other hand, the book may seem overly long, containing too many examples. But as someone else once said, short writing makes long reading. So I hope you will not be put off by the book's length.

The writing style is more casual than it is conventional, and it does not always meet editors' standards as to what is "correct." Therefore I am pleased to take full responsibility for the language.

Despite that this is a text, it contains some new scientific ideas. Those ideas I most hope that you will notice as being original contributions are, first, causality as a concept requiring appropriate operational definition (Chapter 32) and second, the Monte Carlo approach to *basic* statistics (Chapters 27 to 31). Since the first publication of the Monte Carlo methods in this book, there has developed a body of experimental evidence that this radically different way of learning and doing statistics is more effective, easier to understand and more effective than the conventional analytic method (Simon, Shevokas, and Atkinson).

About the sex of pronouns in the book: The first edition used "he" for the unidentified person. That will not pass any longer, and never should have passed. However, I do not wish to clutter up the writing with clumsy "he or she" phrases or to weaken it with annoying circumlocutions. The solution I've chosen is simply to sometimes write "he" and sometimes "she," more or less at random, when I mean an unidentified human being. This practice may seem a bit strange at first, but I trust that it will cause no confusion and will be pleasant and efficient. If this practice seems good to the reader, maybe other writers will adopt it, too.

A personal note: The considerable success of the first edition heartened me in many ways. First—and this may in turn hearten other prospective authors—the skeletal first draft of the manuscript was rejected by fifteen (15) publishers before Hanan Selvin pointed out its potential to Random House. Second, I worried that because the book is not narrowly specialized to a single discipline, each teacher would say that it might be good for others but not for him or her. It turns out, however, that there are a good many instructors who believe in a broad education in research methods; this heartens me because I, too, believe that. Third, I worried that the lack of mathematical notation and "sophisticated" and "rigorous" complexity would deter instructors from adopting the book; but apparently there are plenty of instructors who are more interested in teaching than in impressing students, and that cheers me, too.

In closing, I am grateful for your attention to my thoughts and writing. I benefited from the suggestions and corrections I received from readers of the first edition, and I shall be glad to receive more on this second edition. Thank you.

acknowledgments
to second edition

Hanan Selvin listened to tapes of many chapters for the second edition, especially the new ones, and gave me a flood of useful and delightful comments, only some of which did I have the strength to exploit. Gideon Keren made helpful comments on Chapter 11. And the following long list of people were kind enough to send me evaluations or remarks about the first edition: Marcus Felson, William Ahlhauser, Wayne W. Snyder, Jason Millman, Robert A. Baker, Oleh Wolowyna, Lawrence G. Smith, Lucy W. Sells, Leigh Marlowe, Siamak Movahedi, Michael A. Baer, Joann S. DeLora, Marc D. Magre, Leroy Gruner, John H. Kramer, Jules W. Delambre, Alan C. Acock, Robert W. Shotoln, David M. Krieger, Michael D. Grimes, L. V. Hayes, Robert C. Smigelski, David G. Pfeiffer, Jamie M. Calderon, D. E. W. Holden, David M. Monsees, Jr., L. Fannin, Luther H. Keller, Linda Brookover, Bourque, David Nasatir, Kenneth R. Rothrock, Louis A. Brown, LeRoy Martinson, Gosts Wolff. I am grateful to one and all.

More and more my family and our life together sustains me. Wife Rita and children David, Judith, and Daniel give my days the joy and meaning that enable me to write.

Urbana, Illinois, 1978   J.L.S.

acknowledgments
to first edition

For a hundred and more years ingenious social scientists have faced obstacles to getting the empirical knowledge they sought, devised ways to circumvent the obstacles, and then told others what they learned. I am grateful to them.

Hanan Selvin subjected the penultimate draft of this manuscript to the searching scrutiny that most manuscripts need but few are lucky enough to get. The quantity and quality of his critical comments were an author's dream, and I have in many places appropriated his thought and word without special note. There would be fewer errors and obscurities in the book if I had followed his advice even more diligently.

James W. Carey gave me many exciting and enjoyable hours discussing some of the fundamental concepts. I also benefited from talks with Howard Maclay. Other friends may also recognize their casual observations in these pages. Allen Holmes read the chapters on statistics very carefully and corrected some errors. Dennis J. Aigner was also good enough to look at those chapters. For useful references and suggestions I am grateful to Stanley Friedman, Lewis Goldberg, James H. Lorie, and Louis Schneider.

My greatest debt is to my wife, Rita. Without her encouragement this book would never have been done.

I have tried to cover the wide intellectual area of all the social sciences, and I hope the reader will bear with me when I depart from the substantive fields that I know best. I will appreciate hearing from anyone who can set me straight on any matter or who can give an instructive or interesting example to illuminate a point.

Jerusalem, 1968   J.L.S.

contents

prologue

Cast your mind back 450 years. The Governor of Rodera—a small Asian principality—decided to find out why the country's tax revenues were not greater. Here is a classic problem for research, and much of mathematics and social-science techniques was originally invented to improve tax collection.

The Governor first consulted an adviser who had studied in Europe and had learned something of Aristotelian logic. The adviser reasoned that (a) good citizens willingly pay as much tax as they are able to, (b) the folk of Rodera were very good citizens, and therefore (c) the tax collections *could not* be higher.

The Governor immediately dismissed this syllogistic thinking as pure nonsense because he disbelieved the premises. Even without special training he was smart enough to understand the weakness of bad logic.

Next, the Governor called in the regional tax collectors and put the problem to them, because they were experts in the tax-collection field. After consultation the consensus among the tax collectors was that the people of the country simply *could not afford* to pay any more taxes. To support this statement the tax men stated that they had already used every possible technique to extract higher taxes—raising valuations of property, checking on hidden assets, and the like—and even their best efforts could not raise more money.

The Governor understood the tax men's analysis of the situation as a self-seeking attempt to make themselves seem competent and hard-working, and he therefore disregarded this "expert opinion."

The Governor then concluded reluctantly that he would have to find out the answers for himself. He instructed an aide to bring him a handful of typical citizens. The aide brought in some people who were close at hand. They included a few beggars who had been loitering nearby, plus the aide's brother and two young guards. It was obvious to the Governor that these

people were not representative of the population, and therefore it was useless to question them. To put it in modern terms, the Governor recognized
that he had a badly biased sample.

The aide was therefore instructed to bring in some "typical" peasants
and townspeople, which he did. The Governor then asked them, "Why
don't you pay more taxes?" The first few answers showed the folly of the
question, for what he heard were excuses, complaints, entreaties—everything
except what seemed to be sensible answers.

The Governor then confined his questions to factual matters. He asked
about each person's property, his crops, family size, and the amount he paid
in taxes. Assuming that the answers were true and that he could have them
checked, the Governor thought he was getting somewhere.

The information obtained from such a small handful of people clearly was
not enough, however, because the group did not include any rich men, any
people from the far provinces, any foreign residents, or any representatives
of other important classes of people. Nor could the Governor tell from this
sample how many people in each class there were. Therefore, the Governor
ordered a nation-wide house-to-house census.

Nowadays the data for a complete nation-wide United States census can
be collected in months. But transportation and communications were poorer
then, and few literate people could be found to collect information. The
census therefore required twelve years.

By the fifth year the Governor grew impatient and decided to experiment
with the effect of new pressures to increase tax collections. He ordered that
anyone who did not pay half again as much tax as in the previous year would
have his cattle confiscated. It turned out that the total taxes paid did not
increase. The crops were bad that year, and the Governor could not determine whether the taxes would have been as high or higher than otherwise
if the crop had been normal. The trouble was that his experiment was uncontrolled, because he had not kept the old tax system in effect in some areas
for comparison—that is, his experimental design was incomplete. And worst
of all, many people slaughtered their cattle to avoid confiscation, which
ruined the country's meat supply for several years.

By the time the census data were all in hand at the end of the twelfth
year, the country's situation had changed, and the data collected in early
years no longer meant much. (Nowadays we know how to take samples to
reduce cost and avoid long time lags during which the picture may change.)
Furthermore, after twelve years the tax-census data filled a whole warehouse, and another ten years would have been required to interpret them.
The Governor gave up the task in disgust and retired to his harem.

The point of this story is that knowledge is often not easy to come by
because there are many obstacles in one's path. And common sense alone is
not enough. But by now social science has accumulated a body of tested
experience on how best to overcome the obstacles and acquire empirical
knowledge efficiently and safely. This book presents some of this accumulated experience.

basic research methods in social science

1 introduction

1. Purpose of the Book

This book is primarily for students who have never before studied or done empirical social-scientific research. I hope that the book contains good advice that will help you get your first research project off the ground successfully and increase your efficiency in later work. As for those of you who will not do empirical research, the book may teach you to distinguish good research from poor research and help you to understand why empirical researchers do things as they do them.

People who have had some training or experience in empirical research may also gain from the elementary level of the discussion. Basic concepts often are bypassed as one rushes to learn the methods of particular fields. Coming back to fundamentals can widen the perspective of an advanced student and fill holes in his knowledge. If an advanced student is to gain something from this book, however, he must have the wisdom to realize that the apparent simplicity of the basic concepts is often deceiving. For example, everyone knows that *ceteris paribus*—holding "all other things equal"—is important. But the more research you do, the more you realize how complex is the *ceteris paribus* idea, how difficult it is to choose the right *ceteris paribus* conditions, and how often research is useless because other things really were not made sufficiently equal.

The book is intended for future *producers* of research, of course. But many people who study research methods will never produce research; rather, they will be research *consumers,* in their jobs and as citizens. For this important latter group of people, the aim of the book is to teach how to evaluate research done by others—to know which research is good and which is not; where the weak spots are in a piece of research and how important they are; and whether a research finding, whether presented in the professional literature, in an informal report, or in the popular press, is likely to be valid or not. For example, Volvo recently advertised that "90 percent of the Volvos sold in the last eleven years in the U.S. are still on the road." A good course in research methods is likely to alter your impression of what that claim might mean.

I hope that you yourself carry out some empirical research—no matter how small in scope—as you read this book. It is not enough to study empirical research the way one studies astronomy, economics, psychology, and other academic subjects. Reading about research principles is certainly useful. But research is not entirely an academic subject. Rather, it is largely an art, a how-to-do-it subject like musical composition, writing advertisements, or swimming.[1] You never really know how to do research until you do it, any more than you can know how to swim after only pool-side instruction. You must jump into the water, thrash around, and gradually improve with practice. For the same reason, skill in empirical research requires experience —that is, doing research of your own and criticizing the research of others.[2] For example, when you do a piece of research you cannot fail to learn just how complicated even the simplest research really is.

Eventually you would learn much that is in this book by trial and error. Instruction can only hasten the process and make it less painful by showing what has and has not worked for others. But that is as far as the teaching can go. (Reading what others say about research *can* be enormously profitable, however, *if* you will benefit by the experience of others.)

Now a theme that will recur throughout the book: There is never a single, standard, correct method of carrying out a piece of research. Do not wait to start your research until you find out *the* proper approach, because there are always many ways to tackle a problem—some good, some bad, but probably several good ways. There is no single perfect design. A research method for a given problem is not like the solution to a problem in algebra. It is more like a recipe for beef stroganoff; there is no one best recipe.

For technical matters, too, there may be several satisfactory techniques, and there is no cut-and-dried answer. For example, if you want to do a

1. A great mathematician applies the same analogy to his sort of work, too: "Solving [mathematical] problems is a practical skill like, let us say, swimming. We acquire any practical skill by imitation and practice" (Polya, p. 4).
2. Also valuable are the too-rare accounts of how and why a piece of research was done. Three short descriptions of this sort can be found in W. Wallis and H. Roberts (Chap. 3). Anthropologists often weave such material into their writings; W. Whyte (2nd ed., Appendix A) has a delightful and useful description of this sort. K. Colby's account of Semmelweiss and childbed fever is excellent (pp. 44–50). R. Braidwood's "Biography of a Research Project" is a fascinating description of archaeological research. P. Hammond offers some excellent examples. C. Mills (pp. 199 ff.) interweaves a description of one of his labors with marvelous general advice on craftsmanship and how to get ideas and do social analysis. J. Madge has written a book full of such accounts of sociological research.

questionnaire survey, should you interview by mail, by telephone, or in person? Chapter 13 discusses the pros and cons of each method, but eventually sound judgment is required for this technical decision; no handy rule book can make such decisions for you. Or, should you pay your subjects in an experiment or survey? Again there is no pat answer; instead, this book tries to give you some principles that will help you to make sound technical decisions about your research methods.

In this book the word "method" refers to *empirical* techniques and devices of various sorts. To the philosophers the term refers to "scientific method"—the whole process of getting knowledge, including the theoretical and the empirical steps. But even then it is surely true that there is no single "scientific method." ". . . There is no one scientific method . . . there will be as many different scientific methods as there are fundamentally different kinds of problems" (Northrop, pp. ix, 19). "The scientific method, as far as it is a method, is nothing more than doing one's damnedest with one's mind, no holds barred" (Bridgman, p. 450).

2. What Kinds of Research Are Called "Empirical"?

This book deals with *empirical*[3] research and not with scientific speculation. Much of scientific work consists of thinking up ideas about the nature of the world, generalizing from observed facts to scientific "laws," and developing logical systems that are called "theories" or "models." But simply as a division of labor the speculative part of science is not covered here. The subject of this book is "getting the facts." Of course empirical work goes beyond "mere" observation and description, and it is inextricably intertwined with explaining nature and making predictions about it. But the process of thinking up explanations or hypotheses about nature and its laws is beyond our scope here.[4]

Nor is this book concerned with the logical process of building scientific theories. That is, it does not deal with the process of finding the *logical* relationships between various scientific statements or with the process of developing generalizations or scientific laws. Rather, its subject is the less glamorous craft of producing and examining factual and material evidence and sense data to develop the descriptions, measurements, comparisons, and tests of hypothesized relationships that are themselves part of the speculative side of scientific work.

Lest there be misunderstanding, I emphasize that a good idea is the

3. ". . . [T]he adjective *empirical*, in its combinations with various nouns, appears to denote observations and propositions primarily based on sense experience and/or derived from such experience by methods of inductive logic, including mathematics and statistics" (*The Dictionary of the Social Sciences*, p. 237). The crucial distinction here is between empirical research and *theorizing*, though the two activities are very much interdependent.
4. The elusive phenomenon of scientific *discovery* is discussed at length by many writers. See, for example, J. Young, A. Bachrach (Chap. 1), W. Beveridge (Chaps. 5, 6), C. Mills (Appendix, especially pp. 200–201, 211–217).

keystone of an empirical study. Mere data collection and measurement are worthless unless the subject is important. Theory is often the fount of important ideas for empirical research, and sound theory is of inestimable value in any field. The relationship between theory and empirical research is explored in Chapter 5.

Finally, "empirical research" excludes knowledge obtained by *consulting authorities,* in books or in person.[5] It includes only knowledge obtained from data resulting from first-hand observations, either by you or by someone else. Reexamination of data collected by others, such as U.S. Census data, *is* empirical research, of course.

Most of the examples in this book are drawn from "pure" research. But I also draw examples concerning policy decisions from the "applied" social sciences, and they often have a dollars-and-cents orientation. Applied research *methods* are sometimes more sophisticated than are methods used in pure research (Stouffer, 1950a, pp. 198–9), because it is possible to work up *some* calculation, even though crude, to compare the benefits expected from a research method against the cost of doing the research with that method. Such calculation leads to efficiency in research. (**Pure research** can be defined as research whose social or economic payoff is far in the future, whereas **applied research** is expected to have a quick payoff. But pure research is often done without any thought at all about payoff, just to satisfy the desire to *understand.*)

Here are two examples of how dollars-and-cents calculation in an applied problem helps to make sensible decisions about research: First, an advertiser can calculate whether comparing two advertisements in a split-run test[6] is worth the cost of the test. One can also compare the costs and benefits of a split run against the costs and benefits of other types of advertising research. Second, a candy firm can sensibly calculate its sample size when comparing two new flavors of candy. It can reckon the relevant costs and dollar benefits. It is much harder to determine the sample size sensibly when I. Pavlov, for example, studies how the flow of saliva in dogs can be conditioned to the sound of a bell. The possible benefits of such pure research—some intangible gain in the quality of human life perhaps far in the future or merely the satisfaction of an urge to understand our world better—are less predictable and much more difficult to evaluate in money terms to balance against the money cost of the research. Yet the decisions must be made anyway.[7]

Our examples come from the *social* sciences, not only because the book is

5. But see the section on "expert opinion" in Chapter 14.

6. In a split-run test a magazine or newspaper arranges to print two advertisements so that each appears automatically in *every other copy* in each stack of copies that is sent out. This is the closest thing to a perfect experiment.

7. It is always *conceptually* possible to develop *some* rational calculation of the value of a piece of research and its various outcomes so as to have *some* rational guidelines for research decisions (see Chapter 8; Wilson 86–87; Schlaifer. But in most pure research such calculation is not done because it is so difficult to do meaningfully.

intended for students of the social sciences, but also because empirical scientific methods have been used with greater variety and greater subtlety in the social sciences than in the natural sciences (Chapter 33 defends this claim).

We shall turn frequently to a few such famous studies as Alfred Kinsey's research on sexual behavior, employment and unemployment surveys, Herman Ebbinghaus' learning experiments, Presidential election polls, television-audience ratings, Sigmund Freud's case history of Anna O., the U.S. Surgeon General's Report on *Smoking and Health,* and Ivan Pavlov's work on conditioning reflexes. These studies have been chosen for several reasons: They are inherently interesting; most students have a general knowledge of them from survey courses or general reading; most of the studies have been repeated or scrutinized closely by outside experts (for example, the American Statistical Association appointed three top statisticians to report on Kinsey's methods); and they show us a wide variety of methods and a broad representation from the social sciences.

I also refer frequently to my own work, despite its limitations, because I know exactly what went into the work—the difficulties, decisions, errors, corrections of errors, and the order in which things took place. One cannot have such intimate knowledge of anyone else's work. Yet it is these details and decisions, seldom written about, that are hardest for the novice to understand and master and that one usually learns only by serving as an apprentice (that is, "graduate assistant") or by trial and error in one's own work.

The book emphasizes the design and plan of research, rather than the analysis of research data. Except for studies that reanalyze data collected by others, the most important and interesting decisions arise at the design stage, or at least they *should* arise then. If you postpone these decisions until after the data have been collected, you may suffer heartbreak and wasted expense.

Here are three brief examples of the importance of good design: First, two library scientists sought to determine the proportions of various-sized books in research libraries. So they measured the heights of each of the hundreds of thousands of books in a major library. With a little planning and sound design they would have needed only to measure a fraction of that number of books. And with sound design the results could also have been applied to libraries other than the one they studied.

Second, a family-planning group tested one birth-control propaganda campaign in Village A against another propaganda campaign in Village B, forgetting that subsequent differences in birth rates and contraception-acceptance rates might reflect basic differences between the two villages unconnected to the campaigns, rather than only the differences between the campaigns. Sound planning would complete the design by alternating both campaigns in the two villages or by other methods. The same sort of error has often been made by experimental psychologists and sociologists.

Third, our understanding of voting behavior has been greatly enhanced by the use of the *panel method,* in which the same people are quizzed about their voting behavior *several times* during the same election campaign. These repeated observations make it possible to understand the mechanism of voting and vote shifting in ways that are impossible without the panel design.

Mistakes at the design stage can be mended only at great extra cost, or not at all. By comparison, mistakes at the analysis stage can be remedied at slight or no cost as long as the mistakes have not gotten into print or been acted upon.

Think through the research design carefully in advance. Failing to consider all the necessary details at the design stage because of procrastination or mental laziness is one reason that many researchers get very little done. Of course not everything can be foreseen, especially in exploratory studies, but one should use as much foresight as possible. It is useful to talk to your friends about the design, and to prepare an outline of it; both processes reveal fuzziness in your design thinking.

The design of a piece of research must depend upon the particular purpose that the research is intended to serve; this is a message I shall repeat again and again. For example, the Internal Revenue Service publishes statistics on the amount of advertising done by groups of firms that sell various products, and these statistics include *all* firms' advertising, because the government requires data on the entire economy. But the statistics gathered and published by industry trade associations cover *only the leading firms,* because the industry-collected statistics are designed to meet only the information needs of the industry. For another example, a psychologist studying the relative memorability of beginning, middle, and ending portions of messages will use a different test of memory (perhaps a list of nonsense syllables) than will a psychologist who is studying how many pieces of information a radio operator can remember accurately. *You must ask yourself repeatedly: Exactly what do I want to find out? and why? If you can answer these questions clearly and precisely, you have gone a long way toward creating a satisfactory research design.*

Part One begins with Chapter 2 on the language of science, which is inseparable from science itself. Chapter 3 discusses basic concepts such as variable, function, sampling, and the ideal paradigm for the study of causal relations. Chapter 4 classifies the types of questions that empirical research is asked to answer; this classification aids in deciding what types of research methods are appropriate for any given study. Chapter 5 explores the relationship between theory and empirical research. And Chapter 6 discusses the choice of appropriate empirical proxies (indicators) for theoretical variables.

Part Two gets down to the brass tacks of just how to conduct a piece of research. Chapter 7 provides a checklist of the basic steps one often takes when executing an empirical research project. If you are actually doing a piece of research in conjunction with reading this book—as I very much hope you are—then you should certainly start by reading Chapter 7.

Other chapters in Part Two discuss crucial decisions in the research process—assessing the value of a prospective piece of research (Chapter 8), and whether to choose experimentation or the survey method (Chapters 10 and 13) or other methods (Chapter 14). Other chapters cover efficiency in sampling (Chapter 9), experimental design (Chapter 11), and the procedures of classification and measurement (Chapters 15 and 16). Part Two ends with the discussion of data handling and data adjustment in Chapter 17.

It was a toss-up whether to reverse Parts Two and Three. The reader may choose to read them in either order.

The chapters in Part Three consider the various types of obstacles that nature puts in the way of the fact seeker, and that prevent one from getting valid answers quickly and easily with common sense alone. Ways to surmount each obstacle are also discussed. These ways of surmounting obstacles to knowledge are the warp and woof of research method.

Part Four discusses what to do with your data once they are collected—how to analyze them and how to interpret them statistically (Chapters 25–30). Chapter 31 discusses how to decide on a sample size; it properly belongs in Part Two, but it had to follow after Chapters 25–30. Chapter 32 discusses the crucial concept of causality in social science.

3. The Place of Statistics in the Study of Research Methods

A working knowledge of the basic ideas of statistics and probability helps clarify one's thinking and improves one's capacity to deal with practical problems and to understand the world. And to be efficient a social scientist is almost sure to need knowledge of statistics and probability.

On the other hand, great research has been done by people with no formal knowledge of statistics. And a little study of statistics sometimes befuddles students into thinking that statistical principles are guides to research design and analysis. This mistaken belief only inhibits the exercise of sound research thinking. Kinsey put it this way:

> However satisfactory the standard deviations may be, no statistical treatment can put validity into generalizations which are based on data that were not reasonably accurate and complete to begin with. It is unfortunate that academic departments so often offer courses on the statistical manipulation of human material to students who have little understanding of the problems involved in securing the original data. . . . When training in these things replaces or at least precedes some of the college courses on the mathematical treatment of data, we shall come nearer to having a science of human behavior. (Kinsey, *et al.*, p. 35)

Throughout the book statistical ideas are submerged except as a handmaiden to research methods and research decisions. In addition, Chapters 27–31 offer a new approach to statistics that may have special interest for students who are scared by statistics. This method substitutes "Monte Carlo" experiments for mathematical analysis. It also emphasizes the *reasoning* of statistics—the most important ideas in statistics, which are usually learned only informally. This method has now been shown experimentally to be unusually effective (Simon, Shevokas, and Atkinson).

4. Some General Remarks

A book about how to do research inevitably makes research sound difficult and treacherous. And this book gives special attention to the obstacles to knowledge that one faces in doing research, so as to help you recognize and overcome them.

But please don't let these obstacles cause you to lose heart. Sound and valuable research can be done even by ordinary undergraduates—general research that is worth publishing, and applied research that is of value to organizations and decision makers. All research has flaws, but the flaws need not be so grave as to invalidate the research, even if it is course-work research conducted with a small sample, no money, and a limited budget of time.

Furthermore, research can be enormously exciting and great fun. To find out something about the world that no one has ever known before is a rare thrill. And it is a thrill that almost anyone can experience who will start with a sensible idea, work enthusiastically and hard, and proceed with caution.

Though research can be great fun, I do not like to think of it as a game. Rather, I prefer to remember that sound research can make a valuable social contribution, improving the lives of individuals and communities and enriching our culture. Thinking of research as a game can lead the researcher to focus only on the professional acceptance of one's work and its influence on one's career, rather than on the social and intellectual benefits of the research. Of course we all want to get ahead in the world. But if we want *only* to get ahead, if our eye is on only the main chance professionally, then we will all be losers in the long run.

This book is a textbook. Though some of the ideas in it are new, most are not. Like other textbooks it constitutes a sort of folk wisdom; the folk are the teachers, colleagues, and students who have discussed research with me. Some of this wisdom seems never to have been collected or transcribed from the oral tradition. (For example, the phrase *ceteris paribus* must have a very high spoken frequency among social scientists, yet it does not appear in the index of a single one of the most popular books about research methods in the social sciences.) To collect and discuss this wisdom is the aim of this book.

part one the process of social-science research

2 the language of research: definitions and validity

1. Operational Definitions

A stranger driving a car with California license plates stops you on the street in Urbana, Illinois, and asks "Where is New York?" You, being a lyrical poet with a feeling for the spiritual side of life, tell him, "New York is in the land of the sea, the singers of mercantile songs, and rotten paintings. Why go there?"

The stranger looks annoyed and says, "Come on, buddy, quit the non-sense and tell me where New York is."

"On the East Coast, north of Washington, south of Boston," you answer. He looks bewildered, so you add: "Latitude 40° 40′ North, longitude 73° 48′ West."

He looks outraged. "Will you or won't you tell me what road to take?" he says. "How do I get there?"

What the man really wants is for you to say: "Continue down this street to the first stop sign, about a quarter of a mile. Turn right onto Highway 74. . . ." and so on.

Now you have satisfied him. You have provided *instructions* that he can follow. The instructions are unambiguous (you hope), and, if he follows your instructions exactly, he must arrive exactly where you and he agree he is trying to go—New York, in this case. You have told him what he needs to know—nothing more and nothing less. You have not told him to follow the road around curves, because he needs no instruction to do so. But you have told him which way to turn when he reaches the highway, because you have no reason to assume that he knows whether to go right or left at that point.

Just as with travel instructions, the language of empirical scientific research is made up of instructions that are descriptions of sets of actions or *operations* (for instance, "turn right at the first street sign") that someone can follow accurately. Such instructions are called an "operational definition." An operational definition should contain a specification of all operations necessary to achieve the same result when repeated. It need not specify the obvious operations, however. An example of obvious and unnecessary instructions is found in a child's address on a local letter: "U.S.A., Earth, World, Universe."

The language of science also contains *theoretical* terms (better called "hypothetical terms"), for example, "utility" in economics and "reinforcement" in psychology. The place of theoretical terms is a hotly debated issue in the philosophy of science, which will be discussed in Chapters 3 and 6. Each term that actually enters into the *empirical* work, however, *must* be defined operationally.

Another example: Assume that you are a psychologist and you wish to write to another psychologist to tell her[1] what color stimulus card you used in an animal training experiment, so that she can duplicate ("replicate") the experiment. The word "green" alone might be dangerously imprecise. There are many shades and intensities of green, and your correspondent might choose a color that would lead to different experimental results.

You could ensure that she uses exactly the same color if you send her the stimulus card you actually used. Your operational definition would then be "Use the enclosed color card."

But if it is impractical to send out samples—as it is when you are writing up the experiment for publication—this simple solution will not work. You could improve the chances that another researcher would use the same color if you compared your stimulus card to an interior decorator's color chart, then wrote down the name and number of the matching color and the firm that puts out the color chart. Comparing the stimulus card against the color chart is the *operation* that *defines* the color in question.

Now some actual examples. Army Research Branch scientists in World War II wanted to study "how personal adjustment varied in the army." The key theoretical (hypothetical) term, "personal adjustment," was operationally defined this way:

> With respect to verbal behavior, it is assumed that, *on the average*, men who said that they were in good spirits, that they were more useful in the Army than as civilians, that they were satisfied with their Army jobs and status, and that in general they liked the Army, were better adjusted to the Army than men who were negative in several of these expressions. (Stouffer, *et al.*, I, 83)

1. The pronouns "she" and "he," as noted earlier, will be used interchangeably and more-or-less equally in frequency to refer to the generalized person when it would be too clumsy to use other expressions or circumlocutions.

Notice the words "who said that they were in good spirits. . . ." A question-naire is an essential part of this particular operational definition. Men who answered the questions in one fashion are operationally defined as well adjusted; others are ill adjusted, *by definition*.

Happiness is a concept related to personal adjustment but even more difficult to define satisfactorily. Happiness is perhaps as elusive a concept to define perfectly as it is to achieve. N. Bradburn tackles head-on the problem of operational definition: "One way to find out whether people are happy is to ask them. Respondents were asked to answer this question: 'Taking all things together, how would you say things are these days—would you say you are very happy, pretty happy, or not too happy?' " (p. 2).

Now that operational definitions have been exemplified, a formal opera-tional definition of "operational definition" may be appropriate. "A definition is an operational definition to the extent that the definer (a) specifies the procedure (including materials used) for identifying or generating the definiendum and (b) finds high reliability for [consistency in application of] his definition" (Dodd, in *Dictionary of Social Science*, p. 476). A. Bachrach adds that "the operational definition of a dish . . . is its recipe" (p. 74).

P. Bridgman, the inventor of operational definitions, put it that "the proper definition of a concept is not in terms of its properties but in terms of actual operations." He pointed out that definitions in terms of properties held physics back until Einstein and constituted the barrier that took Einstein to crack (pp. 6–7).

Psychologists have thought more deeply about operational definitions than have other social scientists, because psychology tries to connect what can be observed objectively to what is unobservable inside people's minds. The foregoing definition of "personal adjustment" is an example of what has been done. By contrast, creating satisfactory operational definitions is seldom a problem in economics, for the theoretical concept in economics often points clearly to the empirical variable that should be used. Of course even a concept like "money" is not automatically defined operationally; in some cases the economist includes savings deposits along with cash and checking accounts in the operational definition of money, in other cases not. And the concept "economic backwardness" bristles with such definitional problems as whether a country's present income level or its rate of growth is the more appropriate proxy. Furthermore, putting values on a country's output is a very tricky procedure that affects the relative backwardness of the country and makes one scholar ask "Is [backwardness] an operational term?" (Gerschenkron, p. 42). But seldom is the relationship between theoretical and empirical variables as arguable in economics as is the rela-tionship between, say, the theoretical (hypothetical) concept of love and its operational definition.

Operational definitions are to be distinguished from *property* or *attribute* definitions, in which something is defined by saying what it *consists of*. For example, a crude attribute definition of a college might be "An organization containing faculty and students, teaching a variety of subjects beyond the high-school level." An operational definition of university might be "An organization found in *The World Almanac*'s listing of 'Colleges and Universities.'"

Operational definitions also differ sharply from dictionary definitions. A dictionary definition of "green" is "1a: of the color green (~ jade) b: having the color of growing fresh grass or of the emerald (~ lawns)" (*Webster's Third New International Dictionary* [unabridged], 1971, p. 996). The dictionary definition often gives synonyms, which help you translate the word you do not know into words you already know, or gives *examples* of the word that help you to learn how it is used. But for many words the dictionary definition could not *guide the actions* of one person to correspond exactly to what someone else wanted. A dictionary definition of "New York" would not be at all helpful to your friend who wants to drive there from Urbana. A dictionary definition of "apple strudel" will not guide your grandmother to make exactly the dish that you enjoy. A dictionary definition of "green" will not guide another experimenter to use exactly the same color you did. The dictionary definition of "consumer price index" will not tell you how to reproduce the consumer index used by the United States. The subtleties of these and other nonoperational definitions are discussed later when we define "causality."

There have been heated philosophic arguments about operational definitions and their place in science.[2] The argument is brought out by e. e. cummings (p. 190).

> (While you and i have lips and voices which
> are kissing and to sing with
> who cares if some oneeyed son of a bitch
> invents an instrument to measure Spring with?

In these lines, the poet catches the essence of empirical science, even though he denounces its effects. With ingenious empirical research designs and instruments, meteorologists actually do measure spring. But notice that the researcher must specify which readings on the instruments he will consider to denote spring. That specification is his operational definition.

Another side of the matter is given by W. Kruskal, a statistician turned rhymemaker:

> "You'll care if some four-eyed bastard
> invents a better forceps for the resulting infant,
> or even if, by measuring Spring, the slob
> eventually figures out how to prolong it."

2. What has been said so far does *not* reflect an allegiance to the philosophic position called "operationism." The substitute label "working definition" suggested by Selltiz, *et al.* (p. 43), avoids many unnecessary associations of the term "operational definition." But I shall stick to the common usage.

Numbers and mathematics can be an aid to clarity. But unwise use of mathematical symbolism can make matters more confusing:

> Contrary to common belief it is sometimes easier to talk in mathematics than to talk in English; this is the reason why many scientific papers contain more mathematics than is either necessary or desirable. Contrary to common belief it is also often less precise to do so. For mathematical symbols have a tendency to conceal the physical meaning that they are intended to represent; they sometimes serve as a substitute for the arduous task of deciding what is and what is not relevant; . . . It is true that mathematics cannot lie. But it can mislead.

> However, the dangers of over-indulgence in formula spinning are avoided if mathematics is treated, wherever possible, as a language into which *thoughts may only be translated after they have first been [clearly] expressed in the language of words.* The use of mathematics in this way is indeed disciplinary, helpful, and sometimes indispensable. (Kapp quoted by Georgescu-Roegen, p. 1)

Cummings would have been disturbed if he had known that scientists also measure love—sometimes with the very kisses that he mentioned. "Love" can mean many things, of course, and the operations for measuring any facet of it are far from obvious. Consider, for example, measuring the amount of love between mother and child by the number of times the mother kisses the child. In this case, we certainly have established an operational definition of *something* when we specify counting the number of kisses. But few of us would believe that the number of kisses is a perfect and true index of the amount of "love"; in fact, there may be cases in which number of kisses and amount of love may be inversely related. But for some purposes it might be a *useful* index.

Dispute has arisen because some scientists have taken a position implying that love *is* the kiss count and that the word "love" can have no meaning apart from the description of an operation. Whether or not this general position is wise, a less extreme position is possible; that is, that hypothetical (or theoretical) concepts can certainly be useful in science (and in common language) even though they are not operationally defined. The very fact that one can have in mind a concept that is *not yet* defined operationally but toward which one reaches with an operational definition is proof that concepts can have meaning even though they are not operationally defined. For example, you and I probably can have some meaningful conversation about happiness even though it is a many-sided and imprecise concept to us both. And, when introducing an operational definition of happiness, I may talk about the concept in general terms. That general discussion is a "hypothetical" concept of happiness or, as B. Underwood calls it, a "literary definition" (pp. 54–55).[3]

When you come to execute a piece of empirical research, all the concepts

---

3. A concept may also form part of a deductive theory, even though it is not operationally defined. In that case we call it a "theoretical concept" or an "unobservable."

in the research and all the important words used in the write-up *must* be defined in terms of operations. About this point there should be no argument: If, for example, you are to study love empirically, there must be *something* that you can count or measure that will stand for love; otherwise you simply cannot do any empirical research.

What is the relationship between the operationally-defined kiss count and love? Is there a *logical* relationship between the two? Does "love" mean something apart from a kiss count? Is "happiness" only the answer to a question on a questionnaire? Troublesome disagreement can be avoided by saying that the kiss count stands for love in at least a partial way and that the questionnaire answer is a partial proxy for happiness. We need not assert that the kiss count *is* love or that it is *all* there is to the concept of love. We can agree that there may be *other* measures that stand for other aspects of love, while still making good use of the operational definition. "Basically, an operational definition asserts only that a phenomenon has been reliably measured" (Underwood, p. 62). Whenever you complete the sentence "I measured it by . . . ," referring to a variable, you have provided an operational definition of the variable.

The relationship between the operationally-defined kiss count concept and the hypothetical concept "love" can never be pinned down logically. Rather, the relationship is one of good judgment and scientific artistry. A wise scientist develops operationally-defined concepts that are good "proxies" (that is, that stand for the hypothetical concept). But a proxy can never be perfect and complete; it cannot represent all aspects of the hypothetical term.

Repeatability (replicability) is a major characteristic of scientific research. And operational definitions help make it possible for other researchers to repeat exactly what one researcher has done. This is the key property of operational definitions.

2. Numbers and Operational Definitions

Now let us talk about numbers. Such a suggestion has the unfortunate effect of frightening some of you nearly out of your wits. Relax; this discussion will not trouble you.

"How far is it to New York?" the traveling man asks you next. He is again annoyed when you answer, "a long way," because what is a long way to you might be a short way to him or vice versa. But just putting the distance into numbers is not enough. He will still be confused if you tell him "three short ways."

You might do a little better if you told him it was 3,382,000 cubits to New York—provided he has studied his Bible carefully. The Bible, however, is not clear about the length of a cubit, so describing the distance in cubits might still be confusing. And if the traveling man has never read the Bible he has even less information than if you said, "a long way."

"About 950 miles, or 860 miles on the old road if you want to go that way," is a very satisfactory answer. The traveling man will know what you mean, and he will be able to figure how much time and how much gas it will take him to get there.

Behind every numerical measurement lies an operational definition. A very precise interpretation of "three feet long" is "put three foot rulers end to end, and the distance in question is from one end of the foot rulers to the other." Many years ago, the operational definition of "three feet long" was cruder. It was "Put the heel of your left foot on a mark on the ground, put your right foot directly in front of your left foot, and then your left foot in front of your right foot. Then compare the thing you are measuring against the distance between the mark on the ground and the toe of your left foot."

Now an example. Assume you must determine what proportion of the children in Lincoln County live on farms. How should you go about it? Your first impulse is to answer "Go and look at all the farms." Or if you are slightly wiser you might say, "Look at a sample of the farms." But those are unsatisfactory answers, as we shall see.

For convenience in discussion let us narrow the problem to determining how many children live on just a *single* farm, say the old Carey place. You send a girl to look at it, and she comes back with the answer, "two children." But then you wonder—did she count *all* the children and *only* the children? You had never told her whom she should consider a child, that is, at what age a child stops being a child, and you have never told her whether to count infants as children. Now you must make those decisions. You send her out again, and she returns and says, "Well, there are two children playing on the road near the house but not on the farm land itself." Should you count them or not?

You had never told her whom she should consider a child that is, at what such data collectors), a rule for deciding whether children live or do not live on a farm, in order to cover children visiting on the farm or visiting away from the farm. Then you must instruct her about whether a particular place is to be considered a farm (does the land have to be farmed in order for the place to be a farm?) and so on. You must give her instructions that will cover almost every possible situation in which she may have doubt, plus the important general instruction to ask you for further instructions about any situation that the rules do not cover. Notice that each of your instructions tells her *how to perform an operation.* "Ask 'do you live here?'" is an instruction to perform the operation of asking. The operation to determine whether a farm is being farmed is not obvious; for example, does a small patch of vegetable garden make it a farm?

Other language need not always be as precise as the language of science. The glory of poetry and religious language often is that many meanings are possible, and the reader may find the meaning that satisfies one's own heart. Legal decisions are often purposely ambiguous; sometimes a judge writes a decision that will not bind future generations or reduce their flexibility, using "words that trail rainbows but disguise his meaning," in Oliver Wendell Holmes' lovely description (Rosenfeld).

It is easier to be vague than to be specific or numerical, as you know if you have ever tried to evade a difficult examination question. Vague and empty language, which J. Barzun calls "hokum," may go undetected elsewhere but it is fatal in research.

> Hokum is the counterfeit of true intellectual currency. It is words without meaning, verbal filler, artificial apples of knowledge. . . . Words should point to things, seen or unseen. But they can also be used to wrap up emptiness of heart and lack of thought. (Barzun, p. 25)

J. Locke long ago diagnosed the difficulty:

> . . . [H]e that shall well consider the errors and obscurity, the mistakes and confusion, that are spread in the world by an ill use of words, will find some reason to doubt whether language, as it has been employed, has contributed to the improvement or hindrance of knowledge amongst mankind. . . . This, I think I may at least say, that we should have a great many fewer disputes in the world, if words were taken for what they are, the signs of our ideas only, and not for things themselves. ("Essay on the Human Understanding," Part III, Chapter 10)

As a test of precision, state your research procedure as a written set of instructions to a *layman*. If the average person can follow your instructions and then return to you with the correct data you want to gather, then you have stated your research design well.

A class exercise dramatizes how difficult it is to write even the simplest set of instructions in unambiguous language. Students work in pairs. Each student leaves the classroom for five minutes and counts any set of objects in the rest of the building—perhaps the number of chandeliers on the first floor, the number of doors to the building, the number of stairs in the north staircase, or anything of which there is more than one. Then each student writes a set of instructions for his partner that he hopes will lead the partner to count exactly what he did and to arrive at the same answer. The partners then exchange instructions and carry them out.

The results are often funny. One person counts five statues on the first floor; the partner counts none. Why? The instructions said "black statues," and the partner did not think the statues were exactly black. One person counts fifteen chandeliers on the first floor; the partner counts none. Why? What one partner called the first floor the other called the basement. One person counts eight staircases, and the partner counts two staircases. Why? One person counts the stairs between each floor as a staircase; the other counts the stairs from top floor to bottom floor as a staircase. And so it goes, showing how difficult it is to write *any* set of instructions, that is, an operational definition, that will really be satisfactory.

The language of empirical science has much similarity to the language that a witness is permitted to use in court: no hearsay, no speculation, what the witness himself observed and *only* what he observed. The empirical researcher must transform the vague, the unspecified, the abstract, into the specified and concrete, even though precision is hard work and all of us are lazy.

Trouble with scientific language also arises because of wrong notions about the relationship of words and things. Most people assume that, if there is a word, there is also a thing that corresponds to the word. If that were so, finding the right word would be a matter of searching through dictionaries and rule books until you found the right word for any thing or vice versa. This attitude is fostered by our laws and by the rules that parents must make for children as they are growing up. The state and city ordinances tell you, as they must, exactly what "speeding" is. And our immigration laws are precise about what makes a person "American." But, if you are doing a research study on speeding, the legal definition will probably not help you. Instead, you will have to make your own definition, a definition that is operational, so that you can work with it and communicate it to others. And the definition must fit your particular research needs. And, if you are studying Mexican musicians, you will have to decide whether a pianist born and brought up in Russia but who now holds Mexican citizenship is a Mexican musician. The legal definition of "Mexican" will not suffice; nor can you use an operational definition that someone used in a study of Mexican exports.

The crucial idea is that *you must create your own definitions*—no one can do it for you. And the words do not have meaning—at least for the purpose of your study—until *you* give them meaning. On the other hand, one must try to use words in a manner that other people can understand. It is seldom sensible to coin words or to use familiar words in unfamiliar ways, and whenever possible you should use *exactly* the same operational definitions as previous writers in the field so that your work may be compared with theirs.

In applied research for clients, one often has trouble getting the client to be specific about what he wants to find out. If the client says, "Find out how to improve our advertising operation," the researcher cannot answer him *as a researcher*. (He may act in the role of consultant, but that is not research.) The researcher must find out whether the client wants to know the optimum *amount* of advertising or the best *type* of advertising, or what. The same is true in applied research for government agencies. It should be a *policy* decision whether the City of Los Angeles orders research done on how badly off is a minority group in housing, employment, or both, though the researcher may advise on which of the research projects would be most fruitful and feasible.

Chapter 32 contains further discussion of definitions and takes up the problem of defining the important term "causal."

3. Validity and Reliability

Every piece of research aims to produce an answer to a scientific question. And it is reasonable to ask just *how good* an answer the research provides. This section is about concepts that may be used in judging how good the answer is.

Validity is the overall concept used to refer to how good an answer the study yields. If the answer given by the research is likely to be sound, the research is said to be valid. The concept of validity may be applied to the investigation as a whole, or it may be applied to one or another aspect of the study. The rest of this section and much discussion throughout the book should help you to judge whether a study is valid and its conclusions sound.

Reliability is one of the constituent elements of validity. Reliability is the extent of random variation in the results of the study. Wildly unreliable results cause a study to be invalid. For example, if an intelligence test sometimes yields a high I.Q. score and sometimes a low I.Q. score for the same child, the results of the test are unreliable, and any study that employs the test is invalid.

A subconcept of validity that applies to the research as a whole is *construct validity* or *external validity*. No matter how accurate and error-free the research, the study may be quite inapplicable to the original question. For example, American I.Q. tests may be invalid for measuring the intellectual capacity of children in other cultures. Or a sample of prison convicts is probably invalid for study of the sex behavior of all Americans.

A study may also be invalid because its *internal* procedures are invalid. For example, a study of the effects of early stair-climbing training on a group of infants is invalid unless the results are compared with those from a group of infants who received no training. The results of such a "control group" will indeed reveal that the training has no long-run effect; the untrained group soon catches up with the trained group.

An important cause of overall unreliability—and therefore a cause of invalidity—is a too-small sample. For example, a sample of ten people, no matter how representative, will give unreliable results for a Presidential election poll, because different samples of size ten will give different answers on such a close issue.

The constituent elements of a study may also be described as "valid" or "invalid," "reliable" or "unreliable." Let us concentrate on operational definitions and measuring devices. A specified set of conditions, that is, a definition or a measuring device, is reliable if the same input always leads to the same output. Reliability is roughly the same as *consistency* or *repeatability*. The concept applies to *either* operational definitions or to measuring devices.

A good operational definition is very reliable; that is, applying the definition produces the same result every time. And a weighing scale is reliable if it shows exactly the same reading every time a given iron bar is placed upon it. An I.Q. test is reliable if people get the same score when they are tested twice. Good operational definitions of "children," "live," and "farm" will lead *any* person to count the same number of children at a sample of dwelling places.

It is easy enough to check the reliability of a merchant's scale with repeated weighings of the same iron bar. But checking the reliability of an I.Q. test is more difficult. For example, most people do better the second time they take a given test. One of many ways to check the reliability of the I.Q. test is to split the test into two halves and examine whether the scores on the halves are similar.

An operational definition or measurement can be very reliable but still be worthless. For example, if the weighing scale always reads 10 percent higher than a fair scale, the readings are no good. And if an I.Q. test has excellent split-half reliability but does not give higher scores to the students who later do better in school, the test is not useful. Another example: A thoroughly reliable operational definition for "love" is "Add the weights of a boy and a girl. If their combined weights total over 322 pounds, they will be said to be in love." But this measurement does not correspond at all to the hypothetical concept of love you are trying to measure, and therefore it has no meaning.

All these worthless operational definitions are said to "lack validity." A definition (or a classification or measurement) is valid if it really classifies or measures what you want it to classify or measure. An I.Q. test is valid if it really does measure the future school success of students, because that is what it is intended to measure. A scale weighs validly if its weights agree with the commonly accepted weights of the Bureau of Standards in Washington. A pre-election Presidential poll is valid if it accurately picks the election winner. A count of the gold bars in Fort Knox is valid if it reveals how many bars "really" are there. (The best answer we can get might be off by $20 million in either direction, according to O. Morgenstern.) An operational definition of love is valid if all those people who fit it seem to the experts in the field to be in love.

There is no simple rule for deciding whether an operational definition is valid. Rather, the decision calls upon your judgment and scientific wisdom. Often a good test is whether you can persuade other scientists that the definition is valid. And of course the validity must depend upon the purpose of the study. For example, it is easy to make up a very reliable operational definition of "the faculty of the University of Illinois." You could use any of these definitions: the full professors listed in the staff directory; all assistant, associate, and full professors in the directory; all members of the faculty club; all buildings-and-grounds employees listed in the directory; or any other easily defined group. But if your purpose is to survey "faculty" opinion about an important campus issue, it is not so clear which definition to use. Should you include teaching assistants? research associates? retired professors? and so on. A bad choice will give you an invalid definition. But what is the criterion of validity? The most valid definition in this case probably includes *those people whom your listener or reader will have in mind when you tell him what the faculty opinion is.*

Another example of how validity depends upon purpose: In Chapter 32 we shall see how difficult it is to construct a valid operational definition of "cause and effect." Furthermore, a definition of cause and effect that is valid for a decision maker is *not* necessarily valid for a scientist.

Often there are several possible ways to validate an operational definition, and the validating method is best that gets "closest" to what the definition is intended to define or measure. One can think of a hierarchy among various validating methods. For example, no one would disagree that the *ultimate* validation of an I.Q. test is that it predicts well which students do well in school and which students do poorly. But another approach to validating an I.Q. test is to compare its results to those of well-established I.Q. tests. The latter validation is less powerful than the school-success validation, for it is less direct and therefore more subject to flaw; the well-established tests themselves may not be very valid. One method may be said to provide stronger validation than another method in a given situation; in another situation the relative validation power of the same two methods might be the reverse.

Chapter 6 discusses the specifics of the validation process.

4. Writing Scientific Reports

The "mere" writing up of results may strike you as a minor part of the research process. But do not skip this section; the subject is not trivial at all. The written description of research is part of the very warp and woof of the research itself. For example, in some kinds of research—especially experimental and survey tests of sharply stated hypotheses—you can often write up the report of the research before the data are collected, except for the actual results. This exercise helps you to think through a study and often uncovers difficulties in theory and design that would otherwise appear later and cause trouble.

If you write up the report early and if you write it up well, you have done much of the research job.

Research reports, and research proposals too, must follow the specifications that we have set forth for scientific language. Scientific communication must be *objective*, rather than *subjective*, in both the words and the concepts used. "Subjective" here means the thoughts that are inside one person's head and that are unavailable for checking by other people. "Objective" here means those statements that are *public* and checkable. ("Public knowledge" and "private knowledge" may be better terms respectively than "objective" and "subjective.")

I will not give you a set of step-by-step instructions on how to write up a research project. Such a set of procedures might force all your write-ups into that format whether or not it fits the needs of a particular project. And *no* format will fit *all* research. When preparing to write up a piece of research, read well-done pieces of research in your field, and choose as models one or more that resemble your project. Notice that no one format is used by all writers, even within a single restricted journal in a branch of psychology, say. There may be some very general similarities of format, but the organization of each report is tailored to the particular needs of each research project.

An important issue in many write-ups is how much to generalize from the data or how much to qualify the conclusions. Some researchers are super-cautious about drawing inferences about their work or about hazarding the inferences in print. For example, to report a finding that men have more dreams of violence than women do but to claim that, because the sample all came from Illinois the results cannot therefore be generalized beyond Illinois, is ridiculous. Or, a biologist who finds that cigarette tars cause cancer in rats may refuse to suggest that cigarette tars may well have the same effect in humans. By so doing you may protect yourself from criticism, but you may also lessen the importance of your work by failing to make it relevant to researchers who are interested in cancer in humans. (Furthermore, there is an unattractive hypocrisy in such overcautiousness. We all know damn well that the only reason one studies the effect of cigarette smoking in rats is because of the possible implications for human beings.) Later, and particularly in the section on experiments, there is further discussion of when it is and when it is not reasonable to draw general inferences from samples.

On the other hand, the researcher also has an obligation to keep the reader from jumping the rails and drawing unfounded inferences. A. Kinsey, *et al.*, devoted much of their long explanation of method to limitations of data and method. But the officially appointed statisticians who reviewed the work (Cochran, *et al.*,) gently chided them for not repeating the cautions regularly in the rest of the book so that the casual reader would not be misled.

Sometimes when you have a great many data you must decide how much to include in your report. Err on the side of reporting too much rather than too little, especially in appendixes. You can always cut out the excess.

A word about style in scientific writing. One of the purposes of the founding of the great Royal Society of London in 1660 was to encourage writers on scientific matters not to write special-pleading polemics full of loaded adjectives, but rather to use unemotional and unbiased language. This purpose is indeed admirable, but it has had some unintended and unfortunate consequences. For example, many scientists now refuse to write in the first person, which means that they must often forgo the active voice in their sentences. The passive voice often leads to tortured and ludicrous sentences that resemble a person's contortions when he tries to hide his face from a spotlight; the movement is not graceful. Furthermore, if a writer is artificially restricted from using such linguistic constructions as "I," there are fewer options and fewer tools available, and precision must diminish.

Scientific caution and the desire to avoid criticism also make scientific writing more complicated and sap its vigor and pleasantness. But, when we must make a choice, it is unhappily true that vigor and stylistic grace are the less important of the virtues.

5. Communicating with Yourself

Being precise, specific, and concrete in communicating *with yourself* is also important. To fail to make detailed plans is unwittingly to make important decisions by postponing or ignoring them. Not deciding may mean not doing, and what is not done now may not be possible at a later stage.

Specify as much as you can in advance. Draw up the tables for which you wish to collect data; you will be surprised how hard it is to do this, a sure tip-off that your thinking is too vague. When possible, it is wise to write up the research report prior to collecting data as an aid to good design planning. I cannot overemphasize the importance of doing these and similar exercises *early* in your research work.

One's self-communication is improved by subjecting oneself to the same discipline and requiring the same precision as for communication with someone else. Make liberal use of pencil and paper. Write down what you think you are thinking. You will constantly be surprised at how this method helps to clarify your thinking.

> . . . [V]ery often, a problem seemed settled, everything fixed and clear, till I began to write down a short preliminary sketch of my results. And only then, did I see the enormous deficiencies, which would show me where lay new problems, and lead me on to new work. In fact, I spent a few months between my first and second expeditions, and over a year between that and the subsequent one, in going over all my material, and making parts of it almost ready for publication each time, though each time I knew I would have to rewrite it. . . . I have written up an outline of the Kula institution at least half a dozen times while in the field and in the intervals between my expeditions. Each time, new problems and difficulties presented themselves. (Malinowski, p. 13)

It also helps to ask and answer such questions as "What do I really want to know?" and "What am I really trying to find out?" Returning to these fundamentals when you get stuck often clears up confusions like magic.

Your jottings in the course of the work serve as a better record of your research than your memory does. For example, when you make a decision to exclude or include a subject or datum in the sample, write down why. Later you will need this note when you write up the research. Write down all the other observations of what you see, and note what you did and why you did it. These notes are like the laboratory notebook that is of such crucial importance to natural scientists.

6. Honesty in Scientific Reporting

Scientific research is a human enterprise. And the individual researcher often has a stake in obtaining some particular outcome from the research—

because the particular outcome will confirm his theory, or will be consistent with her ideological biases, or will be sensational and make him famous, or whatever. In this as in all other situations where there are interests at stake, there is pressure to produce the desired outcome, whether or not it can be found in the data.

Some scientific dishonesty[4] is flagrant, as in the example of Cyril Burt, the leading British psychologist of his time. His findings apparently showed that the intelligence of blacks, women, and lower-class Englishmen is lower than that of whites, men, and the British middle class. These findings have had a great influence on psychologists, on the lay public, and on social policy. A few years after Burt's death in 1971, unlikely coincidences were found in the data that led to the discovery of many other discrepancies, and to the judgment that his findings are scientifically worthless. Burt's motive apparently was that he wished to support his personal beliefs about the intelligence of various groups.

Another famous example is that of Piltdown man, the supposed remains of a prehistoric human that was concocted of modified modern remains in 1908 and not exposed until 1953.

Some other well-known recent examples from outside the social sciences include the following:

Item: A scientist at the Sloane-Kettering Institute painted dark patches on white mice to make his colleagues believe he had perfected a way to make skin grafts between non-twins.

Item: The Food and Drug Administration charged a major pharmaceutical manufacturer, G. D. Searle & Company, with falsifying the scientific data upon which claims of the safety of two drugs and an artificial sweetener were based. Searle's research methods, according to an F.D.A. report, were so careless that reliable scientific conclusions could not be derived from them.

Item: A promising student at Harvard University reported experiments showing that something in the blood of one animal can be injected into another, transferring immunity to certain foreign substances. No other research group was able to reproduce the striking results. The line of research was abandoned amid publicly voiced suspicions that the test animals had been tampered with.

Item: A Pennsylvania State University chemist said that he had evidence that the sex scents of insects vary according to what the bugs eat. If true, his "finding" would destroy a major new avenue of research on safe pest controls. His university touted the results loudly. However, the chemist's co-workers examined the same data and repeated the experiments and found no evidence for the claim. The chemist said that he still believed in his theory and would repeat his experiments. (Rensberger, p. 1)

You are not likely to be tempted to commit such out-and-out major frauds. Your temptation may come when your data show a reasonably con-

---

4. The following paragraphs are based on Rensberger.

sistent picture, in accord with the outcome you desire, and then some frag-
ment of conflicting evidence crops up—perhaps an experiment with a few
rats of a different strain, or a sample of data from a census prior to the one
you have been working on, or an analysis using a different mathematical
form that you have assumed to be less appropriate than the line of analysis
you have chosen. Or the conflicting evidence may be results contained in a
forgotten article in an obscure journal by an unknown author that you just
happen to come across.

Then the temptation is simply to convene a short conference with yourself, in which all sides of your mind arrive at a consensus that it would be
scientifically appropriate to ignore the additional and conflicting evidence
on the grounds that it really is not relevant. I doubt that any practicing
empirical researcher is so saintly that such a thought has never crossed his
or her mind. My informal interviewing reveals that nine out of ten researchers admit it, and the tenth is a damned liar. Even Gregor Mendel, the
founder of modern genetics, is now thought not just to have contemplated
touching up the data, but actually, to have falsified them to make them fit
his theory—though the theory was in fact correct.

The prevalence of the problem is suggested by this observation:

Last spring a graduate student at Iowa State University required data of a
particular kind in order to carry out a study for his master's thesis. In order to
obtain these data he wrote to 37 authors whose journal articles appeared in APA
journals between 1959 and 1961. Of these authors, 32 replied. Twenty-two of
these reported the data misplaced, lost, or inadvertently destroyed. Two of the
remaining 11 offered their data on the conditions that they be notified of our
intended use of their data, and stated that they have control of anything that we
would publish involving these data. . . . We met the former condition but refused the latter for those two authors since we felt the raw data from published
research should be made public upon request when possible and economically
feasible. Thus raw data from 9 authors were obtained. From these 9 authors,
11 analyses were obtained. Four of these were not analyzed by us since they
were made available several months after our request. Of the remaining 7
studies, 3 involved gross errors. One involved an analysis of variance on transformed data where the transformation was clearly inappropriate. Another
analysis contained a gross computational error so that several F ratios near one
were reported to be highly significant. The third analysis incorrectly reported
insignificant results due to the use of an inappropriate error term. . . . (Wolins,
p. 657)

Doctoring the data can ruin your reputation, and it can cause you great
suffering from pangs of conscience. On the positive side, some of the world's
great discoveries have come from researchers who took apparently conflicting data seriously and pursued the discrepancy, rather than sweeping it
under the rug, thereby leading to great new findings.

How you conduct yourself about such personal matters as acknowledging
and sharing credit with people who help you or work with you is a related
topic that I will not presume to lecture you about.

7. Summary

Theoretical scientific discussions must be converted into operationally-defined terms when empirical research is performed. One key test of an operational definition is whether readers and subsequent researchers will know exactly what empirical operations you performed, so that these operations can be repeated precisely. This is the test of *reliability*.

A good operational definition must also refer closely to the theoretical concept you are interested in; a reliable but irrelevant operational definition is not *valid* and hence worthless. A good operational definition also has little bias in measurement.

More generally, an empirical study is valid if it yields a reliable answer to the question to which it is addressed, that is, if the research purpose is well met.

Good scientific communication claims neither too much nor too little for the findings of a study. Good scientific writing is clear and vigorous, but relatively objective and unemotional.

EXERCISES

1. An operational definition should suit the purposes of the particular study in which it is to be used. Briefly describe a research project in which each of the following terms might be used, and then create a satisfactory operational definition of the term: "learning"; "part-time job"; "religious rite"; "aggressiveness"; "personal income"; "vacation"; "memory"; "war"; "bartender"; "most popular man on your college campus"; "money" (be careful not to stop with just currency); "tribal loyalty"; "vocational education"; "Negro."

2. Work out an operational definition for the concept "United States resident" for use in a census in this country. Do the same for an underdeveloped African country. Pay special attention to whether a person lives there on the date of the census, and whether that person ordinarily lives there. Explain the reasons for your operational definitions in terms of the purposes of the censuses.

3. Find five examples of good operational definitions in your major field of interest. Then find five examples of poor operational definitions. Tell why they are good or bad.

4. You want to explore the relationship between the amount of attention mothers give to infants and the extent to which one-year-old babies love their mothers. Define "attention" and "love."

5. You want to test the hypothesis that the introduction of universal literacy into underdeveloped countries leads to rapid social and economic development. Define "introduction" and "development."

6. Read the following quotation. How would you go about constructing operational definitions of the 15 major types of headaches?

Heady with victory over gravity, tooth decay and the atom, laboratory science appears to be gearing up for an assault on mankind's oldest ailment—the headache.

The first report from the battlefront by the Ad Hoc Committee of the Classification of Headache of the National Institute of Neurological Diseases and Blindness lists 15 major types of headache, from migraines to cranial neuralgias. (Champaign-Urbana *Courier*, January 26, 1964, p. 33)

ADDITIONAL READING FOR CHAPTER 2

On operational definitions, see Underwood (Chapter 3). Also see Selltiz *et al.,* rev. ed., pp. 42–44.

On the writing of research reports, especially in sociology, see Whitney (Chapter 16) and Selltiz *et al.,* rev. ed. (Chapter 15); for business and economics, see Berenson and Colton.

Useful notes on research procedure and information about papers, libraries, and so on, may be found in Bart and Frankel (especially for sociologists).

To improve your prose, see *The Elements of Style* by Strunk and White, a clear and pleasant summary of the important rules for good writing.

3 basic concepts of research

1. Variables in General

Variables and parameters are the final forms in which you work with scientific terms and concepts. Therefore, the words "variable" and "parameter"—along with "function"—are the most common words in most scientific discussions.

A variable is not just "some quantity that varies." A variable is a quantity *in which you are interested* that varies in the course of the research or that has different values for different samples in your study. Everything changes sooner or later. But a variable is a factor whose change or difference you study.

Perhaps giving specific examples of "variables" will help.[1] Amount of rain is probably a variable to a meteorologist studying precipitation but not to an astronomer who is studying stars—though the rain may be annoying to the astronomer because it makes the stars invisible. Rain is not likely to be a variable to a biologist studying lung cancer. But rain *might* have something to do with air pollution, which might have something to do with lung cancer, in which case rain would indeed become a variable to the biologist. Temperature and humidity are probably not variables for a psychologist studying intelligence in Chicago school children, but they might well be variables to an anthropologist or economist studying the cultural or economic development of primitive peoples.

---

1. Some social scientists use "relevant variable" as "variable" is used here. I think it is less confusing, however, to consider that irrelevant variables are not variables at all.

The researcher chooses his variables, not the other way around; the world about the researcher does not tell him what aspects of it to study. For example, it is entirely a decision of the researcher to study the effects of broken homes on juvenile delinquency rather than the relationship between neurosis and juvenile delinquency. Both choices may be good ones, and the choice is not forced by the nature of reality. Of course, the good researcher does not choose his variables at random or casually; rather, he chooses them with extreme care, for such choices are among the crucial ones he must make. Poorly-chosen variables yield useless results.

2. The Dependent Variable

The dependent variable (actually there may be several dependent variables, but that is unusual) is that quantity or aspect of nature whose *change or different states* the researcher wants to understand or explain or predict.[2] In cause-and-effect investigations, the effect variable is the dependent variable. If you wish to investigate whether there is any relationship between the mother's smoking cigarettes and the weight of the baby, then cigarette smoking is an independent variable.

3. The Independent Variable

The best definition of an **independent variable** is a variable *whose effect upon the dependent variable you are trying to understand*. There may be several independent variables. You may simultaneously investigate the effect of the mother's cigarette smoking, the mother's exercise, parents' weights, and other variables upon the weight of the baby.

In some types of research one cannot label the variables as dependent and independent. For example, a study of the distribution of babies by weight at birth has only the single variable of weight, as long as you do not introduce independent variables to explain why some babies weigh six pounds and others weigh seven pounds. A psychological-anthropological study of the types of personalities found among the Navahos, and the U.S. Census, are other examples of studies without independent variables.

4. Parameters

The concept of parameter is tricky. A parameter is a quantity that has some importance to a study but that remains *unchanged* in the course of the study. This is why some people say frivolously that a parameter is a variable that does not vary.

To illustrate, Figure 3.1 shows the hypothetical relationship between the

---

2. The terms "explain" and "predict," as well as the related terms "causality," "function," and "scientific law," are distinguished and defined in Chapter 32. For the time being, these words are in a crude sense corresponding to everyday usage.

price of scallions and the quantity of scallions that people buy, produced in a given year.

FIGURE 3.1   **Hypothetical Relationship Between the Price and Production of Scallions**

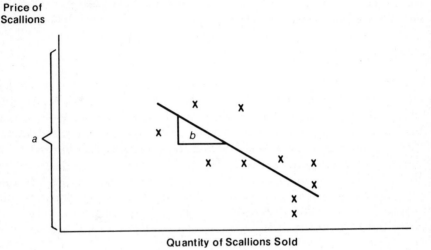

Quantity of Scallions Sold

The crosses represent the quantities sold during periods when various prices prevailed. The straight line is drawn among the crosses as close to as many of them as possible (though there are several ways to do it). The assumption is that each of the crosses may be somewhat in error and that the line represents a better guess than any given observation of how much would be sold at a given price, because the line is based on the information contained in *all* the observed crosses. One might draw curved lines of various shapes also, depending on one's general knowledge of the scallion market, but a straight line is particularly easy to work with.

In algebraic terms, the formula for a straight line is *y* equals *a* plus *bx*. Or, in the example at hand, $q = a + bp$, where q is the quantity of scallions sold and p the price of scallions and where a and b are measured from the diagram or estimated statistically. The algebraic constants a and b are *parameters* for the scallion market and are assumed to stay the same no matter what the price of scallions is. With the help of the parameters, you can predict how many scallions will be sold for any price you pick.

Of course the parameters may change. In another country or another decade, more or fewer scallions might be sold at any given price than the line in Figure 3.1 indicates. But, *for the particular set of circumstances you are working with,* a and b are assumed to be constant, and that is why parameters are called "constant variables."

A parameter is a property of a whole universe[3] and *not* only of the sample

3. See pages 126–127 for a discussion of the meaning of the term "population" or its synonym in research terminology, "universe."

you observe. The term "statistic" is applied to the sample's counterpart of the parameter. For example, if you poll a sample of Kansas voters and find that 56 percent expect to vote Democratic in the next election, that figure is a statistic. On the basis of the sample you might *estimate* that 56 percent of *all* voters expect to vote Democratic, but your estimate of the parameter based on the statistic could be in error. The *actual* percentage of all voters who expect to vote Democratic is the parameter.

5. The Functional Form

The mathematical-logical concept of function is very different from the anthropological-sociological concept of the same name.[4] In the mathematical-logical sense with which we are concerned here, to say that "y is a function of x" means only that the magnitude of y *depends upon* the magnitude of x. The statement implies that y is the dependent variable and x (or several x's) the independent variable(s).

Functional relationships are written in algebraic notation, for example, $y = f(x_1, x_2, x_3)$ if there are three independent variables. This algebra is to be read "y is a function of x_1, x_2, and x_3" or "y depends upon x_1, x_2, and x_3" or "y is the dependent variable whose values (magnitudes) depend upon the values (magnitudes) of x_1, x_2, and x_3."

Another letter, perhaps g or h, could replace f, just as w or z might be used instead of x; the choice of letters is quite arbitrary.

In the scallion example, (quantity of scallions produced) = f (price of scallions) is translated as "the quantity of scallions produced depends upon (is a function of) the price of scallions."

The causal direction of the functional relationship—that is, which variable is put on the left side as the dependent variable, and which is put on the right as the independent variable—is a decision that the researcher makes in light of his or her general knowledge of the subject matter. A given set of variables and data may sometimes be viewed one way, sometimes the other, and sometimes both ways together. For example, in some cases, the price of scallions is seen as the dependent variable, in some cases quantity is seen as the dependent variable, and in some cases—where there is thought to be mutual causation—both are dependent *and* independent variables. More about this later.

The concept and notation of a function are of enormous value in clarifying ideas. The concept is common in all sciences that have reached the stage of investigating relationships, especially cause-and-effect relationships. (But in types of research that really have no independent variables—especially descriptive research of the census type—the functional form is not appropriate or useful.) Algebraic notation is not necessary to express the functional notion that something depends on something else. As we have seen, this idea can be expressed in words alone by simply indicating which are the

4. R. Merton clearly distinguishes these and other senses of functional relationship (Chap. 1).

dependent and independent variables, and many teachers argue that algebraic notation only confuses the student. I am convinced, however, that the exercise of expressing variables in algebraic functional notation is very useful, even if one goes no further with mathematical analysis.

6. Assumption, Theory, Deduction, Hypothesis, Fact, and Law

Assumption, theory, deduction, hypothesis, and fact are commonly used concepts in science, though they are often confused with one another. Their definitions and the relationships among them can best be brought out in the context of a concrete case in economics, the most effective user among the social sciences of a deductive theoretical apparatus.

a. EXAMPLE 1: INTEREST RATES AND GEOGRAPHY

Problem and Fact. It is an observed *fact* that savings-and-loan interest rates on deposits were higher on the West Coast than on the East Coast or in the Midwest in 1977. The *problem* is to predict what would happen to this difference in the future.

Assumptions. We *assume* first that investors will choose the highest available rate of return among investments that have equal risks, that is, that investors are "rational" in this respect. (Notice that this assumption does *not* imply that human beings are generally rational rather than irrational or that all investors will act rationally. Every economist knows that humans are often irrational, just as many free-falling objects, such as leaves and balloons, do not obey the law of gravity. Rather, this assumption is an "abstraction" or an "ideal type," as M. Weber called it.) Second, we *assume* that there are information flows in the real estate market. (In most problems, the economist goes further and assumes *perfect* information.) Third, we *assume* that there are no barriers to moving money from one part of the United States to another. (This assumption would not be made for movement among countries in an international trade problem.)

An assumption is any statement in this form: "If w holds true—and I assume that it does—then z will happen." There are many types of assumptions. One important distinction is between abstract assumptions that are part of the entire theoretical apparatus, of which we have given three examples, and assumptions that are specific to the case under discussion, such as the *ceteris paribus* clause—which means, in this case, that no unusual force is operating to confuse the situation.[5]

Deduction. We then *deduce* that interest rates—savings-and-loan interest rates in this case—will be the same in all parts of the United States. Given the assumptions, this *deduction* can be made as formally as any deduction

5. For discussion of this distinction, see F. Machlup (1955) and J. Melitz.

in geometry. But of course the deduction holds true only *if* the assumptions are well chosen—just as a calculation that uses the formula for a square to determine the area of a plot of land will be correct only if the plot of land has the shape of a square.

The test of a deduction—and of the theory within which it takes place—is that *all* scientists in a given field must be able to agree that the deduction is valid *if* the assumptions are well chosen. A deduction is only an exercise in logic, just as is the arithmetic statement that $3 \times 15 = 45$.

Theory. If there are well-established assumptions in a field, and if there is an apparatus that permits such a deduction as we have made, then one may talk about a body of theory. If so, a speculative statement (conjecture) must be related to this whole body of theory if it is to be called "theoretical." In other fields, any conjecture or deduction from general experience is called **theory.** More about this in Chapter 5.

Hypothesis. We then translate the deduction into a *hypothesis* or *conjecture* that can be tested empirically. In this case, the hypothesis is that interest rates for the same type of deposit will *become* more nearly equal in various parts of the country as time passes. The reasoning is that there must have been some unusual and sudden conditions that created a temporary imbalance among parts of the country. By deduction, the rates will be equal if there is not some continuing reason why they should be unequal, and we assume that there is no such continuing force. Therefore, the interest rates can be expected to become more equal. This is the hypothesis to be tested empirically.

Not all hypotheses are deduced from theories, though most of them rest on facts and assumptions. One might look around and hypothesize that tall girls get married earlier than short girls. This is indeed a scientific hypothesis, but it comes directly from observation and unformalized intuition rather than as a deduction from a body of theory. And a hypothesis is not the same as a theory, though many writers use the two terms almost interchangeably (for example, M. Friedman, pp. 3–46). A hypothesis (conjecture) is a single statement that attempts to explain or to predict a single phenomenon, whereas a theory is an entire system of thought that refers to many phenomena and whose parts can be related to one another in deductive logical form.

An unfortunate confusion in usage pervades this book and others, however. We often talk about "theoretical concepts" when we really mean "hypothetical concepts." For example, when discussing an investigation into people's *happiness,* we called the vague and undefined concept *happiness* a theoretical concept—even though it is not part of any theory—to distinguish it from the *empirical* concept (in this case, people's answers to a questionnaire) that will *stand for* the hypothetical concept. But in view of existing practice, to stick to the better usage would only be confusing here. Furthermore, the terms "empirical concept" and "empirical variable" are both used, though they are synonymous, which adds further confusion.[6]

Law. If an empirical test of the hypothesis confirms the hypothesis, the generalization might be called a *law*, provided that the finding is sufficiently *important*. Even if our hypothesis were to be confirmed empirically, it is insufficiently important to be called a "law."

Another example of the related concepts of fact, theory, hypothesis, and empirical test may be found on page 417.

7. Universe and Sample

A **universe** (or population) is some group of people or objects in which you are interested. The group may exist or not exist, and it may be finite or infinite; for example, the universe of students who will be graduated from college in 2010 and thereafter has not yet been born and is infinite.

A **sample** is some *subgroup* of the universe. The purpose of studying a sample is to make some generalization about the universe. The major reason for taking *only* a sample, rather than studying the entire universe, is *cost*, which is discussed in more detail in Chapter 24; studying the entire universe is almost always prohibitively expensive.

There are many kinds of samples, of which the **random** sample is a very important type. A sample is random if every member of the universe stands the same chance[7] of being included in it. (Read this definition again, and make sure you understand it.) Groups chosen on the basis of the researcher's judgment about their similarity or typicality are another type of sample.

Sampling validity and efficiency will be discussed at length in Chapter 9.

8. The Ideal Causal-Study Design

Much—but not all—of social science is the investigation of causal relationships. Therefore, let us consider what is involved in establishing a causal relationship between some dependent variable y and a particular independent variable x. This section is a preview of much that follows about research design.

Determining a causal relationship would ideally be done as follows: The value of the dependent variable y that is observed for any given subject in the study depends on three elements: first, what the subject was like before it was acted upon by the independent variable; second, the particular level (value or strength or variety) of the independent variable's action upon the subject during the study period; and, third, the particular values of all other

6. Sociologists commonly use a slightly different lingo. This book's "empirical variable" is their "indicator," and this book's "hypothetical concept" is just plain "concept" to them.
7. More precisely, the sampling *process* is random if every member of the universe has a *known* chance of being included in the sample.

variables that act upon the subject during the study period, both those in which you may be interested and those that are just interferences. To put it in algebraic notation (which you may skip if you like but which I believe will help you and should not scare you at all):

$$y_i = f(x_{i,1}, x_{i,2} \ldots x_{i,n}; v_{i,1}, v_{i,2} \ldots v_{i,n}; z_{i,1}, z_{i,2}, \ldots z_{i,n}).$$

In this equation y_i is the observed value of the dependent variable for subject i; $x_{i,1}$ is the value of the independent variable x_1 that subject i is exposed to during the study; $x_{i,2} \ldots x_{i,n}$ are other variables in which you may be interested that act upon the subject i during the study period but that we shall ignore now; $v_{i,1}, v_{i,2} \ldots v_{i,n}$ are the influences that acted upon the particular subject i and formed him or her before the study began; and $z_{i,1}, z_{i,2} \ldots z_{i,n}$ are other influences that may affect the outcome of the research (that is, may affect the observed y for a given subject) but which you are *not* interested in. The z's will be called "interfering" or "confounding" variables or, in some contexts, "parameters." (The definitions of all these terms vary somewhat among the people who use them and the situations in which the terms are used.)

For example, consider a study of the effect of the amount of protein in children's diets upon their ability to learn, as indicated by their ability to memorize nonsense syllables. The symbol y_i represents child i's score on a memory test. The symbol $v_{i,1}$ represents the intelligence of her parents, $v_{i,2}$ the quality of her schooling, and so on for other v's. The symbol $x_{i,1}$ is the independent variable, the amount of protein in child i's diet. The symbol $z_{i,1}$ might represent the amount of exercise the child gets during the study period; $z_{i,2}$ might represent the time of the day the memory test is given; $z_{i,3}$ might represent which tester examines and grades the child; and so on for the many other possible z's.

The ideal study is one in which two (or more) groups of subjects, each made up of subjects with exactly the same v qualities, are subjected to two (or more) different levels of independent variable x_i, *ceteris paribus*, that is, while all the other z influences are kept exactly the same for all the subjects in the study. In the example above, it could mean that, say, two equal groups of children (that is, each group containing children with exactly the same personal-background qualities [v] as those in the other group) would have two different amounts of protein in their diets. All would be tested for memory at the same time of day, all would get the same amount of exercise, and so on.

Now we must ask how the researcher can meet these requirements for the ideal study of causal relationship. *First,* how can the personal-background variables be made equal in the two groups? If you can conduct a controlled experiment, this problem in achieving *ceteris paribus* may be solved perfectly, at least in principle, by calling upon the device of *randomization of the assignment of subjects to treatments.* If you were working with rats instead of children (and testing their memories with a device more appropriate to rats than nonsense-syllable learning), you could start with a large collection of rats and could randomly choose which rats would get the high-protein diet and which the low-protein diet. This could be done by giving each rat a number and then assigning the high-protein diet to the first half of the numbers pulled from a hat. If the sample groups were large enough, all the relevant background characteristics (v's) would then be distributed fairly evenly between the high-protein and low-protein groups (the proof of this is the statistical principle known as the "Law of Large Numbers"). This is why the randomization of subjects is a powerful weapon and a crucial principle in carrying out valid studies of causal relationships.

For several reasons a researcher may not be able to achieve this ideal in equating personal-background characteristics. First, the groups of subjects may be too small in number for the Law of Large Numbers to guarantee a decent split of the various characteristics among the two groups. In that case, you may try to *match* the groups by assigning to the two groups subjects that exhibit the characteristics you deem relevant to as nearly equal a degree as possible. Effective matching of experimental groups is not easy to achieve, as we shall see later.

A *second* force that may prevent random assignment of subjects to groups is that the researcher may not have the power to arrange a controlled experiment; that is, it may just be impossible for you to assign people to groups and then subject the groups to experimental treatment—as may well be the case with protein diets and children. One possible (but treacherous) device is to match subjects *after the fact*, that is, to find apparently similar people who *already* have been subjected to one or another of the treatments and then compare them on the y variable. This device will be discussed at length later.

Now we proceed to the part of the causal study that is usually *hardest* to do well, the handling of the interfering variables (z's) that influence the subjects starting at the time when x_1, the independent variable of interest, begins to act, that is, after the study period begins. The first point to remember is that *each z variable must be taken care of separately and explicitly by the researcher.* This situation is unlike the one with the personal-background variables, in which—if experimentation and random assignment of subjects are possible—you can take care of all of them at one fell swoop by assigning subjects randomly to the experimental groups. In the present instance, if you do *not* properly take care of some important z your research may be ruined.

One way to take care of any z variable is to make it a *parameter*, that is, to "hold it constant" and make it the same for all subjects in all the experimental groups. In the protein-memory example, amount of sleep might affect the subject's performances. This factor can be held constant by putting all the subjects in both experimental groups to sleep at the same time and waking them all at the same time. But some variables cannot be held constant in this fashion; in every piece of research there are several such variables. For example, one might want all the children to eat their meals at the same time of day, to have their memories tested at the same time of day, and to have their memories tested by the same examiner. But suppose that it is physically impossible for each child to begin eating at the same moment because of limited feeding facilities, and some children must wait for others to be tested before it is their turn. And unless there is only one examiner, the children must somehow be divided among different examiners. For any one of these variables that cannot be held constant, an effective alternative is to arrange it so that the members of each experimental group are affected *randomly* by the variable. For example, it should be a matter of a coin toss or dice throw whether each child in each group eats on the early or the late shift. Also the order in which the children are tested, and by which examiner, should be arranged with random drawings. These random arrangements will—if the groups are large enough—accomplish much the same result as holding the variables constant, by ensuring that *on the average* the two groups will be affected reasonably equally by each of the z variables. This device may be termed "randomization of interfering variables to avoid confounding" or just "randomization." When the researcher cannot control these variables experimentally, however, difficulties arise.

Earlier I said that there is no automatic way to achieve *ceteris paribus* and to handle *all* the nonrelevant variables, even if one has complete experimental control. The reason should now be clear. The experimenter must be able at least to *identify* each nonrelevant variable that might influence the results so that she can try to hold it constant or randomize its effect; no blanket mechanism handles *all* these nonrelevant variables. And no one's imagination is active enough to think of *all* the possible interfering (confounding) variables. Furthermore, no one's resources are great enough to be able to deal with every possible interfering variable that has even a slight likelihood of being important.

9. Ceteris Paribus[8]

Theoreticians can ignore the *ceteris paribus* problem, or simply salute it. But to arrange affairs so that other things *are* reasonably equal is perhaps the hardest and most important struggle that the empirical researcher must face.

One of the outstanding characteristics of the social sciences is that the subject matter is not static, not fixed, not immutable. In classical physics or chemistry you can usually be confident that what happens today will also happen tomorrow, that what happens in the East will happen in the West, and that what happens to the contents of one test tube will happen again to those of the next test tube. The chemist or physicist seldom needs to worry

8. *Ceteris paribus* is Latin for "other things being equal."

We reduce to inaction all other forces by the phrase "other things being equal": we do not suppose that they are inert, but for the time we ignore their activity. This scientific device is a great deal older than science: it is the method by which, consciously or unconsciously, sensible men have dealt from time immemorial with every difficult problem of ordinary life. (A. Marshall, p. xiv)

that a sample of matter perversely jumped into the hand to be studied just *because* it is different from other samples of matter. But exactly these things occur in social science studies all the time. All such occurrences are "departures from" or "breaches of" *ceteris paribus*. All of them are conditions that the social scientist must overcome in order to "hold everything else constant."

Here are two glaring examples of breaches of *ceteris paribus* that vitiate comparisons:

> According to the census of January 1, 1910, Bulgaria had a total of 527,311 pigs; 10 years later, according to the census of January 1, 1920, their number was already 1,089,699, more than double. But, he who would conclude that there had been a rapid development in the raising of pigs in Bulgaria (a conclusion that has indeed been drawn) would be greatly mistaken. The explanation is quite simply that in Bulgaria, almost half the number of pigs is slaughtered before Christmas. But after the war, the country adopted the "new" Gregorian calendar, abandoning the "old" Julian calendar, but it celebrates the religious holidays still according to the "old" manner, i.e., with a delay of 13 days. Hence January 1, 1910 fell after Christmas when the pigs were already slaughtered, and January 1, 1920, before Christmas when the animals, already condemned to death, were still alive and therefore counted. A difference of 13 days was enough to invalidate completely the exhaustive figures. (O. Anderson in Morgenstern, pp. 46–47)

Doubling of a pig population over ten years is not biologically remarkable, and the Bulgarian data might well be accepted as fact by a person who is unfamiliar with Bulgarian history. This reminds us that in doing sound research there is no substitute for thorough knowledge of one's subject matter plus wide experience of the world.

> We hear of a museum in a certain Eastern city that was proud of its amazing attendance record. Recently a little stone building was erected nearby. Next year attendance at the museum mysteriously fell off by 100,000. What was the little stone building? A comfort station. (Wallis & Roberts, p. 160)

The enormity of these *ceteris paribus* breaches makes it likely that the researcher will find them out and remedy them. More dangerous are the subtle influences that can ruin the research, like those I. Pavlov described:

> The environment of the animal, even when shut up by itself in a room, is perpetually changing. Footfalls of a passer-by, chance conversations in neighboring rooms, slamming of a door or vibration from a passing van, street-cries, even shadows cast through the windows into the room, any of these casual uncontrolled stimuli falling upon the receptors of the dog set up a disturbance in the cerebral hemispheres and vitiate the experiments. To get over all these disturbing factors a special laboratory was built at the Institute of Experimental Medicine in Petrograd, the funds being provided by a keen and public-spirited Moscow businessman. The primary task was the protection of the dogs from uncontrolled extraneous stimuli, and this was effected by surrounding the building with an isolating trench and employing other special structural devices.

Inside the building all the research rooms (four to each floor) were isolated from one another by a cross-shaped corridor; the top and ground floors, where these rooms were situated, were separated by an intermediate floor. Each research room was carefully partitioned by the use of soundproof materials into two compartments—one for the animal, the other for the experimenter. For stimulating the animal, and for registering the corresponding reflex response, electrical methods or pneumatic transmission were used. By means of these arrangements it was possible to get something of that stability of environmental conditions so essential to the carrying out of a successful experiment. (p. 109)

And H. Ebbinghaus summarized the problem as it faced him in his pioneering study of rates of learning and forgetting:

> He who considers the complicated processes of the higher mental life or who is occupied with the still more complicated phenomena of the state and of society will in general be inclined to deny the possibility of keeping constant the conditions for psychological experimentation. Nothing is more familiar to us than the capriciousness of mental life which brings to nought all foresight and calculation. . . . We must try in experimental fashion to keep as constant as possible those circumstances whose influence on retention and reproduction is known or suspected and then ascertain whether that is sufficient. The material [to be learned] must be so chosen that decided differences of interest are, at least to all appearances, excluded; equality of attention may be promoted by preventing external disturbances; sudden fancies are not subject to control, but, on the whole, their disturbing effect is limited to the moment, and will be of comparatively little account if the time of the experiment is extended, etc. (pp. 11–12)

It was for these reasons that Ebbinghaus used nonsense syllables rather than meaningful words or sentences as the stimuli in his experiments.

The point of the *ceteris paribus* idea is that it is not sensible to compare a sample of apples to a sample of oranges if you are trying to find out the effect of two kinds of fertilizer. How would you ever know whether the apples had an especially good season *because* of fertilizer A, or because it was a good season for apples and not for oranges? Analogously, people in Rochester may differ from people in Syracuse, for many reasons. To compare their reactions to different advertisements is to compare the effects on apples and oranges. All other things in Syracuse are not equal to all other things in Rochester, and therefore the simple comparison is flawed.

Of course, it is true that we can *never* get all the other things equal. Even the people *within* Rochester are not exactly like one another, and no two apples in a basket are perfectly alike. The only way that we could get everything *perfectly* equal would be to try the different fertilizers on the *same* tree or to try the different advertisements on the same person. Even then all else would not be equal because a person is not the same person after being exposed to the first advertisement, and the tree is not the same in two successive growing seasons.

We must resign ourselves to the fact that we shall never get all the other things *exactly* equal. Instead, our job is to get other things *as nearly equal as possible* or at least equal *enough* so that we can proceed with the research without hindrance by unexpected and unknown inequalities in the conditions surrounding the research.

10. Summary

This chapter introduces basic concepts in research.

A *variable* is a factor in which you are interested that varies in the course of the research. The *dependent* variable is the quantity whose variation you wish to explain or predict or understand. *Independent* variables are forces whose effect upon the dependent variables you wish to evaluate.

The term *parameter* has two quite different meanings. In one meaning it is a quantity that may affect the research but that you wish to keep immobilized and unchanged throughout the study. In another meaning a parameter is a property of a universe, in contrast to a *statistic*, which is an estimate of the parameter obtained from a sample.

The *functional form* $y = f(x)$ is the basic logical structure of all cause-and-effect research.

Assumption, theory, deduction, hypothesis, fact, and *law* are often-confusing elements of the meld of theoretical and empirical research. Their meaning and use differs from one social science to another.

A *sample* is a group selected from the *universe* (*population*) for the purpose of describing the population. *Randomly-drawn* samples have great advantages but sometimes they are not practical; sometimes matched or judgmental samples are more appropriate.

The ideal design for the study of cause and effect compares the effect of different independent variables upon the dependent variable in randomly chosen sample groups. Irrelevant factors must be controlled to prevent them from ruining the study; that is, there must be no important breaches of *ceteris paribus.*

EXERCISES

1. Give an example of a quantity that is a variable to one researcher but not a variable to another researcher, though it is part of the "environment" of the second researcher's study.

2. Illustrate the concept of parameter in a context other than economic demand analysis.

3. Illustrate the relationship of the concepts of statistic and parameter for a given universe.

4. Express the essence of any three scientific studies in the functional form $y = f(x_1, x_2 \ldots)$. Or, if you have dug in your heels and resist accepting the algebraic functional form, write down the dependent and independent variables for the three studies.

4 types of empirical research

1. Introduction

Students of psychology often think that experimental investigation of cause-and-effect relationships in human or animal behavior constitutes the whole of social-science research. Many students of economics think that the statistical investigation of the past relationship between price and the amount of commodities sold is the only way to do empirical investigation in economics. Some students of anthropology believe that only participant-observers learn anything worthwhile about the social world we live in. Psychoanalysts sometimes act as if no one can claim to understand anything about human behavior without subjecting it to clinical analysis in depth. Students of market research sometimes think that all research involves finding the relationship between particular personal and social characteristics and purchasing behavior. And the other disciplines have pet methods too.

Each of these beliefs has some basis in fact.[1] But one of the main themes of this book is that there are many types of empirical research and that each may be proper for a particular scientific researcher tackling a particular question. "Mere" description by an anthropologist may seem terribly primitive to a psychophysicist, but a wise psychophysicist may sometimes use a simple descriptive technique to good advantage. Conversely, an anthropolo-

---

1. The best way to define the various social-scientific disciplines may well be in terms of their characteristic methods, whereas it seems to me that the natural sciences tend to cluster around substantive problems.

gist who has an imaginative approach to his subject may one day engage in a simple laboratory experiment to test a theory. One should not let one's discipline determine the choice of method; rather, one should fit the method to the problem.

The task of this chapter is to distinguish among and describe the various types of research *problems,* to help you understand the research possibilities of the research question you select. In order to choose the appropriate research *methods,* one must understand the nature of the research question (see Chapter 18) and also the *obstacles to getting knowledge* to answer the question.

This chapter may seem unsatisfying to you because it introduces a great many topics without discussing them thoroughly. More detailed discussion comes later. The purpose of this chapter is primarily *orientation,* to provide a wide overview of the types of work done in social science.

2. Case-Study Descriptive Research

In the beginning, there is description. When one does not know anything at all about a problem, one must understand it in a *general* way before beginning to make specific inquiries about specific aspects of the subject. For example, the early explorer in a new land writes a general description of the appearance of the country, its geography, climate, people, flora, fauna, and much else. Sea captains and missionaries wrote such descriptions of many exotic lands, though too often their reports were anecdotal and shallow. The early explorer chooses to describe what he thinks to be important and interesting, without any rigid rules of scientific evidence. This first description is important because it serves to focus subsequent studies. Geologists later come to study the peculiar stone formations mentioned in the explorer's report. And anthropologists rush to study with great objectivity the extraordinary patterns of mating with foreigners only hinted at therein.

Descriptive research in the form of case studies[2] is usually the jumping-off point for the study of new areas in the social sciences.[3] S. Freud's case history "Observation 1—Miss Anna O." and similar histories of other patients laid the foundation for modern clinical and personality psychologies. Since Freud's original descriptive explorations, there have appeared many other types of studies of the original theories, including observational and questionnaire surveys and experiments. As Freud put it, "the true beginning of scientific activity consists . . . in describing phenomena and [only] then in proceeding to group, classify and correlate them . . ." (Kaplan, p. 78).

Much anthropological research is descriptive, deliberately setting out to create a rounded picture of an entire culture or some broad aspect of it. In

2. Chapter 14 gives some hints on how to go about doing a case study and discusses further the nature of the case study.
3. Census-type studies may also be considered descriptive research, but we shall discuss them under the heading "Measurement and Estimation."

economics the industry case study continues to be done long after economics has left its infancy, though in contemporary industry studies the economist uses sophisticated theories and statistical techniques of description that encompass the other types of research we shall discuss. (This fact shows the difficulty of classifying types of research. We shall also find descriptive research done within frameworks of classification, cause-and-effect, and other methods.)

A business consultant generally begins work with a general description of the situation. But the "operations research" person often skips this stage, immediately narrows down the problem, and tackles it as a more "advanced" type of research. Sometimes this early narrowing-down is successful, but sometimes it causes the operations researcher to miss the essence of the problem.

Some scientists regard descriptive research as only an early stage of research. There is something to this point of view. Descriptive research does not create laws and conclusions that apply beyond the subject matter described. Rather, it provides *clues* for subsequent research to pin down and generalize.

Nevertheless, I think it is unsound to see descriptive research as only a stage. First, a piece of descriptive research can be of important scientific value for itself, even though it cannot be generalized; a study of the aluminum industry, for example, can provide information valuable for such purposes as antitrust evaluations, even though the findings do not apply to all other industries. And, second, the stage view implies that we know what the later stages of research are. I do not think there is solid evidence for such an evolutionary view of science.

The importance of deciding upon and defining the variables in a research study was emphasized in the previous chapter. But a descriptive study does not have a set of clearly delineated dependent and independent variables. The absence of a limited number of well-defined variables distinguishes case-study descriptive research from other types of research.

Students should not *automatically* shy away from descriptive research. Professors often tout students off descriptive projects, however, because they are harder to do well and easier to do atrociously than are other types of research. Descriptive research does not reveal sloppy and brainless work as glaringly as do more "rigorous" types of research. For this reason, other types of research usually make better training exercises than does descriptive research.

Path-breaking descriptive research, such as that of Freud, is especially difficult because one starts with empty hands—no guideposts, no standards, no yardsticks, no intellectual framework, no categories within which to classify what one sees. The researcher's sole resources are whatever concepts he can borrow from other fields and the ordinary words of the common language. (Every word is indeed a concept but not necessarily a concept especially fitted to the phenomena that the researcher will work with.) He must create his own classification and his own guideposts. He must decide what to look at and what to ignore, what to record and what not to record, which clues to follow up and which to drop, what is important and what is valueless. The early descriptive researcher has great freedom, but such great freedom can be terrifying. Once a tradition of descriptive research is established in a field, however, as is now the case in anthropology, there are standards and concepts that the researcher can use.

Chapter 14 gives you some step-by-step advice to help you do case-study descriptive research.

3. Classification Research

Classification is the process of *sorting out* a collection of people or objects and of developing a set of *categories* among which you divide the collection. No sooner does the scientist see several different examples of a given phenomenon than she begins to say, "This one is like that one and both are different from that other bunch." Then she coins common names for those examples that are like one another. The sorting out may come first and the construction of categories (called "taxonomy") afterward, or the order can be reversed (*a priori* classification). Classification as an end in itself is the subject of this section. More frequently classification is a step in some other type of research.

Bacon was an early "imperialist" in the history of science. He viewed all science as within the domain of his favorite scientific method—classification. Nowadays many scientists are not even willing to dignify classification studies with the name "scientific." But in my opinion classification research is still important and always will be. Again, there is room in the house of science for all kinds of problems and methods.

The work of Linnaeus, a scheme for classifying the entire plant world so as to reveal the family relationships of the various species, is an eighteenth-century classic. And for a long time medical research meant little but classification of diseases by their symptoms. Even now classification is important in the advancement of medicine.

PHOBIAS IN BRITONS FALL INTO 130 TYPES

A half million Britons are afraid of things ranging from blood to barbershops, with some even afraid of being afraid. . . . Britain's phobia victims suffer from at least 130 different types of irrational fear. . . .

The . . . British Medical Association and the National Association for Mental Health, said that one of the largest groups was the agoraphobics—people afraid of open spaces. They number 100,000, many of them women fearful of leaving their own homes. . . .

Fear of spiders, matches, green leaves, pictures of ships in distress, birds and feathers, cats, dogs, mice, frogs, toads, wasps, snakes, blood and thunder were among disabilities haunting people. (*New York Times*, Oct. 14, 1969, p. 13)

Another medical-psychological example classifies types of obesity. "Familial obesity" is one category:

Familial obesity—Snacks at any hour on a social basis. Often is a good cook and enjoys own cooking. Other than housekeeping activities, usually leads sedentary existence. Motivation to reduce is poor. Rapport with doctor is good. Tension infrequent. Caloric pattern often follows pattern of entire family. Food is center of family social life. Prognosis good. (Chicago *Daily News*, January 27, 1964, p. 3)

Important classification research is found in all the social sciences. Freud classified the various psychological defense mechanisms. Sociologists classify various kinds of crowds and riots. Political scientists since Aristotle have classified various forms of government. Economists classify markets, pricing schemes, and devices used as barriers to entering markets.

Some classifications are mere catalogues of more-or-less mutually exclusive categories. Other classifications have more "rational" bases. An example of the latter is Ranganathan's "colon classification" scheme for classifying library books according to five master attributes: personality, matter, energy, space, and time.

The two basic tasks in classification work are: (1) constructing the categories and (2) assigning each observation to the appropriate category (or several categories if the classification is multidimensional). "Numerical taxonomy" (see Sneath and Sokal) is the name of a recent statistical approach to classification that can help systematize the process of making classifications.

What is classification research good for? Here are five uses of a classification scheme:

A classification enables one to deal routinely with individual cases.   After a doctor has decided that a patient has smallpox, the treatment is almost automatic. And the authors of the obesity classification report that it has aided them in diagnosing patients for treatment. Without a classification scheme a doctor would have to do an impossible amount of study on each patient before selecting a treatment; the classification scheme enables her to take advantage of the accumulated store of medical knowledge about which treatments aid which diseases.

A classification aids summarization.   Until a political scientist decides to divide countries into "one-party," "two-party," and "multiparty" systems, he cannot count up how many countries there are of each type. After psychiatrists classify patients as "manic-depressive" or "schizophrenic," a researcher can summarize the number of each type observed in various countries. Summaries of this sort provide knowledge of the group as a whole.

A classification makes other scientists aware of differences among the categories.   Whether the categories be species of plants, types of headaches, or varieties of monopolies, classification often leads the other scientists to understand and explain the differences. For example, after Freud classified the various defense mechanisms, it was natural to inquire into why some people repress, others rationalize, still others project, and so on.

The classification may contain within itself the explanation of phenomena. If the category description says that a person suffering from familial obesity "usually leads sedentary existence," it suggests a reason why the person is fat. The explanation may have been unintentional on the part of the classifier, but such explanations are a frequent valuable by-product of classification.

A classification clarifies one's understanding. Remember how many times you have gotten into an argument that seemed futile and then you (or even the other fellow!) said: "Let's make a distinction between the zilches and the squilches. What you say may be true of the zilches, but it certainly isn't true of the squilches." You may find that the argument has suddenly evaporated and that the two of you agree. (This fifth point is really a summary of the previous four points.)

But the process of putting people or things into categories also has a drawback. (One inevitably loses some information.) For example, assume you have collected "open-ended" free interviews about racial integration. In order to handle the data quantitatively, you classify ("code") the interviews into those for or against integration. You thereby lose all the *shadings* of opinions voiced by the interviewees and the richness and variety of their comments. But, unless you classify in this manner, you cannot handle the people in groups. (Later, however, we shall see how some of the other information can be saved and used simultaneously by *cross-classification*—classification on several dimensions at the same time.)

The loss of individuality in a classification scheme is the basis of a persistent attack on social science. The critic says, "How can you talk as if any two different people in your survey were exactly the same?" or "How can you lump together wholesalers in Vermont and wholesalers in Louisiana when they serve very different markets?" The real question is whether the items are *similar enough* for your purposes; if so, the classification is fruitful. Mineral oil and coffee is the appropriate antidote whether a child who swallows furniture polish lives in Vermont or in Louisiana. In that instance the difference in geography does not matter at all. (But for other purposes the difference in geography is indeed crucial.)

People who refuse to ignore the differences among individuals may avoid erroneous generalizations. But they may also avoid any generalizations at all, which makes science impossible. (Some people criticize classification from a sincere desire for deeper truth; some, to thwart the efforts of others, use anecdotal evidence and exceptional occurrences to throw sand in the gears of scientific conceptualization.)

Classification research is different from other types of research in that one does not usually go out and collect new data for a classification study. Rather one is likely to work with *existing* data, sorting it into a classification that makes sense of it. Therefore, classification research tends to follow after descriptive research in the sequence of scientific stages.

As for the concept of variable in classification research, the classification scheme itself can be viewed as one massive variable *or* as a set of variables, for it is a set of distinctions among a set of related phenomena. But the variable or variables are not "dependent" or "independent," at least until employed in other research. For example, if one wanted to determine whether women are more prone to familial obesity than are men, the obesity classification would be a *dependent* variable; obesity type $= f(\text{sex})$. Or if an economist were to investigate how the presence of monopoly affects economic development, the market classification into monopoly or other forms would be an *independent* variable; rate of economic development $= f(\text{type}$ of market form).

Every collection can be classified in many different ways. For example, I trust that you will not take too seriously the scheme by which research problems are classified in this chapter; one could slice up the research salami in many different ways, some of them more careful and systematic than the classification I use here. My object is to illustrate for you the variety of problems within scientific research, in contrast to the view that all science can be boiled down to a single sort of problem, and the classification-scheme is intended to do this and only this; if it does, it is a good one and, if not, not.

4. Measurement and Estimation

Measurement research seeks to establish the *size* of a phenomenon on one or more of its dimensions: its weight, height, speed, intelligence, number of members, or what have you. Economic data for firms and governments are typical measurements.

Measurement differs from case-study description in these ways: Measurement research focuses on one or a few dimensions, and measures them systematically and in relatively great detail; case study gathers information on many dimensions of the phenomenon, with or without numerical description, and in a more ad hoc fashion.

Among the most frequent subjects of measurement in social science are the following, all of which are described in detail in every elementary statistics text: the total, the central value, the proportion, the distribution by various categories, and the amount of variability.

Deciding *what to measure* and how to draw the definitional boundary lines around the quantity to be measured—translating the theoretical (hypothetical) concept into empirical terms—is a crucial decision in measurement research. An example: When one wants to estimate the cost to

General Motors of producing another hundred thousand automobiles, should one include any of the salaries of the top management in the measurement? The cost accountant will always say "yes," but for some decisions the better answer is "no," as, for example, when General Motors must calculate its costs in connection with a potential sale to a fleet owner of a batch of already-produced trucks.

5. Comparison Problems

Let us consider some examples first. We compare the nation's preferences between two people by means of a presidential election. Market researchers use television ratings to compare the number of listeners that two television shows attract. Psychologists compare the efficiency of teaching machines with the efficiency of conventional classroom instruction. In their interpretation of their data Kinsey, *et al.*, frequently compare the behavior of men with that of women, that of young people with that of old people, and so on. Cultural anthropologists sometimes compare two cultures, to discover differences and similarities. And social anthropologists sometimes compare the kinship systems, say, in a great many different cultures.

Most empirical research in psychology, sociology, marketing research, education, anthropology, political science, and all other branches of social comparison is part of research intended to establish cause and effect. The comparison may be of something against nothing; for example, an hour's tutoring may be compared against no tutoring to see whether the tutoring raises grades at all.

Comparison problems and measurement problems have much in common. In fact, you can have an enjoyable time arguing that comparison problems are really a subtype of measurement problems or, conversely, that measurement problems are really a subtype of comparison problems. The key difference between comparison and measurement is that measurement is against a *known standard*. The standard may be a man's foot or a carob bean or a platinum-iridium meterstick. But the standard is assumed to be *commonly known*, and its common acceptance gives the standard its value as a standard.

Comparison problems, on the other hand, compare two or more entities with one another. In a comparison problem, we are interested in the *relative* measurement of *two or more* phenomena, whereas in measurement problems we are interested only in *one* event relative to a standard quantity. When the psychologist compares two methods of teaching children to read, she is interested in finding the *faster* method; she is not interested in how long either one takes in absolute time. When a network compares the ratings of two television shows, its usual purpose is to identify the *more popular* show. An election seeks to establish which candidate is *preferred* to the other candidates. The difference between comparison and measurement is illuminated by the different types of adjectives used, "fast" versus "faster," the absolute versus the comparative.

Comparison problems are often framed in the logic of statistical hypothesis testing. And discussion of hypothesis testing has dominated the discussion of research methods in the social sciences, and is at the center of classical statistics. But it is very important to recognize that hypothesis testing is only one of several types of research problems, even though it is the dominant type of research in some disciplines. A master survey researcher even generalizes in the other direction:

> At their present stage of development, however, the social sciences cannot insist on this paradigm [hypothesis testing]. Our thinking is rarely far enough progressed to enable us to start out with a sharply formulated hypothesis; most studies are exploratory, directed toward the general examination of a field in order to develop theoretical formulations. (Kendall & Lazarsfeld, p. 133)

Researchers whose experience has been mostly with comparison problems sometimes try to treat *all* problems as problems in hypothesis testing. Violence is done to thought and procedure in the effort to jam all research into the hypothesis-testing mold. For example, it requires intellectual contortions to cast the U.S. Census as a problem in hypothesis testing; the same is true of many other problems in description or measurement. H. Roberts makes this point forcefully about research in business and economics:

> In fields with a highly developed theoretical structure—especially the natural sciences—it is reasonable to expect that most empirical studies will have at least some sharp hypotheses to be tested. This is not true for many areas of business interest, and attempts to force research into this mould are both deceitful and stultifying. "Hypotheses" are likely to be no more than hunches as to where to look for sharper hypotheses, in which case the study might be described as an intelligent fishing trip. (Roberts, p. 2)

Comparisons are usually made on one *dimension* at a time. We might say that one reading-instruction method teaches children *faster* but that the other method requires *less teacher attention*. These dimensions of speed and amount of teacher attention are chosen for comparison because the researcher believes them to be interesting, or important for practical or theoretical reasons, or relevant in some other way.

Comparisons may be made on more than one dimension by *combining the ratings* on several dimensions into a single index. Sometimes this combining is part of the research job, as when one uses several items on a single test. But sometimes it goes beyond the research job. If a school system gives a reading-instruction method two points for excellence in speed of teaching and one point for amount of teacher attention, the over-all comparison must depend on the value judgments of the school board about the importance of teaching speed and teacher attention; these value judgments are the source of the point values.

In the natural sciences and increasingly in the social sciences as they become more mature, comparison studies often give way to measurement because of the existence of better absolute scales against which to measure phenomena. Long ago a foot racer would race only against another runner, and the better and poorer runners would be established by comparison. Now a runner also races against a clock and achieves a time record.

Even with our excellent contemporary timepieces, however, a time record does not always contain as much or more information than does a comparative result. A woman may prove she is a very fast runner by beating other fast runners, even though the recorded time is slow, because the race is held on a slow track and against the wind. Comparative times of race horses on different tracks and against different competition are widely recognized by racing buffs as inconclusive evidence in handicapping a race.

A comparison may be quantitative like "20 percent faster than . . . ," but often the results cannot be expressed any more precisely than "more" or "less" or "equal to." With two paintings you are not likely to go further than asking whether a person likes one of them *better* (although you *might* get more precision by asking whether the interviewee likes painting A "much more than" or "a little more than" painting B).

The *proportion* or *percentage* is the basic descriptive statistic for comparison problems. For measurement problems there is a common standard, and therefore the data can be expressed as *absolute* numbers like "ten inches," "two hours," or "2,150 spectators." But the percentage makes possible quantitative comparisons *between* two or more quantities, even when the absolute value of neither is commonly known. The percentage expresses, for example, *relative* length or popularity, "57 percent as long" or "two-thirds as many spectators."

6. Research That Tries to Find Relationships

The types of research problems we have discussed in previous sections—description, classification, measurement, and comparison—are intended to reveal what phenomena *are;* more broadly, all of these problems are descriptive. Description and measurement studies describe many or a few aspects of one event or one set of events taken as a single entity. Comparison problems describe two (or several) things or groups with reference to each other, and classification studies create devices for more accurate and meaningful descriptions.

Now we shall discuss the first of two types of problems in which we ask how events are *related* to one another. The second type, cause-and-effect problems, is really a subclass of relationship problems.

A few examples should make clear the nature of relationship problems: How well are I.Q. test scores related to future success in school? That is, how well do I.Q. scores *predict* future school success? How well does the behavior of groundhogs on Groundhog Day predict the end of winter? How closely related are income and other indexes of social class? Do rises and falls in the economy follow rises and falls in the stock market?

We shall defer until the next chapter consideration of such problems as whether smoking *causes* lung cancer and whether stock-market movements *cause* movements in the economy.

The investigation of relationships and predictions touches ticklish philosophical arguments like those about the nature of induction and whether it is possible to generalize. We shall, however, sidestep some philosophical arguments and postpone some others until Chapter 32.

An investigation into whether there is a relationship between two occurrences or variables is an attempt to find out whether two (or more) phenomena are part of the *same scheme of things,* that is, whether they are closely associated with each other in nature's cobweb. The cobweb analogy is instructive. If two particles are entrapped close to each other in a cobweb, and if one of them moves, the other will move in close agreement with it. But if the particles are much farther from each other, movement in one will not be *as closely* accompanied by movement in the other. Furthermore, notice that movement in particle A and in particle B can be related even if neither A nor B but rather C initiates the motion.

Of course it is true that everything is related to everything else to *some* extent. If you drop a stone to the ground in Illinois, theoretically there will be an impact in Chile, Ghana, and every other part of the world. But the impact in Chile is so slight that we can ignore it, and no instrument will be sensitive enough to record it. In a psychological context, it is surely true that if some environmental factor causes a change in one aspect of a personality, all other aspects of the personality will be affected to some degree. And if some economic shock in Guatemala causes an inflation in the quetzal there will be *some* related movement in the value of the dollar. Nevertheless, relationships like those in the examples given are so insignificant that we ignore them. We shall confine our interest to *important* relationships between events, relationships that *matter.* And of course relationships must be large enough to be detected by the crude instruments at our disposal. (An atomic explosion or earthquake in Chile can probably be detected in Illinois, though the fall of a stone cannot.)

There are several types of relationships that are not the simple cause-and-effect relationships. Among them are these:

A *third* phenomenon, C, may cause *both* A and B, accounting for the apparent relationship between them. Yet A and B vary together, and we therefore say that there is a relationship between them; to illustrate, tax changes will affect both the stock market and gross national product.

Or A may cause B (or B may cause A), but we may not be able to establish which causes which. Nevertheless, we may be able to establish the extent of the relationship between them. Do you do well in a course because you like the course, or vice versa? Probably both are true. Does a young boy fall in love because a girl asks him to go steady, or vice versa?

Or it may be that A is a partial cause of B and B is a partial cause of A. One such type of interrelationship is "feedback." I hit you, which causes you to hit me. The blow to me is feedback from my blow to you. The going-steady and doing-well-in-course examples might also be examples of feedback.

There can be great value in knowing what relationships exist even if we do not know their nature in terms of cause and effect. Here are some of the uses to which such knowledge can be put:

First, one phenomenon may be used as a *predictor* of another phenomenon of interest. If we believe that the stock market's ups and downs occur six to twelve months earlier than ups and downs occur in the economy, we can then predict what the economy is likely to do six to twelve months hence. We can take action based on this prediction to try to change the behavior of the economy.

The flight of birds close overhead may usually predict rain, even though the flying birds do not cause the rain; when we see the birds, we put up the shutters to avoid being drenched by the oncoming rain.

Second, one phenomenon may serve as a proxy measurement of the other. An advertising researcher may believe that the amount of readership of advertisements in magazines is closely related to the effect of the advertisement in creating sales. If the situation makes it difficult or impossible to measure the *sales* effect of the advertisement directly, the researcher may then measure the amount of *readership* the advertisement gets and use this measurement as an indirect *index* of the sales the advertisement produces.

Third, the relationship between two proxy measurements may be of interest. In the previous paragraph, we discussed the relationship between sales—which is really what the advertiser is interested in—and readership, which the advertiser might wish to use as a proxy index of sales. But the advertiser might also be interested in the relationship between two separate proxy indexes of sales—perhaps readership and the number of coupons that are clipped and returned.

Neither readership nor coupon response is the "real" cause or the "real" effect of sales. But an investigation of the relationship between the two indexes can tell the advertiser whether the firm can reasonably assume that *both* indexes can stand for the same thing. If readership varies with sales, and coupon response varies with readership, the advertiser can expect coupon response to vary with sales.

Educators and educational researchers often look at the relationship of one aptitude test to another aptitude test. If both tests give high and low scores to the same people, then the cheaper and simpler test to administer can be used. Similarly, if the Dow-Jones index of thirty industrial stocks is closely related to the composite of all industrial stocks on the New York Stock Exchange, there is no need to compute the more complete index.

Intelligence tests pose a curious question about indexes. Should we say that a score on an I.Q. test *is* intelligence? This seems to be what people mean when they say "He has a high I.Q." Alternatively, we can think of an I.Q. score as simply a somewhat inaccurate *index* of capabilities that bring about success in the future. For most purposes, it does not matter which way we think of the I.Q. But confusion becomes apparent when we begin to say about someone "He is very bright even though his test scores don't show it." If we interpret the I.Q. score as the *same thing* as intelligence, then the statement would make no sense.

The strategy of research in looking for a relationship is to examine the *patterns of variations* in the two phenomena you seek to relate. If A generally goes up when B goes up, then A and B are related to some extent. Or, for that matter, if A generally goes *down* when B goes up, they are also related but inversely.

A basic way to examine the variations and test for the presence of a relationship is to arrange the data in some form like a table or a graph.[4] For example, if we want to find out whether or not there is a relationship between a man's income and which political party he votes for in a small town, we might record the data from our sample of 200 in this way, in a two-row, two-column ("two-by-two") table, as in Table 4.1.

TABLE 4.1

	Republican	Democrat	Subtotals
Below $10,000	Cell A = 35 (17.5%)	Cell B = 68 (34%)	103
Above $10,000	Cell C = 47 (23.5%)	Cell D = 50 (25%)	97
Subtotals	82	118	

If all the observed people had fallen into cells A and D, it would be obvious that there is a relationship. Similarly, if A and B had equal numbers of people and if C and D also had equal numbers of people, then it would be equally obvious that there is *not* a relationship. But in the social sciences we are rarely so lucky as to have such clear-cut results. Almost invariably the data will show a mixed pattern like that in the table. We therefore have some difficulty in deciding whether there is or is not a relationship between income and political party and, if a relationship does exist, how "strong" it is.

Casting tables into percentages (see the numbers within parentheses in the example) often clarifies whether there is a relationship. But it is always a question which percentages should be computed. In this case, each cell is shown as a percentage of the whole. If there were *no* relationship between income and political party, the *ratio* of the percentages in cells A and B would equal the ratio of the percentages in C and D; the same would be true of cells A and C compared to B and D. That is, percentage A divided by percentage B would equal percentage C divided by percentage D, and percentage B divided by percentage C would equal percentage B divided by percentage D. That these ratios are *not* equal suggests a relationship between income and political party, though we must later check whether such a pattern might be caused by chance.

Statistical theory can help us to draw sound inferences, as we shall see in Chapters 25–30. One common statistical way to measure the extent of a relationship is a *correlation coefficient*, which can be used in place of—or, better yet, in addition to—tables and graphs. It will be discussed in Chapter 30.

4. Consult H. Zeisel (1957) for a clear discussion of how to arrange data in tables and graphs.

7. Finding Causes and Effects

As we have mentioned, cause-and-effect relationships are a subclass of scientific relationships in general; I shall substantiate this claim in Chapter 32. To say *how* cause-and-effect relationships differ from other relationships or, to put it another way, to create a definition of "cause-and-effect relationship" is a difficult matter, indeed, and that is the job of Chapter 32.

Deciding whether to call a particular relationship between two variables, say A and B, a "causal" relationship is sometimes a straightforward matter. If the observed relationship is the result of an *experiment*, there is usually little argument about saying that an observed relationship is a causal relationship, implying that the artificially manipulated independent variable is the cause and the dependent variable whose change is observed the effect. Indeed, one of the best ways to reduce confusion about whether an observed nonexperimental relationship is causal is to subject it to experiment.

As we shall see in more detail later, however, an experimental relationship may *not* deserve to be called a "causal" relationship, usually because there is something wrong with the way that the experimenter has "specified" the independent variable. Consider, for example, the fabled gentlemen who got experimentally drunk on bourbon and soda on Monday night, Scotch and soda on Tuesday night, and brandy and soda on Wednesday night—and stayed sober Thursday night by drinking nothing. With a vast inductive leap of scientific imagination, they treated their experience as an empirical demonstration that soda, the common element each evening, was the cause of the inebriated state they had experienced.

Observed relationships that do *not* spring from controlled experiments are much harder to characterize as causal or noncausal. Various practical devices can, however, assist in safe classification of a relationship as causal. Here is one such device: If you observe a relationship between A and B and if you can establish that A did not cause B, the *likelihood* that B caused A is then greater. For example, years in which the corn price is high are followed by years in which large amounts of corn are grown. We can be quite sure that the high price is not caused by the large supplies because the high price occurs in the *previous years;* causes usually (but *not always!;* see the postscript to Chapter 32) precede the effects. (But this relationship *by itself* is not sufficient to establish causality from B to A; C might cause both.)

Another device that increases confidence that a relationship is causal is cross-classification analysis with tables. If you try out many of the most likely additional variables in a cross-classification and if the original observed relationship between your variables is not affected, you have made a more convincing case that your observed relationship is causal. Examples of cross-classification are given in Chapters 25 and 26.

Some *scientists* react to the difficulties of establishing cause and effect by withdrawing into their shells and refusing to say that the relationships they find are anything more than correlations. (Sometimes this is a safety play to avoid possible criticism, as with some scientists' findings of relationships between smoking and lung cancer.) But *decision makers* cannot avoid making judgments about cause and effect, even if they wish to weasel out of it. If smoking does not *cause* cancer, there is no point in trying to stop people from smoking. If the stock market does not *cause* changes in the economy, there is not much point in trying to control the action of the stock market as an aid to controlling the economy. Therefore, it is often the decision makers who frame research problems narrowly in terms of cause and effect. What causes juvenile delinquency? How can I increase the readership of my furniture advertisements? How does a longer school year affect a child's education? Do television dramas cause violence in children? The decision maker wants to know what to change so that he can achieve the effect he wants.

The decision whether to call a relationship "causal" is indeed a delicate matter. Statistical techniques alone cannot guarantee that an observed nonexperimental relationship is causal. Nor can statistics or other formal reasoning methods guarantee that even an experimental relationship is causal. Statistics would not reveal the flaw in the reasoning that soda causes inebriation. The only protection that the researcher can give himself is to *saturate himself* in the complicated and detailed richness of the phenomenon he is working on. An hour's elbow bending and casual talk about liquor at a neighborhood bar will save you forever from believing that soda is the active ingredient.

8. Mapping Structures

This last type of research problem will be discussed only briefly. Examples include finding the kinship structure of a group, that is, who is related to whom in what ways; determining the structure of an unwritten language; and mapping an economy. Structure (or system) mapping is a sort of description, but it is more highly organized than ordinary description. It is a good deal like putting together a jigsaw puzzle; first, one tries to find a second piece to fit a given piece, then a third piece to fit the first two, and so on until the whole system falls into place. Unlike exploratory descriptions, structure mapping begins with a conceptual structure that the investigator tries to fill in. One knows in advance what one is looking for; for example, the linguist tackles an unknown language knowing that it must have phonemes, morphemes, nouns, verbs, and so on. His job is to identify the various members of the classes and the relationships among them. To put it another way, the structure mapper starts off knowing the generalities of the language; his job is to fill in the specifics.

Taken as a whole, structure mapping encompasses many other types of research, especially classification and comparison—for example, comparing two words that sound similar to see whether a speaker of the language distinguishes between them. Mapping a system is a sequence of trial, observation of the result, deduction of a new hypothesis, trial of the new hypothesis, and so forth.

Structure mapping is important in economics. For example, an input-output analysis is a map of the flows of materials to and from each segment of an economy—where nails from nail factories go and where raw materials for nails come from. But, even though the ultimate objective of most economists is to understand the economic system as a whole, most economic studies deal with single relationships in particular sectors of the economy. Simplification and abstraction of this kind are often necessary in science because systems are often too complex to study as wholes.

Deduction usually plays a large part in structure mapping. For example, when the linguist identifies one word as a noun and then hears another word used directly after the noun, he deduces that the second word is not a noun also, because one noun seldom follows another. And in economic input-output analysis one can deduce useful facts about the inputs of nails to various industries if one knows the total output of the nail industry.

The work of structure mapping re-enacts in microcosm the activities of the various disciplines *taken as wholes*. Whole series of studies follow the same pattern as do the individual steps in structure mapping. An example is a series of related animal experiments in the psychology of learning. The studies form a sequence of experiments, observations, deductions, further hypotheses, and so on. The difference is that in psychology the unit of work is defined as a single experiment, whereas in kinship studies or field linguistics the unit is defined as the mapping of the entire system.

9. Evaluation Research

Evaluation research is *not* another sort of research different from the types of research described above—despite some recent claims to the contrary. Fad, fashion, and catchwordism run wild in science, just as elsewhere in society, especially when money is to be made by being "with it." And with recent demands by the holders of grant pursestrings that social science be "relevant" and "responsive to current social needs," there emerged the label "evaluation research," which seems super relevant and responsive.

Every comparison study in the history of the study of learning is an "evaluation" of one method of learning or teaching compared to another. Every economic study of the effect of a minimum-wage law on employment and earnings of poor people is evaluation research, evaluating the effect of such legislation. Every medical and anthropological study tracing the impact of Western culture on an isolated tribe's physical and mental hygiene is evaluation research. In short, many comparison, measurement, and cause-and-effect studies yield explicit evaluations, and many of the rest yield implicit evaluations; there does not exist a distinct kind of research known as evaluation research.

Much research could be made much more valuable, however, if the researcher would aim to produce results yielding clear-cut evaluations that can be used to improve social judgments. But this is a distinction between a) sound, well-designed research and b) ill-conceived, sloppy work, rather than between "evaluation research" and other research.

In concluding this chapter, I want to repeat that there *are* several types of research problems and that, furthermore, there *ought* to be several types of research problems. Unfortunately, too many scientists in various disciplines assume that the type of problem they attack is all there is and all there should be to scientific research. Some economists think and act as if deduction and statistical analysis of time series is the beginning and end of social science. Some psychologists claim that all scientific research is and should be a process of testing hypotheses by experiments. The danger of such narrow claims is that they lead to stereotyped choices of research methods, which blind the researcher and cut down his effectiveness.

It seems to me that the demand that *all* research be thrust into any one mold, hypothesis testing for instance, is an example of a common and destructive tendency in science—overstating the merits or generality of a theory or method, or "intellectual imperialism" as I choose to call it. This imperialism results in bitter arguments about this theory *or* that theory, rather than agreement that each theory (and method) may do some jobs better than the other theory (or method).

The purpose of this discussion of the various types of research problems has been to lead you to ask yourself: "What type of research problem is the question that I am trying to investigate? Into which class does it fall?" This approach helps one to understand the nature of a research problem and how to go about it.

10. Summary

Each social-science discipline uses some method almost to the exclusion of others. For example, psychology specializes in experiments, sociology in surveys, and economics in statistical analysis of government-produced data. However, other methods sometimes can be more appropriate. The task of this chapter is to describe the various types of empirical research so that you may think of them when you need them.

Descriptive research is especially called for when a field is first opening, to define the problems and to produce clues for further research to follow up.

Classification research makes distinctions among the phenomena under investigation. This may lead to causal explanations of the differences among the phenomena or of the relationships among them. Or the classification may serve as a map of the territory to orient subsequent researchers.

Measurement (estimation) research is a quantitative, and therefore more precise, form of descriptive research, but it is usually less flexible and rich in variety than is qualitative descriptive research. The most common measurements are: counting, central value, proportion, distribution, and variability.

Comparison research is done to find out which alternative is bigger, faster, or perhaps better.

Relationship research attempts to determine whether there is an association between two phenomena. This may be to aid prediction, or to determine whether one variable can be used as a proxy for the other, or it may be a prelude to determining a causal relationship.

Cause-and-effect research can be done with experiments or surveys; best of all is a combination of methods, together with good judgment. Cause-and-effect research attempts to go beyond the existence of an association to determine if one of the variables can plausibly be said to cause the other.

Structure mapping is research that investigates an entire structure, whether it be a kinship group or an economic system. It encompasses other sorts of research as well.

EXERCISES

1. Within one given field, for example, psychology, economics, or anthropology, find examples of each of the seven types of research—description, classification, measurement and estimation, comparison, search for relationships, cause-and-effect, and mapping structures. Some rummaging around in the literature will be necessary to find all seven types.
2. If the class is doing individual research projects, classify each student's project by type of research.
3. Read through the first five *empirical* articles in a professional journal or in a book of readings of empirical research, and classify the studies by type of research.
4. Show how a particular distribution of data would be summarized one way for one purpose and another way for another purpose.

ADDITIONAL READING FOR CHAPTER 4

On exploratory and descriptive studies, see Selltiz (Chapter 4).

For a fascinating firsthand account of participant-observation descriptive study, see the Appendix to Whyte's *Street Corner Society*. More generally, see Denzin (Chapter 9).

Descriptive research in anthropology—that is, field methods—is covered well in Williams' short pamphlet.

Coleman discusses evaluation research for policy purposes, including a discussion of "social audits." Campbell (1969) presents research designs that are particularly appropriate for the evaluation of policy changes.

Tanur *et al.* contains a wide variety of studies showing how quantitative statistical methods can be used for measurement, estimation, comparison studies, and the finding of relationships. Though the book's subject is statistics, no previous knowledge of statistics is required, and the studies are a pleasure and a joy to read. They cover a wide variety of areas from anthropology to business, and from pure to applied research. The studies include both the social sciences and the biological sciences, and some natural sciences as well. Very highly recommended.

5 theory, model, hypothesis, and empirical research

The purpose of this chapter is to throw some light on the confusing relationships among theory, theorizing, models, hypotheses, and empirical research.

The aim of all research—theoretical and empirical—is to get new knowledge. But we can distinguish among quite different types of knowledge that one may be seeking. One may seek better understanding of the social world, that is, a better explanation of some human phenomenon such as racial discrimination or psychological depression. Or one may seek to find the best way to deal with a given class of situations, say, economic recession or psychological depression. Or one may seek to evaluate the effects of a program, say, school busing or psychotherapeutic treatment. There is some—but only some—connection between this variety of aims and the nature of various research problems described in the previous chapter.

The roles of theory and empirical research, and the relationships between them, differ with the types of knowledge one seeks. Here are a few examples to illustrate possible relationships between theory and empirical research:

1) An urban planner may want to know whether the prospective dwellers in a new area will support a shopping mall. The question comes out of the planner's background knowledge. Other than that, theory is nil. Empirical research is the main tool, and its results are the knowledge sought. 2) Malthus deduced from basic principles of economic theory the hypothesis (conjecture) that additional births cause the standard of living to fall. For many years that hypothesis—accepted as part of economic theory—was

regarded as knowledge in itself, without supporting empirical research. 3) In recent years researchers have looked at the data on birth rates and standards of living for various countries, to see if the relationship between birth rate and economic growth rate is consistent with Malthus' hypothesis. Their aim has been two-fold: to elaborate on Malthus' theorizing to produce greater knowledge of the effect of births upon the economy, and to test Malthus' theoretical deduction. Their aim was not, however, to challenge the body of economic theory from which Malthus' deduction was drawn. When the data turned out not to support Malthus' theorizing, three possible conclusions were suggested: Either the Malthusian theory is insufficient and must be improved, or the data and its analysis are not good enough, or both.

1. What Is Theory?

Empirical research was easy to define (see pages 5–6). But theory is harder to nail down, partly because the concept has very different meanings in different disciplines and even at different moments in particular disciplines. In fields such as economics and physics, where there are well-established assumptions and an apparatus for making systematic deductions, then there is said to be a *body of theory.* The theory must cover a substantial portion of the material in a field or subfield, and it must be *systematically organized,* or else one should not say that there is a body of theory in a discipline. To put it another way, there is no theory unless it is a *body of theory.*[1]

The deductions from the theory need not be *correct* for the theory to claim the title of "theory," but people are less likely to honor the claim of a theory that often produces crackbrained hypotheses.

Another requirement of a body of theory is that the same assumptions and the same type of deductive apparatus must be used for many of the problems in the field. One could work out a set of assumptions from which one could deduce *any* single hypothesis. But such a set of assumptions would not be enough to constitute a theory; a set of assumptions must support not just the one hypothesis but many other hypotheses also. The assumptions that make up microeconomics, for example, underlie an enormous body of economic analysis.

In other fields where phenomena cover a wider range of behavior than does economics—sociology, psychology, and anthropology among them—it has not yet been possible to develop an integrated body of propositions, which most writers accept as the basic underpinning for the field as a whole. In such fields the term "theory" has a looser meaning, and may refer to

1. W. Letwin makes this argument very forcefully in his discussion of theory in economics; G. Homans makes a similar point about sociological theory (pp. 11–12). And this point of view is well accepted in the physical sciences. Unfortunately, however, it is far from universal among social scientists; most social scientists continue to use the terms "theory" and "hypothesis" interchangeably. Such usage leaves no room for the important distinction between statements that are logically related to other statements within a deductive system, and statements that are not.

almost any speculative thinking offered as an explanation for some phenomena.

The key element of theory is that it *abstracts* a few characteristics of reality in an attempt to isolate and describe its central features. The rational profit-making firm in economic theory is such an abstraction. Everyone knows that no organization is perfectly rational or perfectly single-minded in the pursuit of a single goal. But the microeconomic theory which is built upon this abstraction, together with other abstractions such as perfect competition and complete information, is useful and hence is retained and used despite the fact that the theory departs from complete realism when it abstracts and focuses on a few key elements.

Theory can be wise in its choice of a key element or elements to focus on, or the theorizing can be foolish and wrong-headed. The test is whether the elements of the theory yield hypotheses that are important, reasonable, and relevant to one's interests. This is not the same as being right or wrong, however—some wise thinking can turn out to be wrong on the facts; yet the theorizing was worthwhile because it led us to learn something of value that we did not know before.

For example, either a sociologist-demographer or an economist-demographer interested in fertility may observe that more education among women is the strongest and most reliable factor associated with lower fertility. And either the sociologist or the demographer, starting with the basics of that field, can arrive at a reasonably convincing theoretical explanation of why more education among women causes lower fertility.

Obviously there are a great many influences other than education—psychological, economic, cultural—that determine whether a given family or community has more or less children. To fully describe in all its richness even one family's process of making a birth decision would require much time and many words. Theoretical speculation abstracts (in this case) the single element of the women's education to examine as a contributing explanation of the decision to have another child. And empirical investigation of this phenomenon will also abstract to women's education alone, or to women's education plus a few other variables, as the explanation of fertility. (The additional variables, however, are likely to reflect whether the researcher is a sociologist, psychologist, or economist.)

2. Models, Theory, and Hypotheses

Some fields and some subfields of any given discipline, are not ready to build an all-embracing body of theory. But imaginative scientists nevertheless put together sets of abstract propositions from which one can deduce some hypotheses. Such a set of propositions that is relevant to one corner of a field or to a few related phenomena is usually called a **model.**

A model is like a mini-theory. It has the same basic nature as a theory because it focuses on a few elements abstracted from all of reality. And the terms "model" and "theory" are frequently used interchangeably.

3. Two Views of Theory and of Science in General

There are two views of the universe that lead to two views about theorizing—and of science in general. One may view the world as a system having inherent order, and the task of the scientist being the discovery of the "true" propositions and relationships in that system. For example, one may think that the speed with which a body falls due to gravity is one of the underlying propositions that characterize our world, and if we diligently seek after such propositions and relationships we can discover them all and then have a complete understanding of the universe. To put this view another way, at the beginning the universe was created or evolved according to a set of equations, and it is our job to discern the equations.

The other view—the one which I find more helpful—is that the universe is not perfectly formless or chaotic—though it may once have been—but that the regularities and generalizations we discover result from our interests and perceptions as well as from the features of the world. That is, we invent and develop the relationships we find, rather than merely discovering them. For example, what shape is the earth? It is round and smooth to a firm that manufactures cheap globes, but is bumpy to a manufacturer of more expensive globes. To a surveyor or farmer, it is flat. Its circumference is greatest at the equator, for some persons. To an aviator, it is an unsmooth, unround set of upcropping mountains. And so on. The earth does not have one shape but many, and the relevant "model"—flat, round, bumpy—depends upon your needs and interests. No "model" of the earth captures all its features—because then it would not be an abstracted model, but the earth itself. As Georgescu-Roegen put it:

> [A]ctuality is a seamless whole we can slice . . . wherever we may please. And, Plato to the contrary, actuality has no joints to guide a carver. . . . Only our particular purpose in each case can guide us in drawing the boundary of a process. So, every scientist slices actuality in the way that suits best his own objective—an operation that cannot be performed without some intimate knowledge of the corresponding phenomenal domain. . . .
>
> No analytical boundary, no analytical process . . . (p. 3)

Just so it is with the familial process of making decisions about whether to have another child; no single statistical model of it is *the* correct one. Rather, different models of the fertility decision will be appropriate for answering different scientific questions, and with respect to different scientific purposes.

4. The Relationship Between Theory and Empirical Research

Now we tackle the tangled relationship between theory and empirical research. In applied research the relationship between hypothesis (there is seldom anything that can be called theory) and empirical research is so close as to be obvious. Consider the research firm that polls the electorate to predict the winner of the presidential election. The relevant speculations are mostly obvious assumptions: the election will really be held, the candidates will stay alive, and so on. That is, there is no real theorizing involved, and the empirical research is the entire scientific task.

In "evaluation" research—such as an evaluation of whether busing affects the attainment and socialization of students—the empirical research also often seems to proceed without theory. But it is worth noting that the reason there is a busing phenomenon to investigate is because of the speculation some years back that school integration *would* affect students' attainments and socialization.

In "pure" research that seeks to explain the human world in general scientific terms, the relationship between theory and research is more complex and difficult. Theoretical speculation and empirical research are two approaches to the knowledge one seeks. And the use of two very different approaches together is much more powerful than one approach alone. If the two approaches give the same answer, then one can feel much more secure with the conclusion than with only one approach. And if the two approaches do *not* yield the same answer, you are alerted that the matter is not so settled and straightforward as one approach alone would suggest. This is true for the combination of research and empirical research just as it is for two separate empirical methods.

The central task in using theoretical speculation and empirical research together is to mold them and sharpen them so that both are addressing the same question, in such manner that their results can reasonably be compared. In this respect the relationship between theory and a given piece of empirical research is no different than the relationship between two pieces of empirical research bearing on a given problem: The two research approaches must be made to deal with the same phenomena, or else their results cannot be compared.

"Operationalization" of the theoretical concepts is the task of finding appropriate empirical proxies for the theoretical variables. "Conceptualization" is the complementary process of finding appropriate theoretical constructs for interesting empirical patterns that turn up. Operationalization and conceptualization work hand-in-hand as the research work progresses. Very often the researcher passes back and forth from conceptualization to operationalization, rather than the one-way flow from theory to empirical work envisioned by the philosophers of science.

A key link in the struggle to have the theoretical statements and the empirical work deal with the same phenomena is sound definition of the variables. On the theory side, there is no special technique except general clear thinking to help define terms clearly. But on the empirical side, the operational definition is a powerful tool in working toward definitions that all researchers can understand and that therefore can be compared against the theoretical terms. This topic is dealt with in Chapter 2, especially pages 12–17.

An example of the connection of theory—assumption, deduction, and hypothesis—with empirical research whose purpose is to test the theory was given on page 34. Here is another example, again taken from economics:

a. EXAMPLE 1: ADVERTISING RATES IN NEWSPAPERS: FACTUAL PROBLEM

It is an observed fact that newspapers charge lower advertising rates to local retailers than to nationally advertised brands of goods. To explain why they do so is a research problem.

Assumptions. We *assume,* first, that businessmen (newspaper owners, in this case) will charge that price to each group of people that will result in *maximum profit.* (This is the "economic man" assumption, the same as the first assumption in the example on p. 34.)

Second, we *assume* that businessmen *know* how groups of customers (retailers and national advertisers) react to various prices. (This is the "perfect knowledge" assumption, the same as the second assumption on p. 34.)

Deduction. We *deduce* that if one customer group is *less sensitive* to a price increase than is another group, it will be profitable to charge a higher price to the less sensitive customer. This can be shown with a standard logical chain of economic deduction.

Empirical Test. There are many possible ways to test this deduction empirically. One could, for example, try to find out whether local advertisers really are more sensitive to a price increase than are national advertisers. This could be investigated by examining the changes in the quantity of local and national advertising following individual price changes in a sample of newspapers. Or, one could relate the aggregate amounts of local and national advertising to the average prices of local and national advertising over a period of years. Or, one might persuade one or more newspapers to conduct controlled experiments with their advertising prices. All these methods examine changes in economic data, and then reason back to the beliefs and behavior of presumably rational decision-makers.

Another approach is to directly examine the beliefs of the newspaper executives. This is the method we shall consider, with the hypothesis and related test as follows:

Hypothesis. We *hypothesize* that, if the deduction is correct, the newspaper publishers *believe* that national advertisers are less sensitive to price changes.

Research Method. The hypothesis can be tested by finding out what the newspaper advertisers believe about the relative sensitivity of local and national advertisers. A questionnaire study found that publishers do indeed believe that national advertisers are less sensitive to price changes and thus confirmed the hypothesis (Simon, 1965d).

b. LOGIC AND THE CONNECTION BETWEEN THEORY AND EMPIRICAL WORK

Philosophers have devoted much effort to analyzing the logic of the scientific process. They have outlined how science begins with a theoretical framework, deduces propositions, and tests the propositions. Scientific publications tend to follow this format, which is also shown in the examples on page 34.

The actual development of a scientific project seldom follows this logic, however. Rather, you may begin with some data, get an idea out of the data, scratch around for some relevant theory, then test the theoretical deduction, find that the theoretical deduction is not confirmed, do some theorizing, get some more data, get new ideas, and on and on. Or the scenario may begin with a casual observation in everyday life, move on to data or to theory, and so forth.

The point is that the route to valuable scientific results tends to be circuitous, unprogrammed, non-logical, intuitive, repetitious, frustrating, surprising, and hence exciting, as Hasburg's map (Figure 5.1) illustrates.

A last point about the connections between theory and empirical research: They go both ways. Just as theory supports empirical research, there also can be no science without empirical research to serve as a bridge between scientific thought and reality, as the source of speculation and as a *test* of hypotheses. Empirical work and hypothesizing shade into one another. When you look out the window, observe rain, and announce "It's raining outside," you are extrapolating that it is raining all around the house and not just outside one window. Empirical and theoretical statements form a continuum.

> . . . [N]o observation is purely empirical—that is, free of any ideational element —as no theory (in science, at any rate) is purely ideational . . . the terms of even the barest description carry us beyond the here-and-now, if only because they must be capable of more than one utterance to have a usage. When I say, "This object is red," I am inescapably relating the present occasion to others in which "red" is properly used. . . . When we see that someone is pleased or angry, we are relying on a whole framework of ideas about cultural patterns in the expression of emotion, just as we understand what is said not just on the basis of what we hear but also in terms of a whole grammar somehow brought to the hearing. (Kaplan, pp. 58–59)

The relationship of theory to research is discussed from a related point of view in the following chapter.

5. Summary

The relationship between theory and empirical research differs from situation to situation. Seldom does the pattern follow the philosophical-logical

FIGURE 5.1

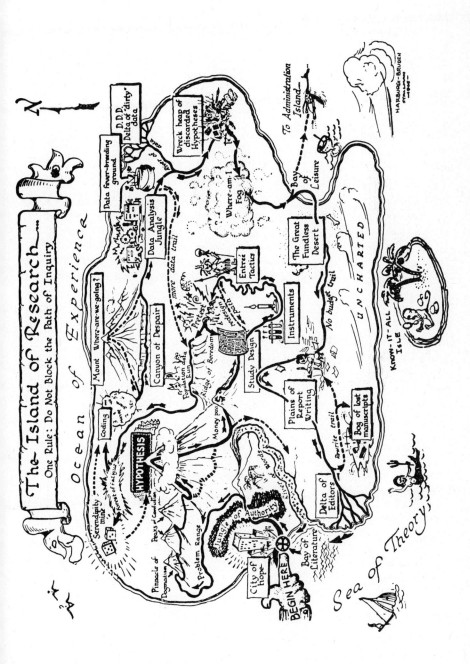

Source: Ernest Harburg, Ph.D. Reprinted by permission.

model beginning with a body of theoretical axioms and proceeding through deduction to empirical testing. Rather, the process may begin at any point—data, curiosity about an observation in daily life, or theoretical deduction—and then it flows back and forth in a web of ideas and empirical testing and theoretical development.

The place of theory differs from discipline to discipline. In some fields the body of theory is strong and well-integrated, whereas in other fields the best that one can hope for is a modest model to guide empirical study. Applied work tends to proceed without theory as such, but rather on the bases of hunches and guesses relevant to a practical need for tested information.

ADDITIONAL READING FOR CHAPTER 5

Selltiz *et al.* (Chapter 2) cover many of the same topics as does this chapter.
Kaplan's *The Conduct of Inquiry* is an excellent treatise on the philosophical basis of social research, and especially the relationship of theory to empirical research.
Kuhn's theory of the development of science has been very influential recently, though somewhat controversial. It is worth getting acquainted with.

6 choosing appropriate proxies for theoretical variables

When the research project begins with abstract theory, you must find one or more reasonable empirical proxies (indicators) for the theoretical variables. Even when the research is "applied" rather than "pure," you must be sure that your empirical variables lend themselves well to the empirical work. This chapter discusses how to choose empirical variables. It follows naturally from the discussion in the previous chapter of the relationship of theory to empirical research and expands on it.

When the theoretical structure is well-defined, the theoretical variable may be confined to a single dimension. But in fields in which the researcher works less with a well-structured theory and more with free-ranging imagination, the theoretical variable is likely to be multidimensional. Lazarsfeld describes this part of the transition from theoretical to empirical variables:

> *Imagery.* The flow of thought and analysis and work which ends up with a measuring instrument usually begins with something which might be called imagery. Out of the analyst's immersion in all the detail of a theoretical problem, he creates a rather vague image or construct. The creative act may begin with the perception of many disparate phenomena as having some underlying characteristic in common. Or the investigator may have observed certain regularities and is trying to account for them. In any case, the concept, when first created, is some vaguely conceived entity that makes the observed relations meaningful.

Suppose we want to study industrial firms. We naturally want to measure the management of the firm. What do we mean by management and managers? Is every foreman a manager? Somewhere the notion of management was started, within a man's writing or a man's experience. Someone noticed that, under the same conditions, sometimes a factory is well run and sometimes it is not well run. Something was being done to make men and materials more productive. This "something" was called management, and ever since students of industrial organization have tried to make this notion more concrete and precise.

The same process happens in other fields. By now the development of intelligence tests has become a large industry. But the beginning of the idea of intelligence was that, if you look at little boys, some strike you as being alert and interesting and others as dull and uninteresting. This kind of general impression starts the wheels rolling for a measurement problem.

Concept Specification. The next step is to take this original imagery and divide it into components. The concept is specified by an elaborate discussion of the phenomena out of which it emerged. We develop "aspects," "components," "dimensions," or similar specifications. They are sometimes derived logically from the over-all concept, or one aspect is deduced from another, or empirically observed correlations between them are reported. The concept is shown to consist of a complex combination of phenomena, rather than a simple and directly observable item.

Suppose you want to know if a production team is efficient. You have a beginning notion of efficiency. Somebody comes and says, "What do you really mean? Who are more efficient—those who work quickly and make a lot of mistakes, so that you have many rejections, or those who work slowly but make very few rejects?" You might answer, depending on the product, "Come to think of it, I really mean those who work slowly and make few mistakes." But do you want them to work so slowly that there are no rejects in ten years? That would not be good either. In the end you divide the notion of efficiency into components such as speed, good product, careful handling of the machines—and suddenly you have what measurement theory calls a set of dimensions. (Lazarsfeld in Brodbeck, pp. 610–611)

Now let us return to one-dimensional variables; further discussion of multidimensional variables is in Chapter 16.

There are several stages in the process of moving from a speculative question about the world to the beginning of the actual empirical work. The first necessary step is to transform the original question into the functional form $y = f(x_1, x_2 \ldots)$. Then you must translate the *hypothetical* (theoretical) variables (concepts) as they appear in your functional form into *empirical* variables ("indicators") that you can work with. The philosophical relationship between hypothetical and empirical variables has already been discussed (Chapter 2). Now we can get down to the actual process of choosing ("specifying") appropriate empirical variables.

The choice of appropriate variables is perhaps the most important decision that the researcher must make. It is at this stage that one finally pins down the vague interest and turns it into concrete operational research: the process by which one moves from "I want to find out how people feel about. . . ." to a researchable statement. Like every other decision in the research process, the choice of variables must depend on just what it is you want to find out and why you want to find it out.

Sometimes the general research question immediately suggests the empirical variables. For example, when one asks about the effect of prosperity on whether Democrats or Republicans win presidential elections, one can easily decide how to measure whether a person is a Democrat or a Republican, though the measure of prosperity is not so obvious. If one asks whether people drink more liquor in summer or winter, it is easy to decide that the Federal Alcohol and Tobacco Tax Unit data are appropriate. But, even in such simple cases, definition of the variables is not automatic and requires some judgment. Are beer and wine counted as liquor? And what about illegal moonshine?

In most research projects, however, one cannot simply plunge in and start measuring an obvious approximation to the theoretical (hypothetical) variables of interest, for one of two reasons: Direct data on the hypothetical (theoretical) variable may not be available, or the hypothetical variable may be a vague concept like love, happiness, welfare, or conformity, none of which immediately suggests empirical counterparts. To put it another way, one cannot find an empirical counterpart about which almost everyone will agree that it really "means" the same thing as the hypothetical variable. Yet in both cases *some* empirical measurement must be done, and it must be done in some way that has meaning. In either case one must create a "proxy" (or "surrogate")—a variable that is different from but stands for the phenomenon in which one is interested. The trick is to create good proxies, proxies that reveal something about the "real" variable in which one is interested.

Better than any single proxy are *several different proxies*. If you use several proxies, and if the results agree, you will reduce doubt about whether you have captured the theoretical variable in your empirical variables. Equally important is that several proxies allow you to draw a more general conclusion from your empirical work, and to map out the domain within which your theoretical proportion does and does not hold.

1. Dependent Variables Whose Referents Are Clearly Defined

This section deals with the type of problem Pogo faces forthrightly in Figure 6.1. Walt Kelly is kidding—but not entirely. When television was young, an engineer in the Dayton, Ohio, Water Department discovered that when the commercials came on the water pressure dropped as people went to kitchens and bathrooms. This measurement of program and commercial popularity is known in research folklore as the "Dayton Water Survey."

Archimedes provided a nice illustration of the substitution of an easily measurable quantity for a quantity that is harder to measure. Archimedes sought to measure the *areas* of various geometrical shapes. But could he do that empirically? It would require cutting up a shape into tiny squares and counting the squares, which would be tedious, to say nothing of difficulties with incomplete squares with curved edges. Archimedes then hit on substituting a process of weighing figures drawn on material of uniform thickness; weight provided a good and handy proxy for area (Mason, p. 51). The same old dodge is still used for estimating the area under curves in, say, radioactivity studies in biology.

The next section discusses such unobservable concepts as beliefs, attitudes, and preferences. In this section we deal with concepts that are measurable *in principle* but not *in practice.* That is, we are talking here about concepts for which we have satisfactory operational definitions but for which we cannot carry out the operations. One can develop quite satisfactory operational definitions of a competitor's advertising expenditures, of China's rice crop, or of a jury's deliberations, even though one is blocked from actually carrying out the operations. On the other hand, there can be no satisfactory operational definitions of such inner states as beliefs and preferences, except in terms of the behavioral proxies that one creates for them.[1]

There are two ways to justify the measurement of a given variable as a proxy for another variable that is clearly defined but cannot itself be measured. The first is to demonstrate an *empirical association* between the proxy and the hard-to-measure variable. The second is to demonstrate a *logical link* with a chain of reasoning between the proxy and the conceptual variable. A combination of the two methods is best. Each of the two ways will be illustrated here.

Many examples of pure empirical proxies can be found in aptitude and vocational testing. One testing organization asks the subject to write as many words as he can, any words at all, in a one-minute period. A person who gets a high score is said to have an aptitude for those jobs that require high creativity. This prediction is based on the supposed fact that people who are successful in creative vocations score higher on this test than do other people. One might be able to find some logical rationale for such a relationship, but basically it is a purely empirical link; if people who are successful in creative jobs were found to score low on this test, a low score would then be accepted as a predictor of success in creative jobs.

Many of the projective tests used by clinical psychologists—like the Rorschach ink-blot test and the Thematic Apperception Test, as well as such personality batteries as the Minnesota Multiphasic Personality Inventory—are "validated" in a purely empirical way. Those responses or "profiles" that are found among people known to be manic-depressive rather than schizophrenic, say, or neurotic rather than psychotic, are then used as "indicators" to predict whether a given person is of one type or another.

1. One might argue that there is no difference between hypothetical (theoretical) concepts for which we have no operational definitions, except in terms of proxies, and concepts for which we have operational definitions that cannot be carried out. If you do not find the distinction useful, ignore it.

FIGURE 6.1

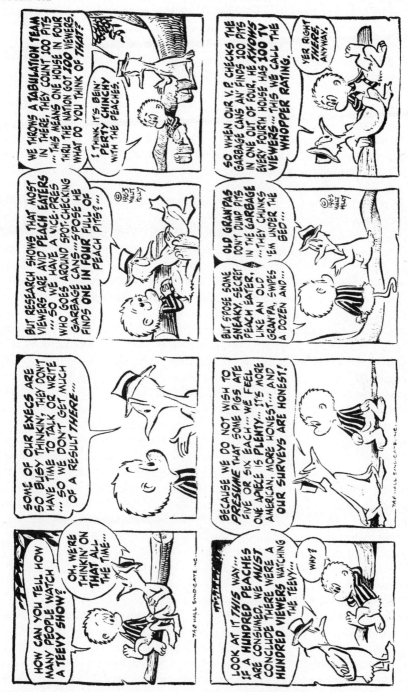

Source: *Pogo*, November 26, 1963, by Walt Kelly; © 1963 Walt Kelly.

In most of the social sciences, the relationship between a proxy and a defined but hard-to-measure conceptual variable is through a *chain of reasoning*. For example, C. Warburton made a fascinating determination of how much liquor was drunk in the United States during Prohibition. The usual measurements of liquor consumption—tax receipts—were not available, so he made the following estimates:

1. amounts used of various possible *ingredients* of liquor (corn sugar; corn syrup and corn starch, corn meal; corn, rye, and other grains; malt syrup; fruits and vegetables), plus estimated amounts of industrial alcohol, medicinal alcohol, and smuggled alcohol
2. *death rates* from alcoholic diseases
3. number of *arrests* for drunkenness.

He then combined these three types of estimate in one grand estimate. The relationship between each of the three estimates and actual consumption could not be directly validated empirically, except perhaps by a survey, and it was too late for that. Warburton's only validation of each of these estimates, and therefore of his combined estimate, was his *reasoning* about the link between drinking and the sources of production, death rates, and arrest rates.

It is sometimes possible to study an invisible phenomenon by finding something visible that is logically linked to it. A famous example in the physical sciences is observation of the Brownian movement of invisible molecules by the use of the "cloud chamber." In this device the molecules become attached to droplets of oil that are of visible size, and the motion of the molecules can then be inferred from the observed motion of the oil droplets.

Business researchers have used many ingenious methods—some ethical, some not so ethical—to obtain sales information that their competitors do not disclose. Retailers who want to know a competitor's sales volume can count the number of customers who enter the competitor's store and then multiply by the estimated size and number of purchases. (Sometimes a retailer takes the more direct method of having agents watch the cash registers in the competitor's store for five minutes at a time and then projecting overall estimates from that sample evidence.) Measuring competitive sales by consumer-purchase panels and by store inventories is a large and flourishing business for many commercial firms.

Information about a competitor's advertising budget is normally obtained by keeping a count of the number and sizes of the competitor's advertisements in all advertising media that the competitor is known to use. Commercial firms and trade associations perform this service for many types of firms in many industries. But the counts are never quite complete. Each firm therefore adjusts its estimate of a competitor's budget by comparing the amount the outside agency estimates for the firm's own expenditures against the firm's own *actual* expenditures, which might be 30 percent to 90 percent greater, and it then makes the appropriate adjustment in the reported figures for its competitor.

Military intelligence officers commonly estimate unavailable magnitudes from what can be observed. Content analysis is frequently used for this purpose. For example, I am told that in World War II the Allies in England counted and measured the numbers of various types of songs played on various European radio stations as an index of changes in German troop concentrations, and deduced from the serial numbers of captured weapons the extent of German war production.

Instruments can sometimes be used to see the invisible. Organisms that are too small to be seen with the naked eye reveal themselves to the microscopist. And geographical features of the moon came close with the aid of the telescope and radiotelescope. But a contrary example also springs to mind. What is the best proxy for whether it is raining outside? On first thought the best proxy is a rain-collecting device that can be read electronically inside the building. But, if you want to go outside in a moment, a better proxy might be to observe how many of the people who walk past the window with umbrellas have them open and how many of the umbrellas are closed. What *other* people are doing about the rain (assuming that they are acting rationally, just as economics assumes the rational economic man) is a good proxy for the variable (rain) that you want to know about. And an observation of umbrellas may be a *better* proxy than the automatic rain collector. You would be better prepared to know how to dress if you knew that 90 percent of the people had their bumbershoots up than if you knew that precipitation was at the rate of .005 something per something per minute.

On the other hand, if you were estimating rainfall for the U.S. Weather Service, an umbrella count would *not* be satisfactory. Here is another example of how purpose and cost/benefit analysis of the information must dictate the choice of method.

To learn about unobservable human behavior, one must usually depend upon the *subject's statements about his behavior* as proxies for the behavior itself, as A. Kinsey did. But we must always worry about how good a proxy "verbal behavior" is for actual behavior. It was not practical for Kinsey to validate the proxy variable directly by observing subjects and then comparing the observed behavior with their statements. Therefore, he used *reliability* checks to determine whether several types of statements by the subject jibed with each other, whether husband's and wife's statements agreed, and whether statements made in later reinterviews jibed with earlier statements.

Kinsey also used the skilled intuition of the interviewer as a measure of validity.

Laboratory experimentation sometimes provides reasonable proxies when subject matter is not accessible. Researchers at the University of Chicago who wished to study the workings of the jury system were denied access to actual jury deliberations for ethical-legal reasons. (After they had obtained permission from one judge to monitor a jury room, a member of Congress became so indignant that he called for a full Congressional investigation even though the cases were minor and the judge and lawyers all had given their permission.) To overcome this obstacle experiments were set up with the cooperation of courts in which people currently on the jury list listened to *recorded mock trials.*

The problem of estimating the characteristics of a group of people *that does not yet exist* illustrates the difference between hypothetical variables that are *conceptually* vague—such as attitudes and beliefs—and those that *in principle* are not vague. How can a university administration estimate what kind of housing the students twenty-five years hence will want when those students have not even been born yet? There is no difficulty in constructing a perfectly satisfactory operational definition of the body of students twenty-five years from now, but the operation obviously cannot be carried out now. (A sensible approximation may be to assume that present-day students are like future students.)

Whenever possible, you should try to validate your empirical variable by comparing it directly with the variable that is of ultimate interest to you. For example, I once developed a method to help marines improve their performance with the .45 caliber pistol. The teaching device was a series of holes in a sheet of metal into which the shooter placed a rod in the barrel of his pistol. The shooter's task was to pull the trigger when the gun was aimed at the target, at which time the rod was within the hole. If he jerked the gun off the target, an electric circuit would ring a buzzer. This method did improve the marines' skills in dry-firing in the laboratory, and it seemed reasonable that skill on the live-ammunition range would also be improved. But would improvement actually show up on the firing range? That would be the ultimate validation. Unfortunately I was transferred before I could compare the empirical dependent variable (performance in the laboratory) with the variable of ultimate interest (performance on the target range).

Generally, the greater the similarity between the proxy and the actual variable, the better the proxy. For example, if you want to find out whether a small child thinks that a dollar bill is worth more than 100 pennies, you will probably do better to ask "Which one do you want for your birthday?" than to ask "Which one is bigger?" or "Which one is worth more?" The Schwerin firm exploits this principle in measuring the effect of advertising. Before and after showing commercials to special movie audiences, Schwerin holds a lottery and offers people the choice of various brands of merchandise if they win. Choice when one may actually receive the merchandise is a more realistic measure of preference than asking "Which brand do you prefer?"

The extent to which attitudes are reasonable proxies for behavior must also be considered carefully. For example, it is common to reason that a woman who says she hates blacks is more likely to discriminate than is a woman who says she likes blacks. Maybe so, but maybe not. But it is surely foolish to pay *no* attention to attitudes and to argue that attitudes are always a worthless measure. For example, it was found in World War II that, among soldiers who had never been in battle, those who said they were confident of their skill in battle, less fearful of getting hurt, and aggressive toward the enemy did indeed perform better in battle later on (Kendall & Lazarsfeld in Merton & Lazarsfeld, p. 179). And, in countries where people say they want relatively few children, they actually have relatively few children (Berelson, 1966).

Just *how* good a proxy an attitude is depends on the situation. Advertisers have had to be sophisticated about this point. For example, consider just a *few* of the possible measurements that relate to the selling power of a magazine advertisement: the number of copies of the magazine sold, the number of people who look at the magazine, the number who look at a particular page, the number who notice the advertisement, the number who read part of the advertisement, the number who remember the advertisement, the number who exhibit more favorable *attitudes* after seeing the advertisement, the number of people who remember selling points about the product, the increase in the number of people who say they *want* the product, the number of people who try out the product, and, finally, the number of people who actually become purchasers.[2] The closer the measurement is to actual purchasing, the better the proxy should be. On the other hand, closer proxies—including actual sales—are often much harder to measure, and therefore a compromise is usually struck. Under the best of conditions the proxy is also validated empirically.

In some situations one selects an emipirical variable that is related to the variable of final interest only by a long chain of reasoning. As an illustration, M. Haire wanted to find out why women did not buy instant coffee. That question is reasonably specific, but it is still a long way from being specific enough to define a piece of research. What Haire had to do next was to specify a set of dependent and independent variables and a functional relationship that he could study empirically.

What he actually did was to conduct an experiment in which he submitted two shopping lists to two groups of women. On the shopping list he gave to group A were many items of food plus "Nescafé instant coffee." On the shopping list for group B were all the same items except that "Maxwell House coffee (Drip Ground)," replaced "Nescafé instant coffee." Haire then asked the women in his groups to say what kind of woman they thought had made out the shopping list. Twenty-four of the twenty-five women in group A, whose list included instant coffee, gave such judgments as "lazy housekeeper." Only two of fifty in group B, whose list included regular coffee, said the woman was a lazy housekeeper.

2. See W. Madow, *et al.* (pp. 41 ff.), for a similar discussion of types of television-audience measurement.

The functional form of Haire's research design was "Judgment about shopping-list maker is a function of whether instant or regular coffee is on the shopping list." But his original purpose was to find out why women do not themselves buy instant coffee. It seems reasonable, then, to ask what the connection is between Haire's original question and the functional form he actually used.

The connection between the basic question of the research and the actual variables and functional form is a *chain of reasoning*. Haire assumed that women could not or would not give the real reasons that they themselves did not buy instant coffee. He further assumed that they might "project" their real reasons onto other people. Therefore, the chain of reasoning was as follows: First, if a woman thinks that she herself is lazy when she buys instant coffee, she will say that *another* woman who buys instant coffee is lazy; second, if a woman thinks herself lazy when she buys instant coffee, she will not buy instant coffee. Haire therefore assumed that if women did judge instant-coffee buyers lazy, he would have evidence that belief in the laziness of instant-coffee buyers really does inhibit purchase. And that is indeed what he found. (Haire then buttressed these findings by a supplementary investigation of which women did buy instant coffee, and, indeed, the women who did *not* say that other instant-coffee users were lazy tended to buy instant coffee themselves.)

A variable that is a good proxy at one time may not be a good proxy years later. Studies that repeated Haire's 1940s experiment in the 1960s and 1970s did not obtain the results he did, probably because of a shift in attitudes toward instant coffee (Arndt).

2. Dependent Variables Whose Referents Are Not Clearly Defined

We have just discussed empirical variables as proxies for concepts that are clearly defined but impractical to measure. Now we shall discuss proxies for which an empirical validation is not only *practically* impossible but also *conceptually* impossible. Nor are logical validations possible for these proxies. They differ from Warburton's example, for *in principle* he might have validated his estimates by taking surveys of how much people drank during Prohibition.

The intelligence test is an interesting example because it illustrates both types of uses of proxies. If the I.Q. test is interpreted as a *prediction of future school success*, it illustrates the first type, because it can be validated by comparing I.Q. scores with later school grades; a high correlation convinces us that the I.Q. test is a good proxy. But, if we interpret the I.Q. test as an empirical proxy for a generalized hypothetical notion of intelligence, we are dealing with the second type, for no empirical or logical validation is possible.

H. Ebbinghaus early gave much thought to the relationship between the inner mental state of memory, which is unobservable, and the behavior of repeating nonsense syllables correctly, which Ebbinghaus observed and measured. It is the experimental use of this observable behavior that gives

. . . a foothold for the application of the method of the natural sciences: namely, phenomena . . . which are clearly ascertainable, which vary in accordance with the variation of conditions, and which are capable of numerical determination. Whether we possess in them correct measures for these inner differences [memory], and whether we can achieve through them correct conceptions as to the causal relations into which this hidden mental life enters— these questions cannot be answered *a priori*. . . . There is only one way to do this [validate the proxy], and that is to see whether it is possible to obtain, on the presupposition of the correctness of such an hypothesis, well classified, uncontradictory results, and correct anticipations of the future. (Ebbinghaus, p. 9)

There is also a close relationship between choosing proxies for vague variables and choosing measurements, as this story illustrates:

GROOMING CODE: SISTER TURNS "FINGER-MAN"

Ferndale, Mich., Feb. 20 (AP)—Too bushy or not too bushy? That is the question at St. James Catholic High School in this Detroit suburb.

Sister Mary Aurilla, school principal, has devised a simple test to answer the question of whether the hair styles worn by the 200 girl students are too bushy. She pushes her index finger into the girl's hair. If her finger tip touches the girl's head and the knuckle doesn't show above the hairdo, then it's too bushy. Girls who fail the finger test are sent home to rearrange the situation. (Champaign-Urbana *Courier*, February 21, 1965)

If business of hair is understood to refer only to the *single dimension of* thickness, then we can view the finger test as a *measurement*. But, if bushiness could mean *other* characteristics in addition to thickness, then the finger test is a one-dimensional proxy chosen to stand for the more complex hypothetical (conceptual) variable.

When your hypothetical variable is vague, you must bull ahead and say "This empirical variable is what I shall call. . . ." When Kinsey wanted an empirical variable to stand for male sexual outlet, he simply said that orgasm would be the proxy, because it seemed reasonable to him and because no other measurable variable seemed more reasonable. If orgasm took place, the act was counted as sexual outlet; if not, not. Kinsey was not asserting that orgasm *is* sexual outlet; most of us would probably agree that in the loose sense there can be sexual outlet without orgasm. Orgasm was simply the best that Kinsey decided he could do for an empirical proxy in the male study. (In the female study, however, orgasm was *not* the proxy for sexual outlet.)

One can validate this type of variable only with *judgment*. The variable has been well chosen if other scientists are willing to accept that the empirical variable gets at the hypothetical variable. Not all empirical variables are well enough chosen to overcome this obstacle, and indeed some proxies are downright foolish. To measure mother love by how often a mother cuddles a child might or might not be satisfactory. To measure mother love by how much the mother *says* she loves a child would probably be worth little or nothing.

One must not forget the distinction between the proxy and the "real" variable, as noted for orgasm and sexual outlet. For another example, running away from home might be a good indicator of unhappiness in adolescents. But one should not therefore think that anyone who runs away from home *is* unhappy. To show such a relationship, a researcher would first have to show an empirical link between running away and *other* indicators that are generally accepted signs of unhappiness.

Can one ever observe the "real" variable directly? Consider again being inside a building and wanting to know whether it is raining outside so that you can decide what you should wear. You are likely to look out the window to see whether you can see raindrops falling. Are you then observing the "real" variable, or are you observing only a proxy variable? Common sense says that you are observing the real variable, as it is the rain itself that you are looking at. But what you observe will depend upon the time of the day and other conditions that affect your vision, so that what you observe is not *just* the real variable. Perhaps what you observe can better be described as the visual impression of the raindrops seen from a distance under certain visual conditions.

Deciding whether you are observing the "real" variable is not likely to be a problem. You will be on safe ground if you describe your observed variable as a close or not-so-close proxy for the phenomenon in which you are interested. If you think that what you are observing is the "real" variable, you might state that there is complete identity between the proxy and the phenomenon you are studying.

Sometimes several research techniques can be strung together to form a logical chain between a proxy and an ill-defined variable. In the library study, for example, we wished to determine the relationship between the scholarly value of given books and the rates of their withdrawal from the library (Fussler & Simon). Therefore, we first investigated the withdrawal of books from the library by studying withdrawal records. Then we investigated the relationship between book use within the library and withdrawals from the library by a questionnaire survey of the unrecorded use of books. Then we related recorded book use to the ultimate value of books, with the aid of judgments by a panel of expert scholars in various fields. Given that validating chain of reasoning, we could reasonably accept the rate of withdrawal of a book as a proxy of its value in the succeeding work.

Students of human emotions often validate by comparing several different proxies. If there is high agreement among them, faith in one or all of them is increased. One may also decide that the proxy that best agrees with all the others is the *best* proxy among them. For example, if I want to measure how happy people are, I might ask them these questions, each of which, I think, tells something about how happy a person is:

1. In general, how would you say you feel most of the time, in good spirits or in low spirits? (Stouffer *et al.*).
   A. I am (was) usually in good spirits
   B. I am (was) in good spirits some of the time and in low spirits some of the time
   C. I am (was) usually in low spirits
2. Taking all things together, how would you say things are these days—would you say that you are (were) very happy, pretty happy, or not too happy? (Bradburn & Caplovitz).
   A. Very happy
   B. Pretty happy
   C. Not too happy
3. How good a life would you say that you yourself have? We're talking about *just* you, and not your family or your community.
   A. Wonderful life
   B. Good life
   C. So-so life
   D. Poor life
   E. Terrible life

If the answers that people give to the three questions are highly correlated, my confidence is increased that singly or together these questions are indeed measuring happiness. (Chapter 17 discusses the combination of separate proxies in composite *indexes.*)

The branch of economics called "welfare economics" offers a particularly interesting and thorny problem of relating the proxy to the theoretical variable. Most economists agree that the aim of welfare economics is to study the effects of various arrangements on the "welfare" of groups of people, and "welfare" is generally taken to be a synonym for "happiness" (Boulding, 1952). But *the amount of goods and services* (purchasing power) is always the proxy used in welfare economics; studies in welfare economics commonly consider what happens to the goods and income of a community under various conditions. Anyone with a grain of wisdom knows that money is not all there is to happiness, however. And quite obviously a particular good does not have the same happiness value for all people. Here is the perennial stumbling block of "interpersonal comparisons": How can we tell the amount of happiness that a loaf of bread will give a poor person compared to the happiness it will give to a rich person?

Some economists have given up on the idea of validating welfare economics by empirical or logical methods. They feel that the reader must *intuitively* accept the "objective function" relationship between goods and happiness if he is to accept welfare economics. Others simply deny that they are talking about happiness and restrict their discussion to *material* welfare. But then welfare economics loses its claim to speak of the ultimate human concern, and it can become arid and without content.

The situation may not be as bad as it seems; some empirical validation may be possible. "Happiness" has been investigated successfully under various other sets of conditions, and there is no *a priori* reason why it is not possible to relate happiness to various economic conditions also. In fact, happiness seems to be positively related to people's incomes (see J. Simon, 1974).[3]

Empirical investigation of the qualities of art is not dissimilar to welfare economics in this respect. In both cases the dependent variable is ephemeral and subjective. Anyone can simply *state* that a particular novel or painting is "better" than another novel or painting without needing any definition or proxy for "better." But to make a *scientific* study of what makes one novel or play better than another, an objective empirical variable is necessary. It is not difficult to find *some* objective empirical variables; for example, the number of copies the novel sells, and the price paid for the painting, may appeal to many businessmen as excellent proxies for excellence of art. Or one might compare how much two novels or two plays move people by measuring various physiological changes associated with emotion—like respiration or sweating—with devices similar to the lie detector. But I doubt that in the near or distant future *any* objective proxy will satisfy critics and artists as a "true" or "self-evident" measure of the value of art. Instead they are wont to say that to measure art is to measure the unmeasurable. (A content analysis [see Chapter 14] might, however, reveal that "good" adventure stories use higher proportions of verbs than do less exciting adventure stories.)

3. Choosing Independent Variables

Most of the proxies discussed in the previous section have stood for *dependent* variables. But difficulties also exist in choosing appropriate independent variables. For example, if you want to investigate the effect of training upon the performance of a rat running through a maze, you must first specify exactly what you mean by "training," and then you must train the rats in exactly that way.

This is a good place to say again that the questions in a questionnaire survey can have a major influence on what answers mean. To exaggerate the point, if you were trying to measure the dependent variable "degree of liking of Jimmy Carter," it would make quite a difference whether an inter-

---

3. Earlier it was noted that economics has relatively little difficulty in validating its variables, however, precisely because they *can* usually be expressed in single-dimension variables like dollars or tons of steel.

viewer says "Do you like that great American Jimmy Carter?" or "Do you like that traitor Jimmy Carter?"

In contrast to specifying dependent variables, choosing independent variables often permits performance of an objective test to see which variable is better. The researcher can often try out two or more independent variables to see which one works best in "explaining" the dependent variable or which one is more closely correlated with the dependent variable. For example, an economist who is studying the demand for autos and other goods may have a choice between using family income or family expenditures in a given year as a variable; the two may differ because families may save some income or spend some savings. The economist may have theoretical reasons for preferring expenditures, say, but he probably will try out both variables to see which gives the best results.

Another problem is *how many* independent variables to use at one time; this problem mostly afflicts the economists and sociologists in their nonexperimental research. We do not really know how to answer this question; at best the answer is complex and not well understood. In crude terms, one keeps on adding more variables to a cross-classification or other multivariate scheme as long as they improve the explanation appreciably. (On the other hand, one must avoid adding variables that are *not* relevant, because adding them introduces error; this is another difficult and little-understood problem.)

The choice of variables is a cousin to classification; in the latter you specify the *dimensions* or *attitudes* (and the *categories* of those dimensions) on which you will measure the events or species or groups of people in which you are interested. Classification is discussed in Chapter 15, as are the related matters of *scaling* and *measurement*.

Making sure that the supposed variables are not *tautologies*—and therefore not usable in empirical research—is a last obstacle in choosing variables. For example, S. Freud's pleasure-pain principle is a tautology as it is usually stated. If one says that a person does what is pleasurable to him and that he does not do what is painful, then *everything* he does is pleasurable by *definition*. And, if so, there is no way of empirically distinguishing pleasurable from painful actions or of using pleasure-pain as an empirical variable. C. Darwin's evolution principle also is often stated as a tautology.

4. Choosing a Level of Aggregation

The world is like a cobweb, I suggested before. Because every filament is ultimately related to every other filament, a movement of any filament will finally be reflected by every other filament. Nevertheless, some filaments are closer to or farther from others, and there will be stronger or weaker association between them. Also, a movement in a given filament y might be caused by the movement in filament x, where the movement is initiated; or the movements in both x and y might be reflecting movement initiated at z (the "third factor").[4]

Now we must consider a more complex view of the world. Consider the question of why people buy automobiles. Just a few strands of this question are shown in Figure 6.2.

The four different *purchase* rectangles represent four different "levels of aggregation." A given scientist might—and some do—try to explain any one of the following:

1. *total* purchases (or changes in total purchases)
2. purchases by particular *groups*, like northerners or blacks or Catholics (or *comparisons* between groups, northerners versus southerners, for example)
3. purchases by *households*, expressed as probabilities
4. purchases by *individuals*.

Economists are mostly interested in total purchases; sometimes they think about the group or individual level of aggregation but primarily as a means for understanding and predicting total purchases. Anthropologists are also mostly interested in total purchases. Sociologists are more likely to be interested in the group level of aggregation. Psychologists are mostly interested in individual purchases. Market researchers are interested in individual purchases when they study advertising appeals related to auto styles, for example; but they work at the group level of aggregation when they study where to locate dealers and where to advertise and at the level of total demand for autos when they advise on how many cars to produce. Most of the market researcher's attention is actually devoted to a level of aggregation not even shown in the diagram—individual purchase of particular *brands* of cars.

These points should be considered when deciding at which level of aggregation to work: First, what level of aggregation are you *interested* in? That is, for which level of aggregation do you want to make decisions, for example the individual or the nation? Or what body of data do you want to explain? If you want to study the causal relationship running from per capita income to literacy or the correlation between per capita income and suicide rates, you want data for individuals and not groups. But you might want to study the relationship between *national* income and literacy if you are interested in the extent to which a high national income produces literacy. The level of aggregation in which you are interested is often influenced by the discipline within which you work, but you should not *blindly* adopt the level of aggregation usually used in your discipline.

4. The scientist's problem is that the connections among filaments do not always seem obvious or sensible. "During World War II, the production of optical instruments was temporarily greatly hampered by a shortage of babies' diapers. The reason was that diapers were an excellent polishing material for lenses" (Morgenstern, p. 133).

FIGURE 6.2 **Some Possible Variables and Levels of Aggregation for Use in Analysis of Auto Purchasing**

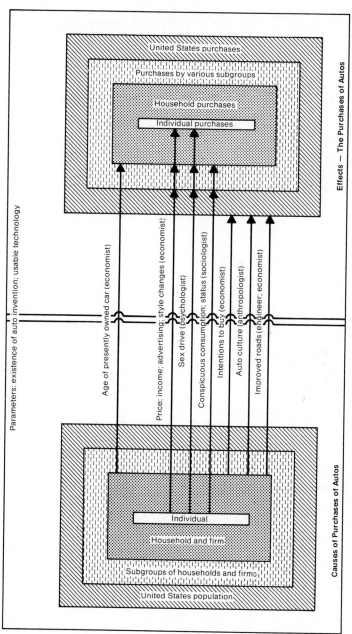

Please Note: The assignment of concepts in this diagram to particular fields may be misleading, especially in these years of the late 1970s when the social sciences seem to be breaking down the partitions among them.

Second, which level of aggregation is it *feasible* to study? Sometimes data are not available at the desired level of aggregation. For example, E. Durkheim studied the relationship between religion and suicide. The religions of people who commit suicide are the relevant data, but all that was available were the numbers of people who committed suicide and the numbers who followed the various religions in countries and states as wholes. Durkheim did as well as he could at this too-high level of aggregation, showing that suicide is more common in places dominated by particular religions. But this tactic also occasionally led him into the ecological fallacy (discussed in Chapter 21).

Sometimes one must go to extra effort to study the subgroups separately so as not to be misled by the aggregate. This is especially true when comparing two or more aggregates that are composed of different proportions of subgroups. For example, the crude death rate among U.S. blacks (that is, the proportion of deaths in a year to total population of U.S. blacks) is lower than the crude death rate for U.S. whites, but the life expectancy at birth for whites is higher than for blacks, as of 1976 (*Population Index*). The explanation is that a larger proportion of whites are in the older age brackets, due to lower mortality and lower fertility in the past. In such a situation one must disaggregate and compare the mortality rates for each age group in order to compare blacks and whites fairly.

Third, sometimes it is easier to understand the whole than to understand all its parts and the relationships among them. For example, it will be much easier and more accurate to determine the effect of a price rise upon auto sales by studying the relationship of *total* auto sales in past years when different prices prevailed than to try to understand the motivations and psychological reactions to a price rise of individuals who might or might not purchase autos. It is particularly sensible to work at the higher level of aggregation (total purchases, rather than individuals, in this case) when there are *many* different motivations and psychological influences that bear importantly upon the individual's response (in this case, response to the price rise).

Sometimes, however, the whole does not equal the sum of the parts, in which case one cannot reason from the parts to the whole, or vice versa. One reason that the whole may behave differently from the parts is that there may be *interaction* among the parts. An example is R. Niebuhr's argument about "moral man and immoral society"; one cannot ascertain the likelihood of a country's starting a war from data on the amount of conflict and hostility among neighbors within the country. J. Keynes' thrift paradox is another case; societies whose citizens save a lot may thereby grow poor instead of rich.[5]

5. Another technical reason that the whole may not equal the sum of its parts is known as the "aggression problem" in economics. The *demand functions* of individual consumers, say, do not sum in any simple way to the demand function for the economy as a whole. The problem is particularly acute in economics because the basic deductive theory concerns individuals, but the data and policy decisions concern higher levels of aggregation like the nation.

Experience and careful thought, then, are the only aids to making correct decisions about levels of aggregation. Often the wisdom of your field will be a good guide but not always; for example, an economist can sometimes do better if he abandons the usual economist's level of aggregation—total demand—and works at the level of individuals (Katona) or subgroups (Morgan in Klein *et al.*). Similarly, a psychologist can often best answer a psychological question by working with groups of people rather than with individuals.

Some people have thought that the lowest level of aggregation must always be best. This view is called "reductionism." The argument against reductionism is mostly not a matter of logic, except to the degree that, because there is always *some* possible lower level of aggregation, *no* level really meets the reductionist requirement. In this view, psychology is more "basic" than sociology, biology is more basic than psychology, chemistry is more fundamental than biology, and so on. It is a simple empirical fact of the history of science, however, that in many cases it has proved more fruitful to work at higher levels of aggregation.

5. Choosing a Level of Explanation

There are many, many variables that one might say are causes of auto purchases. Just a few of these variables are shown on the left side of Figure 6.2. The question is, which of these variables should one choose when investigating the causes of auto purchasing? Deciding among possible alternatives is the central task in specifying variables.

This section deals not with how to *think up* variables, but rather with how to *decide among* variables, that is, how to choose which variables to include and exclude among those you do think up. I assume that you have already completed the thinking-up stage, which you should summarize this way:

> auto purchasing = *f* (the invention of autos, the auto culture per capita, income, income of individual, age of present car, price of autos, style changes of cars, desire for sex mastery, desire to consume conspicuously, desire for high status, stated intentions to buy a car, condition of roads . . .).

This equation is simply an all-inclusive listing of factors that you think might influence purchasing. Writing down the functional form is a crucial step in jogging your imagination and clearing your mind. You may find it easier to write symbols instead of words (for example, S = auto sales), but I find it safer to stick to words at the very beginning.

When you decide at which level of aggregation you will work, some variables will be excluded. For example, the sex drives of the country as a whole do not vary much from year to year, though individuals may change and there may be differences among individuals. Therefore, sex drives are not a useful variable in explaining the variation in auto purchases from year to year. On the other hand, if you are working at the level of individual purchases, the existence of our automobile culture will not help much as a variable, for all individual subjects are part of the culture. The same is true of price and the individual. But there is not an *automatic* relationship between the level of aggregation on the right side and the level of abstraction on the left side. For example, intention to buy is an individual-level variable, but it can be used to predict total purchases. You must think your way through this maze, variable by variable.

Your discipline may supply some guidance on which variables to include on the causal side. For example, social status is a "sociological variable." But on occasion economists and psychologists have also found it useful.

FIGURE 6.3 **The Story of an Accident**

In the community nobody thought much about traffic accidents. There were traffic laws but governing bodies had never put enough money into building roads, training drivers, and supervising traffic.	Public Apathy Funds Not Made Available		Government	Early Causes Neglect and Failure of Many People
Joe was taught by his father. There was no driver training in the schools he attended.	No Organized Driver Training		Educators	
His father stressed the mechanics of the car so that Joe would be able to take care of it himself. As soon as he learned to manipulate the controls, Joe drove by himself.	Failure to Stress Safety in Teaching		Educators	
Some years later, Joe had a car of his own. Every night he drove to the next town to see his girl. One night he was late and had to hurry.				
The highway had been built many years before when cars could not go so fast as Joe's. The curve was too flat and sharp.	Design	Road	Engineers	
On the way, Joe passed a road sign which had once read "Slow—Dangerous Curve" but now it was too faded and dirty to be legible.	Maintenance	Road	Engineers	
Cars of the model of Joe's had cheap window crank knobs which came off with use and left a sharp crank end exposed.	Design	Vehicle	Engineers	
Joe's crank knob had come off. He had meant to have it fixed but had never got around to doing it.	Maintenance	Vehicle	Engineers	
There were too few police to make speed violations much to worry about. Moreover Joe had never been ticketed even when he knew officers had seen him violate. He thought you could talk yourself out of it. Besides, the judges usually let you off easy.	Inadequate Supervision Inactive Personnel	Police Courts	Enforcement Agencies	

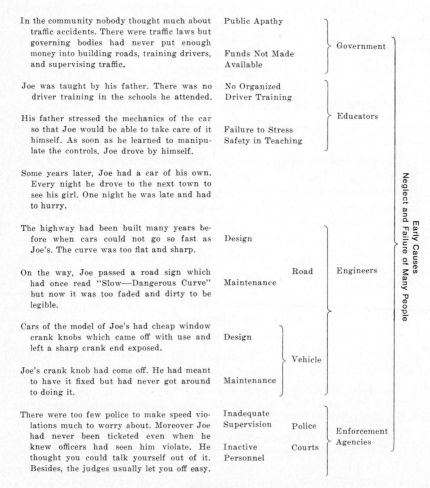

Figure 14.4.

Source: "Framework for Assessment of Cause of Automobile Accidents," pp. 442–3, by J. Stannard Baker, in *The Language of Social Research,* edited by P. Lazarsfeld and M. Rosenberg; copyright © 1955 by The Free Press of Glencoe, a division of The Macmillan Company.

There are also causal relationships among some of the variables on the causal side. If a relationship between two independent variables is very strong, it is not sensible to use both variables because their effects will overlap strongly.

The key point is that no one level of explanation is *inherently* superior to other levels of explanation. Consider also the example of mental illness and the many levels at which it is fruitful to investigate it. Biologists and physicians have studied the physiology and pharmacology of mental illness, and they have discovered valuable physical and chemical treatments. Psycholo-

How and Why It Happened

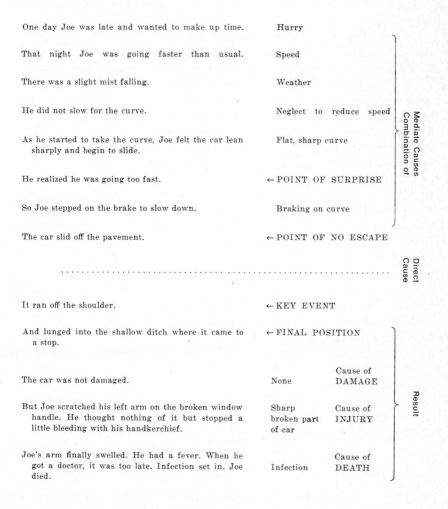

One day Joe was late and wanted to make up time.	Hurry	
That night Joe was going faster than usual.	Speed	
There was a slight mist falling.	Weather	
He did not slow for the curve.	Neglect to reduce speed	Mediate Causes Combination of
As he started to take the curve, Joe felt the car lean sharply and begin to slide.	Flat, sharp curve	
He realized he was going too fast.	← POINT OF SURPRISE	
So Joe stepped on the brake to slow down.	Braking on curve	
The car slid off the pavement.	← POINT OF NO ESCAPE	Direct Cause

It ran off the shoulder.	← KEY EVENT		
And lunged into the shallow ditch where it came to a stop.	← FINAL POSITION		
The car was not damaged.	None	Cause of DAMAGE	Result
But Joe scratched his left arm on the broken window handle. He thought nothing of it but stopped a little bleeding with his handkerchief.	Sharp broken part of car	Cause of INJURY	
Joe's arm finally swelled. He had a fever. When he got a doctor, it was too late. Infection set in. Joe died.	Infection	Cause of DEATH	

gists think about mental disease as a functional disorder that results from a person's early learning and life experience, and they study how to retrain the individual psychologically. Sociologists and social psychologists have studied the various types of home life and environment that lead to mental disease, and perhaps this work teaches us how to reduce mental illness by reducing the conditions under which it arises. Economists have not paid much attention to mental illness, but if they did they would assess its economic effect upon the community and then study the costs of various programs to reduce mental illness; such studies might be valuable (see Fein).

Each of these levels of investigation and explanation of mental illness can be valuable, and we benefit if each person—psychologist, sociologist, or biologist—tackles the problem with those theories and methods that she knows best.

Causation of automobile accidents is still another example. As Figure 6.3 shows, there are many factors that may be considered causal variables or conditions for an accident. The variables that an investigator chooses to study depend upon his discipline and his ability to manipulate particular aspects of the situation. Engineers can manipulate the design of highway and car; therefore they study how various designs affect the accident rate. Educational psychologists study methods of teaching auto safety. And so on. There is potential value in studying many of the listed variables that enter at various points in the causal chain.

Variation in birth rates offers a last example of a phenomenon that can sensibly be studied at many levels of explanation. Aside from biological facts, why do some families have more children than do others? At the psychological level, the effects of personal inadequacy, "ego-centered interest in children," and liking for children have been examined (Kiser & Whelpton). Such social-psychological variables as marital adjustment, conformity to group patterns, and doubling-up of families have been investigated. Sociological variables have included religion, nationality, adherence to traditions, social class, education, and their associated values. Variables with an anthropological flavor include the sacred values of a culture, the extent of structural cohesion and authority in a culture, and the extent of social disorganization (Lorimer, pp. 247–251). And, of course, economic variables, including per capita income, laws governing inheritance of land, business cycles, and tax laws subsidizing or penalizing large families, have long been considered relevant to birth rates. Some of these sets of variables have proved more fruitful than have others, but each level of explanation has certainly been worth the investigation.

6. Summary

Theoretical variables must be made operational if empirical research is to take place. The choice of empirical proxies to represent the theoretical (hypothetical) variables of interest is crucial. The empirical variables must be both observable and relevant.

In some cases the choice of proxy may be straightforward because the hypothetical variable is clearly defined (for example, the number of people watching the Olympics on television). In other cases the theoretical variable may be vague and abstract (for example, happiness).

The ingredients in making a wise choice of proxy are the usual ones: research imagination, experience, and good judgment. Choosing independent variables wisely requires that the investigator understand the material and have sound hunches about the causes of the phenomenon being studied.

An important decision is the level of aggregation of the dependent variable. Should one work with individuals, or small groups, or large groups? If possible, it is best to work at *several* levels of aggregation to see whether the results corroborate each other.

The independent variables may also be considered at various levels of explanation. To some extent the choice depends upon your discipline and point of view, but the choice also should be illuminated by general scientific intuition.

EXERCISES

1. Give examples from your field of five dependent variables for which direct data cannot be obtained but whose conceptual referents (hypothetical variables) are clearly defined.
2. Suggest proxies for the variables you gave in Exercise 1.
3. Give examples from your field of five hypothetical (theoretical) variables that are vague and not clearly defined.
4. Suggest proxies for the variables you gave in Exercise 3.
5. Give a realistic example of how a slight difference in a question might have a large effect on the result.
6. Give an example of a research situation in which one must decide what level of explanation at which to work.
7. Give an example from your field in which the researcher would come up with an erroneous conclusion (the opposite from the right conclusion) by working at the wrong level of aggregation, that is, an example in which the whole does not equal the simple sum of the parts.

part two research decisions and procedures

7 the steps in an empirical research study

How do you start a research project? What do you do first and second and next after that? These are the pressing questions to the novice in research. The aim of this chapter is to tell you how to get started on your research work, step by step.

The procedures described will be loose and unspecific because of my emphasis on the diversity of research types and methods. Once you have reached the point of deciding on the actual method you will use, however, you may wish to examine the specific procedures recommended in books devoted to the problems of research in particular fields.[1] Remember, nevertheless, that any given procedure is not a sacred order that must be obeyed but is rather a series of steps that has often been found useful in a *particular* field.

The following broad discussion of approaching a research problem is intended mainly as a checklist for doing research. It may also be valuable as a checklist in analyzing the research reports done by others. If you are able to ask and answer these questions about someone else's research, you know what the other fellow did and how well he did it.

The steps given here look neatly ordered. In practice, one goes back and forth from one aspect of the research process to another, sometimes with the

1. That is, for economics and business, R. Ferber and P. J. Verdoorn (Chap. 2); for education and social psychology, F. Whitney (Chap. 5); for marketing research, J. Lorie and H. Roberts (Chap. 3); for sociology, C. Selltiz, *et al.* (pp. 12–14).

feeling of getting nowhere. Harburg's map on page 69 dramatizes the variety of paths one may follow in the search for knowledge.

Step 1. Finding a Good Research Problem

This book is about research methods. But the best chosen methods and the fanciest, most rigorous and sophisticated techniques are worthless unless the problem is important. It behooves you, therefore, to invest time, energy, and thought into finding an *important* topic for research. (How to decide which problems are important is discussed in Chapter 8.)

But more. Even if the topic is important, you won't get far unless you are interested in it. So you must try to find a subject that will keep you interested.

We can divide the sources for research ideas into five categories: (1) The scientific literature; (2) fields of your general interest; (3) recognition of social problems; (4) ideas suggested by others; and (5) data collected by you for other purposes. Let us consider them one-by-one.

1. Scientific articles often contain suggestions for further research. But few undergraduate or graduate students are sufficiently familiar with the scientific literature to make this a likely place to hunt for a topic. (Furthermore, it is my opinion that the best topics come not from the literature but from direct observation of people and groups.)

2. You may have a strong interest in Appalachia, or gymnastics, or cooking, or unemployment. If so, you may have run across questions to which you could find no answer. One such question can point to a topic that will interest you.

3. Social problems are perhaps the best source of important problems. For example, thinking about the rampant unemployment of the 1930s led Keynes to his greatest discovery. More likely for a beginner, you may be aware of a local problem such as how to inform students of available health services; perhaps there is an interesting and useful project for you in experimenting with various communications methods to determine which works best. Managers of nonprofit and business enterprises often have problems that need study, and are delighted to work with you.

4. Instructors often have ideas that they are happy to suggest to you. Don't feel bashful about asking, and ask several instructors, so you can have a better chance to choose one that interests you. The best instructors to ask are those that have done a lot of empirical research themselves.

5. An infrequent but important source of research ideas for the professional investigator is the data that the investigator is studying for another purpose. In the course of examining or analyzing a set of data the investigator may notice an unexpected pattern, or a discrepancy from the standard pattern, or simply an interesting observation. This process of unexpected happy discovery of a new scientific lead was labeled "serendipity" by Merton, and the name stuck.

By its nature, you do not *choose* to stumble across new ideas by seren-dipity. But you can increase the probability of such a "lucky" event by reading widely, thinking freely, and spending much time with large masses of data.

Step 2. Ask "What Do I Want to Find Out?"

No matter what type of problem you want to work on and no matter what methods you will eventually use, your empirical work *must* begin with a careful consideration of the research *problem*. You must find out what it is that you are trying to find out. You must ask: What information am I trying to obtain? What is the exact question to which I seek an answer?

It is hard work to specify an intellectual problem exactly. It is much easier to wave your hands in the air and say something vague to yourself or to other people about how "I'm interested in getting some answers about juvenile delinquency." What answers? To what questions? Do you want to know how many juvenile delinquents there are? Or whether parents' incomes affect the rate of juvenile delinquency? Or whether juvenile delinquents enjoy their delinquency? Or what?

And each of those questions is still too vague. If it is the effect of parents' incomes on juvenile delinquency that interests you, do you want to find out whether low income causes increased delinquency? Or whether parents with high incomes can use their money to buy their children out of jams? Or whether children in different income groups are delinquent in different ways? Or what?

Conformity is another example. Eminent social observers—including psy-chologists, psychoanalysts, and sociologists—hand down to anyone who will listen pronouncements that Americans have become more conformist in the twentieth century.[2] Interesting, but is it true? Before anyone can really know, the question must be made more specific. Do Americans join more organizations than they used to? Do we dress and talk more alike than we used to? Is there less variety in our political opinions? There may be great disagreement over *which* specific question or combination of questions is appropriate; one must choose here which operational definitions will stand for theoretical concepts. But there can be no disagreement that if casual observations about conformity are to be proved or disproved, *some* specific operational questions must be substituted for the unspecified term "con-formity."

Economists have trouble with such problems as whether people are "better off" in one economic system or another and in developed or unde-

---

2. "Eventually, he [the industrial worker] is under the influence of our whole cultural apparatus, the advertisements, movies, television, newspapers, just as everybody else, and can hardly escape being driven into conformity, although perhaps more slowly than other sectors of the population. What holds true for the industrial worker holds true also for the farmer." (Fromm, p. 163).

veloped countries. They usually duck these matters by claiming that they are interested only in *economic* welfare and that economic welfare is measured by per capita income, and that is that. Do you think that this attitude is reasonable?

Making a research problem specific robs it of its conversational glamor, of course. But you must do it if you want to be a successful hard-nosed empirical researcher.

Making a problem specific is difficult for the same reason that creating specific operational definitions of scientific terms is difficult. You must *make up the rules yourself*, rather than find out what someone else has in mind. Research is not the same as answering examination questions; it is more like constructing the questions.

Zen Buddhism offers a clue to why specifying research problems is so hard. Read this description of a fictional incident from M. West's *The Ambassador:*

> Sometimes he would lay before me, as a subject of meditation, one of those apparently meaningless propositions which are *kōan*.
> The one which he proposed to me, and to which he returned always with mild persistence was this:
> "What will you do when they ask you to kill the cuckoo?"
> My first reply was a challenge to Musō to define the terms of the proposition. Who, for example, were they? What was the cuckoo, and why should I be asked to kill it?
> Musō smiled and refused the challenge. "You, Amberleysan, *you* must tell *me* what I mean." (West, p. 17)

There are no boundary lines or classifications in nature, and *you* must draw such definitional lines around the part of nature you want to study.[3]

How to *find* problems on which to work is not discussed here; it is primarily a matter of scientific imagination and insight.[4] The research questions that you uncover will depend on your interests, on the gaps in empirical knowledge in the field in which you are working, on what your bosses want to know, and so forth. These and many other factors will determine how, in moments of inspiration, you finish this sentence: "Gee, wouldn't it be interesting to find out . . . ?"

It is helpful to consider *which general type* a research problem is. Is it an attempt to establish a comparison? to find a cause or an effect? to measure

3. The analogy between Zen and science goes further. Zen works to wipe out the conventional categories of everyday life so that one may see the world with fresh eyes. And the good scientist refuses to accept conventional ways of classifying the world and its relationships. As the imagination transcends the old categories, it moves on to new ways of perceiving the world. The end points of Zen and science are completely different, however. The scientist must eventually convert her vision into objective concepts so that they can be communicated to others and enter into the body of science, whereas the Zen adept's vision remains her own.

4. For discussion of this aspect of research, see J. Young; A. Bachrach; W. Cannon; W. Beveridge (especially Chaps. 5 and 6); C. Mills (pp. 200–201, 211–217).

the dimensions of something? Chapter 4 classifies research questions and discusses the types.

Step 3. Establish the Purpose of the Project

Why do you want to know the answers to the research question you are asking? How will the information be used and by whom? The purpose and the destination of the knowledge can be important in deciding how to carry out the research. The U.S. Bureau of the Census uses methods of collecting data that are different from those used by commercial research organizations because the purposes of the two kinds of research are different, although the subject matter may be the same. Compare how you investigate whether it is raining before going on a picnic to the way in which the U.S. Weather Service collects information for farmers to use in deciding when to plant. Television ratings also exemplify how a technical choice depends upon purpose. Such ratings generally measure the number of *households* in which the television sets are tuned to various programs. The household, rather than the individual, is the purchasing unit, and the sponsors who pay for the ratings are interested in purchasing. An educational television station, however, is more interested in which *individuals* watch given shows than in which households.[5]

Your purpose may also determine whether you can use information already gathered by other researchers. For a picnic decision, you can use the Weather Service report. But if you farm in a section of the country that has its own precipitation peculiarities not reported by the Weather Service, you may have to collect your own rainfall data. Another example: educational television stations sometimes feel it necessary to collect their own data on viewing, even when commercial ratings on their stations are available to them.

Step 4. Determine the Value of the Research

Perhaps you have several ideas for research projects. You want to invest your time and energy in the work that will be *most* valuable according to whatever is the relevant measure of value. For example, understanding the economy of the United States is more valuable than understanding the economy of Kankakee, Illinois. And depression is a more important psychological problem than is fear of stuffed pandas. Chapter 8 is devoted to methods of comparing the various candidates for your attention.

Step 5. Saturate Yourself in the Problem

It is important to have a wide and deep understanding of the background of your study, especially in research to determine relationships of cause and

5. See Jessen, *et al.* (U.S. House of Representatives, p. 55).

effect.[6] Notice how R. Benedict saturated herself in her materials at the beginning of an anthropological project:

> . . . [D]uring the period when she was doing the research that led to *The Chrysanthemum and the Sword* . . . she did not evolve her ideas "mystically" from her inner consciousness, but worked very systematically. She saturated herself in Japanese materials of a carefully selected variety: literature, art, projective tests, interviews, etc. After she thought she had detected some highest common factors or least common denominators that constituted, so to speak, implicit premises cutting across bodies of culture content that were quite different, she then wrote down some hypotheses as to what she should find—and should not find—in as yet unexamined data if her initial formulations were correct. She then sought out fresh materials drawn from the same categories and validated, rejected, or reformulated her initial hypotheses and made at least one more trial run. Most American social psychologists, to be sure, would have been appalled at one aspect of her procedure. I once asked her: "But *how many* new novels, for instance, do you think you must read and analyze before you stop?" She told me plainly that this was a silly question. (Lerner, p. 261)

And W. Whyte's experience in "street corner society" taught him the importance of saturating oneself in the situation:

> The ideas that we have in research are only in part a logical product growing out of a careful weighing of evidence. We do not generally think problems through in a straight line. Often we have the experience of being immersed in a mass of confusing data. We study the data carefully, bringing all our powers of logical analysis to bear upon them. We come up with an idea or two. But still the data do not fall in any coherent pattern. Then we go on living with the data—and with the people—until perhaps some chance occurrence casts a totally different light upon the data, and we begin to see a pattern that we have not seen before. This pattern is not purely an artistic creation. Once we think we see it, we must re-examine our notes and perhaps set out to gather new data in order to determine whether the pattern adequately represents the life we are observing or is simply a product of our imagination. (Whyte, pp. 279–280)

W. Caudill committed himself to a mental institution to increase his understanding, though I do not recommend such heroic measures in all cases.

Step 6. Choose Empirical Variables

At this stage the talkers are separated from the fact-getters; it is the stage at which interesting ideas are transformed into empirical research problems. Choosing empirical variables is the extension of Step 1, and we might lump them together, but I think that it is fruitful to separate them.

One of the important functions of teachers is to exhort students to "narrow down the problem to manageable size" (Roberts, n.d.) so that they will finish within a reasonable length of time. Such narrowing-down goes

6. M. Cohen and E. Nagel emphasized the importance of thorough knowledge of the subject matter in formulating hypothesis (pp. 200–202).

hand in hand with thinking through the problem to the point at which the variables are stated in *operational terms.* The struggle to specify variables that can be investigated empirically often forces the researcher to narrow the problem to a sensible size.

At this stage, one formulates the research as a functional relationship, $y = f(x_1, x_2, x_3, \ldots)$; that is, one decides what will be the empirical variables and which are dependent and independent. It is not the final stage of specificity; that comes when one finally decides how to *measure* the variables, a matter discussed in Chapter 6.[7] But the translation of the question into a functional form is a giant stride in the empirical research.

Sometimes the translation into a functional relationship is a simple matter of finding empirical "proxies" to stand for the theoretical concepts and of deciding which variable to consider dependent and which to consider independent. For example, perhaps you have narrowed your area of interest to the point at which you ask "What is the relationship of scallion prices to sales of scallions?" One way—but only one way, and others are possible—to translate your question into functional language is to hypothesize that "quantity of scallions sold = f (price of scallions)." Notice that you could also have formulated the functional relationship as "price of scallions = q (quantity of scallions sold)," if you were primarily interested in explaining changes in price rather than in explaining changes in the amount sold.[8] In either instance, you would still have to specify the actual operational definitions of your variables, for "price" and "quantity" can mean different things, and each can be measured in different ways.

Now let us consider an example in which it is more difficult to translate the original question into the specific form required for empirical research. Your original vague interest is in "finding out what a single person's life is like." An all-encompassing study of all aspects of singles' lives is obviously impossible; therefore, you first narrow the question to "Are singles more or less happy than are married people?" With this question, you can satisfy yourself that you have completed Step 1.

Assuming that you have established the purpose of your project (Step 2) and determined the value of your research (Step 3), you must now reduce your question to functional language. Implicit in the form of the question "Are singles more or less happy than are married people?" is the more specific question "Is there a connection between a person's marital status and his state of happiness?" Therefore, you write the function "happiness of people = f (marital status)." This function expresses a question that you will then

7. The final stage of specificity also requires that the *form* of the functional relationship be specified, that is, whether a graph of the variables would be a straight line or a curve of one sort or another. The most common functional form is the straight line, which is implicit in most simple correlation studies. One can avoid choosing a functional form only if one limits the study to classification.

8. In some cases you might simultaneously investigate *both* these functional forms. But such sophisticated matters need not concern us now.

test with empirical data: Is there a relationship of the sort represented in the equation?

Later you must go further and state the variables in terms that suggest how the variables will be *measured*. The measurement of marital status is fairly easy, but the measurement of happiness is obviously a thorny matter. Some aspects of happiness have been successfully measured with questionnaires (Bradburn & Caplovitz, Stouffer *et al.*, Knupfer, Clark, & Room), and you decide to do so also. Therefore, you write "people's answers to questions about happiness = *f* (marital status)."

But the variables have not yet been specified completely, because operational definitions have not yet been formulated. For example, will you *ask* the person his marital status? Obviously you will. More important, what are the exact questions whose answers will be considered the measures of happiness? Nor has it been decided *at what level of aggregation* the variables will be measured, that is, whether you will deal with group averages of marital status, income, happiness, and so forth, or will work with the data on individuals (discussed in Chapter 6). For now, however, Step 5 has been completed, reducing the question to a functional form.

The more complex the question, the more difficult it is to choose satisfactory variables. Breaking down the issue into several parts is often helpful. One often comes to realize that there are two or more questions. When the questions are separated, the tangle sometimes disappears magically. (This is true in chemistry, too, says Wilson, p. 36.)

A good test of whether the problem is sufficiently specific is to ask whether or not another researcher could take your statement of the variables and probably arrive at much the same outcome as you would if you finished the research project yourself.

Perhaps the necessity of narrowing down the question does not apply with such force to those researchers who embark on descriptive research in totally new areas of investigation. But successful descriptive research requires great competence and is usually done by people who break this rule of narrowing-down only with calculated forethought.

An advantage of research that *tests a theory* is that the theory often suggests a precise hypothesis that can be tested empirically on neatly defined variables. But hypotheses that are not deduced from a body of well-knit theory seldom come in such precise form.

Making clear which universe you want to understand and which universe is practical to work with will help you to reduce the problem to a functional relationship. This decision affects all subsequent decisions about research design. For example, a veterinary researcher interested in the growth of animals in response to hormone injections probably will proceed differently from a researcher whose ultimate interest is the mental growth of humans and who experiments with hormone injections in animals as an intermediate research device.

It is perfectly legitimate to confine your interest to a subuniverse. A. Kinsey studied only white males at first. But do not confine yourself to a subuniverse that is of no interest in itself simply because it would be troublesome to gather data on the larger universe.[9] One reviewer took Kinsey, *et al.*, to task severely on this point:

> The point is simply this: unless one is interested only in the 5,940 women in Kinsey's sample, which of course nobody is . . . then the reader must be able to project the found percentages against *some* kind of meaningful population. Indeed, what on earth is a measurement from a total sample good for, unless it is "more or less representative" of some meaningful population? (Zeisel, 1953, p. 520)

On the other hand, one does not always have to take a random sample of the entire universe in order to generalize to that universe, as we shall see in the discussion of sampling. For example, H. Ebbinghaus generalized to human learning from his study of one subject, himself; and I. Pavlov did not take a random sample of all dogs for his conditioning experiments. The topic of choosing empirical variables has only been introduced here; the next chapter discusses it in detail.

Step 7. Calculate the Benefits of Accuracy and the Costs of Error

What is at stake in the research? One must make explicit what depends upon the results and their accuracy. Estimating the costs of various amounts of error in the conclusions or, conversely, the value of the research at various levels of accuracy is especially difficult in pure research. At least some comparisons are possible, however. For example, we know now, and probably scientists knew even when the first measurements were made, that a 10 percent error in the estimate of the speed of light and a 10 percent error in unemployment estimates are more serious than a 10 percent error in the estimated speed of quarterhorses at a state fair in Montana.

One of the most promising developments in research methods in recent decades has been the theory of the value of information—which information, and how much of it, is of economic value. For example, is it worth drilling a test oil well before the main drilling, or is it a better bet to proceed directly to the main drilling? The answer depends upon the chances of hitting oil with a test and with a main drilling, the costs of the test and the main drilling, and the likely profit from the well.

The estimate of the value of accuracy will affect how one goes about the research and especially how extensive a sample one takes. Correct determination of the winner in the race for the Presidency of the United States is

9. "Universe" and "subuniverse" are relative terms. Every universe can be viewed as part of some larger universe, of course. I use the term "subuniverse" to apply only to a unit that is not itself of ultimate interest but is part of the universe that is the focus of most of our interest. Also one man's subuniverse is another man's universe; one sex researcher might be interested in only white midwestern males, though most people would be more interested in statements about all United States males.

important enough so that every single person who wants to vote is polled on election day—a very expensive survey, indeed. But, to choose the fireworks for a town's Independence Day celebration, the mayor may sensibly begin and end the poll with his own child and the child next door. Chapter 8 covers this topic in detail.

Step 8. Determine the Most Important Research Obstacles

The answers to most research questions are not immediately obvious. The patterns of nature and social life are often obscure. Nature seems to throw stumbling blocks—disruptions, deceptions, long distances, high costs, and so on—under the feet of the scientific inquirer. Of course it is foolish to think that there is an evil genius who foils the investigator, though some scientists offer explanations that would almost imply the presence of such an evil genius.[10] At this stage of the research, you must think ahead and take stock of the obstacles to be overcome. Only after you have spotted them, can you develop a sensible procedure for your research. For example, Kinsey came to realize that some people would not answer questions about sex freely and truthfully and that much previous work on sex behavior was therefore not very useful. Kinsey was forced to create a whole battery of new methods, the development of which was an important part of his work.

Step 9. Choose Methods

Once the important obstacles have been identified, you should select the methods that will surmount the obstacles most efficiently and effectively. Consider *all* the various research methods and combinations of them. This is the time to ask, How shall I gather the information I need?

> Rather than disputing about what is "the" best method, behavioral scientists, it seems to me, should examine dispassionately the advantages and disadvantages of every established technique in terms of the relevant situation and the specific questions that are being asked. . . . (Lerner, p. 259)

For a problem in social psychology one might evaluate the potential of an experiment against that of a survey. For a study of the economics of two-seller competition one might compare a laboratory experiment with a field investigation of two-seller markets. For a problem in market research or sociology one might compare personal interviews with mail interviews. In public health one might compare a questionnaire survey with an examination of hospital records, as in the design of smoking-and-health studies.

Real-estate appraisers use many methods. A house is a house, it would

---

10. To credit the possibility that smoking does not cause health damage but rather that smokers are genetically more predisposed to a whole host of different diseases is almost to believe in a genetic component that has such an evil genius. See J. Simon (1966c) or K. Brownlee.

seem, but, depending upon the circumstances and the information available, an appraiser may value the house mostly on the basis of its past selling prices, by comparison with the selling prices of other houses sold recently in the neighborhood, or by summing the values of such aspects of the house as value of the land, number of rooms, and age. The final appraisal probably takes more than one of these methods into account.

Advertising-effectiveness researchers have an especially wide armamentarium, and it takes good judgment to pick the method that will yield much information at little expense. Among the methods are experimental, survey, and panel measurements of sales; readership scores; lotteries in special theaters that show commercials; attitude surveys; and many more. The history of advertising research illustrates the value of a wide knowledge of methods. But the neglect of sales-evaluation methods also illustrates the ill effects of narrow knowledge. Such neglect occurred because most advertising researchers were trained as psychologists or sociologists and never learned the methods for sales evaluation that are common in the training of economists.

To illustrate the process of considering the merits of various methods, imagine that we want to find out how sensitive the consumption of liquor in the United States is to changes in the general price of liquor, so that we can predict the effect of a liquor-tax increase. If the price goes up, people will drink *somewhat* less liquor, but we want to know how *much* less. If the price goes up 10 percent, will people drink 1 percent less, 5 percent less, 10 percent less, 20 percent less?

It is reasonable, when one wants to know something about people, to think of *asking* them. But people do not tell the full truth about their consumption of liquor, and, furthermore, they probably cannot predict their responses to a price change very well. Therefore we must turn to other methods.

Experimenting with the average price of all types of liquor in a liquor store might give clear-cut and reliable results. It would, however, be difficult to obtain the cooperation of a liquor store for such an experiment. More important, other stores nearby would maintain the old prices, and many people would simply shop elsewhere at the old prices, which would ruin the experiment for our purposes.

We might analyze the sales of liquor in the nation as a whole over a period of years. Indeed, this method was used fairly successfully in England and Sweden (Stone, Prest, Malmquist). But it suffers from the lack of variation in the price of liquor, and the variation is hard to measure in a nation as a whole. Without variations in price we cannot measure the effect of price on consumption. We might compare consumption in countries in which liquor prices differ. My working solution was to compare consumption (actually, sales) before and after *tax changes* caused across-the-board price increases in various states in the United States (J. Simon, 1966a).

At some time one should consider whether or not the question can best be answered through *pure deduction.* Some ancient philosophers believed that they could deduce the answer to *any* question, and they looked down their noses at empirical research. Better to discuss with other wise men how many teeth are in a horse's mouth than to examine the dental equipment of a real live hayburner. Such a narrow attitude is foolish. But there are many situations in which deduction is more appropriate than any empirical method. For example, Chapter 14 discusses why the question of whether or not trading stamps raise food prices can probably be answered more correctly with deduction alone than with empirical studies, given the poor data that are available. Similarly, we shall see that our reasoning about the effect of population growth on economic development is more impressive than is the scanty empirical evidence.

Here is a brief checklist for evaluating alternative research methods:

First, how *relevant* will the results be? An experiment often can promise clear-cut reliable results, but they may not generalize to the universe in which you are interested. For example, animal experiments with tobacco tars are relatively easy to run, but who is to say that tobacco tars affect human beings in the same way as rats? Or again, was Kinsey's sample representative of the entire United States population?

Second, how *clear* and *unmuddied* will the results be? Questionnaire surveys of smoking and health are certainly relevant, but they are muddied by many facets of human psychology and biology that cannot be held constant in the survey. In other words, one must consider whether the method avoids the obstacles to knowledge of the problem.

Third, how much will the method *cost?* The high cost of personal-interview attitude surveys is one of their chief drawbacks, and it often forces substitution of another method or abandonment of the project.

Fourth, how *accurate* is the method? Some methods are more accurate than are others, aside from the matter of cost. In other cases, one must estimate the accuracy of the method at various cost levels, for example, at various sample sizes.

Fifth, how *long* will the method take to produce results? Longitudinal studies of the development of children require observing the *same children* at each stage of their lives. Can you afford to wait so long for results, or will some other technique produce acceptable results in less time?

Sixth, are the necessary personnel and equipment available?

Seventh, is the method ethically acceptable (see Chapter 33)?

Once again, one must avoid limiting oneself to a narrow choice of methods. Too many researchers are stereotyped in their research behavior, following A. Kaplan's Law of the Instrument: "Give a small boy a hammer, and he will find that everything he encounters needs pounding." On the other hand, if one discovers a new technique, seeing how widely the technique can be applied is often fruitful.

Several methods together may provide better and cheaper answers than any single method can. For instance, a cheap burglar alarm and a cheap safe together may constitute much better burglar protection than either a first-class alarm or a first-class safe. Two blankets, each with many moth holes in it, will keep you warmer than one good blanket. A postcard survey to thousands of people, in conjunction with a handful of intensive interviews, may better reveal how people feel about an election than will either method alone. And, in judging whether smoking is injurious to health, the Surgeon General's committee considered the results of animal experiments plus clinical and autopsy studies plus statistical analysis of surveys of the mortality rates of smokers and nonsmokers:

> Each of these three lines of evidence was evaluated and then considered together in drawing conclusions. The Committee was aware that the mere establishment of a statistical association between the use of tobacco and a disease is not enough. The causal significance of the use of tobacco in relation to the disease is the crucial question. For such judgments all three lines of evidence are essential. . . . (U.S. Public Health Service, pp. 27–28)

The virtue of complementary techniques is that one is not subject to the same defects as are the others.

Experiments and surveys complement each other well, especially when the surveys are detailed. The combination of those two methods has been the convincing factor in the cigarette-and-lung-cancer issue. C. Kluckhohn noted the value of a combination of methods in his anthropological work:

> Even when the questions being asked are of the same general nature, different methods may complement each other. During my years of work with Navaho children, I sometimes envied my colleagues in psychology who could bring their subjects into an experimental room where noise and other distractions were eliminated, temperature and other variables perfectly controlled, etc. Nevertheless, I reflected, my psychological colleagues saw the children they were studying for a few hours a week at most and had to depend for an account of what went on the rest of the week upon an interview with the mother or, possibly, both parents. In contrast, my co-workers and I were able to live with a Navaho family in their one-room hut for virtually twenty-four hours a day. Not many family secrets can be concealed for more than a short period under those circumstances. What the psychologists learned, they learned—admittedly—in a more rigorous way. Our knowledge, however, was richer, more ramified, and pertinent to behavior in ordinary daily life settings. (Lerner, p. 260)

Among the striking resemblances between military intelligence and empirical scientific research is that both profit from the use of multiple methods. Thousands of years ago the Chinese military writer, Sun Tzu, pointed out that ". . . the master of intelligence will employ all five kinds of agents simultaneously [native, inside, double, expendable, and living]" (Dulles, p. 14).

Of course, there are also many situations in which you will do best to devote all your resources to a single best method. A first-class safe *or* a first-class burglar alarm *may* be better than a combination of the inferior safe and inferior alarm.

Step 10. Check the Ethics of Your Proposed Research and Method

Sometimes enthusiasm and zeal can lead you to a course of research that is not ethically acceptable, simply because you do not stop long enough to ask the question, "Is this OK ethically?" So do stop and think, and possibly save yourself a heap of trouble with the community and with your conscience.

Ethical standards change over time. The recent spate of articles on the ethics of research (e.g. *Daedalus*) is evidence of the changes in people's outlooks, and of the new concern about the topic. Section 4 of Chapter 33 briefly discusses ethical guidelines in research.

Step 11. Prepare a Detailed Design of the Method

Chapters 9–14 describe the rudiments of design for the major types of methods. Here I offer only a handful of aphorisms and snippets of wisdom.

First, think at length, think in detail, think about everything *before* collecting data. This advice must begin to sound like a broken record, but it is worth the repetition. Time and money spent collecting data before you have done all the thinking possible will be expensive in the short and long run. But of course the future cannot be foreseen perfectly, especially in exploratory research.

Pretests are an important aid to planning. Run little pretests of method, materials, assistants, and everything else, as long as you can do it cheaply. The researcher should stay close to the work at this stage of the game, rather than delegating tasks to assistants. If you will be using a questionnaire, try out the questions on friends or on people in the street. Do not worry that your friends are not a random sample. If the questionnaire is designed for Hottentot infants, your friends' reactions may be meaningless. But in most situations *any* interviewees will reveal whether the questions are unintelligible or anger the interviewees, whether two questions elicit identical answers, and so forth.

If you will be running an experiment, have someone play the experimenter while you are the subject; one never really understands an experiment until he has served as a subject for it. And start off with crude equipment. Do not spend a lot of time and money building finished equipment before you have tried out crude models.

Run pretest after pretest as you continue to make improvements in the method. But, if pretests are very expensive, it may pay to shoot the works the first time—after you have thought the problem through as far as possible.

Pretest the data-record sheets. A well-constructed data sheet is a great help; a poor data sheet can be an awful nuisance. Whenever possible, design your data sheets so that they facilitate later transcriptions, either human coding or machine processing.

Second, many of the decisions one makes at the design stage must be arbitrary. One cannot test everything scientifically in advance. In one study of library use (Fussler & Simon), we had to choose three subject areas out of the many collections in the library as a sample of the library collection as a whole. In advance we could only guess which areas would offer fewest data-collection difficulties and which three areas taken together would provide the widest scope of information. We thought at great length, but eventually the decision had to be made on the basis of judgment and guesswork. We settled on one social science (economics), one natural science (biology), and one area in the humanities (German). Of these three, one was a strong collection, one a weak collection, one a so-so collection. Similarly, when we needed three university libraries as a representative sample of the country for comparative purposes, we picked one in the East, one in the Midwest, one in the Far West. One library was in a huge school, one in a middle-sized school, and one in a smaller school. The libraries were of different strengths. Other characteristics were also taken into account and weighed in the process of arriving at reasoned, but arbitrary, decisions.[11] When there are no rules to follow, you must make your own rules to guide your arbitrary decisions.

The novice often has trouble making the arbitrary decisions. The worst pitfall is to make an arbitrary decision *without recognizing* that it is arbitrary and that other alternatives should be considered. The next worst pitfall is to freeze into paralysis in the face of the alternatives, unable to make a decision because there is no "scientific answer" or because the answer cannot be found anywhere in textbooks on research.

The basic requirement for sound arbitrary decisions is a good set of *reasons*. Often this requirement means setting up reasonable *criteria* for the decisions. In the library subject-area example, one important criterion was based on our wish to know about book use in areas in which the library was strong as well as those in which it was relatively weak. This consideration guided our choice of three areas and gave us a more sensible sample than we would have obtained by picking three areas out of a hat.

Third, draw up in outline the tables and charts that you expect your data to fill. This procedure forces you to think out the details of the research design. Writing the names of the variables across the top and down the side of the tables and charts makes you state the variables explicitly. Ask yourself, What numbers do I want my study to produce? For example, in a comparison study write down the comparisons you would like to make at the conclusion of your research. If you are studying the election process and you want to evaluate the effects of age, sex, and religion on voting, you might end up comparing such groups as "Catholic, male, age twenty-one to twenty-five" with "Jewish, male, age twenty-one to twenty-five." Each of these groups should then constitute a *cell* of your table. A working table with such cells might look like Table 7.1.

11. This sampling procedure would have been a poor choice for *other* purposes, for example, if we had sought to compare libraries in different regions. As always, the procedure and the reasoning must be tailored to the purpose.

TABLE 7.1   Sample Working Table

Percentage Voting Democrat

	Age 21–25	*Age 26–35*	*Age etc.*
Catholic			
Male	? %	? %	etc.
Female	? %	etc.	etc.
Protestant			
Male	? %	etc.	etc.
Female	? %	etc.	etc.
Jewish			
Male	? %	etc.	etc.
Female	? %	etc.	etc.

The best argument for the value of this exercise is the resistance that you feel as you try to draw up the charts and tables. After you try it, you will recognize why this exercise has such power to prevent mistakes and omissions in your study.

Draw up a separate table for each relationship, each comparison, and each measurement that you hope your study will produce. Do not try to cram everything into one master table. And the captions on the blank tables and charts *must be specific*. That is what the exercise is for—to get you to be *specific* about the details of your proposed design and your objectives. On the other hand, do not become so wedded to your preliminary tables that you are blind to other relationships that you may discover in the course of examining your data. These preliminary tables are only a helpful prod to thinking, not a contract that you are obligated to fulfill.

Step 12. Collect the Data

There is little of a general nature to say about the process of collecting data, except that you should exercise *care* in what you do. Sloppiness, especially sloppiness in maintaining data and in recording just what is done at each step, can lead to disaster—the necessity for repeating your work, or scientific error and loss of reputation. See Chapter 17 for detailed discussion of this stage.

Collecting data takes much longer than you think it will. I have never known anyone to do his first research project without being surprised at the number of unexpected and time-consuming snags. The simplest study bristles with minor problems in data collection; no wonder that complex projects can become a life's work.

The great quantity of detail can offer an unexpected temptation. As a student, you try hard to finish school projects so that you can receive course credit and degree; details that delay you are annoyances. But professors who do research under their own direction do not have such externally imposed deadlines to pressure them. Often an academic loses himself in the detailed busy work of a research project because it is comfortable and relatively undemanding. Instead of looking for shortcuts so that he can finish and move on to other work, he sometimes takes a larger-than-necessary sample or submerges himself in doing interviews or experimentation himself or in coding his data. The work is pleasant, he has the satisfaction that he is accomplishing a day's work each day, and he avoids the hard work and decision making involved in writing up the findings and setting up another piece of research. He is using the busy work of research as an escape. (Of course, such practice is not unique to professors. Many people in other lines of work—often those people who refer to themselves as "perfectionists"—fall into the same trap.)

Step 13. Analyze the Data

Chapters 25 and 26 discuss data analysis in considerable detail.

Step 14. Write Up the Research Work

In Chapter 2, pages 23 to 25, there is a discussion of writing up research, the final stage of the work.

The foregoing list of steps for doing research adds up to a good checklist for evaluating and criticizing research done by others:

1. First ask *what* the researcher is trying to find out.
2. Then ask *why* she wants the knowledge.
3. Judge the *value* of her research.
4. Specify exactly *which variables* the researcher uses, if she does not provide an explicit equation.

15. Summary

This chapter lists and describes the main steps in carrying out a research project. This list is also useful in evaluating and criticizing the research of others. Of course such a list does not fit all research situations, but in the main it does apply. The steps are:

(1) Find a good research problem.

(2) Ask "what do I want to find out?" First you must decide what problem you are interested in. Then you must answer this central research question clearly, and keep it in mind as you make decisions throughout the project.

(3) Establish the purpose of the project. Similar research questions can be asked for very different purposes. And you must refer back to your purpose if you are to make sound decisions about variables, data collection, and analysis.

(4) Determine the value of the research. Ask yourself, "Is this research, in my judgment, likely be of greater relative value than other research alternatives?"

(5) Saturate yourself in the problem. Learn the background. Steep yourself in the situation. Range widely for the relevant facts. Only thus can you wisely decide which factors are likely to be important in your research situation.

(6) Choose empirical variables. Select operational proxies for the theoretical (hypothetical) concepts that you wish to investigate.

(7) Calculate the benefits of accuracy and the costs of error. What is at stake in the research? What is the value to researcher and institution and society of reducing the likely error by using more expensive methods on a larger sample? The answer points toward a rational choice of a sample size and sometimes helps you choose among alternative techniques.

(8) Determine the most important obstacles you will face in your research. What difficulties will there be in getting an answer to your research question? Ruminate on these obstacles in advance and make them explicit.

(9) Choose methods. Design your research so as to overcome the main obstacles to knowledge that you face, keeping in mind the constraint of the master obstacle: cost. Choose your methods from the wide variety of techniques in use in the social sciences, rather than limiting your choice to the conventional method of your sub-field. Prefer a combination of two or more methods over a single method.

(10) Prepare a detailed design of the method. Leave nothing vague or unspecified. Run preliminary tests. And prepare the tables and charts you will later fill with data.

(11) Check the ethics of your proposed research and method.

(12) Collect the data—carefully.

(13) Analyze the data—sensibly and imaginatively.

(14) Write up the research work.

EXERCISES

1. Refer to the example of the vagueness of statements on increasing conformity on page 178. Think of another frequent statement about society or human nature that is vague and not easily provable. Give some appropriate ways to make this statement specific, so that it can be tested empirically.

2. Give an example of similar data being collected in different ways for different purposes.

3. How would you measure "friendliness"? "aggressiveness in business"?

4. What are the obstacles to studying the ways in which income influences happiness? to finding out whether a particular advertising campaign for beer is more or less effective than the previous campaign was?

5. Describe a study, and then prepare a working table to show the data that should be produced to fulfill the purpose of the study.

ADDITIONAL READING FOR CHAPTER 7

On the steps in social research, see Selltiz *et al.,* pp. 12–14.

Bachrach provides a short and readable introduction to psychological research, telling what the researcher is up against and how the researcher goes about it.

A breezy but informative introduction to social research is that of Agrew and Pyke.

Hammond's book contains a variety of firsthand descriptions of how some eminent authors did important pieces of research in a variety of fields.

On selecting a research problem, see Selltiz *et al.* (Chapter 3) and Sjoberg and Nett (Chapter 5).

On ethical issues in research, see Cook (Chapter 7 in Selltiz *et al.*), Denzin (Chapter 13), or Smith (Chapter 1). A provocative discussion of ethics and research, urging very strict standards, is that of Kelman.

A fundamental theme of this book is that when quite different research methods produce the same result, the conclusion is all the stronger; and when studies using different methods disagree, it is a clue to retest until the discrepancy can be reconciled. A first-rate article on reconciling the results from experimental and survey studies is that of Hovland.

8 how to assess the potential value of research projects

1. Evaluating the Inputs Required for a Research Project
2. Estimating the Value of Research Projects
3. Summary

To notice an important problem for study that others have not seen is the mark of a pathbreaking scientist. In Zuckerman's interviews with U.S. Nobel winners, "Almost to a man they lay great emphasis on the importance of problem-finding, not only problem solving" (Merton, 1968, p. 60). And beginners in research think it difficult to find *any* research problem for a course or thesis; after you leave school and begin a career in social science, however, you quickly become aware of a great variety of possible projects competing for your time. To a professor or to a researcher in industry or government, the question becomes: *Which one* of the many questions that I might work on would be best? The subject of this chapter is how to choose among possible subjects for research so as to obtain the greatest long-term benefit.

The choice among "pure" research problems is more difficult than among applied problems, as we shall see, so let us talk about the pure-research decision first. One's first impulse is to say that the scientist should work on the "most important" of the research problems that are competing for his attention. But how does one decide which is most important? And should one work on the most important problem even if it is expected to take twenty years, whereas a matter only slightly less important would take only one year or one month?

Whether pure or applied research is in question, the decision about which of several problems to study empirically is much like the businessman's decision about which new business opportunities to invest capital in. In both science and business the solution is to estimate what the benefit-cost ratio (value of output/value of input) promises to be for each of the possible alternatives and then to choose the alternative for which the ratio is highest. Some academics find it repugnant to frame the problem in these "commercial" terms, but if they will examine the basis of their own decisions, it boils down to the same thing. From a philosophical point of view A. Kaplan argues that "These and similar questions cannot be put aside as extralogical, 'merely practical' in import. They arise, whether or not they have been explicitly formulated, in every actual context of inquiry . . ." (Kaplan, p. 252; see his pp. 250–254 for further discussion of this and related points).

The businessman's estimates of this ratio are easier to make than are the scientist's. Both the businessman and the scientist are uncertain about how large the outputs and inputs will be, but at least the businessman can measure cost inputs and profit outputs in the common unit of dollars. It is much more difficult to find measuring rods for the skill and energy the researcher puts into the study and for the value of the knowledge that may come out of the study.

Some scientists say that research need not have any practical effect or social benefit. Nevertheless, A. Einstein, whose work was as "pure" as anyone could wish, felt this way about the matter: "The concern for man and his destiny must always be the chief interest of all technical effort. Never forget it among your diagrams and equations" (Snow, p. 51).

1. Evaluating the Inputs Required for a Research Project

The inputs to a study are of two sorts: first, the time and energy required of the *researcher* and, second, the money costs to the funding foundation or commercial employer or nonprofit client.

A responsible researcher should calculate the cost of the inputs required by a given study from her own point of view *and* from the point of view of the organization that is the source of funds. For pure research one should assume the organizational point of view to be that of the society as a whole.

It is not easy to estimate the time and energy a study will require. The more experienced one is, the more accurate the estimate of the snags and obstacles that will be met and of the resources required to overcome them, just as an experienced building contractor can estimate the time and cost of a building better than a novice.

Any study takes much longer than a novice expects. Sometimes when you read of someone else's work, a project that took a full year seems as if it should not have required more than a couple of weeks. And indeed, if the same woman were to do the work over again, she might well be able to finish in a couple of weeks. But if you or I or anyone else were to try to repeat her work—even with her report to follow—it might require two or three months. And, if we had to start from scratch, as she did, without knowing which path would turn out to be worthwhile and which mistakes to avoid, we would soon find out why it took her a full year. Usually one makes several false starts before developing a satisfactory method, and that takes time.

The time needed to do empirical work varies greatly among researchers. Just as in other trades, there are good research craftsmen and poor research craftsmen, and the difference in their efficiencies can be enormous. The poor research craftsman often takes ten or twenty times as long as the good one does because he lacks a nose for shortcuts; gets hung up on insignificant details; lacks competence in dealing with materials, people, and machines; and does not know when to consider the empirical work complete.

Beware of hidden costs. On first thought, for example, it may seem almost costless to add another question to an interview schedule. But remember to take into account the additional money cost of editing the results of that question and of keypunching it, and—perhaps most important—the time cost to you when you feel you must analyze the results from that question because you have collected the data.

The following qualities make a good research craftsman: experience, which as we know comes only after it is most needed; ingenuity, resourcefulness, and imagination; and an attitude that keeps a person's eyes open for better and quicker methods. Anybody can acquire the last by forcing himself to look around regularly for better and quicker methods, but many people prefer not to take their eyes off the trees to see the forest; it is worth training yourself to keep your eyes open for better methods.

The time a project takes also depends upon the funds available for assistance. Up to a point, the more assistance one can afford, the more quickly the work will go. But, curiously, beyond a certain point *too much* available money can slow down a project. The project director finds himself spending much time hiring workers, checking time slips, and answering questions about exceptions in the work. Often one can get results that are almost as accurate with a smaller sample that requires fewer helpers or even with a shortcut method like using published data instead of creating raw data. In any case, remember that many hands do not always make quick work.

A responsible researcher tries to develop research methods that require a minimum of money. For example, he takes a sample rather than measuring a whole universe. He uses telephone interviews rather than personal interviews if the former are feasible. He mechanizes the job of data processing efficiently. Amazing cost reduction can sometimes be achieved by a touch of resourcefulness. In general, the responsible scientist does not treat outside funds as costless to him and therefore to be spent casually. Not all scientists rate top grades in this respect. For obvious reasons scientists who do applied work in business are usually (but not always) better at economizing than are academic scientists.

2. Estimating the Value of Research Projects

Here are the relevant benefits to the researcher herself from a research project.

1. Her own pleasure and enjoyment. Some kinds of research will be more fun than others, depending on your own likes. Some anthropologists get a bang out of field work with primitive tribes; others cannot stomach it.

2. Short-term professional benefits. The immediate professional payoff may depend upon the moment's fashion in one's academic discipline or upon the needs of the business firm or government bureau. The benefit to you also depends upon the competence of the study, although competence in a researcher is less obvious than it is in a basketball player. And the benefits may depend upon your situation—for example, if you are a student or young scientist you may feel the need to show results quickly, whereas an older researcher may feel less hurried to produce results.

3. Long-term professional benefits. If all's right with the world, the long-run professional benefits will be in proportion to the intrinsic importance of the research, as measured by the influence of the research on a body of thought or on the magnitude of decisions affected by the study.[1]

As an example, an outstanding anthropologist might compare the value of two studies this way. A study of culture 1 would probably require a year, and its probable results would affect perhaps four pages of a basic textbook. A study of culture 2 would probably require twice as much time, and its probable results would affect perhaps five pages of a basic textbook. The output of the first study is four pages per year but for the second only two and a half pages a year, which makes the first a better investment (provided that there are other comparable studies for the researcher to do when the first is complete). Such a calculation may seem too calculating, but pure scientists undoubtedly do such figuring implicitly when deciding what to do next.[2]

A study's potential influence on scientific thought is hard to gauge. Here are some guidelines to help you judge. First, empirical studies that test important theories are themselves important. Examples are the empirical studies that tested J. Keynes' theory of the consumption function (Ackley, Chaps. 10–12), G. Myrdal's explanation of the American dilemma (Westie), and S. Freud's psychoanalytic theories of development (Sears).

Second, the more surprising and unexpected the result of a study, the more valuable is the study—assuming that the surprise does not arise

1. It is depressing to read T. Caplow and R. McGee's contention that scientific achievement and scientific recognition may not always be closely related. But, even if their observation is fair, universities are still more objective in hiring and rewarding scientists than is, say, the political patronage system. Injustice may occur, but *gross* injustice is probably rare.

2. Footnotes and references to a person's work are another quantitative measure of productivity value frequently used to measure eminence. And even the purest in heart find themselves counting their own footnotes occasionally. The Science Citation Index is a systematic and comprehensive measurement of the references to a scientist's work.

from faulty procedure. As information theory points out, a man who hollers to you "Your house is on fire" is usually telling you something more valuable than if he hollers "Your house is not on fire." Studies that showed traditional farmers in underdeveloped countries to be responsive to new ideas and to money incentives were more valuable because the opposite was generally assumed to be true and would have been no surprise (Schultz, Chap. 2).

Third, results that offer the possibility of useful action are more valuable than results that close off the possibility. In the previous example, the finding that traditional farmers are responsive to money incentives opens the door to modernizing a country's agriculture by making it worthwhile for the farmers to change their behavior.

Fourth, the wider the application and the more universal the conclusions drawn from the study, the more important the study is. All research is done on *some* limited collection of people or animals or objects or organizations. For example, an economist might learn that, when a Nigerian family has sufficient money income, it buys first a refrigerator and later a washing machine, rather than vice versa. The implicit side conditions of this study are that the subjects live in Nigeria in the 1960s. The study would have more importance if there were reason to think that the same pattern holds in many countries in any decade.

I. Pavlov's experiments offer another example. If bell-salivation conditioning worked only with dogs and could not be generalized to other species, including humans, Pavlov's work would be much less important than it is.

The generality of the results is also one of the criteria that distinguish between pure and applied research. For example, consider an experiment showing that an argument that includes both the "pro"s and "con"s of smoking is more efficient in preventing smoking than is an argument that recognizes only the negative side of smoking. If this experiment were done solely to find out how to prevent smoking and if there were no reason to believe that the finding would also hold true for other persuasive situations, then the experiment would be applied research. But, if the purpose of the experiment were to investigate persuasive arguments *generally* and if the antismoking campaign were chosen only as a representative example, then the experiment is closer to pure research.

An industrial psychologist might decide between two potential studies in this fashion. Study 1 promises to improve job satisfaction in the baseball-glove industry, which employs x people. Study 2, requiring no more time, would improve job satisfaction an equal amount per person in the steel industry, which employs $10x$ people. Obviously the findings of study 2 would have more generality and therefore more value. Or an educational psychologist might consider doing a study to improve the reading speed of brain-damaged children or a study to improve the reading speed of culturally backward children. The latter study would affect more children and would therefore be more general.

The purest test of generality is the number of theories a given study would affect or the number of prior empirical studies that would appear in a different light after the work is complete. But this is difficult to illustrate in the short compass of space available here.

Fifth, the human importance of a study affects its value. More people suffer from baldness than from leukemia, but the latter is studied more because it is more serious.[3] Similarly, a clinical-psychology study that promises to reduce the anxieties in adolescents' first dates has less value than does a study that promises a way to bring psychotics back to reality.

Sixth, empirical studies that are *intellectually connected* with the rest of a field have greater value than do those that are not connected. By "connected"[4] I mean that a study is related to contemporary arguments and open questions in a particular science or that it extends or contradicts work that has already been done. For example, a study that measures the extent to which two kinds of behavior are similar or widely different in identical twins separated at birth is solidly connected with *several* fields, because it throws light on several open questions. Such a study tells the physiological psychologists about the extent to which behavior is biologically determined; it tells the learning and educational psychologists about the extent to which various types of behavior may be learned; and it helps the sociologist understand the impact of social interaction upon human behavior patterns.

The main shortcoming of many an "operations-research" study in applied science is that often it yields nothing but the answer to one specific operating problem. Examples on which I myself have worked include investigations of which advertisement for a particular product will be most productive, and of how many library books should be in open stacks and how many should be in less-expensive storage units. Solving such problems may certainly be important enough to justify the research work. But the work does not carry much interest for other scientists, for it throws no light on problems in which they are interested (except by accident or because new methods are discovered). That is, these operations-research examples are not connected strongly with the body of any scientific field.

Of course, some of the most valuable studies do not fit into the existing structures of the disciplines at the time the studies are done. Rather the discipline moves to meet them. But the *possibility* that sometime in the future the study will be connected into the body of a discipline is important. There must be a chance that a bridge will be created between the existing body of knowledge in a science and a new discovery once the latter's importance is recognized. For example, the first studies of the concentration of economic power in the United States seemed to have no connection with the body of economics. But, as the importance of the topic has been recognized,

3. This choice of scientists also illustrates that the most dollar-profitable studies are sometimes not preferred. A baldness study would be more rewarding commercially than would a leukemia cure. The structure of nonprofit research grants to scientists may, however, explain the situation.
4. See R. von Mises' *Positivism* (Chap. 6) for an excellent simple explanation of the concept of "connectedness" and its importance in the context of scientific language.

and as growing numbers of studies of this sort have been done, the subject has become connected with the rest of economics, as well as creating its own work tradition, the study of industrial organization.

Estimating the value and future influence of a given study is difficult even after the study is complete. Some men in the field may say "a landmark" and others "a potboiler." Twenty years later one can tell how much influence the study has had on subsequent research. It is educational to read through the older studies that have turned out to be important in any field for clues to what makes important studies important. Books of readings collect those studies for you.

If it is difficult to appraise a study's probable influence right after it is done, it is even harder to appraise it *before* it is done—because you then do not know what will turn out or whether anything at all will turn out.

So much for the likelihood that a study will be influential. What about the likelihood that a study will be *correct?* And how important is it that the results will be correct?

First, decide what is at stake. Kaplan discusses this problem in the context of how big a sample to take:

> What is the stake for which we are playing—that is, what will we do with our estimate when we have arrived at it, and what will it do for us in return? Is there always a winner, and how is he selected—that is, what defines the "best estimate" in this situation? Does the situation allow us to make more than one estimate— can any number of entries be submitted by each contestant? What is the cost of making an estimate—what box tops must accompany the entry? What price must be paid for an error, and how is an error defined? Is the price fixed, or does it vary with the size of the error? Can an error be corrected subsequently—are we playing touch-move or can a bad move be withdrawn? How will the prize be diminished by the range of the estimate made—do we win anything by estimating the length as lying between a thousandth of an inch and a thousand miles? How much will additional measurements cost? How long do we have to make up our minds? How much must be paid—in appropriate units of utility—for the use of a computer and other resources, both human and otherwise, available to the scientific enterprise? . . .
>
> What must enter into such criteria is a specification of the costs of reaching a decision, and of the losses incurred when the decision is a mistaken one. Of particular importance is the relative cost of errors. . . . The scientist invests time and money in his experiments, and if his conclusions are erroneous, damage is likely to be done to society as well as to his own reputation. (Kaplan, pp. 252, 253)

Estimating the danger of error is difficult. But for applied research it can be done (see Goodman, p. 280, for social problems, or Schlaifer for business decisions). And even for pure research, one can arrive at *some* sensible decisions. For example, an error in the results of an influential experiment in nuclear radiation effect or in a study of whether the economy is expanding or contracting is more important than is an error of the same probability in a study of whether people at the picnic like hot dogs better than hamburgers. But it is hopeless to count the cost of not considering some yet-unthought-of alternative.

The *ratio* of the estimates of the outputs and inputs of a particular study should then be compared to the ratio of other alternative studies. The total output of a small-cost project need not be as high as the total output of a long and expensive project for the inexpensive study to be the better investment, because its ratio of output to input may be higher. Furthermore, short studies represent less risk to the beginner, who is more likely to start into blind alleys.

One of the characteristics of research is that you are uncertain about what you will learn from the study at the time you decide whether to do it. Therefore, the evaluation of proposed research must take into account the probabilities you estimate for the various outcomes, as well as their costs and benefits.

In recent years huge strides have been made in quantifying the value of information for use in deciding whether to do research, and in choosing the size of sample to take. Here follows an illustration of such a calculation. Readers[5] who are not familiar with the concept of *expected value*[5] might skip this illustration.[6] But I believe that the importance of this approach to research valuation is sufficiently great that the example is worth including despite its length and complexity:

> The proposed research is an experiment, with incentive payments for non-pregnancy, to be conducted in a sample of Indian villages. The goal is to help reduce the birth rate in those less-developed countries with rapid population growth. In some villages, women would be offered sums ranging from $75 per year, for women in the highest-fertility category, downward to relatively small payments for women in low-fertility categories, for each year they had no children. In other villages, the entire payment schedule would be lower. And still other villages would serve as controls, in which no money incentives would be offered for not having babies.
>
> The situation may be diagrammed as in Figure 8.1. If alternative 1 is chosen and the experiment is carried out, I guesstimate that there is a 50-50 chance that the experiment will yield "positive" results and will be interpreted by social planners and decision makers as indicating that the incentive program is successful in reducing births. And if the experiment *is* successful, I estimate that there is about a 50-50 chance (say, .499, to avoid confusion) that a full-scale program will then be embarked upon; *if* the experiment is *not* successful, I estimate that there is a 1-in-8 (.125) chance that an action program will be undertaken. If *no* experiment is undertaken, I estimate that there is a 1-in-4 chance that a full-scale action program will be undertaken.

5. The expected value of an alternative is the sum of the net values of the events that may occur, multiplied by the probabilities that they will occur.
6. This example is drawn from J. Simon (1972).

FIGURE 8.1

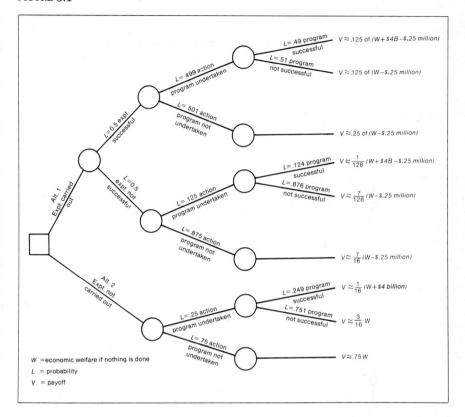

Now for the consequences if an action program *is* carried out: If it is undertaken after a *positive* experiment, it is reasonable to believe that the program has a better likelihood of being successful than would a program carried out after a negative experiment. This is, in fact, the meaning of the information yielded by any piece of research—that the research result can help predict the result of the program itself. The probabilities of program success after positive and negative experiments are roughly estimated by me to be .49 and .124 respectively. And the probability of a successful program (if it is undertaken) *in the absence of experimental information* is estimated to be .249. All this probabilistic structure is summarized in Figure 8.1.

Now let us estimate the economic effects of a successful program. Let us first estimate the number of *fewer* births there would be with a successful incentive action program than with no incentive program. A wild guess for illustrative purposes is that the birth rate would be lower by a fifth if this program is undertaken (and is successful) than if it is not. And let us say that each avoided birth is worth $100–$500 (say, $200) to the rest of the community in India.[7] Avoided births in the future are of less present value than are births now (because of the discounting phenomenon), but as a crude trade-off estimate, let us consider only

7. For a summary of this literature, see Pohlman.

the next five years' births, undiscounted. This quantity is one fifth of 5×20 million expected births, or 20 million births, each multiplied by $200. This gives a total of $4 billion, the benefit we shall count for a successful program. There are no important operating costs to an *unsuccessful* program, because the heart of the program is to give money, and if the program is unsuccessful, no money will change hands. Similarly, there are no important operating costs to a *successful* program. And since the funds paid as incentives are transfers from person to person, they really have little social cost and may be ignored here. The cost of the scientific work involved in the experiment itself might be a quarter or a third of a million dollars, vastly less than the half-billion-dollar expected payoff.

The decision about whether to conduct the experiment depends on a present-value computation of the two alternatives. Denote by W the economic welfare that will result if nothing is done about a no-pregnancy incentive program.

$$
\begin{aligned}
V_{\text{Experiment}} =\ & .5 \times .499 \times .49 \,(W + \$4\,\text{billion} - \$.25\,\text{million}) \\
& + .5 \times .499 \times .51 \,(W - \$.25\,\text{million}) \\
& + .5 \times .501 \,(W - \$.25\,\text{million}) \\
& + .5 \times .125 \times .124 \,(W + \$4\,\text{billion} - \$.25\,\text{million}) \\
& + .5 \times .125 \times .876 \,(W - \$.25\,\text{million}) \\
& + .5 \times .875 \,(W - \$.25\,\text{million}) \\
\approx\ & \$.52\,\text{billion} + W \\[4pt]
V_{\text{No experiment}} =\ & .25 \times .249 \,(W + \$4\,\text{billion}) \\
& + .25 \times .751 \,(W) \\
& + .75 \,(W) \\
\approx\ & \$.25\,\text{billion} + W
\end{aligned}
$$

The V for the experiment alternative is higher, and hence it appears to make sense to undertake the experiment. It is also worth noting that if we perform a "sensitivity test"—changing some of the assumed probabilities and payoffs and observing the resultant changes in V—the experiment continues to make sense even with considerably less "favorable" assumptions.

Of course this analysis is very much simplified and ignores many important factors. Furthermore, the probabilities are only guesstimates. But its value is that it clarifies the issues at stake and provokes us to argue about what is important and what is not.

Even though the foregoing valuation techniques are useful, the process of judging whether it is worthwhile to do a study remains largely a fine art: "It is perhaps the most precious art of the scientist to develop almost a sixth sense, based on deep knowledge of his whole field, that can tell him which researches are likely to be promising and which not" (Price, p. 73). The Nobel prize winners "uniformly express the strong conviction that what matters most in their work is a developing sense of taste, of judgment, in seizing upon problems that are of fundamental importance" (Merton, p. 60).

As a practical matter, the advice of one's elders in science is worth most to students in the choice of problems for term papers and theses. It seems to me that the last and most important gift a professor should make to a student is a subject for a thesis that is likely to turn out well—together with an assessment of the likely costs and benefits of various approaches to the problem, and perhaps some references to readily available data.

3. Summary

The professional researcher always faces the problem of having more alternative research possibilities than he can carry out with the time (and money) at his disposal. A wise choice among the possibilities is much like a business' or society's choice of investments: Which ones offer the highest potential return for the invested time and money?

Like other investments, the choice of research projects has two fundamental elements: (a) an estimate of the inputs necessary for the project, and their costs; and (b) an estimate of the project's likely output, and its value. The latter is the more difficult, but you should at least try to estimate the value of the output of the project even when doing the purest of pure research.

Those projects should be chosen that promise the highest benefit/cost ratio, taking risk and uncertainty into account.

EXERCISES

1. Select at random six articles reporting empirical research in your field, and randomly divide them into three pairs. Assess the relative value of the members of each pair, making explicit judgments based on criteria discussed in this chapter.
2. Consider in each pair the study that you adjudge on an over-all basis to be less valuable. Assume that it took only half as long to do as the better study did. Now which study in each pair represents the better investment of a researcher's time?

ADDITIONAL READING FOR CHAPTER 8

Tull and Hawkins (Chapter 3) explain clearly how one goes about figuring the value and cost of information, using examples from marketing research that may serve as models for all of social-scientific research.

9 sampling

Your aim in taking a sample from a universe (population) is to draw valid conclusions about the universe without the cost and trouble of investigating all the units in that population. The purpose of this chapter is to discuss the *validity* of the conclusions that one is likely to draw from a given sampling method, and the relative *efficiencies* of various sampling methods.

This chapter presents an intuitive introduction to the basic ideas in sampling. This introduction should enable you to draw a sound sample for most scientific and applied purposes. But the drawing of samples for major surveys such as a national census is a highly technical matter demanding calculations that are not taught here. If you should contemplate doing a large-scale and costly sampling operation, by all means call upon the devices of a professional statistician, and *before* you get started.

1. Universe and Sample

A **sample** is the collection of observations for which you have data with which you are going to work. Almost any set of observations for which you have data constitutes a sample.

For every sample there must also be a universe "behind" it. But "universe" is harder to define, partly because it is often an *imaginary* concept. A **universe** (or **population**) is the collection of things or people *from which you want to say that your sample was taken*.[1] A universe can be finite and well defined—"all live holders of the Congressional Medal of Honor," "all presi-

---

1. "Universe" and "population" are perfect synonyms in scientific research. I choose to use "universe" because it seems to have fewer confusing associations.

dents of major universities," "all billion-dollar corporations in the United States." Of course, these finite universes may not be easy to pin down; for instance, what is a "major university"? And these universes may contain some elements that are difficult to find; for instance, some Congressional Medal winners may have left the country, and there may not be any public records on some billion-dollar corporations.

Infinite universes are harder to understand, and it is often difficult to decide which universe is appropriate for a given purpose. For example, if you are studying a sample of schizophrenics, what is the universe from which the sample comes? Depending on your purposes, the appropriate universe might be all schizophrenics now alive, or it might be all schizophrenics who might *ever* live. The latter concept of the universe of schizophrenics is *imaginary* because some of the universe does not exist. And it is *infinite* because it goes on forever.

Not everyone likes this definition of "universe." Others prefer to think of a universe, not as the collection of people or things that you *want* to say your sample was taken from, but as the collection that the sample was *actually* taken from. This latter view equates the universe to the "sampling frame," which is always finite and existent. There is an analogy here to hypothetical and empirical variables; in my view one actually deals with an empirical variable that stands for a hypothetical variable that may itself be difficult to pin down; the other view ignores the hypothetical variable completely when it refuses to deal with imaginary universes. The definition of "universe" offered here is simply the most practical, in my opinion.

2. Random Sampling Basics

Terminology right and wrong: The term **random** refers to the *process* by which a sample is chosen from a universe; the term does *not* refer to a given sample. It may be correct to say that a sample was "randomly chosen," but it is not correct to say that "the sample is random." In the long run and on the average, a random-sampling process produces representative samples, but a given single sample is not likely to be perfectly representative, and hence it is not strictly correct and may be misleading to call a given sample "random." However, like others I often slothfully use the term "random sample," and I hope you will mentally correct this error when you see it.

A randomly-chosen sample is a *fair* sample; that is, it would be a fair bet that any member of the universe would be picked for the sample, compared to any other member of the universe. For example, a bet on any number or color on a *loaded* roulette wheel is not a fair bet, and therefore the loaded roulette wheel does not give you a fair sample. As a matter of fact, the closest we can get to an operational definition of randomness is to call it a property of a sample selected by a carefully balanced roulette wheel.

Your judgment is your best guide to whether a sample is chosen randomly. Is a particular card shuffle random? You must judge whether the cards were shuffled carefully enough so that the game will be fair. How random a shuffle you demand depends upon how high the stakes are, of course. In poker games in the movies, the players are so concerned with random shuffles that they demand brand-new decks of cards frequently.

A magician who forces you to take a particular card is giving you a perfectly *nonrandom* sample, that is, a perfectly *determined* sample. The ultimate test of randomness is whether any member of the universe has been gypped in your opinion. A *biased* sample is a sample that is *not* drawn randomly and that therefore does not represent all parts of the universe. The sample is said to be biased in favor of any member of the universe who has more than a fair chance of being picked for the sample. If the sample is biased in favor of some members, it must be biased against other members. Survey samples are biased against people living on the top floors of walk-up buildings in poor neighborhoods, because interviewers sometimes write down "not home" without even going there.

Whether a sample is randomly chosen, unbiased, and fair is not always obvious.[2] For example, if you put all the names in a phone book into a hat and pick out a hundred of them, the sample will be randomly chosen if you have shuffled well enough. But, if you first put all the A's into a hat and draw one, then put all the B's into the hat and draw one, and so on, the sample will not be randomly chosen, for each person whose name starts with Q, X, Y, and Z has a much better chance of being picked than does a person whose name starts with M, S, or T. (Think about why, if it is not obvious at first.) Similarly, to choose one letter from the hat and then choose a hundred names from all the names beginning with that letter would not yield a fair sample. These samples *could* be made random and might be good tactics in some cases, but these are refinements we discuss later.

If you have a very large sample, you may be able to test whether it was drawn randomly by examining whether any event, or pattern of events, appears more often than it would occur by chance. But if you have a small sample, you are bound to observe patterns of events that appear to be very unusual but that easily could occur, for example, six heads, or head-tail-head-tail-head-tail, in six coin tosses. So for a small sample your only assurance that the sampling process is random must come from careful inspection of the details of the sampling procedure rather than from the sample itself.

Examples of the dangers from a biased sample, and some devices to prevent bias, are discussed in Chapter 21.,

There are two important aspects of obtaining an unbiased sample: taking a sample at random from the sampling frame, and selecting a *sampling frame* that is appropriate for the population in which you are interested.

a. TAKING A SAMPLE RANDOMLY FROM THE SAMPLING FRAME

In theory taking a sample randomly is perfectly easy: Just put all the members of the universe into a hat, shake them well, and take out those to be

2. "Fair" and "unbiased" mean the same thing, except that "unfair" implies that some *person* is getting gypped, for example, in a gambling game.

included in the sample, one by one—either "replacing" the sampled members or not, depending upon the situation (an important decision, which is discussed in Chapters 27–28). Each individual then would have exactly the same chance of getting into the sample. This procedure yields what is known as a *simple* random sample.

But practical difficulties arise in attempting to achieve this theoretical ideal. The first obstacle is that no good sampling frame may be available. A **sampling frame** is the empirical representation of the theoretical universe in which you are interested. For example, if your universe is black students at the University of Illinois, a complete list of such students would constitute an excellent sampling frame. But no such list existed until recently, and therefore it would have taken much work and energy to create a good sampling frame. Now such a list exists, but the researcher must convince a committee before getting access to the list; again this excellent sampling frame may or may not be available.

Another obstacle is that the members of the universe to be studied can themselves seldom be placed into a hat and shuffled. The people in the United States cannot be placed physically into a vessel and mixed well. Instead, one must work with *symbols* that represent these people—their names and the data about them—on paper, rather than in person. Considerable accuracy may be lost in the process of transforming a group of people into a list of symbols.

Even after you have reduced the physical units to symbols on paper, the technique is still not straightforward and automatic. The telephone book may list the names of all telephone subscribers, but you do not want to go to the trouble of cutting apart all the names, one by one, and throwing them into a hat. And, even if you made up such a hatful, how would you shake it so that the units would be mixed perfectly? Such perfect mixing is no easy job, in a hat or otherwise.

In practice, you work out some sort of a rule that will help you draw a sample at random directly from the phone book, say, without cutting and shaking.

Some such rules are bad, some good. The rule to take the first hundred names beginning on a randomly drawn page of the phone book would probably be a bad rule for most purposes, even though the sample is random because every person has the same probability of falling into the sample. Certain national origins and religions are heavily concentrated in some first-letter groups, Z, for instance, and Y. Therefore, your sample will not be *representative*, even though it will be random. Such a procedure violates a basic rule of all sampling, both random and nonrandom: ". . . we want a . . . sample that has a wide representation of experiences" (Klein, p. 4).

A better rule would be to take every fiftieth name, every 125th name, or every "*n*th" name, with *n* standing for the interval necessary to obtain as many names as you need. By this method—yielding a *systematic* random sample rather than a "simple" random sample—you ensure that before the sample is drawn each part of the list has an equal chance of falling into your sample and that no one part of the list will be represented more heavily than will any other. But systematic samples may also have dangers. Taking every tenth house on a street might give you every corner house, and people who live in corner houses are different, at least in income, from the other people on the block. Nevertheless, unless you have some special reason to distrust the systematic every-*n*th sample from the phone book, it probably yields a good random and representative sample.[3]

Another kind of rule that would be a little slower but would avoid the danger of a systematic sample is to select one name randomly from each page, by selecting a random number for each page from a random-number table and then measuring with a ruler instead of actually counting names one by one.

Another danger-free procedure is to pick a page number at random and then a number for a name from that page at random, until you have a large enough sample. But this simple random sampling would be very slow and probably would yield only a slightly more random sample than would systematically taking every *n*th name.

A random-digit table is a great help in taking random samples. The random-digit table is the record of a process like spinning a ten-sided die again and again and again. Instead of spinning the die, you just proceed along a row or down a column (or in a hopscotch pattern if you like) of the random-digit table (see page 412 in Chapter 28). If you want to draw numbers between 0 and 999 instead of between 0 and 9, take groups of three-digit numbers. If you want only numbers between 0 and 63, say, simply ignore any numbers you hit between 64 and 99 and move on to the next pair.

Subtle interferences with randomness can crop up in the most unexpected and surprising ways. For example, it is common practice to take a sample of cards from a card file (library cards, for instance, in a study I worked on) by taking one card each inch or each *n*th inch. This may be done by marking off every inch with a ruler and a sharp pencil and by sampling each card that the pencil mark falls on. But there is danger that old cards may not stick up as high as new ones do or may stick up slightly higher, decreasing (or increasing) the probability that an old card will get into the sample and thereby creating a biased sample.

Extreme vigilance is the only guarantee against such departures from randomness. As D. Huff puts it, "The operation of a poll comes down in the end to a running battle against sources of bias . . ." (Huff, p. 22). And in sampling, as in everything else in research, every technique depends at some point on your experience, general knowledge, and judgment. For example, it is only your judgment that leads you to *reason* that the systematic sample of

---

3. If a systematic random sample is to be used, it always makes sense to use two or more systematic subsamples that have different randomly chosen starting places, rather than a *single* systematic sample twice as large.

the phone book is better for your purposes than taking the first hundred names on the first page.

b. SELECTING THE APPROPRIATE SAMPLING FRAME

Selecting the appropriate sampling frame is like fitting within your camera lens what you really want to photograph. If you want to sample telephone subscribers for the telephone company, the telephone book is a fine sampling frame because it is an almost perfect representation of the population in which you are interested. (But it is not *perfect*. Some names in the phone book represent people who have moved away, some new subscribers are not yet listed, some people have unlisted phones, and some people have several listings. No sampling frame can ever be a perfect representation of the population. Even the Census misses some people—millions of them, especially young black males, as follow-up checks have revealed.) (Miller *et al.*).

If you want to sample the population for a voting study, however, the telephone book may not be a good sampling frame. Some registered voters do not have phones, and they are likely to be lower-income people who have different voting patterns from other registered voters. If you are sampling in a community where almost everyone has a phone, the sampling bias will be tiny, and you can usually ignore it. But, if only a small proportion of the community has phones, the bias in a sample from the telephone book may be enormous.

Nowadays in the U.S., unlisted phones—many of which belong to the higher-income families—are a more important problem than are families without phones. We'll talk shortly about how to deal with this problem with random dialing.

Demographers have used tombstones as a sampling frame in making estimates of the ages at which people died many centuries ago. But there are drawbacks, the most important of which is that the younger the person was when she died, the less likely she was to have accumulated enough wealth so that her heirs could afford to purchase a tombstone. Furthermore, infants were usually buried without any stones. Therefore a sample of tombstones yields a biased estimate of the age distribution at death.

The choice of sampling frame for personal interviews is full of problems.

> The obvious thing is to start with a list of everybody and go after names chosen from it at random; but that is too expensive. So you go into the streets—and bias your sample against stay-at-homes. You go from door to door by day—and miss most of the employed people. You switch to evening interviews—and neglect the movie-goers and night-clubbers. (Huff, p. 22)

The secret of success in choosing a sampling frame is: *Fit the sampling frame to your purpose*. For example, if Rolls Royce wants to gather market information about a change in design, the appropriate sampling frame includes only those people in the income class of present buyers, that is, the rich. But if Rolls Royce were to consider a big price cut to expand their market, then the appropriate sampling frame to learn about the effect of the price drop would include middle-income people.

If you keep in mind the purpose for which you are taking the sample, you will be alert in the choice of sampling frame to potential biases that might prejudice your investigation.

Earlier I mentioned that an important sampling-frame problem in telephone sampling is that many homes have unlisted or new phones—as many as 40 percent in the largest metropolitan areas (Sudman, 1976, p. 65), and 20 per cent for the country as a whole (Cooper, p. 45, Glasser and Metzger, p. 60). One may circumvent this problem by random-digit dialing, which takes advantage of the fact that telephone numbers are concentrated within certain blocks of numbers. An efficient method is: a) Select a systematic sample of telephone numbers from the telephone book; b) Strike out the last three digits of each telephone listing selected; c) Select a three-digit number from a table of random numbers, and append that to the shortened listings selected from the phone book. About half the numbers you obtain in this manner should be usable, and the resulting sample is randomly selected (Sudman, 1976, p. 65).

3. Screening in Sampling

Some studies require a sample of personal interviews with relatively rare individuals—people that have been to Africa, or blind people, or sociologists, or families with four sons. Sending interviewers to a random sample of all homes would be expensive and wasteful because no interview can be obtained in most visits.

You may sometimes circumvent this difficulty by obtaining a list of the rare persons, say, the list of members of the American Sociological Association. But there is no list of families with four sons. In such a case, you may do a screening sample by telephone or mail, asking whether that family has four sons, or a blind person, or whatever. The positive answers then constitute a sampling frame for the personal interview.

4. Efficiency in Random Sampling

Next we turn to various methods of increasing the efficiency of random sampling, that is, of getting a given amount of information for lower cost than would be obtained by a simple random sample. Another way to state the same point is that our aim is to reduce the amount of *sampling error* for a given sampling cost, or, to reduce the cost necessary to achieve a given level of sampling error.

The term **sampling error** refers to the discrepancy between the estimate one obtains from a given sample, and the estimate that one would obtain from a very, very large sample. To illustrate sampling error, flip a given coin many times to check that it is a fair coin. Then flip it ten times. The difference between the proportion of heads in the ten tosses to the 50-50 result obtained in the long run is the sampling error for that particular sample.

The average sampling error for a given sample size, using a particular sampling method, tends to be halved each time you quadruple the sample; that is, quadrupling the sample doubles the information obtained by it, rather than multiplying it by four.

a. SYSTEMATIC SAMPLING

A systematic sample is one in which every *n*th member is chosen from a list or other array of the universe. Taking every tenth house on the street produces a systematic sample, as does taking every twenty-seventh card in a card file. A systematic sampling process is *random* because, if the starting point is chosen randomly (that is, if whichever of the first ten houses or whichever of the first twenty-seven cards in the file the sample begins with is selected by random drawing), each member of the universe has an equal chance of falling into the sample; each house then has a one-tenth chance or each card a one twenty-seventh chance of being sampled.

The convenience of a systematic sample is obvious. Think how much easier it is to take, say, the twelfth name, or the twelfth and seventeenth names, on each page of a telephone book than to take differently numbered names from various pages and to jump around from page to page, some of which would contain many sampled names and others none.

But an even greater benefit of a systematic sample is its gain in precision over a simple random-sampling process. Systematic sampling helps spread the sample evenly over the universe with respect to the dimension on which you are sampling systematically. For example, with simple random sampling the names in the phone book, starting with any given letter—say "B"—will almost surely be somewhat over-represented or under-represented just by chance. But with systematic sampling the number of names selected starting with "B" will be in the same proportion as "B" names are in the universe.

There is the danger in choosing a systematic sample of hitting a *cycle*, such as corner houses on the street. A corner house is usually more expensive and therefore has more affluent occupants than do other houses on the block. But in practice cycles seldom cause difficulty.

Once more, drawing two or more "interpenetrating" samples—that is, two or more systematic subsamples started at randomly-chosen spots—is always superior to taking a systematic sample with a single starting place. Not only does this procedure reduce the danger of an unrepresentative start like corner houses, but it also permits quick inspection to see how much sampling error there is by simply comparing the means of the subsamples. The extra cost of this useful procedure is practically nil.

A systematic sample can also be a convenient device in carrying out the sampling technique we shall mention next, stratified sampling.

b. STRATIFIED SAMPLING

Stratified sampling is used primarily to reduce the cost of attaining a given level of accuracy in estimating the means and other parameters of populations.[4] The key idea in stratified sampling is that already-existing knowledge is used "to divide the population into groups such that the elements within each group are more alike than are the elements in the population as a whole" (Hansen, *et al.*, p. 40). In this way the researcher can reduce the chance of obtaining atypical samples. This idea can best be brought out with an example. Imagine that you want to estimate the average family income in a given town. On the basis of a previous survey as well as from visual observation, you are quite sure that the four equal-sized quarters of the town differ considerably in family income, NW (Northwest) being highest, followed by SW, SE, and NE in that order. If you take a small "unstratified" sample of only forty families, you might get fifteen families in NW, fourteen in SW, six in SE, and five in NE. That sample would probably give a mean income considerably higher than the mean that you would obtain if you included every family in the town. Or you might wind up with fifteen families in NE and a *lower* mean sample income than the average of the town as a whole. But compare this unstratified sample against a sample that is "stratified" to take ten families from each quarter. The stratified sample is likely to be closer to the "actual" mean than the unstratified sample, for it has equal numbers of families in the high- and low-income quarters. (But the stratified sample *could* be farther away from the actual if the unstratified sample happened to include the lower-income families in the high-income quarters and the stratified sample happened to include an atypical bunch of families.)

To repeat, the greater accuracy of the stratified sample derives from the fact that it cannot obtain a disproportionate number of units in the high- or low-income quarters of the town. *This makes it impossible to obtain many of the more nontypical samples that might be obtained by a simple unstratified random sample.* But each family has the same chance of being picked as every other family in the stratified sample, which is the same probability as in the unstratified sample. Therefore, the stratified sample is thoroughly random. If your original information is wrong, however, and the four quarters of the town do not differ in mean income, nothing is lost by the stratification. The results will be just as good as an unstratified sample, though they will be no better if the basis of the stratification (the prior knowledge about mean incomes in each quarter of the town) is wrong.

Stratified sampling only improves the representativeness of the sample with respect to the variable on which you stratify and with respect to other

4. For a very clear and simple explanation of stratified sampling, see M. Hansen, *et al.* (pp. 40–48).

variables closely associated with it. For example, if income is not closely associated with interest in music, then stratification by average income will not improve the sampling efficiency with respect to musical interest. (Income, however, is closely associated with many other social-science variables.)

In actual practice the stratification groups (the quarters of the town, in this case) are not exactly the same size, and the sample therefore takes the same *proportion* of units from each group, which means that each unit in the universe still has the same probability of being chosen. And, of course, each unit (family, in this case) within each group (quarter of town) is drawn by a random process, completing the requirements for a random sample—that each unit have the same (or known) chance of being picked for the sample.

Another use of stratified sampling is in estimating the means (or other parameters) of two or more *subgroups* within the population. Assume that you want to study the smoking habits of cigarette and pipe smokers. If you want equally accurate estimates for the two groups, you need equal numbers of cigarette smokers and pipe smokers in the sample. But, if you take a random sample of all people, you will surely get many nonsmokers, many cigarette smokers, and a few pipe smokers. For any given random-sample size, then, you would either be getting more accuracy than you needed for cigarette smokers or less accuracy than you needed for pipe smokers.

In such a situation, stratified sampling is a device that allows you to achieve more nearly equal accuracy for the different "strata" (cigarette and pipe smokers can each be considered a stratum) at the same total cost; or, put another way, stratified sampling enables you to achieve the same accuracy for the pipe smokers while decreasing the total cost.

It is fairly obvious that you should try to get approximately the same number of cigarette and pipe smokers into the sample; that is, you want to avoid spending money to obtain unnecessary cigarette smokers. For this purpose, you may *sample in different proportions* in the two strata. If you know *in advance* that there are approximately seven times as many cigarette smokers as pipe smokers, and, if you need to sample one in every 10,000 pipe smokers to get a subsample of the necessary accuracy, you must sample one in every 70,000 cigarette smokers ($7 \times 10,000 = 70,000$) to get a subsample of the same size and equal accuracy.

To carry out a program of stratified sampling, you must know something in advance about the relative proportions of pipe and cigarette smokers, of course. But it is reasonably easy to develop good estimates of those proportions with tiny pretests. And, if your estimates are off, no bias will be introduced, though the cost will be somewhat higher than with better estimates of the proportional sizes of the strata.

Sometimes it is necessary to take a 100 percent sample of some subgroups, and the samples may still be too small. For example, if you wished to find out the characteristics of *women* who smoke pipes, you might have to include in your sample every single woman who smoked a pipe.

A major difficulty with stratified sampling is identification of the people who belong in each stratum. If you are taking a sample of library books, it is easy enough to proceed through a card file taking every hundredth book in English and every fifth book in French; there is no difficulty in distinguishing the language a book is in, unless it is an esoteric language. But if you want to take a street-corner sample of every hundredth person who earns more than $10,000 and every tenth person who earns less than $10,000, it is not so easy to pick out people in the right proportions. And, indeed, your sample can be badly biased if you fail to include many well-dressed people who earn less than $10,000 in your sample. More rigorous identification procedures are obviously necessary.

Remember that a stratified sample is a randomly-drawn sample, even though all people do *not* have the same chance of falling into the sample, because the full definition of a randomly-chosen sample is that each member *either* has an equal chance of falling into the sample *or* it is *known* what chance each member has of falling into the sample, so that the unequal chance can be allowed for. As long as it is known that individual pipe smokers have seven times as great a chance of falling into the sample as did cigarette smokers, we can make appropriate allowances. Bias enters only when various members have an *unknown* chance of falling into the sample, or no chance at all. No adjustment is necessary as long as you make separate estimates for the separate strata. If you are estimating the characteristic in the *universe as a whole,* however, *you cannot simply add together all your observations.* Instead, you must weight the different strata in the proportions in which they occur in the universe. This is *crucial;* to fail to weight stratified samples is to commit an elementary but not uncommon blunder. In the example given, to estimate the smoking habits of the population as a whole, you must weight the evidence of each cigarette smoker in your sample seven times as heavily as that of each pipe smoker in your sample, because of your stratifying plan, which gave each pipe smoker a seven-times better chance of getting into your sample.

C. CLUSTER SAMPLING

Cluster sampling is another device to collect more information at lower cost. It works by decreasing the transportation time and costs of interviewers. Assume that you are making a survey to determine the number of people of each religion in a community. You obviously get *less information* by questioning five members of the same family than if you question five members of *different* families. All five members of the same family are likely to have the same religious affiliation, and therefore you know very little more after asking all five than after asking only one and multiplying his answer by five. Of course, you might find *some* differences within families, but you would be spending a lot of interviewing time to find them. *But* it is much *quicker and cheaper* to ask a question about religious affiliation of five people in one house than to go to five separate houses to ask five separate people.

Cluster sampling is a technique that takes advantage of the *decrease in cost per interview* that comes from collecting data on several subjects in the *same physical location,* compared to the cost of traveling from place to place and collecting data on one subject in each place. If the decrease in cost per interview is to result in a real gain, however, there must not be an excessive decrease in the information produced per subject, as there is, for example, when members of the same family are asked about religious affiliation.

The trick is to work out a sampling system in which you can collect considerable data in each collection area but in which there is little homogeneity (large heterogeneity) among the subjects in each area. For example, there will be less similarity in answers about religious affiliation if you ask five people standing in a grocery-store line than if you ask five people in the same house. There will be greater similarity in the answers from the five people in the grocery line, however, than there would be for five people chosen completely randomly from the community at large, because people from the same neighborhood shop at the same grocery store, and people in the same neighborhood have a tendency toward similar religious affiliations. A cluster-sampling design that samples ten people at random in each of fifty randomly-chosen towns (500 interviewees) might give higher accuracy at lower cost than sampling one person at random in each of 200 randomly chosen towns (200 interviewees).

Keep in mind that there is no gain in using a cluster-sampling design unless your subjects are originally spread over a wide geographic area, requiring high costs in transportation and time for interviewers.

The purpose of the foregoing discussions of stratified and cluster sampling is to teach you the basic ideas of these sampling strategies, but they do not tell you much about the *mechanics* of the strategies. If you undertake a large-scale study that might benefit from the use of either technique, call upon a sampling expert for help.

Cluster sampling yields the sometimes useful side-benefit of enabling you to make estimates for the units from which the clusters have been drawn. For example, Lazarsfeld and Thielens drew a sample of professors from U.S. universities. A simple random-sampling process would have scattered the sample among many universities, with few universities having more than one professor sampled. But instead they sampled clusters at a smaller number of universities, and this enabled them to compare the situations at various universities as well as to make estimates for all universities together.

d. SEQUENTIAL SAMPLING

Sequential sampling is another device to reduce sampling costs. Like stratified sampling, it seeks to avoid gathering data that are unnecessary for the level of accuracy you want. Sequential sampling works by *examining the evidence as it comes in* and stopping data collection when enough data are in.

There is no point in examining a sample of 1,000 if a sample of 100 will provide the necessary accuracy. But often it is not possible to guess in advance whether a sample of approximately 100 or 1,000 will be necessary because of lack of knowledge of what the data will be like. Sequential sampling is a device for overcoming this difficulty.

For example, assume that you are the president of a neighborhood political organization and that you want to know whether a majority of your group will approve a gift to you of a golden gavel. You might start down the membership list, call your members on the phone, and ask their opinions. If the first ten members split five and five in their reactions, you may wisely decide that you will have to take a complete poll. But if the first ten people you call are all against it, you can easily decide that a majority of the members is against it and stop your calling right then (provided, of course, that the first ten people were a random sample of your membership and that the name list was not biased!). This is an example of sequential sampling.

Sequential sampling allows you to make a fresh decision from time to time about whether you have collected enough data or need to collect more data. This technique can save you from taking a much bigger sample than you really need. There is further discussion of sequential sampling in Chapter 31.[5]

More generally, doing a series of small studies rather than one huge study allows you to learn from your mistakes and to improve your methods.

5. Nonrandom Samples

If you want to measure some characteristic of an entire population, you must not ignore *any part* of the population. You must make sure to count in all types of people, in the same proportions[6] in which they constitute the population. This is most obvious in political polling. To sample only in the East, say, or only among men or among Protestants would be erroneous. Choosing a representative "sample" is deceptively difficult, as Yates showed.

> A collection of about 1200 stones was spread out on a table, and each of 12 persons was asked to select 3 samples of 20 stones, which should represent as nearly as possible the size distribution of the whole collection. The results showed a consistent tendency, common to nearly all observers, to overestimate the average size of the stones; in fact, only 6 of the 36 estimates were smaller than the true average weight, and 3 of these estimates were made by a single observer. (Hansen, Hurwitz, and Madow, p. 72)

Only a random-sampling process can guarantee you that the sample *approaches* a fair picture of some characteristic of the universe, though how closely depends on the size of the sample, and any *given* sample might be

5. Some caution is required in fixing the sample size by proceeding in several steps. In some cases there may be danger of bias. See Hansen *et al.* (p. 79).
6. Or unequal but *known* proportions, as discussed later.

very odd. Despite this very desirable property of random (probability) samples, a wise scientist does not always decide to take a probability sample. The practical conditions may be such that you cannot obtain a randomly drawn sample at reasonable cost or even at all. Or there may be no need for a probability sample. Let us take the former case first.

As an example in which a nonrandom sample may be better because of cost, consider the case in which we want to find out whether or not people remember the past as happier than the present. A probability sample of the entire United States or world is too expensive. But the cheapest and most convenient sample—college students—might yield a very misleading answer; it might well be true that the felt relationship between adulthood and earlier years is different from, say, the relationship between middle age and the previous periods.

One way to handle this problem is to obtain as many different kinds of easy-to-obtain samples as possible: a parent-teacher association, a retirement club, an immigrant ethnic organization, a minor-league baseball team, a local plasterer's union, a group of waitresses at a restaurant, and so on. If in *each* of these groups people say that they were happier in prior years than at present, an excellent generalization is that people remember the past as happier than the present. The key to effective use of this strategy is to obtain as *varied* a collection of groups (or individuals) in your sample as possible.

Such a collection of diverse groups might be very cheap to obtain for group interviewing. A very much larger sample can be obtained, compared to a probability sample, in which group-administered questionnaires cannot be given.

E. Durkheim, in his famous study of the causes of suicide, used the device of replicating a study in order to strengthen his proof:

> . . . [T]he original finding is re-examined in different groups of subjects—for example, the excess of military over civilian suicides is confirmed for eight different countries of Europe. Durkheim further replicates this finding within the Austro-Hungarian Empire; the military-civilian difference persists in the various military areas. (Selvin, p. 122)

The laws of probability will prevent geographical bias if you draw a sample randomly. But sometimes it is not possible to take a probability sample of the entire population. For instance, a probability sample of the United States was out of the question for the main Kinsey studies, for many reasons. Yet, Kinsey wished to make estimates for the population of *all* United States white males, as well as for each subpopulation. Kinsey's estimates would have been quite wrong had he gathered all his interviews from one part of the country (unless by some fantastic coincidence he had picked one part of the country that was perfectly typical; certain towns in Maine are reputed to be such typical "weather vanes" for national elections, but they are surely not typical for sex studies—and it is almost impossible for any town to be typical if several characteristics are to be studied). Kinsey's data revealed considerable differences in sexual patterns in various parts of the country. New York City, for example, is quite atypical in all respects.

The matched sample is another example of the use of nonrandom groups. In comparison studies, the researcher prefers to compare two or more groups of subjects that are randomly drawn from the same sampling frame and then treated differently in the experiment. But sometimes it is not possible to make up groups of randomly-selected subjects. A political candidate, for example, cannot set up groups of random subjects drawn from the same population on which to test two different political platforms. She may therefore find two cities that are very similar and compare the results in one city with those in the other.

The danger that bias will distort results of a matched-group experiment is very great, however. In one view, "The value of [matching] has been greatly oversold and it is more often a source of mistaken inference than a help to valid inference" (Campbell and Stanley, p. 6). Geographical differences are a frequent obstacle. But worst is the distortion that arises when the independent and dependent variables are confounded, as we shall see in Chapter 23 when we compare people who went to Harvard Business School with people who *seem* equal in all respects except that they did not go to Harvard Business School.

Another situation in which random sampling is not necessarily best is that in which almost any group of individuals can be regarded as a sufficiently fair sample of the population with respect to the characteristics under study.

Though people who live in different places differ in many ways, not every piece of research must take a countrywide or worldwide probability sample. This is most likely to happen when you are studying characteristics that are biological or psychophysical in nature. In such experiments the researcher hopes to find characteristics that apply to all people. I. Pavlov's experiments in conditioning dogs were no less valid because he did not choose randomly from the dog population of Russia. H. Ebbinghaus went even further. He ran one of his pioneer experiments on learning and forgetting on just *one* subject—*himself.* He clearly states the reach and the limits of his method.

> The tests were all made upon myself and have primarily only individual significance. Naturally they will not reflect exclusively mere idiosyncrasies of my mental organisation; if the absolute values found are throughout only individual, yet many a relation of general validity will be found in the relation of these numbers to each other or in the relations of the relations. (Ebbinghaus, p. v)

P. Lazarsfeld, *et al.,* made a similar argument for their choice of Erie County, Pennsylvania, as the place in which to conduct their election study:

> Erie County in 1940 was small, reasonably prosperous, peopled with a homogeneous, friendly group of native Americans engaged about equally in agricultural and industrial work . . . it was not the "typical American county" but for the purposes of this study it did not need to be. We were not interested in *how*

people voted but in *why* they voted as they did. We did not want to predict the outcome of the election but to discover certain processes underlying opinion formation and political behavior. (Lazarsfeld, *et al.*, p. 10)

For similar reasons, as shown in Table 9.1, Peoria, Illinois, has been the site of a great many marketing experiments with new products. But be very careful when you dismiss the possibility of geographical differences. Geography can show up as an important variable even in many biological investigations: In the study of smoking and lung cancer, for example, one might have to consider that the extent of pollution varies from place to place and that such variation might affect lung cancer rates.

TABLE 9.1   Profile of a Test Market—Peoria, Illinois, 1971

	Metro. Peoria	Total U.S.A.
Population:		
Male	49.2%	49.2%
Female	50.8%	50.8%
Children under 18 yrs. of age	35.5%	35.8%
Age Brackets:		
Under 5 years	11.5%	11.3%
5–19 yrs.	26.6%	27.2%
20–34 yrs.	19.1%	18.7%
35–44 yrs.	13.1%	13.4%
45–64 yrs.	20.4%	20.1%
65 & over	9.3%	9.3%
Employment:		
Employed males	53.1%	49.2%
Employed females	21.8%	23.2%
Unemployed males	46.9%	50.8%
Unemployed females	78.2%	76.8%
By occupation:		
Business & professional	9.6%	11.2%
Salaried & semiprofessional	7.8%	8.4%
Skilled	63.7%	59.6%
Unskilled	18.9%	20.8%
Median family income	$5,998	$5,660
Median school years (males, 25 yrs. & over)	10.2 yrs.	10.6 yrs.
Median age (total population)	29.4 yrs.	30.3 yrs.

SOURCE: *Advertising Age,* November 1, 1971, p. 147.

Extreme caution and good judgment are necessary in any nonrandom sampling. For example, it may even matter whether auditory or visual experiments are run on individuals of one particular age group. Even when investigating "universal" phenomena, the researcher should try to take at least a part of his sample from individuals who vary in age, residence, and so forth, as a check that the phenomenon is indeed universal.

Quota sampling is a very important nonrandom sampling method. It may come as a surprise to you that almost all election polls (for instance, those of Gallup) and most other nationwide opinion polls use quota samples, rather than samples chosen on a probability basis. Quota sampling has a superficial resemblance to stratified random sampling. The stratification example given in our discussion would be a quota sample if the town were again divided into the four quarters and one interviewer were sent to each with instructions to interview ten "typical" families about whether they expected to buy a car this year or to vote Democratic. The crucial difference between stratified and quota samples, however, is that the "typical" families chosen by the interviewer for the latter are not likely to be chosen at random; he may avoid homes where there are ferocious-looking dogs, for example. Each family in the universe thus does *not* have the same chance of being chosen, and therefore the researcher cannot use statistical theory to estimate the accuracy of his results, as he can with a random sample.

The quotas are likely to be specified very closely, unlike the strata in stratified sampling. The interviewers are instructed to obtain interviews with fixed numbers of people in each of such categories as age group, color, income bracket, and religion; the proportions for each category are chosen to mirror the proportions in the population at large. Quotas must also be specified for working women, and for interviews done on the weekends and in the evening; unless special attention is given to these hard-to-obtain interviews, serious bias may result. The idea is that, if all the subgroups are given the appropriate amount of representation, the overall sample should then correctly represent the universe. And so it would be if the interviewers managed to choose people *within* each subgroup in a fairly random manner and the survey managed to sample each group in proportion to its actual size. But the survey may obtain too large or too small a proportion of people with little education, for example.

Quota samples are usually cheaper than are random samples of the same size. Some of them yield results of excellent accuracy, but poor construction has led to very inaccurate results in some cases. The excellence of the quota sample depends almost entirely on the skill of the researcher.[7]

Snowball sampling is a method used when members of a universe cannot easily be located by random sampling or by screening, and where the members of a universe know other members of the universe. Each member of the universe who is located is asked for names and addresses of other members. The snowball method has been used, for example, to create a sample of drug users, and to study friendship groups and elites. But the method does not work with blind persons, because they have a low propensity to know each other.

---

7. For empirical studies of the accuracy of quota samples, see F. Stephan and P. McCarthy (Chaps. 7, 8). For detailed analysis of quota sampling in voting polls, see F. Mosteller, *et al.*

An important bias in snowball sampling is that the more others who know a given person as, for example, a drug user, the more likely the person is to be found in the sample. And drug users who are known as such to many other people may be quite atypical of drug users. (For more information see Sudman, 1976, pp. 210–211, and Goodman, 1961.)

6. Summary

A **sample** is a device used to learn about a universe (population) without the expense of studying each member of the universe. A sample is well-chosen if it accurately describes what it seeks to describe, with reasonable efficiency.

Samples can be chosen by random selection or with human judgments. Random selection can depend on the support of probability theory to establish its likely accuracy whereas judgmental sampling cannot, but sometimes judgmental sampling's other advantages outweigh this.

Simple random sampling requires a list of the elements of the universe. Selection of the list—the sampling frame—can be a delicate matter requiring good judgment. From this list a selection is taken with some mechanical technique that seems random; choosing numbers from a table of random numbers is simple and sure if it is feasible, and if a nearly complete list of the universe is available.

Systematic sampling selects every nth element in an ordering of the elements of the universe. It may be easier to execute, and can be statistically more efficient, than a simple random sample. Its only drawback is the possibility that there may be some cycle in the data that systematically affects the nth element, but this danger is usually easy to avoid.

Stratified sampling can improve sampling efficiency by explicitly taking subsamples of fixed size within the important different sections of the universe, proportional to their representation in the universe. This improves the representativeness of a sample of any given size.

Cluster sampling takes several observations in each geographic area. This saves time and money. But each single observation in cluster sampling provides less information than in random sampling. On balance, cluster sampling may or may not be efficient, depending on the distance and time required to travel from one observation to the next.

In **sequential sampling** you continue taking observations until you have achieved the necessary accuracy. This method is in contrast with the procedure of fixing the sample size in advance. Sequential sampling is always preferable when it is feasible, but sometimes it is not practical.

Nonrandom samples cannot guarantee the likelihood of any given level of accuracy, as can randomly-drawn samples. But sometimes samples cannot be drawn randomly, either because one cannot run a controlled experiment on humans, or because a randomly-drawn sample is too expensive. A matched-group sample may be appropriate, but there is always the danger that the matched groups are not similar in some important respect. And a representative-group sample may not really be representative of the universe. Quota sampling is an important technique in public-opinion sampling, but requires remarkable judgment and great experience to carry out well.

EXERCISE

1. The public broadcasting system station in Champaign-Urbana takes a survey of the contributors to the station to determine their listening preferences. How might this choice of sampling frame influence the choice of programming? How might this choice of sampling frame influence the musical offerings available to people who like classical music, including both contributors and noncontributors?

ADDITIONAL READING FOR CHAPTER 9

There are many good readings on sampling. Hansen *et al.* give an excellent general discussion, with their Chapter 1 providing a remarkably clear exposition of the relationship between sample size and accuracy. Another excellent general discussion of sampling is that of Lazerwitz. Isadore Chein gives a straightforward introduction to sampling as Appendix A in Selltiz *et al.* Stephan and McCarthy (Chapters 1–11) offer an easily readable and knowledgeable text, especially about sampling of attitudes for public opinion surveys. Kish provides perhaps the most complete treatment of sampling, both simple and complex, especially sampling for surveys.

For practical guidance in all aspects of sampling, see Sudman (1976). A good description of the sampling process in market research may be found in Chapters 9 and 10 of Boyd, Westfall, and Stasch, 4th edition. On the Bayesian and information-value approach to sampling, see Green and Tull (Chapter 7).

About the sampling frame, see Deming (Chapter 3). This book also contains excellent discussion of the theory of sampling and of other topics in sampling. The examples are drawn largely from business, but because of their emphasis on the value of information and the cost of error, they are very instructive to people in other areas as well. Above all, this is a practical book.

Details on random-digit telephone dialing may be found in Glasser and Metzger and in Sudman (1973).

10 experiments: pro, con, and how to do them

1. The Distinction Between Experiment and Survey

An experiment and a survey are alternative methods of getting knowledge about the relationships between (or among) variables, most especially about the *causal* relationships between variables. This chapter is therefore about research into relationships and is not concerned with description, measurement, or classification research, all of which must usually be done with the survey method. For example, you cannot find out how many people there are in the United States through a laboratory experiment; you must go out and count them. You cannot determine how many people will vote Republican in the next election with any laboratory procedures, nor do you need experimentation; you must take a poll.[1]

The first purpose of this and the following chapters is to teach you what you need to know about methods in order to choose the appropriate method for a given situation. Details of execution of each method are given only secondary treatment; references are supplied to technical works on each method.

The crux of the experiment is that the investigator intentionally manipulates one or more of the independent variables (x_1, x_2 . . .), thus exposing various groups of subjects to the different variables (or to different amounts of the independent variables), and then observes the changes in the depen-

1. S. Stouffer offers a useful schema of the differences between experiments and nonexperimental studies.

dent variables (y_1, y_2 . . .). The experimental groups are usually selected randomly, which further ensures that observed differences among groups really reflect differences in the independent variables. The ideal design was discussed on pages 36–39.

In those situations in which it is possible to experiment with the real-life variables *within the actual real-life situations* in which you are interested, the experiment is *always* a more desirable means of investigating relationships than the survey. The real-life experiment is more desirable because it permits much more certain inference of a causal connection between two variables than does a survey. For example, it may be possible to observe from a survey that, when government spending is high, Gross National Product is high too. But the relationship might be obscured by a hidden third factor, perhaps the quantity of money in circulation, and Gross National Product might be unrelated to government spending except through the same other variable. You would have much stronger grounds for belief in their causal connection if you could (randomly) manipulate government spending to be low or high in various years and then see whether GNP is also low or high in corresponding years. Only then would you know that it is government spending that affects GNP; the randomness of the decision that government spending be high or low in any given year would preclude some other variable from being the cause of both spending and GNP being high and low together; only *you the experimenter* would then be responsible for variations in spending and not some other variable.

For another example, without an experiment we must always recognize a possibility, though not necessarily a high probability (J. Simon, 1966c), that some constitutional (genetic) factor predisposes smokers both to become smokers *and* to die of cancer, heart disease, and other "smoking-caused" diseases. An experiment could reduce the probability by having a random sample of people become smokers or nonsmokers so that (with a big enough sample) there would be no possible relationship between any special genetic factor and both smoking and cancer; *you* would be the only cause of their starting to smoke.

One cannot experiment with government spending or human smoking. But in many real-life situations experimentation is quite possible. For example, if you want to find out which of two methods of teaching reading to first-grade children is better, you can set up a controlled experiment in the real-life situation by trying the two different systems in randomly-selected classrooms. It is a real-life experiment because the methods are tried out under *exactly the same conditions* in which they would actually be put to work. (Remember, however, that even an apparently real-life experiment can be fouled up. For example, a group of students who know that they are being taught by an experimental system might learn faster for just that reason, just as the workers in the Hawthorne factory produced more work under worse conditions just because they knew that they were the subjects of an experiment.)

But wait a minute: Be slow to conclude that an experiment is impossible. For years economists and sociologists have been interested in the effect of taxes on work behavior. They were sure that it was impossible to conduct an experiment in which some people's tax rates were different from others. Then some brash soul decided to press for an experiment anyway. The result was the famous and invaluable set of negative-income-tax experiments of the 1960s and 1970s, where randomly-selected people were given large income supplements, and whose work behavior was then observed.

Similarly, two advertising campaigns can sometimes be studied in a real-life experiment by beaming them to different cities. Medicines are also always tested in real-life experiments before they are released for general use, but only after non-real-life experiments indicate that the real-life experiments probably will not be dangerous.

Whenever real-life experiments are feasible, they are preferable to survey methods. (By "feasible" I mean ethically, physically, and financially possible.) The principle of experimenting when possible seems obvious in the late twentieth century. But, until perhaps a hundred or two hundred years ago, it just did not occur to people to learn about the world by running scientific experiments, that is, by systematically altering some aspects of the world and then observing other aspects to see how they were affected. And, in most parts of the world today, among those people who have not had modern educations, the idea of experimentation is still mostly unknown. Of course, people have always learned about good cooking by informal experiments with various recipes. But, when it came to learning how the world ticks, scholars just did not consider trying to gain knowledge by experimentation or, more generally, by any empirical methods. Remember the story of the philosophers who refused to look into the horse's mouth to find out how many teeth a horse had but preferred instead to debate the issue?

Though a real-life experiment is preferable when feasible, sometimes it is impossible to experiment. Then the investigator must choose between two alternatives: observation of the real-life situation as it unfolds, that is, taking a survey and trying to assess the relationships among the variables, despite the obstacles to doing so; or experimentation with a laboratory imitation of the real-life situation, that is, testing the effects of smoking on rats instead of on humans or subjecting models instead of real buildings to earthquakes. In order to make this choice wisely, you must understand the strengths and weaknesses, advantages and disadvantages of the two methods.

2. The Steps in Experimenting

The beginner always wants a checklist of the steps he should take. You want to know what to do first, what to do second, and so on. Often it is dangerous to satisfy this request, because you may come to think that there really is some "correct" order of procedure; the danger is that you may forget that the procedure for each piece of research must be tailored especially to that research situation—that is, that the procedure should depend on what you want to know, what you know already, and what kind of researcher you are. If you keep in mind, however, that the following checklist is not rigid but is rather a suggested procedure that often fits what people do in experimental work, then it may be safe to put this checklist in your hands.

Let us assume that you have already worked your way through the general steps described in Chapter 7 and that you have arrived at the point of deciding that an experiment will be more effective and appropriate than a survey in providing the knowledge you want. (But, before you make that decision final, read pp. 153–58 on the advantages and disadvantages of experiments and surveys.)

STEP 1: CHOOSE APPROPRIATE VARIABLES

Decide which observable variables will represent the "real" (hypothetical or theoretical) variables in which you are interested. For example, a gymnasium-test score may stand for (be a proxy for) physical fitness as a dependent variable; you are then saying that a score on the gymnasium test is a good measurement of what you mean when you talk about physical fitness in an experiment on fitness-training methods. Or some paragraphs in a foreign language that students read and then are quizzed about may be your measurement of reading comprehension in the language and serve as a dependent variable in an experiment on teaching foreign languages to students. Or, if you want to experiment with how people behave in risk situations, you might give them tiny sums of money and observe how they bet them in a laboratory game. The small sums of money stand for larger sums of money, and the laboratory betting stands for betting behavior in real-life situations.

Variables must have two properties: First, they must be measurable. Physical fitness *per se* is not measurable because it is not operationally defined. You define it operationally by letting something else that is measurable—a gym test, for instance—stand for it. Note that setting up an operational definition really is a matter of letting a measurable empirical magnitude stand for the hypothetical variable in which you are interested. Second, your proxy variable must be a *good* proxy, a "valid indicator," that is, it must have a reasonable and sensible relationship to your hypothetical variable. Height would not be a good proxy for physical fitness, I think you will agree. Selecting appropriate measurable variables is very difficult indeed, and doing a good job of it demands clear thinking and imagination. I discussed the matter in Chapter 6. As has already been noted, it is often wise to observe the effects of several variables in a single experiment.

Deciding *how many* variables with which to experiment is also an important decision. The number of possible variables is limitless, but your time and funds are very much limited. Furthermore, for technical reasons difficult to explain here there must be more subjects in the experiment than

FIGURE 10.1

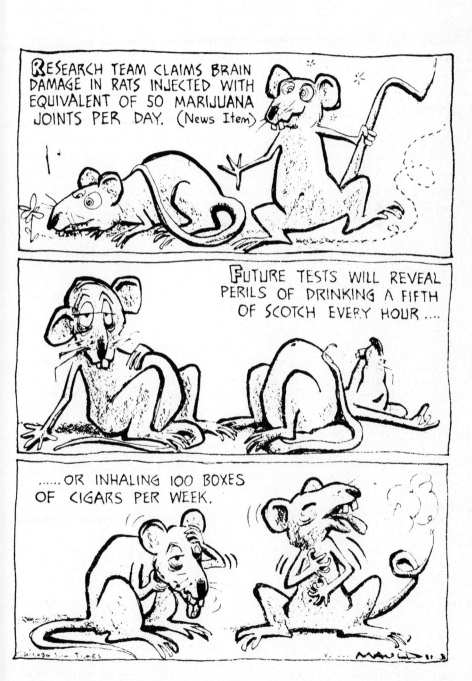

Source: From the Champaign/Urbana Gazette, Aug. 10, 1976. Reprinted by permission.

there are variables, lest the results turn out to be meaningless.[2] Therefore, you must set up priorities among the variables, so that you can vary the most important of them experimentally and hold the others constant. The general logic of the cost and value of research, as described in Chapter 8, should be your guide.

STEP 2: CHOOSE TREATMENT LEVELS

Choose appropriate *levels* at which to test the independent variables. Often the choice is based on plain good sense and is forced by the situation. For example, if a school psychologist wants to see whether longer or shorter reading periods will result in quicker reading advancement, the school will not compare five-hour and five-minute periods with the present sixty-minute periods; rather, the psychologist will choose levels of perhaps thirty minutes and ninety minutes to compare with the present sixty-minute period. The first principle, then, is to vary the stimuli at such levels as are of *practical interest* in the real-life situation. This point is illustrated in Mauldin's cartoon about marijuana research (Figure 10.1). Often one of the levels will be a *control group*, which receives the standard treatment or no treatment at all. The control group provides a base against which to measure the experimental groups.

The second principle is to vary the stimuli in big enough jumps so that you obtain measurable results. The psychologist will not compare sixty-one-minute and fifty-nine-minute reading periods with the present sixty-minute period, for no observable difference is likely to result. Similarly, if General Motors wants to experiment with a price decrease, it will not simply decrease the price of each car a dollar. An example related to this second principle comes from a survey rather than an experiment, a survey of the effects of strategic bombing on German morale in World War II. The first comparison, between groups of people exposed to 6,000 tons and 30,000 tons of bombs dropped, respectively, showed *no difference* in the morale of the two groups. This peculiarity was explained when a group exposed to only 500 pounds of bombs showed higher morale (Hyman, 1955, pp. 184–185).

A third principle in choosing levels of independent variables is to choose *enough* levels of variation so that you will not be fooled by a curvilinear relationship. For example, reading advancement might be related to length of reading period in the fashion shown in Figure 10.2. If you experiment only with levels A and E, you will never find out that the best level is C. Therefore, it pays to experiment at several levels that are quite spread out—like A, B, C, D, and E in the figure. The cost of running treatments

2. This point is very difficult to explain in simple terms. An analogy may help. No *one* number can establish the location of a point on a flat piece of paper; both length and width measurements are required. In a box, which has three dimensions—length, width, and height—*three* measurements are necessary. And, if you can imagine a four-dimensional space or an *n*-dimensional space, it would require four or *n* measurements respectively to establish the location of a single point.

FIGURE 10.2 **Length of Training Periods**

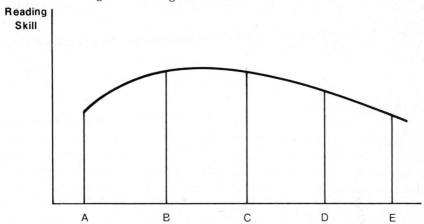

Length of Training Periods

constrains you from running experiments at a very large number of levels, however.

STEP 3: CHOOSE A SAMPLE

Select a sample of subjects for your experiment. The sample should be appropriately unbiased, and it should be drawn from a universe that is a reasonable and sensible representation of the universe in which you are interested.

STEP 4: CONTROL THE EXPERIMENTAL CONDITIONS

Plan the details of the experiment so that the *conditions* are correct. In every experiment there are many factors that can influence the outcome but that you do not want to vary experimentally; they are the *parameters*. You must arrange them to suit your purposes and so that they remain constant during the experiment. For example, if you are conducting psychophysical experiments on how hearing is affected by motivation, you will want your experimental room to be soundproof. Absolute quiet is one of the parameters of the experiment. Not only must you arrange for a soundproof room, but you must also make sure that, during your experiment, the building will not be remodeled with jackhammers and other heavy machinery whose noise will penetrate the soundproofing. I. Pavlov went to great lengths to create experimental conditions that would not disturb the conditioning process in his dogs.

Those conditions that cannot be held *physically* constant must be made to meet the test of *ceteris paribus* in other ways. In an experiment like that of

H. Ebbinghaus on how people learn to memorize nonsense syllables, you would not want to have one group tested in the middle of the night after being awakened from a deep sleep—unless, of course, you were experimenting with the effects of sleep. Rather, you would want time of day to be a *ceteris paribus* condition. If you were trying to find out whether people memorize short nonsense syllables faster than long nonsense syllables, you would not want to have all the long nonsense syllables in the second half of the list. Rather, you would mix up the long and short syllables either randomly in the list or by giving some subjects (randomly chosen) the long syllables first and other subjects the short syllables first. This is nothing but common sense, of course, but such matters are not always so obvious, and violation of *ceteris paribus* conditions causes many experiments to fail.

STEP 5: DIVIDE SUBJECTS INTO GROUPS

Divide the subjects into one or more experimental groups and (usually) a control group. The number of experimental groups depends upon how many different stimuli you want to test or on how many different levels of the independent variable you want to test. Whenever possible, divide subjects into the two groups *randomly;* this is your basic guarantee that the results of the experiment will mean something. Sometimes, however, it is not possible to make up randomized groups. For example, if you are test-marketing an advertising campaign and if you can afford to test the campaign in only four cities, you would probably arrange the cities so that you considered the groups *well matched.* Matching can be very treacherous, however, because you may set up the groups in some way that merely seems convenient to you but that may really bear a relationship to the variables and may thus confound the experiment.

STEP 6: PLAN THE "EXPERIMENTAL DESIGN"

I have placed "experimental design" in quotation marks to indicate that the term has a special meaning in experimentation, apart from the basic plan of the experiment. The phrase refers to the *statistical* scheme by which the variables are related to one another, and the scheme is chosen in such a way as to obtain the greatest validity and efficiency from the experiment. For example, there are many designs in which you vary more than one variable at a time. (See Chapter 11; it is not true that in an experiment you can safely vary only one variable at a time.)

Various experimental designs are discussed at length in Chapter 11.

STEP 7: DETERMINE SAMPLE SIZE

Decide what to do about sample size. Almost always you should begin by taking a small pretest sample that will give you some intuitive feeling for how big a sample you will need and that will also provide necessary data for the estimates of sample size described in Chapter 31. And, whenever possible, plan to take your sample on a sequential basis, gradually increasing the sample until it is large enough, rather than making a firm decision before you begin (Chapter 9). This sequential procedure is impossible in many types of research situations, however.

STEP 8: PRETEST AND REVISE

Conduct a pretest, and then revise your procedure in light of what you learn from the pretest. Run another pretest. Revise again. And so on until your experimental procedure is pat and airtight. Then run the actual experiment.

This is a particularly good time to discuss your work with your fellow students and staff members. Show them a brief write-up of what you are doing and of your preliminary results. One of my own major shortcomings as a researcher is that I do too little of this, largely because I hesitate to ask people. I hope that you are less shy about this than I am, but you should at least recognize that someone is doing you one of the greatest favors it is possible for one person to confer on another when she gives you the benefit of her attention, experience, and critical imagination.

STEP 9: ANALYZE THE DATA

Analyze and interpret your data and draw appropriate conclusions from the data, perhaps with the aid of statistics (Chapters 25–30). This stage is not as large a part of the whole job in an experiment as it is in a survey, because much of your analysis is really built into the experiment as you set it up.

3. Advantages of Experiments

a. ESTABLISHING DIRECTION OF CAUSALITY

The most important advantage of the experiment is that the relationship that you *actually observe* is clear in its causal direction. ("Actually observe" is italicized to emphasize that, if your variables are not good proxies for the hypothetical variables in which you are really interested, the experiment will not be meaningful.) In an experiment it is you, the experimenter, who manipulate the independent variables. If you observe variations in the dependent variable, they must therefore be caused by the variations in the independent variable and not by some other force that is affecting both the independent and dependent variables at the same time. This property of the experiment makes it possible to talk confidently about one aspect of causation. (But your independent variable may not be what you think it is, which may fool you about what is causing the change in the dependent variable.)

b. COST

The absolute cost of a laboratory experiment can often be low compared to that of alternative research methods. For example, an advertiser can pretest the effects of two advertising campaigns in a laboratory situation with a very few people, whereas a field experiment or survey would require actually carrying out advertising campaigns in expensive field tests. For another example, an engineer can make a structural analysis of a building's strength by constructing two-foot models in his laboratory, instead of constructing real buildings experimentally or making exhaustive studies of actual buildings that collapse.

c. CONVENIENCE

An experiment can be run whenever you like, to suit your convenience. If you are going to create a mock riot experimentally, you can pick your time and place so that you will have observers and equipment ready to observe the results. Real riots happen at unexpected times and unexpected places, which is one reason we know so little about riots.

d. ADJUSTABILITY OF VARIABLES AND PARAMETERS

Unlike a survey, an experiment permits you to arrange the parameters and vary the variables in whatever fashion you desire, to look for whatever effects interest you. If you are studying the causes of riots, you can vary the temperature in the place where the riot will occur to see whether people respond more vigorously when it is hot. In real riots, however, you must take the temperature as it comes. In his research on memory of nonsense syllables, Ebbinghaus could first vary the length of the syllable list, then the number of repetitions, then the time between learning and testing, and then the order of the words. Another investigator can then vary the amount of the reward given for correct memorization and so on, until he has systematically explored all the important possibilities. Only an experiment permits such detailed examination.

An experiment often allows you to investigate extremes of the independent variable that are not found in everyday life. It is only in an experiment that you can observe a person who has been awake for four days straight, who has been sleeping only fifteen minutes every four hours, or who has been subjected first to absolute quiet and then to enormous noise. But L. Festinger argues that, in social psychology:

> It is extremely difficult to create in the laboratory forces strong enough for results to be measurable. In the most excellently done laboratory experiment, the strength to which different variables can be produced is extremely weak compared to the strength with which these variables exist and operate in real-life situations. (Festinger, p. 141)

This is not only because experiments are difficult to do, but because "many dangers are present in their execution" (Festinger, p. 141). This comment makes sense when one reflects on the sort of phenomena that social psychologists deal with: race riots, conflict, love, and prejudice.

In experimentation you can systematically refine the relationship you are investigating. Perhaps you have been told by an Indian villager that a particular root has wonderful properties for reducing the blood pressure and tranquilizing excited patients. First you can experiment with samples of the root material. If it works, you probably will want to know exactly what it is in the root that has this medicinal effect. Therefore, your next move might be to experiment with the *juice* from the root. If the juice alone works without the fiber of the root, then next you might try various constituents of the juice. And so on until you have "isolated" the "active principle." Similarly, the researchers in the Hawthorne experiments were able to vary many aspects of the workers' environment, including how much attention the workers got from researchers, and they obtained knowledge of the causes of morale and work output that would have been difficult to learn by survey alone. The key to the Hawthorne research was the ability to try one thing after another, to "sneak up" on the knowledge they sought.

e. REPLICATION

One occurrence is seldom enough to convince you that what you think happened really happened. For example (as noted on pp. 273–75), observers vary from time to time in what they observe. By repeating ("replicating") an experiment, you can obtain an average result; your conclusion is then not based on a single observation that might be unusually high or unusually low. Replication is one of the most useful tools in obtaining valid results, which is why classic experiments are often repeated, sometimes under slightly different circumstances, to ensure that it was not just an idiosyncrasy of the environment that caused the original results—as in our earlier example of the high-pitched sound associated with the air blast, rather than the air blast itself, really causing peculiar behavior in rats.

Study of the jury system was long hampered by the one-time nature of trials.[3] Furthermore, the particulars of cases differ greatly. Therefore, it was formerly difficult to investigate how juries react to various types of cases. In the experimental-jury paradigm invented by Strodtbeck, the experimenter *repeats* the same recorded trial to many juries and thereby obtains a sample of workable size (R. Simon, 1967).

f. UNRAVELING MULTIVARIABLE CAUSATION

If two independent variables are closely related in the world outside the laboratory, a survey cannot easily determine which of them causes variation in the dependent variable. Because the laboratory experiment holds some factors constant as it varies others and then vice versa, the experimenter can

---

3. It might be interesting, however, to study trials that *are* repeated because of hung juries and higher-court reversals.

track down the extent to which each is responsible for change in the dependent variable. (Of course, there are some cases in which it is only the *combination* or *interaction* of the two variables that will cause changes in the dependent variable; experimental designs that vary both variables simultaneously will reveal such interaction, however.)

4. Disadvantages of Experiments

The neatness of an experiment is very appealing, especially when the investigator is frustrated by the annoying shortcomings of survey data. S. Stouffer, who, more than any other one man, was responsible for *The American Soldier*, once wrote, "I would trade a half dozen Army-wide surveys on attitudes toward officers for one good controlled experiment" (1950a, p. 211). But, if pressed, Stouffer would surely have qualified that statement, for the disadvantages of experiments can also be grave.

a. LACK OF "REALITY"

The most important disadvantage of the laboratory experiment (but not of the real-life field experiment, of course) is that you can never be sure that the analogy between the experiment and the real world really holds. In other words, there is always some risk involved in generalizing from what happens in the laboratory to what happens in the real world. Smoking causes cancer in laboratory experiments on rats, but is it correct to reason that the same thing happens with humans? (Chapters 26 and 32 discuss the grounds for safe generalizations.)

The riskiness of a generalization from a laboratory experiment depends on how well you specify your variables. Obviously it makes more sense to generalize about the effects of smoking from a laboratory experiment in which apes smoke tobacco than from a laboratory experiment in which fish are exposed to the smoke from corn silk. On the other hand, much important theoretical work takes place in experiments with very "unrealistic" materials, because more realistic materials are too complicated to allow us to get a simple picture of what happens. From studies with unrealistic nonsense syllables, Ebbinghaus learned much about the learning process that he could not have with such complex subject matter as texts on Shakespeare or physics. It is much harder to run a "clean" experiment with Shakespeare or physics as the materials to be learned, because the subjects' prior knowledge complicates the experiment greatly.

b. UNREPRESENTATIVE SAMPLES

Another danger in drawing conclusions about the universe of interest from the laboratory experiment is that the subjects on whom the experiment is run in the laboratory may be very unlike the people in the real world about whom you wish to draw conclusions. Often it is difficult to persuade a fair sample of the universe to come into the laboratory. Consider these examples: First, economists try to experiment in the laboratory to find out how competing big businesses behave under certain competitive circumstances. But, because it is not possible to lure the presidents of, say, General Motors, Ford, and Chrysler into the laboratory for the experiment, the researchers study the behavior of *students* who are playing a business game. Can one generalize from the students' behavior to that of real executives? Second, a researcher wanted to experiment with the reactions of jurors to a mock trial after they had been given sensational or unsensational newspaper clippings about the trial, to find out the effect of newspaper publicity on the course of justice. But a disproportionate number of the people who agreed to take part in the experiment were from the middle and professional classes. In that study, the unrepresentative sample probably did not affect the direction of outcome (R. Simon, 1966). In another study, however, the same experimenter found it necessary (and possible) to draw subjects from actual jury pools with the assistance of the courts, which ensured representative samples (R. Simon, 1967). Third, a market-research firm runs experiments on people invited by postcard to come to free movies. During the movies commercials are tested. But people who come to free movies in the afternoon are not necessarily typical of the people who might be exposed to the same commercials on television—which is what the advertisers are really interested in.

What is important, of course, is that the subjects be representative *on the characteristics relevant to the experiment*. Pavlov's dogs were not representative of all dogs with respect to size, color, thickness of coat, and so forth, but there was no reason to think that any of those characteristics would affect the outcome of the type of experiment he was doing. Similarly, Ebbinghaus' sample was not representative with respect to his education, intelligence, or nationality, but these characteristics did not make him atypical in his *memory*.

C. EXPENSE

Low cost was listed as one of the possible advantages of the experimental method. But some experiments may be very costly indeed, more costly than other research methods. Some structural testing may require fifty-foot models rather than two-foot models, and fifty-foot models may be expensive to build. A market test of a new product may cost as much as a quarter million dollars. It may be too expensive to gather together as many subjects as are necessary for the conditions of a real riot. Or giving players real money to obtain the necessary realism may be too expensive for some economics experiments.

d. HAZARDOUS OUTCOMES

It may be impossible to experiment with some real-world situations. For example, it is too dangerous economically to run controlled experiments on the national economy. And most sex experiments are unethical or objection-able to good taste. Smoking experiments on human beings violate all civi-lized ethics. (But we let convicts volunteer for hazardous medical experi-ments!)

5. Summary

In an experiment the researcher purposely alters the environment in order to observe the effect of the experimentally altered conditions. This is in con-trast to a survey, in which the researcher observes only what occurs naturally without researcher interference.

Where it is feasible, a real-life experiment is usually preferable to a survey, though the cost may be much greater. A laboratory experiment affords greater control than does a field survey, but it may lack realism.

A major advantage of an experiment is that it helps clarify the causal relationship among the variables.

The steps in running an experiment are as follows:

1) Decide on empirical proxies for the theoretical variables. The proxies must be measurable, and they must be relevant.
2) Choose treatment levels for the independent variables. The levels should bracket the real-life levels you are interested in. There should be enough treatments to catch important differences between the polar treatments, but few enough so that the experiment is cost-efficient.
3) Choose a sample that is as representative of the universe of interest as you can make it.
4) Plan the experiment so that the important non-experimental conditions are well-controlled.
5) Randomly allocate subjects to the various experimental and control groups.
6) Decide on the experimental design, the arrangement of stimuli, groups, and observations.
7) Pretest your procedure, and then revise your plans in light of the pretest.
8) After taking a pretest, determine sample size on the basis of the ex-pected accuracies of various sizes of samples, and of their costs and benefits.
9) Analyze and interpret the data.

EXERCISES

1. One must often choose between a laboratory experiment and a survey. Give one example in which each is preferable, and state why.
2. Give an example of a phenomenon that might be influenced by ten or more variables, and list the variables. Now pick the three that would be most

worth investigating in a laboratory experiment to determine what influences the phenomenon.

3. Illustrate how an experimenter could be fooled by
   a. varying the independent variable over *too narrow* a range
   b. examining the relationship among the independent variables at *too few* values.
4. Describe a study in which one might use an experiment that alters two or more variables at the same time.
5. Give examples from your field in which
   a. field experimentation is not feasible
   b. laboratory experimentation unravels multivariable causation
   c. lack of reality of experiments is a serious problem
   d. representative samples are not necessary for experiments
   e. diaries are a useful technique.

ADDITIONAL READING FOR CHAPTER 10

Aronson and Carlsmith is an excellent introduction to experimentation. General references for experimental procedure are Underwood, and Banks. Campbell (1966) discusses the validity of experiments in social settings. Festinger (1953) discusses laboratory experiments in social psychology, including a discussion of the disadvantages and advantages of experiments.

Experiments with organizations are often thought to be difficult or impossible. Evan presents a collection of studies of such experiments, showing where they are feasible and citing the problems with them in the laboratory and in the field.

11 designing experiments

The key element in an experiment—as compared to other methods of getting knowedge—is the planned, researcher-induced alteration of the situation. The alteration is made for the purpose of producing useful and valid information. Some experiments, however, yield no valid information, and others lead to misleading conclusions. Sometimes this is unavoidable. But more often an experiment fails because the pattern of induced variation—called the "experimental design"—is flawed. The main subject of this chapter, then, is the design of experiments that will produce valid results.

A second subject of this chapter is how to design experiments so that you can get a given amount of information for a lower cost, or a greater amount of information for a given expenditure—that is, experimental efficiency.

1. Simple Uncontrolled Exploratory Experiments

I'll take the liberty of using a very personal example to illustrate this section. Back in 1964 I began to teach my classes in research methods the Monte Carlo method of handling statistics problems, as described in Chapters 27–31. The results apparently were excellent, and I concluded that this is a worthwhile method. Furthermore, the method seemed to have great promise for teaching probability and statistics to high-school students.

To find out more, I then taught this material for six hours to a math class in a local high school. This was an "experiment" in the original meaning of the word, because it was a *test*, an attempt. I altered the usual conditions by teaching new material, and I then observed the results. The high-school students quickly learned to handle both easy and difficult questions that would stump people with many more hours of conventional training in probability and statistics. And the students (and I, their instructor) enjoyed the experience very much.

I was immediately prepared to conclude on the basis of this experiment (together with my previous experience with graduate students) that the Monte Carlo method of doing statistics should be taught in high schools and colleges, together with—or in preference to—conventional analytic methods. But others were not ready to reach the same conclusion on the basis of my experience. They said that my experiment did not prove the efficacy of the method because of at least two loopholes: 1) The good results might have been due to this one teacher's interest and enthusiasm, and might not occur with other teachers; 2) I had no proof that these excellent high-school students in a University high school might not have learned as much if taught conventionally.

Let's consider the second objection. To put it technically, this objection is that my experiment lacks **internal validity;** that is, what I say happened was not proven. I said that the students learned more than they would if taught conventionally. My evidence for this was the result I saw in class *compared to* my general experience with other students. That is, my implicit experimental design was as shown in Table 11.1.

TABLE 11.1   Uncontrolled Experimental Design (University High Experiment)

Stage 1: Choose Groups	Stage 2: Observe Subjects	Stage 3: Experimental Treatment	Stage 4: Observe Subjects
S (selected group, one class in U. High School)	(No formal observation)	X (experimental treatment, my teaching)	O (final exam and informal feedback)
MA (matched hypothetical)	(No observation)	(No treatment)	(No observation)

Others did not accept this design as valid, because they would not accept my implicit comparison to a hypothetical matched group. And this objection has great merit. The tendency of an experimenter to see what he wants to see in a hypothetical comparison is overwhelming. That is, this experimental design is **uncontrolled;** it has no control group against which to validly compare the experimental group.

An experiment is not necessarily valueless because it is uncontrolled, however. *In the early stages of a study, it is often most efficient to proceed without any controls at all.* A controlled experiment demands that you work with only a narrow set of variables, and at the beginning you do not know which variables might be most important and which ranges of the variables to try out. Therefore, you should not rush headlong to the stage of the controlled experiment.

When one first has an idea, one must explore in a loose and casual fashion to make a rough check on the idea and to get more ideas. It is important, however, that this exploratory uncontrolled knowledge-gathering experiment not be offered as proof, but as the exploration that it really is.

Another example: Consider the crucial world problem of people's aversion to new foods. Technology is now available to manufacture "new proteins" (the scarcest part of the diet for most poor people and the most important) at quite low costs and in abundance (Meier, Chap. 2). These new proteins include food yeast, fish flour, algae, and processed peanuts, cottonseed meal, soy beans, and leaves. The proteins can be made to taste like the foods that people ordinarily eat, or they can be made tasteless. But it is not easy to persuade people to use these foods even when they and their children are suffering from terrible protein deficiencies.

Assume that our problem is to persuade people in a particular West African country to purchase and feed a particular new protein—a combination of processed soy bean and cottonseed, say—to their children. (ProNutro in South Africa and Incaparina in Guatemala have demonstrated that it *can* be done and with commercial success; see Belden, *et al.*) It is reasonable to try out various combinations of food tastes and ways of changing people's preferences. At this early stage of the game, it would be unwise to run neat well-controlled experiments comparing, say, finely ground and coarsely ground protein or introduction of the food through tribal chiefs or through parents of small children. At this stage of massive ignorance, it would be wise to try out a great many available forms of the new protein, using a wide variety of communication techniques, to a large number of groups of people without worrying about precise controls, for it would take much too long to try out all the possible variations in well-controlled experiments. Rather, we might send packages of various foods to Peace Corpsmen all over the country and ask them to distribute the foods. Wherever acceptance is reported we could investigate further. Only after such a series of rough trial-and-error stages should we be ready to run controlled experiments to distinguish which are best among the somewhat successful foods and communications techniques.

2. Before-and-After Experiments

Let us leave the Monte Carlo study for a moment and consider another type of uncontrolled experiment, the pretest-experiment-posttest design. In this experimental design, one compares the subjects' behavior before and after the experimental treatment. This design is frequently used in educational and psychotherapeutic research. For example, patients suffering from depression are given a course of therapy, and any change in their mental state is attributed to the therapy. The design for this experiment is as shown in Table 11.2.

TABLE 11.2 Before-and-After Design

Stage 1: Choose Groups	Stage 2: Observe Subjects	Stage 3: Experimental Treatment	Stage 4: Observe Subjects
S (a group of patients suffering from depression)	O (measure extent of depression)	X (therapy)	O (measure extent of depression)

The possible defect of this before-and-after design is, of course, that the change in behavior might have occurred anyway, without the experimental treatment. Depressives tend to get well with or without treatment. And children tend to learn all kinds of things with the passage of time, with or without experimental educational intervention. Furthermore, people may do better in the second test than on the first just because they have greater test experience. Hence the difference in results before and after the experimental treatment cannot safely be attributed to the experimental treatment in this uncontrolled experiment.

3. Matched-Groups Design

Now let us return to the uncontrolled Monte Carlo teaching experiment. The obvious remedy for the lack of internal validity in this case would be to conduct a controlled experiment on two classes, one class taught conventionally and the other taught using the Monte Carlo method. This scheme was therefore planned, with another person to teach both classes (so as to handle the objection that the results depend upon the teacher; more about that later). The design was to teach a class at University High and another similar class of excellent math students at a local high school. That is, this is a **matched-group** design. Our intention was to compare the mathematic aptitude scores of the two groups before the experiment, teach the Monte Carlo method to the less-talented group (if a difference was observed), and afterward, to compare a) the achievements of the two groups, and secondarily, b) the changes in knowledge of each group from before to after. The design would be as seen in Table 11.3.

TABLE 11.3 Matched-Groups Experimental Design

Stage 1: Choose Groups	Stage 2: Observe Subjects	Stage 3: Experimental Treatment	Stage 4: Observe Subjects
M_1 (selected group, one class in U. High School)	O (test math aptitude)	X_1 (conventional teaching)	O (final exam and informal feedback)
M_2 (matched group)	O (test math aptitude)	X_2 (Monte Carlo teaching)	O (final exam and informal feedback)

As happens too often, practical difficulties arose and the matched group was not obtained from the local school. Hence, only the one group (in University High) was taught, by Monte Carlo methods. The results were successful in the teacher's judgment; this increased the *external* validity of the two experiments together, by showing that the good results originally obtained did not depend on a single teacher. That is, the second experiment made the result somewhat more *general*, and generality of the results to other groups and conditions is the test of external validity (more on this to come). But without the matched group, the results were little more valid "internally" than was the first experiment alone. And the design of the second experiment could not be justified as being exploratory, because the exploration had already been done.[1]

Let us consider the meaning of the results if the matched-groups design *had* been carried through. If the Monte Carlo group recorded higher test scores *in spite of* beginning with lower aptitude scores, that would have been strong evidence for the Monte Carlo's methods-effectiveness—but it would not have been *overwhelming* or *conclusive* evidence. In fact, one can *never* obtain conclusive evidence. Rather, one can only build a stronger and stronger case for one alternative as compared to another.

An important loophole in the matched-groups experiment is that the two groups may not really be similar. And even the lower math-aptitude scores of the Monte Carlo group might not resolve this question, because their aptitude for *probability and statistics* might have been higher. Or the time of the day at which they were taught might have been more propitious. Or some other subtle difference between the matched groups might have been responsible for the Monte Carlo group doing better.

What design would be better than matched groups? Probably no design could have been better *for that stage of the work.* We shall shortly discuss designs that yield more valid conclusions, but these more powerful designs require more and different resources than were then available. And such extensive designs only became more appropriate after additional evidence had accumulated that the Monte Carlo method is indeed promising.

4. Simple Randomized-Groups Design

The only way to ensure that the groups in an experiment are truly similar is by selecting the members of the groups by random sampling, as discussed in

1. Because so many students' work slides into this sort of situation, it is worth quoting Campbell and Stanley on the topic (p. 7): "It seems well-nigh unethical at the present time to allow, as theses or dissertations in education, case studies of this nature (i.e., involving a single group observed at one time only). 'Standardized' tests in such case studies provide only very limited help, since the rival sources of difference other than X [the experimental treatment] are so numerous as to render the 'standard' reference group almost useless as a 'control group.' On the same grounds, the many uncontrolled sources of difference between a present case study and potential future ones which might be compared with it are so numerous as to make justification in terms of providing a bench mark for future studies also hopeless."

Chapter 9. Both mathematical logic and overwhelming empirical evidence prove that if two groups are chosen by a truly random selection process from a given population, then as the groups become larger in size they approach average equality in all their characteristics. Of course, two random samples of one person each might be quite unequal, but two random samples of 100 or 1,000 or 10,000 individuals will approach equality in their means and other measures of all their characteristics.

Two separate experiments were run on this simple randomized-groups experimental design by Shevokas and by Atkinson. In both cases, separate sections of the same course were taught by Monte Carlo and by conventional methods. The students were assigned to the sections randomly, although some students requested one section or the other because of class conflicts; this latter element is a breach of strict randomization, but in the judgment of the experimenters—and some such judgment always comes into play somewhere—the breach was not serious. (As a further check, the students' math aptitude scores were compared, and were found to be similar in the various sections in both experiments.)

The experiment of design with randomly-chosen groups—a "true" experimental design—is as shown in Table 11.4.

TABLE 11.4   Simple Randomized-Groups Design

Stage 1 : Choose groups	Stage 2 : Observe subjects	Stage 3 : Experimental treatment	Stage 4 : Observe subjects
R_1 (randomly chosen group)	O_a (observe math aptitudes and math interests)	X_1 (Monte Carlo instruction)	O_b (Final exam and test of math interests)
R_2 (randomly chosen group)	O_a (observe math aptitudes and math interests)	X_2 (conventional instruction)	O_b (Final exam and test of math interests)

The simple randomized-groups design controls all sorts of threats to internal validity. That is, this design assures you that if you repeat the same experiment under the same conditions with subjects drawn from the same population, you will reach the same conclusion, subject only to the variation of sampling error.

A frequently used variation of the simple randomized-groups design was actually used by both Shevokas and Atkinson. They wanted to know what effects the Monte Carlo and conventional methods would have upon students' attitudes toward mathematics. Therefore, the actual design included an attitude test given both before and after the probability-and-statistics instruction. On the one hand, this design, which allows comparison of changes, is very powerful statistically. On the other hand, there is a chance that the attitude test might influence the students' learning in some subtle way. That is, the attitude pretest might have a positive effect on students' learning by one method, and a negative effect on the other method. To put it another way, the results of the achievement-test comparison might be different with or without an attitude test. Therefore, when drawing conclusions about the effects of the two methods on achievement, one must keep in mind all the special conditions of the experiment—the age of the students and the kind of instructor, for example, *and* the presence of the pretest.

This brings us to the *external* validity of experiments such as these. The randomized-groups experimental design assures us that we will obtain similar results if the experiment is repeated with similar people under similar conditions. But what about *different kinds of people under different conditions?* That is, to what extent can we generalize from Shevokas' and Atkinson's experiments the conclusion that the Monte Carlo method produces more learning and better attitudes?

There is no systematic technical device for increasing external validity the way randomization improves internal validity. That is, as Hume taught us long ago (and as discussed in Chapter 32) generalization of results to different kinds of persons and conditions is not a matter of logical deduction but rather of cumulative evidence and sound judgment.

These three aspects of generalizing the Monte Carlo experiments immediately come to mind: 1) Will the Monte Carlo method do better than the analytic method with all sorts of students—bright and slow, old and young, English and non-English speaking? More generally, this is the matter of *generalization to other groups.* 2) Will the Monte Carlo method perform relatively better when taught by teachers who are not especially interested in it? More generally, this is the matter of *generalization to other experimental treatments.* 3) Are the results affected by the testing and other special aspects of the experimental situation?

There will never be a totally conclusive positive answer. But if many experiments are done by different teachers, with different sorts of students under a variety of conditions, using a variety of tests, and if most of the experiments show the Monte Carlo experiments to be relatively better, it will be reasonable to conclude that except under special conditions, it is indeed a better method, and ought to be used in teaching statistics.

5. Some Additional One-Variable Designs

In psychological research one often is interested in whether an experimental treatment has any effect at all, compared to no treatment. The standard design for this situation measures the dependent variable for the experimental group both before and after the experimental treatment. Similar measurements are made for the control group, which receives no experimental treatment but which is selected randomly from the same population as the experimental group. This design may be diagrammed as in Table 11.5.

TABLE 11.5   Simple Design to Test for Presence of Effects

Stage 1 : Choose groups	Stage 2 : Observe subjects	Stage 3 : Experimental treatment	Stage 4 : Observe subjects
R_1 (randomly selected group)	O_{1a} (measure)	X (treatment)	O_{1b} (measure)
R_2 (randomly selected group)	O_{2a} (measure)	—	O_{2b} (measure)

The main comparison is between $(O_{1a}-O_{1b})$ and $O_{2a}-O_{2b}$); that is, the size of the before-and-after differences for the two groups.

This design is very efficient statistically because one can compare *each subject's* before-and-after measurements, which holds consistent the original differences among persons. This quality makes the design very desirable. However, there is always the chance that the pretest measurement influences the extent to which the experimental treatment affects the subjects.

As a check on the effect of pretesting, one can use a design with *four* randomly-chosen groups, two of which are measured twice, and two of which are measured only at the end of the experiment. Comparison among these four groups reveals the effect of the experimental treatment with and without an accompanying pretest. This design may be diagrammed as in Table 11.6.

TABLE 11.6   Design for Control of Pretest Measurement Effect

Group	Observation	Treatment	Observation
R_1	O_{1a}	X_1	O_{1b}
R_2	O_{2a}	X_2	O_{2b}
R_3	—	X_1	O_{3b}
R_4	—	X_2	O_{4b}

6. Multivariate Designs

The experiments discussed until now have all had a single experimental variable. In the statistics experiments, the variable is the teaching method, Monte Carlo or conventional. Of course, there have been other conditions that were not held constant in those experiments, as, for example, the hour of the classes differed among groups in the Shevokas and Atkinson experiments. But only the teaching-method variable was built into the design for systematic manipulation.

This section discusses designs in which *two or more* elements of the experimental situation are systematically altered.

The principle of *ceteris paribus* may at first seem to suggest that the experimenter can vary only one variable at a time, so as to hold all other conditions constant. But we shall see that the experimenter can often gain much by varying *several* variables at the same time in certain prescribed ways and still meet the requirements of *ceteris paribus*. The various designs used to study the effects of several variables simultaneously are called "factorial" designs (or "analysis of variance" designs, because a statistical device by that name is used to determine whether there are real differences between groups when the differences are too small for the answer to be obvious).

The biostatisticians (pre-eminently R. Fisher) have been especially ingenious in developing efficient experimental designs with which they can learn about the effects of various fertilizers, types of water, types of soil, types of seed, and so forth, with the fewest experimental plots.

There are several important and quite different reasons why one might wish to experiment with more than one variable at a time.

a. COST EFFICIENCY

You may be interested in the effects of two or more variables. Hence, you may experiment with them simultaneously in order to reduce the overall costs of experimentation while you gather given quantities of information. For example, a women's track coach (this is being written during the 1976 Olympics) might wish to investigate the popularly accepted coaching lore about the effects of a) the interval between last heavy training, and b) the presence or absence of sex activity on the day before a race. If you have 100 runners available for experimentation, you can simply split them randomly 50–50 on either the time-since-training variable or the sex-activity variable and get information only on that one variable. Or you can split the 100 runners into four groups of 25 runners as in Table 11.7.

TABLE 11.7   Design with Two Independent Variables (Numbers of Subjects Shown in Cells)

		Training Interval	
		Short	Long
Sex on day before race	No	25	25
	Yes	25	25

With this design the researchers can compare two groups of 50 runners each on *both* the time-since-training and the sex-activity variables. Of course, the groups compared on time-since-training are *not* identical in all other ways, differing in sex activity. But the difference in sex activity is *known and controlled*, rather than being haphazard and uncontrolled. Hence, that difference is more likely to be a benefit than a detriment, for reasons to be discussed shortly. So in this design the coach gets more desired information from given resources by experimenting with two variables together rather than just one alone.

There is a wide variety of complex "factorial" designs to help you save money when experimenting with several variables, but that is an advanced topic that few will need to know.

b. GENERALITY AND EXTERNAL VALIDITY

Experimenting with two or more variables simultaneously can strengthen the external validity of an experiment by showing that the result occurs under diverse conditions (if it indeed does so). For example, we might have funds enough to support six comparisons of the Monte Carlo and conventional methods in high schools. We could a) hire one teacher to teach twelve senior classes in one city, or b) we could hire six teachers to teach two classes each, three comparisons in the senior year and three in the junior year, in six different communities. If all the comparisons are favorable for the Monte Carlo method, then we could assert that its success is not limited to one school year or one city or one teacher, but in fact is better under a wide variety of conditions. That is, this latter design increases the generality of the results at little or no additional cost. As Fisher, the master of experimental design, put it:

> There is a third advantage [of a factorial design] which, while less obvious than the former two [efficiency and comprehensiveness], has an important bearing upon the utility of the experimental results in their practical application. This is that any conclusion, such as that it is advantageous to increase the quantity of a given ingredient, has a wider inductive basis when inferred from an experiment in which the quantities of other ingredients have been varied, than it would have from any amount of experimentation, in which these had been kept strictly constant. The exact standardisation of experimental conditions, which is often thoughtlessly advocated as a panacea, always carries with it the real disadvantage that a highly standardised experiment supplies direct information only in respect of the narrow range of conditions achieved by standardisation. Standardisation, therefore, weakens rather than strengthens our ground for inferring a like result, when, as is invariably the case in practice, these conditions are somewhat varied. (Fisher, p. 106)

c. INTERACTION EFFECTS

A phenomenon may depend upon two variables *working together*. This effect is called "interaction." More formally, interaction is present when the effect of one independent variable upon the dependent variable depends upon the values of one or more *other* independent variables. Interaction can best be investigated in experiments that vary more than one variable at a time.

For example, what if sex activity together with no training is better for running races than no sex with no training? You could learn about this *interaction* of sex and training only if you experiment with both variables together. In some cases the influence of the individual variables will be separate and additive, and there will be no interaction effect. For example, it might be that no training on the days before the race may improve running time, no sex may improve running time, and the combination of no sex and no recent training might do best—or *worst*. If the former is the case, there is additivity and no interaction, whereas in the latter case there is strong interaction.

We can diagram the possibilities in Table 11.8, showing running time in seconds.

TABLE 11.8 Illustrative Interactions in a Two-Independent-Variable Design (Running Time in Seconds Shown in Cells)

If the track coach discovers that there is an interactive effect, such as in Box C, this might lead to a best-of-all alternative, say, no recent training and much sex (but please don't generalize, or believe, this hypothetical conclusion).

Similarly, if the statistics-teaching experiment were to be done in both junior and senior years with several teachers, it might show that the Monte Carlo method works better for juniors and worse for seniors. This could be an important piece of knowledge that would not appear if the experiments were done only with students in one year (a piece of information that would be lost and would only blur the overall results, if the experiment were done on both junior and senior students without planning and without checking the effect of the school-year variable). Searching for such interactive effects is an important function of a multivariate experimental design.

7. Experimental Designs to Study Delayed Effects

Implicit in the experimental designs previously described is that all the effects occur immediately. But sometimes the effects of the independent variables occur slowly and are spread out over time. Furthermore, one may want to know about the effects of *various amounts* of the stimulus given over time. This often is the case in medical research and in education and advertising. For example, Random House may wish to know the effects on the sales of the second edition of this book if it advertises in the fall of 1977, *or* if it advertises in fall, 1977 *plus* advertising in spring, 1978, *or* if it does not advertise at all.

The appropriate design experimentally treats the different samples different numbers of times (in separate time periods) and then observes the results *over several periods*. As an example of just one of the many possible designs, Table 11.9 shows that group S_1 (a sample of areas) receives

TABLE 11.9   Illustrative Delayed-Effects Design

	Fall, 1977		Spring, 1978		Fall, 1978	
	Period I_a	Period I_b	II_a	II_b	III_a	III_b
S_1	X (advertise)	O (measure sales)	X	O	——	O
S_2	X	O	——	O	——	O
S_3	——	O	——	O	——	O

advertisements in Fall, 1977, and Spring, 1978; S_2 (another group of areas) gets advertisements in Fall, 1977, and S_3 gets no advertisements. The sales in all three groups of areas are measured not just in the advertising period but afterward as well, to see how much of the effect of the advertising continues into the future. This may be seen, for example, in the sales in Period III of groups S_2 and S_3, both of whom receive no advertising in Period II, though S_2 received advertising in Period I. And by comparison of S_2 sales in Periods II and III, one can determine how the effects of Period I's advertising "decays" over time in group S_2. Comparison of results for S_1 and S_2 will show how much effect the period II's advertising has *in addition* to the effect of advertising in Period I.

8. Summary

It makes sense to take the time and effort at the beginning of a study to create a good sampling or experimental design. This investment can pay off handsomely in the course of your work. The aim of the experimental design is to produce data from which you may derive sound conclusions, and to do so as efficiently as possible. Perhaps the most important element of the experimental design is that any differences in results shown among the various experimental and control groups should arise from differences among the stimuli given to the experimental groups rather than from differences in original composition among the groups. But it is often impractical to achieve the ideal in equalizing the groups—random selection—either because the research is at an early exploratory stage, or because of cost, or because of ethical considerations. The chapter discusses randomized-group designs as well as designs that may be appropriate where random assignment of subjects to groups, or random selection of groups, is not feasible.

Designs that vary more than one experimental element at the same time often have advantages over one-variable designs. Multivariate designs can be cheap, and they can produce more information and greater generality of conclusions, by showing the effect of each variable under a variety of conditions of the other variables; they also can reveal interactions among variables.

A variety of designs can measure delayed effects; most important is to be aware of possible delayed effects and to build them into the design rather than to forget them.

EXERCISES

1. Assume you prepared a list of a sample of people in a midwestern city of 80,000 people, which you considered an excellent random sample of the population, and that you interviewed the people on the list about their voting intentions in a coming election. Several months later another researcher wants to do a market-research study on the entire population of the town. Can he use your old list? Is it or is it not a random sample?

2. Varsity football players at state universities receive lower grades than does the average student. Is this fact a good indication that high athletic ability goes with low scholastic ability in American boys?

3. To show how difficult it is to achieve randomness, have each person in the class pick a number between 0 and 9, and write it down. Then do it again, and a third time, and several more. What patterns do you see? Might they indicate a departure from randomness. (But beware of finding false patterns; see Chapter 30.)

4. How would you compile a random sample of students of Chinese extraction at a university that keeps no records of ethnic background?

5. Specify a purpose for which the telephone book is *not* a good sampling frame.

6. Give an example in which stratified sampling would be a relatively inexpensive way to attain a given level of accuracy. Is there any case in which stratified sampling would be *more* expensive?

7. Show how an estimate can be unbiased, even though sampling units have *different* chances of getting into the sample. (Hint: Remember that probabilities can be *known* even if they are *different*.)
8. Give an example in which cluster sampling provides more accuracy for a given cost than does simple random sampling.
9. Give an example in which sequential sampling is feasible and helpful.
10. Give an example in which matching samples is an appropriate sampling technique.
11. Give an example from your field in which the experimenter could reasonably expect to find interaction between two independent variables.

ADDITIONAL READING FOR CHAPTER 11

Campbell and Stanley's monograph is an outstanding treatment of the subject of experimental validity. The first part of this chapter was inspired by their treatment of the subject. Aronson and Carlsmith also provide useful information on experimental design.

Hyman and Wright, and Greenwood discuss the special problems of experimentation in sociology.

Experimental designs, especially in psychology, are described at length by Wood (Chapters 5–9). Another useful reference concerning experimental design in psychology is Underwood and Shaughnessy.

Boyd *et al.* (Chapter 3) discuss experimental designs in the context of market research.

Hovland *et al.* (Volume 3) is a classic experimental study in social psychology.

Wright and Hyman provide an interesting narrative description of how they went about selecting their design for an evaluation of attitude change in a Summer Camp.

12 non-experimental designs for studying relationships

An experiment has great advantages for studying relationships. But sometimes you cannot experiment, or choose not to. Then you must turn to examining data as nature throws them up to you.

There are two basic strategies for collecting naturally occurring data for the purpose of examining relationships. You may compare data from various periods in the past for the given person or group; this is called a "time series" in economics and sociology, "longitudinal method" in psychology and education, and the "historical method" in anthropology and sociology. Or you may compare *different individuals or groups* at the same time (a "cross section"). The essential ingredient to obtaining valid results with either strategy is that the independent variable(s) in which you are interested must have varied due to reasons unrelated to the nature of the sample periods or sample individuals. For example, perhaps you are interested in the relationship of income to suicide. You might compare income and suicide in (a) the various U.S. states, or (b) various years in the past in the U.S. But it may be that there is some important element in people's makeup that is responsible for *both* low income and low suicide, say, education. This would vitiate both the time series and the cross-sectional approaches—unless you somehow allow for this and other factors that account for changes in the independent variable (income) and that are also related to the dependent variable (suicide). Chapter 23 discusses this obstacle to the use of these non-experimental designs, and how to overcome it.

Though the time series and the cross section sometimes are alternative designs, by far the most compelling conclusions emerge if you are able to use *both* the time series and the cross section, and if their results agree. If the results do *not* agree, this may be a clue to important underlying processes that it will pay to investigate. More about this in Section 4. In some cases, time series and cross sections may be conceptually similar and measure the same phenomenon. For example, one may use a time series and a cross section interchangeably to find out how much taller boys are at ten years of age than at five years of age. We can either measure a group of boys when they are five years old and measure them again when they are ten years of age, or we can measure two different groups of boys at the same time, one "cohort" of ten-year-olds and one "cohort" of five-year-olds. But in some cases time series and cross sections may capture quite different phenomena, as when political cross-section polls reveal a different relationship between income and political-party membership than do time-series data (Brunner and Leipelt).

We shall consider the nature of time series and cross sections in that order. Then we shall take up the special places of the two methods for studying processes that develop only over a period of time. Last, we shall discuss the panel method as a device for studying changes over time.

1. Time Series—The Long View

The usual reason for using the time-series method is that the historical record provides a set of varied observations of the phenomenon in question. That is, past periods constitute a bank of data.

The main drawback of the time-series method is that it is vulnerable to changes in general conditions that may be relevant to the phenomenon you want to study. For example, there have been steady increases in the average height of Americans from generation to generation, and therefore a comparison of the heights of people of different ages from different generations may be blurred by the long-term shifts.

As another example, researchers wanted to learn how the *age* of a book in a research library affects how much people read it, in order to know which books should be kept in expensive locations where people can find them easily. A card in the back of each book revealed how many times it had been used each year for the past fifty years. But fifty years ago there were many fewer people at universities who might have withdrawn *any* book, and therefore the most-read books fifty years ago were read much less than the most-read books now. This increase in university population distorts the picture to make it seem that the difference in the use of a given book now and when it was younger is much less than it really is. (That is, there are more potential readers now to offset the decline in interest.) There were also many fewer books to compete for attention fifty years ago. Though these two major changes affect the use of books in opposite directions, we have no reason to think that they cancel out. Either one of them could distort the picture badly.

In such a predicament the "cross-sectional" method can help. Instead of comparing the use of a given book when it was one year old with its use when it was fifty years old, it was possible to examine the use during *one year* of fifty-year-old books and of one-year-old books. We thus look for the effect of age but under the same conditions of equal numbers of university students and books in the library.

The time-series method can often be statistically efficient because the people being observed serve as their own *controls*. For a crude example, assume that you want to know whether people lose weight during the night. It is intuitively obvious that, if you weigh a sample of people both night and morning and compare each person's night and morning weights, you can obtain the same accuracy with a smaller sample than if you were to weigh one group of people at night and another in the morning. If you weigh the same people twice, the extraneous variables are mostly held constant, whereas different morning and night samples may differ in many ways that require a large sample to "smooth out" the results.

The same principle holds if you compare the use of a sample of books in one year to the use of the *same books* five years later, if you compare the I.Q.s of a group of children at five years of age with the I.Q.s of the *same children* at ten years of age, or if you compare the sales in a group of supermarkets in January to the sales in the *same* supermarkets in February. In each case a much larger sample would be needed if you sampled *two different groups* of books, children, or supermarkets, because of the much greater *variability* that would be introduced.

For simplicity, I have been talking of a time series as a comparison of only two observations of the same universe at different times. Most often a time series is a much larger number of observations—say, monthly observations of store sales over a period of five years, or yearly observations of the U.S. economy over sixty years, or daily observations of people's moods over a period of several months, or hourly observations over a period of weeks. Thus, one has the basis to search for cyclical effects of various lengths as well as trend effects.

2. The Cross Section—The Wide View

Three advantages of the wide view are:

1. The overwhelming advantage of the wide view over the long view is that, because all observations are made at the same time, there is no problem of changes in conditions.

2. Data are often much easier to obtain for a wide view. If you want to find out how the price of a Honda motorcycle depreciates over the life of the motorcycle, you might not be able to obtain data for the prices that particular cycles sold for in previous years or even for the prices of *any* Hondas in

previous years. But it would be easy to obtain price quotations on Hondas of all ages at the present moment.

Or, if you are a demographer, or an actuary working for a life-insurance company, and you wish to construct a "life table" that shows the proportions of a group of people who will die at various ages, it is impracticable to follow the course of a given group of people all their lives. Rather, you examine the proportions of various age groups that die in a given *year* and construct a "synthetic life table."

Again, even if it were decided to compare the use of the *same* books when they were one year old with the use now, when they are fifty years old, most libraries do not have records of the use of particular books that go back fifty years. In that case, unless one were willing to wait another fifty years, there would be no choice but to use the wide view and to compare the use of one-year-old books *this year* with fifty-year-old books *this year*.

3. The wide view can be employed even when the subject matter can be observed only once. For example, you cannot shoot the same rifle cartridge twice in different rifles, to compare the accuracy of the rifles. Instead, you must compare the results of *two different samples* of cartridges. Similarly, asking a person her voting intention in a campaign may alter her subsequent behavior, in which case it will not be safe to ask her her intentions a second time.[1] This danger is probably less with purchase panels, however; there is little theoretical or empirical reason to believe that membership in a panel will eventually bias a person toward brand A and against brand B.

The major disadvantage of the cross-sectional method is that there is likely to be considerable variation among the sampling units that has no connection with the variables of interest. Such variation does not bias the results, but it does require a larger sample size to achieve any given level of accuracy than if there were less irrelevant variation among the subjects.

For example, you might want to study the effect of liquor prices on liquor consumption, and you consider relating the price of liquor in various states to per capita consumption in the states. It is very difficult to study the effect of liquor prices in the United States *as a whole* because the level of liquor prices changes infrequently and raggedly. And one cannot experimentally raise or lower the prices of liquor in the country as a whole, or even in individual states or communities, just for the sake of research. The various states already have different price levels, however, because state legislatures have different revenue policies affecting liquor prices. But it is not possible simply to compare the consumption of liquor in various states that have various liquor prices, because there are differences in consumption from state to state, independent of price. For example, Table 12.1 shows the per capita consumption in a group of states that have identical prices.

There is an analogy between this disadvantage of the wide view and the major disadvantage of the long view. With the long view, conditions change

---

1. But P. Lazarsfeld, *et al.* conclude that this danger does not arise in voting studies.

over the length of the study; with the wide view, conditions are different over the width of the study. Such change may not matter if plenty of data are available at low cost. But sometimes there is not enough data available to compensate for this defect of the wide view. The variability in liquor consumption among the states from such other causes as religion is so great that a cross-sectional sample of perhaps 500 states would be necessary to obtain a reasonably reliable answer—and there are not that many states in the Union.

A solution (J. Simon, 1966a) was to study those instances in which the state changed its revenue policy (and hence the prices of liquor) on a given date and then to compare the consumption patterns *before and after* the price changes in each state separately. The difference between the before and after consumption could then be attributed to the price change. (And, to take account of possible differences *over time* in each state, I standardized by subtracting the changes in consumption over the same periods of time in states in which price remained the same from those in the price-change states. This device allowed for increases or decreases in consumption resulting from religious and cultural changes, tension-level changes, and other society-wide effects.) This design really is a combination of the time-series and cross-section methods, being a cross-sectional sample of changes over time.

The cross-section method is often used successfully in connection with natural geographical differences.

TABLE 12.1

State	January 1962 Price Index (Seagrams 7 Crown)	Per Capita Liquor Consumption in 1961	Gallons of Liquor Consumed per $1 Million of Income
Indiana	4.85	1.26	350
Massachusetts	4.85	2.76	681
Minnesota	4.85	2.22	613
New Mexico	4.85	1.75	506

SOURCE: *Liquor Handbook*, 1962.

For example, the amount of smoking per capita varies greatly from country to country. Researchers therefore collected data from the health records of various countries to see whether the incidence of various diseases is related to the extent of smoking. But this device creates its own new obstacle: A high level of tension in a country might account for *both* the high smoking *and* the high heart-disease rates in the country, rather than the smoking causing the heart disease.

Geographical differences were the core of R. Cavan's cross-sectional study of suicide and anomie. Cavan compared the suicide rates in the various rings of neighborhoods at various distances from the center of Chicago; the closer to the center of the city, the higher the suicide rate.

Communities in the suicide belt.—Chicago has four suicidal areas: the "Loop" or central business district and its periphery of cheap hotels for men and sooty flats over stores (No. 1 on Map VI); the Lower North Side, particularly the central part of this district, which includes a shifting population of unattached men and an equally shifting population of young men and women in the roominghouse areas (No. 64 on the map); the Near South Side linking the Loop on the north with the Negro area to the south and having one-fourth of its population Negro (No. 2 on the map); and the West Madison area, with its womanless street of flophouses, missions, cheap restaurants, and hundreds of men who drift in aimless, bleary-eyed abandon (No. 40 on the map). (*See Figure 12.1*)

D. Schwartzman made clever use of a geographical comparison of the United States and Canada in assessing the effects of monopoly on prices and wages. He compared wages and prices in the United States with those in Canada for those industries that differed in the degree of monopoly in the United States and Canada. He was able to estimate the extent to which a larger share of the market being held by a few firms pushes prices up and wages down. (The effect on prices is economically significant, but not for wages.)

The previous examples dealt with the use of geographical differences. More common is the use of geography on the assumption that the various areas are the *same*. For example, market researchers often take advantage of geographical similarities to test marketing tactics. A company will advertise or distribute coupons in one town, not advertise or place no coupons in another town, and then compare sales in the two towns. Distributing coupons to some people but not to others within a *single* town would avoid geographical differences, but with such a design it would not be easy to measure the *sales* for the coupon group versus the no-coupon group.

Sometimes you can *match* geographic areas on all the *relevant* dimensions. For example, General Foods Corporation matched one city against another or one "test" city against the "normal rest of the United States" on these characteristics:

The test city should contain a cross section of age, sex, education, family size, income, ethnic and religious groups that approximate those of the nation as a whole. No city matches precisely, but some come pretty close. For instance: Columbus, Ohio; Syracuse, N.Y.

Characteristics of the test city's economy are vital. If a city's economy fluctuates with the season, or it is a resort area, an accurate sales picture cannot be obtained for food products.

FIGURE 12.1   Comparison of Suicide and Other Indications of Disorganization in Chicago, by Communities

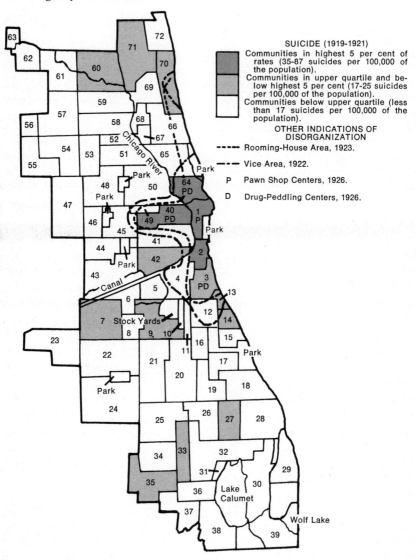

Source: From Ruth S. Cavan, *Suicide*, 1928, p. 81. Reprinted by permission of The University of Chicago Press.

Characteristics of the food trade in the test city are a factor. The ratio of food chains to independent grocery stores is crucial. Some chains feature their own brands; some will not permit auditing. A balance of chains and independents is necessary. Also crucial: Whether the big wholesalers serve several cities from one warehouse. If so, it is hard to enforce limited distribution.

Geographical isolation is also important for advertising considerations. To advertise where there is no distribution is wasteful, and irritates potential customers.

Media availability requirements include at least two television outlets, two newspapers and a Sunday supplement that can handle color ads.

Individual characteristics of a city are equally important. A city that is a good test market for one kind of product may be a poor city for another. Examples: Salt Lake City and St. Louis are unsuitable for testing coffee. Reasons: Salt Lake City is the center of the Mormon religion, which forbids coffee drinking; St. Louis housewives have a strong loyalty to a regional brand. Others: Southern cities are a good place to test new coconut products because home baking is customary; Californians are adventurous about trying new salad dressings, but the state is a bad place to test an artificial orange drink. (*Printers' Ink*, August 27, 1965, p. 30)

Matching cities may be quite a satisfactory tactic. But it always leaves disquieting doubt that perhaps all the important dimensions have not been matched. This doubt gnaws hardest when the experimental differences are relatively small. For example, in one published study (Stewart) the market area that received *no* advertising purchased more of the product than the matched market area that received substantial advertising. It is possible that the conclusion is sound; however, I continue to think that it was the lack of match between the test areas that accounted for such a strange result.[2] (It would be possible to check this by examining the *changes* in sales in the various areas over the experimental period, if data were collected before as well as after the experimental period.)

An improvement is to compare *groups* of geographical areas with one another, selecting areas to be in each group on a random basis. Instead of comparing Rochester with Syracuse, experiment with half a dozen randomly selected towns or with neighborhoods in half a dozen cities, and compare them with another half a dozen towns or with neighborhoods in other cities. The larger the sample, the stronger the protection against geographical bias.

Another tactic is to use each geographical area as its own control. The "criss-cross" is a simple design for situations in which you can control the experiment. For example, first distribute coupons in Syracuse and not in Rochester; then switch. Then you can fairly compare the total redeemed coupons in Rochester with the total from Syracuse.

Studies of matched geographical areas can sometimes be conducted even when experimentation is impossible. C. Mills made a fascinating study of three small cities that had each come to be dominated by one or a few big businesses and of three matched small cities in which smaller businesses mainly supported the local economies (Kefauver, p. 167).

2. J. Gold showed data on the extent of variation among test markets; the extent is either frightening or reassuring, depending on what you are doing.

3. Causes of Differences in Results from Time-Series and Cross-Sectional Studies

Sometimes the results produced by time-series and cross-sectional studies differ greatly, producing apparent paradoxes. For example, within various industrialized countries most cross-sectional studies of the relationship between income and fertility show that lower-income families have more children. On the other hand, time-series studies over the period of a few business cycles show that the *higher* per capita income is, the *more* children people have. And to confuse things further, time-series studies over *long* periods of time—say 100 years—show drops in fertility as per capita income rises.

The fact that the subjects observed sequentially in a time series serve as their own controls, whereas this mechanism is not present in a cross section, sometimes explains a discrepancy between cross-section and time-series results. For example, a simple time series relating national per capita income in various years to fertility (and also to suicide) in those years shows a positive relationship, whereas the same simple relationship is negative in a cross section of states in the U.S. The explanation is that education is systematically and strongly related to income in the various states, whereas in the time series, average education is not related to per capita income. (Of course one may hold education constant statistically in the cross section, and this does indeed change the apparent influence of income or reconcile the difference between time series and cross section; Simon, 1969, 1974; Barnes; this strengthens the basic point.)

Another cause of discrepancy between time-series and cross-sectional results—as seen in studies of the relationship between fertility or suicide and income—is that the cross-sectional studies, and usually the time-series studies too, do not take proper account of the past effects of the relevant variables (income, in this case). The cross section includes data only on people's present incomes, but their past incomes also influence their present behavior, sometimes in ways that counteract the effects of present income. For example, higher-income families give their children more education, which may teach them to want, and how to achieve, smaller families. But the statistical natures of the short- and long-time series and the cross sections are quite different, and they are affected differently by the past. Therefore one must be particularly thoughtful when choosing a wide-view or a long-view method whenever the past may still have influence on the present values of the dependent variable.[3]

Still another cause of discrepancy between time-series and cross-sectional results may be a difference in the "level of aggregation." That is, time series are likely to use national averages as observations whereas cross sections are likely to observe individuals or small groups. For various reasons discussed in Chapter 6, such a difference in *units of observation* can lead to differences in results.

---

3. This argument is developed formally and at length by J. Simon and D. Aigner.

4. Designs for Studying Changes Over Time

People change. A few examples: First, the percentage results of a presidential election would be somewhat different if the election were held a month earlier or later. The results would even differ slightly if the election were a day earlier or later. (Even if during the campaign few people change their minds about which candidate they prefer, the proportion of people who are prepared to vote may well change.) Second, a question asked at the beginning of an interview may get a different answer than if it were asked at the end of the interview, either because of fatigue or because an earlier question may alter the interviewee's knowledge or attitude toward the subject of a later question. Third, at the end of the day chimpanzees may take longer to learn how to reach the banana than at the beginning, or they may learn more slowly during one season of the year than during another. Fourth, in 1890 practically no one smoked cigarettes. Fifty years later half the nation smoked cigarettes. These changes over time are breaches of *ceteris paribus* for studies that use several time periods as samples.[4]

We say that changes occur with time. True enough. But it is not time itself that brings the changes to pass; rather, various processes that occur over time bring change. If people were frozen in such a way as to slow all their bodily processes but not to kill them—as can be done with small cells and human sperm—the passage of time would have no effect. Rather, it is *fatigue* that affects the chimpanzees' performance late in the day. It might be growing annoyance that produces a different answer to a question late in an interview. It is changes in the world situation that alter the election-poll results over time. And it was a shift in tastes as well as improvements in tobacco and cigarette-making technology that caused the increase in United States cigarette consumption in the twentieth century. The word "time" itself is nothing but shorthand for other changes that occur.

Change over time comes in several varieties. A change can be a long-run trend; for example, we believe that the long-run change in our economy will be upward. Change can be cyclical: Each morning the chimpanzees' responses may be faster than in the evening. Or change can be totally unpredictable and without apparent regularity, as is the case with the interest rates on the bond market from day to day (Cootner). (If you *do* find regularities in the bond market that you can predict in advance, be sure to let me know immediately.) Any or all of these kinds of change over time can throw a monkey (chimp) wrench into your research.

Even if a change seems to occur over time—or along with some other change in condition—you often cannot be sure *which* of the other things is not being held constant and is therefore to blame. Early in his interviewing, A. Kinsey found that the incidence of premarital intercourse was 44.9 percent at age nineteen for single males whose educational level was thirteen or

---

4. Whether one can predict the future from the past depends upon whether one can assume *ceteris paribus* from the observed period to the future. This issue is discussed in detail in Chapter 3.

more years, but the incidence was 32.5 percent in later interviews (Cochran, *et al.*, p. 88). This change might result from changes in people's activities over time. But it might *also* reflect changes in interviewing technique, differences in the sampling process, or simply sampling variation (Kinsey, *et al.*, p. 146). The experts who audited the Kinsey work emphasize that the researcher's good judgment is essential in interpreting the result.

The obvious way to study changes over time is to obtain a sample of the subject matter and actually to watch its change. Some famous studies have followed phenomena over a long time. L. Terman, for example, tracked the growth patterns and maturity of a group of exceptional children for almost thirty years. C. Seltzer studied the health and habits of a group of Harvard undergraduates for many years after graduation. And economists have studied the course of some series of agricultural prices for hundreds of years.

But, there are many obstacles to the straightforward application of the long-view method—notably that, unless the data from the past already exist, few of us have the patience to wait around for slow-moving events to unfold themselves. Therefore we must also consider another method as a substitute; sometimes we can study, *in the present,* "cohorts" of people or objects that are of different ages.

What the researcher does about the change over time should depend upon what he is trying to find out and the nature of the situation. Consider the matter of the date on which a presidential election is held. If the date were not automatically set in advance, the government in power might alter the date to suit its own convenience, that is, set a time when it was especially strong, as the government in England sometimes does. In the United States system, the date is fixed long in advance; whether the date is good or bad for the party in power is therefore left to chance.

The political pollster's situation is different. She cannot just pick a day at random to take her poll and then blithely use the result as a prediction of the election results. She knows that the closer to the election the day of the poll is (other things being equal), the better will be the prediction. On the other hand, a poll taken the day before the election does not yield information that is of much benefit to the candidates or of much interest to anyone else.

No matter when she takes her poll, however, the pollster takes *all* her interviews for a given poll on the *same* day (or during a single week) so that she can at least describe the situation correctly at *some* time, and she offers the results as measures of election sentiment *at that time,* rather than as predictions of how the election will turn out. If the purpose of the poll is to aid the decisions of candidates about what to say and where to say it, that interpretation of the results may be quite valid.

The pollster may also poll at *several different times* to see whether there is a "trend." If she thinks she sees a trend, her prediction may contain an adjustment of her latest results to allow for the assumed trend. But one should adjust with great caution, if at all, because there is no sure way of distinguishing a true trend from a wave that rises and recedes or from random fluctuations.

H. Ebbinghaus faced several kinds of time-change problems in his classic study of learning nonsense syllables:

> . . . [C]are was taken that the objective conditions of life during the period of the tests were so controlled as to eliminate too great changes or irregularities. Of course, since the tests extended over many months, this was possible only to a limited extent. But even so, the attempt was made to conduct, under as similar conditions of life as possible, those tests the results of which were to be directly compared. In particular the activity immediately preceding the test was kept as constant in character as was possible. Since the mental as well as the physical condition of man is subject to an evident periodicity of 24 hours, it was taken for granted that like experimental conditions are obtainable only at like times of day. However, in order to carry out more than one test in a given day, different experiments were occasionally carried on together at different times of day. When too great changes in the outer and inner life occurred, the tests were discontinued for a length of time. Their resumption was preceded by some days of renewed training varying according to the length of the interruption. (Ebbinghaus, pp. 25–26)

Sponsors of television rating services generally want to know how many people are watching the program *on the average* throughout the program, rather than at one particular time, because the commercial may come on at any time within the show.[5] And, because the audience of a show varies during the show, it is not sensible to find out how many are watching at any one particular time. The television rating firms therefore take samples of the viewers *throughout* the program, and the ratings are expressed as averages (and totals). The average is an estimate of how many people are watching at any single time within the program.

5. The Panel

The panel is a special type of time-series technique; it measures some attributes of a *given sample* of people at several moments. But it differs from other long-view studies in two ways. First, the panel study is more likely to have truly historical interest than are other long-view studies; it is usually concerned with what has happened at *particular* times; for this aim it is *conceptually* impossible to substitute a wide-view study. For example, a wide-view study at a single moment cannot be used to find out how voters *shift* from candidate to candidate during the campaign or how the market share of a particular brand is faring. There is no substitute for data on September 1, October 1, and so forth.

5. More strictly, sponsors want to know how many people are actually watching when the commercial comes on. But we shall not consider that part of the problem except to note that many more interviewers would be needed to measure the audience at any *given* moment than are needed to measure the average throughout the show.

A panel is *not* the only way to obtain this type of historical information, however. It is possible to take *separate samples* at various points in time instead of collecting data on the single panel sample. For example, if you want to know in *absolute* terms what proportion of the vote your candidate has at different times before the election, then it really does not matter, conceptually, whether you poll 1,000 people two months before the election and *another* 1,000 people one month before or whether you poll a 1,000-person panel twice. There may be *practical* differences between these two strategies, such as the possibility of spoiling the panel by polling them once. But there are not likely to be major cost differences between these two strategies (except perhaps higher costs in finding the same people twice). Similarly, separate samples give conceptually the same television ratings, but for some rating methods—especially those that require placing electronic meters in homes—it is enormously *cheaper* to use panels of the same people for repeated measurements.

A second major difference between the panel and nonpanel long-view techniques is that the panel is much more efficient when you want to measure *changes* from period to period rather than the *absolute levels*. A campaign manager wants to know whether people are shifting toward his candidate, or the soap firm wants to know whether more people are shifting to its brand than away from it. The television executive wants to know whether one episode of a show is *better or worse* than another episode in terms of listenership. For such *comparative* problems the panel method offers great statistical efficiency; there is much less sampling error in the panel, because individuals can be compared to themselves at different moments.

The third—and perhaps most important—difference between the panel and nonpanel long-view methods is that the panel method can reveal much back-and-forth shifting behavior that is otherwise hidden from view. The first important use of the panel method in voting studies was in the Erie County survey in 1940. Lazarsfeld, *et al.*, noted these advantages of the panel method in studying the process by which people decide how they will vote:

> The full effect of a campaign cannot be investigated through a sequence of polls conducted with different people. They show only majority tendencies which are actually the residual result of various sorts of changes—to or from indecision and from one part to the other. They conceal minor changes which cancel out one another and even major changes if they are countered by opposing trends. And most of all, they do not show *who* is changing. They do not follow the vagaries of the individual voter along the path to his vote, to discover the relative effect of various influential factors upon his final vote. (p. 2)

This simple table has a surprising number of implications. Let us assume for a moment that the interviews in October and November had been conducted with different people, rather than with the same people, as was actually the case. Then, the findings would have read as follows: in October 42 percent (167 out

Vote Intention in October

Actual Vote	Republican	Democratic	Don't Know	Don't Expect to Vote	Total
Republican	215	7	4	6	232
Democrat	4	144	12	0	160
Didn't vote	10	16	6	59	91
Total persons	229	167	22	65	483

of 396) of those who had a vote intention meant to vote for the Democratic Party; in November 41 percent (160 out of 392) voted for it. This would have given the impression of great constancy in political attitudes. Actually, however, only the people in the major diagonal of the table remained unchanged: 418 out of 483 respondents did what they intended to do; 13 percent changed their minds one way or another. (p. ix)

A panel study is not always feasible, however. One difficulty is that the events or thoughts may already be long past by the time the researcher begins. Occasionally this difficulty can be overcome by the use of retrospective questions, as illustrated in the question block on happiness in Chapter 22. Memory is not always reliable, however, and indeed one of the panel's major charms is that it avoids memory loss because questions are asked about contemporary behavior and thoughts.

Still a third difficulty of the panel method is "mortality," the loss of respondents from wave to wave of interviewing. And there can also be statistically dangerous mixups in the identities of interviewees from wave to wave.

Another panel difficulty is that the panel questions may affect people's behavior, one of the repetition effects discussed in Chapter 22. And sometimes the cost is high. Nevertheless, the panel can sometimes provide data that cannot be obtained in any other way.

6. Summary

When experimentation is not feasible, one turns to the data that occur without researcher interference. Two such basic research designs are the cross section and the time series.

In some situations, cross sections and time series measure the same phenomena, but in other situations they capture quite different processes. The differences can arise from changes over time, from slow-acting influences, or from differences in the unit of observation and level of aggregation.

Wherever possible, one should try to use *both* a cross section and a time series. If the results agree, the conclusion is strongly supported. If the results disagree, they may point to important underlying processes.

Many of the most important phenomena in social science unfold slowly over a period of years. Changes over time are not caused by abstract time itself but rather by various processes that occur over time. And such changes may be trends or cycles. In some cases you may grapple with changes over time by taking measurements appropriately spaced over the time period. In other cases you may be able to work at a given moment with samples of various ages. As usual, the appropriate tactic must depend upon the purpose of the research.

As a substitute for observing the change over its full period, one may instead examine and compare at a given moment a cross section of people (the "wide view") who are at different stages of the unfolding of the phenomena. The wide view also protects against irrelevant but large changes in general social and economic conditions that always occur over long periods of time.

A very different situation is that in which the researcher wishes to know how people will behave when subjected to a single different condition found in different areas. But so much else also varies from place to place that a reasonable comparison cannot be made. As a substitute for the wide-view comparison, the researcher may turn to a long view from historical records of given people who were exposed to different treatments at different times in their lives.

The panel method offers the best advantages of the wide view and the long view combined, and hence it has enormous research power. It has great statistical efficiency because the same individuals can be compared with themselves at different times, hence reducing extraneous variability, and they can also be compared to each other. Panels require forethought and much organization, as well as expensive observation over the study period. But they are nevertheless the most appropriate method in many research situations.

EXERCISES

1. Give three examples in your field of use of the long-view approach.
2. Give three examples in your field of use of the wide-view approach (that is, the cross section).
3. Give an example of the use of the panel in your field and why it was preferred to other methods.
4. Give an example in which data are easier to obtain for a wide view than for a long view; give a contrary example.
5. Explain why the long-view technique used in one of the examples in Exercise 1 was preferable to the wide-view approach. Do the same for one wide-view example in Exercise 2, in preference to the long-view approach.
6. A university runs a high school for gifted students. You wonder whether the admission system is biased in favor of the children of parents who

work in the school of education at the university. How would you determine whether such a bias shows in the composition of the student body? (Don't forget children whose parents don't work at the university but who are accepted at the university high school.)

7. How would you go about checking whether there is a bias in favor of brothers and sisters who are already at the university high school? That is, does a student with an older sibling have a better than average chance of being accepted?

ADDITIONAL READING FOR CHAPTER 12

Zeisel (Chapter 10) gives a full but simple account of the panel method in public opinion and advertising research. Ferber and Verdoorn (pp. 267–277) discuss consumer-panel use in economics and business. They present a great deal of information on the time-series method and the cross-sectional approach (Chapters 5–9).

For another useful reference on panels, see the man who is the father of panel research, Lazarsfeld (1948).

13 surveys: pro, con, and how to do them

1. The Nature of Surveys

A survey gathers data about variables *as they are found in the world.* The survey can *observe behavior,* as for example whether people are athletes, whether they smoke, whether the money supply is high in some years, and whether there is prosperity in those years. The survey can also collect data on what people *say;* for example, researchers can ask people of various backgrounds for whom they will vote or how much liquor they drink. The important distinction between the survey and the experiment is that the survey takes the world as it comes, without trying to alter it, whereas the experiment systematically alters some aspects of the world in order to see what changes follow. For example, a mother might want to learn the causes of her baby's food rash. She might keep a diary of what foods the baby eats each day and whether he has a rash that day and the next day; that would be nonexperimental observation. Or she could systematically vary the foods that she gives the baby each day, trying first one food alone and then another food alone, noting the days on which the rash occurs; that would be an experiment.

The data for a survey may already exist in the form of records such as the national census or the questionnaire data in the Roper Center repository (Williamstown, Massachusetts) that were collected in the past; or you may need to collect new data especially for your purposes. The logic of the survey method is much the same either way.

The term "survey research" is applied to two very different sorts of investigation. The first aims to learn about relationships between variables, especially causal relationships. Causal-analysis survey research is quite analogous to experimentation, with the single (but overwhelmingly important) difference that the independent variable(s) is not controlled and manipulated by the researcher. Instead the researcher seeks out groups of people that have *already* been exposed to different levels of the independent variable. For example, instead of subjecting randomly-selected groups of people to different amounts of cigarette smoke, the researcher finds people who have smoked various numbers of cigarettes. Or a researcher who wants to study the effect of family income on juvenile delinquency does not choose various groups of families to receive various incomes; rather, he finds and assesses the amount of delinquency in families with different incomes.

The steps in pursuing causal-analysis survey research are much the same as those set forth for an experiment. Furthermore, the obstacles to studying causal relationships with nonexperimental survey research and the methods of overcoming these obstacles contribute much of the subject matter of this book. Therefore, we shall not pursue the matter further in this chapter, except to summarize the advantages and disadvantages of the survey method for causal analysis. After that, we shall focus on surveys that aim to provide quantitative *descriptions* of some aspects of a universe rather than to discover relationships.

2. Advantages of the Survey Method for Relationship Research

First, *with a survey you can get closer to the "real" hypothetical (theoretical) variables than with a laboratory experiment*. You can actually inspect the variables in their real-world setting; for instance, you can examine real cases of lung cancer and real movements of the economy without having to abstract from the real variables to a mock-up laboratory situation. This is the preeminent advantage of a survey over an experiment in those cases in which you want to investigate relationships but in which real-world experiments are impossible.

Second, a survey is often quite *cheap*, especially if you can use already existing records and data. If data exist for the prices and amounts of onions sold each month for several years, using them to explore the relationship between price and quantity is obviously cheaper than setting up a laboratory situation in which people are given quantities of money and opportunities to purchase onions and other foods at varying onion prices.

Third, huge masses of data are often already available or can be culled from existing records—voter-registration lists, for example. This is a major statistical advantage, because the large samples provide high internal reliability. Such huge samples are seldom available in experimentation.

Fourth, surveys can yield a very rich understanding of people—both in breadth by collecting a wealth of information, and in depth by probing people's motives.

3. Disadvantages of the Survey Method for Relationship Research

The major disadvantages described here apply only to causal and noncausal *relationship* research and not to census-type research.

First, the crucial disadvantage of the survey method in causal analysis is the *lack of manipulation of the independent variable*. Because there is no "controlled" variation in the independent variable, it is always possible that the correlation between the independent and dependent variables is not "causal" (see Chapter 23). But it is a mistake to say that survey results never show causation. Whether the results of a survey are causal depends upon many things (see Chapter 32). One short example here: Changes in state liquor taxes are accompanied by changes in the prices of liquor. The effects of these changes in price upon liquor consumption can be studied. The changes in consumption may reasonably be said to be caused by the changes in price because there is no likely connection between consumption and the moment when the legislators decide to raise the tax; the states act in much the same way that an experimenter would if he were randomly selecting when to raise taxes. There is no other likely relationship between the tax raise (and the price change) and the change in consumption, and therefore it is *reasonable* to say that the price change causes the change in liquor consumption.

To repeat the main point, a survey lacks the almost clinching proof of actually trying out the relationship by varying the independent variable to see whether it is indeed followed by changes in the dependent variable.

A second disadvantage of the survey is that *one cannot progressively investigate one aspect after another of the independent variable* to get closer to the "real" cause. One cannot first try out the cigarette, then the cigarette paper and the tobacco separately, and so forth until the ingredient that really causes cancer is isolated.

Third, *statistical devices are not always able to separate the effects of several independent variables* when there is multivariable causation, especially when two independent variables are themselves highly associated. For example, the same people tend to have high incomes and high education; therefore, it is very difficult to tell from survey results whether, say, it is education or income that causes the purchase of books and "high class" magazines.

My final comment on the choice of survey or experiment for causal analysis is old stuff to you by now. Several methods are better than one. If you can seek the knowledge you want with *both* a survey and an experiment and if the results jibe reasonably well, you have a much stronger basis for belief in your results than if your conclusions were based on just one of the techniques.

4. Descriptive Surveys

Now let us discuss surveys that are *not* intended to discover causal relationships but rather aim to *survey*. That is, we might call them *survey surveys* or, more conventionally, *descriptive* surveys, in contradistinction to causal-research surveys. They are surveys whose purpose is to provide true quantitative descriptions of aspects of a universe of people or things.

Because the purpose of the descriptive survey is to obtain an accurate picture of the universe, *random sampling* is particularly important. If the sample is biased in some way, so that it does not cover an important segment of the universe, and if each segment is not sampled in proportion to the relative size of the segment, then the picture of the universe will be distorted and misleading (unless the nonproportional sampling is done purposely and with full knowledge). It is obvious that you cannot find out who will win the next election by asking only Republicans for whom they will vote; yet *The Literary Digest* did almost precisely that when it predicted that Landon would win in 1936. Usually the bias is more subtle, however, and therefore more dangerous. For example, a local civic association decided that it would survey what the people in one city think about the educational system, the work opportunities, and other aspects of the community. The survey was worked out in very nice detail with but one flaw: The sampling plan originally omitted all streets north of the tracks, where most blacks live, because the person running the survey thought that "it would be dangerous for student interviewers." Of course, it is just those blacks who would most likely be dissatisfied with the educational system and other city services. The bias introduced by not taking a random sample *must* have distorted the results to make the picture seem rosier than it is—though perhaps that was what the civic association really wanted.

There are several dimensions of classification that tell us something about the nature of a survey:

1) As already noted, a survey can aim to discover causal relationships or to create accurate quantitative descriptions of one or more aspects of a universe. All subsequent discussion applies only to descriptive surveys.

2) A survey can be a *complete census* of the universe, or it can be a *sample survey* of the universe in microcosm. The advantage of the complete census is accuracy; the advantage of the sample survey is lower cost.

3) A survey need not be a survey of people. You can survey either *people* or *things*. The library study alluded to earlier surveyed the use of *books* in libraries. Or the survey can be of animals (how many cattle are there in Texas?) or of plants (how many acres of corn were planted in Illinois last year?). Most social-scientific surveys are of people, however. And one may survey *groups* as well as individuals. Families are the smallest groups commonly studied. The largest groups are nations; one can survey the nations of the world to discover their policies toward population control by sending questionnaires to the relevant bureaucrats in each nation. Voluntary organi-

zations are forever surveying their local groups as, for example, when they ask for yearly reports on membership and activities undertaken throughout the year.

4) A survey can either *observe* or *ask questions*. All surveys of nonhuman material use the observational method—at least until we find a horse that really does talk. But many surveys of human beings also observe behavior rather than asking questions, as, for example, when we count the passengers who ride buses, observe how many people buy a product at different price levels, or meter the number of television sets tuned to a given program.

5) One borderline technique between observing and questioning is to ask people to observe themselves (the diary technique). Another is to ask them what they have done in the past (A. Kinsey relied heavily on this retrospective technique). Observation by the researcher, his assistants, or mechanical devices is generally preferable to self-observation, but often it is too costly or otherwise impractical, as, for example, in sex surveys. Self-observations can have severe limitations; H. Cantril found that only 86 per cent of people who were interviewed twice at a three-week interval gave the same answer both times about whether they owned a car, and only 87 per cent gave the same answer about how they voted in the 1940 presidential election (Cantril, pp. 102–103). The diary technique can avoid such memory losses, but memory failure is not the only cause of the type of discrepancy found in the second interviews.

Instruments enhance the power of the researcher to observe human behavior. One-way glass enables the psychologist to see without affecting the subject. Fingerprint paper enables the magazine researcher to count the number of people who thumb pages. Infrared dust on people's shoes leaves detectable traces where the subjects walk. The eye camera records eye movements of people as they walk through supermarkets. The camera and tape recorder are invaluable additions to the anthropologist's armamentarium, as M. Mead never ceases to remind us.[1] Instruments can also be used to observe physiological states like blood pressure and galvanic skin response; they are useful in studying levels of emotional responses to various stimuli.

Often the choice between observing and questioning is a matter of convenience and feasibility. But sometimes the types of data that may be obtained by observing or questioning are very different. For example, people's answers to questions about how happy they are constitute one possible proxy for happiness. And observed rates of suicide and lynching constitute another possible proxy for happiness (actually for the opposite of happiness). But the concepts of happiness for which the proxies stand might be considerably different.

This book gives but little treatment to questionnaire surveys (page 195).

---

1. E. Webb *et al.* have collected a great many of what they call "unobtrusive measures" or "oddball measures" of human behavior.

There are several reasons for what may seem a cavalier neglect of the technique that constitutes so much of research in sociology and market research and social psychology. For one, the questionnaire survey is very well covered in an extensive literature. Furthermore, a special treatment of questionnaire surveys leads readers to think that questionnaire research has very special properties that make it entirely different from other kinds of research—which is not so. Also, I want to decrease the likelihood that students will rush blindly to use the questionnaire survey. It is not that I want to discourage its use when it really is appropriate, but too often people do questionnaire research just because they do not realize that there may indeed be much better methods for getting the knowledge they want.

6) Another way of classifying surveys is by the several types of information that they can obtain—to put it another way, by the several sorts of purposes they may achieve. Any given survey may have more than one purpose and may therefore obtain more than one sort of information; most descriptive surveys do. We shall now consider these sorts of information one by one.

A survey may obtain such *demographic data* as population, age, weight, income, and so forth. The U.S. Census is the major illustration of a demographic-data survey. But most other surveys collect some demographic data also, often for purposes of cross-classification to establish different patterns of behavior and attitudes for different groups of people.

Demographic data have been collected as long as there have been governments; information about population and property has always been important to rulers so that they could levy and collect taxes. A. Toynbee (the uncle) quoted this interesting speech about a proposed English census survey, delivered in Parliament in 1753, by Mr. Thornton, Member for the City of York:

> I did not believe that there was any set of men, or indeed any individual of the human species, so presumptuous and so abandoned as to make the proposal we have just heard. . . . I hold this project [a census of population] to be totally subversive of the last remains of English liberty. . . . The new bill will direct the imposition of new taxes, and indeed the addition of a very few words will make it the most effective engine of rapacity and oppression which was ever used against an injured people. . . . Luckily this dire prediction has not come to pass. Moreover, an annual register of our people will acquaint our enemies abroad with our weakness. (Toynbee, pp. 7, 127)

Information about people's *behavior* may also be obtained by surveys. Knowledge of behavior is the main subject and the final goal of much of the behavioral sciences and all of economics; therefore, behavior surveys are of obvious use. Furthermore, information about behavior may also be of interest to us if we are interested in what people *think*, because we can often infer attitudes and beliefs from people's behavior. The behaviorist psychologists go very far in saying that nothing *except* behavior can be meaningful data in psychology (and speech is therefore known as "verbal behavior"). This matter is discussed in a brief note at the end of the chapter.

People's *intentions about future behavior* can sometimes be ascertained by asking them what they plan to do in the future. Important economic data about consumers' intentions to buy durable goods and about businessmen's intentions to invest in plant and equipment are regularly obtained by surveys of intentions. Naturally enough, people do not always do what they have earlier said they intended to do. How well the intentions jibe with the behavior depends upon such factors as the length of time between the survey and the behavior and whether there are unusual occurrences (like a recession) in between. To some extent the errors wash out; some people who intended do not do, and some who did not intend do.

The amount of *information* that people have about various aspects of the world is sometimes the subject of surveys. For government- or business-policy purposes, it may be important to know how many people know that a new recreation area has been opened or that all males must register for the draft or that the income tax has been changed or that Argonaut is now president of the United States. Gallup polls often seek this kind of information.

Opinions, attitudes, beliefs, and interests are often the subject of surveys. I lump all these categories together and call them *thoughts* or *mental contents* because the type of method that is used is quite similar for all of them. This is tricky knowledge to obtain because practically every obstacle enumerated in earlier chapters crops up.

As I have noted, sometimes we survey behavior as a means of inferring what people think. The converse is also true; sometimes we survey people's thoughts in order to learn something about their behavior. The justification given by many social psychologists for surveying attitudes about race relations is that we can infer something about people's behavior from their attitudes. Such inference is hazardous at best, as advertising research tells us with great authority; there is a very tenuous relationship between what people say about a product and their actual purchasing. There must be *some* relationship between the contents of people's minds and what they do, but the relationship is very often not straightforward. Part of the trouble is that there is no one-to-one relationship between what is in someone's mind and what he tells an interviewer.

The reasons people give for their actions are still another subject of surveys: the surveys that ask "why?" Why did you buy a Ford this year? Why did you not go fishing in your neighbor's canoe? Why did you vote for Carter?

Many surveys of other kinds are also intended to discover the causes of human behavior, but in some cases the simple question "why?" can unravel a complex matter with dispatch. This is especially true when one is inquiring into rational actions that are under conscious control, like asking a professor why she gives Jones "F" and Smith "A." The question "why" is also very effective when one is trying to find out a set of social *rules;* for example, if you ask a Japanese why he takes off his shoes when he visits a house, the answer will probably be useful and accurate. But when investigating motivations that are less rational and that depend upon a person's tastes, loyalties, and education, "why" questions are not so likely to produce useful answers. For example, think how confusing it would be if someone asked you why you bought the car you did. To start with, you would not know whether you were being asked why you bought *any* car or why you bought this particular make of auto. And if the latter, you would have difficulty in conveying just why you bought a Ford. For another example, refer back to the discussion of M. Haire's study of why women did not buy instant coffee. The simple question "why?" in that case just could not do the job.

7) Questionnaire surveys are classified by whether they are done *by mail, by telephone, or by personal interviewing.* The *mail survey* is generally cheapest, though sometimes telephone interviewing within a local area can rival it for cost. The main disadvantage of the mail survey is the difficulty of obtaining a satisfactory random sample because some people do not return the questionnaires. Furthermore, those people may well be very different and might give different answers from those people who do respond. (Nonresponse bias is discussed on p. 316.) Sometimes it is possible to increase the response by mailing repeated questionnaires to people. And occasionally the types of information that you seek will not be in danger of bias from nonresponse; a trivial example would be a poll of a professional association's membership about whether the convention should be in New York or Baltimore; there is no reason to believe that the nonresponders would have different preferences from those of the people who do respond. But usually you must investigate the extent and nature of the bias with auxiliary techniques—perhaps with telephone or personal interviews of a sample of the nonresponders—so that you can allow for the bias by adjusting the results of the mail sample.

The rate of response to a mail questionnaire depends very much on who is sending it out, its subject, who receives it, and how easy it is to answer. The response rate can also be influenced by the cover letter sent with the questionnaire and by the inducements offered. Earlier I reported that a 3-cent ballpoint pen doubled responses in a library study (Fussler & Simon). Another report, slightly unbelievable, indicates that 75 percent of a ballpoint-pen group responded, whereas the control-group response was 18 percent (Klein). Sometimes it is worthwhile to purchase people's answers by sending a nickel, dime, quarter, or even dollar with each questionnaire.

The U.S. Bureau of the Census has employed mail questionnaires as the primary method of collecting data on population and housing since the 1970 Census. A test produced a response rate of 83–89 percent for the first mailing, and the Bureau hopes to do better in the future. The biggest problem is creating an accurate mailing list (Cohen, p. 22).

Telephone interviewing can be a remarkably efficient survey method. Until recently it was used only locally because of the cost of long-distance calls, though in some cases long-distance telephone interviewing was efficient. Recently the phone companies have made available various flat-rate plans under which unlimited long-distance calling is possible within wide areas; in some plans the state is the limit, in others the entire United States. These deals are in the process of giving telephone interviewing a vast new importance, I think. Telephone interviewing has been too little used in the past to replace personal interviewing, but now it must come into its own.

There is little difficulty with nonresponse in telephone interviewing, and therefore the sample obtained from a telephone survey is sufficiently random for many purposes. Furthermore, the sample can be taken sequentially; you just keep making more calls until your sample is big enough, which relieves you of having to decide in advance how large it must be. One snag is that the telephone book is not a very random sample; it excludes unlisted phones and people who have moved recently, which together total about 20 percent of the total phones in service (Cooper, p. 45, Glassen and Metzger, p. 60). But random-dialing techniques have been developed that avoid this difficulty, which were discussed on page 128.

The main disadvantages of the telephone interview are these: First, the interview must usually be short; unless you prearrange the interview, it is seldom practical to ask more than a handful of questions. Second, you cannot observe the subject visually; in personal interviews observation can reduce lying. On the other hand, people may not lie or exaggerate as much in a phone interview as in a personal interview because they are not as personally involved with the telephone interviewer. Third, some people do not have phones, but in some areas of the United States such high proportions of people have phones that the worst possible bias from this source cannot be very dangerous.

Personal interviews suffer only from the disadvantage of high cost in money and time. At 1968 costs, personal interviews of a sample of people chosen randomly throughout the United States may cost $25 or more *per interview*, even when carried out by organizations that already have staff facilities set up for interviewing. If you had to start from scratch, the cost would be even higher. Local interviews can be much cheaper, of course.

But personal interviews have some important advantages over mail and phone interviews, which is why they are used despite the high costs. The interview can be long, sometimes several hours; people often enjoy being interviewed. The interviewer can check some information with his own eyes, which may reduce exaggeration; for example, not many people who live in shacks dare report high incomes to interviewers in person. (On the other hand, the personal relationship with the interviewer leads some people to want to impress the interviewer.) Another major advantage of the personal interview is that the interviewer can probe for further information, by asking "What do you mean by that?" and so on, and he can also explain questions that the subject cannot understand; he can even translate into a foreign language for a subject who does not speak English.

The choice among mail, telephone, and personal interviews is delicate and calls for good judgment on the part of the researcher. You must consider all the advantages and disadvantages of the various techniques (summarized in Table 13.1) *as they apply to your particular research project*. The trick is to balance the advantages against the disadvantages to arrive at the best possible technique for the expenditure of time and money.

TABLE 13.1   Relative Merits of Principal Methods of Data Collection

Personal Interview	Mail	Telephone
	Advantages	
Most flexible means of obtaining data	Wider and more representative distribution of sample possible	Representative and wider distribution of sample possible
Identity of respondent known	No field staff	No field staff
Nonresponse generally very low	Cost per questionnaire relatively low	Cost per response relatively low
Distribution of sample controllable in all respects	People may be more frank on certain issues, e.g., sex	Control over interviewer bias easier; supervisor present essentially at interview
	No interviewer bias; answers in respondent's own words	Quick way of obtaining information
	Respondent can answer at his leisure, has time to "think things over"	Nonresponse generally very low
	Certain segments of population more easily approachable	Callbacks simple and economical
	Disadvantages	
Likely to be most expensive of all	Bias due to nonresponse often indeterminate	Interview period not likely to exceed five minutes
Headaches of interviewer supervision and control	Control over questionnaire may be lost	Questions must be short and to the point; probes difficult to handle
Dangers of interviewer bias and cheating	Interpretation of omissions difficult	Certain types of questions can not be used, e.g., thematic apperception
	Cost per return may be high if nonresponse very large	Nontelephone owners as well as those without listed numbers can not be reached
	Certain questions, such as extensive probes, can not be asked	
	Only those interested in subject may reply	
	Not always clear who replies	
	Certain segments of population not approachable, e.g., illiterates	
	Likely to be slowest of all	

SOURCE: *Research Methods in Economics and Business*, p. 210, by Robert Ferber and P. J. Verdoorn; © The Macmillan Company 1962; reprinted by permission of The Macmillan Company.

5. The Steps in Executing a Survey

Step 1.   Follow the procedures outlined in Chapter 7, to the point at which you are ready to decide on a method.

Step 2.   Find out if the data you want to collect already exist in some published study or in one of the "data banks" of some major university research organizations. It is a shame to find out too late that you could have saved hours and dollars with a simple phone call or a letter. Sometimes the existing data are not exactly what you want; for example, the data published by the Internal Revenue Service do not contain fine breakdowns that would often be valuable, and people and firms are classified in categories that may not be ideal for your purposes. Nevertheless, it may be possible to adjust and interpolate the data to make it yield most of the information you want.

Step 3.   From here on, it is assumed that you have *not* been able to find the data you want in existing records but must collect the raw data yourself. Your next step is to *define the universe* that you want to sample or poll. The universe you work with might dictate whether you reach one conclusion or its opposite. For example, assume you want to know if there is any relationship between per capita income and radio ownership or between per capita income and the diets people choose. If you take a sample in a very homogeneous community like Park Forest, Illinois, you will find practically no differences. The range of income is very small, everyone owns a radio, and most people eat steak, drink milk, and eschew caviar. But, if the sample is taken in Chicago, which is more heterogeneous and has a wider income range than Park Forest has, there will be some people poor enough not to own radios, so that some relationship will appear between income and radio ownership. There will also appear to be some relationship between income and menu, for the lower-class black eats collard greens and side meat, and the hillbilly immigrant eats what she ate in the Ozarks. If the researcher wants to obtain a really high correlation, all she has to do is take a world-wide sample. Practically no one of low income in India has a radio.

A similar example exists for drinking behavior and religion. Just because the major religions in the United States do not differ significantly in their stands on drinking, one should not conclude that their point of view is common in all human groups. If the universe includes the Moslem countries, the results will be markedly different. Clearly the universe should be chosen for its relevance to the problem you are interested in and not for how strong a relationship it will yield.

Step 4.   Next, decide on the *sampling procedure* you are going to use. This step includes deciding what list of people or other representation of the universe you will select from, the physical procedure you will use to select names (for instance, systematically by taking every *n*th name or randomly by selecting a random page and then a random name or going to every *n*th house), and then actually making up a list of people (or objects) to be sampled.

Step 5.   Think out and decide upon the procedure that you will actually use in *observing or questioning* your subjects. If you are gathering data with a questionnaire, preparation of the questionnaire is crucial. If you are using an observation survey, you must decide what pieces of behavior you will watch and count; this decision requires classification and definition. If you are studying the first stair-climbing behavior of babies, you must define what will count as climbing motions. If you have already prepared dummy tables, as we suggested on page 111, you will find them an enormous aid in the construction of the questionnaire or observation procedure.

Step 6.   *Test* the questionnaire or the observation procedure in a preliminary run. Look for such things as confusion on the part of respondents about what questions mean and inability to answer within the categories you have provided. Then *revise* the questionnaire or observation procedure. Test again and so on until your procedure does the job it is supposed to do. It pays to iron out all possible difficulties at this stage rather than later.

Step 7.   Collect your data.

Step 8.   Analyze your data. This subject is covered in Chapter 25. Statistical analysis is usually a larger part of survey research—especially that seeking relationships—than of experimentation because the researcher must examine the effect of the variables *analytically* rather than by varying them physically as in an experiment.

Step 9.   *Interpret* the data, and draw sound *conclusions*. Chapters 26–32 cover this work.

6. Summary

A survey gathers data about a population and its characteristics. It observes the population as it exists, without altering it experimentally.

The main advantage of a survey over a laboratory experiment is its realism; and over a field experiment it may have a cost advantage. Its main disadvantages are: a) its difficulty in establishing that two groups being compared are really similar, and b) the difficulty of clarifying causation.

Surveys can gather data by observing or questioning; the data can be demographic characteristics or behavior or intentions or attitudes. Surveys can be done by mail, telephone, or in person; each method has advantages and drawbacks.

The steps in executing a survey are listed in the chapter.

EXERCISES

1. Give examples in which
   a. the higher cost of personal interviewing is warranted
   b. lower-cost mail or telephone interviews make more sense than do personal interviews
   c. an experiment would be cheaper than a survey
   d. a survey would be cheaper than an experiment
   e. observation surveying is preferable to interview surveying
   f. interview surveying is preferable to observation surveying
2. Give examples of surveys that study
   a. behavior
   b. intentions
   c. people's information
   d. attitudes, opinions, beliefs, or interests
   e. reasons given for behavior

ADDITIONAL READING FOR CHAPTER 13

Babbie is a readable general book on survey research methods. Stephan and McCarthy (Chapters 12–22) contain a wealth of useful ideas on the execution of sample surveys. Hyman (1955) is an excellent general work on surveys. And Sudman (1967) helps you execute your survey relatively cheaply; or to put it another way, he helps you get more information for a given expenditure.

On interviewing, see Hyman (1954); Cantril (Chapters 1–4, especially 1–2); Parten; Payne, and almost every textbook in social-scientific and market research. Paul gives an excellent discussion of anthropological interviewing. An article that many have found useful in evaluating the strengths and limitations of field studies is that of Zelditch.

For discussion of "reasons why" analysis, see Zeisel (Chapters 6, 7, 8); Lorie and Roberts (Chapter 17); and P. F. Lazarsfeld (1935).

Sudman (1967) provides a lot of useful information on how to reduce the cost of surveys.

14 some other qualitative and quantitative techniques

Research methods cannot be satisfactorily classified in a one-dimensional, mutually exclusive scheme. Rather, there are several ways that one may classify the technique actually used in any study. For example, the previous chapter examined the difference between the experiment and the survey, and Chapter 12 discusses the difference between the long view and the wide view; a particular survey may use the long-view or the wide-view technique, and an experiment can too. Later in this chapter we shall discuss content analysis. Content analysis can be used in either a survey or an experiment, though it is more likely to be used in a survey.

This chapter covers a few techniques for obtaining knowledge that are not described elsewhere in the book. The first group includes the qualitative methods of deduction and case study—including the psychological depth study—which are neither surveys nor experimental methods. Then we discuss use of expert opinion as a method of obtaining knowledge. Content analysis, which is a quantitative method of working with "qualitative" data, is another topic in the chapter.

1. Deductive Reasoning

The principle of the deductive method for obtaining knowledge is that, *if* A is true and *if* B is true, then *under some specified* conditions one can safely say that C is true. This is the simplest type of deduction, of course. The chains of reasoning can be longer, more complex, and probabilistic, but the same principle holds.

Consider the example of wanting to know whether it is raining outside. Your previous experience tells you that, if people are holding open umbrellas over their heads, it is raining; this observation is premise A. Premise B is what you actually see from your window at a given moment—that almost everyone who has an umbrella with him has it open. You deduce your conclusion C, that it is indeed raining outside.

Notice that whether your conclusion C is correct depends upon the correctness (truth) of your premises A and B. If you are in a country where people hold umbrellas over them to keep the sun off, then premise A is wrong in that case, and your conclusion C will probably be in error. Similarly, if your eyes deceive you about whether people are holding open umbrellas, then premise B is incorrect, and your conclusion will probably be incorrect too.

In one sense, there is nothing "new" in the conclusion C; all the information contained in the conclusion is already contained in the premises. Nevertheless, deduction helps us to know and understand the world about us because it opens our eyes to information that we would otherwise not understand, just as a child learns when an adult points out to her how a bicycle works. Deduction is a device for discovery of the truths that lie concealed within a set of statements. (In this sense, it is like all mathematical analysis.)

In the case of the umbrellas and the rain, the deductive method might or might not be more effective than an empirical investigation. The empirical method of going outside and extending an upturned palm has the advantage of rendering you safe from most false premises. (But notice that the premise that water coming down from above is rain *might* be incorrect; someone might be spraying a hose out a window. In some sense *all* knowledge is deduced, and all knowledge depends upon various premises.) The advantage of the deductive method in this case is that you do not have to go outside and get wet to obtain an answer.

We use deduction all the time as a helpful device. You might have followed this line of thought this morning: Classes meet Monday to Friday; today is Monday; therefore classes meet today. And off you go to class on the basis of your deduction, without telephoning to check that classes are indeed meeting.

Notice that I call the deductive method a "method of getting *knowledge*," in the same way that I have talked about various *empirical* methods of getting knowledge. In one sense empirically established facts have more claim to be called "knowledge" than does a conclusion arrived at deductively, because whenever a deduction and an empirically established fact collide, the deduction must give way: The empirical demonstration is the ultimate test. As someone has said, many a beautiful theory has been slain by an ugly fact. There is a famous example of a World War II navy airplane that theoretically would not fly at all. When a model was made and flown despite the theory to the contrary, the theory had to be revised, for it was in error. When you know that the plane has flown millions of miles, you can afford to disregard the theory telling you that it cannot fly.

The contest between deduction and empirical knowledge is not always so easily settled, however. Often the empirical fact is not so clear-cut because the empirical measurement is uncertain, and in that case a strong deductive argument may be more persuasive. The issue of whether trading stamps raise supermarket food prices is an example. Several empirical studies have apparently shown that trading stamps do not raise prices (Beem; U.S. Department of Agriculture; Bunn). On the other hand, strong deductive economic theory argues that trading stamps *must* raise prices in the long run. (Of *course* trading stamps raise food prices. They make it more difficult for consumers to compare food prices of individual items and of stores as a whole, and this lack of knowledge by consumers dulls the incentive of merchants to set prices to a fine edge of competition. Furthermore, stamps raise the total out-of-pocket costs to the food store; Davis.) And no contrary deduction using other assumptions comes to mind, except possibly that stamp-giving stores reduce their advertising. Furthermore, a reanalysis of the same U.S. Department of Agriculture data that went into the empirical analyses contradicts the original findings (Strotz; but see Beem, 1959). I am therefore inclined to place most credence in the logical deduction and believe that, at least in the long run, trading stamps do raise prices. This example demonstrates that empirical knowledge is not always more conclusive than deductive knowledge or even of a basically different nature.

The effect of population growth upon economic development is another matter in the study of which we put more stock in deduction than in empirical evidence. R. Easterlin sums up the latter: "On the whole, then, simple empirical comparisons between economic and population growth rates are inconclusive. Cases [nations] of high per capita income growth are associated with both high and low per capita income growth" (Easterlin, p. 107). But the empirical analyses are extremely weak, for many reasons. And the theoretical reasons to believe that increased population causes lower income are very strong. Therefore, most scientists advocate population control as a means of speeding economic development, and many nations follow this recommendation—on the basis of deduction and without empirical support.

Note that deduction is not the same thing as theory. Theory is an interlaced *body* of existing systematic knowledge, and it is important just because it is a *source of premises* for deduction (see the discussion in Chapter 3).

We may end this section on deduction with the usual admonition: Do not ignore deduction when it is useful, but do not limit yourself to its use and neglect other methods. On one hand, remember that deduction might give you all the information you need about the effect of trading stamps on prices; on the other hand, do not refuse to look into the horse's mouth to find out how many teeth he has.

2. The Case Study

The case study is almost synonymous with the descriptive type of research discussed in Chapter 4. It is the method of choice when you want to obtain a wealth of detail about your subject. You are likely to want such detail when you do not know exactly what you are looking for. The case study is therefore appropriate when you are trying to find clues and ideas for further research; in this respect, it serves a purpose similar to the clue-providing function of expert opinion.[1]

The specific method of the case study depends upon the mother wit, common sense, and imagination of the person doing the case study. The investigator makes up his procedure as he goes along, because he purposely refuses to work within any set categories or classifications; if he did so, he would not be obtaining the benefits of the case study. These admonitions may be useful: First, work objectively. Describe what is really out in the world and what could be seen by another observer. Avoid filtering what you see through the subjective lenses of your own personality. Second, constantly reassess what is important and what is unimportant. Follow up and record what seems most important. Constantly exercise your judgment on this issue. Third, work long and hard. Saturate yourself in the situation, and keep at it. Some anthropologists believe that case studies of less than several years' duration are likely to be misleadingly superficial (Haring, p. 53). B. Malinowski gives a vivid argument on this point:

> Living in the village with no other business but to follow native life, one sees the customs, ceremonies and transactions over and over again, one has examples of their beliefs as they are actually lived through, and the full body and blood of actual native life fills out soon the skeleton of abstract constructions. That is the reason why, working under such conditions as previously described, the Ethnographer is enabled to add something essential to the bare outline of tribal constitution, and to supplement it by all the details of behaviour, setting and small incident. He is able in each case to state whether an act is public or private; how a public assembly behaves, and what it looks like; he can judge whether an event is ordinary or an exciting and singular one; whether natives bring to it a great deal of sincere and earnest spirit, or perform it in fun; whether they do it in a perfunctory manner, or with zeal and deliberation.

> In other words, there is a series of phenomena of great importance which cannot possibly be recorded by questioning or computing documents, but have to be observed in their full actuality. Let us call them the *inponderabilia of actual life*. (Malinowski, p. 18)

1. See R. Cyert, *et al.* for an interesting example of the case method used in a preliminary exploration of decision making in large organizations.

Sometimes the investigator must choose whether she should carry out one or a few case studies rather than adopting the alternative of doing a survey or an experiment on a larger sample of people. An interesting example is found in market research, in which "motivation research" has competed with survey methods of investigating the reasons people buy. (For the moment we shall apply the label "motivation research" to the psychological case study "in depth" in which a clinical psychologist spends many hours or days "probing" a single person. Sometimes, however, survey methods or experiments are also called "motivation research," when they seek the reasons people buy.) Motivation-research case-study methods were able to produce such insights as that drivers judge auto acceleration by the stiffness of the spring of the accelerator pedal and that men did not want to fly on business trips because of their sense of guilt about dying and leaving their families husbandless and fatherless. On the other hand, an experimental method was able to establish that women did not buy instant coffee because they thought of instant-coffee users as lazy homemakers (Haire, discussed in Chapter 6).

The difference between the two methods is that the insights into feelings about auto acceleration and guilt about flying were ideas produced by the case study but not tested and proved by it. On the other hand, the *idea* about the cause of women's not buying instant coffee was *not* produced by the experiment; the experimenter had to have the idea to start with; he probably got it by introspection or by crude informal case study. But the experiment did test the idea and prove it. Actually, the case study and the survey or experiment are not alternatives but are complementary; they should be used together.

3. Participant Observation

If you wish to understand the full complexity of a case situation in social science, you may have no alternative but to get yourself involved as a person. An example is that of a psychologist such as Freud who wishes to plumb the depths of another person's mind and can only do so by interacting with the person in a human relationship. Another example is that of a white man who wishes to understand black life; Griffith dyed his skin black and traveled as a black in the South. After the participant-observation has been done and key elements of the situation have been identified, research methods that are less dependent on the researcher's personality often can be employed, just as systematic tests of Freud's ideas were made to check on Freud's observations.

When studying a complex group situation, such as Malinowski described on page 295, the researcher is especially likely to conclude that personal involvement is the appropriate strategy. In the words of one experienced participant-observer, in order to understand the richness of individual and group relationships, one aims to "record the ongoing experiences of those observed." And to do so, one must "adopt the perspective of those studied by sharing in their day-to-day experiences" (Denzin, p. 185).

More generally, the participant-observer's strategy is to immerse oneself in all aspects of the situation by using all available sources of information—informal talks with members of the group one is studying, reading letters and other documents, passively observing and listening while simply "hanging around" with the group, and so on. The key difference from other research methods is that the participant-observer *participates with* and has some sort of role in the group, rather than maintaining a distance between the observer and the observed. The great nineteenth-century economist Alfred Marshall said this as well as it has been said:

> [T]he method of le Play's monumental *Les Ouvriers Européens* is the *intensive* study of all the details of the domestic life of a few carefully chosen families. To work it well requires a rare combination of judgment in selecting cases, and of insight and sympathy in interpreting them. At its best, it is the best of all: but in ordinary hands it is likely to suggest more untrustworthy general conclusions, than those obtained by the *extensive* method of collecting more rapidly very numerous observations, reducing them as far as possible to statistical form, and obtaining broad averages in which inaccuracies and idiosyncrasies may be trusted to counteract one another to some extent. (Marshall, p. 116)

It is difficult to observe well while participating in a manner that will aid observation. "Carving out a role" in the group is difficult and treacherous from a scientific standpoint (Denzin, p. 188). There are various possibilities: For example, one can hide one's purpose and pose as a regular member of the group; this raises ethical questions and creates technical difficulties for recording information. Or one can explain one's purpose and try to enlist cooperation. Other difficult choices must also be made according to the exigencies of the situation, such as whether to try to use the same vocabulary as the people whom one is observing. And in one case, how to get oneself released from the insane asylum to which one has gotten oneself committed (Rosenham).

Great wisdom and skill are necessary for success as a participant-observer. But the rewards in ideas and understanding of people and groups can be very great if one succeeds.

4. Expert Opinion

By "expert opinion" I mean the judgments and estimates made by people who have spent much of their time working with a particular subject and who have gathered much general information that has been filtered through their minds and stored in their memories.

At the start, let us distinguish between the use of expert opinion as a source of *general guidance and clues* for getting started in the right direction on a particular research topic and its use as the *final data* on which you base your conclusion. To mention a bad example of the first use, I once

FIGURE 14.1

Source: From the Champaign-Urbana *Courier*, November 5, 1975, p. 9. Reprinted by permission of Newspaper Enterprise Association.

began a study of race horses without soliciting the "expert" opinion of habitual bettors on which variables to study, and the study suffered; on the other hand, it would be total folly to accept expert opinion as your final scientific conclusion on how to predict which horse will win a race. As a positive example of expert opinion as the basis for a conclusion rather than as a source of values, a court often relies upon the judgment of psychiatrists on whether a person is insane (although in perhaps the most important cases the jury has the final say). And, for some purposes of social science, one might accept a psychiatrist's *judgment* that more patients recover from schizophrenia than from depression.

Expert opinion can often be useful as a source of objective information that might be more difficult to collect by other techniques; asking psychiatrists about the recovery rates from schizophrenia and depression is an example. A more crucial use of expert opinion, however, is for judgments that require examination of an entire *context*, that is, taking into account an ill-defined *total picture* rather than a limited number of well-defined factors.

An example is asking a psychologist to judge whether a patient is neurotic on the basis of his *entire profile* on some psychological test battery rather than on the basis of a single score of some type. But L. Goldberg, among others, has shown that simple statistical rules of thumb can make such predictions about as well as the experts.

Expert opinion is indispensable when the judgment involves *human values*. For one example, in the library study our ultimate interest was in creating a scheme that would keep the *most valuable* books in the central library (Fussler and Simon). We developed statistical rules of thumb to make the judgments, but the ultimate judgment of value had to be made by noted scholars in various fields; what they judge as valuable *is* valuable, by definition. Therefore, the best rule of thumb was one that agreed most closely with the expert judges. Another example is scholars' ratings of university graduate departments (Cartter). The scholars' opinions do not simply *stand for* some more objective measure of the quality of a graduate school; their judgments *are* the measure of values. If one believes that more objective data, like the amount of scholarly writing produced by a department, provide the final test of a school's value, one should then collect such information rather than asking for experts' opinions.

Expert opinion can be rendered by a single expert—as is often the case in the courtroom or when a single adviser gives his opinions to policy makers—or many experts can be surveyed. The survey of graduate-school quality is an example of the latter; more than 100 scholars in each field were asked their opinions, for a total of more than 400 scholars. In most cases, a few opinions will suffice, because, if the experts are *really* experts, there will be relatively little variation among their opinions; two well-known economists will surely be in closer agreement on which are the best departments of economics in the United States than will two laymen or two undergraduates or even two well-known psychologists.

The phrase "human yardstick" has been applied to studies in which judges' ratings of psychological phenomena are the measurements with which the researcher works. The agreement among judges is often much higher than the judges themselves think it is; they are often surprised at how little each one's judgment differs from those of the others (Underwood, p. 24).

It is not always easy to draw a sharp dividing line between what is expert opinion and what is first-hand data. In the example of the psychiatrists asked about recovery rates from schizophrenia and depression, is a survey of psychoanalysts a survey of expert opinion or a survey of first-hand data? The analysts keep records, and a survey of such records—even informally through psychiatrists' judgments—is very much like gathering first-hand data in many other surveys.

Here are some points of difference between expert opinion and more formal scientific investigation: First, scientific method generally tries to minimize the human judgment involved in the data-gathering process; a meter reading is the ideal of scientific technique. But when you gather expert opinion, there is much room for human error to creep in, in the form of any of the obstacles to knowledge described in Chapter 19. In expert-opinion studies there is more opportunity for other people's minds to intervene between the researcher and her subject matter than with other techniques.

Second, ordinary scientific studies can be closely replicated, because the researcher specifies exactly how he obtained his data. In expert-opinion studies the researcher can tell you how and what he asked the expert or experts, but he cannot tell you exactly how the experts gathered the information that went into their judgments and estimates.

There is not much to say about how to gather expert opinion. This is the skill that journalists possess, and it is difficult to isolate the elements of the art. All of us spend much of our lives soliciting expert opinion and then deciding what we shall and shall not regard as trustworthy. I think, therefore, that it is not simply ducking the issue to tell you to use common sense in an expert-opinion study and let it go at that.

A sample of experts is probably better than a single expert, and a random sample of experts may be useful. But mere quantity is worthless unless the experts are expert. The statements of a million people about the size of your feet will be less accurate than the statement of the person who just sold you a pair of shoes.

Scientists are wary of conclusions based on expert opinion and perhaps for good reason. A relevant saying of Samuel Johnson's was quoted à propos the university ratings: "A compendium of gossip is still gossip." Nevertheless, expert opinion will always be an important source of knowledge in science as well as in everyday living.

5. Content Analysis

Content analysis is a technique that stands somewhere between the case study and the "open-ended question" in a questionnaire survey.

From one point of view it is reasonable to call content analysis a "qualitative" technique, for the researcher does not make quantitative comparisons between two or more cases. A psychoanalyst may say that one of her patients is "more psychotic" than another patient, but she does not support that statement with a number that counts something. If you ask the psychoanalyst to prove her statement quantitatively, she may reply that you are asking her to measure the unmeasurable. But content analysis is actually a method of measuring the unmeasurable—at least to some extent—and from this point of view it is sensible to call it a "quantitative" technique.

At the other pole, consider the open-ended question. A questionnaire may ask "Why did you leave your last job?" and various answers will be given. The researcher then constructs a classification that may consist of such categories as "Pay too low," "Bad working conditions," "Didn't like the boss," and so on. The researcher reads through each person's answer and "codes" it by deciding that it should go into one or another of the categories. (The original question could have been in the form of a multiple-choice offering these various categories, but there are often sound reasons for giving the respondent freedom to say whatever he wishes, especially at the exploratory stage.) In a sense, such coding is indeed actually measuring the unmeasurable and counting the uncountable, for it converts qualitative answers to quantitative measurements.

The content analyst sets up various classification schemes, which he then applies to speeches or writings. These classifications either count particular *kinds* of words or ideas, or they measure the *amount* of words or time that is devoted to particular ideas. Early examples of formal content analysis were provided by military-intelligence agencies in wartime. Enemy newspapers (and radio stations) were monitored exhaustively, and counts were made of various kinds of references to transportation, obituaries, and so forth. Variations in the numbers of such references from week to week often signify troop movements or other changes that are clues to the intentions and actions of the enemy.

Content analysis has been used extensively in studies of the mass media to determine changes in either the media themselves or in society and culture as time passes. It is a formalization of techniques that have long been used informally. For example, a researcher may count the number of favorable or unfavorable editorials in a country's most important newspaper to see how the political climate has changed over time, rather than merely obtaining an informal impression of the political climate. Or he might count the number of overt references to sex in popular magazines in the Victorian era, compared to the 1960s, to find out whether public attitudes were indeed very hush-hush toward sex in the Victorian era. Or (a study I wish someone would do) he might study the popular press with content analysis to see whether "conformity" has increased as the twentieth century has proceeded. (As I suggested earlier, it would be so hard to define "conformity" meaningfully that, not only would such a study probably be impossible, but also scientific statements about conformity would thereby be revealed as vacuous.)

One of the more adventurous uses of content analysis is D. McClelland's study of the historical relationship between the motivation to achieve among the members of a society and the economic development of the society. He and his associates have measured the frequency of "achievement imagery" in the popular literature of the society at various periods and have related these frequencies to economic indicators. For example, Figure 14.2 shows the close correspondence (with a time lag of about fifty years) between the content-analysis data and coal imports into London from 1550 to 1850. When one considers the multitude of obstacles present in such an investigation, the closeness of the correspondence is startling, and it reassures us that empirical research in social science need not be hamstrung by the less-than-perfect conditions under which we must work.

P. Sorokin used content analysis to analyze the grand cultural changes over millennia. Figure 14.3 shows how the proportion of philosophers of different outlooks has changed from century to century, as a proxy for the sway held by the various systems of truth.

The content of art may also be analyzed systematically, and this technique is the source of much of our understanding of the contacts among cultures and the transmission of knowledge among them. A. Kroeber traces

FIGURE 14.2 **Average *n* Achievement Levels in English Literature (1550–1800) Compared with Rates of Gain in Coal Imports at London 50 Years Later**

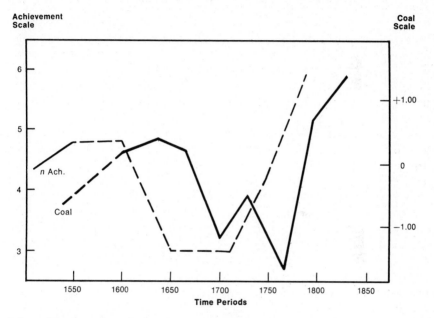

n Ach. = Mean number of achievement images per 100 lines.
Coal = Coal imports at London as deviations from expected in standard-deviation units.

Source: "Need for Achievement and English Industrial Growth," p. 19, by Norman M. Bradburn and David E. Berlew, in *Economic Development and Cultural Change* (October 1961); reprinted by permission of The University of Chicago Press.

the travels of the flying gallop (an invention of artists, because horses do not run that way) as a way of representing a running horse in art:

From the Ukraine, this Scythian style with the flying gallop spread to Hungary; to the Goths who at various times ranged between the Baltic and the Crimea; to the Caucasus and the Caspian Sea; and to southwestern Siberia where a related art maintained itself long after the Scythians were extinct, in fact until around A.D. 500. From this general region our device was communicated to Sassanian Persia (226–641); all earlier Persian art lacks the device, as did the Assyrian and Greek arts by which Persian art was influenced. A farther spread was to

China, where depiction of the flying gallop had become installed by terminal Han times, in the second post-Christian century. The Han dynasty repeatedly sought Western connections, especially in order to obtain heavy cavalry horses from Ferghana in modern Soviet Uzbekistan, so that an avenue was open for import of the stylistic influence.

FIGURE 14.3   **Fluctuation of the Influence in Systems of Truth by Century Periods**

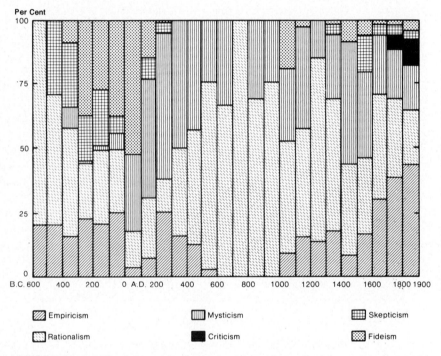

Source: *Social and Cultural Dynamics,* Vol. II, p. 32, by Pitirim A. Sorokin; copyright, 1937, by The Bedminster Press; reprinted by permission of The Bedminster Press.

The Chinese, and following them the Japanese, adopted the flying gallop in their art and have kept it to the present time. . . .

In 1794 it suddenly appeared in an English engraved print of a race horse by Stubbs, followed three years later by a woodcut in the *Sporting Magazine.* It was about twenty-five years more before the new posture made its way into British high-art oil painting. (Kroeber, pp. 500–501)

The most important decision in content analysis involves the choices of categories, which must accurately represent the ideas or concepts that you want to measure. Chapter 15 discusses the issue under the general rubric of "classification."

Computer systems have been developed to speed and refine content analysis. The researcher punches the material onto cards and instructs the computer how to categorize key words. The computer, which is programmed to handle syntactical problems such as tense and number, then scans the material, and lists and counts the words in each category (Stone *et al.*).

6. Simulation[2]

"Simulation" is an ambiguous label that refers to several research techniques. By one meaning any laboratory experiment is a simulation. For example, H. Ebbinghaus' experiment with the learning and retention of nonsense syllables can be called a simulation study of human learning processes. Laboratory experiments with physical models are also called simulation studies by some writers. An example is a laboratory wind-tunnel test of how model airplanes with various characteristics behave under various conditions. Or an engineer might want to know whether there is a chance that a new type of roof for an industrial building might fall in. Because it is impractical to build a full-sized roof and subject it to stress tests and because, for reasons that we shall discuss in the next section, she may not be able to solve the problem with mathematics alone, the engineer will often build a model building with a model roof, table-top size, and then study how much punishment the roof can absorb before it falls in. The Army Corps of Engineers built a scale model to simulate the behavior of tides and river currents in San Francisco Bay—all in a warehouse. These physical experiments are often run when the engineers know how to figure out the answer mathematically but the calculation is too complicated to do easily.

A second type of simulation study is the "game" study, in which people compete in laboratory games to simulate the way they compete in various aspects of real-life competition. Such games have been developed to simulate political relations (Guetzkow); each player might be told that he is a country and that his goal is to make deals with other countries that will get him into the best power position. The researcher then studies what kinds of deals the various countries make under various circumstances. The business games played by students at various business schools are another example. The students are given initial data about their products and the demand for them, their financial resources, and so on. The students then try out various price and marketing strategies to increase their shares of the market and their profits, usually at the expense of their competitors. Such business games might be considered a very complicated form of Monopoly in which

2. H. Guetzkow contains a variety of articles on aspects of simulation, a general bibliography (pp. 191–193), and bibliographies at the ends of individual articles. The article by R. Dawson offers a somewhat different scheme of classifying simulation studies than follows here.

the players have much more control of what happens and much less is left to chance and a roll of the dice. In the case of Monopoly, the purpose of the simulation might be to determine whether at game's end it is usual for one player to have all the wealth or whether the result is a standoff. The hallmark of this type of simulation experiment is that *people interact in the experiment,* usually in competition with one another.

Recently economists have also begun to use some mock-experimental evidence. To gain insight into the way that competing businessmen behave, games have been set up with the players in simulated business situations, and then their behavior has been observed (V. Smith). Games are also used by sociologists to find out how people in small groups interact with one another under various types of circumstances, under stress for example.

A third type of simulation experiment is like the second, except that it is not played with real people but with a computer. The computer is given data about how each unit in the game is likely to act under various conditions, and then the whole thing is set into motion to see where it will come out. The most ambitious simulation of this type is that of G. Orcutt, *et al.,* in which data are put in about how the various units of the economy and society—for example, households and banks—are likely to buy, sell, and perform financial operations. Also put in are the relationships of these groups with one another. Then some starting "shock" is given to the system; for example, the banks are suddenly forced to raise interest rates. The computer then runs through the situations and interactions over and over again very rapidly, so that the researchers can see how things come out at the end of a long series of such situations.

An example of this third type of simulation would occur if the computer were programed for the probabilities of how people would act in various Monopoly situations and then the game were played many times automatically by the computer to determine the outcomes.

This third type of simulation holds great promise for the future. But the value of the results of a simulation depends entirely upon the quality of the input data and relationships.

A simulation's main advantage is the obvious one: the simulation can be done when the real-life conditions cannot be experimented with. A simulation's grave danger also is obvious: the simulation may not resemble the real-life situation in one or more key elements. In the example of the economist's market experiment, one must ask: does the game resemble real life? Do the players act the way people in real-life situations act? Each person who examines the evidence must decide for himself how realistic that particular situation is.

One difficulty in making the simulation realistic is giving the players motivations similar to those experienced in the real-life situations. For example, can a player who is told to play the role of the president of General Motors or the Chief of Staff of the Armed Forces, with billions of dollars or millions of lives at stake, reproduce the same motivations and feelings when playing for pennies or tin soldiers in a lab? Can a person who is given a blindfold and told to play the role of a blind person simulate the feelings of a person who is really blind and who cannot take off a blindfold at the end of the day? Another difficulty in making a simulation realistic arises from the complexity of certain social situations. For example, how can the experiments simulate the conditions of bureaucratic complexity, or the complications of a real man-woman sexual relationship?

One may try to validate the simulation by comparing the results against other sorts of research. For example, if animal experiments with cigarette smoking jibe with non-experimental survey data on humans' smoking, then both results are strengthened. In the case of computer experiments with households and banks, it is difficult to find other data to compare with. In such a case, it is helpful to check the accuracy of the input data about the behavior of the various units and about their relationships. "GIGO: Garbage In, Garbage Out." The input data must first be developed by the classical methods of empirical science—survey and experiment—before a simulation has anything to work with.

In some cases—such as a simulation of competition among two competing organizations (Simon, Puig, and Aschoff)—information neither on other studies nor the input variable may be available. In that case, the only validation method may be to check that the results make sense internally, and that they jibe with theory and general experience.

7. Summary

This chapter describes some methods of getting knowledge other than by traditional experiments and surveys.

If the premises are sound, deductive reasoning can be more accurate than empirical research. But often a scintillating chain of reasoning can be founded on incorrect premises.

Expert opinion can be useful if the experts really know a lot about the topic. But scientific research tackles subjects about which expert knowledge is insufficient.

The case study provides an indispensable overview of a subject when little is known about it. It is generally not a substitute for more formal kinds of research, or vice versa.

Participant-observation can provide rich data on social interrelations. But it cannot be replicated well, and its success depends upon the personal skill of the participant-observer.

Content analysis is a systematic method for measuring attitudes and opinions from written and spoken language. The words and phrases are coded by category of interest.

A simulation can be a laboratory experiment, a gaming study, an experiment with a computer, or any other sort of manipulation of a model. The value of the simulation depends upon the realism of the inputs.

EXERCISES

1. Give examples from your field in which these methods might be useful:
   a. deductive reasoning
   b. expert opinion
   c. case study
   d. content analysis
   e. simulation
2. Give an example in which expert opinion can be gathered in such a way that the study is *replicable* and therefore public and checkable by others.
3. Give examples from your field in which methods a to e in Exercise 1 were used but were *bad* choices.
4. Design a simulation within which you could observe the increasing division of labor and the emergence of "specialists" as the game progresses.
5. Design a simulation that could throw light on how the severity and the surety of punishment influences "white-collar" business crimes.

ADDITIONAL READING FOR CHAPTER 14

Gee (Chapter 7) covers the case study thoroughly and provides many useful references.

On content analysis, Berelson is an excellent general source and contains a comprehensive bibliography of earlier studies. Also see I. De Sola Pool.

The volume of literature on participant observation is enormous. Participant observation and related methods are treated very well in Denzin, especially in Chapters 9 and 10.

Other useful works on participant observation are McCall and Simmons, and Bogdan and Taylor. A readable description of his own adventures and those of other investigators, both in the U.S. and in Latin American contexts, is that of Glazer.

Anthropologists give you the lowdown on participant observation, together with plenty of examples, in Frelich's book. Note especially his introduction. A no nonsense description of *Field Methods in the Study of Culture* is by Williams.

15 classifying, measuring, and scaling

Classification and measurement as types of *research problems* were discussed in Chapter 4; that is, classification and measurement were discussed as *goals in themselves* in some research situations. In research that seeks causal or noncausal relationships and in purely descriptive research, however, classification and measurement are the *means* by which the research proceeds.

Once the variables are chosen for any piece of research, the researcher must decide how to separate the variables into different values; that is, she must "scale" the variables. If she scales a variable *qualitatively*, that is, without numerical relationships, then she is *classifying* the categories of the variable. If she scales a value *quantitatively*, that is, if there are numerical relationships among the categories, then the variable will be a *measurement* scale. Examples to illustrate this distinction will be found later in this chapter.

Three important issues are common to both classifying and measuring: first, choosing the *dimensions* to scale or measure (practically synonymous with choosing variables); second, deciding *which categories* to use in the scales or which *type* of scale; and third, *defining* the categories and drawing their boundary lines. Each of these issues is discussed in the chapter. The topic of scaling human responses is discussed in the next chapter.

1. Classifying

This chapter is about *how* to classify and measure and not about the *nature* of classification. Nevertheless, it is worth devoting a very few words to the nature of the process.

When you classify a group of people or a set of objects, you are putting people into a set of pigeon-hole categories that have different names.[1] The names of the categories have no special scientific significance, though the names may be chosen for convenience; for example, C. Linneaus' two-name system for plants, replacing long and unwieldy names, was convenient and perhaps aided biologists' imaginations in understanding new connections among categories, though the names have no *intrinsic* meaning.

When you place a group of people in a single category, you are asserting that everyone in that category will be treated as similar and that people in different categories will be treated differently in the course of your study. When you classify people by nationality, you will, in your subsequent use of the data, treat all Americans as the same but as different from Chileans, Taiwanese, and other groups. These statements of similarity and difference are only a device to help you to handle the data scientifically, of course, and they say nothing about whether people are "really" equal or unequal, morally or otherwise.

Coding different things or people into the same category inevitably loses some of the information you have about them: Categorization is like converting a color photograph into black and white.

For example, you may have collected some open-ended (unstructured) interviews about people's feelings toward racial integration. In order to handle the data more easily, you might classify (code) each interviewee as either "for" or "against" integration. You thereby lose all the shadings of opinion voiced by the subjects and all the richness and variety of their comments. But, unless you classify the subjects in *some* manner, you will not be able to summarize the data or manipulate them in other objective ways. (Of course, it is possible to classify on *several* dimensions at the same time, so that some more information can be saved and used simultaneously.)

Loss of individuality in observations grouped together in categories is the basis for a persistent attack on science. People say "How can you treat a moderate and a radical as if they were exactly the same in your survey?" or "Why do you lump together wholesalers in Vermont and wholesalers in Louisiana when they serve very different markets?" The real question, however, is not whether the items that you lump together are different in some ways, but rather whether they are similar *for your purposes*. If they are, your classification is perfectly satisfactory. As noted earlier, the same

1. The pigeonholes can also be given identification *numbers* like the numbers on football players or railroad cars. But those numbers usually have little real significance, a point I shall touch on again in the section on measuring.

antidote is appropriate for a child who swallows cleaning fluid in Vermont or in Louisiana.

Sound classification (typology) is a difficult art, as A. Kroeber tells us about the couvade phenomenon:

> The couvade is a custom formerly attributed to the Basques of the Pyrenees, under which on the birth of a child the mother got up and resumed her household duties, while the father went to bed in state and lay in. This piquant habit attracted even more interest when it was found that a good many primitive and backward peoples did more or less the same thing in South America, in Africa, in India and China. These all believed the child would suffer if they did not observe the custom. However, most of them did not go quite as far as the Basques are said to have done: the father lay in, but so did the mother. Cessation from labor by both parents was demanded for the child's health. In still other tribes, both parents refrained from work and certain foods, but the mother refrained more strictly and longer than the father. Among others, the mother alone was under restrictions. And finally, among the southern Ute, where the mother lies still on a bed of hot ashes for thirty days, the father lies with her only for four, and then, after a good meal, must run and hunt as actively as possible for one or several days.
>
> With all this gradation, what constitutes the couvade typologically? The most that it would be possible to give as a definition is: the participation of the father in the period of rest and recuperation that is physiologically natural for the mother after childbirth. In other words, the idea is expressed that it is his child too. Superimposed on this is an endless variety of things prohibited and things required, for the good of the child or for the good of the parents, for a few days or for a full month. And above all, there is every intergradation from the father's sole role, through a joint one, to the mother's alone. No wonder ethnographers have come to talk about "classical couvade," "semicouvade," "pseudo-couvade," and the like, without being able to define the couvade forms so that all specific tribal customs fall unqualifiedly into one or the other class. In short, we have no satisfactory typology for the couvade. Hence in a comparative study we would sometimes be comparing part-comparables, perhaps even noncomparables. The common factor is the name, plus a vague and extremely plastic concept. An exhaustive monograph on the couvade would be almost as near to a train of related but free associations as to a scientific treatise.
>
> The question of whether the couvade has been diffused from a single origin or has had several independent origins can therefore not be answered at present. It is not yet a scientific problem, because the couvade is not a definable recurrent phenomenon. (Kroeber, pp. 542–543)

a. CHOICE OF DIMENSIONS FOR A CLASSIFICATION SCHEME

The dimensions for the classification scheme should be chosen to *fit one's purpose.* You should choose a dimension (variable) for your study that you believe is either of interest in itself or is likely to be helpful in understanding another variable. For example, the U.S. Bureau of Labor Statistics wants to know the situation of labor in the economy. It therefore designates employment-unemployment as a dimension on which it is useful to classify people. When B.L.S. finds out how many people are in each of the categories "employed" and "unemployed," it has developed valuable information for its purposes.

A social psychologist might choose the dimension of employment for entirely different reasons—to help *explain* crimes of violence, perhaps. Counting how many people convicted of crimes of violence were in the categories "employed" and "unemployed" might help to explain why crimes of violence occur or help to predict when and where crimes of violence will take place.

If you are studying only an Amish community in Pennsylvania, the religion dimension will not be useful as a classification. (But Amishness will be a *parameter* of your study.) In most sociological studies in the United States, you *would* use a Protestant-Catholic-Jew dimension. On the other hand, in most countries of the world, you would need additional categories for a religion dimension. And, of course, in many types of studies—of nutrition, say—religion may not be a useful dimension at all. (It might be, though, that an investigator would notice that religion does, indeed, make a difference in the food intake of people. He might then decide to include it in his classification.)

There is no metaphysical all-purpose classification for everything in the world, though some philosophers have spent their lives trying to create one. An illustration of the variety of classification schemes for different purposes is the fact that different types of libraries find different classification schemes best for their various purposes.

F. Machlup provides an example and a discussion of the rationale of economic classification when discussing oligopoly (competition among a small number of firms):

> Hardly any generalizations could be made about the "economic consequences of oligopoly" or about the "causes of oligopoly" unless we first separate different types or kinds of oligopoly. In other words, a classification of oligopoly is needed.

> Of course, an indefinite number of features or conditions could be named as conceivable bases for classification. The problem arises what to select in order to obtain a classification useful for purposes of economic analysis. Distinctions should be made wherever one finds differences suspected of "making a difference" sufficiently important within the chosen frame of reference. It is probably generally agreed that selling prices, output volumes, selling efforts, product qualities are among the major variables considered relevant for our purposes. Hence, the distinctions made in a classification of oligopoly may relate to differences likely to affect these major variables. It will also be agreed that the question of the sources of monopoly power and of the conditions responsible for oligopolistic situations is significant. Hence, a classification may be based on distinctions of the causes of oligopoly. . . .

[N]o single classification [of oligopoly] could possibly serve all purposes. Cross-classification may sometimes be helpful, although the number of possible combinations might become overwhelming. On the other hand, a problem under investigation may be aided by one classification while others are irrelevant. For example, those interested in public policy formation may find it important to know whether an existing big-firm oligopoly is based on definite real-cost advantages or rather on the exploitation of institutional privileges or on the use of coercive or oppressive practices. But they may not in the least be interested in the symmetry or asymmetry of the leadership aspirations of the firms in question. A cross-classification according to leadership and collusion, however, may be significant. For there may be important differences in the effects of collusion without leadership, leadership without (a high degree of) collusion, and collusion enforced by leadership. (Machlup, 1951–1952, p. 160)

More than one dimension is necessary if more than one dimension helps to distinguish various groups or to predict their behavior. But there is no use in having two dimensions if both classify all occurrences in the same way. For example, if all candidates for the baseball team who throw hard *also* throw far and vice versa, either throwing hard or throwing far will be sufficient.

Constructing an appropriate classification scheme is not as simple as it seems, and it requires imagination. A textbook, for example, is largely a classification of knowledge in a particular field. For example, a feature of this book is the classification of obstacles to research in Chapters 18–24.

Dimensions (variables) may be previously chosen by theory or by the direction of your interest, as we have discussed in previous sections on the choices of variables and proxies. But dimensions may also be selected by trial and error, especially in classification research in which the classification scheme is itself the goal of the research.

One usually constructs an empirical classification with several sequences of trial and error, followed by examination of how well the classification works. For example, think how you have arranged the books on your bookshelf. On an *ad hoc* basis, you have placed those books together that seem to *belong* together. You may have begun with some *a priori* elements in the scheme like separation of natural sciences, social sciences, and humanities. But beyond that you probably had no special scheme in mind, and you shuffled and rearranged until the arrangement seemed to make sense. Later on, as you lived with the classification, you may have changed the arrangement as you noticed that some books were used at the same time or that you could find some books more easily if they were nearer psychology than sociology, for example.[2]

2. It is an interesting reflection of U.S. national character that, unlike most other library classification schemes, the Library of Congress system is entirely without theory and is based solely on the pragmatic judgment of which books will be likely to be *used* together. This totally empirical approach may well be the most successful way to deal with the insoluble problem in library classification: that books can be arranged *physically* on only one dimension, even though a *logical* classification would require many dimensions.

Much the same process seems to work for the organization of a college course, book, or paper. My own practice is to write down the various ideas and facts on index cards, along with titles for major sections, and then to spread them on a big table. Then I pick them up and place them in that order that seems to make most sense. The classification seems to evolve satisfactorily in this manner, even though I cannot formulate satisfactory criteria at first.

Some researchers try to play it safe by collecting information on every conceivable dimension. By being supercautious, however, one may spend far more time and money than the information that he *really* wants should cost. The wisest researcher will collect data on those dimensions that she thinks are quite likely to be useful, plus all those dimensions that might conceivably be of use and that she can collect with *very little extra cost*. This selection requires delicate judgment.

b. CHOICE OF CATEGORIES FOR CLASSIFICATION SCALES

Once you decide that you want to employ people's use of umbrellas as your proxy for whether it is raining, your decision about *which categories* to use for this dimension would seem to be an open-and-shut case. But what about "no umbrella"? The answer must depend upon your purpose.

Some of the choosing of categories can be done *after* the data are collected; you can still decide to group several categories together in fewer categories. But the crucial classification work takes place at the design stage. For example, you must decide whether to include the category of "partially employed," in addition to "employed" and "unemployed," and whether to code all subjects into one or the other major category. You must decide whether to classify countries as "highly developed" and "underdeveloped" on the basis of per capita income, to add intermediate categories, or simply to use the continuous variable of per capita income. How sensibly you choose the categories and the dividing lines will determine how useful the variable will be to you. (The next section discusses how to draw the dividing lines and to define the categories.) When constructing a classification scheme, you must be very flexible in accepting new categories (and dimensions) and throwing away existing categories (and dimensions).

The color categories used in various cultures illustrate the effect that one's purposes have upon one's choices of categories.

> Manus children . . . say "yellow, olive-green, blue-green, gray, and lavender as variants of one color"; and while the Ashanti have distinct names for black, red and white, black is applied to any dark color—brown, blue, purple, etc.—while red includes what we differentiate as pink, orange and yellow. (Hallowell, p. 349)

And the Eskimos have many different categories within which to classify ice, whereas to us in the United States all ice is just ice.

If the categories are expressed in words, the scaled variable is often called "qualitative" or "discontinuous." But it is possible to go from words to numbers or vice versa, though the process is not symmetrical. For example, if you have the heights of the people in your sample in feet and inches, you can arbitrarily choose to call everyone over 5 feet 10 inches "tall" and everyone under that height "short." In this way you have converted "quantitative" data into "qualitative" verbal categories. The numerical cut-off points for the categories should be those that are most useful for you. The New York police force establishes a cut-off height of 5 feet 8 inches for policemen because it believes that 5 feet 8 inches is a better cut-off point for its purposes than 6 feet or 5 feet 3 inches, taking into account its need for tall policemen as well as the potential supply of candidates for the job.

Sometimes it is helpful to think of each possible numerical measurement as a category in itself. At first, it seems that there is an infinite number of numerical categories, because, for example, the heights of any two people will differ by at least some infinitesimal amount and no two are exactly the same. But, when you record the heights, you must record in feet and inches, which means that anyone between 5 feet and 6 feet tall can fall into only one of twelve categories at most. Of course, if you used a finer scale—calibrated in sixteenths of an inch, perhaps—there would then be more and smaller categories. But there will always be *some* limit on how small the categories can get, for your measuring instrument will cease to distinguish at *some* degree of fineness; there must always be some point at which the categories are discrete and not continuous.[3] (Notice that it is the *categories* that are discrete, *not* the people's *heights*. It does not make much sense to discuss whether people's heights are continuous or discontinuous, for the argument could be decided only by measurement, which *must* be discontinuous.)

Conversely, it is possible to go from verbal categories to numerical categories. If you have data on people's reactions to a political event, you can designate "like" as "3," "neutral" as "2," and "dislike" as "1." This technique is handy for many purposes, and it must be used whenever you transfer your data to cards or magnetic tape for automatic data processing. But you *must* remember that, just because you have designated "like" as "3" and "dislike" as "1," it does not mean that "like" is three times as great as "dislike," that three "dislikes" equal one "like," or that "like" is as far above "neutral" as "neutral" is above "dislike." You could have picked *any* num-

3. As O. Morgenstern forcefully points out, measurement that is too fine runs the great danger of deluding people into thinking that the data are much more accurate than they really are. Morgenstern quotes N. Wiener that "economics is a one or two digit science," which implies that any numbers that do not round off to one or two digits are misleading (Morgenstern, p. 116). An example is the history of the 1929 potato crop statistic: "First it was raised 2 million bushels, then lowered 30 million, then lowered another million, then boosted 5 million, and recently raised another million. It now stands at 333,392,000. Disregarding the O's, the only digit remaining of the six given in the original estimate is the first, the figure 3!"

bers—"01," "07," and "44," for example, instead of "1," "2," and "3." Unless *you* have decided beforehand, on the basis of some other evidence, that the categories bear some special numerical relationship to one another, you cannot assume any numerical relationship among them. But, if you do decide that two "likes" shall equal one "neutral," then you *can* add them and subtract them at will. Remember, though, that the final answer is dependent upon the numbers that *you* assigned. (Inexperienced or cynical researchers sometimes fool themselves or others by rigging the numbers that they assign so that the outcome is what they want it to be. The Olympic Games provide a lovely example. The United States [unofficially] wants to count 5-3-1 for first, second, and third places; by that scorekeeping it beats the Soviet Union. The Soviet Union counts points 3-2-1 instead, and with that system *it* wins. Who is right? Nobody can be called "right" until we have other reasons to help us judge which system of counting makes more sense.)

C. DEFINING THE CATEGORIES IN A CLASSIFICATION SCALE

After you choose dimensions and categories, you must operationally define the categories. For example, once you have decided that the proportion of umbrellas in use will be your measure of the extent to which it is raining, you must decide whether parasols count as umbrellas. And will a newspaper over the head be counted as an umbrella? Is an open umbrella carried over the shoulder to be counted as an open umbrella?

You must define your categories so that most of your observations will fit into one or another category without too much doubt or arbitrariness in the process. The classification of humans by sex has the useful property that it is easy to designate most human beings as man or woman, though there will be some exceptions who are not easily classifiable.

Different definitions of "employed" and "unemployed" cause argument and confusion. For example, the National Industrial Conference Board estimated unemployment for November 1935 at 9,177,000, whereas the Labor Research Association estimated it at 17,029,000. This enormous difference came from the definition of "unemployed"; the Labor Research Association included farm unemployment and unemployment among professionals, whereas the N.I.C.B. did not. Also for 1935, the U.S. Chamber of Commerce estimated unemployment at a snappy 4 million, but sampling techniques may help to explain this low estimate (J. Cohen, p. 664). In 1949, Soviet official Georgi Malenkov could still estimate United States unemployment at 14 million—using good American data—whereas the U.S. Bureau of the Census was estimating only 4 million unemployed. Malenkov simply classified as "unemployed" anyone who worked "less than full time" (Wallis & Roberts, 1962, pp. 90–91).

Crime statistics sometimes take frightening leaps because the classification scheme has been changed (or because the recording of crimes has been improved). This has also been true of medical statistics; for example, better medical knowledge and practice led to more accurate diagnosis of lung cancer as a cause of death and decreased the number of mistaken diagnoses of tuberculosis and other diseases (U.S. Public Health Service, pp. 127–141).

Here is the sort of definitional decision that must be made in categorizing employment status: If a woman worked twenty-two hours each week during the last month, should you mark her down as "employed" or "unemployed"? Your first reaction might be that the categories were not well selected and that there should be a category of "partly employed," perhaps. Or you might suggest that people should be categorized separately for 0–10 hours, 11–20, 21–30, and so forth. But for *some* purposes, at least, the simple dichotomous classification "employed-unemployed" is useful, especially as a simple index for laymen to watch in the newspapers. So you must classify the woman who worked twenty-two hours one way or the other. Definitional decisions take up much of an empirical researcher's attention. Only the theorist can blithely ignore their existence.

Another example: Should the work that people do at home be counted as employment? Our usual practice is not to consider housewives as part of the labor force. This decision causes certain problems, as is illustrated by the story of the two Englishwomen who hired each other as houseworkers, then fired each other at the end of six months, in order to collect unemployment benefits.

An example of how a given type of obesity is defined for an obesity classification is given on page 47. Each of the characteristics contained in the definition is itself somewhat ambiguous, of course. But the definition is a success if a consensus of doctors would agree upon a decision to classify a given person in or out of that category.

Defining categories is a progressive process. As tough instances come along, you sit down and relate them to your final purpose and then amend your definitions to cover them. In establishing these criteria the important things to remember are as follows: First, have a *reason* for your decision; second, relate the decision to your ultimate purpose; and, third, refer back to your theory for guidance, if you are working with the aid of a strong theory. You must sometimes also throw in a touch of arbitrary reasoning. There will be some observations, for which you are at a total loss how to decide, and you feel as if you could do as well by flipping a coin. Don't. Make yourself *select* one category or the other; that selection will probably be better than a random decision. Hopefully, however, such near toss-ups form only a small part of your sample.

2. Measuring and Scaling

Most of what is true of classifying is true of measuring, for measurement is a type of classification. (Or, if you prefer, classification may be considered a type of measurement, as we shall see.)

The main difference between classification and measurement is the use of *numbers for computational purposes.* (Numbers can also be used simply as labels for categories, as we shall see in nominal scales. But this is still classification by number; labeling does not take advantage of the important properties of the number system.)

a. THE NATURE OF MEASUREMENT

S. Stevens (p. 25) gives a succinct definition of measurement: "Measurement is the assignment of numerals to events or objects according to rule." This is an important definition and worth pondering. It·emphasizes the centrality of numbers in measurement. And it·directs our attention toward the various rules that we may use in measuring.

A **scale** is the operational rule that one uses in a measurement. It is no coincidence that in English the measurement instrument for length is called a rule-r. Our discussion of measurement is largely a discussion of which sets of rules—scales—are best for which kinds of situations.

There are many difficult philosophical arguments about measuring and scaling. The philosophical position that I shall take is the pragmatic one that whatever helps a researcher get on with the business of producing useful knowledge is sound measurement, and whatever in measurement hinders a researcher or causes a researcher to produce trivial though impressive-looking work is unsound.

In the physical and biological sciences, measurement is largely a matter of finding satisfactory *physical instruments* to measure the phenomenon one is interested in—the amount of oxygen on Mars, the speed of transmission of nerve impulses, the number of defects in an airplane wing.

The electron microscope and the electron telescope arc polar examples of such technological advances. But instruments also can help in the social sciences. For example, because psychologists wanted to measure how active animals are under various conditions, they developed running wheels and treadmills that would automatically measure activity. Similarly, timed quick-exposure projectors make possible well-controlled experiments on learning speeds. And anthropologists measure the age of artifacts with the Carbon-14 technique.

In problems that involve counting, simple arithmetic provides all the necessary scales and categories. But it is sobering to remember that this apparently simple mental machinery was not always with us. The number system probably originated with the desire of cattle owners to know how many cattle they owned and to keep track of their herds or flocks (Dantzig, pp. 20–21). Counting the soldiers in an army was another early problem in cardinal measurement. The early rulers of Madagascar counted their army by marching one man at a time through a narrow mountain pass and dropping one pebble in a pile for each man who passed (Dantzig, p. 28). The inventions of numerals and early mathematics were extraordinary advances.

But even after they existed, the crudeness of scales kept measurement inaccurate, as R. Heilbroner points out:

> . . . [T]he early merchant had to settle his accounts by weight of metal, and when a shekel was equal to so many grains from the middle of an ear of wheat and the carat of gold equal to the weight of a carob bean, there were problems enough to tax the skill of a modern arbitrager. (Heilbroner, p. 42)

Social scientists, also, seek better devices to learn about actual events and behavior. For example, estimating the number of houses in a country can be done by census enumerators, airborne photography, infra-red photography, and so on. Or the student of communications who wants to know which pages of a magazine are read can use fingerprint powder. These "nonreactive" measures are appropriate when we are interested in what is outside of people's minds. But when we are interested in the contents or processes of people's minds, we must ask people to respond (react) to stimuli presented to them. It is the peculiar problems involved in constructing scales to measure the contents of people's minds that make scaling an important special topic in social science.

FIGURE 15.1

Source: © 1976/1969 by the New York Times Company. Reprinted by permission.

Please notice that the mere presence of a human being in a scientific measurement situation is not the source of our interest in scaling. If we want to know how hot a room is, and if a person reads a thermometer and records the result, human response is not central; we could replace the person with an automatically read thermometer. But if we ask the person, "How hot do you feel?" under a variety of conditions of temperature and stress, the person's responses are central in our interest. In the latter case we are interested in getting variations in reactions within or among persons as we change conditions, whereas in the former case of thermometer reading we are interested in *avoiding* variations in human responses.

3. Strengths of Scales

This section takes up the various scales according to their "strength" or "power"—both vague words referring to the amount of formal information contained in the scale. Following Stevens, we distinguish four types of scale—nominal, ordinal, interval, and ratio.

a. NOMINAL SCALES

Stevens considers classification to be a type of measurement—a nominal scale—because a number can be assigned to any given classification just as numbers are given to football players or chicken houses. But the numbers then mean no more than do any other names, for instance, "schizophrenia" or "prosperity" or "traditionalism." The number may be useful, but it is unnecessary, and I therefore do not consider classification a type of measurement.

b. ORDINAL SCALES

An *ordinal* scale is exemplified by the street numbers on houses. If I live at 1105 South Busey, you live at 1111, and Bill lives at 1115, we know that you live *between* Bill and me. Notice that this ordinal scale contains *more information* than does classification. If Bill wears 11 on his football jersey, Jim wears 13, and Jack wears 15, you know nothing more about Bill or Jim or Jack than if they wore any other numbers (although their numbers may tell you that all are quarterbacks).

Another ordinal example is the Mohs scale of hardness of minerals. F. Mohs worked out a system by which a given mineral would be rated for hardness *by comparison* with other minerals. Harder stones scratch softer stones, and any given stone is given a rating between a stone it can scratch and one that can scratch it. Note that one stone cannot be said to be twice as hard as some other stone. A stone can be said only to be harder than, softer than, or equal in hardness to another stone. At best, then, stones can only be put in an *order* of hardness, and this sort of scale is therefore called an *ordinal* scale.

Attitude and opinion scales are classic examples of ordinal scales. Here, for example, is an illustration of a brand-attitude scale:

Listed below are several brands of each of two household products. For *EACH* brand place an "X" in the one box which best indicates how much you dislike or like that brand. The more you dislike it, the smaller the number you should give it. The more you like it, the bigger the number you should give it. There are no right or wrong answers. Only your opinion counts.

TABLE 15.1

Products	Dislike Completely 1	Dislike Somewhat 2	Dislike a Little 3	Neither Like Nor Dislike 4	Like a Little 5	Like Somewhat 6	Like Completely 7
Toothpaste							
Brand A	–	–	–	–	–	–	–
Brand B	–	–	–	–	–	–	–
Brand C	–	–	–	–	–	–	–
Scouring cleanser							
Brand D	–	–	–	–	–	–	–
Brand E	–	–	–	–	–	–	–
Brand F	–	–	–	–	–	–	–

(Abrams, p. 193)

A virtue of ordinal scales is that people can often make an accurate judgment about one thing *compared to another*, even when they cannot make an accurate *absolute* judgment. One can often say whether he likes this painting better than that one, even though he cannot say how much he likes either one. To illustrate the accuracy of comparative judgments, you can often tell whether a child has a fever—that is, when the child's temperature is two or three degrees above normal—by touching the child's face to yours and comparing whether her skin is warmer than yours. But you would be hard-put to say whether the temperature outside is 40° or 55° F, or whether a piece of metal is 130° or 150° F.

C. INTERVAL SCALES

An *interval* scale contains even more information than does an ordinal scale. Unless all the lots on the block are the same size, I cannot tell *how far apart* our three houses are by just knowing the house numbers. But if the number on each house represented its *distance* in yards or rods from the bottom of the street, the house numbers would indeed tell us exactly how far apart any two houses are. This type of system is called an *interval scale* because the *interval* between 1 and 2 is equal to the interval between 2 and 3, 3 and 4, or 1105 and 1106. The intervals between numbers on an *ordinal* scale do not have this meaning at all.

d. RATIO SCALES

The example of the house numbers contains an additional kind of information that makes it a *ratio* scale. Ten yards contain twice as many one-yard segments as do five yards, and we can say that the ratio of ten yards to five yards is two to one. We cannot say, however, that 100° F. is *twice as hot* as 50° F., and therefore the Fahrenheit scale is only an interval scale and not a ratio scale. If this statement is not clear to you, reflect on the fact that 50° F. = 10° C. and that 100° F. = 38° C. Very clearly 38° C. is not twice as hot as 10° C. Interval and ratio scales are often known together as *cardinal* scales.

The most common uses of cardinal scales in the social sciences are in *counting*—counting people of various kinds, counting sums of money, counting the number of units of behavior, and so on. For example, H. Ebbinghaus grew dissatisfied with simply classifying people according to *whether* they could remember a given series of nonsense syllables, for he could not then distinguish among *degrees* of memory. Therefore, he tested each subject several times and counted the proportion of times each person correctly remembered the series. Such an approach gave him a cardinal scale to work with (Ebbinghaus, p. 9).

We can illustrate the relationships among these sorts of scales with a single example: You are shown three sculptures. You label them "1," "2," and "3" respectively, thereby creating a nominal scale. You decide that you like #2 better than #3 and #3 better than #1, a nice consistency; your preferences now form an ordinal scale. You decide that you would pay $200 more for #2 than for #3, $100 more for #3 than for #1, and $300 more for #2 than for #1; those willing-to-pay numbers form an interval scale. If you now go one step further and say you're willing to pay $1300 for #2, $1100 for #3, and $1000 for #1, those numbers form a ratio scale. Of course once you have the ratio-scale information in hand you could also go the other way; you could then form an ordinal scale by dropping the dollar figures.

There has been much talk about how one or another sort of scale "requires" or "permits" one or another kind of statistical operation. Such rules do not seem helpful (Guttman, 1971); rather, common sense and basic understanding of what you are trying to do will serve you better than any such rules.

This might be a good place to mention again that measurement is operational definition. To say "stick is long" does not suggest any operation, explicitly or implicitly, and therefore the length of the stick is not well defined and has not been measured. But to say "stick same length my arm" or "stick longer my arm" or "stick two times long my arm" is to state implicitly that the relevant operation is a comparison of the stick with my arm; and, when someone has performed the operation of that comparison, he can know exactly what length of stick you are talking about. "A man's arm" may be a somewhat ambiguous measure, and that is why we have the platinum-iridium meter stick in the U.S. Bureau of Standards, where it is kept at a carefully regulated temperature, so that we have an almost-perfect ultimate standard against which we can measure things.

4. Summary

Classification and measurement are crucial technical operations in research procedure. The theorist can and does ignore these operations, but the excellence of empirical work depends upon one's skill in carrying them out.

With classifications and measurements we make distinctions and we order our knowledge systematically. These operations are fundamental in science.

First one must decide which dimension of the phenomena one wishes to classify or measure. Then one must decide which categories or measurement system to use. Finally one must decide how to classify the phenomena into categories or how to make the measurement. The basic rule for all these research decisions is that they should be made with regard to one's underlying purpose in conducting the research.

EXERCISES

1. Show how information is lost when classifying observations in some research study.
2. Give two research examples in which the subject's sex is an important dimension for classification and two examples in which it is not.
3. For what purpose might it be enough to have two categories of political party in the United States, and for what purposes might more categories be necessary?
4. Give an example from research in your field in which definition of categories presents a major difficulty.
5. Show an example of use in your field of each of the following:
   a. an ordinal scale
   b. an interval scale
   c. a ratio scale

ADDITIONAL READING FOR CHAPTER 15

For excellent discussions of the philosophy of measurement see Stevens, from whom I draw some examples; Kaplan, pp. 171–198; and Coombs.

On the problems and methods of measurement, see Selltiz *et al.* (Chapter 6).

Kerlinger (Chapter 25), 2d ed., treats measurement from the psychologist's point of view.

16 scaling human responses

The term *scale* is one of the most confusing in social science, because of the many ways it is used. Some discussion of "scale" and related terms and concepts is therefore in order.

First let us distinguish *dimension* and *scale*. The concept of **dimension** belongs to the realm of theory. It refers to an aspect or *characteristic* of the phenomenon that you are interested in; for example, happiness or intelligence or productivity. The terms *dimension* and *theoretical component* are often used synonymously.

An *indicator*, or *empirical variable*, is an empirical tool—a proxy for the theoretical dimension—used to capture and represent a theoretical dimension. For example, one question, in a series of questions, about a person's self-judgment of the person's happiness might constitute an operational proxy for happiness. Or one might use the suicide rate as a proxy for the relative happiness of given groups of people. The term "scale" is frequently used as a synonym for *indicator* or *proxy*.

The term "scale" is most frequently used in social science to refer to measurements that involve *judgment*, or *subjective ratings*. The judgment may enter in the process of scaling itself, as when an expert is asked to rate (scale) a group of teachers. Or the judgment may arise when the researcher identifies the scale with the dimension of interest; for example, when the researcher employs a questionnaire to measure happiness. The same sort of judgment is used when the researcher uses the suicide rate as a proxy for happiness, but because suicide data involve less judgment (by the social scientist; the coroner may use a lot of judgment), it is less likely to be called a scale. Physical measuring instruments are seldom called scales in social science, because they involve little judgment.

If the indicator contains several elements—for example, a happiness scale consisting of several related questions—each question is called an *item*. Each item may be thought of as an ordinary variable, and a scale can be composed of two or more simple variables; for example, a baseball player's ability may be scaled based on one point for running ability, one point for throwing ability, and two points for hitting strength.

One of the important roles of scaling procedure is to determine whether two or more measurement scales are measuring the same dimension or are tapping different dimensions; one may use the Guttman-scale procedure (beyond our scope here) or factor analysis (also an advanced topic) for this purpose. This leads into multidimensional scaling, in which responses to several dimensions are measured at once; for example, where a set of questions measure how favorable or unfavorable, how strong or weak, and how active or passive people judge a given stimulus.

Scales to measure human responses come in a bewildering number of varieties. Sorting them according to some important characteristics helps bring some order to the chaos. I shall discuss scales according to these characteristics, and in this order: the type of mental activity the scale is intended to measure; whether you are interested in variations within individuals or differences among individuals; the mathematical strength of the scale (discussed in the previous chapter); and whether the scale is simple or composite.

1. Types of Mental Activity to Be Measured

Let us distinguish these types of mental activity that one may wish to measure: how a person *perceives* a stimulus; what a person knows or thinks about a factual state of affairs (*cognition*); how a person *intends to behave;* what a person's *values, preferences, and attitudes* are; and the extent of a person's *mental capacities.*

a. SCALES THAT MEASURE PERCEPTION

The psychophysicists took the lead in scaling human responses when they began work on how different stimuli are perceived by a person. For example, how is a person's capacity to discriminate between two tones affected by the loudness of the sound? The scales that were invented in the nineteenth century by Weber, Fechner, and others are still in use today for a variety of purposes.

One basic scale of perception, Weber's, repeatedly presents two stimuli to the observer and measures the proportion of the trials in which the person can correctly identify the stimuli. For example, we may present a sound of a given loudness to the subject and then present a series of sounds of other loudnesses (and also the reference sound at appropriate intervals). After each test sound we ask the subject whether it is louder or softer than the reference sound. Then for each test sound's loudness we compute the proportion of trials that the subject got right. The difference between reference and test sounds that is large enough to produce some given proportion of correct responses—say, 75 per cent, because 50 per cent correct is expected purely by chance—is called the "just noticeable difference." The proportions correct for the various loudness differences is a scale that measures accuracy of perception as a function of the differences.

In Fechner's procedure, people are asked to give a number that represents the relative strength of each test stimulus compared to the reference stimulus, e.g., three times as bright, a fourth as bright, and so on. That is, Fechner's procedure works with the relative sizes of individual stimuli rather than with the differences between test stimuli and the reference stimulus, as in Weber's procedure.

b. SCALES THAT MEASURE KNOWLEDGE

Scales to measure cognition (knowledge) are straightforward: One asks the subject, "How many people would you guess live in China?" The resulting data can be compared to the actual figure, and then the distribution of answers can be plotted among individuals.

Tests that measure learning in school are knowledge scales. There are many difficult problems in constructing satisfactory tests of learning, but because they are so special to education we shall not pursue them here.

c. SCALES THAT MEASURE INTENTIONS

Scales that measure intentions are of great importance to all research that aims to change people's behavior. An example is applied research into the effects of marketing variables, such as advertising and price, upon people's purchases; intentions to purchase consumer durables are used as a reasonably close proxy for actual future purchases, both by commercial firms, and by economic analysts when forecasting the near future of the national economy.

Sometimes simple questions about what people intend to do—"Will you buy a car with an airbag?"—can obtain accurate answers directly. In other situations people cannot or will not tell accurately what they will do. If so, one may (a) use composite scales that contain several relevant questions which work from various points of view, to study both the pattern and the number of responses saying "yes" and "no" (more about composite questions later); or (b) substitute other sorts of scales for the intention scale; attitude and preference scales are frequent substitutes, which will be discussed later.

d. SCALES THAT MEASURE INTEREST, ATTITUDES, AND VALUES

Many kinds of research seek to measure whether people respond to particular objects or people negatively or positively. And scaling people's tendencies is usually quite difficult because people have trouble in expressing these tendencies, or are reluctant to do so. Prejudice research is an example; it is hard for any of us to really know our own attitudes toward other racial and religious groups, and we are often reluctant to tell other people about such attitudes.

Attitude research is often used as a lazy man's substitute for intentions research, as when attitudes toward political candidates are used as a proxy for voting intentions, and when attitudes toward or interest in a particular product or brand are used as a proxy for future purchasing behavior. Attitude research at first seems easier to do than intentions research, and hence it is vastly overused.

Evaluative attitude scales usually work on one of the following principles: After presenting the subject with an object or person or concept for the subject's consideration, the subject may be asked: (1) to choose one or more among a set of words to describe the object; (2) to grade the object, numerically or graphically or within a set of categories, as to how well a given word (e.g., "like," "pretty," "nasty," "sweet," "charming," "offensive") represents the subject's attitudes; or (3) to select where, between two opposites (e.g., "approve" and "disapprove"), the subject rates the object. The latter two scales are called "unipolar" and "bipolar," respectively.

e. SCALES OF MENTAL CAPACITY

I.Q. and other tests of mental capacity involve challenging problems of measurement and scaling. Which test items indicate the ability you wish to measure? Which set of items taken together makes up a useful mental scale? In which order should the items be given? Which items stand for which abilities? These issues have led to a large and important body of scaling knowledge called psychometrics, which is too specialized to pursue here.

2. Stimulus and Response Scales

Research can focus on one or another of the elements of the stimulus-response relationship.

a. STIMULUS-ORIENTED SCALES

Psychophysical research focuses on how differences among graded stimuli affect the respondent. The experimenter may present a variety of sounds to a single subject to determine how differences in stimulus intensity are perceived. That is, in stimulus-oriented scaling the researcher is interested in differences among responses *by the same subject to variation among stimuli*.

Stimulus-oriented scaling is found in fields other than psychophysics, too.

Ebbinghaus was interested in the effects of variations in nonsense-syllable presentations upon the learning of particular subjects (and he used only one subject—himself). Or, a sociologist might be interested in which aspects of blacks trigger prejudice by representative whites.

Because the stimulus is under the researcher's control, it can be presented in quantitatively-graded fashion, and quantitatively-graded responses can be obtained, e.g., the proportion of trials in which a subject correctly distinguishes a weight of 1.0 pound from a weight of 1.05 pounds.

b. RESPONSE-ORIENTED SCALES

Some research aims to find how various responses to the *same* stimuli are distributed among a group of people. For example, what proportion of the public wants the town to float a bond issue to improve the schools? What proportions within the groups of Catholics, Protestants, and Jews believe that blacks are naturally superior to whites in athletics? Which segments of the public will be quickest to buy a new health food? Is there a difference among racial groups in ability to distinguish sound intensity? This is research that studies similarities and differences among people and their responses, rather than similarities and differences among stimulus objects and situations.

3. Simple Composite Scales

Scales can consist of a simple item—for example, asking about which tone is louder, which chocolate is preferred, in which order one ranks racial groups by liking, and which candidates one intends to vote for.

Simple single-item scales may not provide sufficient information, however. Therefore one may employ a multi-item composite scale. From such a composite scale one may obtain (a) more accuracy, (b) gradations of intensity, and (c) information on several dimensions of the stimulus or response.

Much of our knowledge about scaling concerns how one may combine items into meaningful composite scales. For example, a one-item I.Q. test cannot give gradations finer than pass-fail. But a ten-item test could permit categorization into ten I.Q. groups, if the test is constructed so that the items are perfectly ordered from easy to hard; that is, if no person would answer a "hard" question correctly after missing an "easier" question. No such perfect I.Q. test scale can be developed, of course, but with a hundred well-chosen questions one may obtain rather fine gradations.

Among the most important composite attitude scaling techniques are those of Guttman, Thurstone, Likert, and Osgood (the semantic differential). All seem complicated upon first acquaintance. But it is their basic principles and not their complex details that are important. You should fight against becoming bewitched by their formal machinery. A complex composite technique can produce useful knowledge only if its basic principle is sound for the particular situation.

a. SUMMED SCALES

The simplest type of composite scale presents several items to the respondent and considers a sum of the responses to the items to be the scale score. Likert scales, which present statements with five possible responses from "strongly approve" to "strongly disapprove," are commonly used in summed scales with numbers attached ranging from, say, $+2$ to -2. The score is the simple sum.

Choosing items sensibly to make up a summed composite scale is critical, of course; the choice can be made with unaided judgment, or a panel of expert judges can be used, or consistency checks can be made on pretest results of a variety of possible items. The Guttman Scalogram is a method for investigating whether the items make up a *cumulative* scale; that is, whether the questions are arranged so that a person who, say, answers "no" to Question Four after answering "yes" to Question 3 will also answer "no" to all questions after Question Four. The underlying idea in the scalogram is to arrange the items in order of their "strengths" so that the step at which the respondent changes from one answer to the other is an index of the degree of the person's attitude.

Sometimes the most effective—and always the simplest—way to handle a set of scale items is to examine which *single* item best predicts the behavior you are interested in, and then to work with this single item alone.

Factor analysis is a statistical device for finding several sets ("factors") of items for which there is high similarity in prediction among items *within* a composite factor, and low similarity in prediction *among the factors*. Some factor analysts have thought that factor analysis is a way of "uncovering fundamental entities" within the human personality, but this claim need not detain us now. For our purposes here, factor analysis is a "sophisticated" device for developing composite scales. Its main danger arises from its "sophistication"; because of the complexity of the method, simple procedural errors are not obvious even when gross, and may pass unnoticed. Another danger is that you may become so entranced with the mathematical possibilities of factor analysis that you forget your original purpose.

4. Choice of Scales

There are numerous types of scales for the study of attitudes, opinions, beliefs, and other mental states. They range from *ad hoc* scales made up specially for single purposes to generalized instruments like the semantic differential, which is a system of many interrelated scales of this sort:

Good———Bad

These interrelated scales have been tested in many types of work, and many of its general properties are known.

Which scale, containing which categories, is best depends wholly on the purpose of the study and the general situation. Consider, for example, the following three scales, all of which were compared (along with the scale shown on page 231) to see which would best relate to women's actual purchasing behavior. Typically, J. Abrams found that *each* of the four scales did best in *some* respect.

Listed below are several brands of each of two household products. For *EACH* brand place an "X" in the one box which best indicates how much you dislike or like that brand. The more you dislike it, the bigger the minus number you should give it. The more you like it, the bigger the plus number you should give it. If you neither dislike nor like it, place your "X" in the 0 (zero) box. There are no right or wrong answers. Only your opinion counts.

Products	Definitely Dislike					Neutral					Definitely Like
	−5	−4	−3	−2	−1	0	+1	+2	+3	+4	+5
Toothpaste											
Brand A	−	−	−	−	−	−	−	−	−	−	−
Brand B	−	−	−	−	−	−	−	−	−	−	−
Brand C	−	−	−	−	−	−	−	−	−	−	−
Scouring cleanser											
Brand D	−	−	−	−	−	−	−	−	−	−	−
Brand E	−	−	−	−	−	−	−	−	−	−	−
Brand F	−	−	−	−	−	−	−	−	−	−	−

Listed below are several brands of each of two household products. For *EACH* brand place an "X" in the one box which best indicates how much you dislike or like that brand. The more you dislike it, the smaller the number you should give it. There are no right or wrong answers. Only your opinion counts.

Definitely Dislike									Definitely Like
1	2	3	4	5	6	7	8	9	10

Listed below are several brands of each of two household products. For *EACH* brand place an "X" in the box that best describes your opinion of that brand. As you'll note, the box on the left represents an unfavorable opinion. The boxes toward the right represent the more favorable opinions. Each box is described for you to help you in expressing your opinion. There are no right or wrong answers. Only your opinion counts.

Below Average	About Average	A Little Better	A Lot Better	One of the Best	None Better

(Abrams, pp. 192–193)

To bewilder you even more, Figure 16.1 provides three other examples of scales that one might use for the scouring cleanser (Green and Tull, p. 180):

FIGURE 16.1

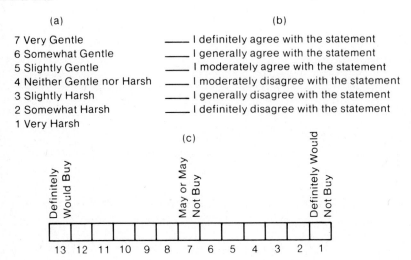

(a)

7 Very Gentle
6 Somewhat Gentle
5 Slightly Gentle
4 Neither Gentle nor Harsh
3 Slightly Harsh
2 Somewhat Harsh
1 Very Harsh

(b)

_____ I definitely agree with the statement
_____ I generally agree with the statement
_____ I moderately agree with the statement
_____ I moderately disagree with the statement
_____ I generally disagree with the statement
_____ I definitely disagree with the statement

(c)

Definitely Would Buy — May or May Not Buy — Definitely Would Not Buy

13 12 11 10 9 8 7 6 5 4 3 2 1

Source: Green, Tull, RESEARCH FOR MARKETING DECISIONS, 3rd. ed., © 1975, p. 180. Adapted by permission of Prentice-Hall, Inc., Englewood Cliffs, New Jersey.

a. SCALE INTERVALS

The intervals on a scale may simply be numbers from 0 to 1, or −5 to +5, or 1 to 10, or any other pair of numbers that serve as poles. The respondent then indicates how far he is from each pole. Poles may be "approve" and "disapprove," "happy" and "unhappy," or whatever. Within the poles numerical intervals can be marked, or there may simply be a line on which the respondent makes a mark.

The intervals on the scale also may be specific categories that seem to form a continuum. An example of a "specific category scale" used to rate white residents of a housing project on their attitudes toward blacks was:

Respect Felt for Blacks in the Project
(Place check at appropriate position on line, or circle X or Y.)

Thinks highly of blacks in project without qualification	Generally respects blacks living in project	Is ambivalent; partly respects, partly feels they are inferior	Generally feels they are inferior	Strongly feels they are inferior
1 2	3 4	5 6	7 8	9

X: Is indifferent to blacks as a group; doesn't think about them.
Y: Doesn't think of blacks as group; considers them as individuals.

(Selltiz *et al.*, p. 404.)

It is desirable that the items in such a specific-category scale be arranged in a reasonable order, and that they measure the same dimension. Various technical methods can help attain those goals; for more information consult a technical work on scaling such as Torgerson, Edwards, or Summers.

One may also try to select categories between which there are *equal-appearing intervals*. This may be approached with the aid of judges and a procedure invented by Thurstone (Thurstone and Chave; Selltiz, *et al.*, p. 414).

Ideally one chooses scales for attitude and opinion surveys by testing alternative scales against actual behavior, as Abrams did with rating scales for household products. In many cases, however, independent testing is impossible, and the researcher must fall back on wisdom and artistry and the advice he can get from other experienced researchers.

But—relax. Don't let the huge number of possible scaling methods paralyze you with fear. The results you get are not likely to be *very* sensitive to which scale you use. And if you try two rather different scales and the results agree, you can feel reassured that you are not likely to be badly in error.

Sometimes the full power of sophisticated complex scaling techniques is necessary and helpful. But such situations are not likely to confront you in your early research work.

5. Summary

Scaling is the term applied to the measurement of human responses to stimuli. Many ingenious scaling methods have been invented to evaluate the individual's response to a variety of related stimuli (psychophysical scaling) and to evaluate the range of responses among a group of people to particular stimuli (attitude measurement). The choice of the appropriate scaling devices requires artistry, good sense, and knowledge of the underlying reality.

Composite scaling devices can help you squeeze information out of data. But the more clear-cut the problem and the better your data, the simpler the techniques you require. And if the data collection was poor in meaning and execution, no amount of fancy techniques will avail.

ADDITIONAL READING FOR CHAPTER 16

An excellent general discussion of scaling is in Selltiz *et al.* (Chapter 12).
Edwards' short book is an excellent text on the special topic of attitude scaling. Summers also provides much useful information about attitude scales.
Torgerson is the classic treatment of scaling from a psychometric point of view, though the book also includes some information on response scales.
On scaling procedures in market research, with special attention given to psychometric techniques, see Green and Tull, 3rd ed. (Chapter 6).

17 data handling, adjusting, and summarizing

Let us pick up the task at the completion of pretesting. Your study design is all set—at least until further modification. Now you must actually collect the data, work them into shape for interpretation, and analyze it. This chapter discusses the process from data collection until you begin the analysis.

1. Data Collection and How to Avoid Disaster

No part of the process of data collection and data handling is safe from human error. Many of the systematic sources of error from observers will be discussed in Chapter 19. But just plain mistakes can creep in anywhere, like the night air. For example, mistakes are made in writing down the data, in transferring them from data sheets to punched cards or tape (human errors though; the machines are nearly fool-proof), labeling the results, and so on.

Unsound decisions about classification and measurement are another major source of error in the data-collection process. Deciding on the exceptional cases and other trivia of the data-collection process is irritating and demanding work.

These decisions about exceptions—many of which occur in the coding of questionnaires, for example—are the soft underbelly of any research project. One of the weakest links in social science is that, when someone reads a published report of a piece of research, he cannot know how wisely or unwisely these decisions have been made. Yet a study can arrive at quite incorrect results if they are made poorly.

The only remedies for the human errors in the data-collection process are eternal vigilance, spot rechecking, checking the data against your intuition, and more checking.

2. Errors in Automatic Data Processing

You should have at least an onlooker's understanding of what computers can do. You should understand how a card or tape serves as a repository of information and how to get information onto and off it. Whether you should program your own work is another question. It may be most efficient to use the services of people who make their livings working with computers. As computers have become more complex, however, they have also become easier to use; you can now learn all the necessary skills of basic programming for social-science research in just a few days.

Whether you do all the work yourself or someone else does it for you, here are some specific pieces of advice for the data-handling process (skip the first four until you have some acquaintance with data-processing procedures and equipment).

First, "clean" (check) the data thoroughly. You should clean to see whether any data appear in columns that should be blank on all cards, in which case you have probably spotted a card on which all the columns have been shifted to the right or left. Clean to see that there are no punches other than the ones that your code allows for, column by column. And so on.

Second, spot-check your data both at the raw stage and at the card stage to see if there are glaring errors. A good way to check is to "print out" all the data and run your eye down the various columns.

Third, check a random sample of the data for minor errors. The number of errors you find will enable you to estimate how many errors there are in the data as a whole. This is a type of quality-control check.

Fourth, at each stage at which you multiply, divide, or otherwise transform your data, print out the results of the transformations and check each calculation. Only experienced researchers can appreciate how many ways there are for transformations to go wrong, mostly through wrong instructions to the programmer or wrong programming. The former director of one of the important computer laboratories swears that the amount of error that takes place in data processing is enormous, dangerous, and mostly unknown to anyone even after the results appear in print.[1]

Fifth, never throw away any original data until five years after you are absolutely sure they have already been useless for ten years; that is, do not ever throw away the data. Especially do not throw away original data if you have transformed them into a more refined form. Transformations (for

1. A. Hoggatt, in conversation.

example, averaging) are often not reversible; sometimes you cannot get back to your original data from the transformed data.

Sixth, if data on other dimensions that just *might* be relevant sometime are available in the data-collection process at only slight extra cost, collect them (but don't go hog wild and swamp yourself with useless data).

Seventh, if your data have idiosyncrasies because of the particular nature of your study, try to collect them in such a way that the idiosyncrasies will not hamstring their use in some future study.

After your first close-up experience with the actual workings of a research project you may be horrified at the inaccuracies and possible errors in the process. This is especially likely to happen after you conduct your first personal interview in a lower-class home, where you quickly find out how much judgment is required of the interviewer, especially when the interviewee does not seem to understand what you are talking about. The coding process can also frighten one into thinking that all research must be worthless. This reaction is similar to the one you experience when you first go into the kitchen of a first-class restaurant: You swear never to eat out again. Still, the number of food poisonings is smaller than the appearances lead you to expect. (But there is no more *excuse* for a sloppy research project than for a restaurant's filthy kitchen—and both *can* be dangerous.)

3. Adjusting the Data

Experiments usually produce nice, clean, orderly data, because what comes out is a product of what is put in and the researcher has considerable *control* of what goes in. Sometimes the experimenter disregards some observations because they are "obviously" in error—perhaps because an earthquake hit at the moment the observation was made—but, aside from such matters, little adjustment is usually done with experimental data.

In non-experimental research the situation is different. The researcher must take what he can get and then patch it up and adjust it. This seems scholarly betrayal to researchers who do mostly experimentation. Yet the adjustment must be done and done well if non-experimental research is to get anywhere at all. Here is an example of adjustments made to the sample in the Survey of Consumer Finances in order to render it suitable for economic analysis:

> *The sample included for analysis.* In keeping with our previous comments about the difficulty both with the data and with their interpretation for spending units involved in some entrepreneurial activity, we decided to exclude from the sample farmers and those who owned a business.

> In any survey, there are some interviews where a relevant item of information is not obtained, e.g., income, assets, or some component of saving. When, as in the Surveys of Consumer Finances, it is intended to publish data and relations pertaining to the nation as a whole, it is best to assign values to these cases by

matching these spending units with others in the sample who are like them in as many respects as possible. The alternative would be to eliminate these interviews entirely, throwing away all the other information, and implicitly assigning them the mean sample values of all the variables (by reweighting the other interviews). However, for our purposes, where we are interested in detailed patterns of relationships and levels of significance, it seemed better to eliminate all these cases and any possibility of spurious relations resulting from the assignment procedure. Hence, we removed from the samples all cases where the amount of income, assets, or saving had been assigned. For the relevant tables we also eliminate the cases where such things as income change, occupation, etc., were not ascertained.

Finally, we made two other types of exclusion: First, we excluded a few cases where there seemed good reason to suspect the reliability of the information. For instance, we took out cases where saving was so large as to indicate a level of expenditure out of proportion with the general economic position of the spending unit. The latter cases usually involved some large transactions where all the money did not seem to be accounted for. Second, there were some cases where extreme saving behavior was clearly present, but it was so extreme and so unusual as to require a separate treatment. (Morgan, pp. 98–99)

M. Friedman emphasizes the importance of wise adjustment of the data:

In seeking to make a science as "objective" as possible, our aim should be to formulate the rules explicitly in so far as possible and continually to widen the range of phenomena for which it is possible to do so. But, no matter how successful we may be in the attempt, there inevitably will remain room for judgment in applying the rules. Each occurrence has some features peculiarly its own, not covered by the explicit rules. The capacity to judge that these are or are not to be disregarded, that they should or should not affect what observable phenomena are to be identified with what entities in the model, is something that cannot be taught; it can be learned but only by experience and exposure in the "right" scientific atmosphere, not by rote. It is at this point that the "amateur" is separated from the "professional" in all sciences and that the thin line is drawn which distinguishes the "crackpot" from the scientist. (Friedman, p. 25)

And one more quotation (this time by a chemist) about this very sensitive issue, which illustrates once again that much of science is art and judgment:

THE REJECTION OF OBSERVATIONS

One of the most difficult decisions which an experimenter has to make is whether or not to reject a result which seems unreasonably discordant. Such results occur, because of accidents or mistakes (Sec. 9.1), with greater or less frequency depending on the skill and care of the investigator. If a mistake of addition is made, it is certainly not reasonable to expect the number obtained to tell very much about the quantity being observed. In particular the use of statistical techniques based on the normal law of error is hardly justified.

Sometimes the reason for a "wild" result is obvious. The operator may know what he did that caused it. These clear-cut cases are not important—if the operator makes a mistake which he knows will spoil the results, he should stop the measurement at that point, or at the least mark it irrevocably for discarding, even if it eventually should come out close to expectations.

On the other hand, the search for specific reasons for rejecting a result after the fact is highly dangerous. It is too easy to find an excuse and too likely that prejudice and emotion will enter. However, if the observer is willing—and strong-minded enough—rejections may be made by the rule that, if a given circumstance is once used to justify discarding a discordant result, the occurrence of the same circumstance must cause rejection whenever it happens and whatever the result.

It is important to look for causes of unusual results; many great discoveries have been made in this way. . . .

There is clearly no magic formula for the rejection of observations. Consideration of the difficulties involved is worthwhile if it leads to the attitude that it is important to be very careful to prevent mistakes and accidents.

With experiments requiring extremely good conditions of observation or extremely high sensitivity on the part of the operator, there is often a desire to disregard negative results on the grounds that conditions were not right or that the operator was not in the right mood. This is undoubtedly responsible for much pseudo science, psychic phenomena, and similar material. If negative results are excluded from a chance sequence, a positive average will naturally result. It is easy to dismiss these cases as mere charlatanism or self-deception, but many educated people do accept such nonsense. (Wilson, pp. 256–257)

One reason that adjustment of the data is so important in nonexperimental work is that the data may be limited. In physiology, chemistry, or experimental psychology, the researcher can repeat the experiment and obtain new data to check whether an observation really is a "sport" (an error of some sort) and should be thrown out of the study. But one cannot simply throw out one year's observation of Gross National Product. (Yet, that is just what is often done with war years!)

Definitional difficulties often lie at the root of discrepancies in the raw data. For example, look at the entries for the population of China in the years 1578, 1661, and 1749 in the "Returned in Census" column in Table 17.1. A. Usher explains these peculiarities to us:

. . . The returns were used as a basis for taxation, and the unit of enumeration has commonly been presumed to be the family. But some enumeration of individuals (mouths) was made as part of the return, and at some periods the return of "mouths" is held to be more trustworthy than that of families. The bias likely to develop from the system of taxation is minimized by the return of both taxable and nontaxable persons. The periods of greatest difficulty are the Sung and early Tsing dynasties. In the Sung period, the basis of enumeration of "mouths" was changed, and males alone were included. In the early reigns of the Tsing Dynasty only males of military age (16–60) were recorded. When adjustments have been made for these divergences of practice, the series of returns becomes essentially self-consistent and conforms to the expectations created by the history of the country. (See "Probable Total" column in Table 17.1; Usher, p. 15)

TABLE 17.1 Population of China (in millions)

Year	Dynasty	Returned in Census	Probable Total
2	Han	59.5	71.0
156	Han	50.0	60.0
606	Tang	46.0	55.0
733	Tang	45.4	54.0
754	Tang	52.9	63.5
1080	Sung	33.3	79.0
1260	Yuen	53.6	65.0
1290	Yuen	58.8	70.5
1381	Ming	60.5	72.5
1393	Ming	58.6	70.1
1491	Ming	56.0	66.0
1578	Ming	63.5	75.0
1661	Tsing	21.0	105.0
1690	Tsing	20.3	101.5
1710	Tsing	23.3	116.5
1749	Tsing	177.4	177.4
1780	Tsing	276.6	276.6
1812	Tsing	360.4	360.4
1842	Tsing	413.0	413.0
1860	Tsing	260.0	?
1885	Tsing	377.6	377.6
1923	Tsing	414.0	414.0

SOURCE: "The History of Population and Settlement in Eurasia," p. 123, by A. P. Usher, in *The Geographical Review*, Vol. 20 (January 1930).

Sometimes, however, one cannot discover *any* reasonable explanation for discrepancies in the raw data. This may be because the data sources are no more than someone's guesses, which are reprinted and passed along as gospel truth. What would you make of the population history of Japan from A.D. 589 to A.D. 1702, from the data in Table 17.2?

Sometimes you may adjust a set of data by *weighting* some data more heavily than others. For example, if you have yearly data on the incidence of mental disease and you want to investigate the relationship between mental disease and religion, you might well pay more attention to the data of the last thirty years than to those from more than thirty years ago, because recent statistics on the incidence of mental illness are more accurate than those from further back. Many scientists are suspicious of such weighting, on the grounds that it is subjective, and properly so, because the method and results of the study cannot be so easily checked by someone else. But *some* such subjective judgments are inevitably part of every study; the researcher has to designate *some* year as the first year she will include in this study, and usually she does so according to the adequacy of the data. The danger, of course, is that the researcher will choose a cut-off date (or weighting scheme) that will prove the hypothesis she wants to prove. There really is not much defense against this fudging danger except making an explicit statement of why you did what you did.

TABLE 17.2   Estimated Populations from the Early Times to the Middle of the Tokugawa Era

Date A.D.	Population	Authorities
589	3,931,151	*Shotoku Taishi Denki*
"	4,031,050	*Taishi Denki*
"	4,988,842	*Taishiden*
610	4,990,000	*Jugan-iko;* Nishikawa-Korinsai, *Nihon Suidoko*
"	4,969,699*	Jurei Suzuki, *Kofutaii*
650–1150[2]	8,833,290*	M. Kimura
710–48[3]	5–6 millions*	G. Sawada
721	4,584,893	*Gyoki Bosatsu Gyojoki*
724–48	2 millions	*Gyoki Shikimoku*
"	4,508,551	*Ibid.,* Differently quoted
"	4,899,620	*Ibid.,* Differently quoted
"	8 millions	*Jugen-Iko* and Nishikawa, *op. cit.*
"	6,631,074	Arai-Hakuseki, *Oritakushiba no Ki*
736	8,631,770*	Ishihara
823	3,694,331*	Y. Yokoyama, *Nihon Denseishi*
859–922[4]	3,762,000*	*Ibid.*
901–22[5]	2 millions*	Hidenori Ino
923	1,128,167*	*Chirikyoku Zasshi*
986–1010[6]	22,083,325*	Hidenori Ino
990–1080[7]	4,416,650*	Yokoyama, *op. cit.*
c. 1155	24–25 millions*	Hidenori Ino
1185–1333[8]	9,750,000*	
1278–87[9]	4,984,828	*Kongyoku Satsuyoshu* and *Ruiju Meibutsuko*
1528	4,916,652	Bishop Shuntei, *Zakkishu*
1553	2,330,996*	*Chirikyoku Zasshi*
1562	4,994,808	Katori Bunsho
1573–91[10]	18 millions*	T. Yoshida, *Ishinshi Nachiko*
1673–83[11]	24 millions	Nishikawa, *op. cit.*
1688–1703[12]	26 millions*	Yoshida, *op. cit.*
1702	24,994,600*	*Chirikyoku Zasshi*

* Indicates estimates by present-day writers.

SOURCE: Ishii, p. 4

Another fix-it operation is collecting more data to beef up an area where your data are too few. For example, in a study like A. Kinsey's you might find upon first inspection of the data in hand that too few men aged fifty-five to sixty-five, Roman Catholic, and members of the middle class have fallen into your sample, perhaps because there are very few people of this sort. If your sample is randomly selected, you can go out and obtain data on more people that meet these specifications; this move is particularly feasible if you are taking your sample in several sequential steps. (But you *must* remember to take account of these resamples when you make estimates for the universe as a whole; see Chapter 9 on stratified sampling for an explanation.)

A last step in the adjustment process is to examine the data to see if the results are reasonable. If the results are not reasonable, there may be an error. Novices laugh when they hear economists or psychologists say, "If the data don't agree with the theory, check the data." But, indeed, the data are often found to be in error when they disagree with the hypothesis. The stronger the theory, of course, the more likely you are to put your money on it when it quarrels with the data.

But watch out—danger ahead! If you recheck your data when they do not agree with your hypothesis and do *not* recheck the data when they *do* agree with the hypothesis, you are loading the dice in favor of getting data that agree with your hypothesis. The only solution is *always* to recheck your data.

4. Estimating Missing Data

Sometimes you need a datum that is not available. You then have two choices: Abandon the study, or estimate the datum. And if you cannot estimate the datum or if the datum represents too large a part of all the data in the study, then you *must* abandon the study.

There are many devices for estimation, all of them involving mostly common sense. In Chapter 21 we will find the example of estimating unavailable advertising expenditures for a given year by assuming that the ratio of 1976 expenditures to 1975 expenditures would be the same as the ratio of 1976 Gross National Product to 1975 Gross National Product. Another example of the same strategy is William Petty's 1687 estimate of the population of London, which took advantage of the fact that the authorities had burned the house of each person who died of the plague of 1666:

> The number of houses which were burnt Anno 1666, which by authentic report was 13,200; next, what proportion the people who died out of those houses bore to the whole, which I find . . . Anno 1666 to be almost 1/5, from whence I infer the whole housing of London Anno 1666 to have been 66 thousand; then finding the burials Anno 1666 to be to those of 1686 as 3 to 4, I pitch upon 88 thousand to be the number of housing Anno 1686. (Letwin, p. 143)

Interpolation and extrapolation are similar devices. If you have data for 1973 and 1975 but not for 1974, it may be reasonable to split the difference and *interpolate* for 1974. (But, if you have the average temperature for Chicago in May and October, do not estimate the average temperature for August by interpolation.) If you have the data for 1974, 1975, and 1976, it may be reasonable to *extrapolate* the trend into 1977. (But do not extrapolate the temperature trend for June, July, and August into September.)

Another trick is to *disaggregate*. It is often easier to estimate for individual parts of a whole and then to combine them for a better overall estimate than to estimate straight-off. For example, perhaps I want to estimate the gross revenue of a particular lunch counter for a year. I have no basis for a direct estimate. But if I sit at the lunch counter for an hour I can count the number of customers in that period of time, estimate the average bill per customer, multiply by the number of hours a day the counter is open (adjusting for busy and slow hours), multiply by the number of stools in the lunch counter, adjust for the time the stool is not in use, and arrive at an estimate. As a matter of fact, I could even estimate the revenue from a single stool without ever going into the restaurant. This kind of disaggregated estimate is a mental sampling process, and it is likely to be closer to the actual figure than if I made a direct estimate for the entire lunch counter.

Another method of estimation would be to watch the cash register for ten minutes, total the receipts, then expand for the whole year.

Another illustration: How tall is the Empire State Building or the tallest building in your town? You know that each floor is eight to eleven feet high, and you can estimate the number of floors. Presto—an estimate.

Valuation estimates can often be improved by disaggregating. For example, when planning a week's riverboat-cruise vacation, my wife and I discussed whether to pay $40 extra for a private shower. The valuation seemed to make sense only after we divided by the number of showers we expected to take and estimated that each private shower would cost between $3 and $4. We could then say to ourselves, "Would I pay $3 to $4 extra to take a shower in the room rather than walk a few doors down the corridor?"

Sometimes it is difficult to get several people to agree about what is the most sensible estimate. A. Enthoven finds that, in government policy research, offering three estimates—high, low, and middle—can often bring agreement: "It is surprising how often reasonable men studying the same evidence can agree on three numbers where they cannot agree on one. In fact, one of the great benefits of this approach has been to eliminate much senseless quibbling over minor variations in numerical estimates of very uncertain magnitudes" (Enthoven, p. 421).

5. Imputation

Chapter 15 referred to the problems in national-income accounting of reckoning the labor value of housewives. This and related problems must be solved by *imputation,* the process of estimating a quantity when there is little or no scientific rationale for the estimate. O. Morgenstern calls imputation (of value) "perhaps *the* classical problem of economic theory" (p. 245). Imputation is also an important problem in other social sciences. I shall discuss three difficult kinds of imputation problems here: dividing combined data into parts, allocating parts of a whole, and evaluating worth in the absence of a standard.

a. SEPARATING COMBINED DATA

I wanted to determine the differences in state tax revenues from distilled spirits in the thirty-four states with private-enterprise liquor stores, compared to the sixteen states in which liquor stores are run by the states and "socialized" (J. Simon, 1966b). But in some states, like Hawaii, the data for beer and wine are lumped together with the data for distilled spirits, and I wanted the revenues for liquor only. Table 17.3 illustrates how the data are lumped together (as well as other complexities that an investigator must unravel if she wants to use such accounting data for scientific purposes).

TABLE 17.3   Liquor-Tax Revenues in Hawaii, 1961

	Number	Amount	
Permit fees			
38 liquor-tax permits at $2.50 (rounded)			$ 95.00
Taxes			
Wholesale		$3,508,524.00	
Retail		6,234.00	
Taxable use		14,742.00	
Total liquor-tax collections			$3,529,518.00
Miscellaneous income			39.00
Total state collections from alcoholic beverages			$3,529,652.00
Costs of collections (estimated)			7,259.00
Net state revenues			$3,522,393.00
Local collections (license fees)			
City and County of Honolulu	649	$ 339,619.00	
County of Maui	134	51,058.00	
County of Hawaii	176	64,379.00	
County of Kauai	83	30,174.00	
Total local collections		$ 485,230.00	
Costs of local collections (estimated)		24.900.00	
Net local collections			$ 460,330.00
Total net state and local revenues			$3,982,723.00

In this case, as in many similar cases, the solution was to refer to states in which the revenues are separate and to assume that the *proportions* would be the same in the states that do not reckon the taxes separately.

b. ALLOCATING PARTS OF A WHOLE

This type of imputation is truly separating the inseparable. For example, how would you decide how much the husband is responsible for the popularity of a given couple and how much the wife is? One tactic would be to investigate the popularity of the husband and the wife in the social relations that they conduct separately. But they may go everywhere together. Furthermore, their popularity or lack of it may stem from how they behave *as a couple,* which may be quite different from how they behave separately; that is, there may be an *interaction effect.*

In the case of this married couple, it may be *meaningless* to impute responsibility for popularity to the husband or the wife. In such cases, you should refuse to try to separate the inseparable. Indeed, if you are studying married couples *qua* couples, there is probably no reason even to try to establish separate responsibility for the popularity of the couple.

In some other cases, however, the problem simply cannot be ducked. The allocation of overhead costs in the U.S. Post Office offers a classic case. Congress sets postal rates for different classes of mail and takes into account the costs of handling the various classes of mail. But how much of the cost of constructing and maintaining the post-office building should be charged to first-class mail, how much to second-class mail, and so on?

One answer is obviously wrong. It would make no sense to charge *each* class of mail as much as it would cost if there were no other classes of mail. If so, the sum of the allocations would be much larger than the actual total cost. Nor is there any particular justification for allocating the costs in proportion to the number of pieces of each class of mail or to the other costs for each class of mail—although these are the answers that accountants would probably offer.

Because there is no agreed-upon or scientific rationale for apportioning these costs, the arguments rage, and the pressure groups scream. The answer is at best a matter of philosophy, judgment, and determination of ultimate purpose. To indicate just one possible line of reasoning, if we assume that the United States *must* have first-class mail and if the other classes of mail are merely riders on the coattails of first-class mail, then it might be sensible to charge to first-class mail *all* the overhead costs for facilities that are used jointly by all the classes of mail. On the other hand, if the object were for the government to make as much profit as possible, the prices would be set purely in terms of what the customers would pay, and no allocation of joint overhead costs would be necessary. If the object is to allocate the costs "most fairly," then the government would probably have to have a national referendum.

6. Imputing Value in the Absence of Standards

The effectiveness of alternative university curricula is notoriously hard to evaluate because there are no agreed-upon standards against which one can rate the graduates of the alternative curricula. You might propose such a measure as "starting salary at graduation" for comparison of graduates of a great-books curriculum and graduates of a free-electives curriculum. But neither this nor any other quick and simple test seems to have any general validity.

A similar problem arises when a university tries to put a value on a piece of its own land—something it *must* do if it is to make wise decisions about where to place which of its buildings. Land for a proposed library site in the middle of the campus obviously has great value, and that value is an important component of the total cost of the building. But what value should be imputed? Only one thing is sure: To impute *zero* value for the land because you have no firm basis for estimation is folly, though this exact course might be suggested by an old-fashioned accountant. (Yet some big companies like Union Carbide still do carry "good will"—the value of their organization and trade name—on their accounting books at $1!)

When there is no empirical source for data but the data are crucially needed, you must somehow make the *most sensible* estimate. Base your estimate on any evidence you can adduce—for example, the cost of similar land as estimated by real estate brokers, if the university had to go out and buy. The most sensible estimate is a delicate piece of judgment in which the skills of the scientist and the knowledge of experienced people (in this case, the economist and the real estate broker) must be combined. Lately there has arisen a body of logical theory—called "Bayesian statistical decision theory"—that provides guidelines for systematically combining such estimates with your other data.

Imputed values can only be tested by judgment. There is no scientific test of the fairness and soundness of an imputed value, and indeed a jury is often required to render a judgment:

LAND PRICE SET BY JURY

A circuit Court jury late Tuesday night returned a verdict of $64,500 for land required by the University of Illinois for the $14.3 million Center for the Performing Arts.

The verdict is the second in the series of condemnation suits by the university to acquire the site bounded by Goodwin Avenue, Gregory Place, Illinois Street, and Oregon Street. The property involved in the latest suit is owned by Albert and Beatrice Gregerson.

The University had appraised the property at between $52,000 and $55,000, and the defendants at between $74,000 and $78,000. (Champaign-Urbana *Courier*, March 25, 1965, p. 3)

The importance of sound imputation is seen in the magnitude of the decisions that are affected. Imputed value judgments of alternative school curricula, not any empirical scientific tests, are the basis of France's nationwide school curriculum decisions. And the imputed "shadow prices" that government agencies pay each other for goods influence the entire makeup of the Soviet economy. (How does the U.S.S.R. decide what price for truck engines the engine factory should charge the truck factory? General Motors has this problem too. One of the possible bases for the Soviet price is the amount the engines sell for in free-world markets. The existence of automatic self-regulating prices, rather than imputed prices, is a key difference between socialism and capitalism.)

7. Standardizing the Data

Before you can compare the two or more events and before you can make estimates about totals, central values, and other measurements—in general, before you can use various pieces of data in some study—you must make them *comparable*. You must *standardize* the data.

Lack of comparability in data is a fertile source of fallacies and lies based on statistical presentation. Often the fallacious implication is not intended to deceive people, but people are deceived nevertheless. For example, the National Safety Council reports that two-thirds of the people killed in automobiles are traveling forty miles an hour or under. But does that figure tell you anything about whether it is safer to travel under or over forty miles per hour? It does not. It would be much more illuminating to know the chances of being killed *per mile driven* at speeds under and over forty miles an hour.

D. Huff gives us the story of the roadside merchant who, when asked how he could sell his rabbit-meat sandwiches so cheaply, replied: "Well, I have to put in some horse meat too. But I mix 'em fifty-fifty: one horse, one rabbit" (Huff, p. 114).

Public-relations men are fond of the noncomparable comparison as a device to make a phony point. A liquor-trade association, for example, wanted to make an argument for "Why Georgia Cannot Afford to Socialize Its Liquor Industry." The brochure purported to show that, if Georgia were to adopt a system like that of Virginia or North Carolina, it would then lose tax revenue. But the flack failed to point out that liquor prices charged by the States of Virginia and North Carolina were at that time far below the average retail prices in Georgia. If the State of Georgia shifted to a system like that of Virginia or North Carolina *and* merely charged the same prices that private retailers had been charging in Georgia *up to that time*, the State of Georgia could increase its revenues enormously. Such a result would be shown if we calculated the amount of state revenue per dollar paid for liquor by consumers, a way of standardizing.

Two newspapers, one for and one against Roosevelt's New Deal, carried these two headlines and stories in the same week, differing in the mode of standardizing:

ELECTRIC OUTPUT IN SEASONAL RISE

Electric power production for the week ended May 28 rose substantially above the total of the previous week. . . .

POWER OUTPUT OFF 10.6% FROM 1937 FIGURES

The production of electricity in the United States in the week ended May 28 was 1,973,000,000 kilowatt hours, a drop of 10.6 per cent from the 1937 week according to the Edison Electric Institute. (Cohen, p. 659)

Another example is the comparison of countries for wealth. The yearly income of India is greater than that of Luxembourg or Holland. But on a per capita basis Luxembourg and Holland are wealthier than India.

But *how* a set of data should be standardized is never obvious. Like every other decision in empirical research, this decision must be made with reference to the purpose of the research. Assume, for example, that you want to compare the average male of two countries for physical strength, as measured by how much weight he can carry for a mile. Should you make a straightforward comparison, man for man, or should you calculate the amount of weight carried *relative to the body weight* of each man? Standardizing men by their own weight is common practice in many of the Olympic games and in collegiate wrestling, boxing, and judo (but not in running and swimming). Or perhaps you should standardize by the amount of food they eat or by any of a dozen other types of standardizing measurements.

The decision must be made with reference to the *universe of interest* that you are trying to investigate. If you want to know how much human male *lifting power* is available in a country, for the purpose of evaluating its labor resources, you would not want to standardize at all. But, if you want to know about the physical *condition* of the men in the various countries and about their "prowess" as we usually think about it, you would standardize by weight, age, and other dimensions.

In experimentation the *control group* is a standardizing device. The control group constitutes a base-line standard against which to compare the experimentally treated group. The key idea is that the experimental group, which is randomly chosen from the same universe as is the control group, would show the same results as the control group *if it had not been treated experimentally*.

Almost every national economic statistic must be standardized. Here is a description of one:

> The US Department of Commerce has developed a new analytical tool to measure economic growth in regions, states, and countries. Its study shows that the "normal" change in the number of workers in an area would have been if its economic conditions had been parallel to the nation's between 1940 and 1960. The difference between actual employment change and "normal" employment change measures the amount by which an area rate exceeded or lagged behind the national rate. This measure is then cross-classified according to the type of industry in the area, and the rates of growth for its industries are compared with the national rates to obtain a measure of relative growth potential.

> As an example of employment shift between 1950 and 1960, jobs in Scranton, Pennsylvania, would have increased by over 9,700 if that city had grown at the "normal" rate. Actually Scranton had a decline of over 8,400 jobs. In effect, this was a net loss of over 18,300 jobs. The study found that the two fastest-growing regions were the Ft. Lauderdale, Florida area, and Anaheim-Santa Ana-Garden Grove, California. These had job gains between 1950 and 1960 of 249 percent and 201 percent, respectively, of their total 1950 employment. The three areas which lost the most jobs were those of Jersey City, New Jersey; Erie, Pennsylvania; and St. Joseph, Missouri, which experienced declines during the decade of over 24 percent each. (*Illinois Business Review,* April 1966, p. 9)

Another common standardizing device for demographic and economic national statistics is the *base year*, in which each year's (or month's) amount is expressed as a percentage of the first or other base year. The deflated dollar is a very useful standardizing device in economic statistics; its purpose is to standardize the *values* of amounts of money earned or paid in years when the values of the dollar were different.

Here is an example of how lack of standardization can turn the world topsy-turvy:

> Many an American youth believed that his life was to be cut off prematurely when the government called him to the colors in 1917 to fight for his country. The fact was that he was really in less danger while fighting for the land that bore him than he was while engaged in his peaceful vocations. Fifty-three thousand-three hundred American soldiers were killed or died of wounds during the nineteen months of our participation in the War, victims of every refinement of modern slaughter; yet during that same period 132,000 persons were killed at home in the performance of the tasks of peace. (*New York Herald Tribune*, January 2, 1927, in Cohen, p. 666)

The *proportion* or *ratio* is a useful device for standardizing data. Its sole purpose is to indicate the *relative sizes* of two quantities to be compared. The percentage is a special kind of proportion; it is a standardization device, for two percentages can immediately be compared to see which is bigger, whereas 22/73 and 18/67 cannot be compared until they themselves have been standardized. All of us have used percentages all our lives, and it is hard to imagine how we would get along without this device. But the percentage is deceptively simple, and it takes a lot of hard thinking to decide which percentage to compute.

Taking out trends is often a necessary standardizing device. Earlier we saw that, if the relationship between auto sales and auto prices is plotted for several decades, it appears as if the two variables go together, leading to the inference that higher prices cause higher sales. Actually, it is the *trends* of higher prices and higher auto sales over the years that confuse the picture. One way to clarify the matter is to consider the *difference from year to year* in sales and prices, which serves to remove some of the effects of trends (of some kinds).

8. Index[2] Numbers

An index number is a device for adding apples and oranges. Everyone knows that you cannot add apples and oranges, but the scientist does it

2. There is confusion in the use of the terms "index" and "index number" in the social sciences. Often *any proxy* (surrogate) is said to be an "index" for the conceptual variable it stands for. But "index number"—often spoken of simply as "index," also—is a special kind of proxy that is a complex of many separate proxies. The distinction will become clear as the section proceeds.

anyway. He simply adds the unaddable.[3] The example is not hypothetical. A newspaper headline said "1964 Crops Near Record in Illinois." But how can one decide easily whether the crop in one year is better than the crop the year before? Perhaps the wheat crop was better but the corn crop worse, the sorghum crop a little worse, the apple crop better, and so on. On what basis do you decide whether the crop as a whole was better or worse? From the point of view of farmers as a whole, the simple cash value of the crops is a good index. But from a wider point of view this index is insufficient, for prices go up when crops are poor. Therefore an *index* is needed that takes into account the amount of each type of crop and weights each of them. And, indeed, the U.S. Department of Agriculture has just such an index, which allows it to say that the "all crops production index as of September 1, 1976 is at 118 percent of the 1967 index used as a standard, down from last year's 122 percent." (AP, September 11, 1976, from C-U *News Gazette*, p. 1)

How do the judges decide who wins a boxing match? Unless one fighter knocks out the other fighter, the judges must take into account several different factors: aggressiveness, number of blows struck, and strength of blows struck, among others. And there must be *some* system to weight the different factors; for instance, number of blows struck is more important than is aggressiveness. The system of weights, and the overall result, is an *index number*. The index number for boxing differs from country to country, and who wins may depend upon the particular system in use.

Wages are another example. How much did wages go up last year? Janitors' wages went up 9 percent, but professors' wages went up 7 percent. Even if the whole world were composed of only janitors and professors, it would not make sense simply to split the difference, because there are more janitors than there are professors.

The stock-market indexes illustrate that conclusions may depend upon how the index is constructed. On a particular day the Dow-Jones Index may go down while the Standard & Poor Index is going up.

Dealing with the index-number problem reaches a peak of frustration when you must decide whether a group of people *taken as a whole* is better or worse off following some social change. A few people may suffer "greatly," and a lot of people may benefit "slightly." But we have no Benthamic "felicific calculus" with which to figure out whether the *total* of human happiness has increased or decreased.

The first principle in making index numbers is to choose items for the index that are representative of the universe whose movement you want to

---

3. By now I have said that scientists measure the unmeasurable, separate the inseparable, and add the unaddable. Scientists also do many other things that are, in someone's theory, impossible, just as we all do these things in our daily life. It is true that all these operations cannot be done *scientifically*. But they can and must be done by scientists in order to get on with the business of obtaining information and knowledge about the world in which we live.

measure with the index. If you are constructing an index of consumer prices, you cannot measure the price changes in *all* items consumers buy; so you take a sample. You might include bread, washing machines, ballpoint pens, men's underwear, and so on. The second principle is to apply weights to the various items according to the items' importance in the universe and also to how well each particular item reflects the movement of all items.

We take published indexes for granted. We forget not only how arbitrary and chancy they are but also how difficult and time-consuming they are to create. All of us think we know which supermarket is the most expensive in town and which is the least expensive. But the price-ranking of a supermarket depends upon thousands of different articles. It took a researcher 300 skilled man-hours to figure out the price ranking of just eight supermarkets in a shopping area (Holdren, p. 68).

Usually we overcome the difficulty of computing indexes by dodging the full complexity of the problem. In the study of liquor prices in various states, I ended up using the prices of just eight brands in the index, weighting all of them equally—mostly because data from only these eight brands were available for most states.

Indexes are made the way all of us implicitly make daily decisions. Consider, for example, the situation of a fellow like Arrowsmith, who has decided to marry one of two girls but has not yet decided which one. Sheila is more beautiful and cooks better, but Victoria is more intelligent and dances better. How is a man to decide? He might make up a scoreboard like this:

	Sheila	Victoria
Beauty	10	5
Cooking	2	0
Intelligence	3	10
Dancing	1	2
Wife index	16	17

Notice that the fellow is giving more weight to beauty and intelligence than to cooking and dancing. Implicitly he is saying that beauty and intelligence are more important than cooking and dancing. The sum of each girl's scores in the four "unaddable" dimensions is her wife index.

Another complication is added if the fellow *does not know* exactly how each girl stacks up on one or more dimensions. Let's say he knows that Sheila is well off and her money is important to him, so he weights it twice as heavily as beauty (and intelligence). He *thinks* Victoria may have money, and, if she does, she has twice as much as Sheila has,[4] he figures the

---

4. I am assuming that twice as much money is twice as desirable, which it usually is not (Galanter, pp. 54–55).

odds are 25 to 75 that Victoria does have the money. The score card is then as follows:

	Sheila			Victoria		
	Points	Odds	Weighted Sum	Points	Odds	Weighted Sum
Beauty	10	× 1 =	10	5	× 1 =	5
Cooking	2	× 1 =	2	0	× 1 =	0
Intelligence	3	× 1 =	3	10	× 1 =	10
Dancing	1	× 1 =	1	2	× 1 =	2
Money	20	× 1 =	20	40	× .25 =	10
Wife index			36			27

This kind of scheme is a formal explicit representation of much of our everyday decision-making process; we would frequently make better decisions if we made explicit scorecards. This is the nature of indexes and the weighting of the components of indexes with "subjective probability" estimates of the odds.

9. Avoiding the Hazards of Hired Help

Other people are not as smart as you are. Even worse, they have only the faintest glimmering of what you are trying to do in your research. And worst of all—though it is perfectly understandable, of course—is that other people do not *care* about your research nearly as much as you do: the performance you get from people depends on their motivations.

These considerations suggest that you should try as hard as possible to (a) involve your assistants in the work, and give them a personal stake in the output; and (b) watch over them with as much vigilance as possible, and tell them that you will check on their work, as, for example, telling interviewers that there will be follow-ups on a randomly selected portion of the interviews. Furthermore, be supercareful about which tasks and responsibility you delegate to assistants. Of course you are not ready to employ assistants yet, but soon you may be. Even more important, this section may lead you to see the potential hazards in research from a different and sobering point of view, both as a producer and consumer of research.

The dilemma is clear: The principal investigator cannot make all the hundreds, thousands, even tens of thousands of nonroutine decisions about data collection in a major study; but delegation is dangerous. And just because it is so irritating, time-consuming, and demanding, you are tempted to leave the decisions to your assistants. But you must not yield to this temptation. You must ride herd on the data-collection process at all points, and you must make all extraroutine decisions yourself until you have trained an assistant and checked his ability. Even thereafter you must check periodically to ensure that he has not strayed. In this periodic checking look for *big* blunders. Check the big items. See if everything looks *approximately* right. If it does not, find out why.

The only possible solution is a managerial solution: Find capable assistants, train them well, and check on them constantly. To be afraid to delegate is to doom yourself to research projects so small that you can do them with your bare hands and to a scientific output a fraction of what it might otherwise be. But to delegate unwisely is to waste all the work that you do.

As a first step in the training of any assistant, have him read, sign, notarize, and swear on his great grandmother's grave that he will follow the instructions listed here. Even following instructions will not guarantee that errors will not occur. But the instructions will give you justification for great righteous anger and outrage when you bawl out your assistant for noncompliance. And *that* may have some effect.

INSTRUCTIONS TO RESEARCH ASSISTANTS (AND TO YOURSELF)

1. When doing a new task, carry out only a small part of the work and then check with your supervisor that the method is correct.
2. Keep a precise and detailed record of exactly how you handle each nonroutine decision.
3. Handle no exceptions without consulting your supervisor.
4. Figure the number of significant digits correctly; if in doubt, ask the supervisor.
5. Perform all computations on paper, not in your head.
6. Throw away nothing—not work sheets, not computations, not unusable data—nothing.
7. Label everything—all data sheets, all work sheets, everything.
8. Indicate the source of each piece of data and computation, whether from published sources or from your own original data.

J. Roth described several instances in which he and other graduate students cut corners when working on research projects. The lapses increased with time on the project, as the workers came to think that they could cheat without affecting the study's results.

When a researcher hires others to do the collecting and processing tasks of his research plan, we often assume that these assistants fit the "dedicated scientist" ideal and will lend their efforts to the successful conduct of the over-all study by carrying out their assigned tasks to the best of their ability. As suggested by my examples, I doubt that hired assistants usually behave this way when they are junior grade scholars themselves. It becomes more doubtful yet when they are even further removed from scholarly tradition and from the direct control of the research directors (e.g., part-time survey interviewers).

It seems to me that we can develop a more accurate expectation of the contribution of the hired research worker who is required to work according to somebody else's plan by applying another model which has been worked out in some detail by sociologists—namely, the work behavior of the hired hand in a production organization. . . .

[W]orkers made the job easier by loafing when the piece rate did not pay well. They were careful not to go over their informal "quotas" on piece rate jobs because the rate would be cut and their work would be harder. They faked time sheets so that their actual productive abilities would not be known to management. They cut corners on prescribed job procedures to make the work easier and/or more lucrative even though this sometimes meant that numerous products had to be scrapped. (Roth, pp. 191–192)

Between you and me—but don't tell your assistant or mine—the errors she does make will sometimes not be very dangerous if they are made *randomly*, in which case they tend to cancel out. This is likely to be true of purely arithmetical errors. For example, in a study of the effects of liquor prices on liquor sales in various states, a clerk made errors, many of them serious, in the calculation of every single one of the state price changes, but correct recalculation arrived at almost the same *median* estimate as did the calculation that contained the errors. On the other hand, even random measurement errors reduce the apparent association between two variables.

If there is any *systematic* bias, however, errors of any kind may damage your study. For example, if interviewers systematically overestimate the values of the homes of whites and underestimate those of blacks, the data on value of homes will be worse than useless for many. Even purely arithmetical errors can be affected by bias; the Internal Revenue Service finds that a large proportion of mistakes in the arithmetic of tax returns are in favor of the taxpayer rather than of the government. And errors in birth records show girls as boys more often than the reverse, and girl babies are more often left out entirely (Wallis & Roberts, p. 95). Whether the error is damaging depends upon the purpose of your study.

10. Summary

This chapter discusses the process of collecting and processing data. These are administrative tasks, calling on the skills of personnel supervision, attention to everyday detail, constant checking for mechanical and human error, and deciding what to do about the innumerable out-of-the-ordinary situations that arise.

Adjusting the data to allow for different origins and reliabilities requires not only wisdom but honesty with yourself to avoid the natural human tendency to jiggle the data so that they show what you expect or want them to show. Making allowances for missing data and allocating portions of aggregated observations require the same honest self-discipline.

Standardizing the data is crucial to a reasonable comparison of groups. The trick is to find a basis of comparison that controls for the main differences among the groups that are not themselves the subject of your interest. Indexes are often useful standardizing devices.

EXERCISES

1. Is there a single most appropriate index for comparing the relative safety of airplane and auto travel? Give one or more indexes along with the purpose(s) for which it is most appropriate.
2. Estimate the number of single men aged seventeen to twenty-five who had no dates in your town or city last Saturday night.
3. Estimate the total market value of all the clothes being worn at this moment by people in your town or city.
4. A professor uses one bedroom of her house for a study, in which she writes books. What cost should she impute for the space when she deducts her expenses for income tax?
5. What standardization devices are used in measuring I.Q.? What standardization devices are reasonable when measuring I.Q.s of boys and girls who grow up in "culturally disadvantaged" homes?
6. Evaluate the cost of eating at four campus eating places, including a college cafeteria. This evaluation requires creating a food index. Then ask a sample of students to rate the eating places in order of cost, and compare what the students think to what your index shows.
7. Estimate the number of students who take the basic courses in psychology and political science in the United States each year. Include night schools and irregular students. State how you built up your estimates.
8. Make *some* reasonable *quantitative* estimate of the comparative value to you of any two courses you might take next semester.

ADDITIONAL READING FOR CHAPTER 17

Mitchell (Chapter 3) presents an excellent discussion of data standardization and related topics in the context of economic data.

See Tintner for a technical discussion of index numbers.

On data processing, see Selltiz *et al.* (Chapter 13).

Schlaifer (1959), pp. 2–13 and Chapter 2, provides a very good discussion of how to combine probabilities and values to arrive at rational decisions. Goodman (1955), pp. 277–281, demonstrates this approach in the context of social policy decisions.

The Census Bureau data error, described as the "Case of the Indians and the Teenage Widows," is worth the reading, by Coale and Stephan. On index numbers, I recommend Suits (Chapter 9).

part three the obstacles to social-science knowledge and ways to overcome them

18 the concept of obstacles in the search for empical knowledge

1. Summary

After the researcher has specified the question that she wants the research to answer, all she has to do is to go out and get the facts. But knowledge can be tricky to obtain, and common-sense knowledge-gathering methods may not be sufficiently powerful. There are often many *obstacles* that prevent you from getting accurate knowledge easily. When I say there are obstacles, I mean that the world is big, complex, numerous, expensive, and tiring to try to understand, not least because human nature is so complex. The resulting complications, as well as the large numbers and vastness of nature that demand time and money, are indeed obstacles to your finding out what you want to find out.

To put it another way, the flaws that occur in other people's research, and for which you criticize them, result from the obstacles that the researchers did not succeed in overcoming. The concept of obstacles to knowledge is perhaps the most important single concept in this book.

In the several years that I have been teaching research design to first-year graduate students no single problem has caused me more persistent anguish than that of trying to organize research errors into a meaningful pattern. I would like (as I think anyone would like) to have a scheme of presentation which is logical and at the same time exhaustive of these research errors. It might be useful too to have a checklist of known errors so that in designing an experiment we could go through and see if we have successfully avoided such errors. (Underwood, p. 89)

The aim of Part Three of this book is to provide such a presentation and classification of obstacles to knowledge and of research errors, as well as to offer methods of overcoming these obstacles. The purpose of this chapter is to introduce the general concept of obstacles to knowledge and to lay the groundwork for the discussions of particular types of obstacles in the chapters that follow.

Examples of obstacles to knowledge are easy to come by. Major obstacles usually exist even for research problems that seem straightforward, as these examples show: How many people in the United States are over six feet tall? You could measure every one of the more than 190 million Americans, but the *cost* of doing so is a major obstacle, an obstacle that you can surmount by *sampling*. Next, how hot is the surface of the moon? Touch your hand to the moon, or hold a thermometer to it. Until you can do so it is necessary to find a method of measuring temperature at *long distance*. Third, what does the Kremlin plan to do about the Middle East? You could ask the Russian Premier, of course. But there is at least a tiny chance that he will not answer your question or will not answer it truthfully. No one has yet developed a satisfactory scientific method to overcome this obstacle. Fourth, how do Americans feel about Thanksgiving? You can ask one or a dozen Americans. But you must find a method to ensure that the people you ask are typical. Fifth, and perhaps most important of all, who will win tomorrow's game between the White Sox and the Tigers? You can easily find out who won yesterday's game. But yesterday does not repeat itself perfectly; there is *variability* in day-to-day scoring. You might look to see who won most of the games between them last year. But team personnel changes from year to year. The obstacles are indeed great.

Sometimes it seems as if nature—and particularly the human aspect of nature that is the realm of social science—diabolically throws sand in the researcher's eyes and leads him to wrong conclusions. Not so. "God is subtle but not malicious," Einstein is reported to have said. If nature did indeed try to fool and foil you, your task would be a lot more difficult even than it is.[1] Subjects who lie purposely to deceive you and communities of people who deceive you purposely are unusual exceptions to this generalization.

My aim in emphasizing the obstacles to knowledge is not to discourage you or make you feel that the game of research is very hard to play well. Rather, I want to convey that overcoming the obstacles is the very essence of the game of research. If there were no difficult obstacles to knowledge, there would be no need for research or for skilled researchers. The obstacles are the challenge, the spice that makes the game fascinating.

H. Ebbinghaus began his study of the learning process by setting forth the two major obstacles that prevent easy application of natural-science method:

1. Those who still believe that genetic factors might be responsible for diseases caused by smoking *and* for smoking behavior implicitly believe in a nature that goes to remarkable ends to confuse scientists (K. Brownlee; J. Simon, 1966c).

In the first place, how are we to keep even approximately constant the bewildering mass of causal conditions which, in so far as they are of mental nature, almost completely elude our control, and which, moreover, are subject to endless and incessant change? In the second place, by what possible means are we to measure numerically the mental processes which flit by so quickly and which on introspection are so hard to analyse? (Ebbinghaus, pp. 7–8)

The most infamous example of an unsurmounted obstacle was the *Literary Digest* presidential poll of 1936. The poll failed disastrously because it did not overcome the obstacle of bias in its sampling procedure; it simply did not succeed in getting a representative sample of the voters, as we shall see later.

Whenever two or more studies of the same question arrive at different answers, one or both of the researchers has failed to surmount some important obstacles. On page 205 there is an example of various researchers who set out to determine whether trading stamps raise or lower the consumer price of grocery products. They reach very different conclusions because important obstacles to knowledge are not overcome in their studies.

Unsurmounted obstacles sometimes go undetected for a long time in pure research. But in commercial research, competition among various firms can be highly effective in revealing errors caused by unsurmounted obstacles. Consider this story from the trade press:

STUDIES YIELD CONTRASTING DATA FOR MAGAZINES

Some SRDS Totals Are Markedly Higher Than Politz's or Simmons'
New York, Aug. 10—SRDS-Data Inc. has released new total audience figures for 27 magazines included in its Consumer/Audience Profile, thereby providing a comparison with figures previously reported by Alfred Politz and W. R. Simmons & Associates.

In some cases the Data Inc. numbers jibe with those from the other two researchers. But for some publications, Data Inc. audience totals range up to 41% higher than Simmons' and 14% greater than Politz's.

Simmons, for example, projected a total audience (of persons age 18 or older) of 10,957,000 for *Woman's Day*, whereas Data Inc. reported 15,543,000, or 41% more and Politz found 13,310,000, or 22% more than did the Simmons organization. . . .

Several factors may account for the different audience totals found by the three researchers: (1) different probability samples; (2) different methodologies in conducting interviews and projecting the figures nationally; (3) not all researchers were in the field at the same time—thereby possibly introducing an audience "seasonality" factor. (*Advertising Age*, August 16, 1965, p. 66)

One must learn how to recognize in advance the various obstacles and know how to surmount each of them efficiently. In this third part of the book, we shall discuss the various obstacles one by one, and in conjunction with each obstacle we shall discuss research tactics to overcome it.

Of course, you cannot spot *all* obstacles in advance. Unexpected obstacles always crop up as you get deeper into your research work, and then you must retreat a bit and modify your method. The entire research process is a cycle of obstacles, methods, new obstacles, modified methods, and so on.

Government intelligence work generally, and spying in particular, resembles research in being a matter of first identifying the obstacles and then finding the appropriate methods to overcome them. "Clandestine intelligence collection is chiefly a matter of circumventing obstacles in order to reach an objective" (Dulles, p. 58).[2]

Some types of knowledge are harder to obtain than are others. It is probably true that the *wider* the scope of the knowledge, the more difficult it is to obtain. It is easy for you to state what magazine *you* read yesterday, although your memory may be faulty. It is a bit harder for your spouse to determine exactly what magazine you read yesterday, and it is decidedly more difficult for a stranger to find out what you read. It is hardest of all for a stranger to find out what magazines *each and every* American or the "typical American" read yesterday.

A newspaper reporter usually has no trouble finding out such facts about a riot as what time it started, how much damage it caused, and how many policemen were on the scene. She has much more trouble in determining "public opinion" about the riot. The difficulties in finding out who started the riot are so great that a reporter who does so successfully may earn a Pulitzer Prize. And the underlying causes of the riot pose a question that bristles with obstacles. After the exhaustive McCone report and innumerable other studies the causes of the 1965 Watts riots are still not clearly known.

This seems an appropriate moment to remind you that *no* empirical knowledge will ever be absolutely perfect and certain—not even your own name. Perhaps there was a case of mistaken identity at birth.

Some obstacles are more likely to appear in some disciplines than in others. But, as with the temperate-zone doctor who occasionally spots a case of tropical disease, a wide acquaintance even with the obstacles that are infrequently found in your area may make the difference between your being a routinely skilled or a really gifted diagnostician of research obstacles.

Skill in recognizing and overcoming research difficulties is a matter of special importance for the statistically trained researcher. (Nonstatisticians may skip the following sentences.) Each assumption that underlies a statistical test is really an assumption that certain obstacles are not present in sufficient degree to invalidate the test or estimating technique. For example,

2. G. Stigler tells us that "business is the collection of devices for circumventing barriers to profits" (Stigler, 1952, p. 435). The business of science is knowledge, and the business of business is profit.

interrelationship among the independent variables is, as we shall see, a common and tricky obstacle, but the assumption that *no* interrelationship exists is necessary for the use of many statistical techniques. If the statistician rushes ahead and applies a statistical technique when the assumptions do not hold or when he has not found some way of rendering the obstacle harmless, his statistical conclusions may fall into serious error. And indeed, not only are statistical techniques often misapplied in this way, but the way the results are stated often obscures the fact that basic assumptions are not valid. Such reports can easily mislead the unwary or less sophisticated reader.

Remembering that there are no standard solutions for obstacles can reduce your frustration and anxiety in designing research. It just is not possible to compile a handbook of research solutions in the style of medical reference books, which indicate one or more specific treatments for each particular disease that you diagnose. Furthermore, as in medicine, there are in research some afflictions that are incurable. For example, the eminent reviewing committee noted that there simply do not seem to be satisfactory methods for overcoming some of the obstacles that A. Kinsey, *et al.*, faced, especially the obstacle of nonresponse (Cochran, *et al.*).

One way that Kinsey and his colleagues tried to surmount the nonresponse obstacle (and others as well) was to compare the results of their study to those of other studies. This is the most general method for surmounting obstacles. But the other studies *also* did not surmount this obstacle and therefore citing them as supporting evidence could only reinforce any error in the findings from this source.

Some obstacles are particularly prevalent in certain social sciences. But, to a surprising degree, most obstacles are found in all the social sciences. Consider economics. Most economists seldom come face to face with the obstacle that people of whom they ask questions may lie to them or rationalize their answers. But that is because most economists work with data gathered by other people—and at *some* point in the data-gathering process *someone* faced these obstacles. For example, a labor economist might work with U.S. Bureau of Labor Statistics unemployment data and take the data at face value, without taking into account that the raw data came from a questionnaire survey of a sample of families, some of whom might have lied, rationalized, or done other human things that present obstacles to getting knowledge. Similarly, almost all the price data that economists work with are or were collected by surveys and question asking and are subject to all the obstacles inherent in that process.

The best general approach to overcoming obstacles to knowledge is to employ two or more *very different* research methods. No single method can overcome all the important obstacles. But different sorts of methods overcome different sorts of obstacles, and together their strengths can cover each other's weaknesses, provided that the results agree. Emphasis on the joint use of two or more empirical methods, together with theoretical speculation, is a basic theme of this book, a strategy called "triangulation" by Denzin.

Please do not allow your awareness of the obstacles to knowledge faced by empirical research to focus you only on the flaws of the research of others, or to conclude that all data and research results are worthless because none can be perfect. Minor flaws need not invalidate research. And if the researcher has a good basic idea and a basically sound research approach, even a good many minor flaws and a small scale of research will not invalidate the research results.

Although the term "obstacle" does not sound attractive, I think we should not complain that knowledge is not perfectly easy to get, just as we should not lament the existence of the phenomenon of friction on earth. To repeat, the obstacles to knowledge are what make the achievement of knowledge interesting. Also, they provide livelihoods for social scientists who sweat for knowledge in universities, government agencies, and business; it is because there are obstacles to knowledge that people will pay to obtain it.

And now, on to the obstacles themselves.

1. Summary

Some factual knowledge about the world comes easily. But the task of empirical social science is to produce the knowledge that cannot be obtained simply and easily by casual observation.

There is a wide variety of obstacles that prevent easy acquisition of reliable knowledge. Sometimes these obstacles keep people from attempting to gather the information; sometimes the obstacles cause information-gathering to yield wrong conclusions.

One of the main tasks of the skilled researcher is to construct the research design in such manner as to overcome these obstacles successfully and efficiently. The battle against nature's complexities is hard and never ending. But this battle is the bread and butter of the empirical social scientist, and it may be won with diligence and ingenuity.

EXERCISES

1. Discuss how each of the three factors listed on page 268 might have accounted for the differences in readership figures for *Woman's Day* estimated by Politz, Simmons, and Data Inc.
2. What are the obstacles to a reporter's finding out who started a riot?

ADDITIONAL READING FOR CHAPTER 18

Obstacles to research are usually discussed in the context of errors and fallacies. See Mead, pp. 45–58, on anthropology; Saiger on medicine; Deming and Hansen *et al.* (Chapter 2) on surveys; Morgenstern (1953), pp. 13–70, on economics; Campbell and Stanley on psychological experiments; Cannon (Chapter 11) on biology. Wallis and Roberts (Chapter 4), Cohen, and Cohen and Nagel, pp. 316–323, are general references that discuss errors and fallacies in social-science research.

Morgenstern's *On the Accuracy of Economic Observation* is a frightening compendium of information on the state of such affairs in economics.

19 obstacles created by the humanness of the observer: appendix on interviewing

1. Observer Variability
2. Observer Bias
3. Cheating by Interviewers
4. Variability Among Observers
5. Observer-Caused Effects
6. Summary
7. Appendix: Personal Interviewing and Interviews

This is the first of the group of chapters cataloguing the obstacles to knowledge and the tactics by which the obstacles may be surmounted. The obstacles described in *this* chapter all arise because the *observer* is a human being rather than a machine. Indeed, if a way could be found to replace the observer with a machine, these obstacles would often be surmounted; that is why data-gathering instruments are used.

To put it another way, obstacles that must be overcome arise because research workers are as complicated as their subjects. This chapter and following ones offer examples of each different obstacle and of methods for overcoming it. You will best understand the nature of the obstacles, however, if you create your own examples from your work and reading.

1. Observer Variability

This obstacle arises from the observer's most human quality—imperfect physical and mental faculties. I am not now talking of bias, which is a *systematic* tendency to deviate from the "true" value in one direction. Rather, I mean the inability of a given observer to *repeat* an observation again and again in exactly the same way with exactly the same result.

Observer variability occurs even when it would seem easy to be objective.

For example, in library-science research it is sometimes necessary to decide whether two similar works by an author are two different works or two editions of the same work. Even an experienced observer will decide differently about the same pair of books from one day to the next. In other words, there will be variability (dispersion) in the observer's judgment from time to time.

Variability of traffic policemen in giving tickets for speeding is part of our folklore. The state of the officer's digestion and the degree of amicability between him and his wife, as well as the sex of the driver, are believed to influence the outcome.

In the physical sciences too—especially in the early stages of a physical discipline—observer variability is an important obstacle. For example, a human laboratory assistant does not read a thermometer perfectly. One important reason is that on repeated trials the observer looks at the thermometer from slightly different angles, giving slightly different readings. The difficulty is compounded if the observer cannot get close to the thermometer, as, for example, when he reads it from inside a window. Many other minor influences also cause variability and prevent precision.

As the natural sciences progressed and as more accurate instrument readings were needed, ingenious researchers developed such ways of surmounting variability in instrument reading as the following:

1. Repeat the observation, and take an average of the observed values. If the observer-variability errors are unrelated to (independent of) one another, the average of the observations is likely to be closer to the actual value than is a single observation.
2. Reduce the variation in the viewing angle with a mechanical device that holds the chin of the observer in a fixed place and thus fixes the location of his eye. Placing a mirror behind the needle is another common device to increase precision in reading instruments.
3. Read and record electronically, and print the reading automatically. But electronics has not completely licked this obstacle. Variability in observing stars is a major difficulty in astronomy, for example.

The social scientist controls observer variability with similar tactics. Observations are repeated and averaged whenever possible, to cancel out random variation. And, analogous to the use of the chin bar in reading thermometers, the social scientist often *reduces the scope* of the observations. If a field worker is to gather data on family income, she can be instructed to determine only *how many* cars are owned, *how many* rooms the house contains, and the occupation of the breadwinner. This list leaves less scope for judgment than would a general instruction to estimate the income level. (Narrowing the scope of judgment may also be considered a step toward operationalizing the definitions the observer works with.)

Reducing scope is a device to restrict the observer to gathering knowledge that he can obtain reliably. Earlier I said that it is easier to state accurately what magazine you yourself read yesterday than to find out what a stranger read or what the average person read. This decreasing accuracy parallels the continuum of confidence you can place in an observer. You rely heavily on her statement of how she herself will vote. You may place considerable credence in her statement of how her husband will vote. You do not have much confidence in her casual statement about how her neighbors will vote. And you are politely skeptical about her prediction of how her state will go in the next election.

Here are two general principles about observer accuracy and the scope of observation: First, the sharper and more measurable the categories, the more accurate the judgments. An observer who estimates the year of a respondent's car will be more accurate about its *age* than if he judges it to be simply "old" or "new." And a judgment of "old" or "new" will be more accurate if he specifies a cut-off point, say three years old. On the other hand, it is a waste to ask for more categories of accuracy than he needs. Second, the less the observer must summarize, the more accurate he will be. He will be more accurate in judging the intelligence of a single person than in judging the average intelligence of a whole group of people.

Learning from experience usually reduces observer variability. Professors often take advantage of this process when they grade exams by reading several exam books and giving only tentative grades before beginning to grade in earnest—and then regrading the exams that were read first. A. Kinsey required a *full year* of practice from his interviewers before he would accept their data. The Kinsey interviewers, however, needed such an extraordinarily long training period because they had to exercise a great deal of judgment.

Mechanical and electronic devices can occasionally be employed in the social sciences to reduce observer variability. For example, College Board Examinations are graded and totaled mostly electronically. Of course, instruments cannot make observations and measurements that require judgment. In educational examinations, this limitation sometimes means ignoring some kinds of complexities in responses and not measuring some kinds of abilities. (In English composition, however, College Board Examinations are graded by judges, and several independent judges provide a consensus.) Tape recorders and cameras are frequently used in anthropology to produce a permanent record that can be reviewed repeatedly, either by the observer himself or by other people, in order to check on and reduce the extent of variability (Mead). And the experimental psychologist uses many gadgets to reduce observer variability—running wheels to measure animal activity, water and food meters to measure intake, and timers of all kinds to ensure exact timing of stimuli.

2. Observer Bias

The tall fellow records a lower temperature than the short fellow because the tall fellow looks down at the thermometer. This innocent propensity to take a lower reading that inheres in the tall fellow we shall call by the ugly name "bias." In scientific usage, bias is merely a tendency to observe the phenomenon in a manner that differs from the "true" observation in some *consistent* fashion.

But usually there is no way to determine the "true" value, especially before the study is complete. Therefore, we assume that *every* observer is biased in one direction or the other. Our job is to determine each observer's bias and to allow for it.

Most biases in the social sciences are *social*. Social-scientific topics and situations stir up and involve the observer's beliefs, emotions, and other mental baggage. For example, sportswriters lament the fate of the noble boxer Battling Siki, who underestimated the problem of observer bias; he fought Mike McTigue for the light-heavyweight championship in Dublin on St. Patrick's Day 1923 and lost by a decision. (No kidding!)

In a survey of anti-Catholicism and anti-Semitism, a Catholic interviewer perceives responses somewhat differently than does a Jewish interviewer. And whether an interviewer's own values are Puritan or libertine may affect a sex survey. In the "Priscilla's Pop" cartoon in Figure 19.1 the interviewer's feminist bias seems to be affecting her survey slightly.

Observer bias creeps in no matter how careful you are. Many scientists have had an experience like this one: I had an idea that professors who had taken their Ph.D. degrees from universities with lesser reputations would be more productive than would colleagues *serving on the same faculty* who had taken their Ph.D. degrees from schools with higher reputations. I therefore began to match up pairs of professors on given faculties who had taken their Ph.D. degrees from different schools in the same year, intending to compare productivity. But I soon found that my desire that my idea be confirmed was causing me to match pairs that would show the results I wanted to see, thereby invalidating the work.

Anthropology has suffered worst and longest from observer bias. Modern anthropologists regard most early anthropological accounts by sea captains and missionaries as almost useless, simply because the authors' perceptions were so warped by their own cultural background. Their bias was often that all non-Europeans were heathen, savage, primitive, and without law or social organization. Even so astute a social scientist as T. R. Malthus fell afoul of this problem:

The prelude to love in this country [New South Wales] is violence, and of the most brutal nature. The savage selects his intended wife from the women of a different tribe, generally one at enmity with his own. He steals upon her in the absence of her protectors, and having first stupefied her with blows of a club, or wooden sword, on the head, back, and shoulders, every one of which is followed by a stream of blood, he drags her through the woods by one arm, regardless of the stones and broken pieces of trees that may lie in his route, and anxious only to convey his prize in safety to his own party. The woman thus treated becomes his wife, is incorporated into the tribe to·which he belongs, and but seldom quits him for another. The outrage is not resented by the rela-

FIGURE 19.1

Source: *Priscilla's Pop*, November 6, 1966, by Al Vermeer: © 1966 by NEA, Inc.; reprinted by permission of Newspaper Enterprise Association (or NEA).

tions of the female, who only retaliate by a similar outrage when it is in their power. (Irwin, ed., pp. 15–16)

Overcoming the obstacle of observer bias in physical problems like thermometer reading is reasonably easy. The simplest tactic is to obtain readings from several observers and to calculate their mean value, on the assumption that their biases will cancel out. (On the other hand, ten blind people see no more clearly than does one blind person.)

The tactics used to reduce variability *within* observers also reduce variability from bias *among* observers. In the thermometer case, such tactics might include careful instructions, devices that put the tall and short men's chins on the same bar, and automatic reading with instruments. Most observer bias in the social sciences is not dealt with so easily, however. (This is one reason why the design of research procedures is often more challenging in the social sciences than in the natural sciences.) Here are some tactics that prove helpful.

First, train observers very carefully. In a famous study of racial bias, G. Allport found that many whites who were shown a picture of a white man and a black man later said that the black was holding a razor, even though it was the white who really held the razor in the picture. The better trained the observer, the less likely he is to make such biased observations. Careful training is the keystone of modern anthropological method.

Second, specify the observer's task as closely as possible, to reduce the area of discretion within which bias may operate. As with observer variability, an observer's bias in estimating family income can be controlled by having him count the age and number of cars owned or the number of rooms in the house.

Third, require observers to refer frequently to detailed instructions. This requirement is a sort of training, for it forces the observer to retrain himself by constantly rereading his instructions. It also reduces his area of discretion by reducing the chance that he will drift away from his instructions.

Fourth, require immediate and detailed reporting whenever possible. Anthropologists try to record their field notes every day, to minimize the chance that their memories will play biasing tricks upon them. Police officers are also trained to take on-the-spot notes, to prevent bias and inaccuracy from creeping in, and courts give special attention to such notes.[1]

Fifth, mechanical devices like the camera and the tape recorder can sometimes reduce the discretion of the field observer. The permanent record can be checked later against the observer's observations, to evaluate bias. This technique has been used extensively in anthropology, market research, and social psychology. The coming of recording devices drastically altered the working habits of anthropologists (Mead, pp. 55–56).

Sixth, have several observers observe the same phenomena, and compare their observations. Note that often all observers must observe at the same

1. J. Hulett advises us that a stubby pencil and a small battered notebook make people less nervous than do more pretentious tools (p. 364).

time, because, for example, an interviewee may answer differently or not at all in a second interview. Complete duplication is usually too expensive, especially in interview studies; in fact, the cost of interviewing is the basic limitation on the size of the study. Comparing the data from several observers to establish their individual biases is usually feasible only on a small part of the study; those biases can then be taken into account when the rest of their data are analyzed. Such a comparison can also test whether the observers have been trained well enough to squeeze their biases out of them. An example is a study in which two well-trained psycholinguists counted the number of pauses of various kinds in a recorded speech. Both of them practiced and compared their counts until these practice counts agreed with each other (Maclay & Osgood). Then each could observe individually without fear of undue bias creeping in. It is often wise to select observers who differ on relevant dimensions, for example, foreign-born and native-born, old and young, white and black, and so on.

This technique of comparing ratings among observers, and of averaging the ratings among observers if the ratings differ, can be especially powerful when the observers themselves are part of the situation and therefore have strong emotional reactions that affect their judgments. For example, the average judgment among a sample of several enlisted men is likely to provide a less biased rating of an officer than will that of just one enlisted man (Selvin, 1960, pp. 31–33); averaging samples of students and patients is likely to provide "better" judgments of teachers and doctors, respectively, than are judgments by just one student and one patient.

The previous examples show how observers can inject bias into what they hear and see and also into their judgments of what they hear and see. But bias can also come from the way that the researcher himself *affects* the human subjects, as we shall see shortly.

3. Cheating by Interviewers

Interviewers have found many ways to avoid their assigned duties (Roth). Some of these deviations are not larcenous; for example, the interviewer may merely skip an interview because the house does not look pleasant from outside. But some of the deviations are pure theft; the interviewer may fill out the questionnaire schedules in her armchair at home, and, worst of all, she may do it with such skill that the answers are hard to distinguish from the real thing without some independent check. (An experienced survey analyst claims, however, that, even though he cannot detect one phony interview, he can tell when a whole group has been falsified by examining the pattern of dispersion among the answers. I hope he is right.)

Prevention and detection of interviewer cheating require a detective's imagination and resourcefulness. Here are some frequently used techniques.

First, the study supervisor may check to see whether the interviewer really carried out the interview by contacting some or all of the subjects by telephone or postcard. This tactic is not feasible if the respondents are guaranteed anonymity. Social scientists do not, however, always act according to the letter of their guarantees and often use key numbers on questionnaires to check against master lists. One hopes that such ethical breaches do not have serious consequences.

Second, someone once told me of a mechanical device that rolls the ques-

FIGURE 19.2

"Our computer analysis of your consumer interviews shows you chickened-out after the second question, Ralph."

Source: Reprinted from *Marketing News* published by the American Marketing Association. June 4, 1976, p. 11. Used with permission.

tionnaire past a writing window, one question at a time and irreversibly. It prevents the interviewer from skipping some of the questions and later filling them out at home.

Third, examination of the answers and analysis of their internal consistency can reveal cheating; this is dramatized in Figure 19.2.

Finally, some researchers claim to have developed special cheat-catcher questions, but they are kept as trade secrets.

If you detect cheating, *find out how much cheating there is,* and report it in your write-up, even though unsophisticated readers of your study or critics with vested interests may seize upon this report as a means of damning the study. In an example of this procedure, F. Evans (1959) found no important personality differences between Ford owners and Chevrolet owners. Commercial motivation researchers raised a howl because this finding threatened their livelihoods, and one of the motivation researchers seized upon Evans' report that one of his interviewers had cheated—which Evans had allowed for by discarding those data—to discredit the study. But sophisticated readers gained confidence from his report because they were reassured that there was no unreported but worrisome cheating.

4. Variability Among Observers

Variability *among* observers is not a special type of difficulty. Rather, it is a combination of variability *within* individual observers and systematic bias differences among observers. Avoiding these two sources of error separately automatically solves the problem of variability among observers.

5. Observer-Caused Effects

The researcher's efforts to study a phenomenon *always* affect the phenomenon and change it. The observer is inevitably a part of the same environment as is the phenomenon she is studying. Therefore, the observer, like all other aspects of the environment, must influence the phenomenon. Sometimes the effect is so slight that it may be ignored, as is usually the case in the physical sciences. For example, the act of measuring the time it takes a ball bearing to roll down an incline affects the ball in some infinitesimal way; there is gravitational attraction between the observer's eyeballs as they roll in her head and the ball bearing as it rolls down the incline, but the attraction is too small to measure. On the other hand, a chemist's breath may well affect a reaction he is running.

The observer effect in medical examinations straddles the physical and social sciences. When a doctor (or especially a young nurse, in the case of male patients) takes a patient's blood pressure, fear or excitement often forces the blood pressure far above the normal level.

More generally, there is the possibility that *every* sort of observation method, whether or not it involves a human observer, may importantly influence the behavior of the subject matter. The most general remedy for this obstacle is to make the observation procedure as "unobtrusive" as possible (see Webb *et al.*). This topic will be discussed in more generality on page 334.

The danger of observer-caused effects is that the researcher may not realize that they are operating and affecting the results. In I. Pavlov's case:

> It was thought at the beginning of our research that it would be sufficient simply to isolate the experimenter in the research chamber with the dog on its stand, and to refuse admission to anyone else during the course of an experiment. But this precaution was found to be wholly inadequate, since the experimenter, however still he might try to be, was himself a constant source of a large number of stimuli. His slightest movements—blinking of the eyelids or movement of the eyes, posture, respiration, and so on—all acted as stimuli which, falling upon the dog, were sufficient to vitiate the experiments by making exact interpretation of the results extremely difficult. In order to exclude this undue influence on the part of the experimenter as far as possible, he had to be stationed outside the room in which the dog was placed. . . . (Pavlov, pp. 108–109)

As H. Spencer pointed out long ago (pp. 66–67), observer-caused effects make trouble in the social sciences because human beings are both the subject of study *and* the observers. The consequent *interaction* between subject and observer must have consequences. We humans spend large parts of our lives learning to pick up and act upon subtle cues given us by people with whom we are in contact. Therefore, even very subtle behavior of the observer can affect the study results. For example, the inflection and tone of voice in which an interviewer asks a question can produce one response or another. A serious charge against the Kinsey study was that the subjects told the interviewers what they thought the interviewers wanted to hear or what they thought would shock the interviewers. But Kinsey's cross-checking techniques satisfied the official reviewers that error from this source was not great (Cochran, *et al.*).

One might argue that in history, economics, or political science there are no observer-caused effects because the research generally takes place after the events are complete. Brutus killed Caesar no matter what the historian says about it now. But might not Brutus' act have been affected by how Brutus thought that future historians might interpret and judge what he did? Furthermore, Brutus' behavior was probably influenced by bystanders, who were really the observers of the event and the sources of the accounts that historians use. And in economics the course of economic events is clearly affected by the kind of *records* that are kept, which are the raw material for the economist later. Someone has argued that Germany was more injured in World War II by unsatisfactory national accounting than by its oil shortage.

We shall consider five kinds of observer-caused effects in social science: first, interviewer effects upon interviewees; second, effects of publicity about study findings; third, time-sequence and repetition effects; fourth, placebo effects; and fifth, experimenter effects.

a. EFFECTS OF INTERVIEWERS UPON INTERVIEWEES

Interviewers' biased perceptions of interviewees and their responses can cause trouble, as we saw earlier. But, even if the interviewer is perfectly unbiased, the interviewee may be affected by her. In both instances, the nature of the observer or her action affects the observation and creates an obstacle. When the observer actually causes change in the phenomenon she is studying, we call the change an "observer-caused effect." But if only what the observer *sees and hears* is affected, we call it "bias." Some people may not care to make the distinction between the two difficulties.

. . . [A] whole series of studies shows that survey results for specialized atti- tudes are affected by the disparities or similarities in the group membership of interviewer and respondent. For example, in two NORC surveys samples of Christian respondents in New York City were asked whether Jews in America had too much influence in the business world. Among those who were inter- viewed by Christian interviewers, 50 percent said the Jews had too much in- fluence, but among those interviewed by Jewish interviewers, only 22 percent said so. In another survey in which respondents were asked whether they agreed with the statement "Prison is too good for sex criminals; they should be publicly whipped or worse," among women respondents who were interviewed by men interviewers 61 percent agreed with this statement; whereas when women were interviewed by women interviewers, only 49 percent agreed. It would seem either that women are less bloodthirsty when they are in the company of their own species or, put more precisely, that they feel more compelled to give the conventional and sanctioned attitude to a male interviewer. In another survey, in which one group of Negroes was interviewed by white interviewers and an equivalent group by Negro interviewers, similar effects were observed. For example, when asked whether the Army is unfair to Negroes, 35 percent of those interviewed by Negroes said "Yes," but only 11 percent of those inter- viewed by whites were willing to express this critical attitude. It is well docu- mented that responses vary with the disparity between interviewer's and re- spondent's sex, class, color, religion, and other group-membership factors. And the systematic direction of these effects is such that one would not attribute them to mere unreliability but to the way in which the respondent alters his behavior in accordance with the kind of person who speaks to him. (Hyman, 1954, pp. 517–518)

Techniques for overcoming this obstacle are much the same as the tech- niques for surmounting observer bias. For example, observer bias in ques- tionnaire surveys is often reduced by handing the subject a written question list. Construction of unbiased questions is a similar problem that we shall discuss later.

The participant-observer method in anthropology is fraught with the diffi- culty of observer-caused effects, and it is not easy for the researcher to decide how to act. W. Whyte experienced these difficulties in an Italian ghetto in New England:

> I had to face the question of how far I was to immerse myself in the life of the district. I bumped into that problem one evening as I was walking down the street with the Nortons. Trying to enter into the spirit of the small talk, I cut loose with a string of obscenities and profanity. The walk came to a momentary halt as they all stopped to look at me in surprise. Doc shook his head and said: "Bill, you're not supposed to talk like that. That doesn't sound like you."
>
> I tried to explain that I was only using terms that were common on the street corner. Doc insisted, however, that I was different and that they wanted me to be that way. . . .
>
> While I sought to avoid influencing individuals or groups, I tried to be helpful in the way a friend is expected to help in Cornerville. When one of the boys had to go downtown on an errand and wanted company, I went along with him. When somebody was trying to get a job and had to write a letter about himself, I helped him to compose it, and so on. This sort of behavior presented no problem, but, when it came to the matter of handling money, it was not at all clear just how I should behave. Of course, I sought to spend money on my friends just as they did on me. But what about lending money? It is expected in such a district that a man will help out his friends whenever he can, and often the help needed is financial. I lent money on several occasions, but I always felt uneasy about it. Naturally, a man appreciates it at the time you lend him the money, but how does he feel later when the time has come to pay, and he is not able to do so? Perhaps he is embarrassed and tries to avoid your company. On such occasions I tried to reassure the individual and tell him that I knew he did not have it just then and that I was not worried about it. Or I even told him to forget about the debt altogether. But that did not wipe it off the books; the uneasiness remained. I learned that it is possible to do a favor for a friend and cause a strain in the relationship in the process. (Whyte, pp. 304–305)

And B. Malinowski, an early developer of the participant-observer method, pointed out:

> . . . [I]f, like a trader or a missionary or an official he [the anthropologist] enters into active relations with the native, if he has to transform or influence or make use of him, this makes a real, unbiased, impartial observation impossible, and precludes all-round sincerity, at least in the case of the missionaries and officials. (Malinowski, p. 18)

b. THE "PUBLICITY" OR "DISCLOSURE OF RESULTS" EFFECT

The public announcement of presidential preelection polls probably affects the election. On the one hand, a poll result might persuade some people that it is a waste of time to throw away their votes on a candidate who is going to lose, and such a reaction might aid a candidate whom the poll shows to be ahead. This is an example of a "self-fulfilling prophecy" (Merton, pp. 179–195). Politicians believe in this poll effect, judging by their screams at election time. P. Lazarsfeld, *et al.* (1948, pp. 107–108), did demonstrate that there is some "bandwagon effect"—people voting for the candidate they expect to win; poll publicity could affect such expectations.

But a poll might help a candidate who is shown to be losing narrowly, by stirring his partisans to rise to the emergency. Perhaps such a self-*defeating* prophecy helped to elect Truman in the 1948 presidential election; the polls showed him slightly behind Dewey. The only evidence on actual election effects that I have seen is that voters who do not vote in the morning may be led not to vote at all by news reports of early election returns (Fuchs).

A forecast of economic inflation may magnify the inflation or even create an inflation that would not have occurred otherwise. People who hear the inflation forecast rush out to make purchases before prices rise. These purchases then actually cause prices to rise. For a contrary example, a forecast of low corn prices may discourage some farmers from planting corn, which may in turn *raise* the price of corn above the level it would have reached without the forecast.

Unlike most other research obstacles, publicity effects can easily be prevented by the researcher. All she has to do is refrain from disclosing the results until events have run their course.

Some studies are done expressly to influence the outcome of the event. The study results are then publicized, withheld, or distorted for tactical reasons. Such use of research is one government weapon against economic recession or inflation. If people are told that prices are coming down, they may refrain from buying and wait for the lower prices. The fall in purchasing may then drive down the prices and curb the inflation.

This phenomenon resembles "feedback," which is discussed on page 351. True feedback, however, does not involve the observer but only the subject; something that the subject herself does affects her own subsequent behavior.

C. SEQUENCE AND REPETITION EFFECTS

One observation sometimes influences the next observation. The farmer cannot afford to break open each egg he sells to see if it is fresh; the next person to examine the egg would then surely find it worthless. Observations that require breaking the egg or the light bulb or the clay pigeon are called "destructive testing," for obvious reasons, and they are one form of repetition effect in which what you do at one time affects the subsequent state of affairs.

Here is an anonymous wag's illustration: You step on a man's toe and then apologize. He accepts your apology graciously. If you then repeat the experiment and step on his toe again, his second response may not be the same as his first.

Sequence effects (also called "position" effects) are a frequent obstacle in psychological studies of learning. We know that the first and most recent stimuli will often be remembered best. For example, if you ask a subject to memorize a list of nonsense syllables, the middle syllables will not get a fair shake. Therefore, if you want to compare the memorization speed of one type of nonsense syllable with the memorization speed of another type of nonsense syllable, you must somehow overcome this obstacle.

A standard technique for avoiding sequence effects is to *vary the sequence* in which the stimuli are presented to different subjects. If there are only three stimuli, one group of subjects may be given stimuli ABC in that order, whereas other groups receive the stimuli in orders BCA, CAB, CBA, ACB, and BAC. The design is "balanced"; that is, each stimulus has an equal chance to be first, second, or third, and the average scores for the stimuli can be compared directly. In other cases in which every stimulus does not have an equal chance, one can determine how much worse the middle (and perhaps last) stimuli did and then make appropriate adjustments. When there are many different stimuli, one can present them to subjects in random order.

Repetition effects are particularly important in panel studies[2] and in any research in which subjects are observed or questioned more than once. Sometimes the subjects are not affected by repetition; there is some evidence that on consumer buying panels the subjects do not "wear out" very rapidly (Sandage; Sobol). But several voting studies have shown differences in the subjects' responses depending upon whether they had previously been asked about their voting intentions. Let us consider these data on the rate of recall for advertisements of a group of women who were interviewed several times:

RECALL AVERAGE

| First Interview | 19.1 |
| Second Interview | 24.9 |

"Respondents were not told on the first interview that they would be contacted again. Yet their interest in advertising was heightened . . . and their retention of commercial messages in the magazine was vastly improved" (Politz, p. 7).

In studies in which there is danger of subjects' being sensitized by earlier observations, the first step is to establish whether there really is a sensitization effect. The simplest way to do so is to compare the second responses of one group against responses of a similar group that has not received a first treatment. In panels, compare a particular set of responses of prior members of the panel with parallel responses from newly recruited panel members. If there is no difference, then you can assume that sensitization is not taking place, and you can accept the panel data at face value (Sudman, 1966).

---

2. In panel studies people are observed or questioned at several different times. Panel studies are discussed in Chapter 20, which includes bibliographical references.

If significant sensitization does occur, you must forgo the repeat-interview or panel technique and employ some other method instead.

d. PLACEBO EFFECTS

Long ago physicians observed that giving a patient a pill—*any* pill, even if it contained only sugar—would often alleviate the symptoms of many diseases. The effect is not limited to those ailments usually regarded as psychosomatic. It includes angina pectoris, which is a type of heart disease; *any* new remedy seems to have the power to alleviate angina symptoms for six or eight months. This is the "placebo effect"; the fake medication is called a "placebo."

Sometimes the fake medication really affects the patient physically. Other times the patient only *thinks* he is getting better and reports the alleviation of symptoms to the doctor even though his underlying condition does not change. This can confuse the investigation of worthless drugs. When medical researchers experiment with the chemical effects of a drug, they must allow for the possible placebo effect, in order not to confuse the two.

The placebo effect brings home to us that medical research is in many ways a social science. It shares many obstacles to knowledge with other social sciences, and it therefore uses many of the same research methods, which is why examples from medical research are included in this book.

One way to avoid the placebo effect is to give the medication without the patient's knowing that he is receiving it—dissolving it in food, perhaps, or mixing it with some other medication that the patient already takes routinely.

The "double blind" experimental design is another method. In the first period group A receives a placebo that looks and tastes like the experimental medicine, and in the second period group A is switched to the real medication. Group B starts with the medication and then is switched to the sugar pill. Neither the doctor nor the patient knows who is getting the placebo; hence the name "double blind." Not only does this design prevent the patient from being affected psychologically, but it also prevents the doctor from reading the symptoms she expects to see. The amount of the placebo effect is then subtracted from the medication effect. One can then infer that any observed differences between the medication effect and the placebo effect may be accounted for by the medication.

e. EXPERIMENTER EFFECTS

The famous Hawthorne effect is another illustration of how the researcher can unwittingly obscure the effect of the variable in which she is interested. A group headed by E. Mayo (Roethlisburger & Dickson; Madge, Chap. 6) working at the Hawthorne plant of Western Electric set out to determine the effects of variations in the intensity of light and working hours on the productivity of a group of women factory workers. To their surprise, they found that *everything* they tried—even worse lighting—seemed to increase productivity. Then an explanation dawned upon the researchers: The increases in productivity were apparently (but perhaps not actually) caused by the *attention* paid to the workers as subjects of research.[3]

The Hawthorne experimenter—attention effect—the subjects performing better (or worse) so as to please (or displease) the experimenter—is only one of many influences that the experimenter can unwittingly have upon the subjects in the experiment. An equally prominent problem is that the subjects may find out what behavior the experimenter expects of them, and then perform as expected (see Rosenthal). This phenomenon is important both for its effects upon research and its effects in operating situations such as the classroom.

An example of expectancy effect in an operating situation is an experiment where teachers were told that certain children "would show unusual academic development" during the school year, though the children so designated were actually chosen at random. Then the children were tested at the end of the year. The effect of the teachers' expectancies can be seen in the results for grades 1 and 2 in Table 19.1.

The expectancies of an experimenter can be transmitted subtly, sometimes so subtly that they are difficult to detect. The story of Clever Hans, the horse who could do arithmetic, brings out the point:

> Clever Hans . . . was the horse of Mr. von Osten, a German mathematics teacher. By means of tapping his foot, Hans was able to add, subtract, multiply, and divide. Hans could spell, read, and solve problems of musical harmony.
>
> Mr. von Osten . . . did not profit from his animal's talent, nor did it seem at all likely that he was attempting to perpetrate a fraud. He swore he did not cue the animal, and he permitted other people to question and test the horse even without his being present. Pfungst and his famous colleague, Stumpf, undertook a program of systematic research to discover the secret of Hans' talents. Among the first discoveries made was that if the horse could not see the questioner, Hans was not clever at all. Similarly, if the questioner did not himself know the answer to the question, Hans could not answer it either. Still, Hans was able to answer Pfungst's questions as long as the investigator was present and visible. Pfungst reasoned that the questioner might in some way be signaling to Hans when to begin and when to stop tapping his hoof. A forward inclination of the head of the questioner would start Hans tapping, Pfungst observed. He tried then to incline his head forward without asking a question

---

3. Here is a digression on the history of social science that carries an important warning. For almost five decades the Hawthorne findings have exerted a powerful effect both on the social sciences—actually creating a whole new research tradition—and on American industrial relations. In 1967 Carey made a persuasive attack upon the Hawthorne work as a whole, arguing that its conclusions in no way follow from the actual data and that the work falls into error because it fails to conform to elementary canons of scientific procedure. And he notes that similar questions were raised shortly after the first Hawthorne reports appeared but were ignored by most social scientists. Carey's charges have not been rebutted, which—together with the strong evidence he and others have offered—suggests that the Hawthorne study conclusions are unfounded in fact. Yet they continue to be taught and quoted. (We can usefully continue to refer to Hawthorne effects here, however, whether or not they really exist in industry.)

TABLE 19.1   Teacher Expectancy Effects: Gain in IQ of Experimental over Control Groups (after eight months)

Initial Ability Level

Grades	Higher	Average	Lower	Weighted Means
1	+11.2	+9.6	+24.8	+15.4
2	+18.2	−2.9	+6.1	+9.5
3	−4.3	+9.1	−6.3	−0.0
4	0.0	+0.2	+9.0	+3.4
5	−0.5	Not obtained	+1.2	−0.0
6	−1.3	+1.2	−0.5	−0.7

Rosenthal, p. 411.

and discovered that this was sufficient to start Hans' tapping. As the experimenter straightened up, Hans would stop tapping. Pfungst then tried to get Hans to stop tapping by using very slight upward motions of the head. He found that even the raising of his eyebrows was sufficient. Even the dilation of the questioner's nostrils was a cue for Hans to stop tapping.

When a questioner bent forward more, the horse would tap faster. This added to the reputation of Hans as brilliant. That is, when a large number of taps was the correct response, Hans would tap very, very rapidly until he approached the region of correctness, and then he began to slow down. It was found that questioners typically bent forward more when the answer was a long one, gradually straightening up as Hans got closer to the correct number.

For some experiments, Pfungst discovered that auditory cues functioned additively with visual cues. When the experimenter was silent, Hans was able to respond correctly 31 percent of the time in picking one of many placards with different words written on it, or cloths of different colors. When auditory cues were added, Hans responded correctly 56 percent of the time.

Pfungst himself then played the part of Hans, tapping out responses to questions with his hand. Of 25 questioners, 23 unwittingly cued Pfungst as to when to stop tapping in order to give a correct response. None of the questioners (males and females of all ages and occupations) knew the intent of the experiment. When errors occurred, they were usually only a single tap from being correct. The subjects of this study, including an experienced psychologist, were unable to discover that they were unintentionally emitting cues.

Hans' amazing talents, talents rapidly acquired too by Pfungst, serve to illustrate further the power of the self-fulfilling prophecy. Hans' questioners, even skeptical ones, expected Hans to give the correct answers to their queries. Their expectation was reflected in their unwitting signal to Hans that the time had come for him to stop his tapping. The signal cued Hans to stop, and the questioner's expectation became the reason for Hans' being, once again, correct. . . . (Rosenthal, pp. 137–138, after Pfungst)

There are a variety of strategies for reducing the danger of experimenter effects, as summarized in Table 19.2. But sometimes it is difficult to overcome this obstacle. In the Hawthorne case, for example, researchers might have varied the intensity of the light without the workers' perceiving that they were the subjects of an experiment. But it would have been next

TABLE 19.2 Strategies for the Control of Experimenter Expectancy Effects

1. Increasing the number of experimenters:
   decreases learning of influence techniques
   helps to maintain "blindness"
   minimizes effects of early data returns
   increases generality of results
   randomizes expectancies . . .
   permits statistical correction of expectancy effects
2. Observing the behavior of experimenters:
   sometimes reduces expectancy effects . . .
   facilitates greater standardization of experimenter behavior
3. Analyzing experiments for order effects:
   permits inference about changes in experimenter behavior
4. Analyzing experiments for computational errors:
   permits inference about expectancy effects
5. Developing training procedures:
   permits prediction of expectancy effects
6. Maintaining "blind" contact:
   minimizes expectancy effects [by avoiding feedback from
   experimenters and subjects]
7. Minimizing experimenter-subject contact [by using screens and
   automated data-collection systems]
8. Giving different expectancies to various experimenters:
   permits assessment of expectancy effects

(Adapted from Rosenthal, pp. 402–404)

to impossible to vary the hours in the work day without the workers' realizing that they were being singled out for special attention. Some other techniques are therefore required.

One way of allowing for observer interference when you cannot prevent it is to vary the amounts and kinds of experimenter behavior, holding all else constant, as suggested in strategy 8 in Table 19.2. At Hawthorne the observers might have varied the amount of time they spent with the workers and whether they acted friendly or unfriendly toward the workers under well-controlled conditions. If such variations on the part of the observer produced *no* differences, then it would be safe to say that the observer is not an important source of variation. As a further control, it is possible to bring the observer into a situation in which nothing else is changed from normal and then measure whether his presence alone would cause any difference. This is like giving one group no pill at all and the other group a placebo, to estimate the effect of the placebo alone.

6. Summary

Observers of human behavior are themselves human, and hence are subject to human errors. These human errors are one of the main obstacles that the researcher must overcome.

Humans vary from moment to moment in how they observe even the same phenomenon. This variability must be controlled as well as possible with instrumentation, instructions, and training. Variability *among* observers may be tackled in similar manner.

Observers often bring their own biases to their work. These biases must be made to affect the observations as little as possible, and what effect does occur should be evaluated and allowed for.

Cheating by observers is a problem to be tackled with checkups and detective work.

Now that you have read through this first of the chapters on the obstacles to knowledge and the devices for surmounting them, you have perhaps concluded that the tactics for overcoming obstacles in research are merely common sense. True. But the study of *other people's* common-sense learning, as embodied in this and other books on the subject, can save you time, money, and heartbreak.

Among the conditions that might be altered to influence experimenter expectancies are: descriptions of the subjects (e.g., as fast learners or slow learners); descriptions of the effectiveness of the experimental variable; and expectations of results predicted by the theory (Rosenthal, p. 404).

7. Appendix: Personal Interviewing and Interviews

Interviewing has always been the main device for obtaining social, psychological, and economic information. And it will certainly continue to be important in the future despite the growth of self-administered questionnaires, self-reports, and automated data collection. Therefore, a few words especially dedicated to the practice of interviewing seem in order, though interviewing is touched upon in many other sections of the book. (A review of the advantages and disadvantages of personal interviewing compared to telephone and mail interviews is given on page 318.)

Perhaps the most important element in good interviewing is that the interviewer not influence the response that the interviewee gives, by word or gesture or general demeanor, as discussed in this chapter. The interviewer must be friendly and pleasant so that the interviewee will be willing to cooperate. But the interviewer should not make the interviewee want to answer in such manner that he or she thinks will please the interviewer. And, the interviewer must not send out signals that will antagonize the interviewee into answering wrongly or perversely as an attempt to foul up the interviewer.

Toward the same end, the interviewee should not indicate in any way what answers the interviewer expects or wants to receive.

In addition to being pleasant and interested in the interviewee, the interviewer can increase the likelihood of obtaining cooperation if she or he dresses more-or-less like the interviewee, though not in a spectacular or "far out" manner.

A good interviewer must know the material thoroughly and follow instructions to the letter. Questions must be read exactly as they are written, in the order in which they are given, and the answers must be rendered faithfully, with as little interpretation as possible. All this requires study and practice before going into the field.

Sometimes interviewers are instructed to go beyond the written questions in order to "probe" for answers and underlying reasons. Good probing requires experience and tact.

The work of hired interviewers must be spot-checked by supervisors to ensure that the interviews were really done, and that the responses are those that the interviewee gave.

Some interviewers are much better than others (Sheatsley; Sudman, 1967, pp. 108–153). Interviewers who have worked at the occupation for a long time are—on the whole—faster, more efficient, and more accurate than newer interviewers. This may be because the poorer interviewers leave the occupation, because people learn, or both.

Education and intelligence also are positively associated with the quality and quantity of work that interviewers produce. National Opinion Research Center's demographic profile of the best interviewer is a married, middle-aged woman, with some college education and previous interviewing experience.

Personality and motivation also are important factors in interviewer success. This includes self-confidence, a positive attitude toward interviewing, and the desire to do a good job—none of which is easy to measure, however, and most of which would make the person an effective employee in *any* position.

Even more important than screening potential interviewers before hiring them is to continually evaluate their performance after they have been hired. An attentive, close-watching supervisor is the basic check. Additionally, coders of the data can supply quantitative estimates of interviewer quality by recording interviewer errors. This is the error-weighting system used by National Opinion Research Center:

Type of Error	Error Weight
1. Answer missing	3
2. Irrelevant or circular answer	3
3. Lack of sufficient detail	2
4. "Don't know" with no probe	2
5. Dangling probe	1
6. Multiple codes in error	1
7. Superfluous question asked	1

(Sudman, 1967, p. 109)

EXERCISES

1. Give examples, from actual research in your field, of these obstacles:
   a. observer variability
   b. observer bias
   c. variability among observers
   d. observer-caused effect on subjects
   e. publicity effects
   f. sequence or repetition effect
   g. Hawthorne (placebo) effect
2. Suggest methods to surmount each of the obstacles in the examples you have given in Exercise 1.

ADDITIONAL READING FOR CHAPTER 19

Observational methods and problems are discussed by Bickman (Chapter 8 in Selltiz *et al.*).

Denzin describes the sociological interview from the "interactionist" perspective (Chapter 6).

Webb *et al.* detail a great many strategies, with accompanying examples, in the use of devices to study people without their knowledge and without interfering with their behavior.

For a discussion of how medical researchers are sometimes fooled, see Loranger *et al.* (1961).

Kornhauser and Sheatsley (in Selltiz *et al.*, pp. 563–574) discuss the art of interviewing concisely.

Additional useful works on interviewing: Gordon; Kahn and Cannell; Richardson; Selltiz *et al.* (Chapter 9).

The basic work on interviewer effects and selection of interviewers is Hyman *et al.* (1975). See also Parten and Payne on this topic, as well as Hyman (1950), pp. 519–523.

An interesting account of interviewing, as perceived by the interviewer, is that of Converse and Schuman.

Rosenthal (1966) is the classic work on experimenter effects in behavioral research.

20 complexities and intractability of the human mind: appendix on questionnaire construction

The obstacles to knowledge that are discussed in this chapter are both the bane and the joy of the social-science researcher—especially of the social scientist who works with questionnaires. These obstacles are the salt of his work, the unique flavor that sets it apart from other scientific work; the chemist or astronomer never faces these obstacles. There is an excellent and voluminous literature on these matters, and you should read extensively in it if you plan to do work in social psychology, economic-data collection, market research, anthropology, or related areas (for example, Ferber & Wales; Hyman, 1955).

1. Lack of Knowledge by the Subject

Much of your own behavior cannot be accurately reported by you. In some cases this is because you do not pay attention to the behavior. For example, if you were asked exactly how many pages you had actually opened a particular magazine to, you would have trouble answering accurately ten minutes later even if you were prompted by being shown all its pages one by one. (One researcher overcame this obstacle by putting little dabs of light glue between each pair of pages of magazines, then examining the copies to see how many glue seals had been broken.)

Another example is the number of television commercials you actually watch, compared to how many you switch stations to avoid or how many you tune out by leaving the room or attending to something else. One's self-report is not likely to be accurate about this behavior. Steiner attacked this problem by having observers surreptitiously watch other members of their families during commercials.

Still another form of this obstacle arises in obtaining data on the *combined* behavior of various people. Even if I know how many pages of a magazine I read, I do not know how many other people have read how many pages of the same copy, even if it is my family copy. One way to overcome this obstacle is to add up the pages looked at by all people (actually, a sample of all people) and divide by the number of copies. A more amusing technique was tried about thirty years ago. A researcher counted the number of fingerprints on magazine copies whose pages had been dusted with special fingerprint powder. (This is another example of the intellectual kinship between detective work and empirical scientific research.)

Businessmen's lack of knowledge of their own behavior is an interesting example. Two economists asked businessmen how they set prices, and many replied that they added fixed markups to their costs (Hall & Hitch). But other analyses that assume prices are set according to what the market will bear explain actual prices better than do the businessmen. Apparently the businessmen fail to recognize when they make adjustments to meet competition and otherwise maximize their profits. One can, however, ask different kinds of questions of the businessmen. A used-car dealer may be able to tell you very intelligently and accurately why he set a price of $2000 on a particular two-year-old Chevrolet even if he cannot tell you how he sets prices *in general*. Still another way is to infer his procedure from his answers to various relevant facts. I asked newspaper executives what they thought their sales to two classes of customers would have been if their prices had been 10 per cent lower or 10 per cent higher. Their answers explained satisfactorily why one class of customers was charged more than the other (J. Simon, 1965d).

An anthropologist must ask "natives" the kinds of questions that the natives can answer knowledgeably, as B. Malinowski points out:

Exactly as a humble member of any modern institution, whether it be the state, or the church, or the army, is *of* it and *in* it, but has no vision of the resulting integral action of the whole, still less could furnish any account of its organization, so it would be futile to attempt questioning a native in abstract, sociological terms. . . .

Though we cannot ask a native about abstract, general rules, we can always enquire how a given case would be treated. Thus for instance, in asking how they would treat crime, or punish it, it would be vain to put to a native a sweeping question such as, "How do you treat and punish a criminal?" for even words could not be found to express it in native, or in pidgin. But an imaginary case, or still better, a real occurrence, will stimulate a native to express his opinion and to supply plentiful information. (Malinowski, pp. 11–12)

Sometimes one group of respondents can answer with more knowledge and accuracy than another group. World War II questioning showed that men who had not yet been in battle were most afraid of air attack, whereas men who had been into battle most feared 88 mm. artillery. To rely more heavily upon the answers of combat veterans seems sensible because their knowledge is greater (Stouffer, *et al.,* II, 235).

2. The Fallibility of Memory

One of the ways that we can learn about human behavior is to ask people how they have acted or what has happened in the past. But it is not news that people sometimes forget things. If you intend to use the products of people's memories as data, you must guard against the inaccuracy of their memories.

A. Kinsey recognized that his subjects might have forgotten what they had done in the past, at what age they had first done it, and how often. To estimate the importance of memory loss he checked up on subsamples of interviewees' memories by various devices. One of these important devices he called "take and retake." Subjects in the take-retake group were asked for their sexual history and then were interviewed again many months later. The two interviews were then compared to see how well the subjects' later statements checked against their earlier statements.

Kinsey was able also to check the quality of subjects' memories by asking questions about their physical development (such as the age of growth of pubic hair) and then comparing those answers against objective physical data. Physical checks of memory were obviously impossible for most parts of the Kinsey study, however.

Kinsey's checks revealed that forgetting differed among types of questions. Forgetting had little effect on the reported *types* of behavior people had engaged in. It had more effect on the reports of *frequency* of behavior. And there was most memory loss about the *age* at which subjects first engaged in various types of behavior.

Several devices offer some protection if you think memory loss may be large. One method of reducing memory loss is to have subjects keep *diaries* of their behavior, so that no remembering is necessary—a common practice in television-viewing research and in market research. No consumer would be likely to remember after a week just what products he had bought the week before and how much of each. But if you get him to write down his purchases *immediately after* he makes them, memory loss can be negligible.

Mechanical counting devices are sometimes useful. For example, if you want to know how often a person on a special diet thinks of food, you can ask her to click a pocket counter. Or, P. Lazarsfeld and F. Stanton developed a "program analyzer" with which a person registered his likes and dislikes of various parts of radio programs by pressing buttons. (Stanton was president of CBS, and I wished he would have put a program analyzer in *my* house.)

In some cases you can circumvent people's bad memories by referring to existing records. For example, you can ask to see their bank books and other financial records instead of asking people how much they have saved (Ferber). In other cases, you must substitute observation techniques for question techniques. The Nielsen Audimeter is a mechanical device that automatically records when a television set is on and when it is off. And another device actually *photographs* people watching the television screen to measure who is actually watching, as well as whether the set is on (Allen).

The type of forgetting euphemistically called "confusion" is a bugaboo of readership research. Show a person a magazine and ask him whether he has read it. He may say "yes" even though he has *not* read it. Actually, memory (or other faculties) plays tricks on people, and they confuse what you show them with something else that they have seen. To overcome this confusion, one group of people is shown a dummy magazine that has never been printed. The proportion that says "yes" to this "placebo" is subtracted from the proportion that says "yes" to the real magazine.

Percentage who say they read actual magazine	42%
Percentage who say they read dummy magazine	12%
Percentage estimated to have read actual magazine	30%

Here is a general precept for dealing with memory loss: It is always good practice to reduce the time period between the event to be remembered and the interview to the shortest possible interval.

Perhaps the simplest memory obstacle to overcome is increasing *fatigue* in the subject. For example, in readership surveys, the interviewer shows the subject page after page of a magazine and asks whether the subject has seen the page. Toward the end of the interview the subject is tired and therefore less likely to remember an article or advertisement. If the interviewer always started at the front of a magazine and worked toward the back, the pages at the back would always be tested on tired people and would therefore be underrated. Readership surveys overcome this difficulty by starting at different places in the magazine with different respondents. In this way, pages at the front, middle, and back have equal opportunities with fresh and fatigued subjects. "Other things" are not equal for any *individual* subject. But for the group taken as a whole, all other things are indeed roughly equal for front, back, and middle advertisements and articles.

3. Cover-Up

There are some factors that people do not want to reveal to strangers (even to intimate friends, or *especially* to intimate friends) because of embarrassment, guilt, shame, or other social motives. The subject may therefore deny, exaggerate, minimize, or otherwise knowingly operate upon the truth to shape it into a form that he feels is more acceptable. Barry Goldwater believed that this obstacle was operating strongly in preelection polls in 1964:

> Senator Goldwater's own polls show that President Johnson has a large lead over him. Sources close to Mr. Goldwater said last week he believes that if his position in the polls does not improve he will be politically dead.

> But the Senator is also said to believe that "subtle impulses," many of which the voters will not discuss candidly with pollsters or with any other questioners, are at work among voters this year and could bring him victory Nov. 3. (*New York Times,* September 4, 1964, p. 2E)

Observation can sometimes operate as a check and prevent misinformation, as, for example, when the subject claims a level of income quite inconsistent with her home or job. Or the researcher can build into the interview internal checks that get at the truth in several different ways and therefore show up inconsistent answers. The take-retake technique can also be used to check on how much cover-up is operating; as cross-examining lawyers know, falsehood can be revealed by discrepant answers to repeated questions when the subject forgets his original lie.

The intuition of a highly trained interviewer can often distinguish truth from falsity. Kinsey's interviewers, for example, were trained to recognize and use the vocabulary of prostitutes in order to elicit responses that would help them to judge whether a woman was really a prostitute. Kinsey relied heavily upon this sort of ability in his interviews. But each of the Kinsey interviewers had a full year's training in these skills. There are few interviewing staffs that can be so well trained and upon whose intuitive capacity it would be sensible to depend to any great extent.

4. Trying to Please the Observer

People like to please other people, and subjects in research studies are no exceptions. Interviewees often answer questions the way that they think the interviewer would like them to answer. And subjects in experiments often act the way they think the observer wants them to act. This is very nice of them, but such genial behavior has a ruinous result unless the researcher does something about it.

Psychologists have given much thought to protecting themselves from subjects who alter their normal behavior during experiments. Psychologists often *camouflage* the experiment and its purpose so that the subject cannot know what the experimenter wants or expects. For example, C. Hull wanted to find out how people learn a concept or make a generalization when they are *not trying* to find a generalization. But human beings are always trying to "solve the problem," especially in psychology laboratories. Hull therefore convinced the subjects that they were participating in a *memory* experiment, and the task was to learn the names of various Chinese characters, whereas in reality the subjects were gradually learning general rules about the names of types of characters. If Hull had not camouflaged the experiment, the subjects would have shown *sudden* learning rather than gradual learning of the concept. I am convinced that it is the very fact of camouflaging or not camouflaging the purpose of the experiment that has caused some experiments to obtain "discontinuous" rather than "smooth" gradual curves of learning concepts in humans. Animals need no such camouflage because (I think) they do not have a whole set of rules of thumb to help them solve problems (Simon, 1953).

In questionnaire surveys, asking the questions in an impartial way so that the interviewer's own prejudices are hidden can help to overcome the obstacle of subjects' trying to please the interviewer.

5. Rationalization and Repression

In the section on cover-up, I discussed conscious distortion of the truth. Freud convinced us, however, that much lies in the human mind that either comes into consciousness as a subconscious distortion of reality or else does not come into consciousness at all because it is repressed.

> [W]hen a group of men who had said that they wanted to avoid serving in the Infantry were asked why, only 8 per cent said that this was because the Infantry "sees too much combat" or because "Its casualty rate is too high." The great majority indicated such reasons as "I don't think I'm physically qualified for it," "It would not give me a chance to do the kind of work I can do best," and "It would not give me training for a better job after the war." The analysts felt that, in a number of cases at least, such responses were rationalizations of the "true" motive—desire to avoid danger. In an effort to determine the extent of such rationalizations, they studied the relationship between reluctance to serve in the Infantry or in overseas combat units and reported worries about battle injuries. They discovered that there was a marked relationship: the great majority of those who said that they worried often about battle injury—79 per cent to be exact—wanted to avoid both the Infantry and overseas combat service. This is in contrast to 37 per cent of those saying that they never worried. Frequently a set of interlocking questions of this type permits an intrinsic check on evasions, and their analysis leads to more convincing results. (Kendall & Lazarsfeld, p. 172)

Digging out the real beliefs and reasons for behavior may involve the use of one or more of the variegated ingenious processes that psychologists have developed. A full description of this armory of techniques for outwitting the unconscious may be found in C. Selltiz, *et al.* (Chap. 8).

6. Deception

The patterns of inanimate nature are difficult to fathom. The quirks and twistings of the human mind add complication. And to top it off, sometimes people try to deceive you for their own purposes. Deception is especially bad because all the usual scientific weapons—random sampling, for example—fail to help. The subject plays against you like an opponent in a game, and she holds many of the winning cards.

There are many wonderful stories of deception by so-called "primitive" tribesmen who tell whoppers about their sex lives to anthropologists and then chortle among themselves at the stupidity of the "civilized" scientist who could believe such nonsense. These reports may be apocryphal; nevertheless, they are instructive.

Tax data are always subject to deception.

> . . . [W]hen in 1711 a census was taken in China in connexion with the poll tax and military service, the total arrived at was 28 millions, but . . . when some years later another census was taken with a view to certain measures for the relief of distress, the total arrived at was 103 millions. (Carr-Saunders, p. A2)

Kinsey's interviewers sometimes heard remarkable lies. Some businesses make a point of releasing false data about their operations, in order to mislead their competitors. Other companies have gone to great lengths to prevent their competitors from gaining useful marketing information. The Federal Trade Commission record in the Clorox case documented instances in which Procter & Gamble concentrated unusual amounts of merchandising effort in markets in which their competitors were testing new marketing techniques, in order to muddle up their competitors' research. In another instance, one magazine sent out vast quantities of free magazines in the weeks that a major readership survey was going on so that the apparent circulation of that magazine would be inflated relative to its competitors.

Deception by national governments to frustrate the intelligence-gathering services of other nations is standard practice. Some acts of deception—feeding wrong information to enemy agents, for example—are very direct. But nations also plant false stories in their own newspapers to throw enemy content analysis off the scent. Nations have falsified national budgets, gold reserves, and production figures: "It is reported that in Russia in the early 1930s the central statistical authorities had worked out 'lie coefficients' with which to correct the statistical reports according to regions, industries, etc." (Morgenstern, pp. 20–21).

American ingenuity is sometimes used to leave an incorrect political impression:

> Gordon D. Hall, a Boston lecturer on extremist groups of both right and left, disputes Birch Society semantics as well as statistics. He said he tried unsuccessfully to get John H. Rousselot, the national public relations director, to accept a bet that the total membership in the nation was less than 25,000.
>
> How the society makes its members seem larger than they really are, said Hall, is shown by the response to an appeal by Welch for a letter-writing campaign against the Xerox Corporation of Rochester, N.Y. . . .

As part of a promotional program in 1964, Xerox contributed $4 million to Tensun Foundation, Inc., without restrictions. The foundation produced a television series on the United Nations, one of the targets of the Birch program.

Because of the flood of mail, Xerox assigned a staff to catalogue the letters. A spokesman said this week that an analysis of 51,279 unfavorable letters had shown them to be written by 12,785 individuals. All of the 12,687 favorable letters received were found to have been written by 12,687 individuals. (Champaign-Urbana *Courier*, March 7, 1965, p. 1)

A dentist told the story of an experiment during the Depression on the effect of an experimental toothpaste on bacterial concentration and tooth decay. Dental students who needed money badly ate candy bars to increase their bacterial concentration, so that they would qualify as paid subjects for the experiment. After the experiment was over they quit eating candy bars, and their bacterial concentration naturally went down. But the experimenter thought that it was his *experimental toothpaste* that had reduced the bacterial concentration. This story illustrates how the medical sciences are troubled by the complexity of the human mind and how experiments are subject to deception, just as surveys are.

There is no simple prescription for dealing with deception. Most important is to be alert to the possibility of deception; research is no place for a sweet belief in the goodness of human nature. Aside from caution and skepticism, your best bet is to make independent checks of the evidence. Kinsey compared answers given by husbands and wives and by pairs of people who could provide information about each other, to determine the extent of deception. His basic technique to overcome deception was the free interview and the trained intuition of his interviewers, who could spot much deception and refuse to be taken in by it.

If deception cannot be avoided or minimized, you may have to shift to working with other subject matter that is less subject to this obstacle. There is no point in doing research that will be wrong because you were fooled while acting in good faith.

7. A Brief Note on Behaviorism

The workings of the human mind are hidden from view. How, then, can we study a person's attitudes, desires, beliefs? One way to learn about mental processes is to assume that a person can really observe her own mental processes and report them accurately. This technique uses the subject as an instrument of the researcher to see what the researcher himself cannot see, a technique that was the basis of the introspectionist school of psychology.

Many psychologists became dissatisfied with using introspective reports by subjects because of the many kinds of distortion and inaccuracy. They turned to observing the *behavior* of subjects and inferring mental processes from it. The behavioral psychologist measures whether a person is hungry by whether she eats, rather than by her statement that she is hungry. This technique has great advantages of *precision* because we can establish with great accuracy whether eating takes place, whereas we cannot verify objectively whether she is "really" hungry. Furthermore, this technique has the bonus advantage that it allows us to study the hunger of animals, whom we cannot ask for verbal reports.

The behaviorist technique consists of watching outward behavior that can readily be observed and then assuming that the behavior is related to the inner states that are not visible for study. The advantages and disadvantages of behaviorism in psychology and related disciplines are a matter of hot dispute. It is certain that there are research situations in which observing behavior is the best possible approach. An advertiser, for example, is supremely interested in whether people really buy his product; information on purchases is more valuable than any reports of such mental processes as attitudes, feelings, beliefs. On the other hand, watching behavior provides far too little information to a psychiatrist who is trying to diagnose a case, though a good psychiatrist will make the most of behavioral evidence too. What *is* very clear is that, although studying behavior may *often* be the best way to infer knowledge about how people's minds work, it is *not always* the best method for doing so.

8. Summary

The complexity of human responses is both the source of our interest as social scientists, and an obstacle to learning about people and their behavior.

The main human-response obstacles that the researcher must contend with are these: (1) Lack of knowledge by subjects about what they do and why they do it. (2) Fallibility of people's memory about their past behavior. (3) Covering up of information that subjects think shameful or do not want to reveal. (4) Trying to say and do things that will please the observer. (5) Rationalization and repression. (6) Deceiving the observer about behavior, attitudes, and motives.

For each of these human-complexity obstacles there is a wide variety of techniques to help you overcome them. Many of these techniques are described in this chapter of the book. Others are learned with research experience.

9. Appendix: Questionnaire Construction

These are key elements in sound questionnaire construction:

1) Keep your study's purpose clearly in mind at all times. This will help ensure that you ask all the questions you want to ask, and leave out questions you don't need answers to.
2) Begin by jotting down the topics you want information about, without worrying about wording or logical order.

3) Number the topics in a logical order, using these principles:
   a. To the interviewee, the organization of the questionnaire should seem sensible and smooth-flowing.
   b. If some questions will affect the answers to others, put the influencing question afterwards.
   c. If there are some questions (such as income) that you may not get answers to, and that may antagonize some people, put them last.
   d. Put the least important questions near the end, in case they don't get answered.
4) Write first approximations of the questions. Use simple language, make each question as short as possible, and use other techniques of effective writing. Devising good questions takes experience and good judgment. Some of the specific obstacles you may encounter are discussed in this chapter. For more detailed guidance, see Payne.
5) Pretest the questionnaire by *personally* going out and asking the questions in an "open-ended" fashion—that is, without a list of answers among which the interviewee must choose. Talk to, say, ten friends and acquaintances (with whom you can feel comfortable) as well as a few members of the target population. Tape-record some of the interviews if you can.
6) Rewrite ambiguous questions, reorganize the questionnaire where necessary, throw out unnecessary or unsuccessful questions, convert some open-end to closed-end questions, and generally tighten up the questionnaire. Attend to the length of the questionnaire: Telephone interviews *must* be short—say, five minutes maximum—and other interviews are cheaper and more effective the shorter they are.
7) Write an introduction that will persuade potential interviewees to participate. If you just say, "Please answer this questionnaire," or "I need it for a course," many people will turn you down or throw away a mail questionnaire—and there is little reason for them not to. But if you tell people how their responses can help society or some particular group or themselves, or how the interview will be an interesting experience, you'll get much greater cooperation. In some cases, it will be best to pay people or give them presents for being willing to be interviewed.
8) Pretest again.
9) Improve the questionnaire again.
10) Go into the field for part of the interviews.
11) Check the preliminary results. If satisfactory, complete the work.

It is well to remember that no one ever becomes perfect at constructing questionnaires. Hanan Selvin, most helpful and generous sociologist-editor of this book and a man of great survey experience, confessed that on a 1974 survey of the faculty of his university, he forgot to ask the respondent's sex, and in 1975 he remembered sex but forgot to ask the respondent's race.

There is no cure for such flaws except extensive pretesting. The experienced "pro" may get into trouble by figuring he or she is so good that pretesting can be skipped. Don't skip or skimp on pretesting; pretest again and again and again and. . . .

> As question worders we need to develop a critical attitude toward our own questions. We must check the tendency to accept the first wording that makes sense to us. We must subordinate any pride of authorship to this critical attitude and should try to substitute clarity for cleverness. Every objection that may be raised about the phrasing should be carefully considered, because that problem may occur many times over in the full-scale survey. If even a single test interview or comment from one of our associates implies any fault in the question, that fault should not be passed over. How many people in the final survey will stumble over the same obstacle?
> The tendency to take things for granted is not easy to correct, simply because it is such a common characteristic of us all. (Payne, p. 17)

There is a vast literature on the construction of appropriate questions and appropriate ways of asking questions (Payne; Hyman, 1954). Many examples show that small differences in the form of the question can make a big difference in the responses. S. Stouffer *et al.*, concluded, on the basis of their vast experience in studying soldiers in World War II, that "error or bias attributable to sampling and to methods of questionnaire administration were relatively small as compared with other types of variation—especially variation attributable to different ways of wording questions" (Payne, p. 5). The danger is greatest when one seeks to learn about people's attitudes and opinions. Consider S. Payne's example of the differences in response to the following questions:

> . . . *Do you think most manufacturing companies that lay off workers during slack periods could arrange things to avoid layoffs and give steady work right through the year?*

> 63% said companies could avoid layoffs,
> 22% said they couldn't, and
> 15% had no opinion.

> . . . *Do you think most manufacturing companies that lay off workers in slack periods could avoid layoffs and provide steady work right through the year, or do you think layoffs are unavoidable?*

> 35% said companies could avoid layoffs,
> 41% said layoffs are unavoidable, and
> 24% expressed no choice. (Payne, pp. 7–8)

The form of the question is not as important when you ask for *factual information*. "What is the name of that traitor who is President?" may get practically the same responses as "Who is that great American who is President?" Sometimes researchers waste their own and other people's energy in nit-picking discussions about which is the best question to use to ask a person's age or whether to ask the question at the beginning or the end of the questionnaire schedule. The form of the question, however, can be enormously important in supposedly factual questions too, as this incident in the measurement of the labor force demonstrates:

> Prior to July 1945 a single question was used. It asked, *Was this person at work on a private or government job last week?* Beginning in that month, two questions were substituted. The first of these merely asked what the person's major activity was during the preceding week. If the major activity was something other than working, the enumerator then asked whether in addition the person did any work for pay or profit during the week.

> The upshot of this change in questions was that in the trial when both versions were used, the new questioning showed an increase of 1,400,000 employed persons over the old wording. About half of these additional workers had worked 35 or more hours during the week under consideration! (Payne, p. 11)

Payne argues that the critical issue in designing questions is "to make sure that the particular issue which the questioner has in mind is the particular issue on which the respondent gives his answers" (p. 9). Trying out your questions to see how they actually work in a pretest is equally important.

> If all the problems of question wording could be traced to a single source, their common origin would probably prove to be in taking too much for granted. We questioners assume that people know what we are talking about. We assume that they have some basis for testimony. We assume that they understand our questions. We assume that their answers are in the frame of reference we intend.
> Frequently our assumptions are not warranted. Respondents may never before have heard of the subject. They may confuse it with something else. They may have only vague ideas about it and no means for forming judgments. (Payne, p. 16)

The *scope* of a question is important. Economics has shunned question-and-answer explanations of economic behavior because, I believe, the few attempts by economists have used questions of too wide a scope. They have asked businessmen "How do you set your prices for liquor?" They would do better to ask the narrower question "Why is your price for Bonny Scotch $32 a case?" or, even better, "What percentage would sales rise if you raised the price of Bonny Scotch to $33?"

In general, writing good questions is an art that usually requires imagination and experience. But my favorite question comes from a college yearbook and is shown in Figure 20.1.

You can obtain some information by asking for it directly. But some information must be obtained by indirection. Income, for example, is a touchy topic, and it is usually asked about by showing the respondent a set of cards with different *ranges* of income, e.g. $10,000–$15,000, and the subject is asked to point to the appropriate income range.

FIGURE 20.1   **Do You Drink?**

Source: *Harvard Yearbook*, 1950; adapted by permission of Harvard Yearbook Publications, Inc.

On some topics people hesitate to make revelations about themselves but are willing to make statements about *other* people. It may be reasonable to assume that such statements are projections of one's views about oneself. For example, R. Simon and I wished to determine the likely effect of possible government subsidies and taxes on people's fertility behavior. People may believe that it is immoral or repulsive to have, or to not have, children for pay. They may resist placing a monetary value on unborn or already-born children. Therefore, people may not reply candidly to direct questions. Their verbal responses to direct questions may cover up their feelings, beliefs, and intentions about their likely behavior. For that reason, we asked both direct and projective questions. The projective questions were intended to ease the sense of repulsion or embarrassment and to allow people to describe their own feelings behind a facade of impersonality. . . .

First we asked:

Please think for a moment about the average family in your neighborhood. How many children do most of the families in your neighborhood have before they stop having children?

Respondents were then asked:

If the government were to give a monthly payment of $50—that is, $600 per year for each child after the second until that child is 18 years old—do you think the average family in your neighborhood would have more children than the (number answered in previous question) children they now have? (R. and J. Simon, pp. 586–587)

Unfortunately there is almost no information on how well projective questions really work, and under which conditions. Therefore, the result of a projective question must be buttressed with other sorts of information to support its standing as scientific evidence.

Even though you may do an excellent job in preparing the questionnaire, some questions will be more effective and easier to answer than others. It is useful to know which questions are superior, as an aid to evaluating your results. D. Twedt (personal correspondence) suggests you ask each interviewer to give two ratings to each question on the schedule, one for understanding and one for cooperation: "To the best of your memory, what percentage of the respondents *understand* the question, and what percentage *cooperated* with truthful, considered answers?"

Another approach is to ask each respondent to indicate for each question how strongly held is the judgment or opinion given. This provides two ratings for each question, one for context and one for intensity. The intensity measure is then used to weight the influence of the substantive answer in the overall result.

EXERCISES

1. Give examples from research in your field to illustrate the following obstacles:
   a. lack of knowledge by the subject
   b. fallibility of subject's memory
   c. cover-up by the subject
   d. trying to please the observer
   e. rationalization or repression
   f. deception
2. Suggest methods of surmounting the obstacles you described in Exercise 1.
3. How could the dentist experimenting with toothpaste (page 301) have protected himself against the possibility of his subjects' deceiving him?

ADDITIONAL READING FOR CHAPTER 20

On questionnaire construction, see Selltiz *et al.* (Chapters 9 and 10) and Kornhauser and Sheatsley (in Selltiz *et al.,* pp. 542–562). Parten is an excellent book on question construction and questionnaires, as is Oppenheim. Questionnaires for use in market research are discussed well in Boyd *et al.* (Chapters 7 and 8). Projective and indirect-question methods are discussed in Selltiz *et al.* (Chapter 10). For examples of the hypothetical-question technique in economics see Gilboy, and Simon (1966b). Paul discusses limited-scope questions in anthropology, as does Malinowski, pp. 11–12.

21 obstacles to obtaining adequate subject matter

If a social scientist is to arrive at sound conclusions, he must have good statistical data in sufficient quantities, good subjects for laboratory experiments, or good respondents for surveys. Computer people have a pungent phrase to describe what happens when a researcher uses poor data input: "GIGO—garbage in, garbage out." This chapter deals with the obstacles to achieving good data—the obstacles of too much and too little data, biased data, and various types of inadequate data.

1. Bias in the Sample

This interchange between G. Shaw and F. Harris illustrates the problem of bias in obtaining a fair sample of subject matter for observation:

> *Shaw:* The first thing we ask a servant for is a testimonial to honesty, sobriety and industry; for we soon find out that these are the scarce things, and that geniuses and clever people are as common as rats.

> *Harris:* The English paste in Shaw; genius is about the rarest thing on earth whereas the necessary quantum of "honesty, sobriety and industry" is beaten by life into nine humans out of ten.

> *Shaw:* If so, it is the tenth who comes my way. (Harris, n.d., p. 358)

Like Shaw and Harris, researchers want to set forth a true description of an entire universe.[1] Shaw and Harris did not go beyond their casual impressions for information about the universe of interest. In the social sciences, however, we often study the universe by taking samples from it. Taking a sample is something like looking at a distant scene through a telescope. The image of the universe that you obtain from the sample will be a true image if your sample represents the entire population. But, if some of the population escapes your sample, the image that you see may be distorted, just as the image of a distant scene will be distorted if your telescope does not cover the whole scene. A sample in which all of the population is not represented or is not represented fairly—without the researcher's knowledge—is called a "biased sample." (But do not leap to the conclusion that all biased samples are *bad* samples. "Bias" is a descriptive title, not a value judgment.)

Sampling bias is one of the two causes of a sample's not being a truthful image[2] of the universe with respect to the characteristic in which you are interested. In technical terms, sampling bias is one of the two sources of difference between the sample estimate and the population parameter. The other cause is *sampling error,* the difference between the sample and the universe that results from the workings of chance; for instance, just by chance the results of ten coin flips might be three heads or five heads or seven heads. Sampling error is discussed in detail in Chapters 9, 27, and 30.

Whether a sample is biased depends upon *which universe you want to describe.* If a newspaperman wants to determine the voting intentions of a city's population, a sample made up of the people he meets at a local bar is likely to be biased. But if he wants to get the reaction of bar patrons to a rise in liquor prices, a sample drawn from a local bar may be unbiased and perfectly appropriate. The danger, always, is that the biased sample may give you an image unlike the image of the universe that you would get if you studied each and every member of the population.

An example is the data that are collected by the American Newspaper Publishers Association on the amount of advertising in United States newspapers. The data cover only 389 daily papers in 146 cities. The cities that are covered are the *biggest* cities. This means, on one hand, that the data cover 60 per cent of all daily circulation but, on the other, that they distort the picture by omitting more than 1,300 smaller newspapers. (Samples are often *purposely* distorted by the researcher, however, for reasons of efficiency.

---

1. "Universe" and "population" are synonyms in the language of scientific sampling.

2. The term "image" is picturesque but somewhat inaccurate. No sample is ever a perfect replica of the universe from which it is drawn, and in fact the sample can safely be very different from the universe in all characteristics other than those being studied. Furthermore, it would be rare for a sample and a universe to have *exactly* the same mean, say, just because of the workings of chance. To put it more correctly, an unbiased sample is one in which the estimates of the characteristics under study have "expected values" equal to the universe parameters.

Such a practice requires that the researcher know where the distortion is *and* that no part of the universe be omitted *completely*.)

The most celebrated fiasco caused by a biased sample and its misinterpretation was the *Literary Digest* polling debacle before the 1936 presidential election. The magazine's news stories convey the flavor of the event.

August 22, 1936

The Digest PRESIDENTIAL POLL IS ON!

Famous Forecasting Machine Is Thrown Into Gear for 1936

The 1936 nation-wide *Literary Digest* Presidential Poll has begun.

Unruffled by the tumult and shouting of the hottest political race in twenty years, more than 1,000 trained workers have swung into their accustomed jobs. While Chairmen Farley and Hamilton noisily claim "at least forty-two States," and while the man in the streets sighs "I wish I knew," the *Digest's* smooth-running machine moves with the swift precision of thirty years' experience to reduce guesswork to hard facts.

This week, 500 pens scratched out more than a quarter of a million addresses a day. Every day, in a great room high above motor-ribboned Fourth Avenue, in New York, 400 workers deftly slid a million pieces of printed matter—enough to pave forty city blocks—into the addressed envelopes. Every hour, in the *Digest's* own Post Office Substation, three chattering postage metering machines sealed and stamped white oblongs; skilled postal employees flipped them into bulging mail-sacks; fleet *Digest* trucks sped them to express mail-trains. Once again, the *Digest* was asking more than ten million voters—one out of four, representing every county in the United States—*to settle November's election in October.*

Next week, the first answers from those ten million will begin the incoming tide of marked ballots, to be *triple-checked*, verified, *five times* cross-classified and totaled. When the last figure has been totted and checked, if past experience is a criterion, the country will know *to within a fraction of 1 per cent* the actual popular vote of forty millions.

As in former years, the *Digest* Poll will be marked by three distinctions:

Impartiality—A half century's reputation as the oldest and greatest news magazine in the world precludes any thought of bias; the *Digest* has no stake in the outcome. . . . Accuracy—The Poll represents thirty years' constant evolution and perfection. Based on the "commercial sampling" methods used for more than a century by publishing houses to push book sales, the present mailing list is drawn from every telephone book in the United States, from the rosters of clubs and associations, from city directories, lists of registered voters, classified mail-order and occupational data.

The list is being constantly revised, so that "dead" addresses do not appear. Fraud is impossible, since the ballots are almost as difficult to reproduce as

Uncle Sam's currency. (Tho in fact, the attempted frauds have thus far been insignificant.)

The "system" is both simple and complex. The master-list represents every vocation, every voting age, every religion and every nationality extraction in the country. It is constantly revolving, so that a certain percentage of names change with each poll.

Thus new voters are included, as well as those who have changed their affiliation between elections.

Trained experts have been constantly keeping that master-list up to date, checking names against the latest directories and organization rosters. Thousands of telephone books piled to the ceiling have been combed through for "revises," and new names have filtered in to keep the total at ten million. Soon, the first of the marked ballots will begin to trickle in, tho the tide reaches thousands upon thousands a day at its peak.

August 29, 1936

Digest POLL MACHINERY SPEEDING UP

First Figures in Presidential Test to Be Published Next Week

In election after election, as the public so well knows, *The Literary Digest* has forecast the result long before Election Day. For this journalistic feat and public service it has received thousands of tributes during many years. To-day the praise is continuing. . . . *The American Press,* . . .

"With the advent of the Presidential election campaign comes *The Literary Digest* Poll—that oracle, which, since 1920, has foretold with almost uncanny accuracy the choice of the nation's voters. . . ."

September 5, 1936

FIRST VOTES IN *Digest's* 1936 POLL

Scattering Returns From Four States Show Landon Leading

Like the outriders of a vast army, the first ballots in *The Literary Digest's* great 1936 Presidential Poll march into the open this week to be marshaled, checked and counted. . . .

More than 24,000 strong, they represent the initial returns from four States— Maine, New Jersey, New York and Pennsylvania.

The Big Parade has started.

Once again the *Digest* is making a country-wide test of political sentiment to find the answer to a national question. This time it is, "Who will win—Roosevelt or Landon?" . . . four States are represented—Maine, New Jersey, New York, President Roosevelt's home State, and Pennsylvania.

In each of the four the early percentages are heavily in favor of Gov. Alfred M. Landon, Republican nominee. Maine gives him 1,831 ballots, to 522 for Roosevelt. New Jersey casts 2,660 votes for Landon and 1,621 for Roosevelt. In all, these four States are represented with 16,056 ballots for Landon, 7,645 for Roosevelt and 754 for Lemke.

October 31, 1936

LANDON, 1,293,669; ROOSEVELT, 972,897

Final Returns in the *Digest's* Poll of Ten Million Voters

Well, the great battle of the ballots in the Poll of ten million voters, scattered throughout the forty-eight States of the Union, is now finished.

These figures are exactly as received from more than one in every five voters polled in our country—they are neither weighted, adjusted nor interpreted. . . .

November 14, 1936

WHAT WENT WRONG WITH THE POLLS?

None of Straw Votes Got Exactly the Right Answer—Why?

In 1920, 1924, 1928 and 1932, *The Literary Digest* Polls were right. Not only right in the sense that they showed the winner; they forcast the *actual popular vote* with such a small percentage of error (less than 1 per cent in 1932) that newspapers and individuals everywhere heaped such phrases as "uncannily accurate" and "amazingly right" upon us.

Four years ago, when the Poll was running his way, our very good friend Jim Farley was saying that "no sane person could escape the implication" of a sampling "so fairly and correctly conducted."

Well, this year we used precisely the same method that had scored four bull's-eyes in four previous tries. And we were far from correct. Why? We ask that question in all sincerity, because *we want to know.*

The *Literary Digest* prediction was not just wrong—it was so *grossly* wrong that it is given credit for the magazine's going out of business not long thereafter.

The most obvious conclusion from this case is that a huge sample is no protection against error. The *Literary Digest* repeatedly trumpeted that its sample was 10 million, one voter in every four, which is very impressive to the layman. But with a sample of only 10,000 the results would have been practically identical. And a well-selected sample of 10,000 or less might have obtained the correct results with good accuracy.

G. Gallup has the right to say what went wrong with the *Literary Digest* poll, because he made a correct analysis *before* the election:

The reasons the *Digest* poll went wrong in 1936 are obvious to anyone who understands modern polling methods. The *Literary Digest* sent out its ballots by mail and, for the most part, to people whose names were listed in telephone directories or to lists of automobile owners. From the point of view of cross section this was a major error, because it limited the sample largely to the upper half of the voting population, as judged on an economic basis. Roughly 40 per cent of all homes in the United States had telephones and some 55 per cent of all families owned automobiles. These two groups, which largely overlap, constitute roughly the upper half or upper three-fifths, economically, of the voting population.

The *Literary Digest* in previous straw vote polls had sent post card ballots to the same groups, but the *Digest* did not reckon with two factors in 1936—the division of votes along income lines which began with Roosevelt's administration in 1932, and the substantial increase in the voting population which took place between 1932 and 1936. These new voters came predominantly from the poorest levels—from income groups which favored Roosevelt.

The *Digest* not only failed to select a proper cross section, but the means by which the magazine reached voters—mail ballots—also helped to introduce error into the findings.

Persons most likely to return mail ballots are those in the higher income and educational levels, and, conversely, those least likely to return their ballots represent the lowest income and educational levels. So, even if the *Literary Digest* had actually used lists of voters throughout the country as they did in a few cities, instead of names selected from telephone books and automobile lists, post card ballots would still have been responsible for a substantial error in the *Digest*'s findings.

The time factor also contributed to the *Digest*'s downfall. The great bulk of ballots sent out were mailed in September. It was, therefore, impossible to catch any change or trend in sentiment taking place during the last two months of the campaign.

In many elections, in fact in most, no trend develops during the course of a campaign toward either candidate. But in some elections there is such a change in sentiment and, therefore, polling must be so timed as to measure this trend from week to week, right up to election day.

The fact that the *Digest* was using faulty methods was obvious long before the election revealed them. As early as July 14, 1936, two months before the *Digest* even began sending out its ballots, the American Institute [Gallup's organization] . . . predicted almost exactly the *Digest*'s final figure and described in detail exactly what was wrong with the *Digest*'s procedures. (Gallup, pp. 73–75)

In summary, Gallup points out how the *Literary Digest* poll was biased. Gallup's own sampling scheme, however, is *also* not a random one. Rather, he samples from carefully selected *quotas*. Such a quota sample may or may not be accurate and unbiased, depending on the wisdom of the sampler. It is only randomly drawn samples (probability samples) that can offer a *guarantee* against bias. But it is not always easy to draw a random sample even if you understand exactly what you are doing. Expense and energy often rule out true probability samples and the researcher may compromise on the closest he can get to a probability sample within his budget of time and energy.

The most frequent compromise with randomness in the social sciences is the use of college students as the sampled universe when the researcher really would like to study the universe of all people or when the entire United States is the "target universe." So many psychological and sociological studies have been limited to college students that some critics of the social sciences claim that we have no general psychology or sociology, but only a psychology and a sociology of American college students, and that we therefore have no psychological or sociological knowledge of people in general.

Limiting a study to college students is not always bad. A psychologist who studies hunger contractions in the stomach or psychophysical functions like hearing and seeing usually need not worry that college students are much different on those characteristics than are other people, just as H. Ebbinghaus and I. Pavlov did not require representative samples for their experiments to be valid. But a study of voting behavior or sexual behavior is surely biased if it is limited to college students but generalizes for all people.

Many studies of sex behavior had been done before A. Kinsey's, but almost all had been limited to college students, and therefore we really knew very little about the sex behavior of Americans in general until Kinsey came along. Kinsey's sampling certainly was not perfectly random or unbiased—for example, half the men in the male survey lived in Indiana, and the lower-income and less-educated classes were very much underrepresented—but Kinsey's study at least came much closer to obtaining a fair sample of the universe than did any previous work. (As a matter of fact, Kinsey's first survey was limited to white males in the United States; the second was limited to white females.)

The consulting statisticians who judged Kinsey's sampling techniques thought that Kinsey had gone far to get a fair sample. They still asked, however, that Kinsey take at least a small truly random sample to validate his other data and to serve as a conceptual bridge to the other data (Cochran, *et al.*).

The danger of sampling bias is not merely a theoretician's nitpick. In addition to the *Literary Digest* case, you have also seen the example on page 268 of the different results in estimates of magazine audiences obtained by three commercial services, all of whom were highly sophisticated and paid great attention to drawing fair samples. Some difference in estimates will occur because of the inevitable sampling error from small samples. But the differences in this case were so great that the three organizations *must* have drawn their samples in different ways, thereby introducing bias into the estimates.

2. Nonresponse: Unavailability of Some Part of the Universe

The preceding discussion of sample bias emphasized that if the researcher wishes to draw sound conclusions about a universe, he must study the whole universe or all its separate parts, although this investigation can be made with samples. If his study does not cover all parts of the universe, he cannot draw conclusions about the entire universe. If you want to study women Ph.D.s, you must study those women who are not now teaching as well as those who are teaching, or you cannot describe the entire universe of women who have Ph.D.s. If you want to draw conclusions about news-papers, you must have information about small-town papers as well as about big-city papers.

One way to bias a sample is to draw it from the universe disproportion-ately and then not make allowances; the *Literary Digest* example is out-standing in this respect. Another major obstacle goes by the special name of "nonresponse bias." By this name I refer to all situations in which some part of the relevant universe (and therefore some portion of a sample drawn from that universe) is not available for study. For example, some people (more at the beginning of the study than later) would not allow themselves to be interviewed by Kinsey. And some people did not answer the questions of the researchers who studied the effects of smoking (U.S. Public Health Service, p. 113). Indeed, in practically every significant study of human beings there will be some people who refuse to cooperate. (Do not condemn people who refuse to cooperate. Sometimes they have a perfectly good reason, one of which may be that it is a nuisance.) In addition, some members of the sample cannot be reached to ask for their cooperation.

Critics of the Kinsey study delight in pointing out that all Kinsey's sub-jects were volunteers. It is common sense that people who are willing to volunteer their sex histories might well have different attitudes and sex histories than do people who are more reticent. And indeed, one study did show that people who are low in self-esteem are both more likely to refuse to volunteer for sex studies *and* more likely to have conventional sexual behavior (Maslow and Sakoda in Himelhoch and Fava). Kinsey data, too, show that the average sex outlet is lower in groups from which Kinsey obtained 100 per cent response than in his basic samples. This finding does indicate that data from volunteers will lead to overestimates for the popula-tion as a whole. (But do not leap to conclusions about the overall validity of the Kinsey study until you have examined its methods *in toto;* see its Chap-ter 3.)

FIGURE 21.1

"Is no wonder capitalist polls can't match ours for accuracy
and dependability!...Imagine asking people instead of
telling them!"

Source: From the *Wall Street Journal*. Reprinted by permission of Herbert Goldberg.

Unlike the Kinsey study, smoking behavior is not a "hot" topic; smoking is not strongly tabooed in our society. Even so, there may be a biasing relationship between refusal to respond to questionnaires, on one hand, and smoking behavior and health, on the other. People in the hospital dying of lung cancer or other diseases may lack the energy to answer a questionnaire, and the absence of their responses will distort the total picture (U.S. Public Health Service, p. 113).

You are not *necessarily* in trouble just because some people refuse to cooperate. Noncooperators may cause no trouble under some circumstances. If you are sampling on a street corner to find out whether people prefer one type of chewy caramel to another type of chewy caramel, a passerby may refuse to try the caramel because she has just come from the dentist. Such a refusal is not likely to cause error (another example of the decisions one must make on the basis of common sense).

Sometimes so few data are available that the study is impossible. A poll of the President's cabinet on its like or dislike of the President's spouse is not likely to turn up many willing subjects.

Having *100 per cent* of the subjects is not necessary; missing just a few subjects is seldom fatal. For example, if you can obtain responses from 90 per cent of your sample in a preelection preference poll and if 65 per cent of your respondents prefer candidate A, you can be absolutely sure that candidate A would be preferred by the majority even if every single one of the unavailable subjects preferred candidate B. Unless you are trying to make a very subtle study, you need not worry much about error in estimating the universe as a whole if you can gain access to *nearly* all your subjects.

Whether the nonresponders can cause error depends upon whether the *reason* for nonresponse or the characteristics of the nonrespondents are related in any way to the information that you seek to collect. Having just come from the dentist is probably unrelated to whether a person would prefer one or another flavor of caramel, though it causes nonresponse. But a surly unwillingness to express a political preference might well be related to which candidate the nonresponder will vote for. For example, if one of the candidates has expressed an aversion to pollsters, his followers may refuse to answer in much greater relative numbers than will followers of the other candidate.

Unless you have *very strong* reasons to believe otherwise, you should assume that the nonresponders do *not* come randomly from the population. Unfortunately for the researcher, the reasons for nonresponse seem to be related to *almost everything.* If there are substantial nonresponse holes in your data, you must employ remedial tactics so that you can make reliable estimates for the universe as a whole. Some of the possible tactics will be described here.

First, you may *work harder to increase the number of subjects who will respond.* One way is to use a "stronger" technique. For example, personal interviewing is a stronger technique than is the mail questionnaire; fewer people will refuse to answer questions in person than when solicited by mail.

Another way to decrease the nonresponse rate is to increase the number of attempts to find the subjects and obtain cooperation. Interview surveys sometimes go back to "not at homes" as many as eleven times in hopes of finding them in. Or, if a person does not respond to a mail questionnaire, you might telephone to ask him to fill out the mail questionnaire. In desperate straits, you might ask a mutual friend to intercede and persuade the subject to cooperate if a single subject is crucial, as is sometimes the case in political-science studies.

When making these secondary attempts to increase your subject coverage, you must be careful not to change the subjects' answers by your further efforts. If you annoy a subject, you may affect what he says; he may give you a wrong-headed answer just to get rid of you.

Sometimes you can increase the response by *persuading* potential respondents to answer. In some cases, you can persuade them to respond by asking them very nicely or by showing them how their responses will benefit themselves or others in the long run; this technique is the same one that advertising copywriters or salesmen use to persuade people to buy. You can do better than just saying "Please answer this questionnaire for me." A related tactic is to have someone important write them to ask for cooperation, on the stationery of a prestigious institution.

Another technique is to offer *gifts or payment* to the respondents. Psychological laboratories are accustomed to paying students by the hour for prolonged sessions. And market researchers often find that dimes, quarters, or dollars will do the trick. Members of consumer panels are usually paid in merchandise. It is often surprising how much effect a small inducement can have. In a library study we attached a ballpoint pen that cost 3 cents to every other short questionnaire put into books in the library stacks. Twice as many of the questionnaires that had had pens attached came back as did questionnaires that had not had pens attached. As always, one must balance the cost of the inducement against the gains. For example, fewer mail questionnaires are needed if a small payment is offered.

A second way to deal with nonresponse is to *assume* that the subjects whom you cannot reach or who refuse to cooperate are similar to the people whose responses you do obtain. You can then estimate the entire universe on the basis of simple proportionality. Interpolation or extrapolation for periods of time about which we have no data is an example of such simple extensions of data. If we have data on Gross National Product for 1975 and 1976 and estimates of advertising expenditures for 1975 but not for 1976, we might estimate the 1976 advertising expenditures by this formula:

$$\frac{\text{GNP 1976}}{\text{GNP 1975}} = \frac{?}{\text{Advertising Expenditures 1975}}$$

If the assumption of simple proportionality is not justified, your estimate will be a bad one. In this example, it is possible that advertising expenditures decreased from 1975 to 1976, even though GNP increased. Your only weapon is good judgment and such supplementary checks as knowledge that advertising expenditures were a constant proportion of GNP in prior years. You have no *scientific* guarantee that the estimation is not wrong. In any case, you must make crystal-clear to your readers just how much of the universe was not accessible to you, the assumptions that you made in taking account of the nonresponders, and how much effect the nonresponders might have on your findings if they were radically different from the rest of your sample.

Third, if your nonresponse is substantial, it is always wise to make a secondary investigation to find out whether the nonresponders differ from your original sample and, if so, *how*. With this information in hand, you can make modifications that will improve your extensions of the original data—or decide to give up the study if the problem is insoluble. Kinsey used many ingenious devices to determine how and in what ways the volunteers were different from nonvolunteers. One technique was to obtain 100 per cent coverage of several groups, including all those members who had originally declined to volunteer but were willing to change their minds when strongly urged. Kinsey then compared the complete-coverage estimates against the estimates he *would* have made if he had only had the original volunteers available. The results were encouraging. The volunteers were not *sufficiently* different from the nonvolunteers to introduce *major* errors into the results. (This statement is oversimplified. For a full discussion of this and other devices used to check on nonresponse, see the early chapters of Kinsey, *et al.* [1948]).

Many different techniques have been used to surmount the nonresponse problem. The common ingredients are ingenuity and common sense.

Nonresponse varies from place to place and group to group. The French are said to be reluctant to participate in research studies. And many middle-class Americans are tired of the repeated requests. In rural Thailand, however, in a study that asked intimate questions about birth-control attitudes and practices, "Of the eligible respondents none refused to be interviewed. Completed interviews number 1,207" (Peng, p. 1).

3. Inability to Experiment with the Subject Matter

Experimentation has strong advantages over nonexperimental methods for research that aims to determine causality and as a device for overcoming many obstacles to knowledge. But an experiment, either in real life or in a realistic laboratory setting, is not always possible. For example, it is not morally permissible for scientists to apply tobacco smoke to the lungs of nonsmokers to see whether cancer develops, which prevents them from making an absolutely airtight case that smoking causes cancer. (With some other human diseases, however, our society has been willing to sanction experiments on such volunteers as convicts.)

If experimentation is impossible we must do the best we can with evidence that comes from observation of *natural variations* in the independent variables. Sometimes these variations occur under conditions that are almost as neat as those the investigator would arrange. These situations are called by a variety of names—"quasi experiments," "*ex post facto* experiments," "natural experiments." The important characteristic of such quasi experiments is that some force *clearly unrelated to the dependent variable* causes the variation in the independent variable.

Nature usually does not arrange her experiments as systematically as a researcher would, and therefore the evidence is harder to interpret. As in the case of smoking and health, however, the natural evidence is often all we can get. Some people already smoke, and we must extract what information we can from the evidence that we obtain from smokers by survey.

If she were running an *experiment* on smoking, the researcher would constitute the smoking and nonsmoking groups randomly, that is, she would choose people to smoke or not smoke by pulling their names out of a hat so that the only differences between the smoking and nonsmoking groups would be the chance of the lottery. In real life, however, the very fact that some people choose to smoke and others choose not to smoke suggests that there are some differences between the groups to start with. Those differences—rather than the cigarette smoke—might be responsible for the higher incidence of lung cancer and other life-shortening diseases in the cigarette-smoking group.

There are several ways to attack this obstacle to knowledge, none of them totally satisfactory. One way is to *simulate* the experiment you would like to do by running an experiment with people and conditions as similar as possible to the real-life conditions that you are interested in and cannot experiment with. This is an age-old device in the engineering sciences, in the form of mock-up experiments, which have been used in engineering ever since Leonardo da Vinci, and probably before, to determine the effects of various stresses. Using models Leonardo experimented with pillars and beams of various sizes, and he developed basic structural formulas based on these experiments (Mason, p. 149). In the life sciences, one often experiments with animals in lieu of people on the assumption that what is true of animals is likely to be true of humans. If, indeed, cigarette smoke causes cancer in rats, then there is some reason to infer that the same effect may occur in humans. But we can never be sure. On the basis of other evidence about the similarity of rats and humans, we must decide how relevant the rat evidence will be in this case. To illustrate:

Moscow, Oct. 10, 1964 (AP)—Soviet scientists have immunized animals against cancer virus, the official news agency Tass said Saturday in Moscow.

It quoted Nikolai Blokhin, president of the Soviet Academy of Medical Sciences as saying, however, that it was too early to tell whether the discovery had any practical application for treating human cancer patients.

Psychologists simulate when, like Ebbinghaus, they run experiments with nonsense syllables to learn about more complex learning situations. And economists sometimes organize laboratory experiments to simulate firms and consumers buying and selling in markets.

Games are also used by sociologists to find out how people interact with one another under various types of circumstances.

The results of such games can be provocative and can provide clues to understanding behavior. But again the crucial question remains: Does the game resemble real life?

The advantage of such simulation studies is that they make it possible to work with sets of data that are too complex to handle mathematically. But a simulation can never be any better than the empirical data about individuals and relationships that are fed into it. Unfortunately, it is rare that one has very good data to use in such studies—even in advertising research, where there are mountains of existing data. Simulation is discussed at length on pages 215–217.

One use of cross-cultural study is to replace experiments. For example, the smoking-and-health researcher looks for two countries that seem alike in most respects, except that in one country cigarette smoking was fortuitously introduced much earlier than in the other. The health records of the two countries can then be compared. It is important to be sure, however, that there was not some special nonrandom reason that caused cigarettes to be introduced earlier in one country than in the other; such a reason might itself be the cause of differences in health in the countries.

Economists have had to develop many specialized statistical methods to use in lieu of experiments because so many aspects of national economies are not subject to experimentation. An economist cannot carry out a systematic and controlled program of experimentation with the various factors that may affect the business cycle in order to increase our understanding of what causes boom and bust. Instead, his only alternative (except for mock-experiment methods) is to interpret the data that history has made available to him with the aid of those statistical techniques called "econometrics," which squeeze the maximum amount of information out of available data. Whether A causes B or vice versa, A and B cause each other, or A and B are causally unrelated is, however, a major difficulty in econometrics; it could be resolved easily if experimentation were possible. An after-the-fact analytic device is seldom as strong as an experiment in supporting a cause-and-effect argument. Nevertheless, if enough evidence of different kinds is available and if such an argument is constructed soundly, the conclusions can come very close to making an airtight case for the existence of a causal relationship. This sort of reasoning was the basis for the unanimous judgment of the Surgeon General's committee that smoking "causes" lung cancer and other diseases.

4. Flaws in Subject Matter and Unreliability of Data

The botanist is sometimes troubled by specimens that are rotten, aged, atypical, or otherwise flawed. The historian spends much of her time making do with unreliable or incomplete records because people in earlier centuries were not as conscientious about keeping records as we now are. The economist often faces the same difficulty as does the historian because the raw material of empirical economics is generally historical records—though often of the recent past.

The historian generally works with nonquantitative data and reports his results in literary rather than statistical fashion. He can therefore bridge gaps in subject matter with his intuition or imagination. The economist, however, must have some kind of numerical data with which to work, even if he must construct and patch together series of data with baling wire and chewing gum, as someone put it. The sociologist, too, is often at the mercy of those who have created the demographic data he works with.

None of us is astonished to hear that there are errors in survey data, even though the magnitude of the errors is often much greater than we would have guessed. Once you read O. Morgenstern's classic book *On the Accuracy of Economic Observations*, you will no longer be the trusting soul you once were. I think it is more surprising to learn that even the published results of laboratory experiments are far from totally reliable. For example, a reanalysis of the data from seven psychological experiments found gross errors in three of them (Wolins, p. 657).

The clear moral is that when you use data that have been collected by other researchers as your raw material, you must take careful precautions to check the accuracy of the data. "Students have to be brought up in an atmosphere of healthy distrust of the 'facts' put before them. They must also learn how terribly hard it is to get good data and to find out what really is 'a fact' " (Morgenstern, p. 305). But all too often researchers close their eyes to this obstacle, assume that published data mean what they seem to mean, and use the data uncritically. Here is the primrose path, dangerous for you and for the consumers of your research results. A famous economist recently was embarrassed publicly by inadvertently using data that had minor errors in it. And consider the enormous differences between two publicly issued statistics about the same thing, the movement of gold from France to England (Ferraris in Morgenstern, pp. 139–140):

Gold Movement from France to Britain
(in millions of francs)

	According to French Export Statistics	According to British Import Statistics
1876–1880	41.5	94.4

Here are some tactics to help you avoid error.

Find out exactly how the raw data were collected. Study the data-collection methods critically to see whether they make sense and fit your needs. Take nothing on faith. Sometimes you will find incredible blunders that have gone undiscovered for a long time. If insufficient description of the data has been published, write to the author and find out how he did the work. Sometimes such correspondence startles you by revealing that some of the data that you assumed to be hard facts were really just estimates by the author. Printed data, like rumors, have the unfortunate property of gaining the appearance of reliability and respectability as they are successively quoted and go from hand to hand.

Consider, for example, the three "authoritative" sets of data—none of which can possibly rest on very solid foundations—given in Table 21.1.

Whenever possible, cross-check available data against other sources of data. If you are working with Gross National Product estimates and if you also have series of employment data available to you, see if the two series bear a sensible relationship to each other. If no other data are available, at least check the data against rules of thumb and common sense. In the gold-movement example, Ferraris checked the British import statistic against the French export figure. The disparity alerted him to danger, even though he could not determine which figures were correct. For another example, a student of unemployment movements should consider the evidence from *both* the Bureau of Employment Statistics series *and* the Bureau of Labor Statistics' *Monthly Report of Labor Force.* For example, notice in Table 21.2 how the up-or-down directions of the two series have differed, as well as the absolute size of the estimates.

A. Schlesinger, Jr., illustrates how a military historian and political analyst goes about cross-checking the available data:

The [New York] *Times* on Aug. 10 described "the latest intelligence reports" in Saigon as saying that the number of enemy troops in South Vietnam had in-

TABLE 21.1   Numbers of Speakers of Selected Languages in 1976

	Information Please Almanac (1976, p. 414)	CBS News Almanac (1976, p. 762)	World Almanac (1976, p. 200)
Arabic	150	100	125
Bengali	95	110	123
Bihari	37	20	22
Cantonese	80	——	47
English	350	300	358
French	80	75	90
German	105	100	120
Mandarin	555	——	650
Portuguese	110	110	124
Russian	140	200	233
Spanish	220	200	213
Tagalog	8	10	21
Tibetan	9	4	7

SOURCE: Almanacs as indicated, 1976; suggested by Wallis and Roberts, p. 96.

creased 52,000 since Jan. 1 to a total of 282,000. Yet, "according to official figures," the enemy had suffered 31,571 killed in action in this period, and the infiltration estimate ranged from 35,000 as "definite" to 54,000 as "possible."

The only way to reconcile these figures is to conclude that the Vietcong have picked up from 30,000 to 50,000 local recruits in this period. Since this seems unlikely—especially in view of our confidence in the decline of Vietcong morale —a safer guess is to question the wonderful precision of the statistics. Even the rather vital problem of how many North Vietnamese troops are in South Vietnam is swathed in mystery. *The* [New York] *Times* reported on Aug. 7: "About 40,000 North Vietnamese troops are believed by allied intelligence to be in the South." According to an Associated Press dispatch from Saigon printed in *The Christian Science Monitor* of Aug. 15: "The South Vietnamese Government says 102,500 North Vietnamese combat troops and support battalions have infiltrated into South Vietnam."

"These figures are far in excess of United States intelligence estimates, which put the maximum number of North Vietnamese in the South at about 54,000."

But General Westmoreland told his Texas press conference on Aug. 14 that the enemy force included "about 110,000 main-force North Vietnamese regular

TABLE 21.2 Unemployment Series: Levels and Changes, 1946–1961 (*in millions*)

	Unemployment		Monthly Changes		% Difference in Series
	1	2	3	4	5
	Census-M.R.L.F.	B.E.S.	Census-M.R.L.F. Monthly Averages	B.E.S.	$\dfrac{Col\ (2) - Col\ (1)}{Col\ (1)} \times 100$
1946	2.3	2.8			21.7
1947	2.4	1.8	0.1	−1.0	−25.0
1948	2.3	1.5	−0.1	−0.3	−34.8
1949	3.7	2.5	1.4	1.0	−32.4
1950	3.4	1.6	−0.3	−0.9	−52.9
1951	2.1	1.0	−1.3	−0.6	−52.4
1952	1.9	1.1	−0.2	0.1	−42.1
1953	1.9	1.1	0.0	0.0	−42.1
1954	3.6	2.0	1.7	0.9	−44.4
1955	2.9	1.4	−0.7	−0.6	−51.7
1956	2.8	1.3	−0.1	−0.1	−53.6
1957	2.9	1.6	0.1	0.3	−44.8
1958	4.7	2.8	1.8	1.2	−40.4
1959	3.8	1.9	−0.9	−0.9	−50.0
1960	3.9	2.1	0.1	0.2	−46.2
1961	4.8	2.5	0.9	0.4	−47.9

SOURCE: *On the Accuracy of Economic Observations*, 2nd ed., p. 225, by Oskar Morgenstern; copyright © 1950, 1963 by Princeton University Press; reprinted by permission of Princeton University Press.

army troops." Perhaps these statements are all reconcilable, but an apparent discrepancy of this magnitude on a question of such importance raises a twinge of doubt. (Schlesinger, 1966, p. 114)

Sometimes one can check reliability by comparing sets of *different* data that must bear a close resemblance to each other. For example, a bell would go off in the mind of the production manager of American Motors if he were presented with very different data on the numbers of auto *bodies* and auto *engines* produced in his factories; there are very few cars with more or less than one body and engine, and therefore the two numbers must bear a close resemblance to each other.

Check the internal reliability of your data. Make sure that the parts add to the totals and that there are no inexplicable large variations from period to period or group to group. Experienced researchers frequently can detect mistakes in their own and other people's raw data just by scanning them and searching out peculiar variations. In "The Case of the Indians and the Teen-Age Widows," A. Coale and F. Stephan describe how they noticed a few peculiar data in the 1950 Census of Population and how they tracked down the cause of the anomalies:

> Our first clue was the discovery in the 1950 Census of Population of the United States of startling figures about the marital status of teen-agers. There we found a surprising number of widowed fourteen-year-old boys and, equally surprising, a decrease in the number of widowed teenage males at older ages. The numbers listed by the Census . . . were 1,670 at age 14; 1,475 at age 15; 1,175 at 16; 810 at 17; 905 at 18; and 630 at age 19. Not until age 22 does the listed number of widowers surpass those at 14. Male divorces also decrease in number as age increases, from 1,320 at age 14 to 575 at age 17. Smaller numbers of young female widows and divorcees are listed—565 widows and 215 divorcees at age 14. These strange figures, even though they appear in a very minor part of the carefully prepared and widely useful data presented in the Population Census, aroused our curiosity and set us to searching for an explanation. (Coale & Stephan, p. 338)

The explanation: In a tiny fraction of the IBM cards the key-punch operators had moved the data one column to the right, and some middle-aged males were thereby transformed into teen-agers. Further investigation turned up related errors that were not so obvious upon first inspection.

If errors like the teen-aged widowers manage to creep into the U.S. Census—which is a remarkably well-run data-gathering operation—errors are much *more* likely in any other data with which you are likely to work.

Checking the accuracy of the raw data does not eliminate all the likely obstacles. You may also hit snags because the available data has been *summarized* in ways that do not fit your purposes. For example, I wanted to estimate how much shorter is the life of the average smoker than the life of the average nonsmoker (four years by my rough estimate) and how many minutes less of life, per cigarette smoked, the smoker lives. (About seven minutes. Do you have a light?) These estimates were hampered by a *lack of comparability* in existing data. One study categorized smokers as "less than 10 a day," "11 to 20," "21 to 39," and "40 or over," whereas another study reported data as "less than 5," "about ½ pack," "about 1 pack," "about 1½ packs," and other studies used such categories as "20 to 34," "35 plus," and "more than 1 pack."

The appropriate tactic was the reverse of one used to overcome nonresponse—the "linear assumption." That is, I assumed that the numbers of smokers who smoke eleven, twelve, thirteen, and so on to twenty cigarettes a day are roughly equal to one another, and then I split the data for "11 to 20" in such a way as to make them comparable with the other data. Or in a case like this one I might have made a graph of the data and interpolated the missing points. This would provide only a crude approximation, but one has to do *something*. The only question is whether some other approximation would be better.

Another obstacle is that the existing data may lump several other categories together with the one category in which you are interested. If you study expenditures for liquor advertising, you will find that the figures reported for magazines lump together the expenditures for beer, wine, and liquor, whereas the data for newspapers cover the categories separately. Chapter 17 discusses this problem in more detail. In this case, you can bring other evidence to bear. If you have data showing that the split between liquor and beer plus wine in newspapers is twenty to eighty, you might assume that the same proportional split would hold for magazines.

The example of liquor advertising is a special case of the more general obstacle of raw data not being *defined* in a manner that is useful for your particular purpose. As an illustration, unemployment statistics are variously defined as the number of people who are listed on the unemployment rolls or as the difference between the total work force and the number of people *employed*. The estimates from these or other methods can differ very greatly (see Morgenstern, Chap. 13, for detailed discussion).

Another obstacle is that the data may be averages for groups, whereas you may need data for the individuals within the groups. In some cases, you can safely use the group averages to describe the individuals, but this approach can lead to what is called the "ecological fallacy." For example, you might want to study the relationship between income and literacy because, perhaps, you want to know how people's incomes will be affected if literacy is raised. If you compared the literacy rates and *per capita* incomes for Kuwait, Austria, and Israel, you might come to think that more literate people have lower incomes. The fallacy, of course, is that in Kuwait a very few people have all the money and most of the people are very poor. So, even though Kuwait is a rich *country*, most of its individual citizens are very poor. Looking only at these countries, high rates of literacy go with low *per capita* incomes. *Within* each country, however, literate people will have *higher* incomes than illiterate people by and large, and, if one raises literacy, one can safely count on raising *per capita* income also. This is one of those cases in which it is an error to consider the relationship between characteristics of countries to stand for the corresponding relationship between characteristics of individuals. Data are therefore needed for individuals and not countries. (In other cases, however, it may be that you are in trouble because you have data on individuals and you want to study the behavior of *groups*. The whole is not always a simple sum of the parts.)

Mechanical and computational errors sometimes introduce significant error into the data that are available to you. Computers are free of many of the errors of human computation, but they suffer from "rounding" error—that is, the computer performs all mathematics in terms of arithmetical operations, and at each stage it must round off. The computer carries the operations to many digits, but nevertheless these errors pile up as the computer does the millions of computations necessary for even simple problems, and you often find that the same calculations done by different computer methods yield somewhat different results.

5. Shortage of Subject Matter

Sometimes there is insufficient subject matter available to support solid conclusions. This obstacle is less likely to appear in experimental work because data can usually be generated in unlimited quantity, subject only to the restriction of cost and available funds (on this point see Chapter 24). But sometimes the subject matter for experimentation is limited too. For example, in the early stages of the nuclear physics of various particles, the amounts of matter available for experimentation were in short supply, as dramatized in the story of the Curies and their radium shortage.

You are most likely to face a shortage of subject matter when experimentation is not possible. Wars may be mercifully few from the point of view of humanity, but the historian must sometimes catch herself wishing there had been more wars of certain kinds so that she would have more material to work with. Similarly, business cycles are always few in number compared to the economist's need for data.

Lack of data sometimes comes as a surprise. For example, it is a shock to fledgling demographers to learn that the United States was for a long time among the most backward of the industrial nations in recording births; collection of birth statistics did not even begin until 1915; it was not until 1933 that birth data were available for the entire country (T. Smith, pp. 284–285). And there were no national-income statistics (for example, Gross National Product) for the United States covering the years prior to the third decade of the twentieth century until S. Kuznets came along and partly remedied the deficiency.

There are many possible reasons for the nonexistence or the shortage of data. In antiquity figures on Greek and Roman commerce and population were seldom collected. But, even when they were collected and recorded, the records that have come down to us often lack the totals because the totals were at the corners or bottoms of the stone tablets—and those are the parts of the tablets most likely to be broken off over time (Jones, p. 2).

When you are faced with a shortage of data, first look for more data. But look in places that are not obvious, as well as in places that are. If you have too few business cycles to work with in United States history, you might try examining business cycles in those other countries whose economies bear at least some similarity to that of the United States. If you want to study how a ban on advertising affects liquor consumption and if only a few states in the United States have bans, hunt up cases of other countries that have banned liquor advertising. Historians often exhibit genius in finding data in out-of-the-way places.

Sometimes physical instruments can fill gaps in the historical record. Anthropology furnishes an example:

> Now in the field of the nonliterate cultures and cultural items, where dates are totally lacking, and where archaeology can hope in general to give us only relative time sequences, it is also interesting to know whether an institution goes back a thousand or ten thousand years, or is older or younger than another institution. But how shall we learn? Now and then some other science comes to our rescue: geology and palaeontology in remote prehistory, botany or tree-ring dendrochronology in a few particular situations. Such outside aids are, however, rare and unusual. In general, cultural anthropology has to help itself. (Kroeber, p. 541)

Since Kroeber wrote the above paragraph, however, atomic physics has come to the rescue. The carbon-14 method is often an enormous help in establishing dates. In many cases, it is a superior substitute for examination of tree-ring patterns.

Another way to squeeze out more information is to divide up the available units of subject matter into smaller units. Economists sometimes use data for three-month rather than full-year periods, to increase the number of available observations, even though the quarterly data are much less accurate than the yearly data. Another example comes from a study of simulated jury deliberations. An enormous number of expensive jury experiments would have been required to obtain a sample of *decisions* large enough for statistical needs. The researcher therefore also collected data about the *individual judgments* of jurors prior to the deliberations, which yielded a sample twelve times as large as the number of jury decisions (R. Simon, 1967).

Though splitting up the data into smaller parcels may increase its information value in one respect, you will probably have to pay a price in diminishing its information value in some other respect—usually in the form of increased error in the smaller units. In the jury study, the researcher had to be careful to emphasize that individual jurors' judgments are not comparable to decisions made by the jury as a whole.

When all else fails, the skills of the statistician can often squeeze extra meaning out of small samples. Anyone can come to a sound conclusion with a sample of millions. But, as we shall see in Chapters 25–30, it takes skill and ingenuity to infer sound conclusions from samples of five, ten, or one hundred observations.

6. High Individual Variability in the Data

Your intuition will tell you that it is easier to compare the monthly salaries of two jobs when the salaries within each of the two vocations are similar. If three people working at job A earn $500, $550, and $600, whereas three people working at job B earn $411, $580, and $640, it is difficult to tell reliably whether there is any difference in the average salaries of the two jobs because there is so much variability. But if all three people on job A earn $540 and all three people on job B earn $570, it seems much clearer that there is a difference between the salaries of the two jobs.

High variability among the subjects is a frequent difficulty in experimental as well as in survey research. Consider the study of whether making cats "neurotic" will increase their intake of alcohol. J. Masserman's design was as follows: First, determine whether "normal" cats choose milk with 5 per cent alcohol content over milk containing no alcohol; second, find out whether giving one group of cats a neurosis increases the likelihood that it will choose milk with alcohol in preference to plain milk. Two of sixteen cats chose milk with alcohol to start with. If ten of sixteen cats that have been given neuroses come to choose alcohol and only two of sixteen that were not given neuroses chose alcohol when retested (as was the case), it is easy to interpret the results. But if four or five of the normal cats had chosen the alcoholic milk to start with and if fewer than ten of the neurotic cats had chosen the alcohol, it would have been much more difficult to determine whether inducing the neuroses made any difference.

High variability within the subject matter is one of the most important characteristics that sets the social sciences off from the physical sciences. Prenuclear physics and chemistry can be said to be almost determinate, because what happens once will happen again. (But do not forget that many facts about human nature are almost as sure as those in the natural sciences. I can predict with practically perfect accuracy that, if I fire a blank revolver in front of your nose, your eyes will blink in a "startle reflex." And luckily the chances are fantastically good that your next-door neighbor will not turn out to be a cannibal or a pathological killer.)

Several tactics other than those suggested in Figure 21.2 can help you to make satisfactory comparisons between groups, despite a high level of variability within the groups. Two of these tactics are described here.

a. INCREASE THE SAMPLE SIZE

Television programing can be considered (and is) an experiment to see which programs are more popular. Even a slight difference in popularity could be detected if you measured the tuning of every one of the millions of

FIGURE 21.2

"Sorry sir, I'm not going to open up seven locks and disconnect the burglar alarm just to tell you what shampoos I favor."

Source: GRIN AND BEAR IT by George Lichty. © Field Enterprises, Inc., 1964. Courtesy of Field Newspaper Syndicate.

network listeners for each of the programs. Such a large sample is not feasible, and a Nielsen sample of 1,200 dwelling units (Madow, *et al.*, p. 127) is generally large enough to measure most differences with acceptable accuracy. If two programs were very close, taking a sample many times as large would help. But remember that if a terrifically large sample is required, the difference probably is not sufficiently important to warrant attention.

b. COMPARE EACH SUBJECT WITH HIMSELF

This tactic can be very powerful in surmounting the obstacle of high individual variability. Assume that you are a campaign manager and that you want to find out the effect of having your candidate give personal talks in small towns. You would face the difficulty of high variability within towns if you tried to compare towns the candidate had visited with towns he had not visited. But if you measured preferences for your candidate before and after his visits to some towns, the variability within the towns would not be so great a difficulty. You would need only to compare each town against itself and then to average the changes. Each town is said to be its own control in this type of design.[3]

Variability within groups often impels critics to claim that it is impossible to make any valid predictions for an *individual* in one group compared to an individual in another group. If a poll predicts that 80 per cent of one group will vote for candidate A, the critic asks, How can you predict that *any given* individual in that group will vote for candidate A?

It is certainly true that we can never make a prediction for an individual with perfect accuracy. *Any* prediction is only a *probability*, and, as a simple pragmatic matter, knowing the probabilities for the group as a whole helps us make a prediction for any individual within the group. The odds are four to one that a *randomly chosen individual* will vote for candidate A if the group she is in is 80 per cent for A. First-place teams in the major leagues sometimes lose games to last-place teams. But even the most naïve bettor will not take even odds that the last-place team will win a *particular game.* (The picture is different, of course, if you know something special about the particular vote or the particular teams—who the pitchers are, in the latter case.)

The more that we know about the various groups with which we can identify an individual, the better will be our prediction for the individual. If we had known before the Kennedy-Nixon election that a particular voter was Catholic, we could have said that the odds were 60–40 that she would vote Democratic. If we had also known that she lived in New York City, our odds might have been 80–20, a stronger prediction. (Sometimes, however, the interaction of two such traits can drive the combined effect in the *other* direction.) In general, the more finely we can subclassify an individual, the better will be our prediction for her. The nature of predictions and how to make them are explored at greater length in Chapters 25, 26, and 32.

7. Too Much Subject Matter

An experienced researcher's first response to the obstacle of too much subject matter is "It should only happen to me." Subject matter is like dia-

3. The statistically trained reader will recognize that the analysis of variance is the appropriate general model for determining whether the "within" variance is satisfactorily small compared to the "between" variance.

monds: a scarce commodity of which you cannot believe that you could ever have too much. But it is possible to be buried in data, just as a person might be buried in a landslide of diamonds.

The data in the U.S. Census, for example, overwhelmed researchers in the late nineteenth century. It took seven years and hundreds of clerks to bring order to the 1880 data and to develop summarizing statistics. It was the difficulty of coping with that great mountain of census data that led H. Hollerith to invent a system of punched cards and machines that would read and sort the data electrically. Machines very similar to those original 1890 machines are perhaps the commonest automatic data-processing machines in use today, and they are the granddaddies of the more sophisticated machines that are also in existence now. Hollerith's firm grew into IBM—all because of the problem of too much data (Halacy, 1969, pp. 2, 41).

Ironically, the very machines that were invented to sort huge piles of data can themselves create new obstacles of masses of data. Everyone who has worked with high-speed computers has suffered fright and frustration when she received literally pounds of paper and hundreds of thousands of numbers as the output of a computer run, even though all she really wanted was a single yes-or-no answer. Then she is again faced with the necessity of boiling down and summarizing the output into some useful and manageable form.

Automatic data processing is one way to cope with too much data. Another tactic is to take a sample of the large masses of data. The sample should be large enough to be sufficiently accurate yet small enough to be worked on easily (Chapters 9 and 31 discuss sampling and sample sizes in more detail). If automatic data processing were not available, it would be necessary to take small samples from the mass of census data collected and make estimates for the country as a whole based on those samples.

Then why not collect census data for only a sample of the population? The answer is that data on the entire population can provide knowledge about *small subdivisions* of the population, as well as about the population as a whole. A small sample of the entire population would tell us with considerable accuracy how many people in the United States as a whole earn less than $5,000 per year. But a small sample of the United States population could not reveal accurately how many people in Elko County, Nevada, earn $5,000.[4]

For accounting purposes, most business firms collect complete financial data on their operations in preference to taking samples of the data. Accountants generally insist on reckoning to the last penny rather than making estimates based on samples, even though the Internal Revenue Service will settle for accounts rounded off to the nearest dollar.

4. In fact the U.S. Bureau of the Census does conduct some of its business with samples. The monthly Current Population Survey quizzes 35,000 people. And only two or three questions in the Decennial Census are asked of everyone; the rest are sampled.

8. Invisibility or Inaccessibility of Subject Matter

There are times when you want to study a phenomenon that you cannot see or that you cannot reach with your measuring instruments as directly as you would like. For example, the United States wants to know how successful China's harvest is, but China does not supply the data, and the United States cannot make an on-the-spot survey. Or a firm wants to know how much a competitor is spending for advertising. Or you want to know exactly what is said inside jury boxes, but the law will not permit you to record the deliberations. Then you must work with a less satisfactory proxy.

9. Interference with Subject Matter by Researcher

When you observe or measure a phenomenon, you inevitably affect it to some extent. At one extreme is the example of von Osten's horse (pages 288–289), where the phenomenon that is observed is entirely caused by the observer. At the other extreme are studies of economic and social history, which employ records of the past; the events of the past are already complete and are not influenced by the observer except in the sense that the *records* of the past may be altered by the historian's activity. Much of social research falls between these extremes—the influence that asking a question may have upon a person's thinking; the influence that watching a child's play may have upon the playing; and the influence of governmental study of an industry's practices upon the practices.

Almost always you will wish to minimize the influence of the researcher upon the subject matter. Therefore you should seek methods of observing and measuring that will have as little effect as possible. The less the subjects notice the process of observing and measuring, the less they are likely to be influenced by it. Therefore it makes sense to make your observations as "unobtrusive" as possible, to use the now-well-known phrase of Webb *et al.* Their book compiles and discusses many such unobtrusive devices; in this book such devices are mentioned throughout, as the theme arises repeatedly in various contexts.

10. Summary

Data, good data, are the researcher's life blood. But you may find it difficult to obtain *any* data. Or you may be unable to experiment with your subjects for ethical or practical reasons. Or the data may be unreliable. Or the sample of data may be biased, rather than being a fair image of the universe that you wish to describe. Or you may even have so much subject matter that you are overwhelmed by it. Or . . . or . . . or. . . . For each obstacle to getting good data there are solutions, partial solutions, or substitutes, many of them mentioned in this chapter. But the ultimate resource is your ingenuity and your creative faculty, building on your experience. Good luck.

EXERCISES

1. Give examples from research in your field to illustrate the following obstacles to obtaining knowledge:
   a. bias in the sample
   b. nonresponse or unavailability of some part of the universe
   c. inability to experiment
   d. flaws in the subject matter
   e. shortage of subject matter
   f. too much subject matter
   g. invisibility or inaccessibility of subject matter
2. Suggest methods for surmounting the obstacles you described in Exercise 1.
3. Find two sets of comparable data from different origins and cross-check
   them. How reliable are they, as indicated by the cross check?
4. Show an internal-reliability check of some data.

ADDITIONAL READING FOR CHAPTER 21

Statistical records, personal documents, and other publicly available data are
   discussed in Selltiz *et al.* (Chapter 11). For a discussion of the use of
   "secondary data"—that is, data that are publicly available—in the context
   of business research, see Boyd *et al.* (Chapter 5), or Schoner and Uhl,
   pp. 180–192. A description of various repositories for publicly available
   social-science data is given by Nasatir.
Webb *et al.* give a remarkable number of examples of ingenious ways to obtain subject matter when the task seems especially difficult. This is a book
   to jog your imagination when you are stymied for lack of ideas on how to
   get information to answer a research question.
A good summary of techniques to overcome nonresponse in interviewing may
   be found in Stephan and McCarthy (Chapter 11). There is a useful short
   bibliography at the end of that chapter.
Moore is an excellent short treatment of errors in economic data.
A useful general discussion of labor-force statistics is Jaffe and Stewart.
Selvin (1965) cogently discusses the ecological fallacy.

22 obstacles to the study of changes over time

1. Summary

Change over time can be an *obstacle* that can becloud the understanding of relationships in which your variables are not time-related. But in some cases change over time is exactly what you are interested in. This chapter discusses the obstacles to understanding what *does* happen over time.

Some non-cause-and-effect research aims to describe a phenomenon as it exists *at a single point in time*. For example, the U.S. Census tries to measure the population of the nation in a given year. Television ratings try to measure the sizes of television audiences at each moment in the television day. A. Kinsey tried to describe and compare sexual behavior of males and females in a particular contemporary period. But many—perhaps most—non-cause-and-effect research studies are concerned with change over time. Most history is a study of change. Much of anthropology is a study of the changes in cultures. The descriptive psychological studies by A. Gesell and others of how children behave at various ages belong in this category, as does the work of L. Terman, who collected data on a group of gifted children year by year over a period of almost thirty years.

Time itself works no changes; time is only a proxy for other processes that operate over time. If a researcher studies the effect of an independent variable on a dependent variable that reveals its change only slowly, it is much the same as if time is used as a proxy. For example, a prolonged period of smoking is apparently necessary to affect health, and the effects may become apparent late in the smoker's life—even if she quits smoking. Or, even less pleasantly, syphilis contracted when young can cause a person to go mad many years later. In these examples of long time lag—or long "latency period"—between cause and effect, it is not *time itself* that produces the delayed effects but rather various series of biological changes that take place unobserved and in interaction with subsequent happenings.

The difference in the short-run and long-run purchase responses to price changes offers another example in which a time variable is a proxy for other changes. If the power company raises the price of electricity, you may do nothing immediately, but next time you buy a stove you may shift to gas.

Sometimes the long run actually *reverses* the short-run direction. For example, when a baby drinks from her mother's breast, she diminishes the milk supply for a while, but this activity stimulates an increase in production that results, several hours later, in a *larger* supply than if the baby had not suckled. These examples emphasize that it is crucial to choose the appropriate time period in which to look at the effect of the independent variable.

In some situations the independent variable takes effect gradually and *cumulatively*. A cigarette advertisement has some immediate effect in cigarette sales, but this year's advertising also has some effect next year, five years hence, and even twenty years hence, because an advertisement may create a brand loyalty that persists for many years. In the pre-World War II cigarette market, fully 80 to 85 per cent of the effect of a given year's advertising took place in the years after the year in which the advertising was run (Telser). The researcher must then find some way of summarizing the effect of a given year's advertising in *all* the following years together— not an easy task.

Sometimes the study of changes over time is really a *comparison of various stages*. For example, if a person wants to know how his weight is changing—perhaps as a result of a diet, or perhaps only as a result of aging—he wants to compare his weight this year with his weight last year. But such comparisons are bedeviled by time-related breaches of *ceteris paribus*. The researcher must separate the change caused by the internal processes of the material, which is what he is interested in, from the *environmental* change effects. Therefore, he must make sure that he works with appropriately chosen time periods. For example, the weight watcher must weigh himself consistently each day. It will not matter whether he weighs himself at the height or at the depth of the daily weight cycle, whether he weighs himself every morning or every night, as long as he is consistent. But, if he sometimes weighs himself in the morning and sometimes at night, the picture will be confused. Similarly, when a businessman wants to compare his sales from year to year to see whether the business is growing, he can safely compare the same month for two or more years, even though that month is an unusually high or an unusually low month in the yearly cycle.

The most formidable and frequent obstacle in research over time is that the change in the dependent variable takes place so slowly, over so long a period of time, that it is not feasible to observe the variable over the full period of change. Research on the development of gifted children, on smoking and health, on syphilis, on cigarette advertising, and on cultural change all exemplify this obstacle. Now we must consider some devices to overcome it.

One way is *not* to overcome the obstacle but rather to wait, as Terman actually did for almost thirty years. Terman's method of observing the children at intervals over a long period of time is an example of the "panel" method. The essence of the panel is that it allows the researcher to observe changes *in the same individual* over time, which vastly reduces problems of individual variability. The panel method is used frequently in voting studies and in market research, because it provides an unexcelled opportunity to observe switching and shifting behavior among individuals, behavior that is much harder to observe in a comparison of one group with another. The panel method is described in more detail in Chapter 12.

In some cases—especially in economics—the researcher need not wait for new data to accumulate. Much economic data on previous years are already available, and economists can use them to examine long-term changes of the economy; this approach is called "time-series analysis." Although there are many sophisticated statistical devices to aid this kind of analysis, the essence of the time-series method is simply the examination of data from many successive periods, in order to find and explain the changes that occurred.

Sometimes it is not obvious whether a time-series study is being done because the researcher is interested in finding out about changes over time or because she is using historical data to find out other relationships. For example, an economist or sociologist might make a graph of the relationship between yearly birth rates and yearly per capita income. She might also notice that the birth rate is falling, that is, that per capita income is the same for two years but the birth rate is lower in the second year. The researcher might take account of the change in the birth rate over time because she is interested in the change *per se*. Or she might be interested *only* in the relationship between birth rate and per capita income, in which case she takes account of the time trend to clarify the relationship between birth rate and income.[1]

One way to find out now what happened long ago is to *ask* people. For example, I wanted to find out how people's happiness changed when their family incomes changed, without waiting many years to collect the information. Therefore I employed questions of this sort:

> Given your present knowledge of yourself and of other people, what proportion of Americans of your age and sex would you say are (were) happier than you are (were)?

1. To put it technically, in the former case the coefficient of the time trend is a parameter of interest, and the researcher is studying economic or social history or development. In the latter case the coefficient of time is simply a constant for which one can make allowances in a static demographic analysis.

A. Less than 10% happier than you
B. 10–25%
C. 25–50%
D. 50–75%
E. 75–90%
F. More than 90% happier than you

_____At present
_____When you were in early grammar school, grades 1 to 4
_____When you were in grammar school, grades 5 to 8
_____When you were in high school
_____When you were age 17 to 22 (or in college)
_____(Skip if under 29) When you were age 23 to 29
_____(Skip if under 39) When you were age 30 to 39
_____(Skip if under 49) When you were age 40 to 49
_____(Skip if under 59) When you were age 50 to 59
_____(Skip if under 69) When you were age 60 to 69

Sometimes one can surmount the obstacle of slow change by artificially speeding up time. The geneticist cannot wait around for the many years between generations of human beings; instead, he studies the genetics of fruit flies or other organisms that reproduce generations very quickly. In a year's time he can trace a genetic change through perhaps thirty successive generations of fruit flies.

Time may also be speeded up artificially with a combination of analytic and experimental devices. For example, earlier we noted that there are too few business cycles in recent United States history to provide economists with sufficient data for study. Another way to handle this situation is to make various assumptions about how typical individuals and institutions of various types in the economy behave—banks, families, steel companies, Federal Reserve Bank, and so forth—and then to "simulate" their interaction on a computer. Instead of taking three years, a business cycle can be run through the computer in minutes. Then the economist can examine what kind of business cycle results from a given set of assumptions. Chapter 14 explores simulation in more detail (also see G. Orcutt, *et al.*).

For studies of child development and aging processes, the *cohort* method—which is called the "wide view" in Chapter 12—is a possible substitute for the panel or historical "long view." For example, there is no *conceptual* difference between comparing the activity rates of each of a group of monkeys when they are one month old with their own activity rates when they are two months old and comparing a one-month-old group of monkeys with a two-month-old group on the same day. There are practical and statistical differences between the two approaches, however; they are discussed in Chapter 12.

Accounting for effects that are spread out over time can sometimes be done effectively with statistical analysis of past data. But it is vastly preferable, where it is possible, to investigate such effects with experiments that permit observations in several successive periods. Such designs are discussed in Chapter 12.

1. Summary

Changes that occur slowly in people are among the most important phenomena. And often these long-run changes are different from short-run changes and cannot be inferred from them.

Sometimes one can find historical data about individuals or groups or economies that can be compared at various dates and with the present. These data may be found in censuses or archives. Frequently people can recollect how things were at various times in the past. Sometimes one may compare people or groups that are now at different ages, on the assumption that different individuals or groups of different ages are analogous to the *same* individuals or groups observed at different periods in their lives.

At times no such devices are satisfactory. One may then resort to a long-term panel study, and wait (and wait and wait) for the results.

EXERCISE

1. Find five research studies of changes over time in your major discipline, and show how the obstacles were (or were not) successfully overcome.

23 obstacles to the search for causal relationships

The ideal design of a study that seeks to establish cause and effect was set forth in Chapter 2. But sometimes the distinction between studies that do and do not establish causal relationships is subtle, confusing, and ambiguous. Chapter 32 tries to sort out the philosophical tangle of such borderline cases. This chapter discusses the *empirical obstacles* in the way of determining whether a relationship is causal and focuses on how to *design* the study to avoid them successfully.

This chapter and Chapters 25 and 32 all deal with the search for causes and effects. Here is the distribution of labor among the chapters: This chapter discusses the practical decisions that you must make at the planning stage of your study to ensure that it will permit you to draw causal conclusions. Chapter 25 discusses how to handle your data after they have been collected, in order to extract the most knowledge about the cause-and-effect relationships. Chapter 32 considers some of the more subtle problems that arise when you must decide whether to refer to an observed association as a cause-and-effect relationship.

One general piece of advice before we tackle the specific obstacles: Get to know all about the circumstances surrounding the causal relationship you seek to establish. Saturate yourself in the relevant facts. It is only in that way that you can protect yourself against the kinds of mistakes about causal relationships that young children make, for instance thinking that the turning on of streetlights makes the sun go down.

Most of the obstacles to establishing causal relationships afflict nonexperimental research most sharply. Therefore, most of what we know about establishing causal relationships comes from sociologists, economists, and historians, rather than from experimental psychologists. But, even if you can experiment with your subject matter, your problem is not automatically solved, as we shall see.

1. Causation by a "Hidden Third Factor"

This section takes up the possibility of coming to believe mistakenly that one variable is causally influential when another variable is "really" the cause—the "hidden third factor" error, also called "spurious correlation" in sociology and social psychology. Sometimes this obstacle is included under the term "confounding" in experimental psychology (Underwood, pp. 89–92); and, along with the obstacle of multivariable causation, it is called "specification error" in economics.

The classic example of the hidden-third-factor error in an experimental context is the case (see Chapter 4) of the gentlemen who, after getting drunk successively on brandy and soda, whiskey and soda, and bourbon and soda, concluded that the soda caused their inebriation. Notice that their deduction was perfectly sound, given only that much evidence. Other knowledge of the world is necessary to set them straight.

The situation is diagramed in Figure 23.1. The objective is to determine the cause of y, the dependent variable—inebriation, in this example—when a relationship (broken line) with an independent variable, x_1 (drinking soda), has been observed. The "real" cause is shown by the solid arrow from w (liquor) to y.

Another example is Mark Twain's cat who sat on a hot stove lid: "She will never again sit down on a hot stove lid; but also she will never sit down on a cold stove any more." Twain's recommendation has merit: "We would be careful to get out of an experience only the wisdom that is in it—and stop there."[1]

Such errors have occurred many times in the history of science, and sometimes the error has temporarily knocked a science off the track. In one famous experiment, a scientist found that rats exhibited unexpected learning behavior, y, when stimulated by a blast of air, x_1. The results turned psychological theory topsy-turvy. Later, it was found that the rats' unexpected behavior was "really" caused by a piercing sound, w, that accompanied the blast of air from the experimenter's apparatus, a sound that affected them the way a squeaky piece of chalk affects many humans.

For another example, medical researchers for many years attempted to graft, y, a vital part of one mammal onto another mammal of the same species, but the operations always failed, despite the delicacy with which the surgeons performed the operations. The medical researchers then con-

1. Thanks to Chuck Linke for this quotation.

FIGURE 23.1   **The Hidden-Third Factor-Error**

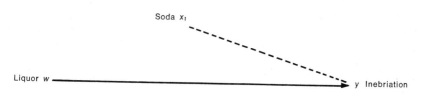

cluded that there were physiological and chemical reasons, x_1, preventing the success of such organ transplantations. Then along came a Russian scientist who claimed to have succeeded in sewing one dog's head onto the side of another dog—and both heads barked for months. It was because his surgical technique, w, was so good that infection did not occur and the operation succeeded. The previously assumed causes of the transplantation failure, antibodies, protein reactions, and so forth, were found not to be the real causes at all.[2]

Sometimes it does not matter whether you know which is the "real" cause. If an ingredient in cigarette smoke causes cancer but must *necessarily* always be part of cigarette smoke, it does not matter much whether we say that cigarette smoking, ingredient X, or still another ingredient in cigarette smoke causes lung cancer.

On the other hand, if there is any possibility that the real cause might ever be *separated* from the other variables that accompany it, then it makes a difference whether we refer to ingredient X or something else as the real cause, for future research may thus be influenced. (Incidentally, finding that tars are the real cause does not weaken the causal status of cigarette smoking but rather *strengthens* it.)

Chemists often can approach progressively closer to real causes. They can now show that the tars contained in cigarette smoke cause some kinds of cancers in animals. Perhaps sometime soon they will be able to show that cigarettes without these factors will not cause cancer (but perhaps may still cause myriad other diseases). They will then have come closer to isolating the "real" cause of cancer.

Remember also how the Curies refined tons of ore and progressively identified many elements as irrelevant until they found that radium alone was "truly" responsible for the radioactive photographic-plate effect that Becquerel had observed with potassium-uranium salt. The chemist and physicist can refine a given sample until it is almost perfectly pure, until it contains practically nothing but one compound or element. It is the *purity* of the specimen that makes us feel that the real cause has been identified. Nevertheless, the chance *always* exists that it is some impurity in the sample

---

2. My friend Stanley Friedman could find no reference in the scientific literature to this event, which was originally reported in the newspapers, so probably it is phony. But the example is still illustrative.

or container—or something else in the environment—that is the real cause of the phenomenon.

The social scientist cannot refine his material with such satisfying progressive logic, but his best strategy is somewhat similar. He should vary every possible condition except that which he regards as the cause, to see whether the variations change the values of the dependent variable. In experimentation, one varies each of the controlled conditions systematically. In nonexperimental research, various types of cross-classification are tried to see whether any other variables seem to exhibit any causal influence (Zeisel, 1957, Chaps. 8, 9, especially p. 192).

Sometimes, however, the hidden factor is tied so tightly to the apparent cause that they cannot be separated. In questionnaire research the possibility always exists that it is some special quirk in the form of the question that forces a particular type of answer, rather than the intended content of the question. But a question must be asked in *some* words, which means that some quirk is always possible. Asking the same question in two different forms offers some check on this problem.

2. Multivariable Causation

This section takes up an obstacle that often afflicts research studies in which you want to establish the effect of one, two, three, or n (n is the standard symbol for some large but unspecified number) particular independent variables on a dependent variable. The difficulty is that the various independent variables do not change independently of one another, at least in the world outside the laboratory. If you want to determine the effect of rainfall, x_1, on crop yield, y, you may have to take account of the fact that, when rainfall is heavy, temperature, x_2, tends to be lower than usual. Therefore, you will not be able to determine, without making some special arrangements, what the simple relationship between rainfall and crop yield is. In other words, the difficulty is to create *ceteris paribus* conditions.

Again it is helpful to diagram the situation (see Figure 23.2). The object in this case is *not* to find *which* variable explains the variations in y, as it was in the previous section. Rather, the purpose is to determine *whether or not*,

FIGURE 23.2   **Multivariable Causation**

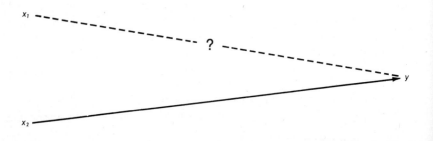

and *how much,* a particular variable x_1 influences y. The obstacle is that, unless the researcher *also* takes account of x_2 (or also x_3, x_4, and so forth), he cannot determine the extent of the causal relationship between x_1 and y, because there is a relationship (though noncausal) between x_1 and x_2.

Another example: Particular departments in department stores spend more for advertising, x_1, during those months when they have especially interesting merchandise. How, then, can you determine the effect of advertising on sales, y? A change in sales might be partly or wholly caused by the excellence of the merchandise assortment, x_2, rather than by the advertising, or it might be caused by both.

Many wonderfully wrong conclusions can be drawn from unwise handling of multivariate problems. For example, auto prices, x, and auto sales, y, both rose from 1932 to 1956 (see Table 23.1) (Suits, 1958). It is unwise, however, to conclude that higher prices cause higher auto sales *or* that high sales of cars cause high prices over a long period of time. When one takes account of such other variables as disposable income, x_2, stock of cars on the road, x_3, credit terms, x_4, and other variables, then the *lower* the price the more cars that are sold, a more sensible conclusion indeed. All the other independent variables are themselves related to price, which is why the simple relationship between price and sales is confusing.

The multivariable obstacle is not simply that many different factors affect the dependent variable. Of course it is true that, beside a lighted match, a cigarette, a hand to hold the match, and air in which to burn are required to cause a lighted cigarette. But the presence of air may generally be treated as a parameter (that is, a condition that does not change in the course of the study); if it does change, the change is not related to the striking of the match. But disposable income and the stock of cars on the road *cannot* sensibly be treated as parameters in a study of the relationship between prices and auto sales.

The nature of the multivariate obstacle, rather, is that the conditions of *ceteris paribus* do not hold. Other things are not equal when the rainfall is high or low, and therefore the differences in crop yield at high and low rainfall may not be attributed simply to the differences in rainfall. If there were no relationship between rainfall and temperature, then it *would* be safe simply to look at the relationship between rainfall and crop yield, for the effects of temperature would average out over the period of the study, and the *ceteris paribus* assumption would hold. The crucial issue in the multivariate problem is that there *is* a relationship between the independent variables x_1 and x_2.

Similarly, if department-store product quality tends to change as the amount of advertising changes, then the conditions of *ceteris paribus* do not hold, and the changes in sales may not be attributed simply to changes in advertising.

If you can *experiment* with the subject matter, you may be able to surmount the multivariate obstacle, because the nature of experiment ensures

TABLE 23.1

Year	Real Retail- Price Index, Passenger Automobiles	Real Disposable Income (Billions of 1947–1949 Dollars)	Stock of Cars January 1 (Millions)	Retail Sales, New Automobiles (Millions)
1932	126.5	83.4	18.7	1.10
1933	128.5	82.6	17.9	1.53
1934	128.5	90.9	18.9	1.93
1935	120.5	99.3	19.4	2.87
1936	117.0	111.6	20.1	3.51
1937	121.0	115.6	21.5	3.51
1938	133.8	109.0	22.3	1.96
1939	131.0	118.5	22.7	2.72
1940	134.3	127.0	23.2	3.46
1941	144.9	147.9	24.5	3.76
1949	186.6	184.9	30.6	4.87
1950	186.6	200.5	33.1	6.37
1951	181.5	203.7	35.7	5.09
1952	195.7	209.2	37.6	4.19
1953	188.2	218.7	39.3	5.78
1954	190.2	221.6	41.6	5.47
1955	196.6	236.3	43.0	7.20
1956	193.4	247.2	47.0	5.90

SOURCE: "The Demand for New Automobiles in the United States," p. 279, by Daniel B. Suits, in *The Review of Economics and Statistics*, Vol. XL (August 1958).

the conditions of *ceteris paribus*. If, instead of examining data on natural rainfall and crops, you artificially *control* the amount of water that each crop plot receives, you can then vary the amount of water among the experimental plots in *random* fashion. If the amount of water varies randomly, you can then be sure that the temperature will not be associated with the amount of water that the plots receive. The temperature will indeed vary also. But, as there will be no *systematic* relationship between temperature and water, you can be sure that the high-water and low-water trials among the plots will *average* the same temperature. If they average the same temperature, then the conditions of *ceteris paribus* hold—for temperature, anyway. Any changes in crop yield may then be attributed solely to changes in water. This example is an application of the crucial device of *randomization* in experimentation.

Sometimes you can arrange to conduct an experiment, even though it does not seem possible to do so at first. A department store may be loath to vary its advertising expeditures randomly in order to isolate the effect of advertising from that of merchandise quality. But you may be able to convince the manager to vary the advertising level *slightly* from week to week, so that the experimental data may be obtained without causing an executive uproar or disturbing the store's basic promotional scheme very much.

TABLE 23.2   Accident Rates of Male and Female Automobile Drivers

	Men %	*Women* %
Never had an accident while driving	56	68
Had at least one accident while driving	44	32
Total	100	100
(Number of cases)	(7,080)	(6,950)

SOURCE: *Say It With Figures,* 5th ed., p. 120, by Hans H. Zeisel; copyright 1947, 1950, 1957, 1968 by Harper & Row, Publishers, Incorporated; reprinted by permission of the publishers.

If experimentation is truly not feasible, all may still not be lost. You may be able to isolate your independent variable by holding the other variable(s) constant *statistically* instead of experimentally. Cross-classification is one statistical device that accomplishes this purpose. A cross-classification allows you to look at the effect of different levels of your independent variable x_1 at the *same* level of the other independent variable x_2, which makes it possible for you to examine the effect of x_1 on y under conditions that approach *ceteris paribus*. For example, perhaps you want to learn the effect of sex upon incidence of auto accidents. The simple tabulation in Table 23.2 apparently shows that women are safer drivers than men. But it seems plausible that amount of driving might affect the picture. And a cross-classification does clarify the issue.

Table 23.3 shows that when distance driven is crudely controlled by dividing the sex groups into more than, and less than, 10,000 miles driven, there is no difference in accident rates. (Furthermore, one can guess from this crude cross-classification that men are *safer* drivers per mile driven, as follows: The distribution of the sexes by amount driven indicates that men drive more miles than women. This implies that *within* both the more-than- and the less-than-10,000-miles-driven groups, men drove more miles than women. If nevertheless the accident rates within distance groups are similar by sex, men have less accidents *per mile*. A finer subclassification would check on this guess.)

The regression is another statistical technique that helps to isolate the effect of the independent variable in which you are interested. The regression is actually something more than a refined type of cross-classification; it takes advantage of the *continuous* gradations in variables, rather than lumping them into a few categories, as does cross-classification. A regression uses the information from all the observations to smooth out the whole set of observations, rather than each observation by itself. These and other analytic devices to accomplish the same purpose will be discussed at greater length in Chapter 25.

A mighty question may have sprung to your mind: How can one know when all the important variables have been taken care of? There is no fully

TABLE 23.3   Automobile Accidents of Male and Female Drivers
by Number of Miles Driven

	Male Drivers		Female Drivers	
	Drove More Than 10,000 Miles %	*Drove 10,000 Miles or Less* %	*Drove More Than 10,000 Miles* %	*Drove 10,000 Miles or Less* %
Had at least one accident while driving	52	25	52	25
Never had an accident while driving	48	75	48	75
Total	100	100	100	100
(Number of cases)	(5,010)	(2,070)	(1,915)	(5,035)

SOURCE: *Say It With Figures*, 5th ed., p. 133, by Hans H. Zeisel, copyright 1947, 1950, 1957, 1968 by Harper & Row, Publishers, Incorporated; reprinted by permission of the publishers.

satisfactory answer. The core of the matter is thorough knowledge of the complexities of that aspect of the real world that you are investigating, as well as extensive trials of the likeliest variables.

This chapter explains what to do about multivariable causation in planning your study; Chapter 25 takes up what to do after you have your data in hand. It is now, at the planning stage, that you should take advantage of your flexibility to choose sound variables. At the design stage you should arrange to collect the data you will need for the cross-classification or the regression. If you are doing an experiment, you should at this stage ensure that all the relevant variables are being held constant. In the crop-yield study you would collect temperature, as well as rainfall and crop-yield, data; if you were experimenting, you would hold the temperature constant. In the department-store study, you would obtain data on excellence of merchandise assortment, as well as on advertising and sales. In political polling, you would collect data on income, age, geography, and anything else that might seem relevant.

You should also consider collecting data in more than one way, so that your results will bolster one another and increase the weight of total evidence. Animal experiments and human surveys on smoking support one another and strengthen the argument for the cause-and-effect relationship with cancer because each method holds constant a different set of the multiple variables.

3. Confounding the Dependent and Independent Variables

Do England's leaders come from Oxford and Cambridge because the instruction at those universities makes leaders of men? Or is it simply that the people who would be leaders anyway are sent to Oxford and Cambridge?

This is a hard question to answer, partly because it is difficult to measure the extent to which a university graduate is a "leader" or "succeeds." Let us instead ask a similar question about a type of educational institution whose graduates' success we can more easily measure—business schools; it seems fair to say that the salaries paid to businessmen are a reasonable proxy for success. We ask, then, does Harvard Business School make good business people? Or do people who would be successful in business anyway go to Harvard Business School?

It will not suffice to compare the salaries earned by graduates of Harvard Business School with the salaries of a group of business people who went elsewhere to business school or who went to no graduate school at all. If the best prospects go to Harvard Business School, then their salaries will be higher, even if they gain nothing at all from the Harvard Business School training.

Attempts to evaluate the effect of psychoanalysis run afoul of a similar obstacle. One cannot simply compare a group of neurotics who have undergone psychoanalysis with another group of neurotics who have had no psychoanalytic treatment. The group that has had psychoanalysis obviously consists of people different from those in the other group to start with, for they *chose* to undertake psychoanalytic treatment. Making such a choice might well indicate a desire to overcome the neurosis that would have resulted in improvement even without treatment. Indeed, there does not seem to be satisfactory evidence for the effectiveness of psychoanalysis.

Still another example is the comparison of life expectancy of people who take exercise with that of people who do not. There is always an important possibility that people exercise because they are healthy, rather than vice versa.

In all these cases we say that there is "confounding" (see Figure 23.3);[3] that is, *both* the independent variable, x_1, in whose effect we are interested (exercise, psychoanalysis, Harvard Business School training) *and* the dependent variable, y (success, mental health, physical health), may be caused by some other personal-background factor, v (brains and drive, natural healing processes, natural good health). The difference between confounding and the hidden third factor is that in the former we are *particularly* interested in whether the specific variable x_1 is a cause of y, whereas in the latter we concentrate on finding out *which* variable causes y. Confounding also differs from the multivariate obstacle; in the former confounding v *causes* x_1, whereas in the latter the relationship between x_1 and x_2 is *not* causal.

Notice the difference between this obstacle and the obstacle of nonre-

---

3. "Confounding" is a word used mostly by psychologists, and they use it to refer to almost any experiment that suffers from insufficient controls or incomplete design (Underwood, pp. 89–90). The definition and usage here are more restricted but still common. Statisticians also use the term when they *purposely* give up some information in order to reduce the size of the experiment.

FIGURE 23.3   **Confounding of Variables**

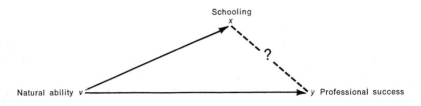

sponse. If there is nonresponse, one cannot get data on one group of people that *may* be special. In confounding, the difficulty is that certain kinds of people *do not exist* or are not known to exist. The people who do not exist are people in every way exactly like those who go to Harvard Business School but who do not actually go to Harvard Business School.

It does not suffice simply to find a group of people who *seem* in every possible way like those who went to Harvard Business School or like those who underwent psychoanalysis or like those who took exercise but who did not *actually* do those things. They would still differ in one crucial way: the thing that kept them from going to Harvard Business School or taking exercise or psychoanalysis. Whatever that thing is may well turn out to be the crucial difference between the groups.

To surmount the obstacle of possible confounding often requires exceptional effort and cost. The only way I can think of to measure fairly the effect of a Harvard Business School education would be to select *randomly* a group of young people who would otherwise not go to Harvard Business School—perhaps from among the entrants to the training programs of large business firms—send them to Harvard Business School, and then over a long period of years compare their careers with those of the rest of the group from which they were drawn randomly.[4]

In the investigation of the effect of exercise, it would be difficult to experiment with a group of people over a period long enough so that the exercise might be considered to make any difference. And, even if it weren't, it would be many years from the beginning of the experiment until the results were available.

Sometimes it is possible to carry out a *quasi experiment*. In the case of relating psychoanalysis to cure, there may be no psychoanalysts in some part of the country. Assuming that problems of geographical differences could be surmounted (see p. 198), one could compare the rate of recovery from neurosis where psychoanalytic treatment is available with that where there are no psychoanalysts. This design might be particularly useful in measuring the effects of psychotherapeutic treatment on psychosis in mental hospitals.

---

4. But difficulties never end. B. Glad pointed out that even this experimental design is subject to an important flaw: People who return from the Harvard Business School program may progress more quickly simply because their superiors are impressed by the degrees, even if the training really has no value.

4. Feedback; Interaction Between Dependent and Independent Variables

In this complicated world of ours, there are many situations in which A and B influence each other. We see this type of mutual influence in most human relationships: The more you love me, the more I love you, the more you love me. You step on my toe, I jab you with my elbow, you hit me on the nose. A change in demand for a product causes a change in the price, which causes a change in the supply of the product, which causes a change in the price, which causes a change in demand, on and on forever. Cause and effect bounce back and forth like a ping-pong ball or an echo in a canyon. This effect is called "feedback" or "mutual causation."

Feedback can be positive, in which case it increases the original effect, or it can be negative, in which case it tends to "dampen" the original effect. Jeremiah describes a feedback reaction involving the Children of Israel: "Thine own wickedness shall correct thee, and thy backslidings shall reprove thee" (Jeremiah 2:19).

The term "feedback" was invented by the radio engineers for circuits in which the output signal is "fed back," to be amplified again. The same idea has proved useful in the social sciences. For example, the basic Keynesian economic model can be shown in the schematic form that electronics engineers use. Figure 23.4 indicates that national income depends upon investment and consumption and that consumption in turn depends upon national income. There is mutual interaction between national income and consumption; the influence of each *feeds back* upon itself.[5]

Another example: In areas where liquor consumption is high, there are many stores that sell liquor. Does the existence of many stores lead to high consumption, as the prohibitionists believe, or vice versa? The influence is likely to run in both directions.

Still another example of mutual causation is the relationship between social status and choice of career. For example, doctors tend to claim that their own specialties have the highest social status among medical specialties. Do doctors choose these specialties because of the high social status, or do they "put a halo" on their own specialties to make themselves feel good? Probably both. When mutual causation exists, it is not easy to ascertain what causes what and to what extent. For example, advertising researchers want to know which advertising causes sales and how much. D. Starch and others have shown that a relationship exists between readership of magazine ads and purchase of the advertised products. Starch developed a system by which he purported to measure the *effect of the advertising* by measuring the difference between rates of sales to readers of the advertisement and to nonreaders of the advertisement. But, although people who read particular

---

5. The equations represented in the diagram are
National Income = Investment + Consumption $\qquad Y = I + C$
Consumption $\quad$ = Constant Multiple × National Income $\quad C = aY$

FIGURE 23.4   **An Example of Feedback**

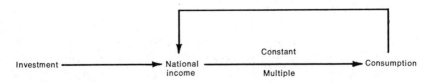

Source: *Mathematical Economics*, 2nd ed., p. 289, by R. G. D. Allen, 1959. Reprinted by permission of Macmillan London and Basingstoke.

advertisements buy more of the products advertised in the ads, it is also true that people who buy particular products are more likely than other people to *read* the advertisements for those products *after* they have purchased the products (perhaps to reassure themselves that they have bought the right car or whatever). If so, to what extent can one say that reading advertisements causes the purchase of the products or that purchase of the products causes reading the ads?

There is no easy answer. In this case one might subtract the effect caused by people who read the ads but who had already bought the products. Sometimes complex mathematical, statistical, or simulation techniques can help to disentangle the relationship (Johnston), but often there is *no* way of disentangling cause and effect in such cases of mutual causation.

In the social sciences other than economics, complete analysis of a system of feedback variables is not likely to be necessary or successful because "systems analysis" functions best when the system is relatively *closed,* as it is with the echo in the canyon and with radio circuits. In the social sciences, the influence of A upon B and of B upon A is almost always mediated by so many other elements that there can be no one-to-one relationship between what A does to B and what B does to A. And so, as a matter of practice, it is almost always the best policy to look at the influence of the variables on one another in *one direction* and *one at a time.* Sometimes the researcher dodges by stating that he will restrict his interest to *establishing a relationship* between the variables, rather than trying to ascertain the amounts and directions of cause and effect. But in some cases, especially in research done to aid policy decisions, the researcher cannot cop a plea that way. For example, we want to know if smoking causes cancer, not merely whether the two are related. Knowledge of a relationship is useful as a beginning, but knowledge of cause and effect is of ultimate interest here as so often elsewhere.

5. Summary

Knowledge of causes and effects is all-important in building a social science. It is also crucial in situations where the aim is to make changes that will improve the quality of life. Causation can never be known in some absolute or ultimate sense. But we can get closer to a useful understanding of causal relationships with astute research.

There are several sorts of obstacles to a sound understanding of a causal relationship: a) A third factor may account for both the hypothesized cause and effect. Systematic testing under a wide range of conditions can reduce the likelihood that such an unknown factor is causing confusion, b) There may be several important variables jointly responsible for the phenomenon in question. Sound multivariate research, experimental or nonexperimental, can appraise the relative importance of the independent variables, c) The line of causation may run from the hypothesized effect to the hypothesized cause. This is most easily checked by experimentation, d) Both variables may influence each other, either simultaneously or sequentially.

Discerning the scheme of causation is a very general problem in social-science research. This chapter suggests some techniques. Others are found throughout the book.

EXERCISES

1. Give examples from research in your field to illustrate the following obstacles:
   a. hidden third factor
   b. multivariable causation
   c. confounding the dependent and independent variables
   d. feedback; interaction between independent and dependent variables
2. Suggest methods of clarifying the causal relationship in each example in Exercise 1.

ADDITIONAL READING FOR CHAPTER 23

There is an excellent simple exposition of cross-classification in Zeisel.

24 the master obstacle: cost

The cost of carrying out a piece of research is the most important obstacle that a researcher must overcome. This obstacle will face (or faze) you in one form or another in every single piece of empirical research you conduct. You must economize to do a satisfactory amount of good research, and your economies must be of money, energy, and time. Logically, this obstacle belongs at the head of the list. But the most logical order of presentation is not always the best pedagogical order, and therefore the discussion of cost as an obstacle has been deferred until now.

Cost is the *master* obstacle because almost all other obstacles can be overcome with large amounts of money and time. For example, if you were studying reading habits and if cost were no object, you could assign a full-time observer to watch and photograph every page that your subject reads or looks at, rather than depending on questions asked of the subject. Or you could reduce experimental bias by having many different experimenters re-run the experiment. Reflection will convince you that most other obstacles could also be overcome with expenditures of money.

Cost is more than an obstacle, however; it is often the very factor that makes research necessary or useful. The information that comes from research often produces profit by reducing cost. Furthermore, scientific empirical research is a more efficient and therefore less costly method of getting knowledge than hit-or-miss methods of gathering knowledge. For example, it is cheaper to pretest a piece of advertising copy in a laboratory than to run an entire advertising campaign to find out whether the copy works well.

There are several kinds of research decisions in which cost is a crucial factor; we shall now discuss them one by one.

1. Procedure to Produce Data for Study

Sometimes an investigator is limited to existing data; for example, one cannot go back and resurvey voting preferences before the election of 1936. And sometimes limited time requires the use of existing data; one cannot always wait for a survey or experiment to be executed and the data processed. Nevertheless, a researcher is often faced with a choice of whether to use existing data or to collect new data. The decision should be dictated by considerations of *cost and accuracy*. But lack of accuracy is itself a cost. To make this decision rationally, then, you must assess the cost that would result from lack of accuracy, as well as the cost of obtaining accuracy. The cost of the inaccuracy caused by flaws in existing data must be weighed against the cost of creating new data. What is most important is that you *make explicit* to yourself just how much you are spending to avoid the flaws in the existing data.

Another data-production choice is between experimentation and field survey. Sometimes a laboratory experiment is cheaper than a survey, but often a survey is cheaper. Again, you must balance the cost of the technique against the higher value of the information produced by the more expensive technique. (If the less expensive technique produces better data, your choice is made for you.)

Social scientists who do survey research must often decide among interviews conducted in person, over the telephone, and by mail questionnaire. In almost every case, the personal interview is more expensive, but sometimes the extra expense is necessary and justified. In surveys like A. Kinsey's in which subjects do not respond easily and straightforwardly, the skill of the interviewer in face-to-face encounter is necessary, especially when there are many questions to be asked. On the other hand, the questions asked in surveys on smoking and health are few, easy to answer, and not likely to be touchy, so the mail questionnaire is quite satisfactory except for the problem of nonresponse. The expense of conducting hundreds of thousands of interviews for the smoking studies would have made those studies impossible.

Research on magazine readership has used all three interviewing techniques. The decisions in particular studies have been based on the exact nature of the information required plus the costs and revenues attached to the various accuracy levels. For example, a large consumer magazine can afford to spend more money on interviewing techniques than can a small trade magazine because positive information would mean a much greater gain in revenue for the large consumer magazine.

2. Sampling and Cost

In 1886 C. Booth sought to find out how many poor people there were in London, because the extent of poverty and misery was a subject for debate in the 1880s (just as the actual number of people in England had been a subject for debate a hundred years earlier) and because he wanted to find out what the causes of this poverty and misery were. Obviously he could not finance the gathering of such a monumental mass of data. Therefore, he turned to "the method of wholesale interviewing," as Beatrice Webb called it (Moser, p. 19)—collecting information from school attendance officers, whose job it was to visit individual homes and children.

In the 1890s Rowntree felt that Webb's method was not sufficiently accurate, and he therefore employed interviewers to go to every wage-earning home. He worked in the city of York, however, which was much smaller than London.

It was an enormous advance in social research when in 1912 Bowley studied living conditions in Reading by means of a sample. Not only was a sample much cheaper than Rowntree's method, but with the smaller data-collection effort Bowley could take more care with such technical matters as nonresponse bias. Hence Bowley's results probably were more accurate than a 100 per cent sample would have produced.

The decisions on whether to sample, how to sample, how large a sample to take, and what sampling method to use are basically cost decisions. If cost were no object, every study would take a very large per cent of the potential subject matter, because accuracy would then be greater and error smaller than in a smaller sample.

The presidential election in the United States is a 100 per cent sample (that is, not a sample) of all American people who want to vote. I do not know whether the nation goes to all this expense to prevent any trace of sampling error because its citizens do not know any better or because the election offers an important ritual of participation. (This 100 per cent sample does not guarantee a perfect survey, however; it was especially unsure in Boston when ballot-box stuffing and repeat voting were well-developed local arts.)

The U.S. Census attempted to be a 100 per cent sample for a long time. In recent censuses, however, some questions were asked of only one person in four, for example, and future censuses will probably go further with sampling. The preliminary reports issued by the U.S. Bureau of the Census for quick information dissemination are also products of a sampling process (but in this case the sample is a sample of the *data*, as distinguished from a sample of people).

3. Sample Size

I have said that the only reason for not taking a 100 per cent sample of the universe is cost. But how big *should* the sample be? The most common ways of choosing a sample size are to find out how big a sample is customary in similar research and to take as big a sample as the budget will allow. Both methods are logically fallacious, but the former contains some grains of practical wisdom. Observation of others' work can help the researcher to take advantage of their trial-and-error learning. For example, Kinsey spent much time in working out appropriate sample sizes, and, if you were to carry on work similar to his, it might be reasonable to imitate his sample sizes.

Fitting your sample size to the available budget funds requires circular reasoning, because the budget has to be fixed on the basis of how large the sample size will be. Someone has to make an independent decision at *some* stage of the game.

The best general advice about sample size is to take a pretest sample that is small by *any* standard and then see whether you can observe any clear pattern of the sort you are looking for. You may find that even such a tiny sample is big enough. If not, the variation within your pretest sample will guide you in deciding how much larger a sample you are likely to need. Chapter 31 gives you detailed rational methods for deciding how large a sample to take.

4. How Many Variables to Investigate

There are always more variables that *might* be important than you have time and money to investigate. Therefore, you must decide which of the variables are promising enough to be worth the cost—a process of economics and good judgment. As R. Fisher put it:

> It is an essential characteristic of experimentation that it is carried out with limited resources, and an essential part of the subject of experimental design to ascertain how these should be best applied; or, in particular, to which causes of disturbance care should be given, and which *ought* to be deliberately ignored. (Fisher, p. 22)

For example, a wise advertising researcher does not bother to experiment with various shades of ink in a direct-mail advertisement; rather, she concentrates on such variables as the advertising message and the offer the advertisement makes. On the other hand, cancer researchers are willing to follow up leads that may seem very trivial at first because the problem is so important and because there are too few good leads of any kind.

There is not much that can be said about this decision except that the researcher must *get into the habit* of asking herself whether an additional variable is sufficiently promising to justify its cost. There just are no scientific or automatic routines to aid in making such decisions.

5. Amount of Tolerable Bias

The Kinsey study made no attempt to achieve a random sample of the population of the United States, because the attempt would have been impossibly expensive. Furthermore, even if astronomical sums had been spent and a random sample had been *attempted*, the *departures* from randomness would still have been very large because of nonresponse. Kinsey's judgment on this matter was mostly approved later by the statistical review board of the American Statistical Association, though the statisticians did call for a small probability-sample test of just how much bias Kinsey's procedure injected into his study (Cochran, *et al.*). Other statisticians were less satisfied, however (Wallis, 1949); this is a matter of judgment on which there is room for competent professionals to disagree.

Cost also affected the geographic pattern of Kinsey's sampling. Half the subjects were from Indiana. But Kinsey judged that the expense of drawing more of his subjects from farther away would not be justified by the probable decrease in bias.

Bias and cost must also be balanced when deciding how much money and effort to spend on converting nonresponders into responders. Should the researcher call back twice? five times? eleven times? The decision must be based on the costs of calling back *and* the costs of inaccuracy caused by the bias.

6. Managerial Cost Efficiency in Research

Some researchers are crackerjack managers. They use the research money at their disposal as efficiently and conscientiously as if it came out of their own pockets. But too many researchers take no pride in cost efficiencies and ignore all reasonable procedures for calculating what should and should not be done.

Scientific accuracy and avoidance of error are important, but one can be too finicky about such things as not using existing data that may not be quite perfect for one's purposes, rather than collecting new data from scratch. Beside appealing to your sense of justice about other people's money, I suggest that economical practices may also be personally efficient for you and help you to accomplish a lot more work in your lifetime.

Having funds available to pay for help may expedite your work. But, beyond a certain level, *too much* money may slow you down by inducing you to magnify the size of your project to the point at which you must do large amounts of administrative and supervisory work. Or an excess of money may lead you to collect too much data and thereby slow down your analysis. Money and the help it buys are useful only if they do not prevent you from traveling light and fast.

Academic scientists sometimes forgo efficient shortcuts out of unnecessary prissiness. For example, market researchers have known for years that it is often cheaper in the long run to pay interviewees and panel members and that such payment can often be made without compromising the research. Yet I know of an academic researcher who put up a monumental battle against giving away a cheap pencil to induce people to answer a questionnaire. (A later test showed that the pencils far more than paid for themselves.)

A slight acquaintance with the basic notions of managerial economics can help a researcher, just as it can help any other administrator, to be more efficient. Consider, for example, a study situation in which you hand out one-question questionnaires in person at a huge convention. It pays to take a sample far larger than any sample size you might reasonably need because the *extra* cost of the extra questionnaires and their distribution is practically nil.

Perhaps this statement by a famous chemist will add weight to the argument:

> In designing a bridge, an engineer naturally chooses the most economical design which satisfies all the specifications, including the aesthetic requirements. In designing an elaborate experiment, questions of cost are all too frequently ignored completely. This is partly because of the great difficulty of making good estimates of the time required to carry out a given investigation, but it is also partly a traditional attitude that somehow science is above vulgar monetary considerations.

> With the increasing cost of research it becomes necessary to take economic factors into account, however difficult this may be. Certainly there is no excuse for doing a given job in an expensive way when it can be carried through equally effectively with less expenditure. It is much more difficult to decide whether a given project should be carried out at all, considering its probable cost. In applied research there sometimes exist fairly definite criteria, such as the possible monetary benefits of a successful research, coupled with a rough estimate of the chance of success.

> In pure science no estimate of monetary value is usually available or in fact desirable. Here cost still enters in deciding between alternative problems. Naturally this is not the only factor, but it is certainly wrong to disregard it altogether.

> Cost estimates should include not only direct expenditures for materials but also salaries and overhead, even if these are not directly charged to the project. (Wilson, p. 6)

Computers and modern data-processing technology have radically changed the economics of research. I mentioned earlier how simple IBM machines were developed to make the U.S. Census cheaper and quicker to analyze. By now machines have reduced the cost of handling data so much that many studies are possible that were out of the question before.

7. Summary

Cost is the master obstacle to getting empirical knowledge, because with large enough expenditures of time and money almost all other obstacles can be overcome. Your task as a researcher is to devise sufficiently efficient ways of overcoming obstacles of all kinds so that with the time and money at your disposal, you can produce relatively much useful knowledge.

Sampling rather than studying the entire population is a basic cost-reducing tactic. Using available data is another. Also, one should use good judgment to avoid collecting unnecessary data on irrelevant variables, and not demand more accuracy than is required by the overall purpose of the research. And it is all-important to *care* about being a good manager of research resources, both because it will make you more productive and because you owe it to whoever—your institution, or society as a whole—is ultimately paying the bill.

EXERCISE

1. Give examples in which
   a. experiment is cheaper than survey
   b. survey is cheaper than experiment
   c. sampling is not used at present but should be
   d. a slightly biased sample may be obtained at a much lower cost than an unbiased sample

part four extracting the meaning of data

25 analysis of simple data: association and regression

After data have been collected, they must be rearranged and fiddled with to make them yield up the information they contain. This is the process of analysis.

Many different processes in social-scientific research are called "analysis," and perhaps the most important job of this chapter is to distinguish among them. What type of analysis a researcher performs should depend upon the type of research question that he seeks to answer, as well as on the method by which he collects the data and the sharpness with which the research question or hypothesis has been formulated.

Descriptive classification and measurement research call for processes that some writers do not call "analysis." There are no independent variables to relate to dependent variables. Rather, there is but one—or several—variable(s) whose relationships are not in question, as in a census or other measurement of multiple variables. The analysis begins with standardizing the data and separating it into convenient or interesting categories, and ends with summarizing statistics or with graphs or tables of the data. The appropriateness of the various summarizing statistics for various types of research question was discussed briefly in Chapter 4. Discussions and illustrations of the logic of tabular and graphic display can be found in almost any elementary statistics book or in H. Zeisel (1957, Chaps. 2, 4). D. Huff (Chaps. 3, 5, 6, 9) shows how you and others can deceive people with tables and graphs.

A good descriptive analysis *shows* the important data in a form such that they will be clearly understood and their meaning grasped by the reader. For example, there should be a separate table or graph for each idea you are trying to communicate, rather than one enormous master compilation in which nothing is obvious.

The more complicated processes of analysis take place in causal- and non-causal-relationship research and in comparison research. There are at least seven major types of relationship analysis: statistical *testing* to determine whether an association exists; characterizing the *form* of a relationship; evaluating the *importance* of the observed differences and relationships; *searching* for new relationships within the data; *digging deeper* into the observed association to make it yield a deeper meaning; *refining* observed associations into causal relationships; *generalizing and predicting* on the basis of the observed data. Each of these processes will now be discussed in turn.

This chapter deals with situations in which you wish to investigate the relationship between two given variables for which the data are already in hand. The following chapter deals with the analysis of data where more than two variables are involved, and where the variables are not already chosen at the time you begin your analysis.

1. Testing for the Existence of Simple Relationships

To distinguish and to establish relationships are the basic tasks of science, and therefore the category and the association are the basic conceptual units in science. To say that there is an association between two variables is to say that when one phenomenon varies, the other is likely to vary in a predictable manner. All the more complicated statements in science—cause-and-effect statements, for example—are built upon the foundation of the association.

This is the question that relationship testing seeks to answer: Is there, or is there not, an association between a particular pair of variables? Sometimes the answer is statistically obvious immediately. For example, J. Masserman observed that, when given a choice of milk with alcohol or without alcohol, only two of sixteen normal cats chose liquor, whereas ten of sixteen neurotic cats chose liquor. It was then reasonably obvious that the difference between two of sixteen and ten of the sixteen indicates a "real" association; that is, if he were to run the experiment over again, the neurotic cats almost surely would choose the liquor more often than the normal cats. Of course, the existence of an association would be even more conclusive if the results had been 20 of 160 versus 100 of 160, rather than 2 of 16 versus 10 of 16. But, even so, no further statistical proof of the association is necessary, and the analysis of Masserman's data is complete. All that is left for him to determine is that the experimental results are not an artifact of bad sampling or some other bias and then to say what the association between neurosis and alcohol *means*—a matter of theorizing that is beyond the scope of this book.

But, if the results for the neurotic and nonneurotic group had been less different than 2/16 and 10/16, Masserman could not have immediately asserted with confidence that there is a relationship between neurosis and liquor drinking. If the research is experimental—as in this case—the best procedure is to repeat the experiment on more subjects (cats); if the same results appear, one's belief in the existence of the relationship will be strengthened. Furthermore, if the study is a survey, it is frequently possible to obtain more data. But, if you cannot increase the size of your sample and if there is doubt about the existence of a difference between two (or more) groups or a relationship between two variables, you must turn to statistical testing for help.

Often your data measure two (or more) characteristics for each observation, and you wish to determine the existence of an association between the two characteristics. Let's say, for example, that you have I.Q. and athletic scores for ten high-school boys, as shown in Table 25.1, and you want to know whether the two abilities are related. A quick and simple test is the "two-way classification." You rank each observation from high to low, as shown in Columns 3 and 4 of Table 25.1. Then you construct a table that shows how often the above-average observations of one characteristic are associated with the above-average observations of the other characteristic, the below-average with the below-average, and so on, as shown in Table 25.2. If there is a strong association, the observations will be piled up in two diagonal cells, whereas if the association is not strong the observations will be scattered equally among the four cells. In this case there appears to be an association, but the matter is sufficiently inconclusive that we need to know how often a 4-4/1-1 split would occur by chance. (A statistical test of that probability is shown in Chapter 28, page 416.)

If the data came in quantitative form rather than simply high or low, you can make a more revealing test by plotting the data quantitatively, as the I.Q.-athletic score data are plotted in Figure 25.1. Now we can see quite

TABLE 25.1 Hypothetical Athletic and I.Q. Scores
for High-School Boys

Athletic Score (1)	I.Q. Score (2)	Athletic Rank (3)	I.Q. Rank (4)
97	114	1	3
94	120	2	1
93	107	3	7
90	113	4	4
87	118	5	2
86	101	6	8
86	109	7	6
85	110	8	5
81	100	9	9
76	99	10	10

TABLE 25.2

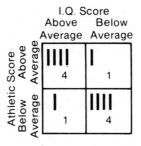

SOURCE: Table 25.1

conclusively that there is a solid positive relationship between I.Q. and athletic score.

It is important to remember that everything said in this chapter applies *only* when you start with a given hypothesis and the data serve to prove or disprove that particular hypothesis. It is a very different situation when you make up a new hypothesis *after* you examine the data—as we shall see in the next chapter.

FIGURE 25.1   **Hypothetical Data for a Class**

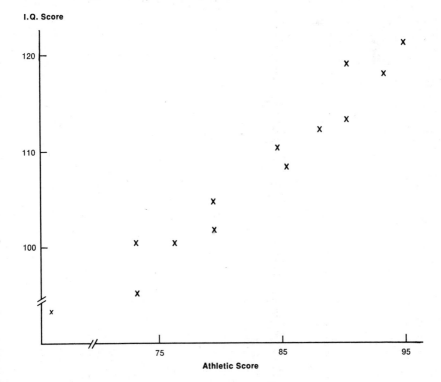

2. Characterizing the Form of an Association

Associations can be of many varieties: positive (direct) or negative (inverse); and straight-line (linear) or curvilinear or oscillating. Complex numerical statistical techniques often obscure the form of a relationship. Hence an invaluable first step when you are investigating the form of a relationship is to *graph* the data. For example, assume that you have data on the birth rate in Yemen for each of the past twenty years. Is the birth rate going up or down or staying the same? It is often surprisingly difficult to make a valid analysis. And a graph is an important first step in determining the nature of the association.

Graphs are generally limited to exhibiting the association between two variables, though a third variable can be shown by plotting two different sets of data on the same graph; for example, the relationship of age to weight can be shown separately for men and women in the same graph. Even when you think the relationship is multivariate, however, it can be illuminating to plot the dependent variable two-dimensionally against each independent variable.

One reason that a visual graph of the data is so important is that some kinds of association become visible that would not appear in various kinds of statistical analysis. For example, data like those shown in Figure 25.2 appear to be curvilinear, but, if you were simply to compare the average values of *y* for the low and high *x* groups, no relationship would show up because the two averages would be similar.

The decision on whether to characterize data as an upward or downward straight line or as a curve of some sort must be a blend of judgment and a branch of mathematical statistics called "curve fitting." For example, in Figure 25.3 the American Council in Education drew a curve through the data of the experts' ratings of economics departments plotted against the amounts of scholarly publications produced by the economics departments. Would you care to argue that a straight line or another shape of curve is not more sensible?

FIGURE 25.2

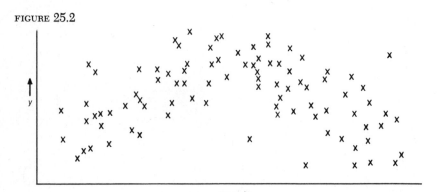

FIGURE 25.3   **Relationship of Rated Quality of Graduate Faculty to Index of Publications, 71 Economics Departments**

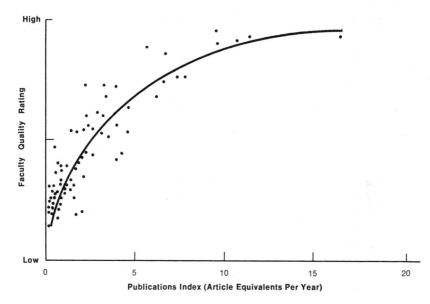

Source: *An Assessment of Quality in Graduate Education*, p. 80, by Allan M. Cartter, 1966; reprinted by permission of American Council on Education.

Deciding whether to treat the data as one group or as a collection of small groups is one of the major issues in characterizing a set of data. If you assume that each of the observations was very certain and there was little or no error in measurement or variability in behavior from trial to trial, then it would be reasonable to assume that each point represents exactly what it shows on the graph and leave the data as in Figure 25.4 without drawing a smoothed curve.[1] This is usually reasonable, however, when each point on the graph stands for repeated observations or for large subsamples, as in Figure 25.5 in which R. Dahl shows how the proportion of New Haven men over twenty-one years of age who participated in gubernatorial elections changed over time.

If you believe that each point contains some variability due to chance—as will almost always be the case—you will want to use the information contained in the observations to help locate the curve at *other* points as well. This process is called "smoothing" the curve. The most modest way of doing so for the raw data shown in Figure 25.6 is by averaging only small groups; this operation does not assume much, and it may be all you need to do if

1. The diagrams for this illustration are all taken from the 1930 edition by M. Ezekiel, who gives an excellent discussion of the issue. This early edition contains much wisdom about statistical analysis.

FIGURE 25.4   **Relation of Speed of Automobile to Distance It Takes to Stop, as Shown by Individual Observations**

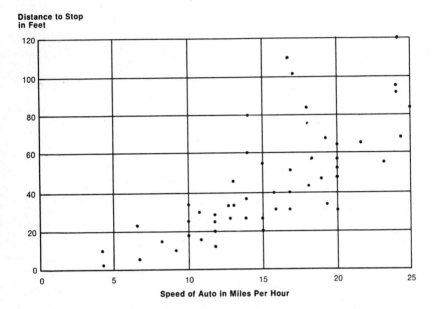

Source: *Methods of Correlation and Regression Analysis,* p. 37, by Mordecai Ezekiel, 1930; reprinted by permission of John Wiley & Sons, Inc.

the number of observations in each small group is large. But as the figure shows, there is still much zigzag. In such cases we often try more radical smoothing, using averages of larger groups, as in Figure 25.7.

One might go even further and fit either a straight line or a curve to these data. (A curve might be especially appropriate if there is another observation at *x* in Figure 25.7.) Either a straight line or a curve uses *all* the data to throw light either on *all* the other data or on the kind of *overall* relationship that is assumed to hold between the variables.

There is more than one way to "fit" a line or curve to a set of data. For now let's limit the discussion to data that seem to fit a straight line rather than a curve; that is, "linear correlation." When you fit a line by eye-and-hand[2] with a straightedge ruler—or better, with a black thread—your intuitive criterion seems to be simply to get the line "as close" to the observation points as possible. But how should one define "close"?

A reasonable criterion is to draw that line which minimizes the sum of the distances between the correlation line and the points; these minimum distances would be measured perpendicular to the correlation line, as seen in Figure 25.8. The usual criterion—chosen simply for mathematical con-

2. Ezekiel's first edition (1930) concentrates on hand-fitting methods, whereas his latest edition (Ezekiel & Fox) concentrates on mathematical fitting methods.

FIGURE 25.5   Total Votes Cast in New Haven in Elections for Governor, as Percentages of Males 21 Years Old and Over, 1813–1850

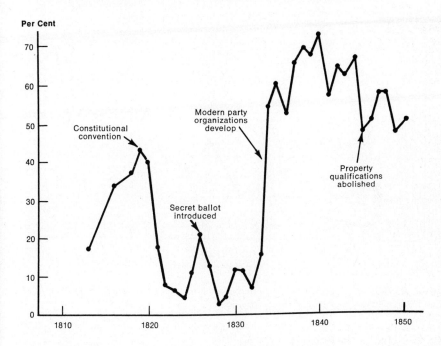

Source: *Who Governs?* p. 20, by Robert A. Dahl, 1961; reprinted by permission of Yale University Press.

venience—is to select the line around which the sum of the *squared* differences between observations and the correlation line is minimum. One can either select the best-fitting line by trial and error, or by using the equivalent handy mathematical shortcuts.

3. Regression Analysis: Characterizing a Causal Relationship

The previous section concentrated on the association itself. Now we consider how to characterize the form of simple associations when it is reasonable to assume that, if there is a relationship, one of the variables (x) causes the other (y). This is called **regression analysis.**

Some associations should not be interpreted causally. For example, one would not suppose that either I.Q. or athletic ability is the cause of the other; rather, both may be caused by other common factors. Or, consider two hypothetical scales of violence on television, the Bash and the Gore scales, constructed by different researchers. Each scale is set to run from 0 to 100 points. One hundred ninety-two "action" programs are rated with both scales. A graph of the results may show close association between the

FIGURE 25.6   Relation of Speed of Automobile to Distance It Takes to Stop, as Shown by Averages of Very Small Groups

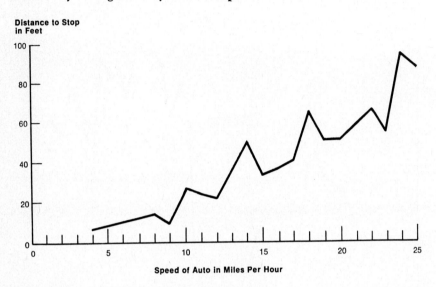

Source: *Methods of Correlation and Regression Analysis*, p. 42, by Mordecai Ezekiel, 1930; reprinted by permission of John Wiley & Sons, Inc.

FIGURE 25.7   Relation of Speed of Automobile to Distance It Takes to Stop, as Shown by Averages of Small Groups

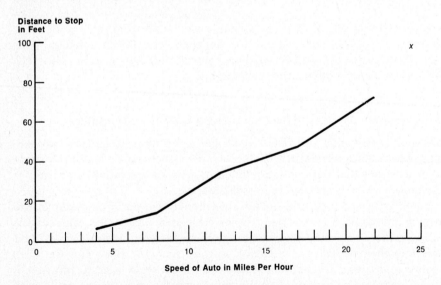

Source: *Methods of Correlation and Regression Analysis*, p. 45, by Mordecai Ezekiel, 1930; reprinted by permission of John Wiley & Sons, Inc.

FIGURE 25.8   **Hypothetical Data for a Class**

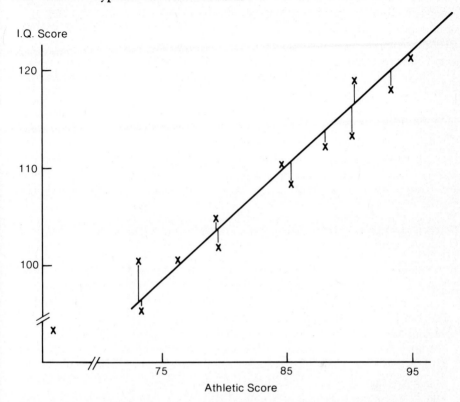

I.Q. Score

Athletic Score

two scales, but clearly there is no causal relationship between the two scales.

Now let us consider the relationship of auto speed to distance required to stop. In an experiment where people are asked to drive at various speeds, it is clear that speed influences stopping distance rather than vice versa. The question we wish to answer is: At each particular speed x_1, what will be the stopping distance y_1? That is, we wish to predict a stopping distance conditional upon a particular speed, as accurately as possible. This implies that— if we assume a straight-line relationship between the data—our aim is to find that line for which the *vertical* deviations between observations and the regression line are as small as possible (rather than the distances *perpendicular to the correlation line,* as seen in Figure 25.8).

We could make the sum of the absolute vertical deviations our criteria. But the standard criterion, chosen mostly for purposes of mathematical convenience, is the sum of the *squared* vertical deviations. (One could imagine situations where the sum of absolute deviations would be the more reasonable criteria, however.) The vertical distances that enter into the "sum of least squares" that we seek to minimize are shown in Figure 25.8.

The best-fitting regression list that minimizes the "sum of squares" can be found by a series of trial-and-error approximations, or commonly by mathematical formula with calculations performed on the computer. What is important is that you understand the "least squares" principle; not one in a thousand people who calculate regression lines with mathematical analysis on the computer could remember the mathematical deviation on the spot, and none needs to.

Curve-fitting by formula has some advantages over curve-fitting by eye, however.

1. Reliability. When data are clean and beautiful . . . , there is little problem about the fitting, but when we have a swarm of points with considerable variation, our eye is not a sure guide in placing the line.

2. Objectivity. Scientists prize repeatable objective methods, because they fear that unconscious bias on the part of an observer may distort the results. [Curve fitting by formula can be repeated by other persons with the same results.]

3. Generalization. It is desirable to have a general method of curve-fitting that can be extended to new and more complicated situations. (Mosteller et al. pp. 385–386)

Whenever there are two variables, one can compute *two* regression lines, since each variable can be x or y. In the early years of this century, social scientists were puzzled by the decision about which line to use, especially in economic studies of supply and demand. For example, if you have data for various years on the prices and quantities of onions sold, should price or quantity be the y variable? One response of economists was to calculate *both* regressions. If both are plotted on a single graph, this means finding one regression line that minimizes the sum of squared *vertical* deviations and another that minimizes the sum of squared *horizontal* deviations. These two regression lines may be seen in Figure 25.9.

Figure 25.9 allows us to see how the line of correlation relates to the regression lines: it bisects them. And that makes intuitive sense, because in correlation there is no implication of a directional relationship in *either* direction between the variables; it makes sense that this nondirectional line should lie halfway between the two causally directed regression lines.

A **regression coefficient** is a measure of the steepness of the linear regression line. It tells how many units of y are associated with a one-unit change in x. The logic of this was discussed on page 370. The regression coefficient tells something about the form of a relationship, but it does not tell about its strength; the latter is discussed in the next section.

The logic of curvilinear regression, as illustrated in Figure 25.3, is the same as that of linear regression. One may fit a curve either by the eye-and-hand method or with mathematical analysis and computers. The usual criterion of fit is still the same, however: minimize the sum of squared vertical deviations from the regression line.

Multiple regression is a common technique, too. It is used when one wants to investigate the influences of more than one independent variable on the dependent variable y. The logic is the same as in simple regression

FIGURE 25.9

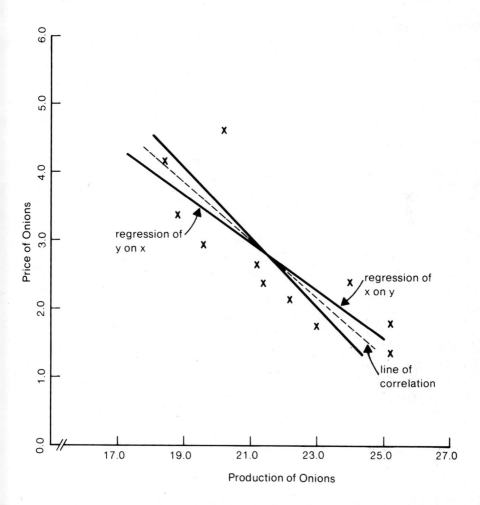

Production of Onions

except that instead of a line on a two-dimensional graph, one minimizes the sum of deviations from a "hyperplane"; for example, the deviations from a two-dimensional plane in three-dimensional space if there are two independent variables and one dependent variable.

4. Evaluating the Strength and Importance of Observed Differences and Relationships

A mail-order advertising man once stated very well the message I wish to convey here: Look for differences that scream, not differences that whisper. His point was that if you have two advertisements that differ little in their selling power, the difference is not important; rather, you should seek to find a new advertisement that is *much* better than the old advertisement.

The development of statistics to test whether differences and relationships exist *at all* has had an unfortunate side effect in this connection. Hypothesis-testing statistics tell people *whether* there is a difference (or relationship). They draw attention away from the *size* of the difference (or the strength of a relationship). The time has come to restore the balance: "The psychologist owes it to himself to determine not only whether an association exists between two variables—an association which may often be so small as to be trivial—but also to determine the probable magnitude of the association" (Dunnette, p. 350).

The size of a difference is obvious: If one type of fertilizer produces 120 bushels of corn per acre and another fertilizer produces 110 bushels at the same cost, the difference is ten bushels. Notice that here it is the *absolute* difference that is important—ten bushels—not the relative difference 10/110 or 10/120.

An example of the phony use of difference data occurred some years ago in the Great Tar Derby in cigarette advertising. *Reader's Digest* tested the quantity of tar in each brand of cigarette and found very slight differences among them. But *some* brand had to be lowest—which Old Golds was. The advertising for Old Golds immediately began to shout that Old Golds was "lowest in tars according to an impartial *Reader's Digest* test." This claim was true, but it was also meretricious and deceptive, for the difference between Old Golds and other brands really amounted to nothing. (A government agency eventually killed this Old Golds advertising, but not before the damage had been done.)

Evaluating the strength of a *relationship* is not so obvious. The best measure is usually the *accuracy of prediction* yielded by the relationshp. If a particular entrance examination predicts with 80 per cent accuracy whether a student will succeed in or flunk out of a given institution and if, without the aid of the examination, you could predict with only 60 per cent accuracy (that is, if 60 per cent of all entering students do succeed), then the relationship between success and test score is big enough to be important. One way of thinking about this difference is in terms of its absolute size: With the examination 20 per cent of the students will be classified correctly who would otherwise be classified incorrectly. Another measure of the test's usefulness is that it improves prediction by $\dfrac{80\% - 60\%}{60\%} = 33\%$. If another test predicts with 81 per cent accuracy, the difference between the two tests is too small to be important (though you certainly should use the 81 per cent accuracy test if there is no other difference between the two tests).

The strength of a *quantitative* relationship between two variables (in contrast to the yes-no relationship of the entrance test) may be measured by the improvement in capacity to correctly predict the dependent variable with the aid of the regression relationship, as compared to predictions made

FIGURE 25.10   One-Variable Versus Two-Variable Analysis
(Hypothetical Data for People on a Block)

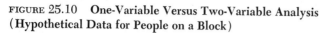

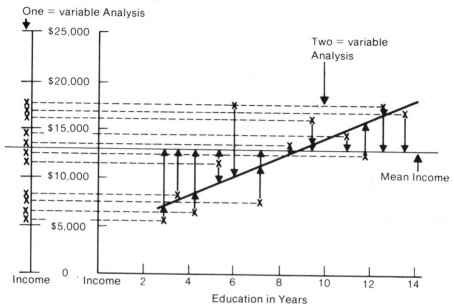

without it. Consider Figure 25.10: If one is to predict income from the distribution of people's incomes alone, the best prediction for a given individual is the mean of the group. The size of the deviations may be seen in the distances measured from each income point to the horizontal mean-income line. With the aid of the regression line, one can predict using it instead of the mean-income line. It is clear from the measured deviations in Figure 25.10 that the differences between people's actual incomes and their predicted incomes are much smaller if one predicts on the basis of their education rather than on the basis of mean income alone.

The improvement in prediction that one obtains from a regression depends on two factors: (1) The steepness of the regression line, and (2) the variation remaining around the regression line. We see in hypothetical Figure 25.11a that even though education explains all of income, the regression analysis does not improve the accuracy of prediction very much because there is relatively little variation in income. In Figure 25.11c education aids prediction of income considerably because there is relatively much variation in income, and much (though not most) of the variation is explained by education. In Figure 25.11b education explains income almost completely, and there is considerable variation in income; in this situation the regression analysis is most useful.

The strength of the regression relationship is usually measured by comparing the amount of variation in the dependent variable explained with the regression to the amount of variation without it.

FIGURE 25.11

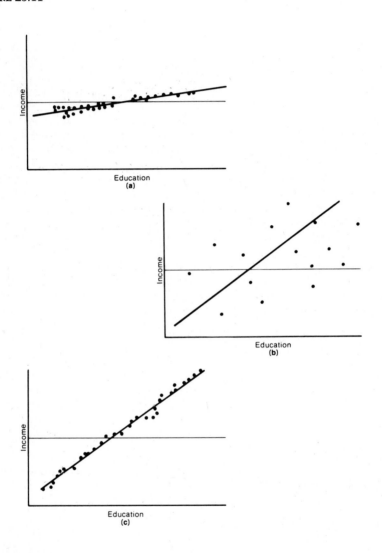

5. Summary

After the data are collected, they must be analyzed. These chapters deal
with the analysis of data that are collected in order to throw light on matters
that are well-defined in advance, and where the main aim is to investigate
the relationship between two variables.

One can look at a pair of variables in several related ways. One may wish
to: (a) test whether any relationship *exists* between them, which is a matter
of statistical probability theory; (b) characterize the *form* of the relationship, which is best done with graphs; (c) evaluate the strength and impor-

tance of relationships, by comparing the results to a real-life context; or (d) determine the degree of causal relationship between the variables.

ADDITIONAL READING FOR CHAPTER 25

On the analysis and interpretation of data, see Selltiz *et al.* (Chapter 14). Rosenberg (1968) is a thorough detailed exposition of the principles of analyzing survey data. Huff and Zeisel are both interesting, readable, and informative books about analysis and misanalysis of social-science data.

A consumer's-eye-view of data analysis and the use of tables is by Wallis and Roberts, pp. 270–279.

An excellent discussion of analysis of small samples with methods such as indexing and subclassification is given by Labovitz.

Ferber and Verdoorn (Chapter 3) is a careful step-by-step introduction to regression analysis that may be particularly useful to a beginner in this area. Almost every statistics book for business and economics contains a section on regression analysis.

Econometricians have developed a wealth of sophisticated regression techniques, which may be learned from any elementary econometrics text. Two good texts are Johnston and Goldberger. An unusually clear and readable introduction to regression and its uses is in Suits (especially Chapters 7–9).

26 searching for relationships: analysis of complex data

1. Searching for New Relationships Within the Data

Relationships that we find among variables help us to explain, understand, control, predict, and so forth. We *know more* about the world when we have established a relationship between two variables. Consider Figure 25.10. When you combine the two variables, income and education, you know more than you know from the income variable alone. This knowledge may or may not be useful or desirable to you, depending upon what your goals are. Later we shall talk more about the meaning of observed relationships.

There are two kinds of analytic activity between which the investigator shuttles back and forth when he seeks to determine causal and noncausal relationships. One is *getting ideas* about relationships, which he then formulates as hypotheses. The other is *examining and testing* the hypotheses. Both searching and testing are done in all sciences, by all scientists, all the time. But the searching activity varies considerably from field to field and at different periods of the development of a field. The three different sources within which a scientist may search for hypotheses follow.

a. OBSERVATION OF EVERYDAY EXPERIENCE

Many of the most important scientific ideas have come to scientists as they casually observed the world about them. Newton's hypothesis of the law of gravitational attraction, which came to him as he sat under a tree, is a legendary example. E. Durkheim's hypothesis that suicide rates are related to such factors as religion probably came about in this way. And early economic thinkers who noticed the relationship between prosperity and the stock of money in circulation surely derived the hypothesis from business and government experience.

The key to informal searching for hypotheses is to keep your eyes open and to ask yourself what important phenomena in the world around you have not yet been explained scientifically. But keeping your eyes open is not enough by itself. A thorough saturation in scientific literature is also necessary to give you a "prepared mind," so that you will notice important relationships.

b. THE BODY OF THEORY

The distinction between theory and hypotheses derived from casual experience is important and hard to grasp. Economics is by far the strongest of the social sciences in possessing a body of theory from which hypotheses can be deduced, but not all economic hypotheses come from theory; an example is the empirical business-cycle research of W. Mitchell. Experimental psychology also has a considerable body of strong theory. Sociology and political science are not so blessed, nor is anthropology. Therefore, in contrast to sociology and anthropology, the former fields generate more of their hypotheses by deduction from theory and then test them in classical fashion, as described in the next chapter. The creation of theory and the deduction of hypotheses from it are beyond the scope of this book.

c. INSPECTION OF DATA COLLECTED FOR OTHER PURPOSES

This third source of hypotheses, which H. Selvin and A. Stuart aptly call "data dredging," is most characteristic of the survey analyst. The data dredger examines data that she has collected for a particular purpose but that contain much more information than she used for the original investigation; or she may examine data collected by government agencies for general purposes—the population census or the census of manufacturers, for instance. She may consider data from public survey agencies like the Gallup and Roper polls, data on prices, freight-car movements, or amounts of employment advertising. This searching for new relationships in existing data is often called "secondary analysis" (Kendall & Lazarsfeld). The purpose of this section is to tell something about how to go about this secondary analysis.

The prepared mind—that is, a wide and thorough knowledge of the field in which you are working—is a prerequisite for successful data dredging, just as it is for generating hypotheses from informal observation. This is why the job of searching for hypotheses cannot be routinized or given to computers. Some of my best friends are electronic computers, but reluctantly I must badmouth them: No computer can sort out your data for you. Once I had the idea that, if a researcher collected enough data on the stock market or the horse races, he could then shovel them into a computer, and the computer would find the useful relationships. But not so. The computer adds when you tell it to add, subtracts when you tell it to subtract, and correlates (for example) income with education when you tell it to do so. But the computer has not the slightest capacity for guessing that the relationship between income and education means anything; nor does a mathematical statistician. This part of the job is strictly yours.

Let us assume that the data you are analyzing are data that you yourself have gathered, rather than published data, so that you have no problems of finding out exactly how they were collected. To begin with, saturate yourself in the raw data. Look and look some more at the original data sheets and at the computer printouts of the data. You should look for any *regularities*. Ask yourself what *might* be interesting about the data. Look for simple facts, because the simple facts are the most important. Your knowledge of your discipline should tell you what facts and patterns are of importance in your discipline, and it is that knowledge that will guide your search.

Certainly you should be looking for *big* differences, especially in a comparison research problem, differences that will be apparent to simple eyeball inspection. Differences that require subtle statistical analysis are usually not so valuable.

Do your looking with pencil and paper in hand. Compute simple estimates for various variables—averages, totals, first-half-versus-second-half calculations, percentages, and so forth. Look at this raw material as if someone had given it to you as pieces cut with a jigsaw and you are to find the key to the puzzle.

Make crude tables and graphs. If you think you see a relationship between two variables, plot them on a graph. Not only will the graph give you an excellent view of whether there is a relationship, but it will also show you the *form* of the relationship, as discussed earlier.

Watch a good researcher just after he has received the first batch of raw data from a piece of survey research. The data will probably be only a small installment on the total because he is anxious to get a first peek at them to see what they show. You will see him poring over the data, sheet by sheet, back and forth, doodling quick crude simple statistics (totals, averages, medians, and so forth) on a pad. It is from such searching activity that new and interesting hypotheses spring.

When there is a huge mass of data and it has gone through various transformations, you must find some way of boiling down the computer output; no one can look for patterns in a stack of I.B.M. printouts a foot thick. One useful practice is to compute the simple correlations (a correlation coefficient is a common measure of the *association* of two variables) between each pair of variables you are working with.[1]

Some apparent relationships are massively supported; for example, insurance data on tens of millions of people show conclusively that women live to be older than men. But this relationship might not seem so conclusive if you were searching through data on only 200 people. Most often you *think* you see a pattern, but there are insufficient data to provide massive corroboration. If you were *testing* a hypothesis generated by theory or by casual observation, you could turn to the classical testing statistics described in the next chapter to determine how likely your relationship is to be a "real" one. But, when you develop hypotheses by searching through data, you *cannot* test the relationships you observe with those statistics (unless you use a fresh batch of data). The following paragraphs tell you why in general terms, and the last part of the next chapter expands on this point and gets more specific.

In any small set of data there will be some apparent regularities. For a sad example, horse-race bettors often make a practice of "analyzing" the results of the races over ten days or a month, and *inevitably* they find that the lightest (or the heaviest) jockey was winning a disproportionate amount of the time, that the older (or younger) horses were outwinning the odds, or even that horses with white muzzle streaks were heavy moneymakers. But then the horseplayers try out their "rule" the next day and find that they come out losers as usual. What they fail to realize is that, if you flip a coin 100 times, interesting-looking runs of several heads and several tails will occur *just as a matter of chance*. And with as many variables as are present in horse races there is even more opportunity for these interesting-looking apparent regularities caused by chance to appear than in the case of coin flipping.

It is possible to determine in advance of tossing the coin the likelihood of a run of, say, twelve heads in a row or a disproportion as great as sixty-five heads out of 100 tosses. But, if you go through the 100-toss routine *many* times, *some* unusual pattern is sure to come up sooner or later. And a mass of data through which you search is like a large but *unknown* number of 100-toss routines. That is why you must expect to find *some* unusual patterns. That is also why you cannot test the patterns in the same way that you would test the patterns in a single 100-toss routine.

What should you do? I have said that, if your sample is enormous, you will not face this problem. A second easy dodge is to write down your pattern and then to test it out on a *fresh* set of data—another set of coin tosses or horse races, data different from the sample in which you found the

---

1. Some investigators condemn this practice because they are rightfully afraid that it leads to spurious correlations caused by chance. But, used with care and some delicacy, this practice need not necessarily lead to abuse—especially if the researcher demands that associations make sense before he pays any attention to them and if he tests all such associations on fresh batches of data.

pattern originally.[2] But what about when you are short of data? There is an almost unlimited supply of old racing forms for the horse-race analyst to examine. But there are only a few business cycles for the economist to work with, only a few civil wars for the historian, only a few twentieth-century presidential elections for the political scientist; you cannot easily manufacture more of these phenomena for inspection. There are two possible answers. First, you can wait for further years to test your hypothesis, but that is seldom an attractive alternative. Second, you can make it a practice not to look at some of the data—perhaps saving out the last few years in the business-cycle example—to serve in a fresh-data test. But this tactic has the disadvantage that you have fewer data in your base sample to look at, an important drawback in many cases. None of these suggestions is wholly satisfactory, but, alas, this is not always a satisfactory world.

2. Reading the Meanings of Data

The problems of reading-the-meaning analysis may best be shown by an extended illustration. Tables 26.1 and 26.2 give the data from an *experiment* in which two tape-recorded mock courtroom trials were played to separate groups of subjects drawn from the regular jury lists of big-city courts. The trials were quite realistic even though abbreviated. It is important to note that the *same trials* were played to many groups of jurors, so that differences in jurors' verdicts could be observed under varying conditions. (The jurors were asked for their *individual* verdicts before the jury deliberations, and those individual verdicts, rather than the group verdicts, are shown in the tables.)

Table 26.1 shows the data for a trial in which the defendant, accused of housebreaking, pleaded guilty by reason of insanity (R. Simon, n.d.). One-third of these jurors were *instructed* by the judge that they might find the defendant not guilty by reason of insanity (N.G.I.) if he "did not know right from wrong" (the famous M'Naghten rule). A second group was instructed that it might find N.G.I. if the crime was "a product of mental illness" (the new Durham rule). The third set of jurors was given no instructions at all.

Table 26.2 shows data for jurors who were similarly divided into different instruction groups but heard another trial, that of a man charged with *incest* who also pleaded "not guilty by reason of insanity" (N.G.I.).

The original hypotheses were that there would be more N.G.I. verdicts under Durham than under M'Naghten; that the uninstructed group would fall in between; and that, the lower a juror's socioeconomic class, the more likely he would be to vote N.G.I. Now then, what can be read from the

2. This approach is not *perfectly* safe, either. If you try out enough chance-caused results on fresh data, a few of them must also be confirmed by the chance process. But trying the relationship on fresh data cuts down severely the likelihood of chance-caused relationships.

TABLE 26.1   Proportions Voting "Not Guilty by Reason of Insanity"
(N.G.I.) in Housebreaking Case, by Occupation (Sample
Sizes in Parentheses)

Rules of Law

Occupational Category	Uninstructed	M'Naghten	Durham	Mean Percentage
Proprietors	79(14)*	27(11)	61(13)	56
Clerical workers	74(35)	50(40)	69(36)	61
Skilled laborers	76(21)	57(21)	33(15)	53
Laborers	87(24)	71(31)	70(30)	76
Housewives	69(26)	76(16)	70(23)	72

* Example of how to read the table: 79 per cent of 14 proprietors who received
no instructions voted N.G.I.

SOURCE: "Jurors' Reactions to Alternative Rules of Law in Defense of Insanity Trials" (unpublished manuscript), by R. J. Simon; reprinted by permission
of the author.

tables? Before reading further, you should inspect them and see what
meanings you read into them, to test your judgment against that of the
researcher.

The first part of the first hypothesis is certainly confirmed; in almost every
cell in each trial the N.G.I. percentage under M'Naghten is substantially
lower than for the same socioeconomic group under Durham or Uninstructed, and in no cell is it substantially higher than in the cells on either
side of it. Thus in Table 26.1, 27 per cent of the eleven proprietors instructed under the M'Naghten rule gave N.G.I. verdicts, which is less than
the 79 per cent (who gave N.G.I. verdicts) of the proprietors who received
no instructions and the 61 per cent who were instructed under the Durham
rule. The consistency of these results suggests that they mean something,
even though the sample in each cell is so small. On the other hand, con-

TABLE 26.2   Proportions Voting "Not Guilty by Reason of Insanity"
(N.G.I.) in Incest Case, by Occupation (Sample Sizes
in Parentheses)

Rules of Law

Occupational Category	Uninstructed	M'Naghten	Durham	Mean Percentage
Proprietors	33(48)	15(39)	33(58)	27
Clerical workers	33(76)	23(66)	32(79)	29
Skilled laborers	43(53)	22(49)	38(50)	34
Laborers	40(50)	29(41)	40(77)	36
Housewives	13(31)	25(40)	24(37)	21

SOURCE: "Jurors' Reactions to Alternative Rules of Law in Defense of Insanity Trials" (unpublished manuscript), by R. J. Simon; reprinted by permission
of the author.

trary to the hypothesis, the Uninstructed cells are *not* lower than the comparable Durham cells; if anything, they are higher in N.G.I. verdicts. Here, then, is an analysis decision to be made: Is Uninstructed higher than Durham? The author's answer was "no," for two reasons: It did not make sense theoretically for reasons argued elsewhere in her book, and the evidence is not overwhelming in that direction.

The author's decision might certainly be disputed by another analyst; in fact, *you* might dispute it. This is the job, then: to find a reasonable way of looking at the data and to draw conclusions that *most* reasonable people would agree with.

(Earlier I said that an advantage of experiments is that they can be repeated on larger samples if the results are inconclusive. This example is an exception; the data were extremely costly to collect, and the analysis that we are considering here was not sufficiently central to the study to warrant further replications.)

Now for the second hypothesis, that socioeconomic status is related to N.G.I. verdicts. The author excluded housewives because the data do not show their husbands' socioeconomic status. She then chose to look at the *mean* of the averages for the three instructions for each socioeconomic group in each trial (last column). (Another analyst might not choose to look at these means.) In the incest trials the proprietors—who have the highest socioeconomic status—are lowest in N.G.I. when we look at the mean percentage for the three types of instructions, and proprietors are second lowest in the housebreaking trial. And laborers, who are the lowest socioeconomic class, have the highest N.G.I. rate in both trials. This much seems to confirm the hypothesis. But what about the clerical workers? In the housebreaking case they vote more N.G.I. than the skilled laborers, but they vote the opposite in the incest case. This leads to two questions: Which of these two groups has the higher socioeconomic status? And are the sample sizes so small that random chance could account for the difference between trials, or is there something in the nature of the trials themselves? The very low N.G.I. figure (33 per cent) for the skilled laborers who were instructed with the Durham rule in the housebreaking case is still another problem.

The author concluded as follows. She ignored the reversal between skilled laborers and clerical workers; instead, she *grouped together* these middle two socioeconomic groups. She assumed that there is a rough socioeconomic-status order as indicated in the order of the rows in the table. And she ignored various peculiarities within instruction groups in the table. She then concluded that there is a rough association between socioeconomic status and likelihood of voting "not guilty by reason of insanity."

Now that you have seen how rough-and-ready this type of analysis is and that it is obviously a game at which anyone can play, what conclusions do you reach? One point is clear: There is no simple statistical testing device that one can apply to the data to determine what "significant" conclusions can be drawn from them.

3. Refining Observed Associations into Causal Relationships

The *association* (relationship) is the basic unit of any science that is past the early exploratory stage. It is all that the data can show directly—which is that two or more variables vary together. But we usually want to know more than that an association exists between two variables. We want to *infer* causes and their effects from relationships. We also would like to know more about the linkage between causes and their effects and under which conditions cause-and-effect relationships take place. The purpose of this section, then, is to describe briefly some devices for learning more about cause and effect than can be inferred from a given observed relationship.[3]

a. EXAMINING FOR SPURIOUS CAUSAL RELATIONSHIPS

On page 342, we discussed the hidden-factor fallacy (spurious causal relationship), in which x does not cause y but in fact z causes the variation in both x and y. The problem, then, is to determine whether some hidden z accounts for an observed relationship between x and y.

In experimentation one tries to eliminate the possibility of a hidden factor by controlling all the conditions of the experiment except the independent variable(s). For example, Pavlov recognized that the presence of an observer in the same room as the dog sometimes affected the dog's response, and therefore Pavlov avoided interference from this hidden factor by moving the observer behind a screen or outside the room.

In survey research, however, the researcher does not have the power to alter the conditions under which the data are collected. The best she can do is to try to hold conditions constant statistically. For example, Table 26.3 shows data on the relationship between candy eating and marital status, as reported by H. Zeisel (1957, p. 198).

There is clearly an association between the two variables. The difference

TABLE 26.3 Percentage Who Eat Candy,
by Marital Status

	Single	Married
Eat candy regularly	75%	63%
(Number of cases)	(999)	(2,010)

SOURCE: *Say It With Figures*, rev. 4th ed., p. 198, by Hans Zeisel; copyright 1947, 1950, 1957 by Harper & Row, Publishers, Incorporated; reprinted by permission of the publishers.

3. This topic is discussed in much greater detail, at a simple level with illustrations, by H. Zeisel (1957, Chaps. 8, 9), by P. Kendall and P. Lazarsfeld (an important original treatment and one of the great essays on the analysis of data), and by T. Hirschi and H. Selvin (1967) in comprehensive detail.

between 75 per cent and 63 per cent, obtained from samples of 999 people and 2,010 people, is obviously not caused by chance; we need no statistical test to prove it. But what does this association *mean?* Candy eating clearly does not cause people to be single. The more sensible question is, Does being single cause people to eat more candy?

Now look carefully at Table 26.4.

TABLE 26.4   Percentage Who Eat Candy, by Age and Marital Status

	Married		Single	
	Up to 25 Years	*25 Years and Over*	*Up to 25 Years*	*25 Years and Over*
Eat candy regularly	81	58	79	60
(Number of cases)	(503)	(1,507)	(799)	(200)

SOURCE: *Say It With Figures,* rev. 4th ed., p. 199, by Hans Zeisel; copyright 1947, 1950, 1957 by Harper & Row, Publishers, Incorporated; reprinted by permission of the publishers.

We have controlled for *age* ("held age constant") by introducing it as a third variable in the cross-classification analysis. That is, we subdivide the married and unmarried groups by age and then note that there is *no difference* to speak of between the married and unmarried groups in either the "up to twenty-five years" or the "twenty-five years and over" category. In other words, when age is held constant, there is no longer a relationship between marital status and candy eating. Age was a hidden third factor.

Does this mean that age causes candy eating? Not necessarily. There may be further hidden factors that will remove the appearance of a causal relationship there also. Therefore, the investigator should try other likely variables to see if any of them removes the observed association.

Which variables should the investigator try? This is a crucial question, to which the answer will seem most unsatisfactory: The investigator chooses those variables that good sense, imagination, and professional knowledge suggest might be hidden third factors (and for which there is data available). In other words, insight.

How *many* variables must you try before you can be satisfied that the observed association is indeed causal? The answer is the same: Only good sense can guide you. You can never try *all* the possible variables. Nor can you ever be *perfectly* sure that some hidden factor really does exist. But, as you try more and more likely variables and the original relationship remains unchanged, you can be progressively surer that the observed relationship is really between cause and effect and is not spurious.

The candy example was worked using the cross-classification technique. But the more sophisticated statistical techniques of multiple regression and multiple discriminant analysis do the job much better from almost every point of view.

b. EXAMINING FOR THE DIRECTION OF CAUSAL FLOW

The data of an observed relationship do not in themselves tell you what causes what. That became clear when we first looked at the simple relationship between candy eating and marital status: Without further information there was no way to decide whether candy eating caused marital status or vice versa (or neither caused the other, which is how it turned out). The further information we brought to bear was general knowledge that made it unlikely that candy eating caused marital status (although candy might make people fat, which might keep them single).

On the other hand, the same uncertainty does *not* exist about the *direction* of the causal flow between age and candy eating. Age causes candy eating, not the reverse. We know this because, if candy eating caused one to be over or under twenty-five years of age (quite unlikely on general grounds!), the original relationship between marital status and candy eating would not have disappeared after age was introduced into the relationship. (This should become clear on reflection.)

There are, then, two complementary ways to determine in which direction causation flows between two variables: reasoning and general knowledge, on one hand, and introducing more variables, as already described, on the other.

Before leaving hidden-third-factor associations—remember that non-causal relationships can be useful as *predictive* indexes.

c. INVESTIGATING FOR CAUSAL INTERMEDIATES

The picture of the hidden-factor situation in Figure 2.3 was like this:

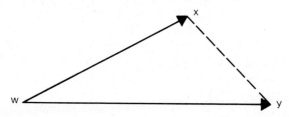

The cross-classification can reveal the existence of the links between w and y and between w and x, as in the candy eating example. But the *direction* of the causal flow is still not revealed by the data themselves. Instead, the appropriate diagram might be like this:

$$x\longrightarrow w\longrightarrow y$$

In other words, w could be an *intermediate* between x and y, rather than the cause of both x and y. If so, it is sensible to call *either* x or w the cause of y. But it is often useful to *understand* that w is an intermediate that links x and y.

The difficulty is that there is no way of telling *from the data themselves* whether the case involves a hidden third factor or a causal intermediate. The flow of causality might "really" run

marital status————→age————→candy eating.

No analysis of the given data can show that this is not the appropriate interpretation.

The only way to distinguish between the hidden-third-factor case and the causal-intermediate case is on the basis of *further knowledge*. In this case, we have the knowledge that getting married cannot change one's age (unless one lies on the marriage certificate), and it is that knowledge and that knowledge only that convinces us that the age is a hidden third factor and not a causal intermediate between marital status and candy eating.

The time at which the various events take place is often sufficient additional knowledge with which to decide which "paradigm" is more appropriate.[4] For example, we know that agricultural operations take place in this order: fertilizing the soil, planting the seed, growth of the plant. Given that knowledge, we know that planting cannot be a hidden third factor that causes both fertilizing and harvesting.

d. EXAMINING FOR MULTIVARIATE CAUSATION

This type of causal analysis seeks to overcome the multivariable obstacle discussed in Chapter 23, that, if you take into account only one of two or more important independent variables, you will come to misleading conclusions. An example given was the relationship between auto prices and auto sales; only after income and stock of cars are taken into account does it correctly appear that higher prices cause fewer rather than more auto sales. Another example was that the single-independent-variable tabulation of accident rates by sex shows that a much smaller proportion of women drivers ever have accidents than do men.

Now we consider *how* to unravel multivariable causation. Table 23.3 (p. 385) shows further cross-classification of the accident-sex data. Now it appears that women are no safer drivers than are men. In another example, Table 26.5 shows the median salaries paid to economists with different amounts of education. With the exception of the Ph.D. degree, it appears that the more education an economist obtains, the less money she will make. This situation seems quite improbable; general experience prompts one to look further into this association. But, in contrast to the hidden-factor case, a new variable (or variables) that will make the association between educa-

---

4. Kendall and Lazarsfeld, Hirschi and Selvin (1966), and others want to make time order the basic and conclusive method of deciding the direction of causal flows, but I argue to the contrary in the postscript to Chapter 32.

TABLE 26.5   Salaries of Economists at Different
Education Levels, 1966

Degree	Median Reported Salary
Ph.D.	$13,500
Master's	12,000
Bachelor's	14,700
Less than bachelor's	16,500

tion and salary *spurious* is not sought. A sensible person would guess that education will still have *some* causal effect on salary when other variables are taken into account. And so it turns out (see Table 26.6).

Table 26.6 cross-classifies by type of employer. *Within* each type of employment, amount of education and salary are *positively* associated. Together, amount of education and type of employment yield a better and more sensible cause-and-effect relationship than does either variable alone.

TABLE 26.6   Salaries of Economists, by Degree and Type of Employer, 1966

Degree; Type of Employer	Median Annual Salary
Educational institutions	
Ph.D. degree	$14,000
Master's degree	10,500
Bachelor's degree	11,900
Federal government	
Ph.D. degree	16,200
Master's degree	13,800
Bachelor's degree	13,400
Other governments	
Ph.D. degree	16,600
Master's degree	11,500
Bachelor's degree	12,000
Nonprofit organizations	
Ph.D. degree	18,500
Master's degree	14,000
Bachelor's degree	14,000
Industry–business	
Ph.D. degree	20,000
Master's degree	14,000
Bachelor's degree	15,000
Less than bachelor's degree	18,000
Self-employed	
Master's degree	18,000
Bachelor's degree	18,000

(One proof that the explanation is better is that the range of salaries among amounts of education *within* each type of employment is greater than the simple range of salaries among amounts of education.)

This example is particularly interesting because the original relationship is *reversed;* the simple association shows an *inverse* relationship between education and salary, whereas the refined association is positive. This example shows the wisdom of further exploration into some negative or "zero" relationships, especially when the observed association does not make very good sense or fit well with theory.

4. Generalizing and Predicting

The analyst is not finished when she has drawn a valid descriptive picture, made correct classifications or measurements, or established valid causal or noncausal relationships. She must also *look beyond* the data with which she has worked to make such generalizations or predictions as her data warrant.

A good principle is that you should generalize from your data if you can reasonably regard them as a fair sample of the universe to which you want to generalize. Everything that we know about bias in samples therefore comes to bear upon the problem. If the sample was randomly drawn from a universe, then you can infer that what is true of the sample is true of the universe. But, when the sample is not randomly drawn from the universe, the generalization is certainly not automatic.

For example, can you generalize a poll of attitudes toward the draft taken in a class of architecture students to the student body as a whole? The answer depends upon what you want to generalize and with what accuracy, as well as upon the relationship of the sample to the universe. If architecture students are 85 per cent against the draft, it is probably safe to generalize that *at least a majority* of all students in the same university are against the draft. It would be a much riskier generalization to say that 85 per cent (or even a majority) of *all* students are against the draft. Obviously a poll of attitudes toward the architecture of the university's buildings would not generalize as well from a sample of architecture students to all students as would a poll on the draft; the architecture students are a less typical sample, more likely to be unrepresentative (I do not want to use the word "biased" in this context) of attitudes toward architecture than of attitudes toward the draft.

You have only your judgment to rely upon when generalizing from your data. The discussion of laboratory experiments makes the same point; that is, whether findings about smoking and cancer in rats can be generalized to humans and whether principles of learning derived from nonsense-syllable experiments can be generalized to complex learning situations depend upon judgment. H. Ebbinghaus argued that, even if it was not safe to generalize absolute rates of learning that he observed in himself, his only subject, at least the *relations* could be generalized:

The tests were all made upon myself and have primarily only individual significance. Naturally they will not reflect exclusively mere idiosyncrasies of my mental organisation; if the absolute values found are throughout only individual, yet many a relation of general validity will be found in the relation of these numbers to each other or in the relations of the relations. (Ebbinghaus, p. v)

Prediction is just a special type of generalization—a generalization from past to future. But prediction is *always* a leap of faith; there is no scientific guarantee that the sun will come up tomorrow. It is purely your judgment and knowledge of your subject matter that supports the analysis that something will happen in the future, based on what happened in the past.

A prediction is reasonable if it is sensible to assume that the past and the future belong to the same universe, that is, if you can expect conditions that hold in the past to remain the same in the future. It is reasonable to predict that next year a poll of architecture students about a military draft will yield much the same results as this year *if conditions do not change radically.* If the United States is attacked or the world is beset with peace during the next year, this year's poll is obviously not going to be a good prediction of next year's attitudes. But, if your judgment tells you that very little change is likely to occur in basic conditions, it is then sensible to predict next year's attitudes on the basis of this year's poll. The prediction that the sun will come up tomorrow morning is implicitly a statement that tomorrow morning comes from the same universe as have all mornings in the past.

Sound predictions can be made even when changes in conditions will certainly occur, *if the changes are orderly and knowable.* In such a case, the prediction will be *different* from one that follows directly from the data used in the prediction. For example, the prediction of the amount of electric power that will be used this year is higher than the amount of power used last year and in previous years. A shorthand way of justifying such a prediction is that there is "an upward trend" over many years. But the fact that power use has increased over many years is not in itself very firm ground for an upward prediction, unless you know that the important conditions that have created the trend are also changing upward. If, however, you know that the number of generating stations is increasing, as is the number of owners of electrical appliances, and that per capita income is rising and the price of electricity is not rising relative to the price of other fuels, you have much better justified an upward prediction for next year. All these conditions did not hold in 1930 or 1931, however, and an automatic extension into the 1930s of the trend of electric power use in the 1920s would then have been an error.

For another example, predictions of trends in voting behavior based on a series of polls must also be done with care. Candidate Smudgin may have 40 per cent of the vote in an August poll, 45 per cent in September, and 49 per cent in October. Nevertheless, there is almost as good a chance that this trend will reverse as that it will continue.

Still another example: A prediction of future sexual behavior based on trends revealed in the A. Kinsey report would be treacherous indeed. One might plausibly argue that social customs related to sex move in cycles, as women's dress fashions move in perhaps fifty-year cycles (Kroeber, pp. 331–336). The Kinsey-revealed upward trends might create resistances that will cause reaction and then downward trends. Trend predictions without further information are unwise indeed.

The important point is that the past is never a guarantee of the future, and prediction should never be a mechanical extrapolation. Merely drawing a graph with time on one axis and on the other axis some variable that shows an apparent consistency in movement is a very dangerous basis for predicting that the next time period will follow the same apparent movement. The safer basis for extrapolation of an observed trend into the future is an *understanding* of the various forces that underlie the process. Gaining such an understanding is more a matter of saturation in the situation than of scientific technique. Prediction shares this property with *all* generalization from the known to the unknown. This is the answer to the logical problem of induction, which is really not a meaningful problem at all because generalization is not a matter of formal logic (see Chapter 32).

One bit of practical wisdom about predicting the future: Give greater weight to recent periods than to periods further back. Last year's results are a better predictor of this year's results than are the results of two years ago or three years ago, in most cases. It makes sense to weight your observations by their recency.

The *best* prediction about a *single individual,* based on your knowledge of a group to which the individual belongs, is that the individual will be *average.* If all you know of a male baby is that he is American, your best prediction of his height is that he will be perhaps 5 feet 9 inches. Similarly, if advertisement A makes seventy-five sales and advertisement B makes sixty sales, your best prediction for the future is that A will make 75/60 as many sales as B. But, if you have some *other* knowledge of the situation, you should alter your prediction to take account of it. For example, if you want to predict a male baby's adult height, there are two groups for reference: all males in the United States (or in the community) and his father (or parents). If his parents are 6 feet 5 inches and 6 feet 2 inches, should you predict that the boy's height will be 6 feet 4 inches or the 5 feet 9 inches average for all men? In this case you probably would predict that the boy will be far taller than average but perhaps not so tall as his parents. And you probably would make a similar prediction, though perhaps somewhat lower, if the baby boy with the tall parents is only average length at birth. A formal scheme for incorporating such further knowledge is called "decision theory," and it is dealt with in most modern statistics books. This branch of statistical theory helps us to decide which is the best among several alternatives, based on predictions of the effects of the alternatives and of the *value* of the various effects—as, for example, that our marriage-bound friend in Chapter 17 should marry Victoria rather than Sheila.

It is a mistake to modify a prediction downward in order to be "conservative." Assume that the *best* estimate of a baby's future height is 5 feet 9 inches. To be "conservative" and estimate 5 feet 6 inches is to be *less accurate*. The only justification for a so-called "conservative" estimate is that the *risk* involved in being under 5 feet 9 inches is different from the risk of being over 5 feet 9 inches. This is the implicit reason for accountants' conservative predictions.

A prediction can be made on the basis of a single observation. If you have no reason to believe that the single observation is unusually high or low, then the prediction should be the same as the observation. If you do have some such outside knowledge, however, modify your prediction accordingly. It is also legitimate and sensible to adjust predictions, even if you have large numbers of observations. Much of the difference between good and not-so-good election pollsters is apparently art and skill in adjusting their data. For example, Gallup is said to have reduced the weight given to Southern straw votes to three-fifths of the weight given to straw votes elsewhere in the 1960 prepresidential election polling. This was supposed to allow for the relatively light voting expected in the South.

There is almost a qualitative difference between predicting the effect of a *small* change in a variable and predicting the effect of a *large* change. This is so, I believe, because it is reasonable to assume *ceteris paribus* for small changes, whereas large changes usually affect the entire structure of the environment in such a way as to render foolish an assumption of *ceteris paribus*. For example, in a town with twenty saloons, one might predict with reasonable certainty the effect of one more saloon on liquor consumption and on social habits. But the effect of a *hundred* more saloons seems much less predictable. A hundred more saloons would change the entire character of the town and might trigger a prohibitionist movement or a mass emigration from the town.

H. Wold puts the matter this way:

When it comes to [the effect of] deepgoing technological innovations such as the industrial revolution, or fundamental changes in the social system, such as the transition from feudal to bourgeois society, we are far above . . . the most attenuated relaxation of the *ceteris paribus* principle. We are then in the wide realm where scientific methods no longer suffice as a basis for forecasting. (Wold, 1966c, pp. 37–38)[5]

An example is the issue of the "optimum population" for a country: whether the United States, say, would be better off with 50 million people, 300 million people, 600 million people in the year 2000. To put it another way, one might ask whether the United States would be better off in 1977 with 100 million or 400 million people, rather than its actual 216 million people. But very many aspects of the situation are interrelated and affect

5. The discussion in Chapter 33 of the limits of social science with respect to historical explanation is closely related.

one another, which makes it impossible to predict on a scientific basis (that is, on the basis of *ceteris paribus* reasoning) what the effect of major changes in population would be. Fewer people imply more available natural resources per capita. But fewer people also imply fewer men in the military to prevent another country from appropriating the natural resources. Fewer people imply smaller markets for businesses to sell to and therefore reduced stimulus to business investment. But many more people may mean reduced spending power per capita, especially for luxuries, and therefore reduced stimulus to business investment. Less business investment implies reduced per capita income in many cases, and so on.

The problem is not just that many things will change at the same time but that we do not know how they will interact and therefore how they will change.

A related example is the effect of various sizes of population upon social organization. If there are very few people in a country and therefore few rules to prevent conflict among them, an increase in the number of people may well increase the amount of conflict. But, if the population increase is *very* great, the increase in conflict may also lead to an increase in rules or in social cooperation that reduces conflict, *or* it may lead to a big conflict that kills off people and reduces the population.

The greater predictability of small changes explains the businessman's willingness to try small changes in price and other variables, whereas he balks at large sudden changes. This concept also fits the United States' pragmatic and meliorist philosophy of government, which implies that the effect of major changes—that is, revolution—is treacherously hard to predict. The logic of this is, I think, that, as with the saloons, a *major* governmental change cannot occur in isolation. A major all-at-once alteration toward socialism, say, must affect not only economic variables but also the forms of justice, international policy, and so on.[6]

5. The Tension Between Facts and Theory or Hypothesis

Sometimes the meeting of facts and hypothesis is a lovely wedding. The facts confirm the hypothesis, which in turn fits into the theory; the scientist is then as happy as a honeymooner.

Less happily, much of the time the facts that you observe do not sharply confirm your hypothesis. Often the situation is rather indeterminate, and you cannot tell whether the data do or do not support the hypothesis. In this case, you may collect more data to clarify the situation.

6. This statement is not an apology for conservatism; certainly there must be *some* situations in which revolution and major change are warranted. All I am trying to do here is to translate and interpret, first, the standard scientific behavior of extrapolating a straight line a short distance and, second, the common realization that it is often easier to work with differences than with absolute values. The subject needs scrutiny by philosophers, especially the issue of how to decide whether a change is small or large, that is, whether to assume *ceteris paribus*.

Even worse (as far as your state of mind goes, anyway), the data may slap your hypothesis smack in the face. And then you have some decisions to make. One possibility is to accept the facts as correct and the hypothesis as incorrect; this may not be a disaster, because the overturning of your hypothesis may itself be an important advance, as is often true in experimental psychology.

Another possibility is to modify your hypothesis so that it takes account of some conflicting facts but still points in the same general direction. For example, I thought I noticed an absence of Cadillacs among the cars in Yellowstone State Park, and I hypothesized that rich people—as characterized by Cadillac ownership—do not go to national parks for vacations. Then my wife and I did a casual count of the proportion of Cadillacs we actually saw, and there were, indeed, Cadillacs to be seen, apparently contradicting my hypothesis. But then I thought I noticed that the Cadillacs we saw were *old* ones. If so, I could salvage my hypothesis for the time being, by amending it to say that rich people, characterized by owning *new* Cadillacs, do not go to national parks.

Amending one's hypothesis can be a useful step. But it can also be a way of fooling oneself. After excluding old Cadillacs from consideration, we again surveyed the cars, and we still noticed some new Cadillacs. But I thought I noticed that the new Cadillacs were *local*, from the State of Montana. By excluding them as atypical, I might still save the hypothesis.

One could continue on this way for a long time, progressively modifying the hypothesis to remove discrepancies between it and the facts. But the final point will probably be either a confirmed hypothesis that is so narrow that it has practically no meaning, or a hypothesis that is confirmed for a small sample but that is specious and not true for a larger sample. More on this last point in the next chapter.

6. Summary

Sometimes the task of analysis is to sort out the relationships among a complex set of data, and sometimes to seek new hypotheses about relationships within a set of data. These tasks, in contrast to the analysis of simple relationships, are the subject of this chapter.

Ideas for new relationships may come from everyday experience, or from the body of theory, or from saturation in a body of data collected for other purposes. One must beware the danger that in any large body of data many apparent relationships may appear by chance.

Finding the meaningful relationships within a complex set of variables requires close study of them. Comparing cross-classifications and regressions that are run in several ways can often throw light on the causal network.

Sound generalization demands that you make sound analogies from your data to other parts of the universe. Accurate prediction of the future requires that your sample of past data be drawn from a universe whose conditions are similar to those within which future events will occur.

EXERCISES

1. Give examples of each type of analysis discussed in the preceding chapter.
2. Find an example in the literature of a relationship that is statistically significant but too small to have any usefulness or interest.
3. Give an example from your field of a curvilinear relationship that a linear correlation analysis would not reveal and that might go undiscovered without graphing.
4. Find a pattern of numbers in the table of random numbers in the next chapter that looks as if it were not the result of chance.
5. Give an example of a situation in which prediction is severely limited by major changes about which it is not sensible to assume *ceteris paribus*.

ADDITIONAL READING FOR CHAPTER 26

Knight lists the many adjustments that various public pollsters have used in election polls.

27 inferential statistics: introduction

1. Types of Statistics

A statistic is a *number*.[1] There are two kinds of statistics, summarization (descriptive) statistics and inferential statistics. The most important summarization statistics are the total, average, range, distribution, and so forth. Those statistics are nothing new to you; you have been using them all your life, and they are discussed in detail in every elementary statistics text.

The second kind of statistics, inferential statistics, is the subject of this chapter and of statistics courses. Inferential statistics can be used for two purposes: to aid scientific *understanding*, by estimating the probability that a statement is true or not, and to aid in making *sound decisions* by estimating which alternative among a range of possibilities is most desirable. The latter type of statistical theory—"decision theory"—is a recent arrival (really a revival) on the intellectual scene but is beyond the scope of this book; it is well-treated by H. Raiffa and by I. Bross among others. This chapter will stick mostly to "hypothesis-testing theory," though there will be comfortably little mathematical theory in our discussion. In the previous chapter, I discussed the types of analysis in which hypothesis-testing statistics are useful. Now we get down to the brass tacks of how to use probability statistics.

---

1. A more conventional definition: "[S]tatistic: a summary value calculated from a sample of observations, usually but not necessarily as an estimator of some population parameter; a function of sample values" (Kendall & Buckland, p. 279).

2. The Nature and Meaning of Probability

What does the term "probability" mean? To say that an event has a high or low probability is simply to make a statement that forecasts the future. In practice, probability is stated as an arbitrary weight between 0 and 1, such that 0 means you estimate that there is no chance of the event happening, and 1 means you are sure it will happen. A probability estimate of .2 means that you think the chances are 1 in 5 (odds of 1 to 4) that the event will happen. A probability estimate of .2 indicates that you think there is twice as great a chance of the event happening as if you had estimated a probability of .1.

The idea of probability arises *when you are not sure* about something; that is, when you do not have enough information and therefore can only *guess*. For example, if someone asks you what your name is, you do not use the concept of probability to answer. To be sure, there is some chance that you do not know your own name, but for all practical purposes you can be quite sure of the answer. If someone asks you who will win tomorrow's ball game, however, there is a chance that you will be wrong, no matter what you say. Whenever the situation is such that there is a chance that you could be wrong, the concept of probability can help you.

A probability statement is always about the future. But one does not know what the likelihoods really are for future events, except in the case of a gambler playing black on an honest roulette wheel, or an insurance company issuing a policy on an event with which it has had a lot of experience, such as a life insurance policy. Therefore, we must make guesses about the likelihoods, using various common-sense gimmicks. All these gimmicks should be thought of as *proxies* for the actual probability. For example, if NASA Mission Control simulates what will probably happen if a valve aboard an Apollo spacecraft is turned, the result on the ground is not the *real* probability that it will happen in space, but rather a proxy for the real probability. If a manager looks at the last two Decembers' sales of radios, and on that basis guesses the likelihood that he will run out of stock if he orders 200 radios, then the last two years' experience is serving as a proxy for future experience. If a sales manager just "intuits" that the odds are 3 to 1 (a probability of .75) that the main competitor will not meet a price cut, then all his past experience summed into his intuition is a proxy for the probability that it will really happen. Whether any proxy is a good or bad one depends on the wisdom of the person choosing the proxy and making the probability estimates.

The concept of probability helps you to answer the question: "What are the odds that . . . ?"[2] The purpose of this discussion of probability statistics

2. A given probability may be expressed in terms of probability, odds, or chances, and I shall use all three terms to help familiarize you with them. If the chances are 1 in 10, the odds are 9 to 1, and the probability is .1. If the odds are 2 to 5, the chances are 5 in 7, and the probability is 5/7. If the odds are 99 to 1, the chances are 1 in 100, and the probability is .01. If the odds are 100 to 1, the chances are 1 in 101, and the probability is 1/101. "Likelihood" is a synonym for "probability."

is to help you to become a *good bettor,* to help you make sound appraisals of true and untrue conclusions (or, in terms of decision theory, to help you to decide which alternatives you should bet on). The concept of probability is especially useful when one has a "sample" from a "universe" and wants to know the probability of various degrees of likeness between the sample and the universe. In other words, one wants to know the probability that the universe's average I.Q., for example, will not differ from the sample's average I.Q. by more than some arbitrarily chosen number of I.Q. points, say, ten points. A related question: What is the probability that a simple was taken from a given universe rather than from another universe, so that one can safely draw conclusions about the universe from the sample evidence?

What "is" probability? Various definitions of the term are useful in particular contexts (see Ayer; Schlaifer, 1961, Chap. 1). The rest of this chapter contains many examples of the use of probability, and, as you work with them, you will develop a feeling for the concept. The following two definitions (which are not always compatible) may be helpful to start you off:

1. The probability that an event will take place or that a statement is true can be said to correspond to the odds at which you would bet that the event will take place. (Notice a shortcoming of this definition: You might be willing to accept a $5 bet at 2–1 odds that your team will win the game, but you might be unwilling to bet $100 at the same odds.)

2. The probability of an event can be said to be the proportion of times that the event has taken place in the past, usually based on a long series of trials. For example, insurance companies use this type of definition when they estimate the probability that a thirty-five-year-old postman will die during a period for which he wants to buy an insurance policy. (Notice this shortcoming: Sometimes you must bet upon events that have never or only infrequently taken place before, and so you cannot reasonably reckon the proportion of times they occurred one way or the other in the past.)

You have been using the concept of probability all your life, in practically every decision you have ever made and in every conclusion you have ever drawn. You place your blanket on the beach where there is a *low probability* of someone's kicking sand on you; you bet heavily on a poker hand when there is a *high probability* that you have the best hand; a hospital decides not to buy another ambulance when the administrator figures that there is a *low probability* that all the other ambulances will ever be in use at once.

How does one estimate a probability? First, let us consider how one can estimate an ordinary garden variety of probability, which is called an "unconditional" probability. Several ways to estimate an unconditional probability can be illustrated with an example from poker.[3] What is the prob-

---

3. I hope you are not offended by the references to gambling games in the discussion of statistics in this and other chapters. Not only was the theory of probability invented to answer questions about gambling games, but gambling games still provide the best examples.

ability of drawing an even-numbered spade from a deck of poker cards?

The first possible source for an estimate of the probability of drawing an even-numbered spade is *experience*. If you have watched card games casually from time to time, you might guess at the proportion of times you have seen even-numbered spades appear, and you might guess "about 1 in 15" or "about 1 in 6" or something like that. (The actual probability is 6 to 52, of course.) You might make an estimate based on your experience if someone asked you the probability that two cards of the same denomination will turn up in the same hand of five cards dealt from a poker deck. General information and experience are also the source for estimating the probability that your team will win tomorrow, that war will break out next year, or that a United States astronaut will reach Mars before a Soviet cosmonaut. You simply put together all your relevant prior experience and knowledge and make a guess.

The second possible source of probability estimates is empirical scientific investigation with repeated trials of the phenomenon—called a "frequency series." In the case of the even-numbered spade, the empirical scientific procedure is to shuffle the cards, deal one, record whether the card is an even-numbered spade, replace the card, and repeat the steps a good many times. The proportion of times you observe an even-numbered spade come up is a probability estimate based on a frequency series. You might reasonably ask why we do not just *count* the number of even-numbered spades in the deck of fifty-two cards. No reason at all. But that procedure would not work if you wanted to estimate the probability of a batter getting a hit or a cigarette lighter lighting.

Observation of frequency series might help you to estimate the probability that a machine will turn out a defective part or that a child can memorize four nonsense syllables correctly in one attempt. You watch and record the results of repeated trials of exactly the same event.

There is no *logical* difference between the sort of probability that the life insurance company estimates on the basis of its "frequency series" of past death rates, and the salesman's seat-of-the-pants estimate of what the competitor will do. No frequency series can speak for itself in a perfectly objective manner. Many judgments go into compiling every frequency series, in deciding which frequency series to use for an estimate, and in choosing which part of the frequency series to use. For example, should the insurance company use only its records from last year, which will be too few to give as many data as one would like, or should it also use death records from years further back, when conditions were slightly different? In view of the necessarily subjective nature of probability estimates, the reader may prefer to talk about "degrees of belief" instead of probabilities. That's fine, just as long as it is understood that we operate with degrees of belief in exactly the same way as we operate with probabilities; the two terms are working synonyms.

(Of course, no two events are exactly the same. But under many circumstances they are *practically* the same, and science is interested only in such "practical" considerations.)

A third source of probability estimates is *counting the possibilities*. For example, by examination of an ordinary die one can determine that there are six different possible numbers that can come up. And one can then determine that the probability of getting a "1" or a "2", say, is $\frac{2}{6}$, or $\frac{1}{3}$, because "1" and "2" are two of six possibilities. One can similarly determine that there are two possibilities of getting a "1" *plus* a "6" out of thirty-six possibilities when rolling two dice, a probability of $\frac{2}{36}$, or $\frac{1}{18}$.

Determining probabilities by counting has two requirements: that the *possibilities* all be known (and therefore limited) and few enough to be studied easily; and that the *probability* of each particular possibility be known. For example, it is known that the probabilities of all sides of the die coming up are equal; that is, equal to $\frac{1}{6}$.

A fourth source of probability estimates is *mathematical calculation*. If one knows by other means that the probability of a spade is $\frac{1}{4}$ and the probability of an even-numbered card (Queen = "12") is $\frac{6}{13}$, one can then calculate that the probability of turning up an even-numbered spade is $\frac{6}{52}$ (that is, $\frac{1}{4} \times \frac{6}{13}$). If one knows that the probability of a spade is $\frac{1}{4}$ and the probability of a heart is $\frac{1}{4}$, then one can calculate that the probability of getting a heart *or* a spade is $\frac{1}{2}$ (that is, $\frac{1}{4} + \frac{1}{4}$). The point here is not the particular calculation procedures but rather that one can often calculate the desired probability on the basis of already known probabilities.

It is possible to estimate probabilities with mathematical calculation *only* if one knows *by other means* the probabilities of some related events. For example, there is no possible way of mathematically calculating that a child will memorize four nonsense syllables correctly in one attempt; empirical knowledge is necessary.

The mathematical theory of probability—with which we shall not deal here—concerns itself with developing ways to reckon complicated probabilities, for example, the probability that an even-numbered spade will come up three out of the next seven cards followed by a red queen followed by an odd heart at least twice in the next five cards, and so forth. These complex calculations are of great importance—for example, no rocket would be put in orbit without many such calculations—but in the social sciences one can usually avoid them, at least while one is a beginner.

a. CONDITIONAL AND UNCONDITIONAL PROBABILITIES

Two kinds of probability statements must be distinguished, *conditional* and *unconditional*.

Let's use a football example to explain conditional and unconditional probabilities. In the year this is being written, the University of Illinois has an unpromising football team. Someone may nevertheless ask what chance the team has of winning the postseason game at the Rose Bowl, to which only the best team in the University of Illinois' league is sent. One may say that *if* by some miracle the University of Illinois does get to the Rose Bowl, its chance would be a bit less than 50–50—say, 40. That is, the probability of its winning, *conditional* on getting to the Rose Bowl, is .40. But the chance of its getting to the Rose Bowl at all is very low, perhaps .01. If so, the *unconditional* probability of winning at the Rose Bowl is the probability of its getting there multiplied by the probability of winning *if* it gets there; that is, .01 × .40 = .004. (It would be even better to say that .004 is the probability of winning, conditional only on having a team, there being a league, and so on, all of which seem almost sure things.) Every probability is conditional on many things—that war does not break out, that the sun continues to rise, and so on. But if all those unspecified conditions are very sure, and can be taken for granted, we talk of the probability as unconditional.

A conditional probability is a statement that the probability of an event is such-and-such *if* something else is so-and-so; it is the "if" that makes a probability statement conditional. Now it is true that in *some* sense all probability statements are conditional; for example, the probability of an even-numbered spade is $6/52$ *if* the deck is a poker deck and not necessarily if it is a pinochle deck or a tarot deck. But we ignore such conditions for most purposes.

Most of the use of probability in the social sciences is *conditional* probability. All hypothesis-testing statistics are conditional probabilities.

The typical conditional-probability question used in social-science statistics is: What is the probability of obtaining sample S (by chance) *if* the sample were taken from universe A? For example, what is the probability of getting a sample of five children with I.Q.s over 100 *by chance* in a sample randomly chosen from the universe of children whose average I.Q. is 100?

The first source of such conditional-probability statements is examination of the frequency series generated by universes like the conditional universe. For example, assume that we are considering a universe of children who average an I.Q. of 100. Write down "over 100" and "under 100" respectively on several slips of paper, put them into a hat, draw five slips several times, and see how often the first five slips drawn are all "over 100." This is the Monte Carlo method of estimating probabilities.

The second source of such conditional-probability statements is mathematical calculation. For example, if half the slips in the hat have numbers under 100 and half over 100, the probability of getting five in a row above 100 is 2^5; that is $2 \times 2 \times 2 \times 2 \times 2$. But, if you do not know the proper mathematical formula, you can come very close with the Monte Carlo method, which is what you will learn here.

3. The Concept of Independent Events

A key concept in the use of probability and statistics is that of *independence* of two events. Two events are said to be independent when one of them does not seem to have any relation to the other. If I flip a coin that I know from other evidence is a fair coin and get a head, the chances of then getting *another* head are still 50–50 (one in two, or one to one). And, if I flip a coin ten times and get heads the first nine times, the probability of getting a head on the tenth flip is *still* 50–50. This is why the concept of independence is characterized by the phrase "The coin has no memory." (Actually the matter is a bit more complicated. If you had previously flipped the coin many times and knew it to be a fair coin, then the odds would still be 50–50, even after nine heads. But, if you had never seen the coin before, the run of nine heads might reasonably make you doubt that the coin was a fair one.)

Nevertheless, people commonly make the mistake of treating independent events as nonindependent, perhaps from superstitious belief. Roulette gamblers say that the wheel is "due" to come up red. And sportswriters make a living out of interpreting various sequences of athletic events that occur by chance and talk of teams that are "due" to win because of "the Law of Averages." For example, if Rod Carew goes to bat four times without a hit, all of us (including trained statisticians who really know better) feel that Rod is "due" to get a hit and that the probability of his doing so is very high—higher, that is, than his season's average. The so-called Law of Averages implies no such thing, of course.

Not all events are independent, of course; far from it. A boy may telephone one of several girls chosen at random. But, if he calls the same girl *again* (or if he does *not* call her again), the second event is not likely to be independent of the first, and the probability of his calling her is *different* after he has gone out with her once than it was before he went out with her.

This observation suggests another way to look at the concept of independence. If the occurrence of the first event *does not change the probability that the second event will occur*, then the events are independent.

4. The Distinction Between "Probability Theory" and "Inferential Statistics"

The term **probability theory** refers to situations in which you know the nature of the system you are working with, and you wish to estimate the likelihood that the system will produce one or more *particular events*. For example, you can assume you know from the start the nature of a deck of bridge cards, and you want to estimate, say, the likelihood that such a deck with 13 spades among 52 cards will produce 10 spades in the first 13 cards dealt.

In contrast, the term **inferential statistics** refers to situations in which you do *not* know the nature of the system you are dealing with, and you want to *infer* the nature of the system from the evidence at hand. For example, someone may deal 10 spades to you in the first 13 cards, and you—not knowing what kind of deck it is—want to estimate how likely it is that the deck has only 13 spades among the 52 cards, or if it has a larger proportion of spades.

To put it another way, in an inferential-statistics situation we want to determine one or more *statistics of the system;* the mean and the median are examples of such statistics that we wish to infer about an unknown system. In contrast, probability theory tells us about the likelihood of particular occurrences within systems whose statistics we already know.

Clearly, probability theory is relevant to situations such as gambling with cards or dice, where the physical nature of the system is known, and to such business situations as life insurance, where the overall probabilities of dying at each age are well known from a great deal of prior experience. (Business situations in which one does not know, but is prepared to assume, the structure of the situation can similarly be dealt with using probability theory.)

Inferential statistical thinking is particularly relevant for scientific investigations. In much of science the researcher tries to determine the nature of an unknown system from the evidence that she collects about it.

5. Translating Scientific Questions Into Probabilistic and Statistical Questions

Science does not begin and end with statistics. Professional statisticians are quite humble about the importance of statistics. But taking a course or two in statistics has a way of going to a student's head, making him think that nothing can be proved without statistics and that anything can be proved if sophisticated statistics are used. This is the fallacy of "statistics is everything."

The fallacy of "statistics is nothing" is also dangerous, however. As M. Dunnette points out, researchers often disregard statistics because their *intuition* tells them that some conclusions *must* be so ". . . on the grounds that they are intrinsically good for humanity and that they need not, therefore, meet the usual standards demanded by scientific verification. . . . [Psychotherapy, for example] continues to survive in spite of a lack of evidence about its effectiveness" (Dunnette, p. 346).

A social-scientific study begins with a general question about the nature of the social world. The scientist then transforms this question into a form that can be studied scientifically. The translation of general questions into scientific questions has been discussed earlier (Chapters 2, 6).

Let us suppose that, by this time, the researcher has not only translated her general question into a scientific question but has also *carried out* her scientific investigation as an experiment or survey. Suppose further that the data that she has collected are not entirely clear-cut in support of firm conclusions. At this juncture, if she does not want to or cannot collect more data, the researcher may turn to inferential statistics to help her.

The first step in using probability and statistics is to *translate the scientific question into a statistical question.* Once you know exactly what kind of probability-statistical question you want to ask—that is, exactly what probability you want to determine—the rest is relatively easy. The stage at which you are most likely to make mistakes is in stating the question you want to answer in probability terms. Though this step is hard, *it involves no mathematics.* This step requires only *hard, clear thinking;* you cannot beg off by saying "I have no brain for math!" To flub this step is to admit that you have no brain for *clear thinking,* rather than no brain for mathematics.

I repeat, the hardest job in using probability statistics, and the most important, is to *translate* the scientific question into the form to which statistics can give a sensible answer. This translation is in the spirit of the discussion in Chapter 2 of the language of science and operational definitions; you must translate scientific questions into the appropriate form for *statistical operations,* so that you know which statistical operations to perform. This is the part of the job that requires hard, clear thinking—though nonmathematical thinking—and it is the part that someone else cannot easily do for you.

The best way to explain how to translate a scientific question into a statistical question is to illustrate the process.

a. ILLUSTRATION A

Are doctors' beliefs about the harmfulness of cigarette smoking (and doctors' own smoking behavior) affected by the *social* groups among whom they live (J. Simon, 1967–1968)? We decide to define the doctors' *reference groups* as the *states* in which they live, because data about doctors are available state by state (*Modern Medicine*). We can then translate this question into an operational and testable scientific hypothesis by asking this question: Do doctors in tobacco-economy states differ from doctors in other states in their smoking and beliefs about smoking?

But what numbers help us to answer this question, and how do we interpret them? We can now ask the *statistical* question: Do doctors in tobacco-economy states belong to the same universe (with respect to smoking) as do other doctors? That is, do doctors in tobacco-economy states have the same characteristics (at least of those we are interested in, smoking in this case) as do other doctors? Later we shall see that the way to proceed is to consider the statistical hypothesis that these doctors do indeed belong to that same universe; that hypothesis and the universe will be called "benchmark hypothesis" and "benchmark universe," respectively, though more conventional usage is "null hypothesis."

If the tobacco-economy doctors do indeed belong to the benchmark universe, that is, if the benchmark hypothesis is correct, then there is a 49/50 chance that doctors in some states *other* than the state in which tobacco is most important will have the highest rate of cigarette smoking. But in fact we observe that the state in which tobacco accounts for the largest proportion of the state's income—North Carolina—has a higher proportion of doctors who smoke than does any other state. (Furthermore, a lower proportion of doctors in North Carolina than in any other state say that they *believe* that smoking is a health hazard.)

Of course, it is possible that it is just *chance* that North Carolina doctors smoke most, but the chance is only 1 in 50 if the benchmark hypothesis is correct. Obviously, *some* state had to have the highest rate, and the chance for any other state was *also* 1 in 50. But, because our original *scientific* hypothesis was that North Carolina doctors' smoking rate would be highest and we then observed that it was highest, even though the chance was only 1 in 50, the observation is interesting and means something to us. It means that the chances are strong—49 in 50—that there is a connection between the importance of tobacco in the economy of a state and the rate of cigarette smoking among doctors living there.

To attack this problem from another direction, it would be rare for North Carolina to have the highest smoking rate for doctors if there were no special reason for it; in fact, it would occur only once in fifty times. But, if there *is* a special reason—and we hypothesize that the tobacco economy provides the reason—then it is *not* rare for North Carolina to have the highest rate; therefore we choose to believe in the not-so-rare phenomenon, that the tobacco economy causes doctors to smoke cigarettes.

b. ILLUSTRATION B

Does medicine CCC cure cancer? You begin with this scientific question and give the medicine to six patients who have cancer; you do not give it to six similar patients who have cancer. Your sample is only twelve people because it is simply not feasible for you to obtain a larger one. Five of six "medicine" patients get well; two of six "no medicine" patients get well. Does the medicine cure cancer? That is, if future cancer patients take the medicine, will their rate of recovery be higher than if they did not take the medicine?

One way to translate the scientific question into a statistical question is to ask: Do the "medicine" patients belong to the same universe as do the "no medicine" patients? That is, we ask whether "medicine" patients still have the *same* chances of getting well from the cancer as do the "no medicine" patients, or whether the medicine has bettered the chances of those who took it and thus removed them from the original universe, with its original chances of getting well. The original universe, to which the "no medicine" patients must still belong, is the benchmark universe. Later we shall see that we proceed by making the benchmark hypothesis that they still belong to the benchmark universe (that is, still have the same chance of getting well as the "no medicine" patients).

We want to know whether the medicine does any good, which is the same thing as asking whether patients who take medicine are still in the same universe as "no medicine" patients or do they belong to a different universe, one which now has different chances of getting well. To recapitulate our translations, we go from (a) Does the medicine cure cancer? to (b) Do "medicine" patients have the same chance of getting well as "no medicine" patients? and finally to (c) Do "medicine" patients belong to the same universe (population) as "no medicine" patients? Remember that "population" in this sense does *not* refer to the population at large but to a group of cancer sufferers (perhaps an infinitely large group) who have a given chance of getting well, on the average. Groups with different average chances of getting well are called "different populations" (universes). Later we shall see how to *answer* this statistical question.

We must keep in mind that our ultimate concern in cases like this one is *prediction of future results* of the medicine; that is, to predict whether use of the medicine will lead to a higher recovery rate than would be observed without the medicine.

c. ILLUSTRATION C

Is method A a better method of teaching reading than method B? That is, will method A produce a higher average reading score in the future than will method B? Twenty children who were taught to read with method A have an average reading score of 79, whereas children who were taught with method B have an average score of 84. To translate this quite satisfactory *scientific* question into a statistical question we ask: Do children taught with method A come from the same universe (population) as children taught with method B? Again, "universe" (population) does *not* mean the town or social group the children come from, and indeed the experiment will make sense only if the children *do* come from the same population, in that sense. What we want to know is whether the children belong to the same population (universe), defined according to their *reading ability*, after they have studied with method A or method B.

Translating from a scientific question into a statistical question is mostly a matter of asking the probability that one or more samples come from some given benchmark universe. Notice that we must (at least for general scientific testing purposes) ask about a *given* universe whose composition we assume to be *known*, rather than about a *range* of universes or a universe whose properties are unknown. In fact, there is really only one question that probability statistics can answer: Given some particular benchmark universe of some stated composition, what is the probability that an observed sample comes from it? A variation of this question is: Given two (or more) samples, what is the probability that they come from the *same* universe? In this latter case, the relevant universe is implicitly the universe whose composition is of the two samples combined.

The necessity for stating the characteristics of the universe in question becomes obvious when you think about it for a moment. Probability-statistical testing adds up to comparison of a sample with a particular benchmark universe and asking whether there is probably a difference between the sample and the universe. To carry out this comparison, we ask *how likely* it is that the benchmark universe would produce a sample like the observed sample. But, in order to find out whether a universe could produce a given sample, we must ask whether some *particular* universe—with stated characteristics—could produce the sample. There is no doubt that *some* universe could produce the sample by a random process; in fact, some universe did. The only sensible question, then, is whether a *particular* universe, with stated (or known) characteristics, is *likely* to produce such a sample. In the case of the medicine, the universe with which we compare the sample who took the medicine is the benchmark universe to which that sample would belong if the medicine had had no effect. This comparison leads to the benchmark (null) hypothesis that the sample comes from a population in which the medicine (or other experimental treatment) seems to have *no effect*. It is to avoid confusion inherent in the term "null hypothesis" that I replace it with "benchmark hypothesis."

The concept of the benchmark (null) hypothesis is hard to grasp.[4] The best way to learn its meaning is to see how it is used in practice. For example, we say we are willing to believe that the medicine has an effect if it seems very unlikely from the number who get well that the patients given the medicine still belong to the same benchmark universe as the patients given no medicine at all—that is, if the benchmark hypothesis is unlikely.

d. ILLUSTRATION D

If one plot of ground is treated with fertilizer and another similar plot is not treated, the benchmark (null) hypothesis is that the corn raised on the treated plot is no different from the corn raised on the untreated plot; that is, that the corn from the treated plot comes from the same universe as the corn from the untreated plot. If our statistical test makes it seem very unlikely that a universe that produced the type of corn from the untreated plot would *also* produce corn such as that from the treated plot, then we are willing to believe that the fertilizer has an effect. For a psychological example, substitute the words "groups of children" for "plot," "special training" for "fertilizer," and "I.Q. score" for "corn."

There is nothing sacred about the benchmark (null) hypothesis of "no difference." You could just as well test the benchmark hypothesis that the corn comes from a universe that averages 110 bushels per acre, if you have

4. The classic discussion of the null hypothesis is by R. Fisher in his *The Design of Experiments* (pp. 18–19), but even that discussion is not at all satisfactory. Another useful treatment is by J. Neyman (Chap. 5), who substitutes the term "test hypothesis" for "null hypothesis," however. The fact is that this concept is among the slipperiest in all scientific research and the hardest to learn. Don't despair if the notion eludes you at first. It will come clear as you work with it.

reason to be especially interested in knowing whether the fertilizer produces more than 110 bushels per acre. But in many cases it is reasonable to test the likelihood that a sample comes from the population that does not receive the special treatment.

So far we have discussed the scientific question and the statistical question. Remember that there is always a generalization question too: Do the statistical results from this particular sample of, say, rats apply to a universe of humans? This question can be answered only with wisdom, common sense, and general knowledge.

6. Summary

This chapter begins with a discussion of the concepts of statistics, probability, independence, sample, and universe. Then it illustrates how scientific questions are translated into statistical questions. The translation is accomplished by specifying the relevant benchmark universe, and then asking the likelihood that the observed sample could have come from that universe. If you can soundly translate your scientific question into a statistical question, you have accomplished the hardest part of the task of statistical inference.

28 probability and hypothesis testing by the monte carlo method

I have said that probability and statistical theory tells us the chance that something will (or will not) happen, expressed in the *odds* that it will (or will not) happen. Now let us see how we can *estimate* the odds of several concrete situations, using a completely new approach to basic problems in probability and statistics, the Monte Carlo method.

1. Introductory Problems

a. EXAMPLE 1: AN INTRODUCTORY PROBLEM—POKER HANDS

Let us begin with a pure problem in odds: What is the chance (what are the odds) that the first five cards chosen from a complete deck of fifty-two bridge (poker) cards will contain two cards of the same denomination?

We shall estimate these odds the way that gamblers have estimated gambling odds for thousands of years. First, check that the deck is not a pinochle deck and is not missing any cards. (Overlooking such small but crucial matters often leads to errors in science.) Shuffle thoroughly until you are satisfied that the cards are randomly distributed. (It is surprisingly hard to shuffle well.) Then deal five cards and mark down whether the hand does or does not contain a pair of the same denomination. At this point, we must decide whether three of a kind, four of a kind, or two pairs meet our criterion for a pair; we decide *not* to count them.

Then replace the five cards in the deck, shuffle, and deal again. Again mark whether the hand contains one pair of the same denomination. Do this many times. (Table 28.1 shows 100 hands, which my good assistant has just dealt.) Then count the number of hands with pairs, and figure the proportion (as a percentage) of all hands. In Table 28.1, 44 per cent of the hands contained pairs, and that is our estimate of the probability that one pair will turn up in a poker hand.

This experimental estimation (called "Monte Carlo estimation" for obvious reasons) does not require a deck of cards. For example, one might create a fifty-two-sided die, one side for each card in the deck, and spin it five times to get a "hand." But note one important part of the procedure: No single "card" is allowed to come up twice in the same set of five spins, just as no card can possibly appear twice in the same hand. If the same "card" did turn up twice or more in a die experiment, one could pretend that the spin had never taken place; this procedure is necessary to make the die experiment analogous to the actual card-dealing situation under investigation. Otherwise, the results will be slightly in error. This type of sampling is known as "sampling without replacement," because each card is *not re-placed* in the deck each time it is dealt (until the end of the hand, that is).

Still another Monte Carlo method uses a *random-number table,* a sample

TABLE 28.1

Trial	1	2	3	4	5	6	7	8	9	10	11	12	13
Results	Y	Y	N	N	Y	Y	N	N	Y	N	N	Y	N

Trial	14	15	16	17	18	19	20	21	22	23	24	25	26
Results	N	Y	Y	Y	Y	Y	N	N	Y	N	Y	N	Y

Trial	27	28	29	30	31	32	33	34	35	36	37	38	39
Results	N	Y	N	Y	Y	N	Y	N	N	N	N	Y	N

Trial	40	41	42	43	44	45	46	47	48	49	50		
Results	N	N	N	N	Y	Y	Y	N	N	Y	N		

Subtotal: 23 Yes, 27 No = 46%

Trial	51	52	53	54	55	56	57	58	59	60	61	62	63
Results	N	Y	N	N	Y	N	Y	Y	N	N	N	Y	Y

Trial	64	65	66	67	68	69	70	71	72	73	74	75	76
Results	Y	N	N	Y	N	N	N	N	Y	N	Y	N	N

Trial	77	78	79	80	81	82	83	84	85	86	87	88	89
Results	N	N	N	N	Y	N	N	N	Y	Y	N	Y	N

Trial	90	91	92	93	94	95	96	97	98	99	100		
Results	Y	Y	N	N	Y	Y	Y	Y	N	Y	N		

Subtotal: 21 Yes, 29 No = 42%

Total: 44 Yes, 56 No = 44%

of which is shown in Table 28.2. Arbitrarily designate the spades as numbers 01–13, the diamonds as 14–26, the hearts as 27–39, and the clubs as 40–52. Then proceed across a row (or down a column), writing down each successive two-digit number, except for numbers outside 01–52, and omitting duplication within sets of five numbers. Then translate them back into

TABLE 28.2   Table of Random Digits

14900	77763	66045	91851	02199	34221	58116	06648	55779	50353	16401
14901	93968	57080	56566	05093	12677	02035	34393	28765	83709	60080
14902	96185	55327	46929	21087	08191	54583	17963	18599	57717	26689
14903	50956	13999	05475	02687	20207	28492	18203	53613	64035	69836
14904	42925	13489	61425	07510	92172	78063	78247	34647	37710	71779
14905	74102	76512	99800	27498	08257	71444	29192	73165	85985	58584
14906	25963	77276	01566	26830	83288	89183	03636	91176	04673	48271
14907	00336	28332	95442	45548	92764	69320	67663	74935	45673	89406
14908	97190	07021	54689	76464	07125	60376	96263	81957	98097	89311
14909	42508	33579	74511	37271	66533	14980	87997	46543	20445	29364
14910	15095	69719	62380	00947	13581	49929	23187	04410	11076	50274
14911	46426	40638	80584	14926	70877	76023	31838	32280	61814	43410
14912	18432	53552	44904	13591	53696	28658	09538	77232	23728	49210
14913	98828	28017	51152	39704	04560	20423	63072	94843	02544	70033
14914	81052	43812	38934	31109	94872	40069	70062	53044	24375	70147
14915	74325	73599	05533	99548	74035	63714	07222	08337	76768	32818
14916	90928	47761	02291	80702	83239	25189	89692	19820	22468	05036
14917	07510	62086	73335	06373	14326	08408	25356	55568	57104	01080
14918	91192	26484	00867	88759	10759	33681	65027	20204	86513	09961
14919	67338	60292	26494	65254	72875	19913	77183	67772	63750	00160
14920	85269	97756	56322	57967	67739	07247	43739	71253	20167	27559
14921	53369	93055	91402	49671	04836	76592	94506	36169	53691	29980
14922	41545	08255	77112	08226	59377	64281	78805	43935	89642	28246
14923	25149	61362	56824	03083	87188	24545	92615	02467	24037	30907
14924	07811	48013	21451	00027	24292	19821	61891	50220	58751	50149
14925	59136	72788	65822	92765	11578	41707	67454	53971	22142	42152
14926	39413	48108	16818	63717	28962	08592	14709	06238	05846	00185
14927	71779	00051	96502	23391	64072	62357	28655	24549	11676	47937
14928	41939	06052	07881	75888	74477	40449	59968	83495	62878	49038
14929	16852	18740	41590	28762	40054	10564	35447	68877	44619	61061
14930	04631	58241	41013	05634	63332	39191	97358	71011	11686	52933
14931	95217	80882	38875	03353	78129	48089	28134	99469	34177	72409
14932	80365	85981	85997	77118	04077	83723	50303	98313	01146	18326
14933	58855	05833	18794	52072	59851	01483	88374	36319	36368	26524
14934	22006	45586	23893	41542	62646	33970	54241	92550	88540	53154

SOURCE: *A Million Random Digits*, p. 299, 1955; reprinted by permission of The RAND Corporation.

TABLE 28.3

	Ace	Deuce	3	4	5	6	7	8	9	10	Jack	Queen	King
Spades	01	02	03	04	05	06	07	08	09	10	11	12	13
Diamonds	14	15	16	17	18	19	20	21	22	23	24	25	26
Hearts	27	28	29	30	31	32	33	34	35	36	37	38	39
Clubs	40	41	42	43	44	45	46	47	48	49	50	51	52

1	10	09	25	33	52
2	01	35	34	36	48
3	17	39	29	27	49
4	45	20	48	05	47
5	42	24	52	40	37
6	20	04	02	29	16

cards, and see how many "hands" of five "cards" contain one pair each. Table 28.3 shows six such hands, of which 2, 3, and 6 contain pairs.

How accurate are these Monte Carlo methods? The accuracy depends on the *number of hands* we deal—the more hands, the greater the accuracy. Mathematical calculations tell us that, if we were to deal millions of hands, 42 per cent would contain a pair each; that is, the chance of getting a pair in the long run is 42 per cent. The estimate of 44 per cent based on 100 hands in Table 28.1 is close, though whether it is close enough depends on one's needs, of course. If you need great accuracy, you should deal more hands.

How many trials (hands) should be made for the estimate? There is no easy answer. The best approach is to run several (perhaps ten) equal-sized sets of trials and then to examine whether the proportion of pairs found in the entire group of trials is very different from the proportion found in the various subgroup sets. If the proportions of pairs in the various subgroups differ greatly from one another or from the overall proportion, then keep *quadrupling*[1] the number of trials until the overall average is not changed much by the additional trials. In this case, Table 28.1 shows that the average of the total of 100 hands is not much different from the average of the first fifty hands, and so we could reasonably quit dealing after 100 hands.

The method of solution just discussed for this problem clearly is not difficult to do or to understand. In contrast, the conventional analytic method of solving this problem requires knowledge of the theory of permutations and combinations, and it is not easy for the average student even though it is a very elementary probability theory. It is even more true in the examples to follow that the Monte Carlo solution is simple and straightforward, whereas the conventional analytic solution is either difficult or impossible for the ordinary student, undergraduate, or graduate.

1. The reason for quadrupling is that *four* times as big a sample gives *twice* as much accuracy (as measured by the standard deviation, the most frequent measurement of accuracy). That is, the error decreases with the square root of the sample size. And a step that doubles accuracy is a comfortable arbitrary step in many cases. But, if you see that you need *much* more accuracy, then *immediately* increase the sample size even more than four times.

b. EXAMPLE 2: ANOTHER INTRODUCTORY POKER PROBLEM

Which is more likely, poker hands with two pairs or with three of a kind? This is a *comparison* problem, rather than a problem in absolute estimation, as was Example 1.

In a series of 100 hands (using random numbers), four hands contained two pairs, and two hands contained three of a kind. Is it safe to say, on the basis of these 100 hands, that hands with two pairs are more frequent than hands with three of a kind? I do not think so. To check, we deal another 300 hands. In this 300, we see fifteen hands with two pairs (3.75 per cent) and eight hands with three of a kind (2 per cent), for a total of nineteen to ten. Although the difference is not enormous, it is reasonably clear-cut. Another 400 hands might be advisable, but we shall not bother.

Earlier we obtained forty-four hands with *one* pair each out of 100 hands, which makes it quite plain that *one* pair is more frequent than *either* two pairs or three of a kind. Obviously, we need *more* hands to compare the odds in favor of two pairs with the odds in favor of three of a kind than to compare those for one pair with those for either two pairs or three of a kind. Why? Because the difference in odds between one pair and either two pairs or three of a kind is much greater than the difference in odds between two pairs and three of a kind. This observation leads to a general rule: The closer the odds between two events, the *more trials* are needed to determine which has the higher odds.

Again it is interesting to compare the odds with the mathematical computations, which are 1 in 21 (4.75 per cent) for a hand containing two pairs and 1 in 47 (2.1 per cent) for a hand containing three of a kind—not too far from the estimate of 3.75 per cent and 2.0 per cent, based on 100 random hands.

We have dealt with these first two examples in an intuitive, unsystematic fashion. From here on, however, we will work in an explicitly systematic step-by-step manner.

c. EXAMPLE 3: FOUR DAUGHTERS AMONG FIVE CHILDREN (TWO-OUTCOME SAMPLING WITH EQUALLY LIKELY OUTCOMES WITH REPLACEMENT)

What is the probability that four of the first five children in a five-child family will be daughters?

The first step is to state the approximate probability that a single birth will produce a daughter as 50-50 (1 in 2). This estimate is not strictly correct because there are 106 male children born to every 100 female children, but the approximation is not too far off for most purposes, and the 50-50 split simplifies the job considerably. (Such "false" approximations are part of the everyday work of the scientist. The question is not whether a statement is "only" an approximation but whether it is a *good* approximation for your purposes.)

The chance of a fair coin's coming up heads is 50-50, as are the odds in favor of the birth of a single daughter. Therefore flip a coin in groups of five flips, and count how often all five of the flips produce *heads*. (You must decide in *advance* whether four heads mean four girls or four boys.) It is as simple as that.

In Monte Carlo estimation it is of the highest importance to work in a careful step-by-step fashion—to write down the steps in the estimation, and then to do the experiments just as described in the steps. (For classroom purposes, it is often sufficient for the student to write down the steps in the experiments, together with a very few experimental trials, rather than doing a full set of trials. The instructor can easily judge whether the student's method is correct.)

Here is a set of steps that will lead to a correct answer about the likelihood of getting four daughters among five children:

Step 1. Using coins, let "heads" equal "boy" and "tails" equal "girl."
Step 2. Throw five coins, and examine whether they fall with exactly four tails up. If so, write *yes* on a record sheet; otherwise write *no*.
Step 3. Repeat Step 2 perhaps a hundred times. Count the proportion of *yeses*. That proportion is an estimate of the likelihood of obtaining exactly four daughters in five children.

The first few experimental trials might appear in the record sheet as follows:

Number of Heads	Yes or No
1	No
1	No
4	Yes
3	No
2	No
3	No

The probability of getting four daughters in five births could also be found with a deck of cards, a random-number table, or a die. For example, half the cards in a deck are black, so the probability of dealing a black card ("daughter") from a full deck is 1 in 2. Therefore, deal a card, record "daughter" or "son," *replace* the card, deal again, and so forth for sets of five cards. Then count the proportion of groups of five cards in which you got four daughters.

Notice that the procedure outlined in the steps would have been different if we had asked about the likelihood of *four or more* daughters rather than exactly four daughters among five children. For *four or more* daughters we would have scored *yes* for either *four or five* heads, rather than just for four heads.

It is important that in this case, in contrast to what occurred in Example

1, the card be replaced *each time,* so that each card is dealt from a full deck. This method is known as *sampling with replacement.* One samples with replacement whenever the successive events are *independent;* in this case, we assume that the chance of having a daughter remains the same (1 in 2), no matter how many sons or daughters the family has previously had.[2] But, if the first card dealt is black and is *not* replaced, the chance of the second card's being black is no longer 26 in 52 (1 in 2) but is only 25 in 51 (less than 1 in 2). If the first *three* cards are black and are not replaced, then the chance of the fourth card's being black sinks to 23 in 49.

To take the illustration further, consider what would happen if we used a deck of only six cards, half (three) black and half (three) red, instead of a deck of fifty-two cards. If the cards were replaced each time, the six-card deck would produce the same results as a fifty-two-card deck; in fact, a two-card deck would do as well. But, if the sampling were done *without* replacement, it would be *impossible* to obtain four "daughters" with the six-card deck because there would be only three "daughters" in the deck. To repeat, then, whenever you want to estimate the probability of some series of events of which each is independent of the other, you must sample *with replacement.*

2. The General Procedure

Until now, the steps to follow in solving particular problems have been chosen to fit the facts of that problem. And so they must. But we can also describe the series of steps in a more general fashion so as to throw light on what we are doing when we construct a series of Monte Carlo problem-solving operations leading up to estimation of a probability. The general steps are lettered rather than numbered here, because more than one step in a particular Monte Carlo experiment *may be* necessary to complete a general step described here.

Step A. Construct a universe of random numbers or cards or dice or some other random generation mechanism that has similar composition and structural properties as does the universe whose behavior we wish to simulate and describe. The universe refers to the system that is relevant for a single simple event.

a) A coin with two sides, or two sets of random numbers 1–5 and 6–0, simulate the system that produces a single male or female birth, when we are estimating the probability of four girls in the first five children. Notice that in this universe the probability of a girl remains the same from trial event to trial event—that is, the trials are independent—which is a universe from which we sample with replacement.

---

2. This assumption is slightly contrary to scientific fact. A better example would be the probability that four mothers delivering in a row in a hospital will all have daughters. But that example has other difficulties.

b) A deck of 25 red and 25 black cards simulates a group of 25 boys and 25 girls from which we draw a sample of five students.

Hard thinking is required in order to decide just what the appropriate real universe is. Once this is done, however, it is relatively easy to choose the appropriate simulation model.

Step B. Specify the procedure that produces a sample that simulates the real-life sample we are interested in. That is, you must indicate the *rules* of procedure by which the sample is drawn from the simulated universe. These rules must correspond to the behavior of the real universe you are interested in. To put it another way, the simulation procedure must produce simple experimental events with the same probabilities that the simple events have in the real world.

In the case of four daughters in five children, the procedure is to draw a card *and then replace it,* if you are using cards. If you are using a random-numbers table, the random numbers automatically simulate replacement.

Recording the outcome of the sampling must be indicated as part of this step—record *yes* if girl, *no* if boy.

Step C. If several simple events must be combined into a composite event, and if the composite event was not described in the procedure in Step B, describe it now.

For the four girls in five children, the procedure for each simple event of a simple birth was described in Step B. Now we must specify repeating the simple event five times.

Recording *yes* or *no,* success or failure, is part of this step. This record indicates which set of events of interest to us—the outcome of the composite event, which is the Monte Carlo trial—occurs.

Step D. Calculate from the outcomes of the Monte Carlo trials the proportion of *yes* or *no,* success or failure, that estimates the likelihood we wish to determine.

There is indeed more than one way to skin a cat (ugh!). And there is always more than one way to correctly estimate a given probability. Therefore, when reading through the list of steps set forth here to estimate a given probability, please keep in mind that a particular list is not sacred or unique; other sets of steps will also do the trick.

a. EXAMPLE 4: THE BIRTHDAY PROBLEM (THE PROBABILITY OF DUPLICATION IN A MULTI-OUTCOME SAMPLE FROM AN INFINITE UNIVERSE)

As an indication of how powerful *and* simple are Monte Carlo methods, consider this famous examination question used in courses on probability: What is the probability that two or more people among a roomful of, say, twenty-five people were born on the same day of the year (for example, Nov. 26)? To answer, we may simply examine the first twenty-five numbers from the random-number table that fall between 001 and 365 (days in the year) and record whether there is a duplication among the twenty-five. Repeat the process enough times to get a reasonably stable probability estimate. Then pose the question to a mathematical friend of yours, watch him sweat for a while, and compare your answer to his. (I think you will find the correct answer very surprising. People who know how this problem works have been known to take advantage of this knowledge by making and winning big bets on it.)

More specifically, here are steps to handle this problem for the case of twenty-five people in the room:

Step 1. Let three-digit random numbers 001–365 stand for the 365 days in the year. (Ignore leap year for simplicity.)

Step 2. Examine the first twenty-five random numbers 001–365 to see if there is duplication (triplicates or higher-order repeats are counted as duplicates). If there is one or more duplicate, record *yes*; otherwise record *no*.

Step 3. Repeat perhaps a hundred times, and calculate the proportion of a duplicate birthday among twenty-five people.

Here is the first experiment from the random-number table on page 412, starting at the top left:

Experiment Numbers	Duplication
1) 021, 158, 116, 066, *353*, 164, 019	Yes
080, 312, 020, *353* . . .	

3. Hypothesis Testing

The previous problems have been problems in probability theory—that is, problems in estimating the likelihood of a composite event resulting from a system in which we *know* the probabilities of the simple events. That is, we have been dealing with systems whose "parameters" we know.

Now we turn to inferential-statistical problems. These are problems in which *we seek to learn and estimate* the probabilities of a system—that is, the probabilities of its simple events and parameters.

This chapter begins a discussion of the group of problems in inferential statistics known as "hypothesis testing" problems. Subsequent chapters continue with hypothesis testing, and chapters that follow take up estimation of the *strength* of a relationship between two or more variables.

a. EXAMPLE 5: DOES IRRADIATION AFFECT THE SEX RATIO IN FRUIT FLIES?
(WHERE THE BENCHMARK UNIVERSE MEAN IS KNOWN, IS THE MEAN
OF THE POPULATION AFFECTED BY THE TREATMENT?)

You think you have developed a technique for irradiating the genes of fruit flies so that the sex ratio of the offspring will *not* be half males and half females. In the first twenty cases you treat, there are fourteen males and six females. Does this result confirm that the irradiation does work?

First convert the scientific question—whether the treatment affects the sex distribution—into a probability-statistical question: Is the observed sample likely to have come from a universe in which the sex ratio is one male to one female? The benchmark (null) hypothesis, then, is that the treatment makes no difference and that the sample comes from the one-to-one universe. (The concept of the benchmark hypothesis was discussed on page 405.) Therefore, we investigate how likely is a one-to-one universe to produce a distribution of fourteen males to six females.

A coin has a one-to-one (one out of two) chance of coming up tails. Therefore, we might flip a coin in groups of twenty flips and count the number of heads in each twenty flips. Or we can use a random-digit table. These steps will produce a sound estimate:

Step 1. Let heads = males, tails = females

Step 2. Flip twenty coins and count the number of males. If 14 or more males occur, record *yes;* if 13 or less, record *no.*

Step 3. Repeat Step 2 perhaps 100 times.

Step 4. Calculate the proportion of *yes* in the 100 trials. This proportion estimates the likelihood that a fruit-fly population with a mean of 50 per cent males will by chance produce as many as 14 males in a sample of 20 flies.

Table 28.4 shows the results obtained in twenty-five trials of twenty flips each.

In two of the twenty-five trials (8 per cent) there were fourteen or more heads, which we shall call "males," and in one of the twenty-five trials (4 per cent) there were fourteen or more tails ("females"). We can therefore estimate that, even if the treatment does *not* affect the sex and even if the births over a long period are really one to one, we would get fourteen or

TABLE 28.4

Trial of 20 Coin Flips	Number of Heads	Trial of 20 Coin Flips	Number of Heads	Trial of 20 Coin Flips	Number of Heads
1	11 = No	10	10 = No	18	12 = No
2	12 "	11	10 "	19	13 "
3	8 "	12	10 "	20	10 "
4	12 "	13	9 "	21	11 "
5	12 "	14	9 "	22	14 Yes
6	7 "	15	12 "	23	9 "
7	9 "	16	7 "	24	7 "
8	8 "	17	14 Yes	25	10 "
9	6 "				

more of one sex or the other in three out of twenty-five times (12 per cent). Therefore, finding fourteen males out of twenty births is not overwhelming evidence that the treatment has any effect, though it is suggestive.

How accurate is the estimate? Seventy-five more trials were made, and of the total 100 trials ten contained fourteen or more "males" (10 per cent), and seven trials contained fourteen or more "females" (7 per. cent), a total of 17 per cent. So the first twenty-five trials gave a fairly reliable indication. As a matter of fact, a mathematical computation (not explained here) shows that the probability of getting fourteen or more females out of twenty births is .057 and, of course, the same for fourteen or more males from a one-to-one universe, a total probability of .114 of getting fourteen or more males *or* females.

Notice that the strength of the evidence for the effectiveness of the radiation treatment depends upon the original question, whether the treatment had *any* effect on sex. But if there were reason to believe at the start that the treatment could increase only the number of *males,* then we would focus our attention on the fact that in only two of our first twenty-five trials were there fourteen or more males. There would be only a 2/25 probability of getting the observed results by chance if the treatment really has no effect, rather than the weaker odds against obtaining fourteen or more of *either* males or females.

Therefore, whether you decide to figure the odds for just fourteen or more males (what is called a "one-tail test") or for fourteen or more males *plus* fourteen or more females (a "two-tail test"), depends upon your advance knowledge of the treatment. If you have no reason to believe that the treatment will have an effect *only* in the direction of creating more males, and if you figure the odds for the one-tail test anyway, then you will be fooling yourself. Theory comes to bear here. If you have a strong hypothesis, deduced from a strong theory, that there will be more males, then you should figure one-tail odds, but if you have no such theory you should figure the weaker two-tail odds.[3]

"Significance level" is a common term in probability statistics. It corresponds roughly to the probability that the observed sample does not come from a particular universe by chance. The results of Example 5 can be phrased as follows: The hypothesis that the radiation treatment affects the sex of fruit-fly offspring is accepted as true at the 17 per cent "level of significance." (A more common way of expressing this idea would be to say that the hypothesis is *not rejected* at the 17 per cent level of significance. But "not rejected" and "accepted" really do mean much the same thing, despite some arguments to the contrary.) This kind of statistical work is called *statistical testing.*

The question of *which* significance level should be said to be significant is

3. If you are very knowledgeable, you may do some in-between figuring (with what is known as "Bayesian analysis"), but leave this alone unless you know exactly what you are doing.

difficult. How great must a coincidence be before you refuse to believe that it is only a coincidence? It has been conventional in social science to say that, if the probability that something happens by chance is less than 5 per cent, it is significant. But sometimes the stiffer standard of 1 per cent is used. Actually, *any* fixed cut-off significance level is an arbitrary construction. (And even the entire notion of saying that a hypothesis is true or is not true is sometimes not very useful.)

Before leaving this example, let us review our intellectual strategy in handling the problem. First we observe a result (14 males in 20 flies) that differs from the mean of the population (50 per cent males). Because we have treated this sample with irradiation and observed a result that differs from the untreated population's mean, we speculate that the irradiation caused the sample to differ from the untreated population. We wish to check whether this speculation is correct.

When asking whether this speculation is correct, we are implicitly asking whether future irradiation would also produce a proportion of males higher than 50 per cent. That is, we are implicitly asking whether irradiated flies would produce more samples with male proportions as high as 14/20 than would occur by chance in the absence of irradiation.

If samples as far away as 14/20 from the population mean would occur frequently by chance, then we are not impressed with the experimental evidence as proof that irradiation affects the sex ratio. Hence we set up a model that will tell us the frequency with which such samples as 14 males out of 20 births would be observed by chance. Carrying out the Monte Carlo procedure tells us that perhaps a tenth of the time such samples would be observed by chance. That is not frequent, but it is not infrequent either. Hence we would probably conclude that the evidence is provocative enough to justify further experimentation, but not so strong that we should immediately believe in the truth of this speculation.

b. EXAMPLE 6: DO ANY OF FOUR TREATMENTS AFFECT THE SEX RATIO IN
FRUIT FLIES? (WHEN THE BENCHMARK UNIVERSE MEAN IS KNOWN,
IS THE MEAN OF THE TWO-OUTCOME POPULATION AFFECTED BY
ANY OF THE TREATMENTS?)

Suppose that, instead of trying just one type of radiation treatment on the flies, as in Example 5, you try *four* different treatments, which we shall label A, B, C, and D. In treatment A you get fourteen males and six females, but in treatments B, C, and D you get ten, eleven, and ten males, respectively. It is immediately obvious that there is no reason to think that treatment B, C, or D affects the sex ratio. But what about treatment A?

A frequent and dangerous mistake made by young scientists is to scrounge around in the data for the most extreme observation and then to treat it as if it were the only observation made. (This matter is discussed in more depth on page 276.) In the context of this example, it would be fallacious to think that the probability of the fourteen males–six females split observed for treatment A is the probability that we figured for a *single* experiment in Example 5. Instead, we must consider that our benchmark universe is composed of *four sets* of twenty trials, each trial having a 50–50 probability of coming out male. We can consider that old trials 1–4 in Example 5 constitute a single new trial, and each subsequent set of four old trials constitutes another new trial. We then ask how likely is a new trial of four sets of twenty flips to produce *one* set with fourteen or more of one or the other sex.

Let us make the procedure explicit, but using random numbers instead of coins this time:

Step 1. Let 1–5 = males, 6–0 = females
Step 2. Choose four groups of twenty numbers. If for *any* group there are 14 or more males, record *yes;* if 13 or less, record *no.*
Step 3. Repeat Step 2 perhaps 100 times.
Step 4. Calculate the proportion of *yes* in the 100 trials. This proportion estimates the likelihood that a fruit-fly population with a mean of 50 per cent males will produce as many as 14 males in at least one of four samples of 20 flies.

We begin the trials with data from the previous example.

Trial Number	Group A	Group B	Group C	Group D	Yes/No
1	11	12	8	12	No
2	12	7	9	8	No
3	6	10	10	10	No
4	9	9	12	7	No
5	14	12	13	10	Yes
6	11	14	9	7	Yes

In two of the six trials, a sample shows 14 or more males. And another trial shows 14 or more *females*. Without even concerning ourselves about whether we should be looking at males or females, or just males, or needing to do more trials, we can see that it would be very common indeed to have one of four treatments show fourteen or more of one sex just by chance. This discovery clearly indicates that a result that would be fairly unusual (3 in 25) for a single sample is commonplace in one of four observed samples.

C. EXAMPLE 7: A PUBLIC-OPINION POLL (IS THE MEAN OF A POPULATION GREATER THAN A GIVEN VALUE?)

A municipal official wanted to determine whether the *majority* of a town's residents were for or against the awarding of a cable-television franchise, and he asked you to take a poll. You judged that the telephone book was a fair representation of the universe in which the politician was interested, and you decided to interview by telephone. Of a sample of fifty people who expressed opinions, thirty were for the plan and twenty were against it. How conclusively do the results show that the people in town want cable television?

The benchmark (null) hypothesis is that 50 per cent of the town does not want the plan. (This statement really means that 50 per cent or *more* do not want the plan.)

This problem is very much like the one-group fruit fly-irradiation problem in Example 5. The only difference is that now we are comparing the observed sample against an arbitrary value (50 per cent in this case, because that is the cut-off point in a situation where the majority decides), whereas in the fruit-fly example we compared the observed sample against the normal population mean (also 50 per cent, because that is the normal proportion of males). But it really does not matter why we are comparing the observed sample to the figure of 50 per cent; the procedure is the same in both cases. (Please notice that there is nothing special about the 50 per cent figure; the same procedure would be followed for 20 per cent or 85 per cent.)

In brief, we designate 1–5 as *no* in the random-number table, 6–0 as *yes*. We count the number of *yes* and *no* in the first fifty numbers and repeat for perhaps a hundred trials. Then we count the proportion of the trials in which a 50–50 universe would produce thirty or more *yes* answers.

In operational steps, the procedure is as follows:

Step 1. 1–5 = no, 6–0 = yes
Step 2. In 50 random numbers, if 30 or more are *no*, record it as *against*.
Step 3. Repeat Step 2 perhaps 100 times.
Step 4. Calculate the proportion of experimental trials *against*.

This estimates the likelihood that as many as 30 *nos* would be observed by chance in a sample of 50 people, *if* half (or more) are really for the plan.

In Table 28.5 we see the results of twenty trials; in 4 of 20 trials (20 per cent) 30 or more *nos* were observed by chance.

This is the probability that as many as thirty of fifty people would say yes by chance if the population were "really" split evenly. (If the population were split so that *more* than 50 per cent were against the plan, the probability would be even *less* that the observed result would occur by chance. In this sense, the benchmark hypothesis is conservative.)

This example suggests that the mayor would be wise not to place very much confidence in the poll results, but rather ought to either act with caution or take a bigger sample.

TABLE 28.5

Trial	Number of "No"s	Number of "Yes"es
1	23	27
2	25	25
3	26	24
4	22	28
5	22	28
6	20	30
7	25	25
8	21	29
9	28	22
10	19	31
11	28	22
12	19	31
13	18	32
14	23	27
15	34	16
16	27	23
17	22	28
18	26	24
19	28	22
20	27	23

d. EXAMPLE 8: COMPARISON OF POSSIBLE CANCER CURE TO PLACEBO EFFECT (DO TWO TWO-OUTCOME POPULATIONS DIFFER IN THEIR MEANS?)

Example 5 used an observed sample of male and female fruit flies to test the benchmark (null) hypothesis that the flies came from a universe with a one-to-one sex ratio. Now we want to compare *two samples with each other*, rather than comparing one sample with a hypothesized universe. That is, in this example we are not comparing one sample to a benchmark universe, but rather asking whether *both* samples come from the *same* universe. The universe from which both come, *if* both come from the same universe, may be thought of as the benchmark universe in this case.

The scientific question is whether pill P cures cancer. A researcher gave the pill to six patients selected randomly from a group of twelve cancer patients, of whom five got well. She gave an inactive placebo to the other six patients, and two of them got well. Does the evidence justify a conclusion that the pill has a curative effect?

(An identical statistical example could be constructed with an experiment on methods of teaching reading to children. But in such a case the researcher would respond to inconclusive results by running the experiment on more subjects, though in cases like the cancer-pill example the researcher often cannot obtain more subjects.)

The answer is to *combine* the two samples and then test both samples against the resulting combined universe. In this case, the universe is twelve subjects, seven (5 + 2) of whom got well. Given such a universe, then, how likely would it be to produce two samples as far apart as five of six and two of six patients who get well? In other words, how often will two samples of six subjects each, drawn from a universe in which $\frac{7}{12}$ of the patients get well, be as far apart as $5 - 2 = 3$ patients in favor of the sample designated "pill"? This is obviously a one-tail test, for there is no reason to believe that the pill group might do less well than the placebo group.

Construct a twelve-sided die, seven of whose sides are marked "get well." Or use pairs of numbers from the random-number table, with numbers 01–07 corresponding to "get well," numbers 08–12 corresponding to "not get well," and all other numbers omitted. (If you wish to save time, you can work out a system that uses more and skips fewer of the numbers.) Designate the first six subjects "pill" and the next six subjects "placebo."

The more specific procedure might be as follows:

Step 1. 01–07 = get well, 08–12 = not get well

Step 2. Select two groups, "Pill" and "Placebo," of six random numbers from 01 to 12.

Step 3. Record how many "get well" in each group.

Step 4. Subtract the result in experimental placebo group from that in experimental pill group (the difference may be negative).

Step 5. Repeat Steps 1–4 perhaps 100 times.

Step 6. Compute the proportion of trials in which the pill is better by three or more cases. In the trials shown in Table 28.6 in three cases (12 per cent) the difference between the randomly drawn groups is three or greater. Apparently it is somewhat unusual for this universe to generate "pill" samples in which the number of recoveries exceeds the number in the "placebo" samples by three or more. Therefore the answer to the scientific question, based on these samples, is that there is some reason to think that the medicine does have a favorable effect. But the investigator might sensibly await more data before reaching a firm conclusion about the pill's efficacy, given the 7 to 1 (12 per cent) odds.

This method is not the standard way of handling the problem; it is not even analogous to the standard analytic difference-of-proportions method. Though the method shown is quite direct and satisfactory, there are *many other* Monte Carlo methods that we might develop to solve the same problem. You should by all means invent your own statistics, rather than simply trying to copy the methods described here; the latter only illustrate the process of inventing statistics rather than offering solutions for all classes of problems.

TABLE 28.6

Trial	Pill	Placebo	Difference
1	4	4	0
2	3	5	−2
3	4	3	1
4*	5	2	3
5	4	3	1
6	2	5	−3
7	4	4	0
8	4	5	−1
9	4	4	0
10*	5	2	3
11	4	5	−1
12	5	3	2
13	3	5	−2
14	3	2	1
15	3	4	−1
16	5	4	1
17*	6	3	3
18	4	5	−1
19	3	4	−1
20	2	3	−1
21	4	4	0
22	4	4	0
23	3	5	−2
24	3	3	0
25	3	3	0

* The total of the asterisked trials is 3 differences as great
as 3 in favor of pill.

e. EXAMPLE 9: DO FOUR PSYCHOLOGICAL TREATMENTS DIFFER IN
EFFECTIVENESS? (DO SEVERAL TWO-OUTCOME SAMPLES DIFFER
AMONG THEMSELVES IN THEIR MEANS?)

Consider now, not two but four different psychological treatments designed
to rehabilitate juvenile delinquents. Instead of a score, there is only a *yes* or
a *no* answer as to whether the juvenile has been rehabilitated or has gotten
into trouble again. Label the treatments *P, R, S,* and *T,* each of which is
administered to a separate group of twenty juvenile delinquents. The number of rehabilitations per group is P, seventeen; R, ten; S, ten; T, seven. Is it
improbable that all four groups come from the same universe?

This problem is like the placebo-vs.-cancer-cure problem, but now there
are more than two samples. It is also like the four-sample irradiated-flies
example, except that in this case we are *not* asking whether any or some of
the samples differ from a *given universe* (50–50 sex ratio in that case).
Rather, we are now asking whether there are differences among the samples
themselves. Please keep in mind that we are still dealing with two-outcome

(yes-or-no, well-or-sick) problems. Later we shall take up problems that are similar except that the outcomes are "quantitative."

If all four groups come from the same universe, that universe has an estimated rehabilitation rate of

$$\frac{17 + 10 + 10 + 7}{20 + 20 + 20 + 20} = \frac{11}{20} = \frac{55}{100}$$

because the observed data *taken as a whole* constitutes our best guess as to the nature of the universe from which they come—if they all come from the same universe. (Please think over this matter a bit because it is important though subtle. It may help you to notice the absence of any *other* information about the universe from which they all have come, if they have come from the same universe.)

Therefore, select twenty two-digit numbers for each group from the random-number table, marking *yes* for each number 1–55 and *no* for each number 56–100. Conduct a number of such trials. Then count the proportion of times that the difference between the highest and lowest groups is larger than the widest observed difference—that between P and T $(17 - 7 = 10)$. Table 28.7 shows that none of the first six trials shows anywhere near as large a difference, suggesting that it would be rare for four treatments that are "really" similar to show so great a difference. There is thus reason to believe that P and T differ in their effects.

The conventional way to approach this problem would be with what is known as a "chi-square test."

f. EXAMPLE 10: IS ONE PIG RATION MORE EFFECTIVE THAN THE OTHER? (TESTING FOR A DIFFERENCE IN MEANS WITH A TWO-BY-TWO CLASSIFICATION)

Each of two new types of ration is fed to twelve pigs. A farmer wants to know whether ration A or ration B is better.[4] The weight gains for pigs fed

TABLE 28.7

Trial	P	R	S	T	Largest Minus Smallest
1	11	9	8	12	4
2	10	10	12	12	2
3	9	12	8	12	4
4	9	11	12	10	3
5	10	10	11	12	2
6	11	11	9	11	2

4. The data for this example are drawn from W. Dixon and F. Massey (p. 117), who offer an orthodox method of handling the problem with a *t* test.

on ration A are 31.0, 34.0, 29.0, 26.0, 32.0, 35.0, 38.0, 34.0, 30.1, 29.1, 32.0, and 31.0. The weight gains for pigs fed on ration B are 26.0, 24.0, 28.0, 29.0, 30.0, 29.0, 32.0, 26.0, 31.0, 29.0, 32.1, and 28.0.

The *statistical* question is whether the pigs fed on the different rations come from the same universe with respect to weight gains.

One approach is to adopt a strategy similar to that previously used in Example 9—though we now require a bit of arbitrariness. We can divide the pigs into two groups, those twelve with the higher weight gain, and those twelve with the lower weight gain. Then we check whether an unusually large number of high-weight-gain pigs were fed on one or the other of the rations.

We can make this test by ordering the twenty-four weights from high to low this way: 38.0 (ration A), 35.0 (A), 34.0 (A), 34.0 (A), 32.1 (B), 32.0 (A), 32.0 (A), 32.0 (B), 31.0 (A), 31.0 (B), 31.0 (A), 30.1 (A), 30.0 (B), 29.0 (A), 29.0 (A), 29.0 (B), 29.0 (B), 29.0 (B), 28.0 (B), 28.0 (B), 26.0 (A), 26.0 (B), 26.0 (B), and 24.0 (B).

Among the twelve high-gain pigs, nine were fed on ration A. Is this further from an even split than we are likely to get by chance?

Take twelve red and twelve black cards, shuffle them, and deal out twelve cards. Count the proportion of times in which one color comes up nine or more times in the first twelve cards, to reflect ration A's appearance nine times among the highest twelve weight gains. More specifically:

Step 1. Constitute a deck of twelve red and twelve black cards.

Step 2. Deal out twelve cards, count the number of reds, and record *yes* if there are nine or more of *either* red or black.

TABLE 28.8

Trial	Black	Red	Trial	Black	Red	Trial	Black	Red
1	7	5	19	5	7	37	6	6
2	7	5	20	5	7	38	5	7
3	6	6	21	4	8	39	7	5
4	6	6	*22	9	3	40	5	7
5	6	6	23	7	5	41	6	6
6	4	8	24	5	7	42	4	8
7	6	6	25	5	7	43	7	5
8	6	6	26	7	5	44	5	7
9	5	7	27	6	6	45	8	4
10	8	4	*28	9	3	46	5	7
11	6	6	29	7	5	47	5	7
12	7	5	30	7	5	48	6	6
13	8	4	31	8	4	49	6	6
14	5	7	*32	3	9	50	6	6
15	6	6	33	5	7			
16	7	5	34	6	6			
17	8	4	35	5	7			
18	8	4	36	5	7			

Step 3. Repeat Step 2 perhaps fifty times.

Step 4. Compute the proportion of *yes*. This estimates the probability sought.

Table 28.8 shows the results of fifty hands. In three (marked by asterisks) of the fifty (6 per cent) there were nine or more either red or black cards in the first twelve cards. Again the results suggest that it would be *slightly unusual* for the results to favor one ration or the other so strongly just by chance if the universe is really the same.

4. Summary

This chapter demonstrates how problems in probability and hypothesis testing may be solved using the experimental Monte Carlo method. A systematic procedure is given and then illustrated in the handling of a variety of problems.

EXERCISE

1. Find an example of a misleading statistic in a newspaper or magazine.

29 hypothesis testing with measured data

The previous chapter discussed testing a hypothesis with data that are already in dichotomized form or data in situations where you have measurements but it is convenient to dichotomize the data. Now we move on to hypothesis testing with measured data.

a. EXAMPLE 11: THE PIG RATIONS AGAIN, USING MEASURED DATA (TESTING FOR THE DIFFERENCE BETWEEN MEANS OF TWO EQUAL-SIZED SAMPLES OF MEASURED-DATA OBSERVATIONS)

Another way to approach the pig-ration problem does not require converting the quantitative data into qualitative data and therefore loses no information. The term "to lose information" can be understood intuitively. Consider two sets of three sacks of corn each. The first set includes sacks weighing, respectively, one pound, two pounds, and three pounds. The second set includes sacks of one pound, two pounds, and a hundred pounds. If we *rank* the sacks by weight, the one-pound and two-pound sacks have ranks one and two in both cases, and their relative places in their sets are the same. But if we know not only that the one-pound sack is the smallest of its set and the three-pound or hundred-pound sack is the largest, but *also* that the largest sack is three pounds (or a hundred pounds), we have more information about the set than if we know only the ranks. The rank data are known as "ordinal" or "ranked" data, whereas the data in pounds are known as "cardinal" or "measured" data. Converting from cardinal (measured) to ordinal (ranked) data loses information but may increase convenience.

We begin by observing that if the two rations are the same, then each of the observed weight gains came from the same universe. This is a basic tactic in our statistical strategy. We say that if the two rations came from the same universe, our best guess about the composition of the universe is that it is composed of weight gains like those of the twenty-four pigs we have observed. Since ours is a sample from an infinite (or at least very large) universe of possible weight gains, we assume that there are *many* weight gains in the universe just like the ones we have observed, in the same proportion as we have observed them. For example, we assume that $\frac{2}{24}$ of the universe is composed of 34-pound weight gains, as seen in Figure 29.1.

Of course, we recognize that weight gains other than the exact ones we observed are possible, and in fact certainly would occur. And we could assume that the "distribution" of the weight gains would follow a regular "smooth" shape such as in Figure 29.2. But deciding just how to draw Figure 29.2 from the data in Figure 29.1 requires that we make some assumptions about unknown conditions. And if we were to draw Figure 29.2 in a form that would be sufficiently regular for conventional mathematical analysis, we might have to make some *strong* assumptions, going far beyond what we have observed.

If it were necessary to make such assumptions and draw a smooth curve such as Figure 29.2 from the raw data in Figure 29.1, it might well be done satisfactorily—if done with wisdom and good judgment. But there is no necessity to draw such a smooth curve, in this case or in most cases. We can proceed by assuming only that the benchmark universe—conventionally called the "null" or "hypothetical" universe, and which is the universe we shall compare our samples to—is composed only of elements similar to the observations we have in hand. We thereby lose no efficiency and avoid the probability of making misleading assumptions.

To execute our tactic, we write down each of the twenty-four weight

FIGURE 29.1

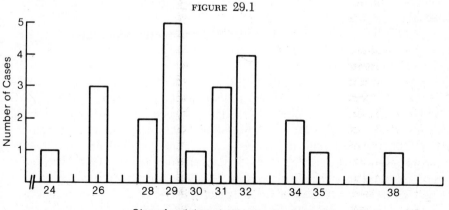

Size of weight gain in pounds, observed

FIGURE 29.2

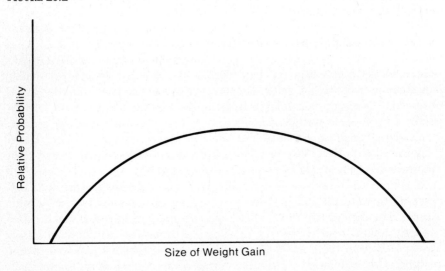

gains on a separate, blank index card. We then have one card each for 31, 34, 29, 26, and so on. (Drop the decimal points that were arbitrarily added in Example 10 to break ties.) Shuffle the twenty-four cards thoroughly, and deal two hands of twelve cards each. Call the first "ration A" and the second "ration B." Reckon the average weight gain for the two hands, and record it as in Table 29.1. Reshuffle, and repeat several times.

In operational steps:

Step 1. Write down each observed weight gain on a card, such as 31, 34, 29, and so on.

Step 2. Shuffle and deal out groups A and B of 12 cards each. Calculate the mean weight gain of each group.

Step 3. Subtract the mean of group A from the mean of group B and record. If the figure is more positive than 3.08 or more negative than 3.08, record "more" or "less," respectively.

Step 4. Repeat Step 3 fifty times, and calculate the proportion of "more." This estimates the probability sought.

In none of the first ten trials did the difference in the means of the random hands exceed the observed difference (3.08 pounds, in the top line of the table) between rations A and B. (The difference between group *totals* tells the same story and is faster, requiring no division calculations.) Ordinarily I would quit dealing at such a point, confident that a difference in means that great is not likely to happen by chance. (Using the quick multiplication rule described on page 417, we can estimate the likelihood of such an occurrence happening by chance as $\frac{1}{2} \times \frac{1}{2} \times \frac{1}{2} \ldots = (\frac{1}{2})^{10}$ $= \frac{1}{1024} \approx .001 = .1\%$, a small chance indeed.)

Table 29.1 shows fifty trials of which only one (the thirty-ninth) is as "far out" as the observed samples. These data give us an estimate of the probability that the two rations do not come from the same universe—approximately $49/50$, or 98 per cent. (Compare this estimate with the probability of roughly 99 per cent estimated with the conventional t test—that is, a significance level of 1 per cent.) On the average, the test described in this section yields a significance level as high as such mathematical-probability tests as the t test; that is, it is just as efficient, though the test described in Example 10 is likely to be less efficient because it converts measured data to ranked, or classified, data.[1]

This example illustrates how the *dispersion within samples* affects the difficulty of finding out whether the samples differ from each other. For example, the average weight gain for ration A was 32 pounds, versus 29 pounds for ration B. If *all* the ration A-fed pigs had gained weight within a range of, say, 29.9 to 31.1 pounds, and if all the ration B-fed pigs had gained weight within a range of 28.9 to 29.1 pounds—that is, if the highest weight gain in ration B had been lower than the lowest weight gain in ration A—then there would be no question that ration A is better, and even fewer observations would have made this point clear. Variation (dispersion) is thus of great importance in statistics and in the social sciences. The larger the dispersion among the observations *within* the samples—as measured by the mean absolute deviation (the average absolute difference between the mean and the individual observations, treating both plus and minus differences as positive); the variance (the average *squared* difference between the mean and the observations); the standard deviation (the square root of the variance); the range (the difference between the smallest and largest observations); or some other device—the larger the *sample size* necessary to make a conclusive comparison between two groups or to make reliable estimates of summarization statistics.

Are you performing your tests by hand rather than by computer? In a few years everyone will be using computers right at his desk for such tasks. But in the meantime you might prefer to work with the median instead of the mean, for the median requires less computation. Simply compare the difference in medians of the Monte Carlo twelve-pig samples to the difference in medians of the actual samples, just as was done with the means. The only operational difference is to substitute the word "median" for the word

---

1. Note to statisticians: The test described in this section is nonparametric and therefore makes no assumptions about the shapes of the distributions, which is well because we would be on soft ground if we assumed normality in the pig-ration case, given the sample sizes. This test does not, however, throw away information as to the rank and median tests illustrated earlier. And indeed, this test proves to be more powerful than the other nonparametric tests. After developing this test, I discovered that its general logic follows the tradition of the "randomization" tests based on an idea by R. Fisher and worked out for the two-sample case by E. Pitman (1937). But the only mentions of *sampling* from the universe of possibilities are in M. Dwass and in J. Chung and D. Fraser. I am grateful to J. Pratt for bringing the later literature to my attention.

TABLE 29.1

(1)	Mean of First Twelve Observations (First Hand) (2)	Mean of Second Twelve Observations (Second Hand) (3)	Difference (4) = (2 − 3)	Greater or Less Than Observed Absolute Difference
Actually Observed	381 ÷ 12 = 31.75	344 ÷ 12 = 28.67	3.08	
Trial				
1	368 ÷ 12 = 30.67	357 ÷ 12 = 29.75	.87	Less
2	364 ÷ 12 = 30.33	361 ÷ 12 = 30.08	.25	ʺ
3	352 ÷ 12 = 29.33	373 ÷ 12 = 31.08	−1.75	ʺ
4	378 ÷ 12 = 31.50	347 ÷ 12 = 28.92	2.58	ʺ
5	365 ÷ 12 = 30.42	360 ÷ 12 = 30.00	.42	ʺ
6	352 ÷ 12 = 29.33	373 ÷ 12 = 31.08	−1.75	ʺ
7	355 ÷ 12 = 29.58	370 ÷ 12 = 30.83	−1.25	ʺ
8	366 ÷ 12 = 30.50	359 ÷ 12 = 29.92	.58	ʺ
9	360 ÷ 12 = 30.00	365 ÷ 12 = 30.42	−.42	ʺ
10	355 ÷ 12 = 29.58	370 ÷ 12 = 30.83	−1.25	ʺ
11	359 ÷ 12 = 29.92	366 ÷ 12 = 30.50	−.58	ʺ
12	369 ÷ 12 = 30.75	356 ÷ 12 = 29.67	1.08	ʺ
13	260 ÷ 12 = 30.00	365 ÷ 12 = 30.42	−.42	ʺ
14	377 ÷ 12 = 31.42	348 ÷ 12 = 29.00	2.42	ʺ
15	365 ÷ 12 = 30.42	360 ÷ 12 = 30.00	.42	ʺ
16	364 ÷ 12 = 30.33	361 ÷ 12 = 30.08	.25	ʺ
17	363 ÷ 12 = 30.25	362 ÷ 12 = 30.17	.08	ʺ
18	365 ÷ 12 = 30.42	360 ÷ 12 = 30.00	.42	ʺ
19	369 ÷ 12 = 30.75	356 ÷ 12 = 29.67	1.08	ʺ
20	369 ÷ 12 = 30.75	356 ÷ 12 = 29.67	1.08	ʺ
21	369 ÷ 12 = 30.75	356 ÷ 12 = 29.67	1.08	ʺ
22	364 ÷ 12 = 30.33	361 ÷ 12 = 30.08	.25	ʺ
23	363 ÷ 12 = 30.25	362 ÷ 12 = 30.17	.08	ʺ
24	363 ÷ 12 = 30.25	362 ÷ 12 = 30.17	.08	ʺ
25	364 ÷ 12 = 30.33	361 ÷ 12 = 30.08	.25	ʺ

"mean" in the steps previously listed on page 432. You may need a somewhat larger number of Monte Carlo trials when working with medians, however, for they tend to be less precise than means.

b. EXAMPLE 12: IS THERE A DIFFERENCE IN LIQUOR PRICES BETWEEN STATE-RUN AND PRIVATELY RUN SYSTEMS? (TESTING FOR DIFFERENCES BETWEEN MEANS OF UNEQUAL-SIZED SAMPLES OF MEASURED DATA)

The pig-ration example dealt with equal numbers of pigs in each litter. The general technique demonstrated in Example 11 is quite flexible, however, and can be used with unequal-sized samples. Consider the 1961 data for the price of a fifth of Seagram 7 Crown whisky in the various states. (Some

(1)	Mean of First Twelve Observations (First Hand) (2)	Mean of Second Twelve Observations (Second Hand) (3)	Difference (4) = (2 − 3)	Greater or Less Than Observed Absolute Difference
26	359 ÷ 12 = 29.92	366 ÷ 12 = 30.50	−.58	''
27	362 ÷ 12 = 30.17	363 ÷ 12 = 30.25	−.08	''
28	362 ÷ 12 = 30.17	363 ÷ 12 = 30.25	−.08	''
29	373 ÷ 12 = 31.08	352 ÷ 12 = 29.33	1.75	''
30	367 ÷ 12 = 30.58	358 ÷ 12 = 29.83	.75	''
31	376 ÷ 12 = 31.33	349 ÷ 12 = 29.08	2.25	''
32	365 ÷ 12 = 30.42	360 ÷ 12 = 30.00	.42	''
33	357 ÷ 12 = 29.75	368 ÷ 12 = 30.67	−1.42	''
34	349 ÷ 12 = 29.08	376 ÷ 12 = 31.33	2.25	''
35	356 ÷ 12 = 29.67	369 ÷ 12 = 30.75	−1.08	''
36	359 ÷ 12 = 29.92	366 ÷ 12 = 30.50	−.58	''
37	372 ÷ 12 = 31.00	353 ÷ 12 = 29.42	1.58	''
38	368 ÷ 12 = 30.67	357 ÷ 12 = 29.75	.92	''
39	344 ÷ 12 = 28.67	381 ÷ 12 = 31.75	−3.08	More
40	365 ÷ 12 = 30.42	360 ÷ 12 = 30.00	.42	Less
41	375 ÷ 12 = 31.25	350 ÷ 12 = 29.17	2.08	''
42	353 ÷ 12 = 29.42	372 ÷ 12 = 31.00	−1.58	''
43	357 ÷ 12 = 29.75	368 ÷ 12 = 30.67	−.92	''
44	363 ÷ 12 = 30.25	362 ÷ 12 = 30.17	.08	''
45	353 ÷ 12 = 29.42	372 ÷ 12 = 31.00	−1.58	''
46	354 ÷ 12 = 29.50	371 ÷ 12 = 30.92	−1.42	''
47	353 ÷ 12 = 29.42	372 ÷ 12 = 31.00	−1.58	''
48	366 ÷ 12 = 30.50	359 ÷ 12 = 29.92	.58	''
49	364 ÷ 12 = 30.33	361 ÷ 12 = 30.08	.25	''
50	370 ÷ 12 = 30.83	355 ÷ 12 = 29.58	1.25	''

states are omitted for technical reasons.) The question is whether the price is systematically different in the sixteen "monopoly" states in which the state government owns the retail liquor stores, compared to the twenty-seven states in which retail liquor stores are privately owned, or whether the observed differences might have occurred by chance. The prices for the sixteen monopoly states are $4.65, $4.55, $4.11, $4.15, $4.20, $4.55, $3.80, $4.00, $4.19, $4.75, $4.74, $4.50, $4.10, $4.00, $5.05, and $4.20.

The prices for the private-enterprise states are $4.82, $5.29, $4.89, $4.95, $4.55, $4.90, $5.25, $5.30, $4.29, $4.85, $4.54, $4.75, $4.85, $4.85, $4.50, $4.75, $4.79, $4.85, $4.79, $4.95, $4.95, $4.75, $5.20, $5.10, $4.80, and $4.29.[2] Now

2. The data are from *The Liquor Handbook* (1962, p. 68). Eight states are omitted for various reasons.

write each of the *forty-two* prices on a separate card, to constitute the benchmark universe. The logic is the same as in Example 11: If the two samples do come from the same universe, then our best guess about the contents of that universe are the observations we have from it; the fact that the samples are of unequal size in this case makes no difference, if in fact they are from the same universe. From this universe we repeatedly deal out sixteen cards. The probability that monopoly states' prices are "really" lower than those of the private-enterprise states is estimated by the proportion of times that the sum (or average) of the sixteen prices dealt is less than (or equal to) the sum (or average) of the actual sixteen prices.

The steps:

Step 1. Write each of the 42 prices on a separate card.

Step 2. Deal out groups of 16 and 26 cards. Calculate the mean price of each group.

Step 3. Calculate the difference between the groups in Step 2, and compare the experimental-trial difference to the observed mean difference of $4.84 − $4.35 = $.49; if it is as great or greater, write *yes,* otherwise *no.*

Step 4. Repeat Steps 2 and 3 a hundred times.

Step 5. Calculate the proportion of *yes,* which estimates the probability we seek.[3]

This is another example of a Monte Carlo test used in a situation in which a *t* test is conventionally done.

---

3. Various tests indicate that the difference between the groups of states is highly significant. See J. Simon (1966b).

30 correlation and other statistical issues

1. Correlation and Association

The questions in the previous examples have been stated in the following form: Does the independent variable (irradiation; type of pig ration) have an effect upon the dependent variable (sex of fruit flies; weight gain of pigs)? Another way to state this question, however, is: Is there a *causal relationship* between the independent variable(s) and the dependent variable?

A causal relationship cannot be defined perfectly neatly, as discussed in Chapter 32. Even an experiment does not determine perfectly whether a relationship deserves to be called "causal" because, among other reasons, the independent variable may not be clear-cut; for example, even if cigarette smoking experimentally produces cancer in rats, it might be the paper and not the tobacco that causes the cancer.

It is clear, however, that in any situation where we are interested in the possibility of causation, we must *at least* know whether there is a relationship (correlation) between the variables of interest; the existence of a relationship is necessary for that relationship to be judged causal even if it is not sufficient to receive the causal label. And in other situations where we are not even interested in causality, but rather simply want to predict events or understand the structure of a system, we may be interested in the existence of relationships quite apart from questions about causation. Therefore, our next set of problems deals with the likelihood of there being a relationship between two measured variables—variables that can take on many values (say, the values on a test of athletic scores) rather than just two values (say, whether there has been irradiation).

Another way to think about such problems is to ask whether two variables are independent of each other—that is, whether you know anything about the value of one variable if you know.the value of the other in a particular case—or whether they are not independent but rather are related.

a. EXAMPLE 13: IS ATHLETIC ABILITY DIRECTLY RELATED TO INTELLIGENCE? (IS THERE CORRELATION BETWEEN TWO VARIABLES OR ARE THEY INDEPENDENT?)

A scientist often wants to know whether two characteristics go together; that is, whether they are correlated (related or associated). For example, is athletic ability correlated with high I.Q.? That is, do youths with high athletic ability tend also to have high I.Q.s?

Physical-education scores of a group of ten high-school boys are shown, ordered from high to low, in Table 30.1, along with the I.Q. score for each boy. The ranks for each student's athletic and I.Q. scores are then shown in columns 3 and 4.

We want to know whether a high score on athletic ability tends to be found along with a high I.Q. score more often than would be expected by chance. Therefore, our strategy is to see how often high scores on both variables are found by chance. We do this by dissociating the two variables and making two separate and independent universes, one composed of the athletic scores and another of the I.Q. scores. Then by drawing pairs of observations from the two universes at random, we can consider the experi-

TABLE 30.1 Hypothetical Athletic and I.Q. Scores for High-School Boys

Athletic Score (1)	I.Q. Score (2)	Athletic Rank (3)	I.Q. Rank (4)
97	114	1	3
94	120	2	1
93	107	3	7
90	113	4	4
87	118	5	2
86	101	6	8
86	109	7	6
85	110	8	5
81	100	9	9
76	99	10	10

mental patterns to occur by chance, and can compare them to what actually occurs in the world.

The first testing scheme we shall use is similar to our first approach to the pig rations—splitting the results into just highs and lows. We take ten cards, one of each denomination from ace to ten, shuffle, and deal five cards to correspond to the first five athletic ranks. The face values then correspond to the I.Q. ranks. Under the benchmark hypothesis the athletic ranks will not be associated with the I.Q. ranks. Add the face values in the first five cards in each trial; the first hand includes 2, 4, 5, 6, and 9, so the sum is 26. Record, shuffle, and repeat perhaps ten times, as in Table 30.2.

Then compare the random results to the sum of the observed ranks of the five top athletes, which equals 17.

The following steps describe a slightly different procedure from that just described, because this one may be easier to understand:

Step 1. Convert the athletic and I.Q. scores to ranks. Then constitute a universe of spades, ace to 10, to correspond to the athletic ranks, and a universe of hearts, ace to ten, to correspond to the I.Q. ranks.

Step 2. Deal the well-shuffled cards into pairs, each pair with an athletic rank and an I.Q. rank.

Step 3. Locate the cards with the top five athletic ranks, and add the I.Q. rank scores on their paired cards. Compare this sum to the observed sum of 17. If 17 or less, indicate *yes*, otherwise *no*. (Why do we use "17 or less" rather than "less than 17"? Because we are asking the likelihood of a score *this low or lower*.)

Step 4. Repeat Steps 2 and 3 forty times.

Step 5. Calculate the proportion of *yes*. This estimates the probability sought.

TABLE 30.2

Observed score: 17

Trial	Sum of I.Q. Ranks	Yes or No	Trial	Sum of I.Q. Ranks	Yes or No	Trial	Sum of I.Q. Ranks	Yes or No	Trial	Sum of I.Q. Ranks	Yes or No
1	26	No	11	35	No	21	30	No	31	30	No
2	23	No	12	36	No	22	31	No	32	21	No
3	22	No	13	31	No	23	35	No	33	25	No
4	37	No	14	29	No	24	25	No	34	19	No
*5	16	Yes	15	32	No	25	33	No	35	29	No
6	22	No	16	25	No	26	30	No	36	23	No
7	22	No	17	25	No	27	24	No	37	23	No
8	28	No	18	29	No	28	29	No	38	34	No
9	38	No	19	25	No	29	30	No	40	26	No
10	22	No	20	22	No	30	31	No	39	23	No

In Table 30.2 we see that the observed sum is lower than that in all but one (trial 5) of the ten random trials, which suggests that there is a good chance (9 to 1) that the five best athletes will not have I.Q. scores that high by chance. But it might be well to deal some more to get a more reliable average. We add thirty hands, and thirty-nine of the total forty hands exceed the observed rank value, so the likelihood that the observed correlation of athletic and I.Q. scores would occur by chance is about 2.5 per cent. In other words, the odds are 39 to 1 against there being no association between athletic ability and I.Q. score, and it therefore seems reasonable to believe that high athletic ability tends to accompany a high I.Q.

Some explanation is required for the procedure of adding ranks for the first *five* athletes and comparing them with the second five, rather than comparing the top three, say, with the bottom seven. We could indeed have compared the top three, two, four, or one with the rest. The first reason for splitting the group in half is that an even split provides fuller information and therefore greater efficiency. (I cannot prove this to you, but perhaps it makes intuitive sense.) A second reason is that getting into the habit of looking at an even split reduces the chances that you will pick and choose in such a manner as to fool yourself. For example, if the I.Q. ranks of the top five athletes were 3, 2, 1, 10, and 9, we would be kidding ourselves if, after looking the data over, we drew the line between athletes 3 and 4.

A simpler but less efficient approach to this same problem is to classify the top-half athletes by whether they were also in the top half of the I.Q. scores. (Of the first five athletes actually observed, *four* were in the top five I.Q. scores.) Then shuffle five black and five red cards and see how often four or more (that is, four or five) blacks come up with the first five cards. The proportion of times that four or more blacks occurs in the experiment is the likelihood that the observed scores come from the same universe—that is, the likelihood that there is no association between the two characteristics. Table 30.3 shows a proportion of five *yes* out of twenty trials, yielding a much weaker result than did the previous method.

We have proceeded on the theory that, if there is *any* relationship between athletics and I.Q., then the better athletes have higher rather than lower I.Q. scores. The justification for this assumption is that past research

TABLE 30.3

Observed score: 4

Trial	Score	Yes or No	Trial	Score	Yes or No	Trial	Score	Yes or No	Trial	Score	Yes or No
1	4	Yes	6	2	No	11	3	No	16	3	No
2	2	No	7	4	Yes	12	1	No	17	2	No
3	2	No	8	3	No	13	3	No	18	2	No
4	2	No	9	3	No	14	3	No	19	2	No
5	3	No	10	4	Yes	15	4	Yes	20	4	Yes

suggests that it is probably true. But, if we had *not* had the benefit of that past research, we would then have had to proceed somewhat differently; we would have had to consider the possibility that the top five athletes could have I.Q. scores either higher *or* lower than those of the other students. The results of the "two-tail" test would have yielded weaker odds than those we observed.

b. EXAMPLE 14:

Example 13 investigated the relationship between I.Q. and athletic scores by ranking the two sets of scores. But ranking of scores loses some efficiency because it uses only an "ordinal," rather than a "cardinal," scale; the numerical shadings and relative relationships are lost when we convert to ranks. Therefore, it is worth considering a test of correlation that uses the original cardinal numerical scores.

First a little background: Figures 30.1 and 30.2 show two hypothetical cases of very high association among the I.Q. and athletic scores used in previous examples.

FIGURE 30.1 **Hypothetical Data for a Group of Boys**

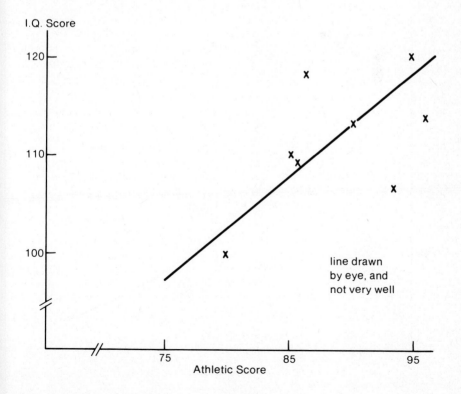

Figure 30.1 indicates that the higher the I.Q. score, the higher the athletic score. Knowing a boy's athletic score, you can thus predict quite well his I.Q. score by means of the hand-drawn line—or vice versa. The same is true of Figure 30.2, but in the opposite way. (Notice that, even though athletic score is on the x axis (horizontal) and I.Q. score is on the y axis (vertical), the athletic score does not cause the I.Q. score. It is an unfortunate deficiency of such diagrams that *some* variable must arbitrarily be placed on the x axis, whether or not you intend to suggest causation.)

In Figure 30.3, which plots the scores as given in Table 30.1, the prediction of athletic score given I.Q. score, or vice versa, is less clear-cut than in Figure 30.2. On the basis of Figure 30.3 alone, one can say only that there *might* be some association between the two variables.

Now we can use a handy property of numbers. Consider the cases in Table 30.4, in which there is a perfect (linear) association between x (Column 1) and y_1 (Column 2), and between x and y_2 (Column 4); the numbers shown in Columns 3 and 5 are those that would be consistent with perfect associations. Notice the sum of the multiples of the x and y values. It is higher (xy_1) and lower (xy_2) than for any other possible way of arrang-

FIGURE 30.2   **Hypothetical Data for a Group of Boys**

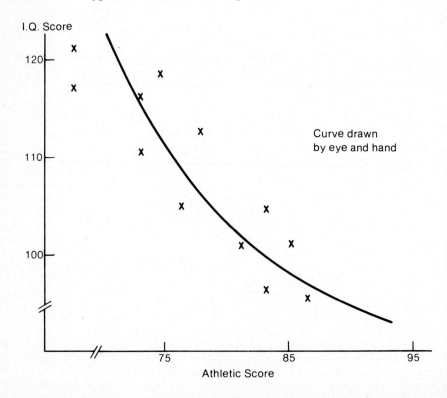

FIGURE 30.3   **Hypothetical Data for a Class**

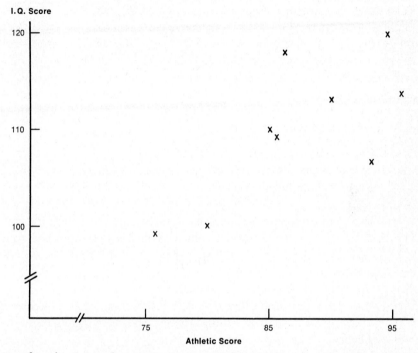

ing the y's. Any other arrangement of the y's (y_3, for example, chosen at random), when multiplied by the x's (for example, xy_3), produces a sum that falls somewhere between the sums of xy_1 and xy_2, as is the case when y_3 is also less correlated with the x's. Column 7 in Table 30.4 shows how the sum of the products of another less-regular set of I.Q. scores multiplied by athletic scores (Column 7) is *between* the sums that would occur if the I.Q. scores were ranked from best to worst (Column 3) and worst to best (Column 5). The extent of correlation (association) can thus be measured by whether the sum of the multiples of the observed x and y values is relatively high or low compared to random sums.

TABLE 30.4

1	2	3	4	5	6	7
x	y_1	xy_1	y_2	xy_2	y_3	xy_3
2	2	4	10	20	4	8
4	4	16	8	32	8	32
6	6	36	6	36	6	36
8	8	64	4	32	2	16
10	10	100	2	20	10	100
		220		140		192

Now we attack the I.Q.–athletic-score problem in a different fashion. First multiply the x and y values of the observations, and sum them (95,759) as in Table 30.5. Then write the ten I.Q. scores on cards, and assign the cards in random order to the ten athletes, as shown in Column 1 in Table 30.6. Multiply by the x's, and sum. If the I.Q. scores and athletic scores are *positively* associated—that is, if high I.Q.s and high athletic scores go together—then the sum of the multiplications for the observed sample will be higher than for most of the random trials. (If high I.Q.s go with low athletic scores, the sum of the multiplications for the observed sample will be *lower* than for most of the random trials.)

Step 1. Write the ten I.Q. scores on one set of cards, and the ten athletic scores on another set of cards.

Step 2. Pair the I.Q.- and athletic-score cards at random. Multiply the scores in each pair, and add the results of the ten multiplications.

Step 3. Compare the experimental sum in Step 2 to the observed sum, 95,759. If the experimental sum is as large or larger, record *yes,* otherwise *no.*

Step 4. Repeat Steps 2 and 3 twenty times.

Step 5. Compute the proportion of *yes,* which estimates the likelihood that an association as strong as that observed would occur by chance.

The sums of the multiplications for 20 trials are shown in Table 30.7. No random-trial sum was as high as the observed sum, which suggests that the probability of an association this strong happening by chance is very low,

TABLE 30.5

1 Athletic Score	2 I.Q. Score	3 Column 1 × Column 2	4 I.Q. Score	5 Column 1 × Column 4	6 Actual I.Q.	7 Column 1 × Column 6
97	120	11640	99	9603	114	11058
94	118	11092	100	9400	120	11280
93	114	10602	101	9393	107	9951
90	113	10170	107	9630	113	10170
87	110	9570	109	9483	118	10266
86	109	9374	110	8460	101	8686
86	107	9202	113	9718	109	9374
85	101	8585	114	9690	110	9350
81	100	8100	118	9558	100	8100
76	99	7524	120	9120	99	7524
		95859		95055		95759

TABLE 30.6

Athletic Score	1	2	3	4	5	6	7	8	9	10
97	114	109	110	118	107	114	107	120	100	114
94	101	113	113	101	118	100	110	109	120	107
93	107	118	100	99	120	101	114	99	110	113
90	113	101	118	114	101	113	100	118	99	99
87	120	100	101	100	110	107	113	114	101	118
86	100	110	120	107	113	110	118	101	118	101
86	110	107	99	109	100	120	120	113	114	120
85	99	99	104	120	99	109	101	107	109	109
81	118	120	114	110	114	99	99	100	107	100
76	109	114	109	113	109	118	109	110	113	110

Athletic Score	11	12	13	14	15	16	17	18	19	20
97	109	113	101	109	107	100	99	113	99	110
94	101	110	114	118	101	107	114	101	109	113
93	120	120	100	120	114	113	100	100	120	109
90	110	118	109	110	99	109	107	109	110	99
87	100	100	120	99	118	114	110	110	107	101
86	118	99	107	100	109	118	113	118	100	118
86	99	101	99	101	100	99	101	107	114	120
85	107	114	110	114	120	110	120	120	118	100
81	114	107	113	113	110	101	109	114	101	114
76	113	109	118	107	113	120	118	99	113	107

approaching zero (an empirically observed probability is never actually zero).

C. EXAMPLE 15: IS THERE A RELATIONSHIP BETWEEN DRINKING BEER AND BEING IN FAVOR OF SELLING BEER? (TESTING FOR A RELATIONSHIP BETWEEN COUNTED-DATA VARIABLES)

The scores for athletic ability and I.Q. were measured data. Therefore, we could use them in their original "cardinal" form or split them into "high" and "low" groups.

TABLE 30.7

Trial	Sum of Multiplications	Trial	Sum of Multiplications
1	95430	11	95406
2	95426	12	95622
3	95446	13	95250
4	95381	14	95599
5	95542	15	95323
6	95362	16	95308
7	95508	17	95220
8	95590	18	95443
9	95379	19	95421
10	95532	20	95528

Often, however, the individual observations are recorded only as *yes* or *no*, which makes it more difficult to ascertain the existence of a relationship. Consider these answers to two public-opinion survey questions: "Do you drink beer?" and "Are you in favor of local option on the sale of beer?"[1]

Here is the question: Is a person's opinion on local option related to whether he drinks beer? There are seventy-eight respondents, fifty-seven of whom approve local option and twenty-one of whom do not. Therefore, write *approve* on fifty-seven index cards and *disapprove* on twenty-one index cards. Now take *another* set of seventy-eight index cards, preferably of a different color, and write *yes* on fifty-two of them and *no* on twenty-six of them, corresponding to the numbers of people who do and do not drink beer in the sample. Now lay them down in random *pairs*, one from each pile.

If there is a high association between the variables, the observations will bunch up in the two diagonal cells on either diagonal. Therefore, subtract one sum of two diagonal cells from the other sum for the observed case: $(37 + 6) - (20 + 15) = 8$. Compare this difference to those found in random trials. The proportion of times that the trial differences do not exceed the observed difference is the probability that the observed association is not caused by chance. (Notice that, in this case, we are working on the assumption that beer drinking is *positively* associated with approval of local option and not the inverse. We are interested only in differences that are equal to or exceed $+8$ when the northeast-southwest diagonal is subtracted from the northwest-southeast diagonal.)

Step 1. Write *approve* and *disapprove* on 57 and 21 red index cards, respectively; write *drink* and *don't drink* on 52 and 26 white cards, respectively.

Step 2. Pair the cards randomly, and count the numbers of the four possible pairs: *approve-drink, disapprove-don't drink, disapprove-drink,* and *approve-don't drink.* Record the number of these combinations, as in Table 30.9, where columns 1–4 correspond to the four cells in Table 30.8.

Step 3. Add Column 1 plus Column 4. From this figure, subtract the sum of Column 2 plus Column 3. If the difference is equal to or greater than 8, record *yes*, otherwise *no*.

Step 4. Repeat Steps 2 and 3 perhaps a hundred times.

Step 5. Calculate the proportion of *yes*, which estimates the likelihood that an association this great or greater would be observed by chance.

1. These data are from an example in W. Dixon and F. Massey (p. 242), in which the problem is tackled with a conventional test (the chi-square).

TABLE 30.8

Are You in Favor of Local Option on the Sale of Beer?	Do You Drink Beer?		
	Yes	No	Total
Approve	37	20	57
Disapprove	15	6	21
Total	52	26	78

A series of ten trials in this case (see Table 30.9) indicates that the observed difference is very often exceeded, which suggests no relationship between beer drinking and opinion.

Though the test just described may generally be appropriate for data of this sort, a second thought casts doubt about whether it is appropriate in this case. Even if the test showed that an association existed, would we believe the test result to be meaningful? I think not. In Table 30.10 we see that nonbeer drinkers have a *higher* rate of approval of allowing beer drinking, which does not accord with experience or reason. Hence, without additional explanation we would not believe that a meaningful relationship exists among these variables even if the test showed one to exist. (Still another reason to doubt that a relationship exists is that the absolute differences are too small—there is only a 6 per cent difference in disapproval between *drink* and *don't drink* groups—to mean anything to anyone. On both grounds, then, it makes sense simply to act as if there were no difference between the two groups and to run *no test*).

The lesson to be learned from this is that one should inspect the data carefully before applying a statistical test, and only test for "significance" if the apparent relationships accord with theory and general understanding.

TABLE 30.9

Trial	Approve Yes (1)	Approve No (2)	Disapprove Yes (3)	Disapprove No (4)	(Column 1 + Column 4) − (Column 2 + Column 3)* (5)
1	33	24	18	3	$36 - 42 = -6$
2	38	19	14	7	$45 - 33 = 12$
3	39	18	13	8	$47 - 31 = 16$
4	38	19	14	7	$45 - 33 = 12$
5	35	22	17	4	$39 - 39 = 0$
6	35	22	16	5	$40 - 38 = 2$
7	38	19	14	7	$45 - 33 = 12$
8	40	19	12	9	$49 - 31 = 18$
9	40	17	12	9	$49 - 29 = 20$
10	37	20	15	6	$43 - 35 = 8$

* In absolute figures.

TABLE 30.10

	Percentage Approve	Percentage Disapprove	Total
Beer drinkers	71%	29%	100%
Nonbeer drinkers	77%	23%	100%

2. Advantages and Disadvantages of the Monte Carlo Method

With card and dice experiments one can make many statistical tests without the mathematical theory of probability. But figuring the answer analytically is often *quicker*, especially for problems with many observations. For example, imagine that you want to know how often you will get two aces if you deal out hands of only two cards. A random experiment would take a while, but one can figure the answer in a hurry by multiplying $\frac{1}{13} \times \frac{1}{13} = \frac{1}{269}$, which tells us that, on the average, we shall get two aces in a hand of two cards once in 269 hands.

Mathematical methods can also be useful in more complex problems, though there are many problems that are *so* complex that mathematicians resort to random experiments for estimating the probabilities, using computers rather than cards or dice to run the experiments in a hurry.

Mathematical methods make handling cardinal quantitative data easy. But, as we demonstrated in the pig-ration example, sometimes card and dice experiments can also be run with quantitative data, without assuming as much as is necessary for the use of mathematical methods.

Though analytical methods may get an answer quicker than the Monte Carlo method, a person who does not expect to use probability statistics very often might find that, in the long run, it is more efficient to spend extra time on slow Monte Carlo trials than on studying the mathematical methods. On the other hand, anyone who plans to work in scientific research should eventually study probability statistics, especially because that study deepens one's *intuition* about scientific and mathematical relationships.

A major advantage of the Monte Carlo method is that everything that you do is very explicit and you must think through each step. Such discipline reduces the probability of erroneous calculations from blindly plugging in the wrong method and formula.

It is an apparent disadvantage of the Monte Carlo method executed by hand that large sample sizes are clumsy to work with, as are very small probabilities; for example, it is difficult to work with data on the viewership of educational television stations because the probability of a given person watching may be only 1 in 1,000. But testing problems arise only when the samples are small; with large masses of data the conclusions are obvious without probability statistics. Furthermore, computers can easily be programmed to handle Monte Carlo methods.

One can avoid the tedious work of Monte Carlo experiments by getting the help of a statistician who will use mathematical methods. But—and it is a huge "but"—to be sure that the answer the statistician gives you is the answer you want, you must describe the Monte Carlo trial you would otherwise run to test your results. Then and only then can you be sure that the mathematical test the statistician performs is the right one. If you simply go to her and say, "I want to test whether these two samples are different," you are much more likely to get a misleading answer than if you describe to her a Monte Carlo experiment and then ask her merely to perform the same task with mathematical analysis.

If you can say exactly what kind of Monte Carlo trial will give the test you want, you have performed 90 per cent of the work—and the hardest 90 per cent. It takes very hard, very clear thinking. Again, the job is *not* mathematical; if you tell yourself that you cannot do these and similar probability-statistical tests because you do not understand mathematics, you are fooling yourself. If you cannot do correct tests of the type described in this chapter, it is because you are not willing to think hard and clearly. And you cannot shift the burden to a statistician, because then *he* will have to do the hard, clear thinking for you, and he does not know what your study needs as well as you do. Furthermore, mathematical statisticians develop formulas to imitate the Monte Carlo trials you want to run, but they have no special training in deciding which Monte Carlo trials to perform. To repeat, that is the hard, clear thinking that you must do for yourself.

3. The Multiplication Rule

You should be familiar with two basic calculations in mathematical statistics, and you should know when they are applicable. The first calculation is the *rule of addition*. It states that, when two events are mutually exclusive, the probability of one event *or* the other event (*or* both) is the *sum* of the probabilities of each event happening alone. For example, the probability of drawing a spade is $1/4$, and the probability of a heart is $1/4$, and both cannot occur in the draw of one card. The probability of drawing *either* a spade *or* a heart is $1/4 + 1/4 = 1/2$. Remember that the rule of addition should be used whenever you use the words "either . . . or (or both)" in the question.

The *multiplication rule* is the most important handy calculation in everyday statistical work. It is used whenever the question is, What is the probability that A *and* B will happen? For example, the probability of having a daughter the first time *and* a daughter the second time is $1/2 \times 1/2 = 1/4$ (on the assumption that the sex of each newborn child is independent of that of the preceding ones). The probability of having four daughters in a row is $1/2 \times 1/2 \times 1/2 \times 1/2 = 1/16$, as we approximated earlier with card shuffling. If you want a more precise estimate using the data that 106 males are born for each 100 females, the appropriate calculation would be $(100/206) \times (100/206) \times (100/206) \times (100/206)$. The multiplication rule is very handy for quick estimates of whether data result from chance. For example, if you compare the advertising effectiveness of large versus small firms in five separate years and if the small firms do better in each of the five years, the probability that this performance results from chance is $(\frac{1}{2})^5 = \frac{1}{2} \times \frac{1}{2} \times \frac{1}{2} \times \frac{1}{2} \times \frac{1}{2} = \frac{1}{32}$ (if you hypothesized that small firms do better). (If the data show that the smaller firms do better in seven years out of eight, however, you will need a more complicated calculation than the multiplication rule, and you had best use a Monte Carlo method.)

Another example: If the chance of my wife getting a job at a given university is .2, and my chance of getting a job at the same university is .15, then the chance of *both* of us getting jobs at that university is .2 $\times$ .15 = .03.

4. Evaluating the Significance of "Dredged-Up" Relationships

In all the previous examples of hypothesis-testing statistics, we have assumed that the researcher had a specific hypothesis before examining the raw data and making the test. But there are other types of analysis, like secondary analysis, in which the researcher searches through the raw data in hopes of "dredging up" some relationships. Dredged-up relationships must *not* be tested with the probability apparatus described earlier in this chapter.

There are two ways to go astray in searching through raw data. The first is to seize upon the extreme observation of a *large* randomly generated sample distribution and to consider it unusual when in reality it is to be expected sometime. An example is the birth of ten daughters in a row. When you wonder whether it reveals something biological about a particular family, keep in mind that a pattern of ten girls in a row is no more and no less rare than a pattern of boy-girl-boy-girl-boy-girl-boy-girl-boy-girl. The second way to go astray results from the *smallness* of the sample rather than from its largeness: finding specious patterns that exist simply because *some* patterns must apparently occur. An example is bettors' finding patterns in a series of horse races. We shall take up these two fallacies in order.

a. "UNUSUAL" OCCURRENCES IN LARGE SAMPLES

If you are the dealer in a game of bridge and you deal yourself the ace, two, and three of spades; the four, five, and six of diamonds; the seven, eight, and nine of hearts; and the ten, jack, queen, and king of clubs, you probably will not think much of it. Now, will you think that there is a *pattern* (that is, a nonrandom deal) if you get thirteen spades? You will not think so if you yourself are dealing, because you will know that you did not cheat. But if *someone else* deals thirteen spades to himself, you may be suspicious and think the deal is a nonrandom (that is, cheating) deal. The point is that whether you think there is a pattern depends on more than the observed data; it also depends on what else you know—in this case, that you dealt and did not rig the cards.

To push the example further, remember that the first bridge hand we described did not surprise you much. But, if one of the players had *predicted* that you would get exactly that hand, you would be very surprised indeed. You would think that the hand was nonrandom and that the other person had either fixed the cards or was possessed of extrasensory perception. Again, your surprise depends on what you knew in advance—in this case, that your friend had predicted the exact hand.

Here is another example of the same sort:

. . . On 16 May 1965, reading the San Francisco *Sunday Chronicle* I noticed an article on page 22 entitled "Ancient Men on the Nile." In scanning this story, I saw the phrase ". . . the expert appraisal of Philadelphia anthropologist Dr. Carleton S. Coon." To anyone who had been an undergraduate student at the University of Chicago in the early 1930s, this unusual name would call up nostalgic memories of another Carleton Coon and his partner, Joe Sanders, whose popular Coon-Sanders dance band was then playing at the Blackhawk. So I found myself thinking about Joe Sanders, very probably for the first time in 30 years.

Less than five minutes later, having turned the pages of the paper to page 33, I saw an obituary notice headed "Joe Sanders." It read, ". . . died Friday. . . . [W]ith the late Carleton Coon . . . organized the Coon-Sanders band." These two closely spaced recollections of a person forgotten for 30 years, with the second event involving a death notice, is in the classical pattern; but it is obvious that no causal relationship could have existed between the two events.

The probability of a coincidental recollection of a known person in a 5-minute period just before learning of that person's death can easily be calculated, to within a factor of 10. Let us take a 30-year period, and assume that an average person would recognize the names of 3000 different people who might die in that period of time. . . . We assume that our subject will learn of the death of each of these persons at some time in the 30 years. If we restrict our attention to the time when our subject learns of the death of a particular person, we can then ask how probable it is, that in the 5 minutes just preceding that exact time of learning of the death, an unrelated recollection that is unique to the 30-year period will occur. This probability, to within a factor of 2, is the ratio of a 5-minute interval to a 30-year interval, or 3×10^{-7} [$\frac{3}{10}$ million]. (It is clear that if one thinks of the particular person once a year rather than once every 30 years, the probability will rise by a factor of 30, to about 10^{-5} [1/100,-000].) The probability that one will have such an experience when learning of the death of any one of the 3000 recognizable persons is clearly 10^{-3} [1/1000] in a 30-year period, or approximately 3×10^{-5} per year. If we take the sample of 10^8 [100 million] adults in the United States, 3×10^3 [3000] experiences of the sort related above should occur per year, or about 10 per day. . . . With such a large sample to draw from, it is not surprising that some exceedingly astonishing

TABLE 30.11

	Psychological Characteristic I		Psychological Characteristic II		Psychological Characteristic III	
Brand of Men's	%		%		%	
Suit Purchased	High	Low	High	Low	High	Low
A (26 buyers)	38(10)	62(16)	35(9)	65(17)	50(13)	50(13)
B (21 buyers)	38(8)	62(13)	71(15)	29(6)	57(13)	43(9)
C (7 buyers)	43(3)	57(4)	43(3)	57(4)	43(3)	57(4)
D (14 buyers)	43(6)	57(8)	43(6)	57(8)	28(4)	72(10)
E (19 buyers)	37(7)	63(12)	47(7)	53(10)	47(9)	53(10)
F (27 buyers)	48(13)	52(14)	52(14)	48(13)	41(11)	59(16)
Don't know (15 buyers)	27(4)	73(11)	20(3)	80(12)	47(7)	53(8)

coincidences are reported in the parapsychological literature as proof of extra-sensory perception in one form or another. (Alvarez, p. 1541)

Still another example of the attribution of meaning to far-out observations occurs on the stock market from time to time. *Someone* must be lucky in a series of consecutive stock-market transactions, just by chance. When it happens, the fellow who hits it right by chance a large number of times assumes that the good results result from his *knowledge* and his method of stock analysis. Thereupon, he writes a book called *How I Made My Fortune in Stocks* and makes *another* small fortune in book royalties.

The data in Table 30.11 illustrate this problem as it often appears in social-science research. The investigator collected data on three psychological characteristics of seven groups of people who exhibited different purchasing behavior, hoping to find characteristics that would distinguish the various groups. None of the three characteristics is *consistently* different for all seven groups of people.[2] But the investigator noticed a split of 71 per cent to 29 per cent in favor of the buyers of brand B on characteristic 2. *If* one treats this comparison as if it were the *only* comparison under examination, it appears to be very significant statistically and unlikely to occur by chance. The investigator offered the split as a valid finding from the data.

But there are twenty-one possible comparisons in the table (seven purchasing groups by three characteristics), which means that the likelihood of *one* comparison appearing to be significant is *much* higher than if only one comparison were examined (refer to Example 6 in Chapter 28). The investigator argued that, for *a priori* theoretical reasons, this was the only one of the twenty-one comparisons that he *expected* to be significant, and a confirmation of his expectation would strengthen his case for the finding's significance. But the reader is entitled to be skeptical of such *post facto* discussion, and skepticism is reinforced by the small number of subjects in the comparison—only twenty-one.

2. Statistical tests conducted by the investigator indicate that none of the three characteristics in the seven groups is significant at the .05 level.

To determine whether any meaning should be attached to the apparently unusual event is not easy. At the very least, one should remain alert to such events and explore them, rather than ignoring them; it would be foolish to shrug off a bridge dealer who twice deals himself a perfect hand. "An erroneous rejection of extreme observations profoundly affected the course of history when, shortly after seven o'clock on the morning of December 7, 1941, the officer in charge of a Hawaiian radar station ignored data solely because they seemed so incredible" (Wallis and Roberts, p. 170).

The examination of such "unusual" observations is known as "analysis of deviant cases" (Kendall and Lazarsfeld, p. 167), and it is an important source of scientific knowledge. For two examples, if a country has an unusually low rate of lung cancer or if an individual lives through a plague in which everyone else dies, an investigation of the causes of such an unusual occurrence may be instructive, *or* it may reveal only that the apparent exception is the result of random chance. One should consider the unusual event as a clue that *may* lead to an explanation. And certainly keep your eyes open for a repetition of the event, just as you watch a card dealer whom you suspect.

But pay attention only to those events that have some importance; there is no sense in doing more than exclaiming about a card hand that has a peculiar combination of numbers but no special significance in the game.

A second way of dealing with an unusual event is to calculate just how unusual it really is. That is what L. Alvarez did with his memory of Joe Sanders, and he found that the event was not very unusual, considering all possible opportunities for it to happen in the United States. But, if the same thing had happened to Alvarez three times on successive days, the probability of the sequence's happening to anyone anywhere would be astronomically small, and he would not be likely to reason it away as he did. One could also calculate the probability of observing a split as wide as 15 to 6 for a single comparison among the twenty-one comparisons in Table 30.11. That calculation is rendered muddy, however, by the argument about the theoretical basis for that observation, as well as by the presentation of still other tables and data in the same study.

A third—and most important—way to evaluate unusual dredged-up events is to see if the same thing happens elsewhere. In Illustration A in Chapter 27, North Carolina was seen to have both the biggest stake in tobacco growing *and* the highest rate of doctors' smoking. Assume that one had merely *noticed* this fact, rather than having sought these data to test a hypothesis. This observation *could* be a coincidence. But we can look to see if the same relationship holds elsewhere—as indeed it does for the other major tobacco-economy states—confirming our belief that the observed association for North Carolina is not just a fluke (J. Simon, 1967–1968). And in the study of psychological characteristics and purchasing behavior, the investigator should repeat the test on another sample from the group in question, to see if the same sort of finding appears again, before he places much confidence in the finding.

b. PATTERNS IN SMALL SAMPLES

A second error in data dredging is reading a pattern into too small a sample. This is the error horse-racing fans frequently fall into. They look over the back records of races and find what they think is a pattern—say, that jockey A has been winning *every other race*. They then bet him to win after he loses his next race, and they are surprised when the "pattern" does not continue. Their error lies in not understanding how easy it is to think there is a pattern when there really is none, just as patterns apparently appear with randomly thrown dice or cards or random numbers.

Statistics offer little help in deciding whether a newly discovered pattern really means anything. If there were some way to calculate how many possible patterns might appear, then one might estimate the likelihood that *some* pattern of a particular strength would appear. But the possibilities of the human imagination in generating possible patterns are almost limitless, so even this statistical hope goes aglimmering.

The only safe test is to find the pattern *first* and then to see if it repeats itself in *different data*—data that you have not seen when you found the original pattern. If the pattern does repeat, you can use probability statistics to determine how likely the data would have been to repeat the pattern *had you predicted it in advance on the basis of finding your first pattern*.

Such a procedure points up the importance of theory once again. If you have a general theory about some subject matter, you can deduce specific hypotheses from it and then ask whether the data show the expected pattern. Without the theory your hypothesis will not be very strong, and therefore it will be more difficult to ask and answer a clear-cut question about whether the pattern of the data means anything.

c. NUMERICAL ARTIFACTS

Still another way to go astray in examining data is to discover artifacts—apparently interesting findings *that could not be otherwise*. An example is the children's teaser: "Did you know that exactly the same number of men got married last year as did women?" Sometimes this sort of artifact is not so obvious. Consider the observation that "Even though in the United States there are many fewer women than men with Ph.D. degrees, the data show that there were almost as many women with Ph.D. degrees who married men with Ph.D. degrees as men with such degrees who married women with such degrees." (Think about it!)

The famous "regression fallacy" is an artifact that occasionally slips into the work of even the wisest scientists. The regression fallacy takes its name from F. Galton's observation that the height of the population was "regressing to the mean." That is, Galton thought that the heights of people were becoming more uniform because the sons of the tallest fathers and of the shortest fathers were closer to the average than their fathers had been. What

Galton overlooked was that in each generation sons of *other* fathers are by chance much taller or shorter than are their fathers, so that each generation has equal numbers of very tall and very short people. One can avoid the regression fallacy by considering *all* the members of the universe (or sample) and not simply looking at selected members, for example, the sons of the tallest or shortest fathers.

Economics is often afflicted with the regression fallacy. Consider this conclusion based on the data that follow it:

> . . . [S]ome pretty big variations in advertising-sales ratios between different industries seem to be narrowing. For example, a spread of 0.49% in 1948 between metalworking machinery and equipment, and fabricated structural metal products, had been reduced to 0.32% by 1962. (The metal-working ad-sales ratio declined from 1.03% to 0.91% during the period, while fabricated structural gained from 0.54% to 0.59%.)

> Similarly, the advertising-sales ratios of other industries, such as pulp, paper and paperboard, have moved closer to the levels of other groups . . . the ratios [are] "quickly approaching the level of stability."

Industry	Advertising Expenditures-Sales Ratio	
	1948	*1962*
Primary metals	0.21%	0.39%
Fabricated structural metal products	0.54	0.59
Cutlery, hand tools and general hardware	1.91	3.28
Heating apparatus & plumbers' supplies	1.14	1.06
Miscellaneous fabricated metal products	0.54	0.92
Stone, clay & glass products	0.63	0.78
Construction, mining & material handling machinery and equipment	0.71	0.85
Metalworking machinery & equipment	1.03	0.91
Electrical generating, transmission, distribution & industrial apparatus	1.27	1.51
General industry machinery & equipment	1.02	1.09
Special industry machinery	0.77	0.94
Office, computing & accounting machines	1.25	0.72
Professional, scientific & controlling instruments, photographic & optical goods	1.93	2.15
Industrial organic & inorganic chemicals	0.72	1.24
Pulp, paper & paperboard	0.33	0.87
Converted paper & paperboard boxes	0.87	1.07
Motor freight transportation and warehousing	0.30	0.32

But, viewed in their entirety, the data do *not* show that the advertising ratios are moving together. One measure is the ratio of the range to the median:

$$\frac{1.93 - 0.21}{0.77} = 2.2 \text{ for the year 1948, and}$$

$$\frac{3.28 - 0.32}{0.94} = 3.2 \text{ for the year 1962.}$$

(Another measure of dispersion, the ratio of the standard deviation to the mean, is also higher in 1962 than in 1948.) To conclude that the ratios are "approaching stability" is therefore not reasonable.

I suspect that the regression fallacy is at the roof of many doubtful observations about changes in society over time. Consider, for example, the common observation that people are becoming more conformist with successive generations. (Put aside for now the difficulty of defining and measuring conformity.) Perhaps the writers who make this statement have themselves been nonconformists in their lives. It is likely that their own children are more conformist than they are, as the laws of chance would predict. Therefore, the writers observe a "trend toward conformity." But they are ignoring the nonconformist children that come out of conformist homes, children whom the writers do not see but yet who probably make up a generation that contains as many nonconformists as other generations do.

5. Summary

This and the previous chapter discuss statistical problems of determining whether there is a correlation between variables, and how to determine the strength of relationships, using the Monte Carlo method. Advantages and disadvantages of the Monte Carlo method are compared.

How one may evaluate the significance of relationships that are "dredged up" from a body of data is also discussed.

EXERCISES

1. What would be the probability of having three daughters in a row, if the probability of a girl child were 0.4?

2. You employ ten interviewers to ask people whether they prefer candy bar A to candy bar B. Each interviewer interviews twenty people and the preferences for candy bar A were 10, 14, 4, 16, 7, 3, 2, 15, 14, 5. Are the differences among interviewers those that might be expected by chance, or is there reason to believe that the interviewers differed in what they did?

3. Pick a problem randomly from a set of randomly chosen exercises in any basic statistics book, and solve the problem with Monte Carlo methods.

4. Three merchandising plans were tried out on a random sample of stores. Plan A raised sales by 2, 1, 0, 2, and 1 units in the five stores, respectively. Plan B raised sales by 1, 0, 0, 1, and 0 units in five stores. Plan C raised sales by 2, 0, 0, 0, and 1 units in five stores. What is the probability that plan A is "really" better than plans B and C?

5. What is the probability that four of your first five children will be daughters, assuming that you will have five children? What is the probability that you will have either four boys or five girls among your first five children?

6. What are the odds that three or more cards of any one suit (for instance, spades) will appear in a five-card poker hand from a well-shuffled deck? Give a numerical answer, as well as showing the steps by which you got the answer.

7. John tells you that with his old method of shooting foul shots in basketball his average (over a long period of time) was .6. Then he tried a new method of shooting and scored successes with nine of his first ten shots. Should he conclude that the new method is really better than the old method?

8. "If six fair coins are tossed, what is the probability that exactly three of them turn up heads?" (Adler, 1963, p. 92)

9. A football team played nine games during last season. It won the first, lost the next three, and then won the last five. A sportswriter concluded that the team had improved during the season. Is that a good conclusion? Or is there a good chance that the team had the same six in nine chance of winning each game throughout the season? (This is a very tricky problem to set up.)

10. "If seven accidents occur at random on a highway during one week, what is the probability that one occurs each day of the week?" (Adler, 1963, p. 92)

11. Two different diets were tested on a randomly selected group of overweight people. The weight losses in pounds were:

Diet A   0 5 10 9 6 4 1 3 8 7 3 4
Diet B   4 6 4 1 1 3 2 8 5 9 1 2

Judge whether diet A is better for losing weight than diet B is. Outline a procedure, discuss the logic of your procedure, and estimate.

12. Each of ten people secretly chooses a number between 1 and 100. What is the probability that at least two of them will choose the same number? State a procedure and an estimate.

13. What are the odds that two cards of the same denomination will appear in a five-card poker hand from a well-shuffled deck?

14. "On the average, how many times must a die be thrown before it comes up 6?" (Mosteller, 1965, p. 1)

15. There are ten boys in a grammar-school class, three black and seven white. In a foot race the order of finishing is, from first to last (B = black,

W = white), BWBWBWWWWW. Should one say that black boys are faster afoot than white boys are?

16. If I sent the manuscript of this book to five publishers chosen more or less randomly and if all five rejected it for publication, what would be a sensible probability that a sixth publisher (chosen in the same way) would accept it? (Hint: A sensible solution requires that you assume some additional information. This is what Mosteller calls a "problem without structure.")

17. You show me a jar that only you know has 4,322 stones in it, and you ask me to guess the number of stones. Estimate the probability that I shall guess correctly. (This is another problem without structure.)

ADDITIONAL READING FOR CHAPTER 30

You may read more about "data-dredging" procedures in survey analysis in the article by Selvin and Stuart.

31 how big a sample?

Sometime in the course of almost every study—preferably early in the planning stage—the researcher must decide how big a sample to take. Deciding the size of sample to take is likely to puzzle and distress you at the beginning of your research career. You have to decide somehow, but there are no simple, obvious guides for the decision.

For example, one of the first studies I worked on was a study of library economics (Fussler and Simon), which required taking a sample of the books from the library's collections. Sampling was expensive, and we wanted to take a "correct" sized sample. But how large should the sample be? The longer we searched the literature, and the more people we asked, the more frustrated we got because there just did not seem to be a clear-cut answer. Eventually we found out that, even though there are some fairly rational ways of fixing the sample size, most sample sizes in most studies are fixed simply (and irrationally) by the amount of money that is available or by the sample size that similar pieces of research have used in the past.

The rational way to choose a sample size is by weighing the benefits you can expect in information against the cost of increasing the sample size. In principle you should continue to increase the sample size until the benefit and cost of an additional sampled unit are equal.

The benefit of additional information is not easy to estimate even in very applied research, and it is extraordinarily difficult to estimate in basic re-

1. R. Schlaifer (1961) attacks the sample-size problem in the wider context of decision making, costs, and benefits. The statistically knowledgeable reader can find an excellent discussion of sample size in M. Hansen, *et al.* A. Mace gives many examples of the appropriate calculation in an engineering framework.

search, as discussed in Chapter 8. Therefore, it has been the practice of researchers to set up target goals of the *degree of accuracy* they wish to achieve, or to consider various degrees of accuracy that might be achieved with various sample sizes, and then to balance off a degree of accuracy with the cost of achieving that accuracy. The bulk of this chapter is devoted to learning how the sample size is related to accuracy in simple situations.

In complex situations, however, and even in simple situations for beginners, you are likely to feel frustrated by the difficulties of relating accuracy to sample size, in which case you cry out to a supervisor, "Don't give me complicated methods, just give me a rough number based on your greatest experience." My inclination is to reply to you, "Sometimes life is hard and there is no shortcut." On the other hand, perhaps you can get more information than misinformation out of knowing sample sizes that have been used in other studies. Table 31.1 shows the middle (modal), 25th percentile, and 75th percentile scores for—please keep this in mind—*National Opinion Surveys* in the top panel. The bottom panel shows how subgroup analyses affect sample size.

Pretest sample sizes are smaller, of course, perhaps 25–100 observations.

TABLE 31.1   Most Common Sample Sizes Used for National and Regional Studies, by Subject Matter

Subject Matter	National			Regional		
	Mode	Q_3	Q_1	*Mode*	Q_3	Q_1
Financial	1000+	—	—	100	400	50
Medical	1000+	1000+	500	1000+	1000+	250
Other behavior	1000+	—	—	700	1000	300
Attitudes	1000+	1000+	500	700	1000	400
Laboratory experiments	—	—	—	100	200	50

Typical Sample Sizes for Studies of Human and Institutional Populations

Number of Subgroup Analyses	People or Households		Institutions	
	National	*Regional or Special*	*National*	*Regional or Special*
None or few	1000–1500	200–500	200–500	50–200
Average	1500–2500	500–1000	500–1000	200–500
Many	2500+	1000+	1000+	500+

SOURCE: From *Applied Sampling*, by Seymour Sudman, pp. 86–87. Copyright 1976 by Academic Press, reprinted by permission.

Samples in research for Master's and Ph.D. theses are likely to be closer to a pretest than to national samples.

Once again, the sample size ought to depend on the proportions of the sample that have the characteristics you are interested in, the extent to which you want to learn about subgroups as well as the universe as a whole, and of course the purpose of your study, the value of the information, and the cost. Also, keep in mind that the *added* information that you obtain from an additional sample observation tends to be smaller as the sample size gets larger. You must quadruple the sample to halve the error.

Now let us consider some specific cases. The first examples taken up here are from the descriptive type of study, and the latter deal with sample sizes in relationship research.

1. Samples in Descriptive Research

a. EXAMPLE 16

What proportion of the homes in Countryville are tuned into television station WCNT's ten o'clock news program? That is the question your telephone survey aims to answer, and you want to know how many randomly selected homes you must telephone to obtain a sufficiently large sample.

Begin by guessing the likeliest answer, say 30 per cent in this case. Do not worry if you are off by 5 per cent or even 10 per cent, and you will probably not be further off than that. Select a first-approximation sample size of perhaps 400; this number is selected from my general experience, but it is just a starting point. Then proceed through the first 400 numbers in the random-number table, marking down a *yes* for numbers 1–3 and *no* for numbers 4–10 (because 3/10 was your estimate of the proportion listening). Then add the number of *yes* and *no*. Carry out perhaps ten sets of such trials, the results of which are in Table 31.2.

Based on these ten trials, you can estimate that if you take a sample of 400 and if the "real" viewing level is 30 per cent, your average percentage error will be 1.375 per cent on either side of 30 per cent. That is, with a sample of 400, half the time your error will be greater than 1.375 per cent if 3/10 of the universe is listening.

Now you must decide whether the estimated error is small enough for your needs. If you want greater accuracy than a sample of 400 will give you, increase the sample size, using this important rule of thumb: To cut the error in half, you must *quadruple* the sample size. In other words, if you want a sample that will give you an error of only 0.55 per cent on the average, you must increase the sample size to 1,600 interviews. Similarly, if you cut the sample size to 100, the average error will be only 2.75 per cent (double 1.375 per cent) on either side of 30 per cent. If you are distrustful of this rule of thumb, run ten or so trials on sample sizes of 100 or 1,600, and see what error you can expect to obtain on the average.

TABLE 31.2

Trial	Number "Yes"	Number "No"	% Difference From Expected Mean of 30% (120 "Yes")
1	115	285	1.25
2	119	281	0.25
3	116	284	1.00
4	114	286	1.50
5	107	293	3.25
6	116	284	1.00
7	132	268	3.00
8	123	277	.75
9	121	279	.25
10	114	286	1.50
Mean			1.375

If the "real" viewership is 20 per cent or 40 per cent, instead of 30 per cent, the accuracy you will obtain from a sample size of 400 will not be very different from an "actual" viewership of 30 per cent, so do not worry about that too much, as long as you are in the right general vicinity.

Accuracy is *slightly* greater in smaller universes but *only* slightly. For example, a sample of 400 would give *perfect* accuracy if Countryville had only 400 residents. And a sample of 400 will give *slightly* greater accuracy for a town of 800 residents than for a city of 80,000 residents. But, beyond the point at which the sample is a *large fraction* of the total universe, there is no difference in accuracy with increases in the size of universe. This point is very important. For any given level of accuracy, *identical* sample sizes give the same level of accuracy for Podunk (population 8,000) or New York City (population 8 million). The *ratio* of the sample size to the population of Podunk or New York City means nothing at all, even though it intuitively seems to be important.

The size of the sample must depend upon which population or subpopulations you wish to describe. For example, A. Kinsey's sample size would have seemed large, by customary practice, for generalizations about the United States population as a whole. But, as Kinsey explains: "The chief concern of the present study is an understanding of the sexual behavior of *each segment of the population,* and it is only secondarily concerned with generalization for the population as a whole" (Kinsey, *et al.,* 1948, p. 82, italics added). Therefore Kinsey's sample had to include subsamples large enough to obtain the desired accuracy in *each* of these subuniverses. The U.S. Census offers a similar illustration. When the U.S. Bureau of the Census aims to estimate only a total or an average for the United States as a whole—as, for example, in the Current Population Survey estimate of unemployment—a sample of perhaps 50,000 is big enough. But the decennial census aims to make estimates for all the various communities in the country, estimates that require adequate subsamples in each of these subuniverses; such is the justification for the decennial census' sample size of so many millions.

Television ratings illustrate both types of purpose. Nielsen ratings, for example, are sold primarily to national network advertisers. These advertisers on national television networks usually sell their goods all across the country and are therefore interested primarily in the total United States viewership for a program, rather than in the viewership in various demographic subgroups. The appropriate calculations for Nielsen sample size will therefore refer to the total United States sample. But other organizations sell rating services to *local* television and radio stations for use in soliciting advertising over the local stations rather than over the network as a whole. Each local sample must then be large enough to provide reasonable accuracy, and, considered as a whole, the samples for the local stations therefore add up to a much larger sample than the Nielsen and other nationwide samples.

b. EXAMPLE 17

This example, like Example 16, illustrates the choice of sample size for estimating a *summarization* statistic. Later examples deal with sample sizes for *probability* statistics.

Hark back to the pig-ration data in Chapter 28 (Example 10). Assume that our purpose now is to estimate the average weight gain for ration A, so that the feed company can advertise to farmers how much weight gain to expect from ration A. If the universe is made up of pig weight gains like those we observed, we can simulate the universe with, say, 1 million weight gains of thirty-one pounds, 1 million of thirty-four pounds, and so on for the twelve observed weight gains.[2] Or, more conveniently, as accuracy will not be affected much, we can make up a universe of say, thirty cards for each thirty-one-pound gain, thirty cards for each thirty-four-pound gain, and so forth, yielding a deck of 30 × 12 = 360 cards. Then shuffle, and, just for a starting point, try sample sizes of twelve pigs. The means of the samples for twenty such trials are as in Table 31.3.

Now ask yourself whether a sample size of twelve pigs gives you enough accuracy; there is a 50–50 chance that the mean for the sample will be more than .66 or .93 pound (the two median deviations) from the "real" mean of the universe, which is 31.76 pounds. Is this close enough? That is up to you to decide in light of the purposes for which you are running the experiment.

To see how accuracy is affected by larger samples, try a sample size of forty-eight pigs dealt from the same deck. (But, if the sample size were to be much larger than forty-eight, you might need a "universe" greater than 360 cards.) The results of twenty trials are in Table 31.4.

2. Only twelve weight gains are involved, because we are now estimating the variation for ration A only.

TABLE 31.3

Trial	Mean	Absolute Deviation of Trial Mean from Actual Mean	Trial	Mean	Absolute Deviation of Trial Mean From Actual Mean
1	31.77	.01	11	32.10	.34
2	33.27	1.51	12	30.67	1.09
3	31.75	.02	13	32.42	.66
4	30.83	.93*	14	30.67	1.09
5	30.52	1.24	15	32.25	.51
6	31.60	.16	16	31.60	.16
7	32.46	1.00	17	32.33	.57
8	31.10	.66*	18	33.08	1.32
9	32.42	.34	19	33.01	1.25
10	30.60	1.16	20	30.60	1.16

Actual Mean = 31.76

* Indicates medians of trials.

In half the trials with a sample size of forty-eight the difference between the sample mean and the "real" mean of 31.76 will be .36 or .37 pound (the median deviations) or more. Again, is this too little accuracy for you? If so, increase the sample size further.

The attentive reader of this example may have been troubled by this question: How do you know what kind of a distribution of values is contained in the universe *before* the sample is taken? The answer is that you guess, just as in Example 16 you guessed at the mean of the universe. If you guess wrong, you will get either more accuracy or less accuracy than you expected from a given sample size, but the results will not be fatal; if you obtain more accuracy than you wanted, you have wasted some money, and,

TABLE 31.4

Trial	Mean	Absolute Deviation of Trial Mean from Actual Mean	Trial	Mean	Absolute Deviation of Trial Mean From Actual Mean
1	31.80	.04	11	31.93	.17
2	32.27	.51	12	32.40	.36*
3	31.82	.14	13	31.32	.44
4	31.39	.37*	14	32.07	.69
5	31.22	.54	15	32.03	.73
6	31.88	.12	16	31.95	.19
7	31.37	.39	17	31.75	.01
8	31.48	.28	18	31.11	.65
9	31.20	.56	19	31.96	.20
10	32.01	.25	20	31.32	.44

Actual Mean = 31.76

* Indicates medians of trials.

if you obtain less accuracy, your sample dispersion will tell you so, and you can then augment the sample to boost the accuracy. But an error in guessing will *not* introduce *error* into your final results.

The guess should be based on *something*, however. One source for guessing is your general knowledge of the likely dispersion; for example, if you were estimating male heights in Rhode Island, you would be able to guess what proportion of observations would fall within 2 inches, 4 inches, 6 inches, and 8 inches, perhaps, of the real value. Or, much better yet, a very small pretest will yield quite satisfactory estimates of the dispersion.

c. EXAMPLE 18

This is the first example of sample-size estimation for *probability* (testing) statistics, rather than the summarization statistics dealt with in Examples 16 and 17. Recall the problem of the sex of fruit-fly offspring discussed in Chapter 28 (Example 5). The question now is, How big a sample is needed to determine whether the radiation treatment results in a sex ratio other than a 50–50 male-female split?

The first step is, as usual, difficult but necessary. As the researcher, you must *guess* what the sex ration will be if the treatment *does* have an effect. Let's say that you use all your general knowledge of genetics and of this treatment and that you guess the sex ratio at 75 per cent males and 25 per cent females *if* the treatment alters the ratio from 50–50.

Look at the random-number table, and let 1–25 stand for females and 26–00 for males (0 stands for 10, 00 for 100 and so forth, when all 10, all 100 and so forth, numbers are being used). Take twenty successive pairs of numbers for each trial, and run perhaps fifty trials, as in Table 31.5.

In Example 5 we found that, if a sample of twenty flies contained fourteen or more males, we could estimate the odds at 23 to 2 (92 per cent) that the ratio is not "really" 50–50. Now Table 31.5 tells us that, if the ratio is really 75–25, then a sample of twenty will show fourteen or more males forty-two of fifty times (84 per cent of the time). If we take a sample of twenty flies and if the ratio is *really* 75–25, we will make the correct decision by deciding that the split is not 50–50 84 per cent of the time.

Perhaps you are not satisfied with reaching the right conclusion only 84 per cent of the time. In that case, still assuming that the ratio will really be 75–25 if it is not 50–50, you need to take a sample larger than twenty flies. How much larger? That depends on how much surer you want to be. Follow the same procedure for a sample size of perhaps eighty flies. First work out for a sample of eighty, as was done in Chapter 28 for a sample of twenty, the number of males (or more) out of eighty that you would need to find for the odds to be, say, 9 to 1 that the universe is not 50–50; your estimate turns out to be forty-eight males, say. Then run fifty trials of eighty flies each on the basis of 75–25 probability, and see how often you would not get as many as forty-eight males in the sample. Table 31.6 shows the

TABLE 31.5

Trial	Females	Males	Trial	Females	Males	Trial	Females	Males
1	4	16	18	7	13	34	4	16
2	6	14	19	3	17	35	6	14
3	6	14	20	7	13	36	3	17
4	5	15	21	4	16	37	8	12
5	5	15	22	4	16	38	4	16
6	3	17	23	5	15	39	3	17
7	7	13	24	8	12	40	6	14
8	6	14	25	4	16	41	5	15
9	3	17	26	1	19	42	2	18
10	2	18	27	5	15	43	8	12
11	6	14	28	3	17	44	4	16
12	1	19	29	8	12	45	6	14
13	6	14	30	8	12	46	5	15
14	3	17	31	5	15	47	3	17
15	1	19	32	3	17	48	5	15
16	5	15	33	4	16	49	3	17
17	5	15				50	5	15

results I got. No trial was anywhere near as low as forty-eight, which suggests that a sample of eighty is bigger than necessary if the split is really 75–25.

It is obvious that, if the split you guess at is 60–40 rather than 75–25, you will need a bigger sample to obtain the "correct" result with the same probability. For example, run some eighty-fly random-number trials with 1–40 representing males and 51–100 representing females. Table 31.7 shows that only twenty-four of fifty (48 per cent) of the trials reach the necessary

TABLE 31.6

Trial	Females	Males	Trial	Females	Males	Trial	Females	Males
1	21	59	18	13	67	34	21	59
2	22	58	19	19	61	35	17	63
3	13	67	20	17	63	36	22	58
4	15	65	21	17	63	37	19	61
5	22	58	22	18	62	38	21	59
6	21	59	23	26	54	39	21	59
7	13	67	24	20	60	40	21	59
8	24	56	25	16	64	41	21	59
9	16	64	26	22	58	42	18	62
10	21	59	27	16	64	43	19	61
11	20	60	28	21	59	44	17	63
12	19	61	29	22	58	45	13	67
13	21	59	30	21	59	46	16	64
14	17	63	31	22	58	47	21	59
15	22	58	32	19	61	48	16	64
16	22	58	33	10	70	49	17	63
17	17	63				50	21	59

TABLE 31.7

Trial	Females	Males	Trial	Females	Males	Trial	Females	Males
1	35	45	18	32	48	34	35	45
2	36	44	19	28	52	35	36	44
3	35	45	20	32	48	36	29	51
4	35	45	21	33	47	37	36	44
5	36	44	22	37	43	38	36	44
6	36	44	23	36	44	39	31	49
7	36	44	24	31	49	40	29	51
8	34	46	25	27	53	41	30	50
9	34	46	26	30	50	42	35	45
10	29	51	27	31	49	43	32	48
11	29	51	28	33	47	44	30	50
12	32	48	29	37	43	45	37	43
13	29	51	30	30	50	46	31	49
14	31	49	31	31	49	47	36	44
15	28	52	32	32	48	48	34	46
16	33	47	33	34	46	49	29	51
17	36	44				50	37	43

cut-off at which one would judge that a sample of eighty really does not come from a universe that is split 50–50; therefore, a sample of eighty is not big enough if the split is 60–40.

Reviewing the main principles of this example: First, the closer together the two possible universes from which you think the sample might have come (50–50 and 60–40 are closer together than are 50–50 and 75–25), the bigger the sample needed to distinguish between them. Second, the surer you want to be that you reach the right decision based upon the sample evidence, the bigger the sample you need.

d. EXAMPLE 19

Referring back to Example 7, on the cable-television poll, in Chapter 28, how large a sample *should* you have taken? Pretend that the data have not yet been collected. You need *some* estimate of how the results will turn out before you can select a sample size. But you have not the foggiest idea of how the results will turn out. Therefore, go out and take a very small sample, maybe ten people, to give you some idea of whether people will split quite evenly or quite unevenly. Seven of your ten initial interviews say they are for CATV. How big a sample do you now need to provide an answer of which you can be fairly sure?

Using the techniques of the previous chapter, we estimate roughly that from a sample of fifty people at least thirty-two would have to vote the same way for you to believe that the odds are at least 19 to 1 that the sample does not misrepresent the universe, that is, that the sample does not show a majority different from that of the whole universe if you polled everyone. That estimate comes from the Monte Carlo experiment whose results are in Table 28.5, page 424. That table shows that, if half the people (or more) are against cable television, only one in twenty times will thirty-two (or more) people of a sample of fifty say that they are for cable television; that is, only one of twenty trials with a 50–50 universe will produce as many as thirty-two *yes*es if a majority of the population is against it. Therefore, designate numbers 1–30 as *no* and 31–00 as *yes* in the random-number table (that is, 70 per cent, as in your estimate based on your presample of ten), work through a trial sample size of fifty, and count the number of *yes*es. Run through perhaps ten or fifteen trials, and reckon how often the observed number of *yes*es exceeds thirty-two, the number you must get for a result you can rely on. In Table 31.8 we see that a sample of fifty respondents, from a universe split 70–30, will show that many *yes*es a preponderant proportion of the time—in fact, in fifteen of fifteen experiments; therefore, the sample size of fifty is large enough if the split is "really" 70–30.

e. EXAMPLE 20

How large a sample is needed to determine whether there is any difference between the two pig rations in Examples 10 and 11 in Chapters 28 and 29? The first step is to guess the results of the tests. You estimate that the average for ration A will be a weight gain of thirty-two pounds. You further guess that twelve pigs on ration A might gain thirty-six, thirty-five, thirty-four, thirty-three, thirty-three, thirty-two, thirty-two, thirty-one, thirty-one, thirty, twenty-nine, and twenty-eight pounds. This set of guesses has an equal number of pigs above and below the average and more pigs close to the average than farther away. That is, there are more pigs at thirty-three and thirty-one pounds than at thirty-six and twenty-eight pounds. This would seem to be a reasonable distribution of pigs around an average of thirty-two pounds. In similar fashion, you guess an average weight gain of twenty-eight pounds for ration B and a distribution of thirty-two, thirty-one, thirty, twenty-nine, twenty-nine, twenty-eight, twenty-eight, twenty-seven, twenty-seven, twenty-six, twenty-five, and twenty-four pounds.

Let us review the basic strategy. We want to find a sample size large

TABLE 31.8

Trial	No	Yes	Trial	No	Yes
1	13	37	9	15	35
2	14	36	10	9	41
3	18	32	11	15	35
4	10	40	12	15	35
5	13	37	13	12	37
6	11	39	14	14	36
7	13	37	15	17	33
8	7	43			

enough so that a large proportion of the time it will reveal a difference between groups big enough to be accepted as not attributable to chance. First, then, we need to find out how big the difference must be to be accepted as evidence that the difference is not attributable to chance. We do so from trials with samples that size from the benchmark universe. We state that a difference larger than the benchmark universe will usually show is not attributable to chance.

In this case, let us try samples of twelve pigs on each ration. First we draw two samples from a combined benchmark universe made up of the results that we have guessed will come from ration A and ration B. (The procedure is the same as was followed in Example 11 on page 430.) We find that in nineteen out of twenty trials the difference between the two drawn groups of twelve was three pounds or less. Now we investigate how often samples of twelve pigs each, drawn from the *separate* universes, will show a mean difference as large as three pounds. We do so by making up a 25- or 50-card deck for *each* of the twelve hypothesized A's and each of the twelve B's, with the ration name and the weight gain written on it; that is, a deck of, say, 300 cards for each ration. Then from each deck we draw two sets of twelve cards at random, record the group averages, and find the difference. The differences in the fifteen trials turn out invariably to be four pounds or larger. Therefore, two samples of twelve pigs each are clearly large enough, and, in fact, even smaller samples might be sufficient if the universes are really like those we guessed at. If, on the other hand, the differences in the guessed universes had been smaller, then twelve-pig groups would have seemed too small, and we would then have had to try out bigger sample sizes, say forty-eight pigs in each group and perhaps 200 pigs in each group if forty-eight were not enough. And so on until the sample size is large enough to promise the accuracy we want. (In that case, the decks would also have to be much larger, of course.)

If we had guessed different universes for the two rations, then the sample sizes required would have been larger or smaller. If we had guessed the averages for the two samples to be closer together, then we would have needed bigger samples. Also, if we had guessed the weight gains *within* each universe to be less spread out, the samples could have been smaller and vice versa.

I hope that the examples in this chapter have not seemed unpleasantly complex or tedious. One cannot estimate necessary sample size without going through procedures like those we have illustrated, though mathematical methods can speed up the tedious shuffling-and-dealing phase. There is just no easy answer to the question of how large a sample to take.

2. Step-Wise Sample-Size Determination

Often it is wisest to determine the sample size as you go along, rather than fixing it firmly in advance. In sequential sampling, which was discussed briefly in Chapter 9, you *continue* sampling until the split is sufficiently even to make you believe you have a reliable answer. Related techniques work in a series of *jumps* from sample size to sample size. Step-wise sampling makes it less likely that you will take a sample that is much larger than necessary. For example, in the cable-television case, if you took a sample of perhaps fifty you could see whether the split was as wide as 32–18, which you figure you need for 9 to 1 odds that your answer is right. If the split were not that wide, you would sample another fifty, another 100, or however large a sample you needed until you reached a split wide enough to satisfy you that your answer was reliable and that you really knew which way the entire universe would vote.

Step-wise sampling is not always practical, however, and the cable-television telephone-survey example is unusually favorable for its use. One major pitfall is that the *early* responses to a mail survey, for example, do *not* provide a random sample of the whole, and therefore it is a mistake simply to look at the early returns when the split is not wide enough to justify a verdict. If you have listened to early radio or television reports of election returns, you know how misleading the reports from the first precincts can be if we regard them as a fair sample of the whole.[3]

Stratified sampling is another device that helps reduce the sample size required, by balancing the amounts of information you obtain in the various strata. Chapter 9 discussed the general idea of stratified sampling. (Cluster sampling does not reduce the sample size. Rather, it aims to reduce the cost of obtaining a sample that will produce a given level of accuracy.)

3. Summary

Sample sizes are too often determined on the basis of convention or of the available budget. A more rational method of choosing the size of the sample is by balancing the diminution of error expected with a larger sample, and its value, against the cost of increasing the sample size. The relationship of various sample sizes to various degrees of accuracy can be estimated with Monte Carlo methods, which are illustrated here.

3. See J. Lorie and H. Roberts (pp. 155–157) for more discussion of the limitations of sequential sampling. And M. Hansen, *et al.*, warn against the danger of increasing the sample size in this fashion:

> The investigator examines the returns from an initial sample to determine whether they appear acceptable to the investigator; if they do, he uses the results as they are; if they do not, he discards the sample results [or keeps the old sample] and draws a new sample, perhaps by a different method, in the hope that he will obtain a result more nearly like the one he expected. Such an approach can be utilized to obtain almost any results desired, or can "prove" any point even when unbiased or consistent methods of selecting the sample and making the individual estimates are used if the initial results are subject to relatively large sampling errors. (Hansen, *et al.*, p. 78)

ADDITIONAL READING FOR CHAPTER 31

Tull and Hawkins (Chapter 6) summarize various approaches to determining sample size, but you must know a little about elementary conventional statistics to understand that chapter.

32 the concept of causality in social science, with notes on prediction, law, explanation, and function

What *is* a cause-and-effect relationship? The main purpose of this chapter is to establish a workable definition of "causality";[2] the chapter also explores the related ideas of prediction, law, explanation, and function.

1. Causality

The task boils down to a search for an *operational* definition of "causality." This is perhaps the most important point of all and the hardest to understand and accept. Of course, the operational definition must be a reasonably valid one. That is, it must fit social scientists' hypothetical conception of causality. Furthermore, it ought to accord with common scientific usage;

1. The first part of this chapter on causality owes a debt to H. Wold. It was two unpublished manuscripts of his (1966a, 1966b) that provoked me to develop this view in apparent opposition to his. And subsequent correspondence has made clear to us both that our views are complementary and refer to different aspects of the subject. Discussions with J. Carey have also been helpful in clarifying these ideas.
2. "Causality," "causation," and "causal relationship" are used as synonyms in this chapter.

that is, the definition should fit situations in which scientists commonly do say that something causes something else or that something is an effect of something else. This definition need *not* also fit the everyday speech of laymen, which is what has led many philosophers into trouble, I believe.

A definition of "causality" seems unnecessary in everyday life. No one is in much doubt about whether to say that a baseball causes a window to break or that yeast causes the cake to rise. And, even when we say we do not know whether two events are causally related—for example, whether walking under a ladder causes bad luck or night air causes disease—our doubt seems to be about our knowledge of the world and not about the meaning of the word "cause."

It is useful to speculate on why the term "cause" and the causal concept are *not* puzzling or vague in everyday life. Much of the explanation is probably that we use causal terms all day long in our common speech—not only the term "cause" itself, but also synonyms like "influence," "produce," and "create" and related words like "smash," "build," and "fix." This common conversational practice teaches us quite accurately *what these terms mean to other people.* Our sure-footed use of the term in everyday speech— as contrasted with our confusion in scientific speech—may also stem from the one-to-one quality of most everyday relationships called "causal." We are not so concerned with whether baseballs cause windows to break but rather with whether *that* baseball caused *that* window to break. In our everyday speech we are not so concerned with general statements about groups of events—for example, whether a rise in price causes fewer people to buy or heat causes riots[3]—as we are in social science.

For the most part, defining causality is not a troubling problem when the scientist can run an experiment. As we shall see, the actual experiment is itself *close* to a complete operational definition of causality—though it is *not* a complete definition. It is when the scientist cannot experiment but must deal instead with the data as the world presents them to him that an operational definition of "causality" is most acutely needed—and most difficult to create. That is the job of this chapter. To create a satisfactory operational definition of "causality" for nonexperimental situations, we must, first, trace some philosophic history; second, go further into the nature of definitions to see why we seek an *operational* definition; and, third and most important, explore the use of the causality concept in the social sciences, in order to find out what a *valid* operational definition of causality should be.

To explicate the term "causality" and the concept for which it stands in social-scientific usage, we must start with the most basic notion in science— the observed *association* or *correlation* or *relationship,* all of which are synonyms. To say that there is an association is simply to say that, when A has occurred in the past, B has also occurred more often than would have

---

3. But notice that I am not saying that everyday relationships are completely determinate or nonprobabilistic. A tumbler does not shatter *every* time it is dropped, but we do not have difficulty saying that a given fall *did* cause it to break.

been expected from chance. Or to put it another way, an association is shown if B has occurred more often when A was present than when A was not present.[4]

This definition of an association does not necessarily exclude historical statements, even though they refer to single occurrences of A and B. There is nothing logically wrong with saying that war with Japan in 1941 occurred more often than it would have if Japan had not bombed Pearl Harbor.

The rest of this chapter is simply (!) a subclassification of various types of observed associations (relationships) into those that can also be called "predictions," "causal relationships," "laws," "functional relationships," and so forth. These categories are not intended to be mutually exclusive, even in principle.

Causation and prediction have often been confused, so we must first talk a bit about prediction. Many—but not all—observed associations can be interpreted as bases for *predictions*. A prediction is the expressed belief that an association will also hold in the future; a person predicts if he believes that the general background conditions will not change drastically from the observation period to the prediction period. For example, if one observes that sales of drug D have been associated with the number of cases of angina pectoris in previous years, one may predict that, if angina pectoris cases rise this year, sales of drug D will also rise—unless one has reason to doubt *ceteris paribus*. But, if one learns that some important condition no longer holds—for example, that a new drug for angina pectoris has been introduced—one will no longer interpret the past observed association as basis for a prediction. One is willing to make a prediction if one believes that the future is an unbiased sample from the same universe as that of the past period on which the prediction is based. (See Chapter 26 for more discussion of the assumption of *ceteris paribus* in predicting.)

Notice that the basis for the interpretation of an association as prediction *cannot be found in the data themselves*.[5] Rather it is in one's general knowledge of the situation. This is the reason for the word "belief" in our definition of prediction.

It is at this point that David Hume makes his mighty entrance. Hume argued that all that one can know is that there has been an association—a "constant conjunction"—in the past. He asserted that there is no *logical* basis for prediction of the future on the basis of the past; one can never prove an induction in any formal logical fashion. And our definition of a prediction is in agreement with that point of view. But then Hume also

4. The definition is framed in terms of dichotomous presence-absence variables only for convenience, and it can easily be generalized to quantitative variables. It uses the past tense to emphasize that it refers only to events that have already been observed and excludes predictive elements.

5. Nor is there basis for the prediction in an operation, as is the case with generalizations on the basis of randomly drawn samples. The generalization to the colors of balls in an urn based on a random sample from the urn is based on the operation of drawing the sample randomly. But we can never draw the future randomly from the past.

stated that to call an association a "causal relationship" is to assert nothing more than constant conjunction.[6] He argued that no one could ever demonstrate a "necessary connexion" between a cause and an effect. In other words, he denied that anyone could show a material or "ontological"[7] relationship between a cause and an effect, and therefore he argued that it is not sensible to say that something is a "real" cause of something else.

One reason why it is impossible to make an air-tight case for an ontological causal relationship is that the possibility of a third factor always exists, and that possibility cannot be dismissed logically. Equally important, there are always conceptual intermediates. If one person says that the bicycle pedals make the bicycle go, another can argue that it is the linkage of the chain and sprockets that makes the bicycle go. Someone else can argue on the level of friction, another on a molecular level, and so on. One simply cannot demonstrate a "real" cause-and-effect relationship in a material sense. That is why an actual experiment is not a *complete* operational definition of a cause-and-effect relationship.

This view of the causal relationship is called a "subjective" view because it asserts that the connection between the two events is a product of the mind of the observer. It asserts that *it is the observer who pairs the two events and calls the relationship a "causal" relationship.* The Humean view does *not* assert that there is *not* a material relationship between A and B. Rather, it asserts that we can never determine and isolate some *unique* material relationship between them that we should call "causal." Also, the label "subjective" may be confusing; the word does not imply that the pairing of two events is strictly private and unknown to other people. The Humean view is quite compatible with the possibility of a wide consensus that the association between a particular pair of events should be called a "causal relationship." "Subjective" simply implies that the pairing is a result of people's *perceptions* and that many people can share a common perception—or at least say they do.

The central point of the Humean view is that, when someone says "A causes B," she expresses some *reflection in her mind* of the material objective world and not the material world directly. It is as if she is talking of a moving picture of a footrace or a landscape, rather than of the footrace or landscape itself. The moving picture can be very public, and almost all of us might agree on what the picture is "of," just as a prediction that the sun will come up tomorrow is quite public and agreed upon. But the moving picture is man-made, just as the association or prediction is man-made, in the sense that it requires an observer to notice the association or to interpret the association in a prediction.

I am *not* saying that there is not a real world in which things grow, push one another, and decay; in which air inflates balloons, baseballs crack win-

6. "We may define a cause to be an object, followed by another, and where all the objects similar to the first are followed by objects similar to the second."

7. By "ontological" I mean physical, material, existential, being *qua* being.

dows, people hurt one another, babies make mothers laugh, and so on. What I am saying is that, when a scientist *observes* an association and abstracts from the real world to make a scientific statement, that statement is not the *same* thing as what he is observing; it is a product of his mind or a picture of the world filtered through his perception, if you like. This is true not only of causal statements; it is true also of every association. Furthermore, every *word* in the language is such a picture of the world and represents such an abstraction from the world.

To repeat, then, a discussion of cause-and-effect relationships, or of associations generally, is a discussion of how people use language in response to various kinds of situations that confront them. This discussion is about language and not about the material world. It is the confusion between those two levels of discussion that is responsible for the confusion about the term "causality."

We must ask, What does "causality" *mean?* R. Braithwaite is outstanding in his clear view that this is indeed the issue for study. When we ask what a word means, we are asking *what people refer to* when they use the word. The definition can never be perfect, of course, because there are always borderline cases, even for such relatively clear-cut words as "chair." Is a stool a chair? Not all people will classify the same instances in the same way. The test of a definition is whether there is some *consensus* among people in their use of the word and whether an operational definition can be formulated that will capture the basis of that consensus. That is the task of this book with respect to the word "causality."

The conclusion of the unamended Humean view is that there is no difference between statements of cause and effect and all other statements of association, or, as this view is propounded today by M. Friedman in economics, that there is no difference between predictions[8] and cause-and-effect statements. But this unvarnished Humean view is not very satisfactory, for social scientists talk and act as if some associations are of a different sort from other associations and as if some predictions are of a different sort from other predictions. A statement that the flight of birds overhead precedes rain seems to be a different sort than the statement that activating the starter of the automobile precedes the starting of the engine; indeed, we react very differently toward these two statements.

There seems to be a difference between the statement that, when one clock's minute hand reaches twelve, another clock strikes the hour, and the statement that, when you remove the plug from the socket, the electric clock ceases to run.

For an economics example, we sense a difference between the observed association between prices on the Dutch stock exchange and the number of

---

8. M. Friedman talks about predictions and associations almost interchangeably, as if predictions were automatically implied by associations (pp. 7–13). In fact, the link between associations and predictions is not logically dissimilar to the link between associations and cause-and-effect statements.

houses built in the United States, on one hand, and the observed association between mortgage interest rates in the United States and the number of houses built in the United States, on the other. Similarly, in sociology there seems to be a difference between a statement that the birth rate is high in districts in Europe where there are many storks and the statement that the birth rate is high where child mortality is high.

2. The Problem of Definition

The *nature* of the differences between these statements is something of which I have so far said nothing. I have only asserted that we seem to act and talk *as if there are* such differences.

A detour about definitions is necessary now. Several sorts of definition of a term are possible, and some are relevant here. First, one can define a term by giving synonyms for it. For example, H. Blalock says that "causality is conceived [in his discussion] as involving the notion of production, that is, causes produce effects . . ." (p. 173). "Production" is a synonym for "causation." Giving synonyms like this one can be useful in clarifying for a foreigner what the word "cause" means in English or in explaining the term to a child. But synonymization obviously does not suffice to solve basic scientific problems of causal labeling.

Second, one may define by *naming some properties* of the concept one is trying to get at. This sort of definition aims to say what causality *is*. It is an "ontological" definition in terms of material properties of the world. Such definitions can help one person to convey to another a general feeling of what she is talking about. They are also often used successfully with children or foreigners—or even in making clearer to another scientist what one has in mind. An example is saying that "an automobile is a device with four wheels, an internal combustion engine, and so on" or "conformity is the act of patterning one's behavior to make it like the behavior of the group." This type of definition of causality has been tried by philosophers for thousands of years, with a notable lack of success. And, as noted in Chapter 2, Bridgman argued that it was because physicists had defined their words in terms of properties that there had grown up the wall to understanding that Einstein shattered—by achieving definitions in terms of *operations* to substitute for definitions in terms of *properties*.

What Hume did was to demonstrate the flaws in an ontological definition of causality. But he did not offer a substitute definition in terms of operations. Rather, he suggested that the term "causality" was useless and ought to be dispensed with. This has been the prevailing view among the most influential of twentieth-century philosophers, including B. Russell.

Third, definition by *denotation* can be helpful under some circumstances. Most of the definitions of terms in this book have been defined denotatively, that is, with examples. But again, we need more than denotation to clarify the scientific notion of causality.

Fourth, when scientists disagree about the application of a term and wish to increase the likelihood that they will apply the same terms to the same empirical phenomena, they *must* turn to operational definitions. The entire purpose of this chapter is to develop useful operational definitions of "causality" and related terms. We shall see that, if experimentation is possible, an operational definition of causality is reasonably easy with the following procedure.

1. Vary the stimulus and observe the variations in the response.
2. Try many other stimuli to see if the same response occurs.
3. If both steps yield appropriate results, call the relationships between stimulus and response "causal."

Furthermore, we must also try to define "causality" operationally in nonexperimental situations. Success of this endeavor is measured in two ways: Does the operational definition result in many scientists reaching the same judgment on whether to apply the term "causal" in a given situation? And does the definition accord with common usage and intuitive "property definitions" held by social scientists? That is, does the proposed operational definition fit closely the hypothetical concept of causality held by most scientists?

I think it is sensible to say that causal relationships are a subclass of associations, that is, that all causal relationships are associations but that not all associations are causal relationships. This is a slight (but important) amendment of the point made by Wold (1966b) that causal relationships are a subclass of *predictions.*

A cause-and-effect statement is a type of scientific *explanation,* but not all explanations are causal statements, as I interpret common usage.

It is at this point that the real work begins. After we have said that causal relationships are a subclass of associations and that each causal statement is a man-made concept, just as are all words and ideas, then what? *How does one distinguish between those associations that are and those that are not within the subclass of causal statements?* To make that distinction effectively is our task. This is the job of creating an operational definition of causality.

There have been various attempts to find a method for deciding whether a particular association should be called "causal," that is, a method for partitioning the class of associations into causal and noncausal associations. But none of the authors has described his proposed method as an "operational definition of causality." I shall briefly mention some of the attempts.

First, many writers have said that all those associations that can be *verified experimentally* deserve to be called "causal"—and no others. This is quite congenial to the scientific intuition, and it has been a very useful rule in much of science. But it is not a perfect rule—that is, it does not work in every case—for at least two reasons: In any experiment a hidden third factor, rather than changes in the presumed independent "test variable," might account for the changes in the dependent variable; and in many situations experimentation is not possible.

Because a hidden third factor may always turn out to be the "real" cause, a single experiment does not provide a *complete* operational definition of causality. Rather, one must also run related experiments varying various parameters of the situation, and only when one has exhausted the important possibilities should he say that the experimental stimulus causes the experimental response. In the Hawthorne experiment, for example, a single experiment varying light intensities and observing work output was not sufficient; the researchers also had to vary such parameters as their own presence in the work situation to establish a causal relationship.

To restate, then, the operational definition of "causality" when experimentation is possible is this: If the response follows the experimental stimulus and if this experimental relationship persists when other elements of the situation are varied, the experimentally observed relationship may be called "causal."

From here on the discussion will be concerned with the case in which no experiment is possible and in which therefore the test of experimental confirmation does not suffice as a principle for defining causal statements. This is common in some of psychology, most of sociology, and almost all of economics and anthropology. It is here that the stickiest questions about causal statements occur.

A second proposed method is that of Wold, who attempted to bring nonexperimental situations within the reach of the experimental-verification principle by asking whether a nonexperimental situation is a "fictitious," or "hypothetical," experiment, meaning that the natural situation has most of the elements of an actual experiment (Wold, 1966b). But this conceptualization has two shortcomings. To begin with, the essence of the experiment as an operational definition of causality is that it is the actual observed results of a real experiment that serve to determine whether the relationship is called "causal." The other shortcoming is that one might say that the very act of choosing to label a relationship as causal is an operation that defines "causality." But such an operational definition has little validity because it does not go far toward resolving disagreements among people on what should be called "causal." That is, it carries us little further than the present ill-defined situation.[9]

A third approach is that of logician-philosophers who have tried various combinations of conditional statements of the "if-then" variety, what they

9. G. Orcutt's extension of the pragmatic point of view to the definition of causality is related (1952a, 1952b). Orcutt argues that a relationship should be called "causal" only *if the relationship can be manipulated for policy purposes.* By this test, the relationship between the money supply and inflation might be called "causal" because the money supply can be manipulated to influence inflation. This point of view has much in common with the experimental-validation test for causality, but it does not demand experimental validation *before* calling the relationship "causal." Also, it does not permit us to refer to a relationship as "causal" if the investigator is interested in the phenomenon just for "pure science" and not for immediate policy manipulation.

call "counterfactual conditionals," and discussions of necessary and sufficient conditions. They have attempted to find some *logical* formulation that successfully distinguishes between causal and noncausal associations. But D. Shapere's assessment that this quest has so far failed completely is surely fair and accurate (Shapere, p. 24). I think the failure results from the philosophers' failure to recognize that an *operational* definition is needed.

Fourth, another type of attempt has recently been made by H. Simon, H. Blalock, and others, abstracting from original work by P. Lazarsfeld. This group has investigated how the correlations between and among three or more variables can help one sort out which of these variables can be said to "cause" which. This is an amplification and formalization of the analysis presented in Chapter 26 to investigate whether a hidden third factor is "responsible" for the correlation between two other variables.[10]

The study of "causal ordering," as it is called, is useful and important, but it does not do the whole job, as H. Simon points out (p. 41). For example, if the investigator starts out with three variables, none of which should really be said to be the "cause" of another, the analysis can tell us nothing about whether the relationship between two given variables should be called a "causal" relationship. These schemes for labeling relationships as "causal" or "noncausal" depend upon the use of *outside knowledge* to help sort out the relationships, for example, the knowledge that one event precedes all the others in time and therefore cannot be the result of all the others. This position boils down to the assertion that a relationship is causal unless proved not causal by tests for spuriousness. Such an analytic scheme does *not* provide an operational definition that indicates whether a *given* relationship should be called causal; at best, it tells us that, within a set of variables and relationships, one relationship is "more causal" than another.[11]

In the course of our later discussion the nature of each of these previous attempts at definition of causality will emerge more fully. For now it is necessary to note only that no definition has been created that fits customary scientific usage, even though this is the stated aim of all of them (H. Simon, p. 60; Wold, 1966b, p. 267). On reflection, it is not surprising that no perfect or near-perfect definition of "cause-and-effect relationship" has yet been created. It is difficult to create perfect automatic rules for discriminating even such generally understood concepts as "chair" and "tree" and "money"; even the best operational definition does not lead everyone to classify all examples of such concepts in exactly the same way; there are always excep-

---

10. H. Hyman (1955) and T. Hirschi and H. Selvin (1967) have gone far beyond the formal Lazarsfeld analytic scheme in somewhat the same direction that we are going here. Part II of the Hirschi-Selvin volume is the most painstaking and perceptive discussion of causality extant, though I do not agree with its point of view entirely. Its strength is its firm root in empirical material, though its limited focus on juvenile delinquency will turn away many who could profit from it. I regret that the book did not reach me in time to influence the writing of this chapter.

11. Wold has recently explored a related and important area. *Assuming* that a given variable *is* causal, Wold investigates which econometric transformations do and do not permit subsequent causal inference (1966a).

tions at the borderline. It is natural, then, that such a term as "cause and effect," which is so much more complex and abstract than are the other terms, will be much harder to define satisfactorily and will have many more borderline cases on which people disagree when classifying situations as causal and noncausal.

In order to develop a definition of "causality" that is *valid* as well as *operational*, we must examine actual scientific usage. Therefore, let us consider a set of situations relating to sales in department stores, to see how the causal concept is used.

a. EXAMPLE 1. INCOME AND TOY DEMAND IN DEPARTMENT STORES

Assume that per capita income in a community rises from period 0 to period 1. *Ceteris paribus*, a rise in the *sales of toys* probably will also occur between periods 0 and 1. This is merely the statement of an association.

Should one say that increased income causes an increase in toy demand? My observation is that, except for those who completely reject the use of the causal concept, no economist will boggle at saying that increased income causes increased toy demand.

Upon casual examination, this relationship seems to have three elements that seem to fit intuitive notions of causality:

1. high predictive reliability
2. a set of theoretical links—the economic theory of consumer preference, in this case—gives us the feeling that we "understand" the relationship
3. few or no qualifications to the statement seem to be required.

For now these are only clues; later we shall examine them with care.

This example was chosen because of its extreme simplicity and the general acceptance of the causality of this kind of relationship.

b. EXAMPLE 2. SEASONAL TOY DEMAND IN DEPARTMENT STORES

I hypothesize that a Chicago department store will sell more toys in December than in January, subject only to such further conditions as that the store stays in business, no natural calamity like war or earthquake occurs, and so forth. I do *not* specify that advertising or price be held constant because variation in them does not change the pattern enough to render the statement untrue. The (hypothetical) observed association is between sales and the calendar months. To put the hypothesis in other words, if the store is in business and unless there is a calamity, there is an overwhelmingly high probability that the demand for toys will be higher in December than in January, and the probability of any such condition as a calamity or the store's not being in business is very small.

How might this situation be characterized in terms of the causality concept in normal economic usage? In the policy-making situation, the manager of the store acts upon this knowledge when she orders more toys for December than for January because she expects higher demand in December. One could say that the manager uses the association as a predictive device; such Humean language is the simplest and least restrictive interpretation of the situation. Furthermore, the manager would act in the same way if she believed that there were a real and material connection between December and demand or if she believed that December was only a predictive index like birds that predict rain. The distinction does not matter to the manager because she cannot manipulate the independent variable. But we would not be surprised if she used causal language and said that December causes toy demand to be higher than does January.

An economic analysis that provides information about relative demand in December and January is certainly of value to policy makers, and therefore the pragmatist should approve the label "causal." It is not, however, a situation in which the independent variable (the calendar change from month to month) is subject to human control. Therefore, Orcutt's pragmatic definition of "causality" does not seem to fit this example. Nor does this situation fit the requirement that a relationship labeled "causal" should be a reasonable analogy to an experiment. It is difficult even to conceptualize an experiment that might test whether the relationship would hold if the "causal" variable were manipulated. How does a researcher manipulate December or seasonality?

An economist might also study the pattern of seasonal demand merely because it is interesting and he wants to understand it, rather than because he wants to help department stores make sound decisions. Or he might wish to estimate seasonal demand for use in seasonal adjustments. If this economist is addicted to causal language, he may say that the seasonal pattern "causes" demand to be higher in December, even though he knows that Christmas and various religious and social beliefs and attitudes mediate between seasonality and toy demand; by using the word "cause" he surely does not mean to imply "complete and ultimate cause," and therefore his knowledge of intermediate links does not weaken the claim of the seasonal patterns to be called "causal."

This example offers good ground for a discussion of time, antecedence, and the causal concept. I have written as if the *time period* called "December" (or the change from December to January) might be called the "cause" of the changed demand, but time itself is only a matrix in which the real cause is embedded, and therefore it is questionable that time can ever be called a "cause," an issue discussed in a postscript to this chapter.

c. EXAMPLE 3. THE HOURLY PATTERN OF TOTAL
DEPARTMENT-STORE DEMAND

In this example, we shall discuss the hypothesis that in a department store the total demand for all goods (and for every good) *after* the store doors have been unlocked is greater than the demand before the doors are unlocked. This example and those that follow may seem trivial or bizarre, because more realistic examples are harder to handle briefly. It is worth noting, however, that these examples are nowhere near as trivial as the usual examples in logical discussions, for instance, "John wears his raincoat because it rains."

The hypothesized association between door unlocking and increased sales presupposes various normal conditions, for instance, that the door opens within thirty minutes of 8:30 A.M., that no strike is in progress, and that the day is not Sunday. In other words, unlocking the door will be followed by a sudden increase in demand *if a good many other conditions are specified.* Side conditions were also specified in Example 2 (for example, the store's being in business), but the present example differs in that the side conditions might very well not be met a good part of the time (for instance, it is often Sunday) and could be changed arbitrarily (for example, the management might decide not to stay open Wednesday). Another difference is that the "cause" variable (unlocking the door) could be put into operation quixotically, for instance, by a drunken manager. We do not know what the probability is that a given door-unlocking event will take place when the various inputs hold. A compulsive janitor may unlock and relock the doors every hour on the hour, with no sales resulting.

This situation differs from those in Examples 1 and 2 in that neither a decision maker nor a scientist is likely to consider the relationship between door unlocking and increased demand a causal relationship. The reasons are instructive. The difference between Example 3 and Examples 1 and 2 that would seem to explain the difference in the appropriateness of the causal concept is that many of the side conditions necessary for the association in Example 3 to be highly predictable are themselves not very predictable and are subject to change. To put it another way, *given* the various conditions, the association is highly predictable. But, *without knowledge* of whether the various side conditions hold, the association of Example 3 is much less predictable than are those in Examples 1 and 2, and it is more difficult to determine whether the side conditions hold in Example 3 compared to Examples 1 and 2.

It should be noted that the difference between Examples 2 and 3 is *not* that Example 3 is a case of multicausation; if anything, the opposite is true. In Example 3, but *not* in Example 1, it is possible to hold everything constant, vary only the "independent" variables, and observe the association.

d. EXAMPLE 4. THE EFFECT ON DEMAND OF A WARNING BUZZER

In a particular department store, a buzzer is sounded in all employees' spaces as warning that the doors will open in five minutes. The hypothesis that we shall discuss in this section is that sales in the hour starting ten minutes after the bell sounds will be greater than sales in the hour before the bell sounds. Again this statement requires that we specify further conditions, including the same ones specified in Examples 2 and 3, as well as some others: that the buzzer is never buzzed except to warn employees of the beginning of the business day, except to test it; that the situation described is not a test; and so forth.

In this example there are two major possibilities. The first is that the buzzer would be activated only in conjunction with an unlocking of the door. If so, the probabilities are *exactly the same* as those for unlocking alone, as in the previous example. There is also, however, a second set of possibilities in which the buzzer and the lock would *not* be activated together. If it should prevail, there is no reason to believe that demand will be higher or lower after the buzzing; that is, the association will then not hold.

Example 4 is a classic hidden-third-factor situation (that is, an example of spurious correlation or specification error). It is not possible to specify (as one could in Example 3) even a very limited set of conditions under which experimental control can be applied with a high degree of probability—*unless* a condition (unlocking) is specified that can *also* be interpreted as the "active" variable in the experiment. Then the latter variable will have an identical observed association with buzzing, provided that one more condition (unlocking) is specified for the buzzing association than for the unlocking association. (Speaking loosely, this distinction gives us a criterion for choosing *between* two variables which one we should call the "more real" cause. The more real cause does not include the other as a side condition, but the other does include the more real one.)

In general, the buzzing example has the same characteristics as does the unlocking example but to a greater degree, because there is no reason to think that we can guess accurately what the conjunction or disjunction of lock and buzzer will be. This important change could take place quixotically and arbitrarily, a characteristic that surely disqualifies the association as a causal relationship. Yet the association can be manipulated experimentally and under rigidly specified conditions. The outcome can be predicted with such high accuracy as to be almost a fully determinate relationship rather than a "mere" statistical relationship.

It is illuminating to make a few more assumptions and then to consider how a person without the usual experience and knowledge might react. Assume that the door locks are electric and are activated by a central switch. Assume also that the switch is wired so that it is pushed to buzz the warning buzzer and that, after a five-minute delay, the doors are automatically unlocked. Because she is from another planet or merely from some "backward" country, the person who pushes the switch thinks that it activates the buzzer, and she does not know about the door-unlocking action. In her perception, the state of demand for toys under each set of conditions will be exactly the same as ours for door unlocking, except that she will believe that the buzzing of the buzzer is the immediate predecessor of increased toy demand. (Stranger *post hoc ergo propter hoc* superstitions have been held, both by B. Skinner's pigeons and by humans.) Note that in this case the relationship can be manipulated and apparently tested experimentally. To reveal this specification error there is no recourse except to subject-matter knowledge; for example, doctors used leeches for a long time because no one did any satisfactory empirical investigation to determine their effectiveness.

3. Generalization About the Meaning of "Cause and Effect"

Now it is time to see what reasonable generalizations can be drawn from the examples. Whether a situation is closely analogous to a controlled experiment clearly does not provide a complete definition of causality. Example 4 could be studied experimentally by varying the time of unlocking the door, whereas it would be difficult to carry out a validating experiment for the seasonal effects of Example 2. Yet it is Example 2 that economists probably will consider causal, rather than Example 3.

Furthermore, even in the controlled experiment there is often no help for specification error except subject-matter knowledge. In the example of the men who got drunk successively on bourbon and soda, scotch and soda, and brandy and soda (p. 342) and concluded that soda causes drunkenness, nothing except substantive knowledge or scientific intuition would have led them to the recognition that it is the alcohol rather than the soda that made them drunk, *as long as they always took soda with their drinks.* And no statistical procedure can suggest to them that they ought to experiment with the presence and absence of soda. If this is true for an experiment, it must also be true for an uncontrolled study, a point illustrated by Examples 3 and 4.

Surety of prediction is not a satisfactory definition of causality. In Example 3, one may predict that increased demand will follow door unlocking with a probability closely approaching 1.0, but the situation is not one that would be considered causal. One important reason why accuracy of prediction is not a complete test of causality is that the scientist can and does arrange side situations in various ways that change the observed and theoretical probabilities. More specifically, by fixing enough side conditions an investigator can force probabilities very high, but the fixing of many side conditions reduces the claim of the relationship to be called "causal."

I hazard the following as a working definition. A causal relationship is expressed in a statement that has these important characteristics: It is an association that is strong enough so that the observer believes it to have a predictive (explanatory) power great enough to be scientifically useful or interesting. For example, he is not likely to say that wearing glasses causes (or is a cause of) auto accidents if the observed correlation is .07, even if the sample is large enough to make the correlation statistically significant. In other words, unimportant relationships are not likely to be labeled causal.

Various observers may well differ in judging whether an association is strong enough to be important and therefore "causal." And the particular academic field in which the observer works may affect this judgment. This is an indication that whether a relationship is dubbed "causal" involves a good deal of human judgment and is subject to dispute.

(2) The side conditions must be sufficiently *few* and sufficiently observable so that the relationship will apply under a wide enough range of conditions to be considered useful or interesting. In other words, *the relationship must not require too many "if"s, and"s, and "but"s in order to hold.* For example, one might say that an increase in income caused an increase in the birth rate if this relationship were observed everywhere. But, if the relationship were found to hold only in developed countries, among the educated classes, and among the higher-income groups, then it would be less likely to be called "causal"—even if the correlation were extremely high once the specified conditions had been met. A similar example can be made of the relationship between income and happiness.

(3) For a relationship to be called "causal," there should be good reason to believe that, even if the control variable were not the "real" cause (and it never is), other relevant "hidden" and "real" cause variables must also change *consistently* with changes in the control variables. That is, a variable being manipulated may reasonably be called "causal" if the real variable for which it is believed to be a proxy must always be tied intimately to it. (Between two variables, v may be said to be the "more real" cause and w a "spurious" cause, if v and w require the same side conditions, except that v does not require w as a side condition.) This third criterion (nonspuriousness) is of particular importance to policy makers. The difference between it and the previous criterion for side conditions is that a plenitude of very restrictive side conditions may take the relationship out of the class of causal relationships, *even though the effects of the side conditions are known.* This criterion of nonspuriousness concerns variables that are as yet *unknown and unevaluated* but that have a *possible* ability to *upset* the observed association.

Examples of spurious relationships and hidden-third-factor causation are commonplace. For a single example, toy sales rise in December. There is no danger in saying that December causes an increase in toy sales, even though it is "really" Christmas that causes the increase, because Christmas and December practically always accompany each other.

Belief that the relationship is not spurious is increased if *many* likely variables have been investigated and none removes the relationship. This is a further demonstration that the test of whether an association should be called "causal" cannot be a logical one; there is no way that one can express in symbolic logic the fact that many other variables have been tried without changing the relationship in question.

(4) The more tightly a relationship is bound into (that is, deduced from, compatible with, and logically connected to) a general framework of theory,

the stronger is its claim to be called "causal." For an economics example, observed positive relationships between the interest rate and business investment and between profits and investment are more likely to be called "causal" than is the relationship between liquid assets and investment. This is so because the first two statements can be deduced from classical price theory, whereas the third statement cannot. Connection to a theoretical framework provides support for belief that the side conditions necessary for the statement to hold true are not restrictive and that the likelihood of spurious correlation is not great; because a statement is logically connected to the rest of the system, the statement tends to stand or fall as the rest of the system stands or falls. And, because the rest of the system of economic theory has, over a long period of time and in a wide variety of tests, been shown to have predictive power, a statement connected with it is cloaked in this mantle.[12]

The social sciences other than economics do not have such well-developed bodies of deductive theory, and therefore this criterion of causality does not weigh as heavily in sociology, for instance, as in economics. Rather, the other social sciences seem to substitute a weaker and more general criterion, that is, whether the statement of the relationship is accompanied by other statements that seem to "explain" the "mechanism" by which the relationship operates. Consider, for example, the relationship between the phases of the moon and the suicide rate. The reason that sociologists do not call it causal is that there are no auxiliary propositions that explain the relationship and describe an operative mechanism. On the other hand, the relationship between broken homes and juvenile delinquency is often referred to as "causal" in large part, because a large body of psychoanalytic theory serves to explain why a child raised without one or another parent or in the presence of parental strife should not adjust readily.

Few social-scientific statements except those in economics can claim to be unambiguous deductions from generally accepted principles because the disciplines do not meet W. Letwin's test:

> . . . [I]f the explanation and prediction follow necessarily from a few principles that explain many other phenomena as well, it is nevertheless [even if inaccurate] a scientific theory. On the other hand, the more isolated statement of one of those principles, or even an exhaustive list of all of them, is not a scientific theory. . . .[13] (Letwin, p. vi; see also Homans, p. 11–12)

12. E. Wilson (p. 160) makes a similar point about "generalizations" in physics and chemistry.

13. This is certainly not a claim that the nonexperimental social sciences are scientifically inferior to economics. This writer believes that, for example, sociology's relative lack of success in developing a deductive structure is a necessary result of the complexity of the subject matter sociologists deal with and especially of the irreducible multiplicity of motives that influence the human behavior they want to study. Braithwaite makes a similar point about psychology, though in my limited knowledge of the fields, it is not as true of recent psychology as of sociology:

The aesthetic defect of psychological theory as a scientific deductive system is that it

This operational definition of "causality" is long, involved, and imprecise, demonstrating my central argument that there is not, and cannot be, *any* simple test or definition of the term. Rather, there must be several criteria, and they cannot be very objective but must be as subjective as each person's own background and experience. It is on such a subjective basis—though presumably guided and influenced by some reasonably clear idea of what the causality concept means to other people—that each person must render her own judgment on whether to *call* a given scientific statement "causal."

To describe the definition of "causality" in another way, we can say that causal relations are a subclass of associations that meet several qualifying tests or conditions. The job of the definition is to establish appropriate tests, which are the conditions a relationship must meet to be considered causal.

The term "causal" has, and probably should have, different meanings to the decision maker and to the scientist. The decision maker will call a relationship "causal" if he expects to be able to manipulate it successfully. Cigarette smoking may be considered causal by the decision maker who wishes to reduce deaths from lung cancer and other diseases statistically related to smoking, which was the meaning of the Surgeon General's committee's use of the word "cause." But to the scientist *qua* investigative scientist the word "cause" is likely to mean that the situation does not require further and deeper exploration; in the case of cigarettes, perhaps only one ingredient in the cigarettes does the damage, and the scientist searching for this ingredient may choose to withhold the word "cause" from the cigarettes themselves.

The difference in meaning and use of the causal concept between decision-making and "pure" investigative situations is just one illustration of the general proposition that the attribution of causality depends upon one's purpose.[14] Not only may the particular *occasion* of the term's use differ between policy makers and "pure" investigators, but also the frequency of its use may differ, for there seems to be a difference in the *necessity* of the causal concept for people in these different roles. The causal concept is perhaps most necessary for a policy maker, especially when he is considering changing one variable in hopes of achieving change in another variable. The classification of causal versus noncausal is an attempt to discriminate

---

has a vast number of separate highest-level hypotheses; up to the present [1949] it has succeeded hardly at all in unifying itself by the use of colligating concepts, as physical theory did in the seventeenth century. (Braithwaite, p. 307)

F. Northrop tells us why economics meets this aesthetic and scientific requirement:

Any deductive theory in any subject whatever must possess relations as well as elements among its primitive concepts. The fundamental entities of economic theory are economic goods, or wants, or valuations. Its fundamental relation is that of "preference." (Northrop, p. 239)

14. This proposition is the subject of a major debate among legal scholars. The question is whether a question of negligence can or should be broken up into a neutral question about the material facts of causation and a legal question about whether the causal act is negligent. It seems to me that the much better arguments belong to those who argue that it is impossible to ask a neutral and "nonevaluative" question about causality.

between situations that he believes allow such control and those that do not. On the other hand, the causal concept is not at all necessary for the forecaster, for he has no interest in trying to manipulate the independent variables. The causal concept may or may not be necessary to the "pure" investigator; B. Russell and most contemporary physicists apparently believe that it is neither necessary nor useful in the physical sciences. Many nonpolicy scholars in the social sciences, however, seem to find the concept useful in classifying situations for future research.

The difference among disciplines in the variables to call "causal" also illustrates how causal labeling depends upon purpose. In those cases in which the variables are complementary—like the achievement motive and capital investment in discussions of economic development—it is perhaps unnecessary for either the economist or the psychologist to deny the causal label to one variable in order to apply it to another variable. But, when the variables are hierarchical—for example, badly designed auto, slippery highway, going too fast, braking too sharply on curve (see p. 91)—then the variables may be causally incompatible, and particular investigators and disciplines must then choose which level to study and call "causal" on the basis of the level they consider most fruitful.

We began by saying that, to find out what "causality" means, we had to investigate how social scientists use the term. That we have done. I believe that there is considerable consensus among scientists on which relationships are causal and which are not, and I believe that we have isolated the most important characteristics of the causal relationships. Given that the characteristics listed earlier successfully distinguish causal from noncausal relationships, one can use these characteristics as guides to labeling associations. It is important to use language in accord with accepted scientific usage, and causal language is no exception. These characteristics, then, are prescriptions, as well as descriptions.

Before leaving the subject of causality, let us try out the definition on disputes about the causal status of some variables associated with juvenile delinquency.[15] Many investigators have found the following variables correlated with juvenile delinquency: broken homes, poverty, poor housing, lack of recreation facilities, poor physical health, race, and working mothers. All these variables were long considered causes of delinquency, but recently the causal status of each has been called into question.

First, each of these variables, alone and in combination with other variables, predicts delinquency with some success. None is perfectly correlated with delinquency, of course, but to demand such a perfect prediction would be a false criterion of causality, as Hirschi and Selvin point out. Therefore, each of these associations meets the first criterion given.

Second, each of these variables except race has been shown to be associated with delinquency in a wide variety of conditions. The range of these conditions is certainly wide enough so that the associations are of interest to

15. This section draws heavily upon material presented in Hirschi and Selvin's "False Criteria of Causality in Delinquency Research."

both "pure" sociologists and policy-oriented sociologists and social workers. But in those conditions in which no other variable in the list is favorable for delinquency—especially poverty and broken homes—race is *not* associated with delinquency, and therefore race fails to meet the second test of causality: that the relationship holds under a wide variety of conditions.[16] The other variables do meet this test, however.

The third test is that of spuriousness and the certainty of connection between the given variable and the "more real" variable. Consider the matter of working mothers, for example. It is reasonable to suppose that *lack of the mother's interest and attention* is the "real" variable (more real than the working-mother variable) associated with delinquency. Mothers who are highly motivated to spend maximum time with their children will be less likely to go to work than will other mothers, even when financial need is great. Another possible connection is that the very fact that she works necessarily reduces the attention a mother can pay to her children. So both these chains are relevant:

interest and attention → going to work   → delinquency
going to work   → interest and attention → delinquency

But in any case we need not worry about the relationship between the mother's working and her interest and attention. The former is a thoroughly reliable proxy for the latter. If the amount of attention the mother devotes is high, she will not be working. As the real variable is not likely to be dissociated from the variable in question (working mothers), we do not disqualify the working-mothers variable from being called "causal." All the other variables except race seem to pass this test, though considerable discussion would be required to demonstrate these relationships.

The fourth characteristic of a causal statement in economics is that the statement be tied in with the rest of formal deductive theory. In sociology, however, this test can seldom be met, if ever. Instead, some sociologists demand that the two variables in the association must be related with intervening variables, that is, that the relationship can be explained with *ad hoc* theory. For example, one might suppose that lack of recreational facilities is associated with delinquency because recreation can occupy adolescents' leisure time and thereby keep them out of trouble. All the variables under consideration can be explained in this fashion. The trouble is that it is too easy to concoct such *ad hoc* explanations for almost any relationship, and one must therefore be uneasy about the causal status of all the variables in question.[17]

A fifth point is relevant for decision makers more than for pure scientists. Race, unlike the other variables, cannot be manipulated by a social planner

16. Hirschi and Selvin do not agree with this test of causality and, consequently, with any judgment on the causal status of race.
17. Again, Hirschi and Selvin would not agree that the causal status of these variables is thereby weakened.

who wants to reduce delinquency. Therefore, the policy maker is not likely to consider the association between race and delinquency a cause-and-effect relationship.

Let us recapitulate what we have said about the troublesome causality concept. The question is, What *is* causality? Definitions using ontological properties are a dead end, and definitions referring to logical properties have failed and must always fail. What is needed is an operational definition of causality.

Here is the operational definition I propose: A statement shall be called "causal" if the relationship is close enough to be useful or interesting; if it does not require so many statements of side condition as to gut its generality and importance; if enough possible third-factor variables have been tried to provide some assurance that the relationship is not spurious; and if the relationship can be deductively connected to a larger body of theory or (less satisfactorily) be supported by a set of auxiliary propositions that explain the mechanism by which the relationship works.

This definition is a checklist of criteria. Whether a given relationship meets the criteria sufficiently to be called "causal" is not automatic or perfectly objective; the determination requires judgment and substantive knowledge of the entire context.

Now let us move on to another troublesome concept, that of *function* or *functional relationship*, which is a particular type of association important in anthropology, sociology, social psychology, and clinical psychology. It has nothing to do with the functional form, $y = f(x)$, with which it shares only the label. Rather, this concept refers to such statements as "A function of the bus driver is to drive the bus."

Some writers (for example, Homans; Hagen, pp. 512–513) believe that *no* set of data should be said to demonstrate a functional relationship, for the data *by themselves* can never show more than an association. This argument is perfectly analogous to the argument that no data should be called "causal." It is quite correct that function cannot be expressed in formal symbolic logic, but associations that sociologists, anthropologists, and psychologists call "functional" do have some characteristics in common, just as causal statements do; and a statement of these characteristics constitutes a meaningful definition of "functional relationship." These characteristics are all contextual, that is, they depend upon general knowledge of the situation under investigation, the sort of knowledge that cannot be expressed or proved in formal quantitative terms.

Here are a set of criteria for a functional relationship.[18]

18. These criteria were not developed from a direct empirical inspection of sociological and anthropological statements labeled "functional" but rather from the following paragraph in R. Merton's "Manifest and Latent Functions." The rest of Merton's remarkable essay contains a good linguistic analysis of the functional concept.

If the logic of this approach is stated in its more general terms, the following interrelated sequence of steps becomes evident. First of all, certain functional requirements

First, a functional relationship is an association between the survival or nonsurvival (or effectiveness) of a group or individual and any other variable. For example, there is an association between the survival, continued existence, and effectiveness of Boy Scout troops and the presence of an adult leader. The association is statistical, of course, and there may be exceptions.

Second, the association must meet all the criteria spelled out for causal relationships; the relationship is always that survival (or efficiency) is the effect variable and the other variable is the cause.[19] It may often seem awkward to say that the independent variable causes survival; it is more natural to say that the absence of the independent variable causes the death (or diminished efficiency) of the group organization or the individual. For example, the absence of an adult leader causes the Boy Scout troop to fall apart.

Third, one important condition might be that some compensating mechanism is not working. For example, the absence of a bus driver will not stop the bus if a passenger jumps into the driver's seat or if an automatic piloting mechanism goes into operation. To demonstrate that a relationship is functional in such a case, it must be demonstrated that the association *will* hold if the compensating mechanism is prevented from operating and that under some actual conditions the compensating mechanism would fail to operate. For example, sometimes no passenger will jump into the bus driver's seat, and then the bus will not move.

Fourth, the statement of the association must be accompanied by a full account of the workings of the mechanism through which the independent variable exerts its influence in maintaining the existence of the group organization. This requirement is closely allied to the requirement for causality that the statement be connected with the body of theory, though in sociology or anthropology the requirement for a deductive theoretical framework is not as strong as in economics.[20]

The anthropological-sociological concept of function is patterned after the same concept in biology, as R. Merton emphasizes. In social science, however, it is much more difficult to define the terms "survival" and "efficiency" without troublesome value terms. For example, one might say that the func-

---

of the organisms are established, requirements which must be satisfied if the organism is to survive, or to operate with a given degree of effectiveness. Second, there is a concrete and detailed description of the arrangements (structures and processes) through which these requirements are typically met in "normal" cases. Third, if some of the typical mechanisms for meeting these requirements are destroyed, or are found to be functioning inadequately, the observer is sensitized to the need for detecting compensating mechanisms (if any) which fulfill the necessary function. Fourth, and implicit in all that precedes, there is a detailed account of the structure *for which* the functional requirements hold, as well as a detailed account of the arrangements *through which* the function is fulfilled. (Merton, p. 48)

19. R. Brown (p. 110) makes the same point.

20. But functional statements do appear in economics. G. Stigler tells us that "the function of a market is to bring together buyers and sellers," or words to that effect. And one of the most famous passages by F. Knight is entitled "Social Economic Organization and Its Five Primary Functions" (pp. 3–14).

tion of the fiddler is to make a successful party. But some people might call the party a success even without fiddling, though it might be a different sort of party. Nor can one say that it is a compensating mechanism that keeps the party from failing, for the compensating mechanism would have to be defined so loosely that the definition means nothing at all.[21]

Functional statements may have either of two purposes. One purpose may be to inform a policy maker which elements of a situation are necessary for it to continue to exist (or "function") or which elements should be removed if he wishes to break up the group (or individual). The second purpose is to increase scientific understanding of the conditions of social survival, efficiency, and equilibrium.

To summarize, the relationships among the most important types of statements found in the social sciences, as I interpret common scientific usage, are shown in Figure 32.1.

First, *associations* are a very general type of scientific statement. Important subclasses of associations are cause-and-effect statements, predictions, empirical generalizations (laws), and functional relationships.

Second, some *explanations* are not associations; they are the logical (tautological) and nonempirical explanations, for example, the explanation[22] of why $(a + b)^2 = a^2 + 2ab + b^2$. Motivational explanations are another nonassociation type of explanation. For instance, to the question "Why did you go out?" one answer might be "I wanted to go to the drug store." Explanations are statements that make one understand, which associations do not always do; that is why some associations do not furnish explanations, for example, the association between moon cycles and murders.

Third, not all *facts* are associations, either, for example, such descriptive one-variable statements as that there are 200 million people in the United States. Conversely, not all associations are facts; hypothetical associations are important statements, but they are not factual.

Fourth, *cause-and-effect relationships* are a subclass of associations. They include only those associations that meet the criteria specified earlier in this chapter.

Fifth, relationships that yield *predictions* are another subclass of associations, those that are taken as forecasts for time periods later than the time of prediction. Not all predictions are causal; empirical generalizations that do not explain a phenomenon can often be used for successful predictions of the phenomenon. And not all causal relationships yield predictions, because the situation to which the causal relationship applies may change.

Sixth, *functional relationships* are a subclass of causal relationships. They include only those causal relationships that refer to survival or efficiency of equilibrium systems and that meet the criteria just spelled out.

---

21. Homans goes further in damning the concept of survival in functional sociological theory (pp. 812–813).

22. Example from A. Kaplan (p. 336). I follow him in this distinction between explanation and association.

FIGURE 32.1   The Interrelations Among Types of Scientific Statements (For instance, cause-and-effect statements are a subclass of association statements in common scientific usage, as interpreted by the author of this book.)

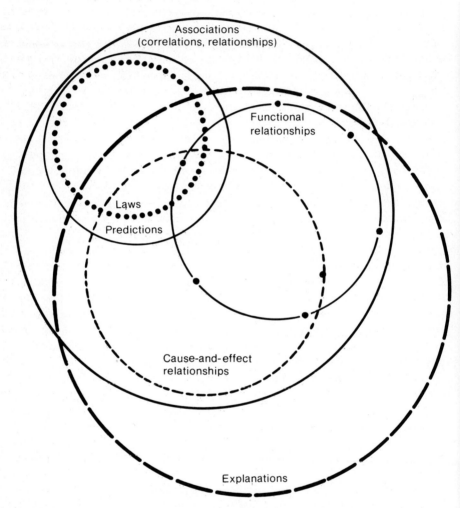

Seventh, *laws* are empirically observed, factual associations. They need not be causal relationships. Conversely, hypothetical associations are not laws because they have not been established in fact.

4. Postscript: Time, Antecedence, and Causality

This chapter has been primarily concerned with *whether* there is a causal relation, rather than with the *direction* of causality, and arguments of time order arise mainly in the latter issue. But time order can also be relevant to issues of *whether* a relationship is causal. For example, if it is otherwise assumed that causality in the relationship discussed is possible only in one direction, time order might then be adduced as an argument that even an otherwise possible causal relationship is impossible.

Many writers state that, even if there are no other logically conclusive tests of causality, time precedence may be considered a satisfactory test on logical grounds. Wold, for example, says, "There is usually a lapse of time between cause and effect, and in any event the effect cannot precede the cause in the flow of time" (Wold, 1967b). The task of this postscript is to show that time order is not a logical golden key to causality but rather that it is a frequently useful hypothesis that must itself be supported with other subject-matter knowledge.

The first problem with time order as the test of causal direction is that it is often difficult to make a practical determination of which event comes first. Even H. Hyman, who is a strong supporter of the time-order test of causality, notes that "guesses [about time order] on the basis of inspection of the nature of the variables are dangerous. The complexities of behavior are such that bizarre time orders are possible" (Hyman, 1955, p. 194). And Hyman notes several types of variables that give special difficulties (pp. 195 ff.). It is especially difficult to make sound judgments of time order in anthropology and archaeology.

A second problem is that, when the two variables are repetitive, and one does not *already* know which causes which, one does not know which events in the repetitive series are relevant for dating. For example, we know that there is a relationship between the price of corn in the fall and the amount of corn planted in the spring. But which causes which, and which comes first? The 1966 corn planting precedes the 1966 corn price, but the 1966 corn price precedes the 1967 corn planting. Time order alone will not establish the direction of causality in such cases.

Third, there may be several possible proxies for the "real" cause or effect, and these proxies may have very different dates. For example, refer to the toy-demand situation, except that now the hypothesis is that *wholesale* demand for toys in *November* will be higher than it was in *October*. It is reasonable to explain this relationship causally by saying that it is really *Christmas* that causes the upsurge in toy demand in November. That would be a satisfactory explanation except that Christmas follows November (or at least the Christmas that we refer to follows November). If one wishes to regard Christmas as the cause, and I see no logical reason not to do so, then cause *follows* effect rather than preceding it. This seems to indicate that time dating cannot be an automatic test of the direction of causal influence.

As always when there are apparent empirical deviations from a law, there are two possible ways to respond: We can junk the law, or we can explain the deviations in such a way as to leave the law intact though more restricted. The abandonment of the phlogiston theory in the face of new evidence is an example of the one possibility; the retention of the law of gravity in the face of evidence that balloons rise and leaves fall more slowly than Newton's law predicts is an example of the other possibility. In the Christmas-toy-demand example, it is possible to maintain the law of time order and causality by using some *other* proxy (Christmas is itself a proxy for the desire to give gifts), especially by arguing that "expectations" or "anticipations" of Christmas precede the demand. This might not be a very difficult explanation to swallow if, as H. Simon suggests, the concept of the future is applied only to human beings. But not so. A bird may be said to build its nest because it is expecting young. Even plant life and mechanical things can be usefully anthropomorphized by having expectations attributed to them. What we have, then, is an avoidance of reverse time data by a device that cannot be tested empirically (except possibly for humans). Because this device can be used to explain anything, it explains nothing. Therefore, it might be better, because of such examples, to drop the law of time order and causality, rather than to try to amend it.

Fourth, in a very formal way we can always say that, if an event occurred at time *t*, then the absence of the event (which has the same *logical* nature as the event itself) prevailed before time *t*. For example, we could say that a woman goes to the maternity ward because she has *not yet* had the baby. In a similar way we can *always* find a negative event to precede another occurrence; we can pick and choose events and their negatives to set up any time order we want—thereby vitiating time order as an automatic test of causality.

Fifth, nor does a discussion of time itself give any reason to believe in a useful logical relationship between time order and causality. Appropriate time dating of a variable or the choice of a combination of a variable and a time system seems to depend *upon the information that is available to us.* As W. Ashby points out, complete knowledge of the present state of a system renders unnecessary any reference to past states to explain the system's behavior. It is "only if a determinate system is only partly observable, and thereby becomes (for that observer) not predictable, the observer [would then want] to restore predictability by taking the system's past history into account . . ." (Ashby, p. 114).

Of course one cannot consider all determinants of an effect as being *simultaneous* with the effect, or the system would never be able to change. But one can think of the proximate cause in the time-order sequence as *approaching* simultaneity with the effect, just as the segment of rope that is proximately causal of the tension at point *p* is the infinitesimal segment that is infinitely close to point *p;* that is, if there is no tension in the infinitely close segment, there cannot be tension at point *p*, even if there is tension in more distant segments.

If we accept that time order is not an *automatic* logical test of causality, where does it leave us? Just because there is no *logical* connection, it does *not* follow that time lags are of no help in establishing causality. First, we must recognize that to use a time lag to infer the direction of causality in a particular relationship is, as Orcutt puts it, to make "use of one of the most general inferences that has been made from all the experimentation that has been done: namely, that actions taken in the present do not *appear* to modify the past" (Orcutt, 1952b, p. 310; italics added). But this is a statistical empirical hypothesis with known exceptions, as we have discussed. Therefore, to make *sensible* use of this inference, one must offer additional reasons why the hypothesis (or "law") should be believed to apply in the particular case. Consider the relationship between market price in year t and crop planting in year $t + 1$. We are willing to accept a normal time order as a test of causality, that is, that price causes planting, rather than vice versa. But we accept time order as a test only because we have no reasons arising from our knowledge of the *subject matter* not to accept it *in this case*. Ultimately, then, time order as a clue to causality has no logical superiority over other subject-matter clues but must itself be considered as subject-matter information, with the possible imperfections that all subject-matter information must have in a complex world.

5. Summary

Causality is a key concept in science, and a most confusing one. Following in the line of Hume, the key to removing the confusion is to understand that causality is not an intrinsic property. The basis for an interpretation of causality cannot be found in the data themselves, even in an experiment, but rather depends upon our general understanding of the situation together with our research purposes. That is, the label "causality" is a judgment.

What we need, then, is a good operational definition of "causality." I hazard the following as a working definition:

First, it is an association that is strong enough so that the observer believes it to have a predictive (explanatory) power great enough to be scientifically useful or interesting.

Second, the side conditions must be sufficiently *few* and sufficiently observable so that the relationship will apply under a wide enough range of conditions to be considered useful or interesting. In other words, *the relationship must not require too many "if's," "and's", and "but's" in order to hold.*

Third, for a relationship to be called "causal," there should be good reason to believe that, even if the control variable were not the "real" cause (and it never is), other relevant "hidden" and "real" cause variables must also change *consistently* with changes in the control variables. That is, a variable being manipulated may reasonably be called "causal" if the real variable for which it is believed to be a proxy must always be tied intimately to it. (Between two variables, v may be said to be the "more real" cause and w a "spurious" cause, if v and w require the same side conditions, except that v does not require w as a side condition.) This third criterion (nonspuriousness) is of particular importance to policy makers. The difference between it and the previous criterion for side conditions is that a plenitude of very restrictive side conditions may take the relationship out of the class of causal relationships, *even though the effects of the side conditions are known.* This criterion of nonspuriousness concerns variables that are as yet *unknown and unevaluated* but that have a *possible* ability to *upset* the observed association.

Fourth, the more tightly a relationship is bound into (that is, deduced from, compatible with, and logically connected to) a general framework of theory, the stronger is its claim to be called "causal."

In brief, one can never decide with perfect surety whether in any given situation one variable "causes" a particular change in another variable. At best, given your particular purposes in investigating a phenomenon, you may be safe in judging that very likely there is causal influence. It is correct to say (as it is so often said) that correlation does not prove causation—if we add the word "completely" to make it "correlation does not *completely* prove causation." On the other hand, causation can *never* be "proven" *completely* by correlation *or any other* tool or set of tools, including experimentation. The best we can do is make informed judgments about whether to call a relationship causal.

EXERCISES

1. Discuss the following statement:
   Somebody once went to a good deal of trouble to find out if cigarette smokers make lower college grades than nonsmokers. It turned out that they did. This pleased a good many people and they have been making much of it ever since. The road to good grades, it would appear, lies in giving up smoking; and, to carry the conclusion one reasonable step further, smoking makes dull minds. (Huff, p. 87)
2. Give two examples in your field of close relationships between two variables that turn out not to be causal because a "hidden third factor" explains them both.
3. Give two examples of relationships in your field that you believe ought to be called "causal," and show how they fit the operational definition of causal given in this chapter; that is, justify applying the label "causal" to the relationships.
4. Give an example of a functional relationship in your field. Justify its being called "functional."
5. Give an example of a relationship that cannot be tested for causality by examining to see which variable occurred first.

ADDITIONAL READING FOR CHAPTER 32

Hirschi and Selvin convey an excellent understanding of the nature of causation, supported by a great many examples from delinquency research. Their analysis of the nature of the causal concept has much in common with that presented here but also diverges from it significantly.

part five **epilogue**

33 the nature, powers, and limits of social science

This chapter is a grab bag of topics. It is something of an indulgence for me because—except for the pages about the necessity of knowing the purpose of the research—it does not have the practical aim of helping you to do empirical research better. With this warning, you can decide whether to read or skip, though I do hope that these topics that I think important will seem important to you too.

1. What Makes an Investigation Scientific?

First of all, scientific research is a form of learning, a way of increasing one's knowledge about the world. And it is a type of *rational* learning; it depends upon the human *reasoning* powers. Though we value rational learning and it seems to be useful in many cases, we should not deprecate other modes of human knowledge. Such nonrational (but not irrational) mental states as artistic feeling, emotion, and spiritual feeling are not competitors of rational learning. I do not urge you to seek rational answers to all important questions. What I do urge is that, *if* you want a rational answer, scientific methods can help you to get it; this book has tried to help you to apply empirical scientific methods.

Second, not all rational attempts to "get the facts" by observing nature are scientific. All of us learn a great deal about the world around us by hit-or-miss methods, rather than by formal scientific investigation. You find out what a restaurant is serving by asking the waitress or looking at the menu. You find out whether it is raining by sticking your hand out the window. As a baby, you learn that the stove may be hot by getting your hand burned and that your parents will usually come when you cry. These common-sense[1] methods of obtaining factual knowledge are generally quite satisfactory for our purposes.

Common sense has limitations, however, sometimes such severe limitations that it produces misinformation or no facts at all. Common-sense observation is often the basis of misleading superstition. And common sense breaks down when the question you want to answer is very complex or is otherwise difficult to investigate.

Scientific research takes up where common sense is forced to leave off. Scientific research is an *extension* of everyday methods of getting information, rather than a replacement for them. Furthermore, common-sense general knowledge is frequently an important point of departure for the good researcher, and an important test of his results. Scientific research must always simplify, which is both its major advantage and an important disadvantage in comparison with common sense. If common sense contradicts your scientific findings, check your scientific findings again. Sometimes you will find that, indeed, your common sense is dead wrong.[2] But sometimes you will find that common sense and your sound intuition prevent scientific mistakes. For example, if a complicated statistical technique tells you that half the smokers will quit if the price of a pack of cigarettes goes up 2 cents, your good common sense will refuse to accept these results and will save you from a major error.

How can you judge whether a piece of empirical research is scientific? The judgment is never open and shut. It is better to ask whether a piece of research is more or less scientific, rather than whether it is or is not scientific. Here are some of the marks of scientific empirical research:

In scientific research you describe the empirical work in such a way that other people could repeat exactly what you did. If you have not described what you did sufficiently clearly and specifically and if subsequent researchers cannot expect to get the same results, then we cannot call the research "scientific."

As an example, consider a newspaperman's public-opinion research. Often a reporter will try to find out what "the man in the street" thinks by going out into the street and asking people. There are many ways the reporter could select people to ask, and the opinions she gets will often depend on

1. I won't bother to define "common sense," but, as some wag has said, it is not always sensible and never common.
2. A fascinating illustration of how fallible our common sense can be and of how what seem to be obvious findings of the social sciences are often not so obvious at all is given by P. Lazarsfeld (1949). He fools the reader by listing several very obvious findings from the famous study of *The American Soldier* (Stouffer, *et al.*, 1949) and then points out that the *opposites* were really found to be true. The findings were not so obvious after all, and common sense was not enough to arrive at the correct answers.

the way she selects people. Unless you know exactly how she selected the people, it is not likely that you can go into the street and arrive at the same conclusions as she does.

The more that the observer *interprets* what he sees, the less repeatable is the study. Sociology has largely worked its way beyond relying on impressions and judgments of the observer, but anthropology has not yet gotten so far. For example, different observers of the Zuñi Indians reached entirely different assessments of the kind of people the Zuñi are, because of different impressions gained in living with the Zuñi. And an impartial observer cannot either examine the raw data to reach his own conclusions or go to the Zuñi and repeat exactly what the prior observers did.

But repeatability alone is not sufficient to make research scientific. If I am trying to find out whether men or women are safer drivers, I can ask my wife for the answer, and I can tell you exactly how I got my answer, namely, by asking my wife. You can surely repeat exactly what I did, by also asking my wife, but *neither* of us will be doing scientific research.

A second mark of a scientific investigation is that it fits in with work that is being done by other scientists. In other words, we are more likely to say that a study is scientific *if it means something to other scientists* than if it has no connection with what anyone else is doing or with the thinking of any field. This may seem unfair or parochial to you at first, but take my word for it (just this one time!). And, of course, we should not be dogmatic about denying the label "scientific" to purely applied studies whose results have only practical value and no implication for science. An example would be a market-research study of which color package sells more detergent. In other words, if work uses scientific methods, that is sufficient for me to call it "scientific," even if its goals are not the goals of the scientific enterprise and the scientific community.

A third mark of a scientific study is that it conforms with established research procedures and avoids the obstacles to knowledge.[3]

2. What Can Empirical Research Do?

Let us now summarize what the knowledge derived from empirical research can and cannot do. Thoughts that appeared in many places throughout the

3. This whole definition of "scientific" research is very crude. Philosophers of science give much more subtle definitions; see, for example, M. Cohen and P. Nagel (pp. 391 ff.). But this definition will serve for most of the unsubtle problems that we shall meet. Just as only the thorny legal problems go to the Supreme Court, we need call upon the philosophy of science only when we are forced to deal with the subtleties. For the rest, our justice-of-the-peace definition will suffice. H. Reichenbach points out that "indifference to philosophy has turned out to be a wholesome attitude for the scientist, though perhaps only as a matter of good luck. Success is often with those who act rather than reflect about what they should do" (Reichenbach, p. 93). A. Kaplan also makes the same point vigorously (pp. 22–24). But this may be truer at some stages in the history of a science than at others. Also, because *indifference* to philosophy has sometimes turned out well, *ignorance* of scientific philosophy is foolish and dangerous. In my opinion, Kaplan's book is by far the best introduction to philosophy of science for the student of social science.

book now can be drawn together. Empirical research can increase our knowledge of nature and its workings and can be a source of power for individuals and institutions. For example, knowledge of the workings of the weather helps you to decide whether to go on a picnic. The Rothschilds increased their power in financial negotiation because they developed a clever system of collecting information in Europe and transmitting it across the Channel to England by lights at night. An army increases its military power when it increases the skills of its intelligence sections. And obviously, advances in medical research increase the physician's power to control the physical human condition. The power in all these examples stems from increased ability to plan future actions.

Much social-science research aims to help make better decisions. Research is used for planning in advertising and national propaganda. Judges, bureaucrats, and legislators often ask for research on which to base judgments, regulations, and legislation.

Empirical research also serves as part of the general scientific enterprise. Empirical facts are inextricably entangled with conceptualization in science, as we mentioned earlier. Hypotheses most often follow from *some* observations about nature, whether from formal or informal research.[4] Furthermore, *after* the theoretical scientist has stretched his imagination to make interesting guesses about what's what, empirical research serves to determine whether the guesses are sound.[5] It is widely accepted among scientists and philosophers that, unless a scientific idea is *capable* of being tested, it has no meaning.[6] Of course, an idea is immensely more valuable after it *has* been tested and found to be in accord with the empirical facts.

Still another use of research fits the classically romantic notion of science: to satisfy a man's curiosity. But do not worry if at first you are not consumed with curiosity about the outcome of your research. Your interest will often mount as your work continues, and the moment when at last you examine your results can have high drama and excitement.[7]

In this discussion of what scientific research can do, it is appropriate to say something about the limitations of research. Laymen sometimes overestimate the power of scientific study and underestimate the difficulty of finding things out, as do students when they begin their first research project. Consider this comment by a medical expert on testing drugs: "Very few people, be they laymen or practicing physicians, have any . . . comprehen-

---

4. An important practical aside: When you cannot come up with satisfactory hypotheses and you feel stumped, go back to your original observation or your raw data, and soak yourself in them. Pore over the pages of your statistical data until you notice some relationships. Or go out and talk casually to people about what you are interested in, if your problem is one of human behavior. And ideas *will* come!

5. I do not mean to suggest that the theoretician and the empiricist should be separate people. I. King claims that every great astronomer has been both a theorist and an empiricist.

6. Kaplan criticizes this concept very sharply and with point (pp. 39–42).

7. Curiosity is necessary to a researcher in the long run, however. As A. Einstein said, "If you don't itch, you can't scratch."

sion of the extraordinary complexity and the great difficulty of establishing even the smallest scientific fact . . ." (Bean, p. 267).

A case in point is my investigation of whether liquor prices are higher or lower in the sixteen states in which the stores are state-owned than in the other states, where liquor is sold in privately owned stores. Apparently this is the simplest possible task, especially as the prices of many individual brands are easily available for most states. Nevertheless, this simple task took weeks and weeks and some fancy statistical analysis. For example, the prices for only eight brands were available in published form, the price of no single brand was available in *all* the states, and for some states there were no published data at all. This meant that some further data had to be obtained from liquor firms and state liquor-control boards, and, even so, some states' price levels had to be estimated on the basis of the price of one brand and others' on the basis of prices of other brands. (And of course the work had to come to grips with the fact that the price level estimated on the basis of one brand or eight brands is not, by a long shot, a perfect estimate of the average price level for *all* liquor sold in a state.)

It is useful to understand the limitations of a particular branch of science at a particular time. Much error, trouble, and argument result from scientists' trying to overgeneralize a theory, that is, trying to squeeze too many phenomena within the compass of the theory. It is not well for a science to be too modest and for scientific thinking to be nothing but a collection of anecdotes. On the other hand, it is not well to be too ambitious and to try to explain too much with a theory. It is my experience that, when two social scientists vehemently disagree on whether a hypothesis is correct, the argument can often be settled by showing that the hypothesis holds for some part of the universe—which is the part the hypothesis maker had in mind—and does not hold for the part of the universe that the objector was thinking of. Often the argument hinges on differing *purposes* that the arguers have in mind for the hypothesis—for instance, policy decisions versus pure understanding.

An example from communications research: The famous two-step flow-of-influence hypothesis suggests this process of modifying people's behavior or attitudes through the mass media: A few opinion leaders are affected directly by the media; then most other people who are affected at all are influenced by the opinion leaders, rather than directly by the media. Evidence to confirm the hypothesis was found in the drug-prescribing habits of physicians in a small city. But many communications theorists talk as though *all* the mass media's effects take place in two steps. This is demonstrably not true for, say, the sales of marriage books by mail order from advertisements in magazines; in fact, the very "one step" privacy of the sale stimulates purchasing ("in plain brown wrapper"). The simple fact is that some behavior is acquired from the media in two steps, other behavior in one step. Furthermore, acknowledgment of this fact can help eliminate the arguments over whether the two-step flow hypothesis is or is not valid.

To drop down one level of abstraction so that a theory fits the facts much better is what R. Merton, for example, has in mind when he talks about "sociology of the middle range," in contrast to "grand theory." It can often be a creative and useful accomplishment in all disciplines to show how a theory can be vastly improved and an argument settled with a qualification or two—though this accomplishment is seldom applauded by anyone.

> Time and again the industrial development of Europe has been described in terms of a general pattern constructed upon the empirical material gleaned from English history. Such an approach is not without merit. Precisely because there are common features in all industrializations, it possessed and still possesses some explanatory and even predictive value. To concentrate upon these general aspects of industrialization may be quite useful for some purposes. But it is equally true, as always when the level of generality is pitched very high, that as one moves deeper and deeper into the subject one is bound to come across things in one area or another that do not fit the general model. When that happens, the historian, after he has refused to ignore the uncomfortable irregularities, is faced with two alternatives. He may regard those things as exceptions and treat them as such. Or else he can attempt to systematize the deviations from the original pattern by bringing them into a new, although necessarily more complicated, pattern. (Gerschenkron, p. 41)

Good science is not only limited; it is also messy. Scientific reports are logical and neat, as they ought to be, but the work process that leads up to them is much less logical and neat. In many cases the researcher cannot clearly state the problem when she begins her work. The research seldom follows the neat stages discussed by philosophers of science (for instance, Northrop, pp. 28–29). Often the results of the first experiments or surveys are muddy and inconclusive. And often the researcher must make technical decisions with insufficient information. In short, scientific research is not a sacred ritual with strict rules of procedure laid down in an official dogma. Rather, it is a body of useful methods to go beyond common sense when common sense is not good enough.

3. The Necessity of Knowing the Purpose of the Research

Scientists often like to characterize their work as a disinterested search for objective truth. But I shall argue that this goal is not enough; one must also have the knowledge for some *purpose*, and the purpose must go beyond curiosity.[8] My argument is not on grounds of social value but on practical ones; I believe that a specified purpose is necessary in order to do useful and meaningful research.

I shall develop this point of view through the example of the relationship of income to family size. As noted earlier, the various relevant studies have

---

8. Kaplan (pp. 42–47 and elsewhere) argues this point of view very well, but he labels it "pragmatism," which—as he notes—is a misleading name because of the common too-narrow interpretation of the pragmatist's requirement that the knowledge be related to some purpose and intended action.

shown both positive and negative relationships between fertility and income. The approach of most recent writers has been to try to clear away as many other variables as possible in order to get at the "pure" relationship of income to fertility. They have sought objective estimates of the "structural parameter" relating income and fertility. But, even if the investigator does succeed in this abstracting process, she will not necessarily have a useful answer. That is, even if "ideally" the "direct effect" of an increase in income is to raise fertility, there almost surely are important classes of nonideal situations (for instance, the presently underdeveloped countries) in which an increase in per capita income has an overall effect (direct and indirect) in the direction of *reducing* fertility.

Unraveling the puzzle and choosing a sensible conclusion require that you first decide what your purpose is. For example, perhaps you want to estimate the effect on the birth rate of giving family-allowance payments to all parents in the United States. Or perhaps you want to forecast the effect on the birth rate of the likely rise in per capita income in the underdeveloped countries of Africa. Or perhaps you want to know whether the ratio of children born to upper-income families to those born to lower-income families will change as knowledge of contraception is more widely diffused in Latin America. Or perhaps you want to know how the birth rate will be affected if education increases along with per capita income in Africa.

In any of these exemplary situations, you want to know the relationship between income and family size, but the answer differs from situation to situation. It is not sufficient for the researcher to seek disinterestedly the structural parameters of the general system of income and family size. Rather, he must decide in advance which system of income and family size he is interested in among the many possible that he could explore. And he can make that decision sensibly only if he first clarifies his purpose, which most often means asking what kind of a decision depends upon the knowledge he develops, for instance, whether family-allowance payments are contemplated. The system the investigator chooses to explore should be most analogous to the situation about which the decision will be made.

This is a problem not only in survey research. The experimenter, too, makes decisions that affect the estimates she obtains, the most important of which are the choices of the *range* over which she varies the stimulus and of the *conditions* under which she runs the experiment. At one degree of food deprivation, the rat may run faster when made even hungrier. At another degree of deprivation, further deprivation may slow him down. Furthermore, it may matter whether the experiment is run in a heated or a cool room. Earlier we saw a similar example in the effect of aerial bombing on German morale (p. 150).

The fact is that nature has no parameters to be estimated. Some researcher must mark off boundaries around some chunk of nature and must specify particular characteristics to be considered before any parameter can be estimated. To search for structural parameters is tantamount to denying that the parameters will be different, depending upon the choice of system and its boundaries. And, given that we must make a rather arbitrary choice about which system to study, it makes sense to refer to one's larger purpose for criteria on which system to work with.

Some scientists argue that one should explore the most universal system possible. But this cannot be a sufficient criterion. What would be encompassed in the most universal estimate of the relationship of income to family size—all people who ever lived or who ever will live? Even if one could obtain such an estimate, it would be irrelevant, not only for most practical decisions that one might make, but also for almost any theoretical purpose. "In my view a useful model will usually be appropriate only in particular circumstances and, even then, only for the analysis of particular problems. Clearly, where greater generality can be achieved without loss of content, we must approve of it—but this can rarely be possible" (Baumol, p. 3).[9]

The argument of this section is still another example of a very general idea that has appeared in various guises throughout the book: The scientist's world is very much what she makes of it, and her results depend heavily upon what she chooses to look at and how she chooses to look at it. One important example was the definition of causality, in which I suggested that a judgment of causality depends upon the scientist's purpose and point of view.

Sociologists and psychologists have been more sophisticated and less confused by this aspect of science than have economists; indeed, this confusion has caused serious problems in economics. An example is the hassle over whether "utility" can be measured, which has been a roadblock in the development of welfare economics. This confusion is interwoven with economists' impatience with discussions of scientific philosophy and method (as distinguished from statistical method). And economists' preoccupation with the analogy of their discipline to what they think is objective physical science helps to account for this unsound point of view. It is therefore instructive to note that, even in physics since Einstein and Gibbs, there has taken place ". . . a shift in the point of view of physics in which the world as it actually exists is replaced in some sense or other by the world as it happens to be observed, and the old naïve realism of physics gives way" . . . (Wiener, p. 20).

4. The Special Powers and Limitations of Social-Science Research

At this point in the history of social science it is unnecessary to discuss whether the social sciences are real sciences. What is more interesting now is whether the social sciences are *more* scientific than are the natural sciences;

9. This statement should not be construed as an argument against idle curiosity as a wellspring of science. The very best of work may well originate in a scientist's desire "to know how it works." But, in the course of her development of the idea, a more disciplined scientific purpose usually emerges, and that emergent purpose serves to guide decisions on research strategy.

as far as methodology[10] goes, I think there is good reason to think that the social sciences are far ahead of the natural sciences. The reason is that social scientists have to fight harder to achieve procedures and results that are satisfactorily scientific. P. Samuelson puts it this way:

> A physicist or chemist need not be much of a methodologist: his disciplines have a logic of their own which often will unobtrusively point the way. It is otherwise with the "softer" social sciences. So little spontaneous guidance is provided by the subject matter, that in some of these disciplines substantive research is displaced by repetitious and inconclusive discussion of methodology. (Samuelson, p. 189)

A simple example: A physicist rarely has to worry about his experiment being contaminated by his own bad mood on the day of the experiment, by the occurrence of a newspaper strike or a war that day, or by his having inadvertently given his subjects too much information—and on and on. But those and many, many other such factors must be carefully controlled to ensure that a social scientist does not foul up his research.

It is worth recapitulating a few of the properties of the subject matter that offer special problems for social science. First, the results are statistical, rather than of an all-or-nothing kind. Of course, *no* research is perfectly determinate; if a chemist mixes hydrogen and oxygen, he might *rarely* fail to get water for various experimental reasons, but it is fair to say that getting H_2O from H and O is practically invariable. But the results of a social-science study seldom are so clear-cut. A new method of teaching reading may work better than the old method did with 60 per cent of children. Or middle-sized business firms may produce more inventions per dollar size than do small or large firms but by only a small margin. These small percentage differences make it much harder to make fair comparisons.

Second, social-science problems usually involve more than one important variable, and often it is very difficult to disentangle the variables to study their effects separately. The difficulty is especially great—and sometimes insoluble—when these multiple variables go hand in hand and also cannot be subjected to experiment. For example, when people receive more education they usually achieve higher incomes also. Therefore it is difficult to determine whether highly educated people travel more than other people do because of their education or because of their income or because of both together.

Third, the researcher herself frequently affects the subject matter, thereby changing the whole situation.

A further difference between the natural and social sciences is that a complete *system* can seldom be constructed fruitfully in the social sciences other than economics. An electronic engineer can discuss and set up equa-

10. Notice that this is the first time I use the word "methodology" in this book and also one of the last. One of the less attractive features of the social sciences is occasional pretentiousness, a symptom of which is the addition of three extra and mostly incorrect syllables to the perfectly good word "method."

tions for the entire system in which electrons flow in a radio circuit. And a refrigeration engineer can follow the refrigeration in an air conditioner back and forth from cycle to cycle. But communications among people, for example, cannot be described so easily in this manner.[11] This is because human systems are constantly *open* to new and disturbing influences. That is, social-science systems *leak* so much that it is seldom possible to predict a long-time course of events from the starting point. Once the refrigeration cycle begins, nothing much affects it except some loss of energy; that is, the system is *closed*, except for loss of energy. But, when human beings interact with one another, a great many new influences come into play with each interchange. It is therefore difficult to describe more than one or two steps at a time, and the idea of system is rendered less useful.

Sometimes it seems as if social scientists labor very hard to bring forth only small mouselike pieces of knowledge. To the extent that this is so, there may be two causes that, like scissor blades, slice from both directions. On one hand, many of the biggest problems of human civilization have barely been scratched: Why do wars occur? What influences will reduce human anxiety? What factors will be efficient in getting underdeveloped countries on the road of development? What is consciousness? Why do people retreat into their own skins as they grow older and have less intimate contact with other people? Of course, the social sciences have made vast gains in some fields like smoothing out business cycles and reducing unemployment. But many huge problems in social science are still almost untouched.

The other scissors blade is that we learn so much about our social world in very simple fashion. Most social questions can be answered very easily. Why have most coal mines in Illinois closed? Because their veins have been worked out. Why don't blacks go to a particular restaurant? Because they know they will be insulted or not served or thrown out. Why are there fewer buses after midnight? Why is the factory shut down on Sunday? These and many other *important* questions can be answered quite well either by consulting our own experience or by asking others. Notice that these questions are *not* trivial, but many of them have single clear answers; in each case, a single factor accounts for what happens, to an overwhelmingly large degree. In the natural sciences it is a major task to unravel even those problems that have single sharp answers: why colds end after five days, or how the genetic code carries information. These questions are much harder to answer than is one about why the factories are closed on Sunday.

Because the easy-to-solve problems do not demand scientific methods, those that are left for social science are all tough problems. It is this that makes social science seem weak and powerless.

Beside the questions that are tough but soluble *in principle*, there is a class of questions that *may* lie beyond the reach of social-scientific techniques. These are questions of the causation of major historical events. A. Schlesinger, Jr., argues that:

11. For a valiant conceptual effort to do so, see J. Carey.

. . . there seem to me two main troubles with this effort—with an effort, for example, to solve quantitatively the problem of the causes of the Civil War. One is that most of the variables in an historical equation are not susceptible to commensurable quantification; the other is that the observer is too mixed up with the phenomena observed to eliminate the subjective element. (Schlesinger, 1962, p. 770)

Furthermore, such historical events are nonrepetitive, in the sense that it is usually not sensible to put the American Civil War in a category with other civil wars and to treat them all as a homogeneous group. Without a sample of some reasonable size, social-science investigation is helpless.

The limits of social science in explaining historical events are related to the limits on social science's ability to predict large changes, as discussed in Chapter 26.

Nor are these historical questions trivial. As a historian, Schlesinger tries to restore the balance:

The *mystique* of empirical social research, in short, leads its acolytes to accept as significant only the questions to which the quantitative magic can provide answers. As an humanist, I am bound to reply that almost all important questions are important precisely because they are *not* susceptible to quantitative method. What he denies is that it can handle everything which the humanist must take into account; what he condemns is the assumption that things which quantitative methods can't handle don't matter. I would suggest that these are the things that matter most. (Schlesinger, 1962, p. 770)

5. The Ethics of Research

For many kinds of problems empirical social-scientific methods can be very powerful. But just because they can be powerful does not mean that they and their findings are automatically good. The sciences may have justifiably scourged some of the superstitious aspects of religion, like miracles and amulets. But, as already noted, the importance of religion and other non-rational aspects of life is not obviated by science, though some people may choose to make a type of substitute religion out of science itself. Also, social-science research can at times have ill effects on aspects of social and personal life that we value.

The possible ill effects of social-science research are of many kinds.[12] Research might affect the results of elections by publicizing correct or incorrect poll estimates before the election. Research can affect the lives and mental welfare of subjects in some psychological experiments and surveys (Kelman; Bachrach, pp. 93–108), and governmental fund-granting agencies have already recognized this problem to the extent of requiring certain safeguards and approval for some types of research. Here are some relevant excerpts from a report by an august group convened to study the subject:

12. For extended discussion of this topic see E. Shils.

. . . The right to privacy is the right of the individual to decide for himself how much he will share with others his thoughts, his feelings, and the facts of his personal life. . . .

From our examination of the relation of behavioral science research to the right to privacy, we have been led to the following conclusions.

1. While most current practices in the field pose no significant threat to the privacy of research subjects, a sufficient number of exceptions have been noted to warrant a sharp increase in attention to procedures that will assure protection of this right. The increasing scale of behavioral research is itself an additional reason for focusing attention in this area.

2. Participation of subjects must be voluntary and based on informed consent to the extent that this is consistent with the objectives of the research. It is fully consistent with the protection of privacy that, in the absence of full information, consent be based on trust in the qualified investigator and the integrity of his institution.

3. The scientist has an obligation to insure that no permanent physical or psychological harm will ensue from the research procedures, and that temporary discomfort or loss of privacy will be remedied in an appropriate way during the course of the research or at its completion. To merit trust, the scientist must design his research with a view to protecting, to the fullest extent possible, the privacy of the subjects. If intrusion on privacy proves essential to the research, he should not proceed with his proposed experiment until he and his colleagues have considered all of the relevant facts and he has determined, with support from them, that the benefits outweigh the costs.

4. The scientist has the same responsibility to protect the privacy of the individual in published reports and in research records that he has in the conduct of the research itself. . . . (Panel on Privacy and Behavioral Research Report, pp. 535–538)

There is much more that can be said about the ethics of research (e.g. Cook, *Daedulus*, Spring, 1969). But better than—or best of all, in addition to—consideration of the ethical principles involved is a discussion of your proposed work with colleagues and laymen. If all agree that what you plan to do is ethical, then you can feel reasonably secure, even though standards and ethical consciousness do change from decade to decade.

The results of empirical research might lead to manipulation and exploitation by government and private firms.[13] It is a scientific disadvantage of free societies that governments respect the wish of individuals and private institutions to keep their records private. The Soviet Union has much more complete economic data of many sorts than does the United States. And data that the United States government does collect—Internal Revenue tax

13. See Chapter 13 for an eighteenth-century warning against the dangers of a census.

data, for example—are available broken down only for *groups* of firms. This confidentiality is very frustrating to the social scientist at times. On the other hand, totalitarian societies keep much data secret for what they consider to be reasons of state security. This is equally frustrating.

6. The Present and Future of Social-Science Research

The very extent of public-opinion research gives one pause. Lerner estimates that "more than half of the American annual expenditure on all types of social research—in business, government, universities—is now spent on attitude research. So crucial, for our mode of self-observation, is information about the will of the governed" (Lerner, p. 26). This large volume of research may affect us directly by conveying our wishes so that what is offered to us "is the result of the demand on the part of the public," as learned through preference surveys, says the president of General Motors (Kefauver, p. 100). On the other hand, surveys can help firms force upon us what we have no special preference for but what we can be induced to accept. The president of American Motors put it thus:

> A small company could not have made the wraparound windshield a successful thing because when you get right down to the guts of it, it has no basic advantages over the straight windshield, and yet through advertising and promotion you can make an item of that type become absolutely the hallmark of a modern car, if you have got a large enough percentage of the total market to do it. (Kefauver, p. 101)

It is interesting to speculate why it was not until the last hundred years or so that scientific methods were applied to social and behavioral questions. Unlike the development of the natural sciences, the development of social science was not held back by the lack of measuring instruments or the absence of sophisticated theories; the obvious ingredients existed for surveys and experiments to have been conducted 2,000 years ago. Why, then, was social-science research not done then?

Actually, censuses and descriptive social science have been carried on almost as far back as history was first recorded (Carr-Saunders, p. A2). It is *relationship* research, and especially research into cause and effect, that has not been done until recently. I hazard as part of the explanation that, until recently in the Western world, most people have not thought about the possibility of changing the structure of their social world for the better, except for the possibility of overthrowing a government or waging a war. The kinds of changes that people contemplated were not the kinds of changes that science can easily evaluate. Most especially, these kinds of changes did not lend themselves to study by experimentation. In sum, then, the rise of social science probably awaited the idea of progress.

The future of social science is not clear to me. Certainly there will be increasingly more social-science research of the kind that is done today. But what else? Will social science also break entirely new ground and try to solve different sorts of problems entirely? I wish I knew.

As to whether social science will help create better lives for the world's people, my crystal ball is murky. One question is whether the new problems we cause for ourselves—especially, more fiendish ways of killing one another without improved political safeguards—increase faster than our ability to handle the problems. Another question is whether an easier world is a better world. All one can do is hope—and I hope that it will be a more *human* world.

EXERCISES

1. What is your guess about the future of social science?
2. Give three research examples from your field in which *deception* is unethical and three examples in which it is ethically acceptable. Give other examples of ill effects of social-scientific research.
3. Give an example in which common sense corrected a wrong finding of social-science research.
4. Should a newspaperwoman collect public opinion in such a manner that her procedure will be replicable?
5. What problems in your field *cannot* be solved by social-science research?
6. What do you think of the proposal to collect much available information about United States citizens in a central repository as a "data bank" for research?

ADDITIONAL READING FOR CHAPTER 33

Lerner presents a collection of interesting articles about the nature of social science.

For more on the place and purpose of research, see Selltiz *et al.,* pp. 1–11).

Barber analyzes the relationship of science to society in an illuminating fashion.

Kaplan's Part V on "values in research" clarifies many important ideas.

On the ethics of research, Cook (in Selltiz *et al.*) is excellent. For a wider-ranging discussion, see the spring 1969 issue of *Daedalus.* A provocative discussion of ethics and research, urging very strict standards, is that of Kelman.

An interesting discussion of what was to have been a large U.S. government-funded research project to study revolution and various countries, Project Camelot, is discussed by Horowitz. This project caused it to abort.

bibliography

Abrams, Jack. "Evaluation of Alternate Rating Devices for Consumer Research." *Journal of Marketing Research*, 3 (May 1966), 189–193.

Ackley, Gardner. *Macroeconomic Theory*. New York: Macmillan, 1961.

Adelman, Irma. "An Econometric Analysis of Population Growth." *American Economic Review*, LIII (June 1963), 414–439.

Agnew, Neil McK., and Sandra W. Pyke. *The Science Game*. Englewood Cliffs, N.J.: Prentice-Hall, 1969.

Allen, Charles L. "Photographing the TV Audience." *Journal of Advertising Research*, 5 (March 1965), 2–8.

Allen, R. G. D. *Mathematical Economics*, 2nd ed. New York: St. Martin's, 1959.

Allport, Gordon W. *The Nature of Prejudice*. Cambridge, Mass.: Addison-Wesley, 1954.

Alvarez, Luis W. "A Pseudo Experience in Parapsychology." *Science*, 148 (June 18, 1965), 1541.

Arndt, Johan. "Haire's Shopping List Revisited." *Journal of Advertising Research*, 13 (October 1973), 57–62.

Aronson, Elliot, and J. Merrill Carlsmith. "Experimentation in Social Psychology," in Gardner Lindzey and Elliot Aronson (eds.). *Handbook of Social Psychology*, 2nd ed. Vol. II. Reading, Mass.: Addison-Wesley, 1968, pp. 1–79.

Ashby, W. Ross. *An Introduction to Cybernetics*. London: Chapman & Hall, 1968.

Ayer, A. J. "Chance." *Scientific American*, 213 (October 1965), pp. 44–54.

Babbie, Earl R. *Survey Research Methods*. Belmont, Calif.: Wadsworth, 1973.

Bachrach, Arthur J. *Psychological Research: An Introduction*, 3rd ed. New York: Random House, 1972.

Backman, Carl, and P. Secord (eds.). *Problems in Social Psychology*. New York: McGraw-Hill, 1966.

Bakan, David. *On Method*. San Francisco: Jossey-Bass, 1969.

Baker, J. Stannard. "A Framework for Assessment of Causes of Automobile Accidents," in Paul F. Lazarsfeld and Morris Rosenberg (eds.). *The Language of Social Research*. New York: Free Press, 1955, pp. 438–448.

Banks, Seymour. *Experimentation in Marketing*. New York: McGraw-Hill, 1965.

Barclay, George W. *Techniques of Population Analysis*. New York: Wiley, 1958.

Barron, Milton L. (ed.). *Contemporary Sociology: An Introductory Textbook of Readings.* New York: Dodd, Mead, 1964.

Bart, Pauline, and L. Frankel. *The Student Sociologist Handbook.* Cambridge, Mass.: Schenkman, 1975.

Barzun, Jacques. *Teacher in America.* Garden City, N.Y.: Doubleday, 1954.

Bassie, V. Lewis. "The Graphic Method of Curve Fitting." Urbana: University of Illinois Bureau of Business and Economic Research (mimeographed), 1967.

Bauer, Peter T., and Basil S. Yamey. *The Economics of Underdeveloped Countries.* New York: Cambridge University Press, 1967.

Baumol, William J. *Business Behavior, Value, and Growth.* New York: Macmillan, 1959.

Bean, William B. Testimony Before the Subcommittee on Antitrust and Monopoly of the Committee on the Judiciary, Part I (1961), p. 267.

Becker, Gary S. "An Economic Analysis of Fertility," in Ansley J. Coale (ed.). *Demographic and Economic Change in Developed Countries.* Princeton, N.J.: National Bureau of Economic Research, 1960, pp. 209–231.

Beem, E. R. "Who Profits from Trading Stamps?" *Harvard Business Review,* 35 (November–December 1957), 123–136.

———. "On Being Fooled by Statistics: The Case of Professor Strotz." *Journal of Business,* 32 (July 1959), 279–282.

Belden, G. C., *et al. The Protein Paradox.* Boston: Management Reports, 1964.

Bentham, Jeremy. *The Principles of Morals and Legislation.* Darien, Conn.: Hafner, 1970. Originally published in 1789.

Berelson, Bernard. *Content Analysis in Communications Research.* New York: Free Press, 1952.

———. "KAP Studies on Fertility," in Berelson *et al.* (eds.). *Family Planning and Population Programs.* Chicago: University of Chicago Press, 1966, Chapter 51.

Berliner, Joseph. "The Feet of the Natives Are Large: An Essay on Anthropology by an Economist." *Current Anthropology,* III (February 1962), 47–61.

Bernstein, Jeremy. *The Analytical Engine.* New York: Random House, 1964.

Beveridge, W. I. B. *The Art of Scientific Investigation,* 3rd ed. New York: Random House, 1960.

Blalock, Hubert M., Jr. *Causal Inference in Non-Experimental Research.* New York: Norton, 1972.

Booth, Charles (ed.). *Labour and Life of the People of London.* 17 Vols. London: Macmillan, 1889–1902.

Boring, E. G. "The Logic of the Normal Law of Error in Mental Measurement." *American Journal of Psychology*, XXXI (1920), 1–33.

Boulding, Kenneth E. "Welfare Economics," in B. F. Haley (ed.). *A Survey of Contemporary Economics*, Vol. II. Homewood, Ill.: Irwin, 1952.

————. *Economic Analysis*, 3rd ed. New York: Harper, 1955.

Bowley, Arthur L., and A. R. Burnett-Hurst. *Livelihood and Poverty*. London: Bell, 1915.

Boyd, Harper W., Jr., and Ralph Westfall. "Interviewers as a Source of Error in Surveys." *Journal of Marketing*, 19 (April 1955), 311–324.

————., and Stanley F. Stasch. *Marketing Research: Text and Cases*, 4th ed. Homewood, Ill.: Irwin, 1977.

Bradburn, Norman M. "Summary of *In Pursuit of Happiness*." Chicago: (mimeographed), 1963.

Bradburn, Norman M., and David E. Berlew. "Need for Achievement and English Industrial Growth." *Economic Development and Cultural Change* (October 1961), pp. 8–20.

Bradburn, Norman M., and David Caplovitz. *Reports on Happiness*. Chicago: Aldine, 1965.

Braidwood, Robert J. "The Biography of a Research Project." *Chicago Today*, II (Autumn 1965), 14–27.

Braithwaite, Richard B. *Scientific Explanation*. New York: Harper, 1953.

Breuer, Joseph, and Sigmund Freud. *Studies in Hysteria*. Boston: Beacon, 1961.

Bridgman, P. W. *The Logic of Modern Physics*. New York: Macmillan, 1927.

————. "The Prospect for Intelligence." *Yale Review*, XXXIV (Spring 1945), 444–461.

Brodbeck, May (ed.), *Readings in the Philosophy of the Social Sciences*. New York: Macmillan, 1968.

Bross, Irwin. *Design for Decision*. New York: Free Press, 1965.

Brown, Robert. *Explanation in Social Science*. Chicago: Aldine, 1963.

Brownlee, K. A. "Smoking and Health." *Journal of the American Statistical Association*, 60 (September 1965), 722–739.

Brunner, Ronald D., and Klaus Liepelt. "Data Analysis, Process Analysis, and System Change." *Midwest Journal of Political Science*, XVI (November 1972), 538–569.

Bunge, Mario. *Causality*. Cambridge, Mass.: Harvard University Press, 1959.

Bunn, Vern A. "Trading Stamps and Retail Food Prices, 1960–1965." New York: S & H Company (mimeographed), 1967.

Campbell, Angus, and Charles A. Metzner. "Books, Libraries and Other Media of Communication," in D. Katz *et al. Public Opinion and Propaganda.* New York: Dryden, 1954, p. 235.

Campbell, Donald T. "Factors Relevant to the Validity of Experiments in Social Settings," in Carl Backman and P. Secord (eds.). *Problems in Social Psychology.* New York: McGraw-Hill, 1966.

————. "Reforms as Experiments." *American Psychologist,* 24 (April 1969), 409–429.

————, and Julian C. Stanley. "Experimental and Quasi-Experimental Design for Research in Teaching," in N. L. Gage (ed.). *Handbook of Research in Teaching.* Chicago: Rand McNally, 1963.

Cannon, Walter B. *The Way of an Investigator.* New York: Consortium Press, 1965. Reprint of 1945 edition.

Cantril, Hadley. *Gauging Public Opinion.* Port Washington, N.Y.: Kennikat Press, 1971.

Caplow, Theodore, and Reese McGee. *The Academic Marketplace.* New York: Basic Books, 1958.

Carey, Alex. "The Hawthorne Studies: A Radical Criticism." *American Sociological Review,* 32 (June 1967), 403–417.

Carey, James W. "Communication Systems and Social Systems." Unpublished doctoral dissertation, University of Illinois, 1963.

Carr-Saunders, A. M. *Population.* London: Oxford, 1925.

Cartter, Allan M. *An Assessment of Quality in Graduate Education.* Washington, D.C.: American Council on Education, 1966.

Caudill, William A. *The Psychiatric Hospital as a Small Society.* Cambridge, Mass.: Harvard University Press, 1958.

Cavan, Ruth S. *Suicide.* Chicago: University of Chicago Press, 1928.

Chapanis, Alphonse R., Wendell R. Garner, and Clifford T. Morgan. *Applied Experimental Psychology: Human Factors in Engineering Design.* New York: Wiley, 1949.

Chapin, F. Stuart. "Explaining Consumer Behavior—On What Level?" in Nelson N. Foote (ed.). *Household Decision-Making.* New York: New York University Press, 1961.

Chernoff, Herman, and Moses E. Lincoln. *Elementary Decision Theory.* New York: Wiley, 1959.

Chung, J. H., and D. A. S. Fraser. "Randomization Tests for a Two-Sample Problem." *Journal of the American Statistical Association,* 53 (September 1958), 729–735.

Churchill, Gilbert A., Jr. *Marketing Research: Methodological Foundations* (Hinsdale, Ill.: Dryden, 1976).

Coale, Ansley J., and F. F. Stephan. "The Case of the Indians and the Teen-Age Widows." *Journal of the American Statistical Association,* 57 (June 1962), 338–347.

Cochran, William C., Frederick Mosteller, and John W. Tukey. "Statistical Problems of the Kinsey Report." *Journal of the American Statistical Association,* 48 (December 1953), 673–716. Excerpted in Jerome Himelhoch and Sylvia Fleis Fava. *Sexual Behavior in American Society.* New York: Norton, 1955.

―――. "Principles of Sampling." *Journal of the American Statistical Association,* 49 (March 1954), 13–35. Reprinted in Dennis P. Forcese and Stephen Richer (eds.). *Stages of Social Research: Contemporary Perspectives.* Englewood Cliffs, N.J.: Prentice-Hall, 1970, pp. 168–186.

Cohen, Jerome B. "The Misuse of Statistics." *Journal of the American Statistical Association,* 33 (December 1938), 657–674.

Cohen, Morris R., and Ernest Nagel. *An Introduction to Logic and Scientific Method.* New York: Harcourt, 1962.

Cohen, Stanley E. "U.S. Tests Use of Direct Mail in Data Gathering for 1970 Census." *Advertising Age* (February 22, 1965), p. 82.

Colby, K. M. *An Introduction to Psychoanalytic Research.* New York: Basic Books, 1960.

Conant, James Bryant. *Two Modes of Thought.* New York: Pocket Books, 1965.

Converse, Jean M., and Howard Schuman. *Conversations at Random.* New York: Wiley, 1974.

Cook, Stuart W. "Ethical Issues in the Conduct of Research in Social Relations," in Claire Selltiz, Lawrence S. Wrightsman, and Stuart W. Cook. *Research Methods in Social Relations,* 3rd ed. New York: Holt, 1976, Chapter 7.

Coombs, Clyde H. "Theory and Methods of Social Measurement," in Leon Festinger and Daniel Katz (eds.). *Research Methods in the Behavioral Sciences.* New York: Holt, 1953, Chapter 11.

Cooper, Sanford L. "Random Sampling by Telephone—An Improved Method." *Journal of Marketing Research,* 1 (November 1964), 45–48.

Cootner, Paul (ed.). *The Random Character of Stock Market Prices.* Cambridge, Mass.: M.I.T. Press, 1964.

Cronbach, Lee J., and Goldine C. Gleser. *Psychological Tests and Personal Decisions,* 2nd ed. Urbana: University of Illinois Press, 1965.

Croxton, Frederick E., and Dudley J. Cowden. *Applied General Statistics.* Englewood Cliffs, N.J.: Prentice-Hall, 1939.

Cummings, E. E. *Poems 1923–1954.* New York: Harcourt, 1954.

Cyert, R. M., Herbert A. Simon, and D. B. Trow. "Observations of a Business Decision." *Journal of Business,* 29 (October 1956), 237–248.

Dahl, Robert. *Who Governs?* New Haven: Yale University Press, 1961.

Dantzig, Tobias. *Number: The Language of Science,* 4th ed. New York: Free Press, 1967.

Davis, O. A. "The Economics of Trading Stamps." *Journal of Business,* 32 (April 1959), 141–150.

Dawson, Richard E. "Simulation in the Social Sciences," in Harold Guetzkow (ed.). *Simulation in Social Science.* Englewood Cliffs, N.J.: Prentice-Hall, 1962.

Deming, W. Edwards. "On Errors in Surveys." *American Sociological Review,* 9 (August 1944), 359–369.

————. *Sample Design in Business Research.* New York: Wiley, 1960.

Denzin, Norman K. *The Research Act.* Chicago: Aldine, 1970. (a)

————. *Sociological Methods: A Source Book.* Chicago: Aldine, 1970. (b)

Distilled Spirits Institute. *Public Revenues from Alcoholic Beverages, 1961.* Washington, D.C.: Distilled Spirits Institute, 1962.

Dixon, Wilfred J., and Frank J. Massey, Jr. *Introduction to Statistical Analysis,* 3rd ed. New York: McGraw-Hill, 1968.

Dublin, Robert. *Theory Building.* New York: Free Press, 1969.

Dulles, Allen. *The Craft of Intelligence.* New York: New American Library, 1965.

Duncan, Otis Dudley, Ray P. Cuzzort, and Beverly Duncan. *Statistical Geography.* New York: Free Press, 1961.

Dunnette, Marvin D. "Fads, Fashions, and Folderol in Psychology." *American Psychologist,* 21 (April 1, 1966), 343–352.

Durkheim, Emile. *Suicide.* Translated by J. A. Spalding and G. Simpson. New York: Free Press, 1951.

Dwass, Meyer. "Modified Randomization Tests for Nonparametric Hypothesis." *Annals of Mathematical Statistics,* 28 (March 1957), 181–187.

Easterlin, Richard. "Effects of Population Growth in the Economic Development of Developing Countries." *Annals of the American Academy of Political and Social Science,* 369 (January 1967), 98–108.

Ebbinghaus, Hermann. *Memory: A Contribution to Experimental Psychology.* Translated by H. A. Ruger and C. E. Bussenius. New York: Columbia University Teachers College, 1913.

Edwards, Allen L. *Techniques of Attitude Scale Construction.* New York: Appleton, 1957.

Enthoven, Alain C. "Economic Analysis in the Department of Defense." *American Economic Review,* LIII (May 1963), 413–423.

Erikson, Kai. "A Comment on Disguised Observation in Sociology." *Social Problems,* 14 (Spring 1967), 366–373. Reprinted in Billy J. Franklin and Harold W. Osborne (eds.). *Research Methods: Issues and Insights.* Belmont, Calif.: Wadsworth, 1971, pp. 66–74.

Evan, William M. (ed.). *Organizational Experiments.* New York: Harper, 1971.

Evans, Franklin B. "An Analysis of Automobile Purchasers: The Discriminatory Efficacy of Objective and Psychological Variables." Unpublished doctoral dissertation, University of Chicago, 1959.

————. "Correlates of Automobile Shopping Behavior." *Journal of Marketing,* 26 (October 1962), 74–77.

Ezekiel, Mordecai. *Methods of Correlation and Regression Analysis.* New York: Wiley, 1930.

————, and Karl A. Fox. *Methods of Correlation and Regression Analysis,* 3rd ed. New York: Wiley, 1959.

Fein, Rashi. *The Economics of Mental Illness.* New York: Basic Books, 1958.

Ferber, Robert, and P. J. Verdoorn. *Research Methods in Economics and Business.* New York: Macmillan, 1962.

Ferber, Robert, and Hugh G. Wales. *A Basic Bibliography on Marketing Research.* Chicago: American Marketing Association, 1963.

Festinger, Leon. "Laboratory Experiments," in Festinger and Daniel Katz (eds.). *Research Methods in the Behavioral Sciences.* New York: Holt, 1953, pp. 140–146. Reprinted in Billy J. Franklin and Harold W. Osborne (eds.). *Research Methods: Issues and Insights.* Belmont, Calif.: Wadsworth, 1971, pp. 325–330.

Fisher, R. A. *The Design of Experiments,* 8th ed. New York: Hafner, 1971.

Flesch, Rudolph. *The Art of Clear Thinking.* New York: Harper, 1951.

Forcese, Dennis P., and Stephen Richer (eds.). *Stages of Social Research: Contemporary Perspectives.* Englewood Cliffs, N.J.: Prentice-Hall, 1970.

Fouraker, Lawrence E., and Sidney Siegel. *Bargaining Behavior.* New York: McGraw-Hill, 1963.

Franklin, Billy J., and Harold W. Osborne (eds.). *Research Methods: Issues and Insights.* Belmont, Calif.: Wadsworth, 1971.

Freedman, Deborah. "The Relation of Economic Status to Fertility." *American Economic Review,* LIII (June 1963), 414–426.

Freilich, Morris (ed.). *Marginal Natives: Anthropologists and Work.* New York: Harper, 1970.

Friedman, Milton. "The Methodology of Positive Economics," in Friedman. *Essays in Positive Economics.* Chicago: University of Chicago Press, 1953, Chapter 1.

Fromm, Erich. *The Sane Society.* New York: Holt, 1955.

Fuchs, Douglas A. "Election Day Newscasts and Their Effects on Western Voter Turnout." *Journalism Quarterly,* XLI (Winter 1965), 22–28.

Fussler, Herman H., and Julian L. Simon. *Patterns in the Use of Books in Large Research Libraries.* Chicago: University of Chicago Library, 1961.

Galanter, E. H., quoted in S. S. Stevens. "Measurement, Psychophysics, and Utility," in C. W. Churchman and Philburn Ratoosh (eds.). *Measurement: Definitions and Theories.* New York: Wiley, 1959, Chapter 2.

Gallup, George. *A Guide to Public Opinion Polls.* Princeton, N.J.: Princeton University Press, 1948.

Gamson, William. *Simsoc.* New York: Free Press, 1972.

Garfinkel, Harold. *Studies in Ethno-Methodology.* Englewood Cliffs, N.J.: Prentice-Hall, 1967.

Gee, Wilson. *Social Science Research Methods.* New York: Appleton, 1950.

George, W. H. *The Scientist in Action: A Scientific Study of His Methods.* London: Williams & Norgate, 1936.

Georgescu-Roegen, Nicholas. "The Economics of Production." *American Economic Review,* LX (May 1970), 1 ff.

Gerschenkron, Alexander. *Economic Backwardness in Historical Perspective: A Book of Essays.* New York: Praeger, 1965.

Gilboy, Elizabeth W. "Demand Curves by Personal Estimate." *Quarterly Journal of Economics,* XLVI (1931–1932), 367–384.

Glasser, Gerald J., and Dale D. Metzger. "Random-Digit Dialing as a Method of Telephone Sampling." *Journal of Marketing Research,* 9 (February 1972), 59–64.

Glazer, Myron. *The Research Adventure: Promise and Problems of Fieldwork.* New York: Random House, 1972.

Glazer, Nathan. "The Rise of Social Research in Europe," in Daniel Lerner (ed.). *The Human Meaning of the Social Sciences.* New York: Meridan, 1959, pp. 43–72.

Gold, Jack A. "Testing Test Market Predictions." *Journal of Marketing Research,* 1 (August 1964), 8–16.

Goldberg, Lewis R. "The Effectiveness of Clinicians' Judgments: The Diagnosis of Organic Brain Damage from the Bender Gestalt Test." *Journal of Consulting Psychology,* 23 (February 1959), 25–33. Reprinted in B. Murstein (ed.). *Handbook of Projective Techniques.* New York: Basic Books, 1965.

Goldberger, Arthur S. *Econometric Theory.* New York: Wiley, 1964.

Goodman, Leo A. "Generalizing the Problem of Prediction." *American Sociological Review,* 17 (October 1952), 609–612. Reprinted in Paul F. Lazarsfeld and Morris Rosenberg (eds.). *The Language of Social Research.* New York: Free Press, 1955, pp. 277–281.

———. "Snowball Sampling." *Annals of Mathematical Statistics,* 32 (March 1961), 148–170.

Gorden, Raymond L. *Interviewing: Strategy, Techniques, and Tactics.* Homewood, Ill.: Dorsey, 1969.

Gould, Julius, and William L. Kolb (eds.). *A Dictionary of Social Sciences.* New York: Free Press, 1964.

Granovetter, Mark. "Network Sampling: Some First Steps." *American Journal of Sociology,* 81 (May 1976), 1287–1303.

Green, Paul E., and Donald S. Tull. *Research for Marketing Decisions,* 3rd ed. Englewood Cliffs, N.J.: Prentice-Hall, 1975.

Greenwood, Ernest. *Experimental Sociology.* New York: King's Crown, 1945.

Griffin, John Howard. *Black Like Me.* Boston: Houghton Mifflin, 1962.

Guetzkow, Harold (ed.). *Simulation in Social Science.* Englewood Cliffs, N.J.: Prentice-Hall, 1962.

Guilford, Joy Paul. *Psychometric Methods,* 2nd ed. New York: McGraw-Hill, 1954.

Guttman, Louis. "Measurement as Structural Theory." Presidential address to the Psychometric Society, 1971.

Hagen, Everett E. *On the Theory of Social Change: How Economic Growth Begins.* Homewood, Ill.: Dorsey, 1962.

Hagstrom, Warren O. *The Scientific Community.* New York: Basic Books, 1965.

Haire, Mason. "Projective Techniques in Marketing Research." *Journal of Marketing,* 14 (April 1950), 649–656.

Halacy, D. S., Jr. *Computers: The Machines We Think With,* rev. ed. New York: Harper, 1969.

Hall, R. J., and C. J. Hitch. "Price Theory and Business Behavior." *Oxford Economic Papers,* II (1939), 12–45.

Hallowell, A. Irving. "Psychological Leads for Ethnological Field Workers," in Douglas G. Haring (ed.). *Personal Character and Cultural Milieu,* 3rd ed. Syracuse: Syracuse University Press, 1956, pp. 341–388.

Hammond, Philip E. (ed.). *Sociologists at Work.* New York: Basic Books, 1964.

Hansen, Morris H., W. N. Hurwitz, and W. G. Madow. *Sample Survey Methods and Theory,* Vol. I. New York: Wiley, 1953.

Haring, Douglas G. "Comments on Field Techniques in Ethnology," in Haring (ed.). *Personal Character and Cultural Milieu,* 3rd ed. Syracuse: Syracuse University Press, 1956, pp. 53–65.

Heilbroner, Robert L. *The Quest for Wealth: A Study of Acquisitive Man.* New York: Simon & Schuster, 1956.

Heise, David R. *Causal Analysis.* New York: Wiley, 1975.

Hirschi, Travis, and Hanan C. Selvin. "False Criteria of Causality in Delinquency Research." *Social Problems,* 13 (Winter 1966), 254–268.

————. *Delinquency Research.* New York: Free Press, 1967.

————. *Principles of Survey Analysis.* New York: Free Press, 1973.

Holdren, Bob R. *The Structure of a Retail Market and the Market Behavior of Retail Units.* Englewood Cliffs, N.J.: Prentice-Hall, 1960.

Homans, George C. "Bringing Men Back In." *American Sociological Review,* 29 (December 1964), 809–818.

Horowitz, Irving Louis. "Life and Death of Camelot." *Trans-action,* 3 (November–December 1965), 3–7, 44–47. Reprinted in Billy J. Franklin and Harold W. Osborne (eds.). *Research Methods: Issues and Insights.* Belmont, Calif.: Wadsworth, 1971, pp. 75–92. Also reprinted in Dennis P. Forcese and Stephen Richer (eds.). *Stages of Social Research: Contemporary Perspectives.* Englewood Cliffs, N.J.: Prentice-Hall, 1970, pp. 228–243.

Hovland, Carl. "Reconciling Conflicting Results Derived from Experimental and Survey Studies of Attitude Change." *American Psychologist,* 14 (January 1959). 8–17. Reprinted in Norman K. Denzin. *Sociological Methods: Source Book.* Chicago: Aldine, 1970 (b), pp. 476–494.

Huff, Darrell. *How to Lie with Statistics.* New York: Norton, 1954.

Hulett, J. E. "Interviewing in Social Research: Basic Problems of the First Field Trip." *Social Forces,* XVI (March 1938), 358–366.

Hull, Clark L. "Quantitative Aspects of the Evolution of Concepts: An Experimental Study." *Psychological Monographs,* 28 (1920).

Hume, David. *An Enquiry Concerning Human Understanding.* London: 1758.

Hyman, Herbert H. *Interviewing in Social Research.* Chicago: University of Chicago Press, 1954.

————. "Problems in the Collection of Opinion-Research Data." *American Journal of Sociology,* 55 (January 1950), pp. 362–370. Reprinted in Milton L. Barron (ed.). *Contemporary Sociology: An Introductory Textbook of Readings.* New York: Dodd, Mead, 1964, pp. 513–523.

————. *Survey Design and Analysis*. New York: Free Press, 1965.

————. *Secondary Analysis of Sample Surveys: Principles, Procedures, and Potentialities*. New York: Wiley, 1972.

Ishii, Ryoichi. *Population Pressure and Economic Life in Japan*. London: P. S. King, 1937.

Jaffe, A. J., and Charles D. Stewart. *Manpower Resources and Utilization*. New York: Wiley, 1951, pp. 62–73. Reprinted in Paul F. Lazarsfeld and Morris Rosenberg. *The Language of Social Research*. New York: Free Press, 1955, pp. 28–34.

Jennings, Norman H., and Justin H. Dickins. "Computer Simulation of Peak Hour Operations in a Bus Terminal," in Harold Guetzkow (ed.). *Simulation in Social Science*. Englewood Cliffs, N.J.: Prentice-Hall, 1962.

Johnston, J. *Econometric Methods*, 2nd ed. New York: McGraw-Hill, 1972.

Jones, Arnold Hugh Martin. *Ancient Economic History: An Inaugural Lecture Delivered at University College, London*. London: Lewis, 1948.

Kahn, Robert L., and Charles F. Cannell. *The Dynamics of Interviewing*. New York: Wiley, 1967.

Kaplan, Abraham. *The Conduct of Inquiry*. San Francisco: Chandler, 1964.

Katona, George. *The Powerful Consumer*. New York: McGraw-Hill, 1960.

Kefauver, Estes. *In a Few Hands: Monopoly Power in America*. Baltimore: Penguin, 1965.

Kelman, Herbert C. "Deception in Social Research." *Trans-action*, 3 (July–August 1966), 20–24.

Kendall, Maurice, and William R. Buckland. *A Dictionary of Statistical Terms*. London: Oliver & Boyd, 1957.

Kendall, Patricia L., and Paul F. Lazarsfeld. "Problems of Survey Analysis," in Robert K. Merton and Paul F. Lazarsfeld (eds.). *Continuities in Social Research*. New York: Free Press, 1950, pp. 133–196.

Kinsey, Alfred C., Wardell B. Pomeroy, and Clyde E. Martin. *Sexual Behavior in the Human Male*. Philadelphia: Saunders, 1948.

————, and Paul H. Gebhard. *Sexual Behavior in the Human Female*. Philadelphia: Saunders, 1953; New York: Pocket Books, 1965.

Kiser, Clyde V., and P. K. Whelpton. "Resume of the Indianapolis Study of Social and Psychological Factors Affecting Fertility." *Population Studies*, 7 (November 1953), 95–110. Reprinted in J. J. Spengler and O. D. Duncan (eds.). *Demographic Analysis*. New York: Free Press, 1956, pp. 256–271.

Klein, D. "Short Notes." *The Reporter of Direct Mail Advertising* (February 1965), 4.

Klein, Lawrence R. (ed.). *Contributions of Survey Methods to Economics.* New York: Columbia University Press, 1954.

———. *An Introduction to Econometrics.* Englewood Cliffs, N.J.: Prentice-Hall, 1962.

Kluckhohn, Clyde. "Common Humanity and Diverse Cultures," in Daniel Lerner (ed.). *The Human Meaning of the Social Sciences.* New York: Meridan, 1959, pp. 245–284.

Knight, Frank H. *The Economic Organization.* New York: Harper, 1951.

Knight, Robert P. "Polls, Sampling and the Votes." Columbia: University of Missouri School of Journalism Freedom of Information Center Publication 168, September 1966.

Knupfer, Genevieve, Walter Clark, and Robin Room. "The Mental Health of the Unmarried." *American Journal of Psychiatry,* 122 (February 1966), 841–851.

Kroeber, A. L. *Anthropology.* New York: Harcourt, 1948.

Kuhn, Thomas S. *The Structure of Scientific Revolutions.* Chicago: University of Chicago Press, 1962.

Labovitz, Sanford I. "Methods for Control at Small Sample Size." *American Sociological Review,* 30 (1965), 243–249. Reprinted in Dennis P. Forcese and Stephen Richer (eds.). *Stages of Social Research: Contemporary Perspectives.* Englewood Cliffs, N.J.: Prentice-Hall, 1970, pp. 273–282.

———, and Robert Hagedorn. *Introduction to Social Research,* 2nd ed. New York: McGraw-Hill, 1976.

Lazarsfeld, Paul F. "The Art of Asking Why." *National Marketing Review* (now *Journal of Marketing*), I (Summer 1935), 26–38.

———. "The Use of Panels in Social Research." *Proceedings of the American Philosophical Society,* 92 (November 1948), 405–410. Reprinted in Billy J. Franklin and Harold W. Osborne (eds.). *Research Methods: Issues and Insights.* Belmont, Calif.: Wadsworth, 1971, pp. 407–417.

———. "The American Soldier—An Expository Review." *Public Opinion Quarterly,* XIII (Fall 1949), 377–404.

———. "Evidence and Inference in Social Research." *Daedalus,* 87 (1958), 99–129. Reprinted in May Brodbeck (ed.). *Readings in the Philosophy of the Social Sciences.* New York: Free Press, 1968, pp. 608–634.

Lazarsfeld, Paul F., Bernard Berelson, and Hazel Gaudet. *The People's Choice: How the Voter Makes Up His Mind in a Presidential Campaign.* New York: Columbia University Press, 1948.

Lazarsfeld, Paul F., and Wagner Thielens, Jr. *The Academic Mind: Social Scientists in a Time of Crisis.* New York: Free Press, 1958.

Lerner, Daniel. "Social Science: Whence and Whither?" in Lerner (ed.). *The Human Meaning of the Social Sciences.* New York: Meridan, 1959, pp. 13–42.

Letwin, William. *The Origins of Scientific Economics*. Garden City, N.Y.: Doubleday, 1967.

Lieberman, Bernhardt (ed.). *Contemporary Problems in Statistics: A Book of Readings for the Behavioral Sciences*. New York: Oxford University Press, 1971.

Llewellyn, Karl. "Legal Tradition and Social Science Method—A Realist's Critique," in Llewellyn. *Essays on Research in the Social Sciences*. Washington, D.C.: Brookings, 1931.

Loranger, A. W., C. T. Prout, and M. A. White. "The Placebo Effect in Psychiatric Drug Research." *Journal of the American Medical Association*, 176 (June 17, 1961), 920–926.

Lorie, James H., and Harry V. Roberts. *Basic Methods of Marketing Research*. New York: McGraw-Hill, 1951.

Lorimer, Frank. *Culture and Human Fertility*. New York: Columbia University Press, 1954. Relevant portion reprinted in J. J. Spengler and O. D. Duncan (eds.). *Population Theory and Policy*. New York: Free Press, 1956, pp. 395–399.

Lucas, Darrell B., and Steuart H. Britt. *Measuring Advertising Effectiveness*. New York: McGraw-Hill, 1963.

Lyon, Herbert C., and Julian L. Simon. "The Price Elasticity of Demand for Cigarettes Estimated by Quasi-Experiment." Urbana: (mimeographed), 1967.

McCall, George J., and J. L. Simmons (eds.). *Issues in Participant Observation*. Reading, Mass.: Addison-Wesley, 1969.

Mace, Arthur E. *Sample Size Determination*. New York: Reinhold, 1964.

Machlup, Fritz. "The Characteristics and Classifications of Oligopoly." *Kyklos*, V (1951–1952), 145–165. Reprinted in Machlup, *The Economics of Sellers' Competition*. Baltimore: Johns Hopkins Press, 1952.

————. "The Problem of Verification in Economics." *Southern Economic Journal*, XXII (July 1955), 1–21.

McLain, Garvin, and Erwin M. Segal. *The Game of Science*. Belmont, Calif.: Brooks/Cole, 1969.

Maclay, Howard, and Charles E. Osgood. "Hesitation Phenomena in Spontaneous English Speech." *Word*, XV (April 1959), 19–44.

MacMahon, Brian, Thomas F. Pugh, and Johanne S. Ipsen. *Epidemiology*. Boston: Little, Brown, 1970.

McNemar, Quinn. *Psychological Statistics*, 4th ed. New York: Wiley, 1969.

Madge, John. *The Origins of Scientific Sociology*. New York: Free Press, 1962.

Madow, W. G., H. H. Hyman, and R. J. Jessen. *Evaluation of Statistical Methods Used in Obtaining Broadcast Ratings*. Washington, D.C.: American Statistical Association, 1961.

Malinowski, Bronislaw. *Argonauts of the Western Pacific.* New York: Dutton, 1961.

Malmquist, S. *A Statistical Analysis of the Demand for Liquor in Sweden.* Uppsala, Sweden: University of Uppsala, 1948.

Malthus, Thomas. *Principle of Population,* 5th ed. Homewood, Ill.: Irwin Paperback Classics in Economics, 1817–1963.

Marshall, Alfred. *Principles of Economics,* 9th (variorum) ed. New York: Macmillan, 1961.

Maslow, Abraham H., and James M. Sakoda. "Volunteer Error in the Kinsey Study," in Jerome Himelhoch and Sylvia Fleis Fava. *Sexual Behavior in American Society.* New York: Norton, 1955.

Mason, Stephen. *A History of the Sciences,* rev. ed. New York: Collier, 1962.

Masserman, Jules H. "Neurosis and Alcohol: An Experimental Study." *American Journal of Psychiatry,* 101 (November 1944), 389–399.

Mead, Margaret. *People and Places.* New York: Bantam, 1963.

Meier, Richard L. *Science and Economic Development,* 2nd ed. Cambridge, Mass.: M.I.T. Press, 1966.

Melitz, Jack. "Friedman and Machlup on the Significance of Testing Economic Assumptions." *Journal of Political Economy,* 73 (February 1965), 37–60.

Merton, Robert K. *Social Theory and Social Structure.* New York: Free Press, 1949, enlarged and revised edition, 1957.

———. "The Matthew Effect in Science." *Science,* 159 (January 1968), 56–63.

Miller, D. *Handbook of Research Design and Social Measurement.* New York: David McKay, 1970.

Miller, S. M. *et al. America's Uncounted People.* Washington, D.C.: National Academy of Sciences, 1972.

Mills, C. Wright. *The Sociological Imagination.* New York: Oxford University Press, 1959.

Mises, Richard von. *Positivism: A Study in Human Understanding.* Cambridge, Mass.: Harvard University Press, 1951.

Mitchell, Wesley. *What Happens During Business Cycles: A Progress Report.* New York: National Bureau of Economic Research, 1951.

Modern Medicine, March 2, 1964, and *Modern Medicine* press release of February 24, 1964.

Moore, Geoffrey H. "Accuracy of Government Statistics." *Harvard Business Review,* 25 (Spring 1947), 306–317.

Morgan, J. N. "Factors Relating to Consumer Saving When It Is Defined as a Net-Worth Concept," in Lawrence R. Klein, *et al. Contributions of Survey Methods to Economics.* New York: Columbia University Press, 1954, pp. 89–156.

———, F. Andrews, and J. Sonquist. *Multiple Classification Analysis.* Ann Arbor, Mich.: Institute for Social Research, 1967.

Morgenstern, Oskar. *On the Accuracy of Economic Observations,* 2nd ed. Princeton, N.J.: Princeton University Press, 1963.

Moser, C. A., and G. Kalton. *Survey Methods in Social Investigation,* 2nd ed. New York: Basic Books, 1972.

Mosteller, Frederick. *The Pre-Election Polls: Report to the Committee on Analysis of Pre-Election Polls.* New York: Social Science Research Council, 1949.

———, Robert E. K. Rourke, and George B. Thomas, Jr. *Probability with Statistical Applications,* 2nd ed. Reading, Mass.: Addison-Wesley, 1970.

———, and David L. Wallace. "Inference in an Authorship Problem." *Journal of the American Statistical Association,* 58 (June 1963), 275–309.

———. *Inference and Disputed Authorship: The Federalist.* Reading, Mass.: Addison-Wesley, 1964.

Myrdal, Gunnar. *An American Dilemma.* New York: Harper, 1944.

Naji, S., and R. Corwin (eds.). *The Social Context of Research.* New York: Wiley–Interscience, 1972.

Nasatir, David. "Social Science Laboratories." *American Sociologist,* 2 (November 1967), 207–212. Reprinted in Billy J. Franklin and Harold W. Osborne (eds.). *Research Methods: Issues and Insights.* Belmont, Calif.: Wadsworth, 1971, pp. 290–301.

Neibuhr, Reinhold. *Moral Man and Immoral Society.* New York: Scribners, 1936.

Neyman, Jerzy. *First Course in Probability and Statistics.* New York: Holt, 1950.

Niskanen, William A. "The Demand for Alcoholic Beverages." Unpublished doctoral dissertation, University of Chicago, 1962.

Noltingk, B. E. *The Art of Research.* New York: Elsevier, 1965.

Northrop, F. S. C. *The Logic of the Sciences and the Humanities.* Cleveland: World, 1965.

Oppenheim, A. N. *Questionnaire Design and Attitude Measurement.* New York: Basic Books, 1966.

Orcutt, Guy H. "Toward Partial Re-direction of Econometrics." *Review of Economics and Statistics,* XXXIV, No. 3 (August 1952), 211–213. (a).

————. "Actions, Consequences, and Causal Relations." *Review of Economics and Statistics*, XXXIV, No. 4 (November 1952), 305–313. (b)

————, et al. "A Stochastic Microanalytic Model of a Socioeconomic System," in Orcutt *et al. Microanalysis of Socioeconomic Systems: A Simulation Study.* New York: Harper, 1961, Chapter 2. Reprinted in R. E. Frank, A. A. Kuehn, and W. F. Massy (eds.). *Quantitative Techniques in Marketing Analysis.* Homewood, Ill.: Irwin, 1962, pp. 481–501.

Palda, Kristian. *The Measurement of Cumulative Advertising Effects.* Englewood Cliffs, N.J.: Prentice-Hall, 1964.

Panel on Privacy and Behavioral Research. "Report." *Science,* 155 (February 3, 1967), 535–538.

Parten, Mildred Bernice. *Surveys, Polls, and Samples: Practical Procedures.* New York: Harper, 1950.

Paul, B. D. "Interview Techniques and Field Relationships," in Alfred L. Kroeber (ed.). *Anthropology Today: An Encyclopedic Inventory.* Chicago: University of Chicago Press, 1953.

Pavlov, Ivan Petrovich. *Essential Works of Pavlov,* edited by Michael Kaplan. New York: Bantam, 1966.

Payne, Stanley L. *The Art of Asking Questions.* Princeton, N.J.: Princeton University Press, 1951.

Pearson, Karl. "Historical Note on the Origin of the Normal Curve of Errors." *Biometrika,* 16 (May–December 1924), 402–404.

Peng, J. Y. "Thailand: Family Growth in the Pho-tharam District." *Studies in Family Planning,* No. 8 (October 1965), 1–7.

Pfungst, Otto. *Clever Hans, The Horse of Mr. Van Osten.* Translated by L. L. Rahn. New York: Holt, 1911.

Pitman, E. J. G. "Significance Tests Which May Be Applied to Samples from Any Population." *Journal of the Royal Statistical Society,* Supplement 4 (1937), 119–130.

————. "Significance Tests Which May Be Applied to Samples from Any Population: III. The Analysis of Variance Test." *Biometrika,* 29 (June 1937), 322–335.

Pohlman, Edward. *Incentives and Compensations in Birth Planning.* Chapel Hill, N.C.: Carolina Population Center, 1971.

Politz, Alfred. *Reach and Frequency.* New York: Politz Research, Inc., Communication Report 4, 1964.

Polya, G. *How to Solve It,* 2nd ed. Garden City, N.Y.: Doubleday, 1957.

Pool, Ithiel de Sola (ed.). *Trends in Content Analysis.* Urbana: University of Illinois Press, 1959.

Pool, Ithiel de Sola, and Robert Abelson. "The Simulmatics Project." *Public Opinion Quarterly*, XXV (Summer 1961), 167–183.

Prest, A. R. "Some Experiments in Demand Analysis." *Review of Economics and Statistics*, XXXI (February 1949), 33–49.

Price, Derek J. DeSolla. *Science Since Babylon*. New Haven: Yale University Press, 1961.

Printer's Ink (August 27, 1965), p. 30.

Raiffa, Howard. *Decision Analysis*. Reading, Mass.: Addison-Wesley, 1968.

Rand Corporation, The. *A Million Random Digits*. New York: Free Press, 1955.

Reichenbach, Hans. *The Rise of Scientific Philosophy*. Berkeley: University of California Press, 1951.

Reichmann, W. J. *Use and Abuse of Statistics*. London: Methuen, 1961.

Rensberger, Boyce. "Fraud in Research Is a Rising Problem in Science." *New York Times* (January 23, 1977), pp. 1, 44.

Richardson, Stephen A., et al. *Interviewing: Its Forms and Functions*. New York: Basic Books, 1965.

Riley, Matilda. *Sociological Research*. New York: Harcourt, 1963.

Roberts, Harry. "Dissertations with Fewer Tears." Chicago: University of Chicago (mimeographed), c. 1957.

Roethlisberger, F. J., and W. J. Dickson. *Management and the Worker*. Cambridge, Mass.: Harvard University Press, 1949.

Rosenberg, Morris. *The Logic of Survey Analysis*. New York: Basic Books, 1968.

Rosenfeld, Leonora D. *Portrait of a Philosopher: Morris R. Cohen in Life and Letters*. New York: Harcourt, 1962.

Rosenham, D. L. "On Being Sane in Insane Places." *Science*, 179 (January 1973), 250–258.

Rosenthal, Robert. *Experimenter Effects in Behavioral Research*. New York: Century, 1966.

Roth, Julius. "Hired-Hand Research." *American Sociologist*, 1 (August 1966), 190–196.

Rowntree, B. S. *Poverty: A Study of Town Life*, 2nd ed. London: Macmillan, 1902.

Saiger, George L. "Errors of Medical Studies." *Journal of the American Medical Association*, 173 (June 11, 1960), 678–681.

Samuelson, Paul A. "What Economists Know," in Daniel Lerner (ed.). *The Human Meaning of the Social Sciences*. New York: Meridan, 1959, pp. 183–213.

Sandage, C. H. "Do Research Panels Wear Out?" *Journal of Marketing,* 20 (April 1956), 397–401.

Schlaifer, Robert. *Probability and Statistics for Business Decisions: An Introduction to Managerial Economics Under Uncertainty.* New York: McGraw-Hill, 1959.

———. *Introduction to Statistics for Business Decisions.* New York: McGraw-Hill, 1961.

Schlesinger, Arthur, Jr. "The Humanist Looks at Empirical Social Science." *American Sociological Review,* 27 (December 1962), 768–771.

———. "A Middle Way Out of Vietnam." *New York Times Magazine* (September 18, 1966), pp. 47–49.

Schultz, Theodore W. *Economic Crisis in World Agriculture.* Ann Arbor: University of Michigan Press, 1965.

Schwartzman, David. "The Effect of Monopoly on Price." *Journal of Political Economy,* LXVII (August 1959), 352–362.

———. "Monopoly and Wages." *Canadian Journal of Economics,* XXV (August 1960), 428–438. (a)

———. "The Burden of Monopoly." *Journal of Political Economy,* LXVIII (December 1960), 627–630. (b)

Scott, William A., and Michael Wertheimer. *Introduction to Psychological Research.* New York: Wiley, 1962.

Sears, Richard R. *Survey of Objective Studies of Psychoanalytic Concepts.* New York: Social Science Research Council, 1951.

Selltiz, Claire, Lawrence S. Wrightsman, and Stuart W. Cook. *Research Methods in Social Relations,* 3rd ed. New York: Holt, 1976.

Seltzer, Carl C. "Morphologic Constitution and Smoking." *Journal of the American Medical Association,* 183 (February 23, 1963), 639–645.

———. "Morphological Constitution and Smoking: A Further Validation." *Archives of Environmental Health,* 17 (July 1968), 143–147.

Selvin, Hanan C., *The Effects of Leadership.* New York: Free Press, 1960.

———. "Durkheim's Suicide: Further Thoughts on a Methodological Classic," in Robert A. Nisbet (ed.). *Emile Durkheim.* Englewood Cliffs, N.J.: Prentice-Hall, 1965.

———, and Alan Stuart. "Data-Dredging Procedures in Survey Analysis." *Journal of the American Statistical Association,* 61 (June 1966), 20–23. Reprinted in Dennis P. Forcese and Stephen Richer (eds.). *Stages of Social Research: Contemporary Perspectives.* Englewood Cliffs, N.J.: Prentice-Hall, 1970, pp. 326–332.

Shaler, Nathaniel. "How Agassiz Taught Me to See," in S. Rappaport and H. Wright (eds.). *Science: Method and Meaning.* New York: Washington Square Press, 1964.

Shapere, Dudley. *Philosophical Problems of Natural Science.* New York: Macmillan, 1965.

Sheatsley, Paul. "An Analysis of Interviewer Characteristics and Their Relationship to Performance" in Seymour Sudman. *Reducing the Cost of Surveys.* Illinois: National Opinion Research Center, 1967, pp. 105–106.

Shils, Edward A. "Social Inquiry and the Autonomy of the Individual," in Daniel Lerner (ed.). *The Human Meaning of the Social Sciences.* New York: Meridan, 1959, Chapter 5, pp. 114–157.

———— (ed.). *Criteria for Scientific Development: Public Policy and National Goals.* Cambridge, Mass.: M.I.T. Press, 1968 (especially "Criteria for Scientific Choice" by Alvin M. Weinberg).

Sidman, Murray. *Tactics of Scientific Research.* New York: Basic Books, 1960.

Sielaff, T. J. (ed.). *Statistics in Action.* San Jose, Calif.: Lansford, 1963.

Simon, A., and E. Boyer (eds.). *Mirrors for Behavior.* Philadelphia: Communication Materials Center, 1974, III.

Simon, Herbert A. *Models of Men.* New York: Wiley, 1951.

Simon, Julian L. "Testing Concept Formation." Unpublished bachelor's thesis, Harvard College, 1953.

————. "Discipline and the Division." *U.S. Naval Institute Proceedings,* 81 (October 1955), 1111–1115.

————. "Cigarette Advertising and the Nation's Welfare." *Illinois Business Review,* 21 (May 1964), 6–8. Reprinted in *Congressional Record* (October 11, 1965).

————. *How to Start and Operate a Mail-Order Business.* New York: McGraw-Hill, 1965 (a), 2nd ed. 1976.

————. "Are There Economies of Scale in Advertising?" *Journal of Advertising Research,* 5 (June 1965), 15–19. (b)

————. "A Simple Model for Setting Advertising Appropriations." *Journal of Marketing Research,* 2 (August 1965), 285–292. (c)

————. "The Cause of the Newspaper Rate Differential: A Subjective-Demand-Curve Analysis." *Journal of Political Economy,* LXXIII (October 1965), 536–539. (d)

————. "The Demand for Liquor in the U.S., and a Simple Method of Determination." *Econometrica,* 34 (January 1966), 193–205. (a)

————. "The Economic Effect of State Monopoly of Packaged Liquor Retailing." *Journal of Political Economy,* LXXIV (April 1966), 188–194. (b)

———. "A Reply on 'Smoking and Health,'" *American Statistician* (October 1966), 35–36. (c)

———. "Doctors, Smoking, and Reference Groups." *Public Opinion Quarterly,* 3 (Winter 1967–1968), 646–647.

———. "The Health Economics of Cigarette Consumption." *Journal of Human Resources* (Winter 1968).

———. "Business Ethics, Business Ideology, and Business Behavior." *Business and Society,* 7 (Spring 1967), 18–32. (a)

———. "Some Principles of Practical Welfare Economics." *Management Science,* 13 (June 1967), B621–629. (b)

———. *Patterns of Use of Books in Large Research Libraries* (with Herman H. Fussler). Chicago: University of Chicago Press, 1969.

———. *Issues in the Economics of Advertising.* Urbana: University of Illinois Press, 1970.

———. *The Management of Advertising.* Englewood Cliffs, N.J.: Prentice-Hall, 1971.

———. "Toward Formal Evaluation of Scientific Research Projects: A Case Study in Population Control." *Policy Sciences,* 3 (July 1972), 177–181.

———. *The Effects of Income on Fertility.* Chapel Hill, N.C.: Carolina Population Center, 1974.

———. *Applied Managerial Economics.* Englewood Cliffs, N.J.: Prentice-Hall, 1975.

———. *The Economics of Population Growth.* Princeton, N.J.: Princeton University Press, forthcoming.

———, and Leslie Golembo. "The Spread of a Cost-Price Business Innovation: The Case of the January White Sale." *Journal of Business,* 40 (October 1967), 385–388.

Simon, Rita. "Murder, Juries, and the Press." *Trans-action,* 3 (May–June 1966), 40–42.

———. *The Jury and the Plea of Insanity.* Boston: Little, Brown, 1967.

———. Unpublished ms. N.d.

Sjoberg, Gideon, and Roger Net. *A Methodology for Social Research.* New York: Harper, 1968.

Smith, H. W. *Strategies of Social Research.* Englewood Cliffs, N.J.: Prentice-Hall, 1975.

Smith, T. Lynn. *Fundamentals of Population Study.* Philadelphia: Lippincott, 1960.

Smith, Vernon L. "An Experimental Study of Competitive Market Behavior." *Journal of Political Economy,* LXX (April 1962), 111–137.

————. "Effect of Market Organization on Competitive Equilibrium." *Quarterly Journal of Economics,* LXXVII (May 1964), 181–201.

Sneath, Peter H. A., and Robert R. Sokal. *Principles of Numerical Taxonomy,* 2nd ed. San Francisco: Freeman, 1973; first ed. 1963.

Snedecor, George W. *Statistical Methods,* 6th ed. Ames: Iowa State University Press, 1967.

Snow, C. P. "On Albert Einstein." *Commentary,* 43 (March 1967), 45–55.

Sobol, M. G. "Panel Mortality and Panel Bias." *Journal of the American Statistical Association,* 54 (March 1959), 52–68.

Sorokin, Pitirim A. *Social and Cultural Dynamics,* Vol. II. New York: Bedminister, 1937.

Spencer, Herbert. *The Study of Sociology.* New York and London: Appleton, 1912.

Starch, Daniel. *Measuring Product Sales Made by Advertising.* Mamaroneck, N.Y.: Daniel Starch, 1961.

Steiner, Gary A. "The People Look at Commercials: A Study of Audience Behavior." *Journal of Business,* 39 (April 1966), 272–304.

Stephan, Frederick J., and Philip J. McCarthy. *Sampling Opinion,* 2nd ed. New York: Wiley, 1963.

Stevens, S. S. "Measurement, Psychophysics, and Utility," in C. W. Churchman and Philburn Ratoosh (eds.). *Measurement: Definitions and Theories.* New York: Wiley, 1959, pp. 18–63.

Stewart, John B. *Repetitive Advertising in Newspapers.* Boston: Harvard Graduate School of Business Administration, 1964.

Stigler, George. "The Kinky Oligopoly Demand and Rigid Prices," in George Stigler and Kenneth E. Boulding (eds.). *Readings in Price Theory.* Homewood, Ill.: Irwin, 1952, pp. 410–435.

————. *Essays in the History of Economics.* Chicago: University of Chicago Press, 1965.

Stone, Philip J., Dexter C. Dunphy, Marshall S. Smith, and Daniel M. Ogilvie. *The General Inquirer.* Cambridge, Mass.: M.I.T. Press, 1966.

Stone, Richard. *The Role of Measurement in Economics.* Cambridge, Mass.: Harvard University Press, 1952.

Stouffer, Samuel B. "Afterthoughts of a Contributor," in Robert K. Merton and Paul F. Lazarsfeld (eds.). *Continuities in Social Research.* New York: Free Press, 1950, pp. 197–211. (a)

————. "Some Observations on Study Design." *American Journal of Sociology,* 55 (January 1950), 355–361. (b) Reprinted in Stouffer. *Social Research to Test Ideas.* New York: Free Press, 1962, pp. 200–299.

————, *et al. The American Soldier,* Vols. I–IV. Princeton, N.J.: Princeton University Press, 1949.

Strotz, R. H. "On Being Fooled by Figures: The Case of Trading Stamps." *Journal of Business,* 31 (October 1958), 304–310.

Strunk, William, and E. B. White. *The Elements of Style,* 8th ed. New York: Macmillan, 1972.

Stuart, Alan. *Basic Ideas in Scientific Sampling,* 2nd ed. New York: Hafner, 1976.

Stycos, J. M. "Sample Surveys for Social Science in Underdeveloped Areas," in R. N. Adams and J. J. Preiss (eds.). *Human Organization Research.* Homewood, Ill.: Dorsey, 1960.

Sudman, Seymour. "On the Accuracy of Recording of Consumer Panels." *Journal of Marketing Research,* 1 (May 1964), 69 ff.

————. "New Uses of Telephone Methods in Survey Research." *Journal of Marketing Research,* 3 (May 1966), 163–167.

————. *Reducing the Cost of Surveys.* Chicago: Aldine, 1967.

————. "The Uses of Telephone Directories for Survey Sampling." *Journal of Marketing Research,* 10 (May 1973), 204–207.

————. *Applied Sampling.* New York: Academic Press, 1976.

Suits, Daniel B. "The Demand for New Automobiles in the United States." *Review of Economics and Statistics,* XL (August 1958), 273–280.

————. *Statistics: An Introduction to Quantitative Economic Research.* Chicago: Rand McNally, 1963.

Summers, Gene F. *Attitude Measurement.* Chicago: Rand McNally, 1970.

Tanur, Judith M., *et al.* (eds.). *Statistics: A Guide to Unknown.* San Francisco: Holden-Day, 1972.

Telser, Lester G. "Advertising and Cigarettes." *Journal of Political Economy,* LXX (October 1962), 471–499.

Terman, Lewis M. *Genetic Studies of Genius,* 2nd ed. Stanford, Calif.: Stanford University Press, 1976.

Thomas, William I., and Florian Znaniecki. *The Polish Peasant in Europe and America: Monograph of an Immigrant Group.* New York: Knopf, 1927.

Thurstone, L. L., and E. J. Chave. *The Measurement of Attitudes.* Chicago: University of Chicago Press, 1929.

Tintner, Gerhard. *Econometrics.* New York: Wiley, 1965.

Tolles, N. A., A. H. Jones, and E. Claque. "The Structure of Economists' Employment and Salaries 1964." *American Economic Review,* LV (December 1965), supplement.

Tomasson, Richard. "Why Has American Fertility Been So High?" in Bernard Farber (ed.). *Kinship and Family Organization.* New York: Wiley, 1966.

Torgerson, W. S. *Theory and Methods of Scaling.* New York: Wiley, 1958.

Toynbee, Arnold. *The Industrial Revolution.* Boston: Beacon, 1956. First published 1884.

Tull, Donald S., and Dell I. Hawkins. *Marketing Research: Meaning, Measurement and Method.* New York: Macmillan, 1976.

Underwood, Benton J. *Psychological Research.* New York: Appleton, 1957.

———, and John J. Shaughnessy. *Experimentation in Psychology.* New York: Wiley, 1975.

U.S. Department of Agriculture, Marketing Research Division, Agricultural Marketing Service. *Trading Stamps and Their Impact on Food Prices.* Washington, D.C.: U.S. Department of Agriculture, December 1958.

U.S. House of Representatives, Committee on Interstate and Foreign Commerce. *Evaluation of Statistical Methods Used in Obtaining Broadcast Ratings: Report of the Committee on Interstate and Foreign Commerce Pursuant to Section 136 of the Legislative Reorganization Act of 1946, Public Law 601, 79th Congress, and House Resolution 108, 87th Congress, 1st Session, 1961.* Washington, D.C.: U.S. Government Printing Office, 1961.

U.S. Public Health Service. *Smoking and Health: Report of the Advisory Committee to the Surgeon General of the Public Health Service.* Washington, D.C.: U.S. Department of Health, Education and Welfare, 1964.

Usher, Abbott Payson. "The History of Population and Settlement in Eurasia," in J. J. Spengler and O. D. Duncan (eds.). *Demographic Analysis.* New York: Free Press, 1956, pp. 3–25. Originally published in *Geographical Review,* 20 (January 1930), 110–132.

Walker, Helen M., and Joseph Lev. *Statistical Inference.* New York: Holt, 1953.

Wallis, W. Allen. "Statistics of the Kinsey Report." *Journal of the American Statistical Association,* 44 (December 1949), 463–484.

———. "Some Useful Nonparametric Methods." Chicago: University of Chicago (mimeographed), October 1957.

———. "How to Read a Table," in Billy J. Franklin and Harold W. Osborne (eds.). *Research Methods: Issues and Insights.* Belmont, Calif.: Wadsworth, 1971, pp. 418–432.

———, and Harry V. Roberts. *The Nature of Statistics,* rev. ed. New York: Free Press, 1966.

Warburton, Clark. *The Economic Effects of Prohibition.* New York: Columbia University Press, 1932.

Warwick, D., and C. Lininger. *The Sample Survey: Theory and Practice.* New York: McGraw-Hill, 1975.

Wattenberg, Ben J., in collaboration with Richard M. Scammon. *This U.S.A.: An Unexpected Family Portrait of 194,067,296 Americans Drawn from the Census.* Garden City, N.Y.: Doubleday, 1965.

Weaver, Warren. *Lady Luck.* New York: Anchor, 1963.

————. "The Imperfections of Science," in S. Rappaport and H. Wright (eds.). *Science: Method and Meaning.* New York: Washington Square Press, 1964, p. 16.

Webb, Eugene J., *et al. Unobtrusive Measure: Nonreactive Research in the Social Sciences.* Chicago: Rand McNally, 1966.

Webb, Sidney, and Beatrice Webb. *Methods of Social Study.* London: Longmans, 1932.

West, Morris. *The Ambassador.* New York: Dell, 1965.

Westie, Frank R. "The American Dilemma: An Empirical Test." *American Sociological Review,* 30 (August 1965), 527–538.

White, A. R. (ed.). *The Philosophy of Action.* London: OUP, 1968.

Whitney, Frederick L. *The Elements of Research,* 3rd ed. New York: Prentice-Hall, 1950.

Whyte, William Foote. *Street Corner Society: The Social Structure of an Italian Slum,* 2nd ed. Chicago: University of Chicago Press, 1961.

Wiener, Norbert. *The Human Use of Human Beings,* rev. ed. Garden City, N.Y.: Doubleday, 1954.

Williams, Thomas R. *Field Methods in the Study of Culture.* New York: Holt, 1967.

Williamson, J., D. Karp, and J. Dalphin. *The Research Craft.* Boston: Little Brown, 1977.

Wilson, E. Bright. *An Introduction to Scientific Research.* New York: McGraw-Hill, 1952.

Wold, Herman O. A. "The Approach of Model Building," in Wold (ed.). *Model Building in the Human Sciences.* Monaco: Centre International d'Etude des Problèmes Humains, 1966. (a)

————. "On the Definition and Meaning of Causal Concepts," in Wold (ed.). *Model Building in the Human Sciences.* Monaco: Centre International d'Etude des Problèmes Humains, 1966. (b)

————. "Time as the Realm of Forecasting." Paper presented at Symposium on the Interdisciplinary Perspectives of Time, New York Academy of Sciences, January 20, 1966. (c)

Wolins, Leroy. "Responsibility for Wrong Data." *American Psychologist,* 17 (September 1962), 657–658.

Wood, Gordon. *Fundamentals of Psychological Research.* Boston: Little Brown, 1974.

Working, Holbrook. "Price Relations Between May and New-Crop Wheat Futures in Chicago Since 1885." *Wheat Studies of the Ford Research Institute.* Stanford, Calif., 1934, p. 10.

Wright, Charles R., and Herbert H. Hyman. "The Evaluators," in Philip E. Hammond (ed.). *Sociologists at Work.* New York: Doubleday Anchor, 1964–1967, pp. 140–163.

Young, James Webb. *A Technique for Producing Ideas,* 4th ed. Chicago: Crain Communications, 1977.

Young, Pauline V. *Scientific Social Surveys and Research: An Introduction to the Background, Content, Methods, and Analysis of Social Studies,* 4th ed. New York: Prentice-Hall, 1966.

Zeisel, Hans. "Review of *Sexual Behavior in the Human Female.*" *University of Chicago Law Review,* XXI (1953), 517–525.

―――. *Say It with Figures,* 5th ed. New York: Harper, 1968.

Zelditch, Morris, Jr. "Some Methodological Problems of Field Studies." *American Journal of Sociology,* 67 (1962), 566–576. Reprinted in Dennis P. Forcese and Stephen Richer (eds.). *Stages of Social Research: Contemporary Perspectives.* Englewood Cliffs, N.J.: Prentice-Hall, 1970, pp. 246–258. Also reprinted in Norman K. Denzin. *Sociological Methods: A Source Book.* Chicago: Aldine, 1970 (b), pp. 495–511.

―――, and William M. Evan. "Simulated Bureaucracies: A Methodological Analysis," in Harold Guetzkow (ed.). *Simulation in Social Science.* Englewood Cliffs, N.J.: Prentice-Hall, 1962.

Zielske, Hugh A. "The Remembering and Forgetting of Advertising." *Journal of Marketing,* XXIII (January 1959), 239–243.

index